National Accountability for International Crimes in Africa

Emma Charlene Lubaale ·
Ntombizozuko Dyani-Mhango
Editors

National Accountability for International Crimes in Africa

palgrave
macmillan

Editors
Emma Charlene Lubaale
Faculty of Law
Rhodes University
Grahamstown/Makhanda
South Africa

Ntombizozuko Dyani-Mhango
Faculty of Law
University of Pretoria
Pretoria, South Africa

ISBN 978-3-030-88043-9   ISBN 978-3-030-88044-6 (eBook)
https://doi.org/10.1007/978-3-030-88044-6

This Palgrave Macmillan imprint is published by the registered company Springer Nature Switzerland AG
The registered company address is: Gewerbestrasse 11, 6330 Cham, Switzerland

Foreword

International crimes such as genocide, war crimes, crimes against humanity and aggression shock human conscience and necessitate action from individual states and the international community of states as a whole. Sadly, there is a historical account of these atrocities occurring in the African Continent. Therefore, national accountability for international crimes remains high on Africa's agenda. However, it remains a concern whether African states are committed to preventing and halting these crimes from occurring in their respective territories as reports of atrocities in Tigray, Ethiopia, Mozambique and Eswatini, just to mention a few, are ongoing. These concerns necessitate a critical reflection on the progress made, challenges encountered and the prospects for accountability for international crimes in Africa.

With close to two decades since the establishment of the International Criminal Court (ICC) when states ratified the Rome Statute, and considering that 60% of African states have ratified it, it became important to embark on such a reflection by the editors of this volume. As the ICC exercises jurisdiction over perpetrators of international crimes based on the complementarity principle, this volume provides a comprehensive analysis and latest research, from a perspective of African scholars, on national accountability for international crimes in Africa.

This edited volume brings together original material from diverse perspectives developed by legal practitioners, political scientists, criminal justice experts and scholars from different criminal justice traditions operating on the African Continent. Case studies from West, East, Central, North and Southern Africa have been reviewed, thus making the edited volume a comprehensive collection of continent-wide perspectives on the topic. The volume blends the use of case studies and doctrinal legal research approaches that adopt the current approaches to the subject of accountability for international crimes in Africa. In addition to case studies, the volume has adopted a comparative approach that highlights the gaps and good practices in a manner that provides a rich authoritative source for promoting an intra-African dialogue about international criminal justice in Africa. Given the dearth of research in the thematic focus of this volume and the unique African lens through which the volume is approached, the volume makes a worthwhile contribution to literature on national accountability for international crimes. Effectively, the volume ensures that the African voice is heard on issues pertaining to the application of the complementarity principle in Africa.

The contextual insights, practices and accounts on the application of the complementarity principle in Africa will help to inform research and practice-based reforms to law and policy on issues of international criminal justice in Africa. Therefore, this edited volume will be relevant to international criminal justice practitioners on the continent, the ICC and other international criminal tribunals. The volume will also be a valuable resource for academics and research students of international criminal justice, political science, international law, African legal studies and criminal justice generally.

States in whose territory the alleged international crimes have been or are being committed will find this volume useful as it explores ways to not only hold the alleged perpetrators responsible for committing the crimes, but it also suggests various ways in which these states can achieve justice for the victims, and national healing, reconciliation and lasting peace.

The focus of the book and the voices emerging from the various chapters make this a very timely publication since in 2022 the Rome Statute's complementarity regime will have been in existence for two decades. Chatting the way forward at this juncture is critical in debates pertaining to national accountability for international crimes in Africa and this volume offers just that. I, therefore, strongly recommend this volume edited and authored by these scholars from Africa. I am certain that many will find it useful.

July 2021

Professor Tawana Kupe
Vice-Chancellor and Principal
University of Pretoria
Pretoria, South Africa

Acknowledgements

The editors of this book (Professor Lubaale and Professor Dyani-Mhango) wish to extend their gratitude to all the authors for their commitment to this project from the time of inception to its conclusion. Their patience adherence to strict deadlines and openness to engaging with the comments made by the independent/blind reviewers of chapters made this project worthwhile. Special thanks go to the team at Springer Nature for their courtesy emails and dedication to ensuring that the book is published on time. We also appreciate the encouragement and invaluable support we received from our colleagues at the Faculty of Law at Rhodes University, the Faculty of Law at University of Pretoria, and the various leadership structures in these two institutions. Sincere appreciation is also extended to the academics and experts in international criminal law who took time to read through drafts of this volume and writing blurbs on it. Importantly, the chapters in this book could not have been finalized without the independent reviewers' incisive comments. We acknowledge the vital role of all these reviewers:

Advocate Tekane Maqakachane
Doctor Michael Addaney
Doctor Simangele Daisy Mavundla
Doctor Martha Bradley
Doctor Sylvie Namwase
Doctor Rufaro Mavunga
Doctor Bonita Meyersfeld

Doctor Itumeleng Shale
Doctor Carol Chi Ngang
Doctor Nomalanga Mashinini
Doctor Mispa Roux
Doctor Kesolofetse Olivia Lefenya
Doctor Dr. Khulekani Moyo
Doctor Sanele Sibanda
Doctor Robert Doya Nanima
Doctor Akinola Akintayo
Doctor Caroline Nalule
Doctor Mwiza Nkhata
Doctor Ellah Siang'andu
Doctor Dr. Swikani Ncube
Ms. Angela Mudukuti
Ms. Samantha Barkley
Mr. Audu Mgbede Echono
Professor Jeremy Julia Sarkin
Professor Bonolo Dinokopila
Professor Angelo Dube
Professor Funmi T Abioye
Professor John-Mark Iyi
Professor Mtendeweka Mhango
Professor Avitus Agbor
Professor Lilian Chenwi
Professor Ouma Ba
Professor Vinodh Jaichand

Contents

Notes on Contributors

Muyiwa Adigun holds an LL.B. (First Class Honours) and an LL.M. (Distinction) both from University of Ibadan, Ibadan, Nigeria. He received his Doctor of Philosophy degree in law from the University of the Witwatersrand, Johannesburg. His research interests include jurisprudence, public law, international law and comparative law. He is the author of: *The International Criminal Court and Nigeria: Implementing the Complementarity Principle of the Rome Statute* (Abingdon, UK: Routledge/Taylor and Francis 2018). Between 2007 and 2015, he was in private legal practice as a Barrister and Solicitor of the Supreme Court of Nigeria. He was also a Post-doctoral Research Fellow, Department of Public and International Law, School of Law, University of Venda, Thohoyandou, South Africa between 2019 and 2020. He is currently a Senior Lecturer in the Faculty of Law, University of Ibadan, Ibadan, Nigeria.

Kasaija Phillip Apuuli is an Associate Professor of Political Science in the Department of Political Science and Public Administration, Makerere University Kampala. He holds a Doctor of Philosophy (D.Phil.) degree in International Law, University of Sussex at Brighton, UK. He was a British Academy Visiting Scholar at African Studies Centre, University of Oxford (2010); and a Fulbright Scholar-in-Residence, University of South Florida (St Petersburg) and Stetson School of Law (Gulfport), Florida, USA (2016). He specialized in the areas of International Criminal Law, Conflict Mediation, and Regional Integration (especially the

AU and EAC). He is the author of several book chapters and articles in refereed journals including *African Security Review*; *Criminal Law Forum*; *Journal of International Criminal Justice*; *Leiden Journal of International Law*, *African Security*; *African Yearbook of International Law*; and *Journal of Contemporary African Studies* among others.

Evelyne Owiye Asaala is a Lecturer of law at the University of Nairobi, she holds a Ph.D. from the University of Witwatersrand (South Africa), a Master of Laws degree from the University of Pretoria (South Africa) and a Bachelor of Laws degree from the University of Nairobi (Kenya). Evelyne has published widely in the area of international criminal law. She has previously consulted with the Trust Fund for Victims of the International Criminal Court, Saferworld International, the International Nuremberg Principles Academy, Truth Justice and Reconciliation Commission of Kenya (TJRC) and the Bail and Bond Task Force in Kenya.

James Carkeek obtained his Bachelor of Arts degree from Rhodes University, he then went on to complete his Honours degree jointly at Rhodes University and Utrecht University before returning to Rhodes to complete his LL.B. He went on to complete his Masters of Advanced Studies in Transitional Justice, Human Rights and the Rule of Law at the Geneva Academy. He has worked as an Intern and then later an Independent Contractor at the International Criminal Court and is currently a Pupil Member of the Pretoria Society of Advocates. His research interests include International Criminal Law, Human Rights Law and Rule of Law Jurisprudence in African states.

Ntombizozuko Dyani-Mhango holds LL.B. and LL.M. degrees from the University of the Western Cape (UWC) and Doctor of Juridical Science (SJD) degree from the University of Wisconsin-Madison. She is a Full Professor and Head of the Department of Public Law at the Faculty of Law of the University of Pretoria. She is rated as an established researcher by the National Research Foundation of South Africa. She is also an Admitted Advocate of the High Court of South Africa. Until recently, she held academic positions up to Associate Professorship at the University of the Witwatersrand teaching public international law, international criminal law and constitutional law to both undergraduate and graduate students. She has also clerked for former Chief Justice Ngcobo at the Constitutional Court of South Africa and was an intern (legal research) in the Chambers Section at the International Criminal Tribunal for Rwanda. It, therefore, is no surprise that her areas of specialization fall under International Law and Constitutional Law, with a focus on African Union Law, in particular member states obligations in international criminal justice, and South Africa's international and constitutional obligations. She has published widely and presented papers in about 30 international and national conferences in these areas. She is a sole contributing editor of a well-received Special Issue (book formatted) titled Twenty-First Century Constitutional Jurisprudence of South Africa: The Contribution of Former Chief Justice S Sandile Ngcobo, published in the *Southern African Public Law* 2017 (issues 1&2) volume. Dyani-Mhango was recently appointed as an inaugural fellow of the Pan African Scientific Research Council. She is also a member of the Law and Society Association (a member of its Governance Committee 2019-2021) and the African Society of International Law. She is a Managing Editor for the *South African Chapter— International Association of Women Judges Law Journal* to be launched in late 2021, a member of the Editorial Committee of the *Comparative & International Law Journal of Southern Africa*, and of the Editorial Board of the *Southern African Public Law*. She is also a member of the Advisory Board of the African Centre for Transitional Criminal Justice based at UWC's Faculty of Law. Dyani-Mhango was recognized as one of South Africa's *Mail & Guardian* Top 200 Young South Africans in 2013.

Ikebundu Francis Ekene studied Law at University of Nigeria, Nsukka (UNEC), in 2010. He was called to Nigerian Bar in 2012. Francis served the National Youth Service Corps (NYSC), Ilorin, Kwara State, upon the completion of service year he joined the firm of Chief Ayo Ajomole & Co. Chambers where he rose to become the Head of Chambers (HOC). He holds an LL.M. in common Law from University of Ilorin and currently a Ph.D. candidate under the supervision of Dr. Azubike Chinwuba Onuora-Oguno.

Christopher Gevers teaches international law and legal theory in the School of Law, University of KwaZulu-Natal. His research focusses on Black Internationalism, Third World Approaches to International Law, Critical Race Theory, and Law and Literature. Since 2015 he has been a faculty member of the Institute for Global Law & Policy at Harvard Law School and has been a visiting Fellow at the University of Oxford and Harvard Law School. His most recent publications appear in Craven,

Pahuja & Simpson (eds.) *International Law and the Cold War* (2019), Heller et al. (eds.) *Oxford Handbook of International Criminal Law* (2020) and the *London Review of International Law*.

Emma Charlene Lubaale is an Associate Professor at the Faculty of Law of Rhodes University. She has previously taught law at the University of Venda. Prior to this, she taught and researched law in the capacity of a Post-doctoral Research Fellow at the University of Pretoria's Institute of International and Comparative Law in Africa. She holds LL.D. and LL.M. degrees from the University of Pretoria. She obtained an LL.B. from Makerere University, a post-graduate diploma in legal practice from Uganda's Law Development Center and a post-graduate diploma in Higher Education from the University of KwaZulu-Natal. Her current areas of interest are: criminal law, international human rights law, international criminal law, women and children's rights. She is currently a member of the Organization of Women in Science for the Developing World, a member of the South African Young Academy of Science (SAYAS), a rated researcher by the National Research Foundation (NRF) of South Africa, a Fellow with the African Science Leadership Program and a member of the Research and Publication Committee of the Black Lawyers Association of South Africa. In January 2020 she was appointed by the NRF to serve on the NRF Standing Panel for the Humanities and Social Sciences (HSS) from 2020 to 2023. She has served as a law reviewer for publishers including Springer Nature, the Pretoria University Law Press, the *Journal of Sexual Aggression, Speculum Juris, De Jure, South African Crime Quarterly* and *Journal of Law, Society and Development*. She is widely published and has made several presentations at national and international conferences on critical issues in her fields of interest.

Suzgo Lungu has over 17 years of professional experience in the provision of legal advice to government in the area of public international law including international criminal law, international humanitarian law, international trade law, development law and international human rights law and various contexts of domestic law at both national and international levels. He has experience of working in 11 SADC countries on international criminal justice and business and human rights. He is currently a Programme Consultant for the Southern Africa Litigation Centre (SALC) in the International Justice and Business Human Rights Programme. Suzgo holds a Doctorate of Philosophy in Law from the University of

Witwatersrand, an LL.M. in Commercial Law (Cardiff University, UK), an LL.M. in International Human Rights Law (Notre Dame, USA), a Bachelor of Laws (Hons) degree (University of Malawi) and a certificate in Parliamentary Drafting (International Law Institute, Uganda). Suzgo is an appointed public notary and prescribed Legal Practitioner. He was called to the Malawi bar in 2003. He has litigation experience at both domestic and international settings including Courts of Malawi, South Africa, Zambia, Lesotho and Zimbabwe and also before international tribunals including the International Criminal Court and the African Court on Human and People's Rights. Suzgo's expertise includes contract and treaty negotiations and analysis, legal research and advisory, programme development or design and implementation. His research interests are in the area of public international law, international human rights law, development law, international humanitarian law, international trade law and international criminal law.

Siphosami Malunga is the Executive Director of the Open Society Initiative for Southern Africa (OSISA) and a human rights lawyer with extensive experience in justice and governance in Africa. He took the helm of OSISA in August of 2013; having previously worked with the United Nations Development Program (UNDP) as the senior governance advisor and regional program manager in the Regional Bureau for Africa. He managed UNDP's democratic governance program for Africa providing policy analysis and intellectual leadership to governance advisors in UNDP's Africa offices. Malunga joined the Department of Peacekeeping Operations in the UN's Transitional Administration in East Timor in 2000 as an advisor to the transitional minister of justice, and later as senior defence trial attorney with the UN Serious Crimes Tribunal. From 2003 to 2006 he worked with the UN in Afghanistan to rebuild the justice sector, before moving to UNDP's Governance Centre in Oslo where he led UNDP's effort to integrate conflict prevention in democratic governance policy and programming. In 2008, he moved to Johannesburg to work in UNDP's East and Southern Africa office until 2011. Malunga earned his LL.B. at the University of Zimbabwe in 1994 and a Masters in International Law (Cum Laude) from the University of Oslo, Norway in 2007. He is currently studying towards a doctoral degree in law (LL.D.) at the University of Witwatersrand. He is regular contributor on political and economic governance as well as human rights and accountability issues in national, regional and global publications.

Innocent Mung'omba is a Legal Assistant at Musa Dudhia and Company, a top tier law firm in Zambia which is part of the Africa Legal Network. He has a Bachelor of Laws Degree from the University of Zambia. As an emerging writer in the area of International Law, he continues to take keen interest in issues regarding the prosecution of international crimes on the African Continent. His 2019 undergraduate dissertation titled "The Application of Universal Jurisdiction in Africa: Exploring the Implications of Hissene Habre's Conviction in Senegal" has been hailed as a "great piece of scholarly writing" by academicians at the University of Zambia. Notable among these academicians are Dr. Ellah Siang'andu, the principal lecturer of International Law at the University of Zambia and Dr. O'Brien Kaaba, the Assistant Dean for legal research at the University of Zambia.

Linda Mushoriwa is a Post-doctoral Research Fellow at the University of Johannesburg, affiliated to the South African Research Chair in International Law. She obtained her Ph.D. degree from the University of KwaZulu-Natal. Her research interests are international criminal justice; international legal theory; postcolonial theory; women and children's rights and law and literature.

Josephine Ndagire is a Lecturer at the School of Law, Makerere University. Dr Ndagire worked with a number of local and international organizations, most recently, as Head of Training at the International Nuremberg Principles Academy (Germany), Director of Legal Services at the Foundation for Human Rights Initiative (Uganda) and as a Senior Researcher at the Max Planck Institute for Foreign and International Criminal Law (Germany). Her publications include a book titled *National Redress for 'Gendered' International Crimes: Uganda, Germany and the International Criminal System*, Verlag Dr. Kovac, Hamburg, 2015.1 She also conceptualized and co-published *Cooperation between Civil Society Actors and Judicial Mechanisms during Prosecution of Conflict-Related Sexual Violence: Guiding Principles and Recommendations*, International Nuremberg Principles Academy, April 2017. She holds a Doctor of Juridical Science (SJD) degree from Emory University (US), a Master of Laws (LLM) degree from the University of Notre Dame (US) and a Bachelor of Laws degree from Makerere University.

Oluwabunmi Niyi-Gafar is currently a Senior Lecturer at the department of Jurisprudence and International law, in the Faculty of Law,

University of Ilorin, Ilorin Kwara state. Bunmi, as she is commonly referred to, holds an LL.D. (2017) from the University of Pretoria, South Africa and an LL.M. (2008) from the University of Ibadan, Oyo State Nigeria. Her areas of research interest are access to domestic water in Africa, Disability Rights, International Human rights and Criminal Justice.

Azubike Chinwuba Onuora-Oguno holds an LL.D. from the Centre for Human Rights at the University of Pretoria. He is a graduate of the Prestigious LL.M. in Human Rights and Democratisation in Africa at the University of Pretoria. Azubike was a former law clerk in the Information and Evidence Unit of the Office of the Prosecutor, International Criminal Court. He is fellow of the Visiting Professional Program at the OSgoode Hall Law School Canada. He delivered the Dean's Lunch time Lecture at the Thurgood Marshal Law School, Houston, Texas and a Speaker at the American Society of International Law. Azubike coordinates an International Research Collaboration group of the Law and Society Association. He is the Secretary General of the International Public Law Society, Nigeria Chapter and the Assistant Secretary of the Nigerian Society of International Law. He is currently a Senior Lecturer at the Department of Jurisprudence and International Law, Faculty of Law University of Ilorin and a teaching research fellow at the International Institute of Social Studies, The Netherlands.

Daniel Ronald Ruhweza is a Ugandan and UK trained Attorney and Lecturer at Law. Daniel obtained his Bachelor of Laws Degree from Makerere University, Master of Laws Degree from the University of Cambridge in England and Doctor of Philosophy from the University of Kent at Cambridge in England. He also received a Higher diploma in Peace and Security from Uppsala University in Sweden. He is a Lecturer with the Department of Law and Jurisprudence at law at Makerere University where he teaches constitutional law, international law and the law of treaties. He serves as the Chair of the Committee of Rule of Law and Strategic Litigation of the Uganda Law Society as well as representing the Uganda Law Society on the Committee on Legal Education and Training of the Uganda Law Council.

Charmika Samaradiwakera-Wijesundara is a Lecturer at the University of the Witwatersrand, Johannesburg (Wits) School of Law. Prior to which she was a Research and Teaching Associate at the Wits School of Law and associated researcher of the Business and Human Rights Programme of the Centre for Applied Legal Studies. She completed her articles of clerkship in the Corporate and Commercial Law Department of Edward Nathan Sonnebergs Inc (subsequently ENSafrica) and is an admitted attorney of the High Court of South Africa. She graduated her LL.B. (with distinction) and LL.M. (by dissertation) at Wits. She is currently a Ph.D. candidate on a joint programme with Wits and the International Institute of Social Sciences in The Hague. She was the vice-president of the Law Students' Council and awarded the Law School Endowment Appeal Prize by Wits. She is an Abe Bailey Fellow, member of the Golden Key International Honour Society and a graduate of the Robben Island Young Leaders Academy.

Abbreviations and Acronyms

AC	African Commission
ACJHPR	African Court of Justice and Human and Peoples Rights
AFISM-CAR/MISCA	African-Led International Support Mission in the Central African Republic
African Charter	African Charter on Human and Peoples Rights
APII	Protocol Additional to the Geneva Conventions of 12 August 1949 and Relating to the Protection of Victims of Non-International Armed Conflicts
ARCSS	Agreement on the Resolution of the Conflict in the Republic of South Sudan
ASP	Assembly of State Parties to the Rome Statute
ATCS	Alien Tort Claims Statute
AU	African Union
AU PSC	AU Peace and Security Council
AZAPO	Azanian People's Organization
BHR	Business and Human Rights
CAR	Central African Republic
CC	Constitutional Court
CFRN	Constitution of the Federal Republic of Nigeria
CID	Criminal Investigation Department
CIO	Central Intelligence Organisation
CNT	National Transitional Council
CoM	Committee of Ministers
CPA	Criminal Procedure Act
CSOs	Civil Society Organizations
DEIC	Dutch East India Company

DRC	The Democratic Republic of the Congo
EAC	Extraordinary African Chambers
ECCAS	Extra-Ordinary Summit of Heads of State and Government of the Economic Community of Central African States
ECOWAS	Court for the Economic Community of West African States
ECtHR	European Court on Human Rights
EIC	East India Company
GoU	Government of Uganda
HCSS	Hybrid Court for South Sudan
HRW	Human Rights Watch
HURIWA	Human Rights Writers Association of Nigeria
IActHR	Inter-American Court of Human Rights
ICC	International Criminal Court
ICCPR	International Covenant on Civil and Political Rights
ICD	International Crimes Division
ICJ	International Court of Justice
ICL	International Criminal Law
ICRC	International Committee of the Red Cross
ICTJ	The International Centre for Transitional Justice
ICTR	International Criminal Tribunal for Rwanda
ICTY	International Criminal Tribunal for Former Yugoslavia
IDPs	Internally Displaced Persons
IGAD	Intergovernmental Authority on Development
IHAT	Iraq Historic Allegations Team
IHL	International Humanitarian Law
ILC	International Law Commission
IMT	International Military Tribunal
IMTFE	International Military Tribunal for the Far East
LOCJ	Law on the Organization, Functioning and Jurisdiction of the Courts
LRA	Lord's Resistance Army
Malabo Protocol	Protocol on Amendments to the Protocol on the Statute of the African Court of Justice and Human Rights
MINUSCA	United Nations Multidimensional Integrated Stabilization Mission in the Central African Republic
MoI	Memorandum of Intent
MONUSCO	Mission in the Democratic Republic of the Congo
MOSOP	Movement for the Survival of the Ogoni People
MP	Member of Parliament
NCFR	National Commission for Refugees

NDPP	National Director of Prosecutions
NEMA	National Emergency Management Agency
NGOs	Non-Government Organisations
NIACs	Non-International Armed Conflicts
NPA	National Prosecuting Authority
NPC	Nigerian Petroleum Company
NPRC	National Peace and Reconciliation Commission
OAS	Organisation of American States
OAU	Organization of the African Unity
OTP	Office of the Prosecutor
PRC	Permanent Representative Committee
PTC	Pre-Trial Chamber
RDP	Royal Dutch-Petroleum
RNC	Royal Niger Company
Rome Statute/Statute	The Rome Statute of the International Criminal Court, 17 July 1998, came in force on 1 July 2002, United Nations, Treaty Series, vol. 2187, No. 38544
RoSS	Republic of South Sudan
RPE	Rules of Procedure and Evidence
RS	Rome Statute
RTGoNU	Revitalized Transitional Government of National Unity
SADC	South African Development Community
SCC	Special Criminal Court
SEMA	State Emergency Management Agency
Shell	Royal Dutch Shell
SPDC	Shell Petroleum Development Corporation
SPLM/A-IG	Sudan People's Liberation Movement/Army-In Government
SPLM/A-IO	Sudan People's Liberation Movement/Army-In Opposition
STL	Special Tribunal of Lebanon
TRC/TC	Truth and Reconciliation Commissions (also known as Truth Commissions)
UAC	United Africa Company
UFDR	Union of Democratic Forces for Unity
UK	United Kingdom
UN	United Nations
UNC	United Nations Charter
UNCAT	United Nations Convention against Torture and Other Cruel Inhuman or Degrading Treatment or Punishment, 1984
UNICEF	United Nations Children's Emergency Fund
UNMISS	The United Nations Mission in South Sudan

UNSC	United Nations Security Council
USA	United States of America
UTMs	Urgent Temporary Measures
WTO	World Trade Organisation
WWII	World-War II
ZANU	Zimbabwe African National Union
ZAPU	Zimbabwe African Peoples Union
ZNA	Zimbabwe National Army

Introduction: Relevance of Debates on National Accountability for International Crimes in Africa

Emma Charlene Lubaale and Ntombizozuko Dyani-Mhango

1 Introduction

> In this new age of accountability, those who commit the worst of human crimes will be held responsible. Whether they are rank-and-file foot soldiers or military commanders … whether they are lowly civil servants following orders, or top political leaders … they will be held accountable.[1]

[1]See, United Nations General Assembly, *Secretary-General's 'Age of Accountability' address to the Review Conference on the International Criminal Court*, Kampala, 31 May 2010, SG/SM/12930L/3158, available at https://www.un.org/sg/en/content/sg/speeches/2010-05-31/address-review-conference-international-criminal-court-age (accessed on 11 July 2021).

E. C. Lubaale (✉)
Faculty of Law, Rhodes University, Grahamstown, South Africa
e-mail: e.lubaale@ru.ac.za

N. Dyani-Mhango
Faculty of Law, University of Pretoria, Pretoria, South Africa
e-mail: ntombizozuko.dyani-mhango@up.ac.za

E. C. Lubaale and N. Dyani-Mhango (eds.), *National Accountability for International Crimes in Africa*,
https://doi.org/10.1007/978-3-030-88044-6_1

These are the words of the then United Nations (UN) Secretary-General, Ban Ki Moon, uttered in Kampala, Uganda, when Assembly of States Parties to the Rome Statute of the International Criminal Court (ICC) met in the review conference of the Rome Statute. These words echo the international criminal justice expectation for individual criminal responsibility of perpetrators including commanders and subordinates,[2] and confirming that international crimes are not perpetrated by abstract entities but by individuals.[3] International criminal tribunals,[4]

[2] See, for example, arts 25 (on individual criminal responsibility) and 28 (on the '[r]esponsibility of commanders and other superiors') of the Rome Statute of the International Criminal Court, 17 July 1998, 2187 U.N.T.S. 90 (entered into force on 1 July 2002) (Rome Statute).

[3] See, *IMT* Judgment (1947) 41 *American Journal of International Law* 172 221, holding that '[c]rimes against international law are committed by men, not by abstract entities, and only by punishing individuals who commit such crimes can the provisions of international law be enforced'.

[4] The International Criminal Tribunal for the former Yugoslavia (the ICTY) was established to prosecute 'Persons Responsible for Serious Violations of International Humanitarian Law Committed in the Territory of the Former Yugoslavia since 1991,' S.C. Res. 827 (25 May 1993). The Statute of the ICTY is contained in UN Doc. S/25704, Anne, x (3 May 1993), and the International Criminal Tribunal for Rwanda (the ICTR) was established for the 'Prosecution of Persons Responsible for Genocide and Other Serious Violations of International Humanitarian Law Committed in the Territory of Rwanda and Rwandan Citizens Responsible for Genocide and Other Violations in the Territory of Neighboring States, between 1 Jan. 1994 and 31 Dec. 1994,' SC Res. 955 (8 Nov. 1994). The Statute of the ICTR is attached to SC Res. 955 as an annex. The notable cases from the ICTY are *Prosecutor v Dusko Tadic,* Judgment, IT-94-1-T, 7 May 1997 (war crimes and crimes against humanity); *Prosecutor v Kunarac*, Judgment, IT-96–23 &-IT-96–23/1-A, 12 June 2002 (war crimes, crimes against humanity in the form of torture and rape); and *Prosecutor* v *Furundžija*, IT-95–17/1-T, Judgment, 10 December 1998 (war crimes in the form of rape and torture); and the notable cases of the ICTR are *Prosecutor v Akayesu*, Judgment, 2 September 1998, ICTR—96-13-T (convicted of genocide and crimes against humanity including rape); and *Prosecutor v Ferdinand Nahimana, Jean-Bosco Barayagwiza, and Hassan Ngeze*, Judgment, 3 December 2003, ICTR-99-52-T (convicted of genocide and crimes against humanity).

special courts[5] and the International Criminal Court (ICC)[6] have held accountable perpetrators of these crimes. But that is just one side of national accountability for international crimes. States are also accountable to their citizens by ensuring that the perpetrators of international crimes are prosecuted and convicted, and to prevent their reoccurrence. In his explanation of the meaning of accountability in relation to those who exercise public function, Okpaluba opines that.

> [accountability] means an obligation that one is bound in law or in justice to perform. In effect, accountability is an elastic, all embracing word such that where a functionary is said to be accountable, it means that they must be answerable and responsible both politically and legally as well as being morally bound. Above all, the functionary is liable in terms of the law...[7]

At the heart of national accountability for international crimes is the principle of complementarity that is found in the Rome Statute provisions. Newton has argued that this principle 'is designed to serve as a pragmatic and limiting principle rather than an affirmative means for an aggressive prosecutor to target the nationals of states that are hesitant to embrace ICC jurisdiction and authority'.[8] Accordingly, the ICC acts as a supranational court as the principle of complementarity gives states

[5] The Special Court for Sierra Leone (the SCSL) was established through an agreement between the United Nations and the Government of Sierra Leone by UN Security Council Resolution 1315 (2000), 14 August 2000, S/RES/1315 (2000), 'to try those who bear the greatest responsibility for serious violations of international humanitarian law and Sierra Leonean law committed in the territory of Sierra Leone since 30 November 1996' (art 1(1) of the Statute of the SCSL). The notable conviction from the SCSL is *Prosecutor v Charles Ghankay Taylor*, Judgment, 26 September 2013, SCSL-03-01-A (war crimes including rape).

[6] See, for example, *Prosecutor v Bosco Ntaganda*, Judgment, 8 July 2019, CC-01/04-02/06-2359 (war crimes and crimes against humanity, including rape and sexual slavery).

[7] CM Okpaluba 'The Constitutional Principle of Accountability: A Study of Contemporary South African Case Law' (2018) 33(1) *Southern African Public Law* 1, 7.

[8] MA Newton '*The Complementarity Conundrum: Are We Watching Evolution or Evisceration?*' (2010) 8 *Santa Clara Journal of International Law* 115, 123. See also Xavier Philippe 'The principles of universal jurisdiction and complementarity: how do the two principles intermesh?' (2006) 88: 862 *International Review of the Red Cross* 375, 381, where he explains the complementarity principle as 'a means of attributing primacy of jurisdiction to national courts but includes a "safety net" allowing the ICC to review the exercise of jurisdiction if the conditions specified by the Statute are met'.

primary jurisdiction[9] to deal with the prosecution of international crimes dependent on certain conditions as outlined in the Rome Statute.[10]

As the court of last resort, the ICC makes the final determination on the inadmissibility of the case before it.[11] There are three factual scenarios the ICC will look at when making its determination. Firstly, the ICC will determine whether 'the case is being investigated or prosecuted' by the state in question.[12] Secondly, the ICC will determine whether '[t]he case has been investigated by [the state concerned] and the [s]tate has decided not to prosecute the person concerned'.[13] Lastly, the ICC will determine whether 'the person concerned has already been tried for conduct which is the subject of the complaint'.[14] The first two scenarios follow a two-prong process: firstly, the ICC determines if there is an investigation or prosecution, and whether once the investigation was done the state decided not to prosecute. If the answer is in the affirmative, the second stage moves to determine whether the state in question is 'unwilling or unable genuinely to carry out the investigation or prosecution',[15] or 'the decision resulted from the unwillingness or inability of the State genuinely to prosecute'.[16] This two-prong process was confirmed in the *Katanga Appeal Judgment*.[17]

The third scenario applies when the state in question has already tried a person in its jurisdiction for an international crime. The ICC determines whether the trial in question dealt with a similar conduct as that which

[9] See art 1 of the Rome Statute, which further reinforce that the national courts will be given primacy over the ICC to deal with perpetrators of international crimes.

[10] See art 17 of the Rome Statute titled: 'Issues of admissibility'.

[11] Art 19(1) of the Rome Statute enjoins the ICC to 'satisfy itself that it has jurisdiction in any case brought before it' and 'may, on its own motion, determine the admissibility of a case in accordance with article 17 [of the Rome Statute]'.

[12] Art 17(1)(a) of the Rome Statute.

[13] Art 17(1)(b) of the Rome Statute.

[14] Art 17(1)(c) of the Rome Statute.

[15] Art 17(1)(a) of the Rome Statute,

[16] Art 17(1)(b) of the Rome Statute.

[17] *The Prosecutor v Germain Katanga and Mathieu Ngudjolo Chui, Judgment on the Appeal of Mr. Germain Katanga against the Oral Decision of Trial Chamber II of 12 June 2009 on the Admissibility of the Case*, Case No. ICC-01/04-01/07 OA 8, 25 September 2009, para 78.

is under an investigation by the ICC Prosecutor. In this regard, the ICC Appeals Chamber in the *Gaddafi Admissibility Judgment* explained that:

> The real issue is, therefore, the degree of overlap required as between the incidents being investigated by the Prosecutor and those being investigated by a State - with the focus being upon whether the conduct is substantially the same. Again, this will depend upon the facts of the individual case. If there is a large overlap between the incidents under investigation, it may be clear that the State is investigating substantially the same conduct; if the overlap is smaller, depending upon the precise facts, it may be that the State is still investigating substantially the same conduct or that it is investigating only a very small part of the Prosecutor's case. ... Alternatively, they may be very minor when compared with the case as a whole.[18]

The ICC may also consider issues of due process such as shielding the perpetrator; undue delays; and judicial independence and impartiality to determine whether the affected state is unwilling to prosecute.[19] The above discussion demonstrates that there are specific circumstances under which the ICC may claim jurisdiction over alleged perpetrators. Other than those circumstances, states have primacy to investigate and prosecute perpetrators of international crimes.[20]

The principle of complementarity makes logical sense from a practical point of view. Notably, national criminal jurisdictions are better placed to preside over proceedings considering their proximity to evidence, witnesses and the scenes of crimes in comparison with the ICC. And as Oko aptly submits, 'nothing emphasises legitimacy of a new regime and deepens the rule of law more than criminal prosecutions undertaken in venues where the crimes occurred'.[21] Moreover, the ICC does not have the resources to prosecute all the international crimes committed globally. As Kleffner has argued, accountability for international crimes

[18] *Gaddafi Admissibility Judgment "Judgment on the appeal of Libya against the decision of Pre-Trial Chamber I of 31 May 2013 entitled 'Decision on the admissibility of the case against Saif Al-Islam Gaddafi'", ICC-01/11-01/11-547- Red,* para 72.

[19] Art 17(2) of the Rome Statute.

[20] See Preamble to the Rome Statute which 'affirm[s] that the most serious crimes of concern to the international community as a whole must not go unpunished and that their effective prosecution must be ensured by taking measures at the national level'.

[21] O Oko 'The Challenges of International Criminal Prosecutions in Africa' (2007)31 *Fordham International Law Journal* 372.

under the Rome Statute can hardly be realised if states leave the burden of prosecution to the ICC.[22]

Worthy to note, the establishment of a permanent international criminal court meant that the Court's intervention in the affairs of African states was imminent. This brought sharply into focus the issue of state sovereignty.[23] While the Court's intervention at first glance came as a threat to state sovereignty, these concerns were soothed by the principle of complementarity which balanced sovereignty with the ICC's intervention. The strong presumption in favour of states exercising jurisdiction over crimes in their territories meant that there would be limited interference by an international criminal court into the affairs of a state as long as there was commitment to investigation and prosecution of crimes in national jurisdictions. Stahn explains that states were open to the idea of a permanent international criminal court under the Rome Statute regime because the ICC would remain a court of last resort, with the bulk of prosecutions taking place in national courts.[24] In this regard, Okuta describes the notion of complementarity as a tool that 'aims to recognise but at the

[22] J Kleffner 'Auto-Referrals and the Complementary Nature of the ICC' In C Stahn and G Sluiter, *The Emerging Practice of the ICC* (2009) 41–53.

[23] The right to exercise criminal jurisdiction within a state's territory is a key element of state sovereignty. It must be noted; however, that this right is subject to exceptions, with states' commitment to the Rome Statute being one such instance when this right may be limited. Moreover, state sovereignty comes with obligations towards citizens and responsibilities regarding protection of citizens. On this see F Deng et al., *Sovereignty as responsibility* (1996); R Cyer 'International Criminal Law vs State Sovereignty: Another Round?' (2005)16 *European Journal of International Law* 979–1000. However, see works of authors who conceptualise international criminal justice as antagonistic to state sovereignty. B Broomhall, *International Justice and the International Criminal Court: Between Sovereignty and the Rule of Law* (2003) viii and 215; Lattimer, M and Philippe S (eds) Justice for Crimes Against Humanity (2003) xv and 512; Nadya SL *The International Criminal Court and the Transformation of International Law: Justice for the New Millennium* (2002) xviii, 566; Sands, P (ed) *From Nuremberg to the Hague: The Future of International Criminal Justice* (2003) 192; Ward, I *Justice. Humanity and the New World Order* (2003) 183; M Alkrisheh & W Mahameed 'The International Criminal Court Statute and State Sovereignty: The Implicit Impact of the Complementarity Principle' (2020) *6 Multicultural Education* 1–7.

[24] C Stahn, 'Complementarity: A tale of Two Notions' (2008)19 *Criminal Law Forum* 87–113.

same time set limits to state sovereignty.'[25] This position finds confirmation in the Report of the Ad-Hoc Committee on the Establishment of the ICC providing that:

> The principle of complementarity reconciles two competing features and jurisdictions. The first is State sovereignty, which claims national jurisdiction over its citizens or those crimes committed on its territory, even though these crimes are of an international character and may fall under the international jurisdiction. The second feature only functions in exceptional circumstances and gives an international tribunal jurisdiction over these heinous crimes.[26]

Based on the premise that ICC would only intervene when there was no accountability at the national level, the complementarity framework was well-received by states, including those on the African continent. Complementarity became a motivation for states' commitment to and support for the Rome Statute regime. Indeed, African states played a key role in the establishment of the ICC. They featured prominently in the ratification of the Rome Statute which saw the ICC come into operation in 2002. Senegal is on record for being one of the countries that first ratified the Rome Statute.[27] Several other African states followed suit, and currently, 33 African states (representing 60% of the African continent) are party to the Rome Statute.[28] With such wide ratification, Africa also has the biggest representation of parties to the Rome Statute globally.

Demonstrating their preparedness to make the Rome Statute regime operational in national courts, several African states such as Uganda, Kenya and South Africa have taken steps to domesticate the Rome

[25] AA Okuta, *Smallest share of the pie? Accountability for international crimes at the domestic level: case studies of Kenya, Uganda and Côte d'Ivoire* (2016 PhD Thesis Amsterdam Center for International Law) 46.

[26] Report of the Ad-Hoc Committee on the Establishment of an International Criminal Court, UN GAOR, 50th Session, Supp No 22, at p. 50, UN Doc. A/50/22(1995), 905.

[27] International Criminal Court, "The States parties to the Rome Statute", https://asp.icc-cpi.int/en_menus/asp/states%20parties/pages/the%20states%20parties%20to%20the%20rome%20statute.aspx, (accessed on 8 July 2021).

[28] As above.

Statute.[29] A considerable number of African states have also established judicial structures for the prosecution of international crimes, with proceedings ongoing in some states.[30] For example, Uganda established a judicial structure devoted to prosecution of international crimes, namely the International Crimes Division of the High Court.[31] The division has jurisdiction over crimes including genocide, war crimes, crimes against humanity, terrorism, piracy and human trafficking.[32] The case against Thomas Kwoyelo, a former Lord's Resistance Army commander, is thus far before the International Crimes Division. The Central Africa Republic also established a judicial structure in the form of the Special Criminal Court, and South Africa has been confirmed to be capable of investigating and prosecuting international crimes in her territory.[33]

African states have also shown support for the work of the ICC by referring cases to the ICC for trial.[34] Uganda's referral of its situation to the ICC, for example, was one of the cases that gave life to the operations of the ICC in its early stages.[35] While the intentions of African states in referring cases to the ICC may be questionable, it is undeniable that African states have, in this regard, cooperated with the ICC.[36] Africa's commitment to supporting the ICC and the Rome Statute regime, at

[29] See, e.g., domesticating laws of Uganda, Kenya and South Africa, i.e. The International Criminal Court Act 2010 of Uganda, International Crimes Act 2008 of Kenya and the Implementation of the Rome Statute of the International Criminal Court Act 27 of 2002 of South Africa.

[30] See, e.g., the International Crimes Division of the High Court of Uganda established in 2008 and the Hybrid Special Criminal Court of the Central African Republic established in 2015.

[31] International Crimes Division of the High Court (formerly War Crimes Division), established by an administrative decree in 2008, Legal Notice Number 10 of 2011.

[32] High Court (International crimes Division) Practice Direction, 2011 para 6.

[33] *National Commissioner of the South African Police Service v Southern African Human Rights Litigation Centre and Another* 2015 (1) SA 315 (CC); 2015 (1) SACR 255 (CC).

[34] International Criminal Court, Situations and cases, (2021), https://www.icc-cpi.int/pages/situation.aspx (accessed on 8 July 2021). As per the ICC website, up to 5 situations before the ICC including Uganda's, the Democratic Republic of the Congo's, the Central African Republic's, Mali's and Cote d' Ivoire's are self-referrals.

[35] As above.

[36] O Ba *States of Justice: The politics of the international criminal court* (2020 Cambridge University Press) 8. Ba is of the view that 'most of the ICC cases in African states were initiated by the states themselves, when their respective governments approached the Court to self-refer cases to the ICC prosecutor. This illustrates the fact

least in its early stages, is therefore uncontested. This is significant as absence of commitment from states parties would render the Rome Statute and the ICC meaningless with regard to the fight against impunity for international crimes.

States parties are also expected to cooperate with ICC requests to arrest and surrender suspects to it should they not be able to prosecute those alleged perpetrators.[37] However, there has been tensions between the AU (and its member states) and the ICC, which stem from the ICC's indictment of sitting heads of state not party to the Rome Statute.[38] As a result, the AU adopted several resolutions condemning this move by encouraging its member states not to cooperate with ICC requests[39]

that the ICC was in any case bound to be a political tool at the hand of states—not only great powers, but also African states—in their attempt to settle scores.

[37] See article 86 of the Rome Statute on cooperation by states parties. For further discussion on states parties failure to cooperate see, N Dyani-Mhango 'The ICC Pre-Trial Chamber's Decision on South Africa's Failure to Arrest and Surrender South Africa: South Africa Escapes 'Sanctions'' 2017 *African Yearbook of International Humanitarian Law* 37; and S Lungu & N Dyani-Mhango 'Ensuring that State Parties to the Rome Statute Co-operate with ICC Requests to Arrest and Surrender Suspects: Reflecting on the Role of the Security Council through the Lens of the Responsibility to Protect (R2P)' (2018) *African Yearbook of International Humanitarian Law* 119'.

[38] See, for example, *Prosecutor v Omar Hassan Ahmad Al Bashir*, ICC-02/05-01/09; *Prosecutor v Omar Hassan Ahmad Al Bashir*, ICC-02/05-01/09-1, Warrant of Arrest, (Mar. 4, 2009); *Prosecutor v Omar Hassan Ahmad Al Bashir*, ICC-02/05-01/09-95, Second Warrant of Arrest, (July 12, 2010); and *Situation in The Libyan Arab Jamahiriya, Warrant of Arrest for Muammar Mohammed Abu Minyar Gaddafi*, ICC-01/11-13, 27 June 2011.

[39] See, for example, *Decision on the Implementation of the Assembly Decisions on the International Criminal Court*, Assembly of the Union, Seventeenth Ordinary Session, EX.CL/670(XIX), Assembly/AU/Dec.366(XVII) (July 1, 2011) (where the AU Assembly instructed the AU member states not to cooperate with the execution of the arrest warrant of Gaddafi and reaffirmed that by receiving President Al Bashir, Kenya and Djibouti were discharging their obligations under art 23(2) of the AU Constitutive Act of the African Union art. 6(1) & (2), July 11, 2000, 2158 U.N.T.S. 3; *Decision on the Application by the International Criminal Court Prosecutor for the Indictment of the President of the Republic of the Sudan*, Assembly of the Union, Twelfth Ordinary Session, Assembly/AU/Dec.221(XII) para 1, (where the AU Assembly expressed 'its deep concern' of the ICC Prosecutor's indictment of President Al Bashir; *Decision of the Meeting of African States Parties to the Rome Statute of the International Criminal Court*, Assembly of the Union, Thirteenth Ordinary Session, Assembly/AU/13 (XIII), para 10; see also *Decision On The International Criminal Court, Assembly of the Union*, Twenty-Sixth Ordinary Session, EX.CL/952(XXVIII), Assembly/AU/Dec.590(XXVI) paras 3–4 (where it commended South Africa 'for complying with the Decisions of the Assembly

and a withdrawal strategy.[40] Consequently, the ICC has found several African states, who are also party to the Rome Statute in breach of their international obligations to arrest and surrender suspects to the ICC.[41] Literature on these ICC decisions[42] and the tension between the AU and

on non-cooperation with the arrest and surrender of President Omar Al Bashir of The Sudan and [decided] that by receiving President Bashir, [South Africa] was implementing various AU Assembly [d]ecisions on the warrants of arrest issued by the ICC against President Bashir and that South Africa was consistent with its obligations under international law [and reiterated] its decision on the need for all Member States to comply with the Assembly [d]ecisions on the warrants of arrest issued by the ICC against President Al Bashir of The Sudan pursuant to Article 23 (2) of the Constitutive Act of the African Union and Article 98 of the Rome Statute of the ICC').

[40] See, African Union, Assembly of States, *Decision on the International Criminal Court*, Doc/EX.CL/1006 (XXX), Twenty-Eighth Ordinary Session, 30–31 January 2017, Addis Ababa, Ethiopia. See also, PI Labuda 'The African Union's Collective Withdrawal from the ICC: Does Bad Law make for Good Politics?' EJIL: Talk! 15 February 2017, available at https://www.ejiltalk.org/the-african-unions-collective-withdrawal-from-the-icc-does-bad-law-make-for-good-politics/ (last accessed on 12 July 2021).

[41] See, for example, the *Corrigendum to the Decision Pursuant to Article 87(7) of the Rome Statute on the Failure by the Republic of Malawi to Comply with the Cooperation Requests Issued by the Court with Respect to the Arrest and Surrender of Omar Hassan Ahmad Al Bashir*, ICC-02/05-01/09-139-Corr, 13 December 2011; *Decision Pursuant to Article 87(7) of the Rome Statute on the Refusal of the Republic of Chad to Comply with the Cooperation Requests Issued by the Court with Regard to the Arrest and Surrender of Omar Hassan Ahmad Al Bashir*, ICC-02/05-01/09-140, 13 December 2011; *Decision on the Non-Compliance of the Republic of Chad with the Cooperation Requests Issued by the Court Regarding the Arrest and Surrender of Omar Hassan Ahmad Al Bashir*, ICC-02/05-01/09-151, 26 March 2013; *Decision on the Cooperation of the Federal Republic of Nigeria Regarding Omar Al Bashir's Arrest and Surrender to the Court*, ICC-02/05-01/09-159, 5 September 2013; *Decision on the Cooperation of the Democratic Republic of the Congo Regarding Omar Al Bashir's Arrest and Surrender to the Court* ICC-02/05-01/09-195, 4 April 2014; *Decision on the non-compliance by the Republic of Djibouti with the request to arrest and surrender Omar Al-Bashir to the Court and referring the matter to the United Nations Security Council and the Assembly of the State Parties to the Rome Statute*, ICC-02/05-01/09-266, 11 July 2016; and, *Decision on the Non-Compliance by the Republic of Uganda with the Request to Arrest and Surrender Omar Al-Bashir to the Court and Referring the Matter to the United Nations Security Council and the Assembly of States Parties to the Rome Statute*, ICC-02/05-01/09-267, 11 July 2016; *Decision under article 87(7) of the Rome Statute on the non-compliance by South Africa with the request by the Court for the arrest and surrender of Omar Al-Bashir*, ICC-02/05-01/09-302, 06 July 2017; and *Prosecutor v Omar Hassan Ahmad Al Bashir (Decision under article 87(7) of the Rome Statute on the non-compliance by Jordan with the request by the Court for the arrest and surrender of Omar Al-Bashir)*, ICC-02/05-01/09-309, 11 December 2017.

[42] See, for example, N Dyani-Mhango 'South Africa's Dilemma: Immunity Laws, International Obligations and the Visit by Sudan's President Omar Al Bashir' (2017) 26

the ICC and how the ICC (mis) treats or targets African leaders in the last decade is immeasurable.[43]

For non-state parties like Libya and Sudan, the situation is somewhat complex. Article 13(b) of the Rome Statute permits the UN Security Council to refer a situation which involves a non-state party to the ICC and thereby trigger the ICC jurisdiction.[44] This has also been the subject of scholarly debates.[45] The ICC Appeals Chamber in the *Kingdom of Jordan Appeals Case* has made a final determination on this debate as it

(3) *Washington International Law Journal* 535; D Tladi 'The Duty of South Africa to Arrest and Surrender Al Bashir under South African and International Law: A Perspective from International Law' (2015) 13 (5) *Journal of International Criminal Justice* 102; D Tladi, 'The ICC Decisions on Chad and Malawi: on Cooperation, Immunities and Article 98' (2013) 11 (1) *Journal of International Criminal Justice* 199; N Dyani-Mhango, 'The ICC Pre-Trial Chamber's decision on South Africa's failure to arrest and Surrender President Al Bashir: South Africa escapes 'sanctions'! (2017) *African Yearbook of International Humanitarian Law.* 37; N Dyani-Mhango 'The ICC Pre-Trial Chamber's decision on Malawi regarding the failure to arrest and surrender President Al Bashir of Sudan: An opportunity missed' (2013) 28 SA Public Law 106; D Akande 'ICC Issues Detailed Decision on Bashir's Immunity (... At Long Last ...) But Gets the Law Wrong' Blog of the European Journal of International Law, 15 December 2011, available at http://www.ejiltalk.org/icc-issues-detailed-decision-on-bashir%E2%80%99s-immunity-at-long-last-but-gets-the-law-wrong/ (accessed on 15 March 2018); and Dov Jacobs 'A Sad Hommage to Antonio Cassese: The ICC's Confused Pronouncements on State Compliance and Head of State Immunity' Spreading the Jam, 15 December 2011), available at https://dovjacobs.com/2011/12/15/a-sad-hommage-to-antonio-cassese-the-iccs-confused-pronouncements-on-state-compliance-and-head-of-state-immunity/ (accessed on 15 March 2018).

[43] See, for example, contributions in VO Nmehielle (Ed) *Africa and the Future of International Criminal Justice* (2012), and in particular, N Dyani 'Is the International Criminal Court Targeting Africa? Reflections on the Enforcement of International Criminal Law in Africa' in Nmehielle as above, 185; and D Chuter 'The ICC: A Place for Africans or Africans in their Place?' in Nmehielle as above, 161.

[44] See art 13(b) of the Rome Statute, which stipulates 'The [ICC] may exercise its jurisdiction with respect to a crime referred to in article 5 in accordance with the provisions of this Statute if: (b) A situation in which one or more of such crimes appears to have been committed is referred to the Prosecutor by the Security Council acting under Chapter VII of the Charter of the United Nations'. See, also, S.C. Res. 1593, para 1 (31 March 2005), where the Security Council resolved to refer the Darfur situation to the ICC.

[45] See, for example, the debate between Paola Gaeta 'Does President Al Bashir enjoy immunity from arrest?' (2009) 7 *Journal of International Criminal Justice* 315; and Dapo Akande 'The legal nature of the Security Council referrals to the ICC and its impact on Al Bashir's immunities' (2009) 7 *Journal of International Criminal Justice* 333, where these authors debate the consequences of the Security Council referral to the ICC.

held that Sudan is under obligation to comply with the ICC demands in terms of the UN Charter despite it not being party to the Rome Statute.[46] It can be argued that this position by the ICC on Security Council referrals of non-state parties has had a catalysing effect on states that are not party to it, as these non-state parties have set up institutions that may effectively bar the ICC from exercising jurisdiction over international crimes committed in their territories.

Earlier writings predicted that the coming into force of the ICC would have a catalysing effect on states but it remained to be seen how this would play out when non-state parties to the Rome Statute were involved.[47] The Security Council's referral of the Libyan situation to the ICC has demonstrated the reality of this with national criminal proceedings in Libya being testament. For example, in challenging the admissibility of the case against Al-Sennusi, Libya submitted, among others, that it had a functional justice system to prosecute those responsible for the atrocities committed during and after the Gadhafi regime.[48] Demonstrating its commitment to accountability for international crimes, Libya was open to the ICC's seizure of the matter were it to fail to foster criminal accountability in its national courts.[49] Not coincidentally, Libya has since prosecuted and convicted Al-Sennusi for the atrocities he allegedly committed during the Gaddafi era.[50] A similar catalysing effect is evident in Sudan. In 2007, Sudan amended the Armed Forces Act by,

[46] *Judgment in the Jordan Referral re Al-Bashir Appeal*, 06 May 2019, ICC-02/05-01/09-397-Corr., para 140, holding that Sudan was under the obligation to cooperate fully with the ICC as the Security Council Resolution's language was strong to equate Sudan to a party to the Statute.

[47] See generally J Kleffner, *Complementarity in the Rome Statute and National Criminal Jurisdiction* (2008 Oxford University Press) J Kleffner and G Kor (eds) *Complementary Views on Complementarity* (2006 Cambridge University Press); M El Zeidy, *The Principle of Complementarity in International Law: Origin, Development and Practice* (2008). For more recent discussions, see generally S Nouwen, *Complementarity in the Line of Fire: The catalysing Effect of the International Criminal Court in Uganda and Sudan* (2014).

[48] *Prosecutor v Saif AL-Islam Gadhafi and Abdullah Al-Senussi*, Decision on the admissibility of the case against Abdullah Al-Senussi ICC-01/11-01/11-466-Red, 11 October 2013 | Pre-Trial Chamber I, paragraph 214 and 312.

[49] As above.

[50] Human Rights Watch Report, 'Libya: Flawed trial of Gaddafi officials', 28 July 2015, https://www.hrw.org/news/2015/07/28/libya-flawed-trial-gaddafi-officials (accessed on 8 July 2021).

amongst others, criminalising international crimes.[51] Effectively, Sudan set in motion a legal framework for prosecuting those responsible for the atrocities in Darfur.

Close to two decades since the coming into force of the Rome Statute establishing the ICC,[52] there is no doubt that concrete developments have taken place on the African continent on issues of accountability for international crimes. However, the implication of these developments for actual accountability for these crimes remains questionable. With the aim of informing current and future discourse on international criminal justice on the African continent, this edited volume provides a timely interrogation of important issues in pursuance of national accountability for international crimes in Africa. Many questions have been raised. Are African states capable of invoking the complementarity principle and exercising their primary jurisdiction over alleged perpetrators of international crimes in their respective territories? What role can the AU play in ensuring that there is national accountability for international crimes in Africa? Can hybrid courts, special courts or international crimes divisions of domestic courts be effective in prosecuting alleged perpetrators of international crimes domestically? What options are available to ensure national accountability for international crimes, while at the same time fostering national reconciliation, healing and long-lasting peace? Are states who are party to the Rome Statute and yet have failed to deal with historical international crimes capable of dealing with post-Rome Statute crimes? These and related questions remain unanswered, thus, the timeliness of this volume.

2 A Roadmap: Issues and Challenges Addressed in This Volume

With the above background in mind, this edited volume comes in four parts that deal with various themes that address the questions above. There are fifteen (15) chapters (Chapters 2–16) in addition to the introduction (Chapter 1) and conclusion (Chapter 17) chapters. Part I (Chapters 2–5) addresses the AU's perspectives on the complementarity

[51] See amendment to Sudan's Armed Forces Act, 2007.

[52] The Rome Statute was adopted on 17 July 1998 in Rome (Italy). It entered into force on 1 July 2002.

principle in Africa to give a brief overview of the issues. The first chapter of Part I, Chapter 2 by Gevers and Mushoriwa 'Unable or unwilling? An assessment of the African Union's perspective on the application of the complementarity principle by the International Criminal Court' gives a historical account of how the African region—Organisation of African Unity (OAU) and now AU—have always supported the idea of a permanent international criminal court to prosecute perpetrators of international crimes such as apartheid. The authors acknowledge that the OAU was instrumental in the adoption of the Apartheid Convention and the Convention on the Non-Applicability of Statutory Limitations to War Crimes and Crimes Against Humanity. However, the authors argue that African states lost faith when it comes to the international community's commitment to the eradication of international crimes and holding perpetrators to account in the African regime as evidenced by the International Court of Justice's judgment in the *South West Africa Cases*,[53] which had '"deeply shaken [their] faith in the rule of law" and "placed in question the very existence of the Court"'.[54] Hence, Gevers and Mushoriwa demonstrate that the problems that the AU has with the ICC that led to the adoption of the Malabo Protocol and the ICC Withdrawal Strategy are not new. The AU has been frustrated with the way the international community treats its concerns about the ICC. Gevers and Mushoriwa caution against the international community's continued ignorance of the AU's concerns in relation to the ICC as this will further drift them apart causing 'to the detriment of both an "effective" ICC and noble ideal of the "highest standards of international justice"'.[55]

Still in keeping with the AU's contribution to international criminal justice, in Chapter 3 titled 'Cooperation as complementarity: A legal appraisal of the AU's Malabo Protocol', Lungu discusses the Malabo Protocol, which, if it comes into force, will establish the International Crimes Division of the African Court on Human and Peoples' Rights as an alternative to the ICC. Lungu does not discuss the viability of this new division, but he is forward-looking as he interrogates this purported

[53] *South-West Africa Cases (Ethiopia v South Africa; Liberia v South Africa),* Second Phase, ICJ Rep, 1966, p.6. Judgment of 18 July 1966.

[54] Gevers & Mushoriwa 'Unable or unwilling? An assessment of the African Union's perspective on the application of the complementarity principle by the International Criminal Court'.

[55] As above.

Court's cooperation regime. Like the ICC, the International Crimes Division will not have police force to arrest and surrender perpetrators to it. Instead, states are expected to cooperate and arrest and surrender perpetrators to the Court. In this regard, Lungu identifies weaknesses with the current cooperation regime of the proposed Division and proposes ways to strengthen it by taking lessons from the ICC and what transpired in relation to states' obligations to cooperate.

In Chapter 4 titled 'Universal Jurisdiction as a tool in promoting accountability for international crimes in Africa: Exploring the Significance of Hissène Habré's Conviction', Mung'omba invokes Senegal's conviction of Hissène Habré as an example to highlight the significance of the exercise of universal jurisdiction by African states to hold perpetrators of international crimes accountable. He argues that this conviction signifies that universal jurisdiction 'can be a powerful tool' to bring perpetrators to justice.[56] He proposes that African states adopt the AU Model Law on Universal jurisdiction to keep momentum after the Habré conviction. He maintains that this initiative would demonstrate to the international community that the African community takes the international crimes seriously and does not tolerate impunity. However, Mung'omba stresses the importance of giving states primacy to deal with the perpetrators of international crimes in their territory unless if they are unable or unwilling to prosecute.

Concluding Part I is Samaradiwakera-Wijesundara's Chapter 5, 'Complementarity and criminal liability of companies in Africa: Missing the mark?', which focuses on a different perspective of national accountability for international crimes by addressing corporate responsibility for international crimes. Like Gevers and Mushoriwa's contribution, Samaradiwakera-Wijesundara's Chapter is grounded on giving historical context to the role played by corporations in the perpetration of international crimes using the examples of South Africa and Nigeria. This discussion is then followed by responding to the question, 'who or what is a corporation?'[57] In answering this question, Samaradiwakera-Wijesundara acknowledges that corporations are not homogeneous, however, she concludes that corporations, just like other juristic persons such as states,

[56] I Mung'omba 'Universal Jurisdiction as a tool in promoting accountability for international crimes in Africa: Exploring the Significance of Hissène Habré's Conviction'.

[57] C Samaradiwakera-Wijesundara 'Complementarity and criminal liability of companies in Africa: Missing the mark?'.

are 'the product of political, economic, and social power' that could be held accountable.[58] She argues for the expansion of crimes against humanity to include poverty and inequality. Samaradiwakera-Wijesundara does not advocate for the amendment of the Rome Statute, instead she argues that article 7(1)(k) of the Rome Statute[59] is broad enough to include poverty and inequality as 'causing great suffering, or serious injury to body or to mental or physical health'. She also argues that if these acts were to be 'committed as part of a widespread or systematic attack', they would satisfy the requirements for crimes against humanity. Samaradiwakera-Wijesundara proposes several reforms to hold corporations accountable for international crimes before national courts and regional courts, in particular, the proposed African Court with an international crimes' division. Using the African philosophy of *Ubuntu/Botho* as a basis, she argues that the best option would be a regional court 'with shared regional given the power of concerted and collective action, underpinned by shared values, to counter the operations of realpolitik and pervasive colonial and imperial dynamics of power'.[60]

Part II (Chapters 6–8) addresses the prospects of the complementarity principle and looks at alternative approaches to hold perpetrators of international crimes accountable. Starting the debate in this Part is Chapter 6 titled 'Towards lasting complementarity among the International Criminal Court, regional and national criminal justice systems in Africa', where Asaala advocates for the expansion of the scope and practice of the principle of complementarity. She argues that a broad interpretation approach to the principle of complementarity would reinforce the ICC and African states' 'efforts towards national prosecution of international crimes through a well-established structure of institutionalised complementarity'.[61] She anticipates an involvement of several players such

[58] As above.

[59] Article 7of the Rome Statute stipulates that '[f]or the purpose of this Statute, "crime against humanity" means any of the following acts when committed as part of a widespread or systematic attack directed against any civilian population, with knowledge of the attack: (k) Other inhumane acts of a similar character intentionally causing great suffering, or serious injury to body or to mental or physical health'.

[60] C Samaradiwakera-Wijesundara 'Complementarity and criminal liability of companies in Africa: Missing the mark?'

[61] E Asaala 'Towards lasting complementarity among the International Criminal Court, regional and national criminal justice systems in Africa'.

as the Assembly of States Parties, the Office of the Prosecutor, civil societies ad states in the establishment of this structure. The aim is to 'ensure that the criminal justice system of every state is ready to prosecute international crimes whenever they occur'.[62] Asaala's proposal is supported by Lubaale and Carkeek's Chapter 7, 'African Restorative Justice Approaches as Complementarity: The Case of Libya'. Here, the authors consider the restorative justice approaches as part of the complementarity regime. They criticise the ICC's narrow interpretation of the complementarity principle, and its focus only on individual criminal responsibility of perpetrators who bear the greatest responsibility, while those who did the actual attack are left behind on the streets with the victims. Lubaale and Carkeek, therefore, argue for traditional justice mechanisms that are generally restorative in nature. Using Libya as an example, the authors draw on traditional justice mechanisms such as the *gacaca* courts in Rwanda, the *Mato Oput* in Uganda, and the three-prong justice mechanisms in Colombia as mechanisms Libya could adopt. The authors argue that by embracing these traditional justice mechanisms developed by African practices, the ICC may no longer be seen as a tool of imperialism.

In her own interpretation of the ICC's cooperative regime, with Sudan as an example, Lubaale, in Chapter 8, 'Now Available But Still Not Accessible to the ICC: Al Bashir And Africa's Politics' discusses the difficulties of expecting the 'perpetrator State' to cooperate with the ICC in apprehending and surrendering the suspect to the ICC. Lubaale argues that even though Al Bashir was successfully toppled and subsequently arrested and convicted of crimes in Sudan, it would be highly unlikely for Sudan to cooperate with the ICC to surrender him to it in order to face trial for the international crimes he is accused on in the ICC. Her reason for this scepticism is that those who were in power with Al Bashir are still leaders within the post-Al Bashir regime. Using the example of Uganda, where the Museveni government self-referred situations to the ICC, Lubaale highlights how the referred situations involve the opposition groups in Uganda. She demonstrates how Museveni's cooperation with the ICC Prosecutor was rested heavily on the ICC's non-involvement in government's atrocities. Lubaale concludes that there is a need to evaluate how politics play a role within the cooperation regime of the ICC and how

[62] As above.

these difficulties can be resolved to ensure accountability for international crimes.

Part III (Chapters 9–13) addresses the ongoing prospects and challenges of national accountability for international crimes in Africa. The focus is on national accountability for international crimes. How have African states fared in ensuring that perpetrators of international crimes are held accountable? What are the gaps, and how are these gaps going to be filled? In this regard, several authors have looked at specific states. Adigun in Chapter 9, 'Complementarity and federalism: Prosecuting international crimes under the Rome Statute complementarity principle in Nigeria as a federal state', examines the prosecution of perpetrators of international crimes in Nigeria. He engages discusses how Nigeria's federal system challenges the application of some models of complementarity. In essence, Adigun explores the relationship between the complementarity principle and federalism. He discusses different layers involved in the complementarity regime and in federalism. He argues that 'there are five models of the principle of complementarity. That while each of these models is distinct, their operation in practical terms may manifest like any of the others and that they may find expression between a central government and federating units in a federal state'.[63] In particular, Adigun examines Sect. 12 of the Nigerian Constitution of 1999, which deals with treaty implementation and argues that the said provision could accommodate various complementarity models between the Federal Republic of Nigeria and any of the States within the Federation. Adigun also anticipates that Nigeria will be capable of reporting to the ICC on the progress made by its states within its federation.

The second contribution focusing on Nigeria is Chapter 10, 'Accountability For Violations Against Internally Displaced Persons In Nigeria: Finding A Nexus Between International Criminal Justice And Human Rights Violations' which looks at the accountability for the violation of the rights of internationally displaced persons (IDPs). Onuora-Oguno et al. argue that violations of the rights of the IDPs by the Nigerian security agencies constitute crimes against humanity. The authors discuss the link between human rights and crimes against humanity in general terms. While their discussion does not the link the violations of IDPs' rights to crimes against humanity, they describe the atrocities committed by

[63] M Adigun 'Complementarity and federalism: Prosecuting international crimes under the Rome Statute complementarity principle in Nigeria as a federal state'.

these security agencies including sexual violence against women and the possibility of them falling within the ambit of crimes against humanity. We have seen the international criminal tribunals holding perpetrators accountable for crimes against humanity in the form of sexual violence,[64] with the recent victory in this regard being the ICC judgement of 4 February 2021 against Dominic Ongwen.[65] The authors also argue that the Nigerian government has either been unwilling or unable to hold the perpetrators of these atrocities to account. Therefore, they call for the ICC to exercise jurisdiction over perpetrators of these crimes based on the complementarity principle since Nigeria is a party to the Rome Statute.

Apuuli's contribution in Chapter 11, 'The establishment of the Hybrid Court For South Sudan and the Special Criminal Court For Central African Republic: Challenges And Prospects', addresses accountability for international crimes committed in South Sudan and the Central African Republic with a focus on the Hybrid Court for South Sudan (HCSS) and the Special Criminal Court (SCC) for the Central African Republic. The author addresses the question of establishing tribunals to deal with the prosecution of perpetrators of atrocities arising from internal conflicts in the respective states while the conflicts are still ongoing. He remarks that these tribunals established to deal with these atrocities are an epitome of the liberal-prosecution theorists who prioritise prosecution before national reconciliation. He argues that such prosecutions are unable to halt mass atrocities. Apuuli then discusses the challenges faced by the SCC and argues that it is likely that the HCSS would face the same challenges once it becomes operational. Although the SCC was established in 2003, it had only become operational in 2018 with no indictments to date. Equally, the HCSS is also not operational even though it was proposed over six years ago. The author therefore argues that instead of prioritising the prosecution while the conflict is still ongoing, it is important for these states to first deal with the cause for the conflict which is mostly due to politics. While highlighting the importance of eradicating impunity,

[64] *Prosecutor v Akayesu* (note 4 above); *Prosecutor* v *Furundžija* (note 4 above); and *Prosecutor v Charles Ghankay Taylor* (note 5 above). For a thorough discussion on the status of the prohibition of sexual violence in international law, see N Dyani-Mhango 'The *Jus Cogens* nature of the prohibition of sexual violence against women in armed conflicts and state responsibility' (2016) 27(1) *Stellenbosch Law Review* 112.

[65] *Prosecutor v Dominic Ongwen*, Situation in Uganda, Trial Chamber IX, Trial Judgment, ICC-02/04-01/15, 4 February 2021.

Apuuli argues that the respective states must first promote reconciliation before dealing with criminal prosecutions. Apuuli's contribution takes us back to the peace versus justice, and whether these two can ever be achieved at the same time. Apuuli's main concern is the attainment of national healing, reconciliation and lasting peace, alongside delivering justice for victims by punishing perpetrators.

Part III also has two contributions that focus on Uganda and accountability for international crimes. In her contribution in Chapter 12, 'A Critical Assessment of the International Crimes Division of the High Court of Uganda', Ndagire makes a critical assessment of Uganda's International Crimes Division of the High Court (ICDHC). She highlights the challenges faced by the ICDHC in the prosecution of perpetrators of international crimes in Uganda. She notes that the ICDHC's jurisdiction is limited to atrocities perpetrated after 25 June 2010 and as to the perpetrators it can deal with as the National Director of Public Prosecutions (NDPP) must consent to the prosecution of international crimes. According to Ndagire, this means that high ranking government officials may never be brought before the ICDHC as the NDPP is a political appointee. This is also confirmed by the fact that the ICC Act which incorporates the Rome Statute recognises customary international law immunities to which high ranking state officials are entitled. Like Lubaale, Ndagire argues that the ICDHC is meant to prosecute those who oppose the current government. She illustrates this by discussing the Kwoyelo trial which has been ongoing for more than 10 years impacting on both the accused's trial rights and the rights of the victims. Ndagire adds that despite the establishment of a mechanism in Uganda to prosecute international crimes, 'in real terms, the mechanism faces significant structural and systemic hurdles' that continue to undermine victims' access to justice.[66] Ndagire also observes that hopes of holding government officials complicit in the commission of some of the alleged atrocities remains elusive.

Taking from Ndagire's page, in Chapter 13 titled 'Wild Goose Chase, Or A Quest for Genuine Prosecution? Lessons From Uganda's Ongoing Trial of Thomas Kwoyelo', Ruhweza discusses the trial of Thomas Kwoyelo and the subsequent delays in its finalisation. As Ruhweza demonstrates, the entire trial process is testament to the fact that the

[66] J Ndagire 'A critical assessment of the International Crimes Division of the High Court of Uganda'.

court is not equipped to exercise the task before it. Interestingly and in his historical analysis of the Kwoyelo trial, Ruhweza revisits the justice versus peace debate. He, therefore, argues for an 'effective amicable settlement processes or mechanisms that have been accepted by both the victims and the perpetrators as a way of burying the hatchet and mending broken ties'.[67] He places reliance on states in his quest to ensure that there is a pursuit of holistic justice and peace in post-conflict societies.

What of atrocities that occurred before the ICC was established? Can we truly call for the adherence to the obligations that arise from the Rome Statute if the states have never dealt with international crimes of the past in their territories? How do states hold accountable perpetrators of international crimes committed during the struggle for freedom, or during the struggle for power after freedom was achieved? The contributions on South Africa and on Zimbabwe deal with these questions, respectively, in Part IV (chapters 14–16). In Chapter 14, 'South Africa's Accountability for International Crimes: Revisiting the (Non) Prosecution of Perpetrators of Apartheid for Crimes against Humanity', Dyani-Mhango addresses the unfinished business of apartheid crimes that constitute international crimes and the failure of South Africa's prosecuting authority to prosecute. This failure to prosecute disregards international and constitutional obligations to which South Africa must adhere. Dyani-Mhango demonstrates how apartheid is considered a crime against humanity both in international law and in domestic law, and such a crime is prohibited both in treaty law and in customary international law and the prohibition is considered a peremptory norm. However, despite this confirmation, Dyani-Mhango highlights that there is yet to be a conviction on apartheid as a crime against humanity in South Africa and elsewhere since international law also recognises the exercise of universal jurisdiction in relation to this crime. Dyani-Mhango also discovers that failure to prosecute is a result of political interference in the National Prosecuting Prosecution (NPA)'s exercise of its prosecutorial duty by the executive branch of government. She then investigates how the NPA and the executive branch of government may be held accountable for failure to prosecute and for political interference, respectively. She argues that even though Parliament has the power to hold the executive to account, some political parties represented in Parliament have an interest in not seeing these

[67] D Ruhweza 'Wild Goose Chase, Or A Quest for Genuine Prosecution? Lessons From Uganda's Ongoing Trial of Thomas Kwoyelo'.

prosecutions as their members may be held to account for atrocities they perpetrated during the apartheid era and the fact that the TRC Act does not make a distinction between atrocities perpetrated by those who fought against apartheid regime and those who perpetrated apartheid crimes in the name of the apartheid regime such as De Klerk, the last apartheid president of South Africa. Dyani-Mhango concludes that there can never be accountability for international crimes perpetrated post the establishment of the ICC and post-apartheid South Africa without first dealing with the perpetrators of apartheid and prosecute them for crimes against humanity.

Equally, Malunga's two chapters discuss the atrocities committed by the post-independence Zimbabwean government and the governing political party, Zanu PF in the 1980s against its own citizens, especially the Ndebeles. In Chapter 15 titled 'A History of Atrocity: Patterns, Perpetrators and Prospects for Accountability for International Crimes in Zimbabwe', Malunga gives a historical account and patterns of atrocities committed by Zimbabwe African National Union-Patriotic Front (Zanu PF) and the Zimbabwean government against its citizens in the past four decades since Zimbabwe gained its independence in 1980. Malunga argues that the Zimbabwean government 'has politicised and racialised atrocities and targeted opposition supporters of the Zimbabwe Unity Movement (ZUM), the Movement for Democratic Change (MDC), white farmers, civil society, human rights, media and democracy activists'.[68] He argues that the atrocities committed and continue to be committed by the Zimbabwean government against its citizens amount to international crimes such as war crimes, crimes against humanity, genocide and torture. It must be recalled as Dyani-Mhango also explains in her contribution that the South African Constitutional Court confirmed that the South African Police Service has a duty to investigate the claims of torture committed against the Zimbabwean citizens by the Zimbabwean officials in the exercise of universal jurisdiction as contemplated in the ICC Act. Malunga, therefore, calls for the prosecution of the known perpetrators for international crimes by exercising universal jurisdiction. In Chapter 16, 'Unpacking Gukurahundi Atrocities Against the Ndebeles of Zimbabwe: What Are the Possibilities for Individual Criminal Responsibility of the Perpetrators Under International

[68] S Malunga 'A History of Atrocity: Patterns, Perpetrators and Prospects for Accountability for International Crimes in Zimbabwe'.

Criminal Law?', Malunga focuses on the Gukurahundi atrocities against the Ndebele population in Matebeleland in Zimbabwe. He classifies the conflict in Matebeleland as a non-international armed conflict as rules of international humanitarian law so provide. He then argues that the atrocities constituted international crimes as they included ethnic cleansing, mass murder, enforced disappearance and torture. He therefore called for international criminal responsibility.

Dyani-Mhango and Lubaale's Conclusion (chapter 17) addresses the contentious issues addressed in the contributions to be explored for future research.

The contributions in this edited Volume have raised more concerns than providing answers. This provides an opportunity for researchers, policymakers, civil societies and governments to come together and find solutions to eradicate atrocities in Africa and to hold those responsible for these international crimes accountable. Needless to say, this edited volume will be of great value to academics, research students, government officials, policymakers and civil societies.

Acknowledgements I acknowledge funding from the National Research Foundation (Funding to EC Lubaale, Grant No: 127504) toward the funding of writing retreats that informed the conceptual development of my contributions to this book. Support from the Rhodes University Research Committee Grant is also acknowledged.

References

Akande, D 'The legal nature of the Security Council referrals to the ICC and its impact on Al Bashir's immunities' (2009) 7 *Journal of International Criminal Justice* 333

Akande, D "ICC Issues Detailed Decision on Bashir's Immunity (… At Long Last …) But Gets the Law Wrong" Blog of the European Journal of International Law, 15 December 2011, available at http://www.ejiltalk.org/icc-issues-detailed-decision-on-bashir%E2%80%99s-immunity-at-long-last-but-gets-the-law-wrong/ (accessed on 15 March 2018)

Alkrisheh, M and Mahameed, W 'The International Criminal Court Statute and State Sovereignty: The Implicit Impact of the Complementarity Principle' (2020) 6 *Multicultural Education* 1

Ba, O *States of Justice: The politics of the international criminal court* (2020 Cambridge University Press)

Broomhall, B *International Justice and the International Criminal Court: Between Sovereignty and the Rule of Law* (2003 Oxford University Press)
Chuter, D 'The ICC: A Place for Africans or Africans in their Place?' in Nmehielle, VO (Ed) *Africa and the Future of International Criminal Justice* (2012)
Corrigendum to the Decision Pursuant to Article 87(7) of the Rome Statute on the Failure by the Republic of Malawi to Comply with the Cooperation Requests Issued by the Court with Respect to the Arrest and Surrender of Omar Hassan Ahmad Al Bashir, ICC-02/05-01/09-139-Corr, 13 December 2011
Decision on the Implementation of the Assembly Decisions on the International Criminal Court, Assembly of the Union, Seventeenth Ordinary Session, EX.CL/670(XIX), Assembly/AU/Dec.366(XVII) (1 July 2011)
Decision on the Application by the International Criminal Court Prosecutor for the Indictment of the President of the Republic of the Sudan, Assembly of the Union, Twelfth Ordinary Session, Assembly/AU/Dec.221(XII)
Decision of the Meeting of African States Parties to the Rome Statute of the International Criminal Court, Assembly of the Union, Thirteenth Ordinary Session, Assembly/AU/13 (XIII)
Decision on The International Criminal Court, Assembly of the Union, Twenty-Sixth Ordinary Session, EX.CL/952(XXVIII), Assembly/AU/Dec.590(XXVI)
Decision on the International Criminal Court, Doc/EX.CL/1006 (XXX), Twenty-Eighth Ordinary Session, 30–31 January 2017, Addis Ababa, Ethiopia
Decision Pursuant to Article 87(7) of the Rome Statute on the Refusal of the Republic of Chad to Comply with the Cooperation Requests Issued by the Court with Regard to the Arrest and Surrender of Omar Hassan Ahmad Al Bashir, ICC-02/05-01/09-140, 13 December 2011
Decision on the Non-Compliance of the Republic of Chad with the Cooperation Requests Issued by the Court Regarding the Arrest and Surrender of Omar Hassan Ahmad Al Bashir, ICC-02/05-01/09-151, 26 March 2013
Decision on the Cooperation of the Federal Republic of Nigeria Regarding Omar Al Bashir's Arrest and Surrender to the Court, ICC-02/05-01/09-159, 5 September 2013
Decision on the Cooperation of the Democratic Republic of the Congo Regarding Omar Al Bashir's Arrest and Surrender to the Court ICC-02/05-01/09-195, 4 April 2014
Decision on the non-compliance by the Republic of Djibouti with the request to arrest and surrender Omar Al-Bashir to the Court and referring the matter to the United Nations Security Council and the Assembly of the State Parties to the Rome Statute, ICC-02/05-01/09-266, 11 July 2016
Decision on the Non-Compliance by the Republic of Uganda with the Request to Arrest and Surrender Omar Al-Bashir to the Court and Referring the Matter

to the United Nations Security Council and the Assembly of States Parties to the Rome Statute, ICC-02/05-01/09-267, 11 July 2016

Decision under article 87(7) of the Rome Statute on the non-compliance by South Africa with the request by the Court for the arrest and surrender of Omar Al-Bashir, ICC-02/05-01/09-302, 06 July 2017

Deng, F et al., *Sovereignty as responsibility* (1996 Brookings Institution Press)

Dyani, N 'Is the International Criminal Court Targeting Africa? Reflections on the Enforcement of International Criminal Law in Africa' in Nmehielle, VO (Ed) *Africa and the Future of International Criminal Justice* (2012)

Dyani-Mhango, N 'The ICC Pre-Trial Chamber's Decision on South Africa's Failure to Arrest and Surrender South Africa: South Africa Escapes 'Sanctions'' 2017 *African Yearbook of International Humanitarian Law* 37

Dyani-Mhango, N 'South Africa's Dilemma: Immunity Laws, International Obligations and the Visit by Sudan's President Omar Al Bashir' (2017) 26 (3) *Washington International Law Journal* 535

Dyani-Mhango, N 'The ICC Pre-Trial Chamber's decision on South Africa's failure to arrest and Surrender President Al Bashir: South Africa escapes 'sanctions'! (2017) *African Yearbook of International Humanitarian Law* 37

Dyani-Mhango, N 'The ICC Pre-Trial Chamber's decision on Malawi regarding the failure to arrest and surrender President Al Bashir of Sudan: An opportunity missed' (2013) 28 *SA Public Law* 106

Dyani-Mhango, N 'The *Jus Cogens* nature of the prohibition of sexual violence against women in armed conflicts and state responsibility' (2016) 27(1) *Stellenbosch Law Review* 112

El Zeidy, M *The Principle of Complementarity in International Law: Origin, Development and Practice* (2008 Martinus Nijhoff Publishers)

Gaddafi Admissibility Judgment, Judgment on the appeal of Libya against the decision of Pre-Trial Chamber I of 31 May 2013 entitled 'Decision on the admissibility of the case against Saif Al-Islam Gaddafi, ICC-01/11-01/11-547- Red

Gaeta, P 'Does President Al-Bashir enjoy immunity from arrest?' (2009) 7 *Journal of International Criminal Justice* 315

Human Rights Watch Report, 'Libya: Flawed trial of Gaddafi officials', 28 July 2015, https://www.hrw.org/news/2015/07/28/libya-flawed-trial-gaddafi-officials (accessed 8 July 2021)

IMT Judgment (1947) 41 *American Journal of International Law* 172

Implementation of the Rome Statute of the International Criminal Court Act 27 of 2002 of South Africa

International Criminal Court, "The States parties to the Rome Statute", https://asp.icc-cpi.int/en_menus/asp/states%20parties/pages/the%20states%20parties%20to%20the%20rome%20statute.aspx (accessed on 8 July 2021)

International Criminal Court, Situations and cases, (2021), https://www.icc-cpi.int/pages/situation.aspx (accessed on 8 July 2021)
International Criminal Court Act 2010 of Uganda
International Crimes Act 2008 of Kenya
International Crimes Division of the High Court (formerly War Crimes Division), established by an administrative decree in 2008, Legal Notice Number 10 of 2011
Jacobs, D 'A Sad Hommage to Antonio Cassese: The ICC's Confused Pronouncements on State Compliance and Head of State Immunity' Spreading the Jam, 15 December 2011), available at https://dovjacobs.com/2011/12/15/a-sad-hommage-to-antonio-cassese-the-iccs-confused-pronouncements-on-state-compliance-and-head-of-state-immunity/ (accessed on 15 March 2018)
Judgment in the Jordan Referral re Al-Bashir Appeal, 06 May 2019, ICC-02/05-01/09-397-Corr
Kleffner, J 'Auto-Referrals and the Complementary Nature of the ICC' In C Stahn and G Sluiter (eds), *The Emerging Practice of the ICC* (2009 Martinus Nijhoff) 41
Kleffner, K *Complementarity in the Rome Statute and National Criminal Jurisdiction* (2008 Oxford University Press)
Kleffner, J and Kor, G (eds) *Complementary Views on Complementarity* (2006 Cambridge University Press)
Labuda, PI 'The African Union's Collective Withdrawal from the ICC: Does Bad Law make for Good Politics?' EJIL: Talk! 15 February 2017, available at https://www.ejiltalk.org/the-african-unions-collective-withdrawal-from-the-icc-does-bad-law-make-for-good-politics/ (accessed on 12 July 2021)
Lattimer, M and Philippe S (eds) *Justice for Crimes Against Humanity* (2003 Hart)
Lungu, S & Dyani-Mhango, N 'Ensuring that State Parties to the Rome Statute Co-operate with ICC Requests to Arrest and Surrender Suspects: Reflecting on the Role of the Security Council through the Lens of the Responsibility to Protect (R2P)' (2018) *African Yearbook of International Humanitarian Law* 119
Nadya, SL *The International Criminal Court and the Transformation of International Law: Justice for the New Millennium* (2002 Transnational)
National Commissioner of the South African Police Service v Southern African Human Rights Litigation Centre and Another 2015 (1) SA 315 (CC); 2015 (1) SACR 255 (CC)
Newton, MA '*The Complementarity Conundrum: Are We Watching Evolution or Evisceration?*' (2010) 8 *Santa Clara Journal of International Law* 115

Nmehielle, VO (Ed) *Africa and the Future of International Criminal Justice* (2012)

Nouwen, S *Complementarity in the Line of Fire: The catalysing Effect of the International Criminal Court in Uganda and Sudan* (2014 Cambridge University Press)

Oko, O 'The Challenges of International Criminal Prosecutions in Africa' (2007)31 *Fordham International Law Journal* 343

Okuta, AA *Smallest share of the pie? Accountability for international crimes at the domestic level: case studies of Kenya, Uganda and Côte d'Ivoire* (2016 PhD Thesis Amsterdam Center for International Law)

Okpaluba, CM 'The Constitutional Principle of Accountability: A Study of Contemporary South African Case Law' (2018) 33(1) *Southern African Public Law* 1

Philippe, X 'The principles of universal jurisdiction and complementarity: how do the two principles intermesh?' (2006) 88: 862 *International Review of the Red Cross* 375

Prosecutor v Dusko Tadic, Judgment, IT-94-1-T, 7 May 1997 (war crimes and crimes against humanity)

Prosecutor v Kunarac, Judgment, IT-96–23 &-IT-96–23/1-A, 12 June 2002 (war crimes, crimes against humanity in the form of torture and rape)

Prosecutor v *Furundžija*, IT-95–17/1-T, Judgment, 10 December 1998 (war crimes in the form of rape and torture)

Prosecutor v Akayesu, Judgment, 2 September 1998, ICTR—96-13-T

Prosecutor v Dominic Ongwen, Situation in Uganda, Trial Chamber IX, Trial Judgment, ICC-02/04-01/15, 4 February 2021

Prosecutor v Ferdinand Nahimana, Jean-Bosco Barayagwiza, and Hassan Ngeze, Judgment, 3 December 2003, ICTR-99-52-T

Prosecutor v Charles Ghankay Taylor, Judgment, 26 September 2013, SCSL-03-01-A

Prosecutor v Bosco Ntaganda, Judgment, 8 July 2019, CC-01/04-02/06-2359

Prosecutor v Germain Katanga and Mathieu Ngudjolo Chui, Judgment on the Appeal of Mr. Germain Katanga against the Oral Decision of Trial Chamber II of 12 June 2009 on the Admissibility of the Case, Case No. ICC-01/04–01/07 OA 8, 25 September 2009

Prosecutor v Omar Hassan Ahmad Al Bashir, ICC-02/05-01/09; *Prosecutor v Omar Hassan Ahmad Al Bashir*, ICC-02/05-01/09-1, Warrant of Arrest, (4 March 2009)

Prosecutor v Omar Hassan Ahmad Al Bashir, ICC-02/05-01/09-95, Second Warrant of Arrest, (12 July 2010)

Prosecutor v Omar Hassan Ahmad Al Bashir (Decision under article 87(7) of the Rome Statute on the non-compliance by Jordan with the request by the Court

for the arrest and surrender of Omar Al-Bashir), ICC-02/05-01/09-309, 11 December 2017

Prosecutor v Saif AL-Islam Gadhafi and Abdullah Al-Senussi, Decision on the admissibility of the case against Abdullah Al-Senussi ICC-01/11-01/11-466-Red, 11 October 2013 | Pre-Trial Chamber I

Report of the Ad- Hoc Committee on the Establishment of an International Criminal Court, UN GAOR, 50th Session, Supp No 22, at p. 50, UN Doc. A/50/22(1995)

Rome Statute of the International Criminal Court, 17 July 1998, 2187 U.N.T.S. 90 (entered into force on 1 July 2002)

Sands, P (ed) *From Nuremberg to the Hague: The Future of International Criminal Justice* (2003 Cambridge University Press)

Situation in The Libyan Arab Jamahiriya, Warrant of Arrest for Muammar Mohammed Abu Minyar Gaddafi, ICC-01/11-13, 27 June 2011

Stahn, C 'Complementarity: A tale of Two Notions' (2008) 19 *Criminal Law Forum* 87

South-West Africa Cases (Ethiopia v South Africa; Liberia v South Africa), Second Phase, ICJ Rep, 1966, p.6. Judgment of 18 July 1966

Sudan's Armed Forces Act, 2007

Tladi, D 'The Duty of South Africa to Arrest and Surrender Al Bashir under South African and International Law: A Perspective from International Law' (2015) 13 (5) *Journal of International Criminal Justice* 102

Tladi, D 'The ICC Decisions on Chad and Malawi: on Cooperation, Immunities and Article 98' (2013) 11 (1) *Journal of International Criminal Justice* 199

United Nations General Assembly, *Secretary-General's 'Age of Accountability' address to the Review Conference on the International Criminal Court*, Kampala, 31 May 2010, SG/SM/12930L/3158, available at https://www.un.org/sg/en/content/sg/speeches/2010-05-31/address-review-conference-international-criminal-court-age (accessed on 11 July 2021)

United Nations Security Council, *Statute of the International Criminal Tribunal for the Former Yugoslavia,* 25 May 1993, as established by resolution 808/1993, 827/1993

United Nations Security Council, *Statute of the International Criminal Tribunal for Rwanda,* 8 November 1994, As established by Security Council Resolution 955 (1994) of 8 November 1994

United Nations Security Council, *Statute of the Special Court for Sierra Leone*, 16 January 2002, As established by Security Council resolution 1315

Ward, I *Humanity and the New World Order* (2003 Ashgate)

PART I

African Union's Perspectives on the Complementarity Principle in Africa

'An Effective Complement to National Criminal Justice Systems, Operating Within the Highest Standards of International Justice'? African States, the International Criminal Court & Complementarity

Christopher Gevers and Linda Mushoriwa

1 Introduction

The opening article of the Rome Statute of the International Criminal Court states that the 'Court…hereby established…shall be a permanent institution and shall have the power to exercise its jurisdiction over persons for the most serious crimes of international concern…, and shall be complementary to national criminal jurisdictions'.[1] This 'principle of

[1] Article 1, Rome Statute of the International Criminal Court. See further Rome Statute Preambular Paragraph 10.

C. Gevers (✉)
University of KwaZulu-Natal, Durban, South Africa
e-mail: gevers@ukzn.ac.za

L. Mushoriwa
University of Johannesburg, Johannesburg, South Africa

E. C. Lubaale and N. Dyani-Mhango (eds.), *National Accountability for International Crimes in Africa*,
https://doi.org/10.1007/978-3-030-88044-6_2

complementarity' is given effect to by article 17, which states that the International Criminal Court (ICC or 'the Court') 'shall determine that a case is inadmissible where [it] is being investigated or prosecuted by a State which has jurisdiction over it, unless the State is unwilling or unable genuinely to carry out the investigation or prosecution'.[2] The 'complementarity regime' has been described as the cornerstone of the Rome Statute without which it might not have received sufficient ratifications to become operational. On the opening day of the Rome Conference in 1998 the late Dullah Omar told the assembled delegates, on behalf of the Southern African Development Community (SADC)[3]:

> [The ICC] should be an effective complement to national criminal justice systems, operating within the highest standards of international justice. ...[and] should contribute to furthering the integrity of States generally, as well as the equality of States within the general principles of international law.

On this understanding, shared by African states at Rome in 1998, the role of the complementarity regime was to ensure respect for both the sovereignty ***and equality*** of all states, and it was *the ICC* that was enjoined to be effective and operate 'within the highest standards of international justice'. Over the past two decades later, however, complementarity has arguably come to work in precisely the opposite fashion. Not only has it operated to undermine the sovereignty of (some) states, but its uneven application has come to further undermine the equality of all states; in part because the Rome Statute has (in most instances) been re-interpreted to empower the ICC to scrutinise whether ***domestic proceedings*** are 'effective' and meet 'the highest standards of international justice'.

In this chapter, we consider these double standards claims against the background of the centrality of the 'complementarity regime' to African states' support for the establishment of the ICC, as well as the shifts on complementarity by the Office of the Prosecutor (OTP), the Court and the 'international justice' community at large since 1998. The

[2] Article 17(1)(a) Rome Statute.

[3] As reported in United Nations Diplomatic Conference of Plenipotentiaries on the Establishment of an International Criminal Court, Official Records, Volume II, A/CONF.183/13 (Vol. II), ('Rome Proceedings') 65.

chapter proceeds in four parts: it begins by placing African states' support for the ICC's 'complementarity regime' in proper historical context, by thickening of the account of their participation in the drafting of the Rome Statute to include their concerns about sovereignty, equality and 'international justice' (misgivings which, the chapter argues, have largely come to pass). Part 3 of the chapter then sets out the shifts in the understanding of complementarity since 1998—as McAuliffe puts it—from the *horizontal* framework contained in the Rome Statute that was 'rooted in State consent and deferential to the State's primacy of action regarding criminal prosecutions, towards a *vertical* framework in terms of which 'the Court enjoys priority over the national jurisdiction, incorporating notions of superior supranationality as an international body and implying a relationship of authority by intervening in the domain of domestic affairs'.[4] Against this background, Part 4 of the chapter turns to consider the OTP's recent decision not to investigate international crimes committed by British soldiers in Iraq[5]—its first substantive 'complementarity assessment' of a non-African state—and argues that it suggests that African states have not only been subject to a *higher* standard when it comes to complementarity, but a *double* standard. The chapter concludes by illustrating that the double standards claim is longstanding, and likely to persist for as long as the ICC continues to uncritically accept and reflect the power disparities within the international order.

2 African States at Rome, Revisited

The history of African states' engagement with International Criminal Law long pre-dates the negotiation and adoption of the Rome Statute in the 1990s.[6] However, even if one accepts a foreshortened history of

[4] P McAuliffe 'From Watchdog to Workhorse: Explaining the Emergence of the ICC's Burden-Sharing Policy as an Example of Creeping Cosmopolitanism' (2014) 13 *Chinese Journal of International Law* 259, 259–260. See further F Megret, 'In Search of the "Vertical": Towards an Institutional Theory of International Criminal Justice's Core' in C Stahn & L Van der Herik (eds) *Future Perspectives on International Criminal Justice* (2010) 178–224.

[5] ICC Office of the Prosecutor *Situation in Iraq/UK: Final Report* (9 December 2020) ('*Situation in Iraq*').

[6] See generally C Gevers 'Africa and International Criminal Law' in K Heller, F Megret, S Nouwen, J Ohlin & D Robinson (eds), *The Oxford Handbook of International Criminal Law* (2020) 154.

this relationship, it is instructive to 'thicken out' the typically superficial accounts of African states at Rome in 1998, beyond registering their 'astonishing enthusiasm'[7] and pointing out that Senegal was the first signatory to the Rome Statute (often as a prelude to jeremiads about Africa's fall from grace). One way to do so is by setting out the understandings under which African states supported the ICC's establishment, contained in the common positions of African states and statements made by their representatives and those of the Organisation of African Unity, namely: (1) the Prosecutor would be both independent and impartial; (2) the influence of the 'Great Powers', chiefly through the Security Council, would be limited; (3) the ICC would act in the interests of *both* peace and (criminal) justice; and (4) the ICC would *complement* national justice systems.[8]

The complementarity regime was central to mitigating all of these concerns in 1998, both directly and indirectly. In addition to insisting that the ICC should 'be an effective complement to national criminal justice systems',[9] African states had reason to believe that the complementarity regime would serve as an indirect safeguard against the realisation of their concerns regarding Prosecutorial independence and 'Great Power' influence and ensure the promotion of peace. For example, the fear of a Court too eager to prosecute crimes committed in 'weaker' states was allayed by the proviso that, in such instances, the complementarity regime would give preference to 'national criminal justice systems'. Similarly, the fear of a Court not eager enough to pursue crimes in 'strong' states was somewhat allayed by the proviso that, at the very least, the Security Council could not simply 'veto' a prosecution; as some of its members had initially envisioned it would.

Before turning to consider how this complementarity regime 'evolved' over the past two decades, it is worth pointing out that the broader concerns of African states in 1998, against which the complementarity regime was to serve as a safeguard, have largely come to pass.

[7] WA Schabas 'The Banality of International Justice' (2013) 11 *Journal of International Criminal Justice* 545, 548.

[8] See Rome Proceedings (n 3 above) 69 (Lesotho), 74 (Tanzania), 84 (Burkina Faso), 87 (Namibia), 108 (Swaziland), 108 (Malawi), 111 (Nigeria), 112 (Democratic Republic of the Congo), 117 (Angola), 118 (Burundi), 127 (Egypt) & 128 (Benin).

[9] Statement by the late Minister Dullah Omar on behalf of SADC, Rome Proceedings (n 3 above) 65.

The Office of the Prosecutor (OTP), particularly the first Chief Prosecutor, has displayed an eagerness to pursue cases in 'weaker' states, and overwhelmingly African states, going so far as to solicit 'self-referrals' notwithstanding the 'principle of complementarity'. As Dugard points out,[10] with the exception of Darfur and Libya, all of the situations being investigated and prosecuted by the ICC were chosen by the OTP who is under no obligation to accept state referrals. This includes the so-called self-referrals, such as in the Democratic Republic of the Congo (DRC), Uganda, the Central African Republic and Mali. These situations were therefore as much *selected* by the first prosecutor Luis Moreno-Ocampo for investigation as the *proprio motu* investigations in Kenya, Côte d'Ivoire, Georgia and Burundi. Moreover, as Ocampo's successor Fatou Bensouda took the position that she was also under no obligation to accept Security Council referrals under article 13(b), this means that the OTP effectively *chose* the Libyan and Sudanese situations as well.

Notably, the OTP's freedom to choose cases was something that African states had fought for at Rome in 1998.[11] However, they did so on the understanding that the OTP would act independently and impartially, 'without interference from States or the Security Council or being prejudiced by political considerations'.[12] However, not only has the OTP been *too eager* to pursue cases in weaker states, but it has also not been eager *enough* to pursue potential cases in, or that implicate, stronger states. Over the past two decades, the OTP has directly and indirectly decided not to pursue several non-African cases and to systematically 'slow-walk' them when they became unavoidable.

A telling example of the 'slow-walking' of an investigation—by the OTP, the Presidency, and the Pre-Trial Chamber—can be seen in Afghanistan, which has been within the jurisdiction of the ICC since it signed up to the Rome Statute in 2003 and has been the sight of alleged international crimes throughout this period at the hands of Afghan and foreign actors, particularly the United States. In January 2007, the

[10] J Dugard 'Palestine and the ICC: Institutional Failure or Bias?'(2013) 11(3) *Journal of International Criminal Justice* 563.

[11] See Southern African Development Community's 'Common Position'; and the Dakar Declaration for the Establishment of the International Criminal Court, adopted in February 1998.

[12] Rome Proceedings (n 3 above) 65.

OTP publicly announced that it had opened a preliminary examination, however it took almost seven years for the Prosecutor's preliminary examination to move beyond the initial 'jurisdiction' phase.[13] Only in November 2017, more than a decade after the preliminary examination began, did the Prosecutor request permission from the Pre-Trial Chamber (PTC) to officially open a formal investigation (*proprio motu*) into crimes committed on the territory of Afghanistan since 1 May 2003. Further delays followed, this time at the hand of the Presidency which in March 2018, nearly four months after Pre-Trial Chamber III had begun considering the matter (and had already twice requested further information from the Prosecutor), reassigned the situation to Pre-Trial Chamber II.[14] In April 2019 the PTC then decided to refuse the OTP's request to open a formal investigation into crimes committed in Afghanistan, not for lack of evidence, but on the basis that it would not be in the 'interests of justice'. This was partly as a result of the 'particularly long' preliminary examination.[15] In March 2020 the Appeals Chamber reversed that decision and authorised the Prosecutor's investigation but did so on a technicality; finding that the 'interests of justice' were not relevant to the Pre-Trial Chamber's assessment under article 15(4). As such, it skilfully avoided the question of whether the investigation of crimes in Afghanistan was in fact in the 'interests of justice'.[16]

[13] ICC Office of the Prosecutor, *Report on Preliminary Examination Activities: 2013* (November 2013) 10.

[14] ICC *Decision Assigning Judges to Divisions and Recomposing Chambers* ICC-Pres-01/18 (16 March 2018).

[15] ICC *Decision Pursuant to Article 15 of the Rome Statute on the Authorisation of an Investigation into the Situation in the Islamic Republic of Afghanistan* ICC-02/17-133 (12 April 2019) para. 92. The Pre-Trial Chamber based its determination on the implications for the 'paramount objectives of the Statute and hence the overall credibility of the Court, as well as its organizational and financial sustainability' (para. 88) and took note of 'changes within the relevant political landscape both in Afghanistan and in key States [i.e., the US] .... [would] make it extremely difficult to gauge the prospects of securing meaningful cooperation from relevant authorities for the future, whether in respect of investigations or of surrender of suspects' (para. 94).

[16] ICC *Judgment on the appeal against the decision on the authorisation of an investigation into the situation in the Islamic Republic of Afghanistan* ICC-02/17 OA4 (5 March 2020), para. 46.

What emerges from the Afghanistan situation (and a similar pattern can be seen in the Palestine situation and, as discussed below, in Iraq)[17] is an initial strategy of non-selection of 'hard' cases involving Great Powers and their allies; then, once they become unavoidable, a further strategy of 'slow-walk[ing] ... preliminary examination[s] into oblivion ... when superpowers are involved'.[18] Here, as Heller points out, the comparison between the progress of African and non-African situations through the different preliminary examination stages is particularly telling: consider the time it took the Afghanistan situation to proceed through the *jurisdiction* phase (seven years) compared to that of Guinea (four years) and Nigeria (three years). Even once permission to open a formal investigation is requested by the Prosecutor, different standards seem to apply. Compare the Pre-Trial Chamber's treatment of requests by the Prosecutor to open formal investigations in respect of Burundi and Afghanistan, submitted within months of each other in late 2017. A little over a month and a half later, the Burundi investigation was authorised,[19] whereas the Afghanistan authorisation decision was handed down a year and a half later.

The avoidance and slow-walking of 'hard cases' by the Prosecutor has been compounded by the willingness of the OTP and the ICC's supporters to operate within the shadow of the Security Council's power or; as Schabas puts it, how the ICC has become 'shackled to the priorities of the Security Council, with all that this entails, including the veto', and '[march] in lock step with the permanent members'.[20] As such, there is much to suggest that African states' concerns in 1998 were well-founded and have largely come to pass. Moreover, they have done so as a result of the decisions (and non-decisions) of not only individual Chief Prosecutors, but the OTP, Judges and other court functionaries, as well as

[17] See further M du Plessis & C Gevers 'The Role of the International Criminal Court in Africa: The Epic Fails?' in J Sarkin & E Siang'andu (eds) *Africa's Role and Contribution to International Criminal Justice* (2020).

[18] K Heller 'The ICC in Palestine: Be Careful What You Wish For' *Justice in Conflict* 2 April 2015 https://justiceinconflict.org/2015/04/02/the-icc-in-palestine-be-careful-what-you-wish-for/ (accessed on 24 May 2021).

[19] ICC *Public Redacted Version of 'Decision Pursuant to Article 15 of the Rome Statute on the Authorization of an Investigation into the Situation in the Republic of Burundi'* ICC-01/17-X-9-US-Exp (25 October 2017).

[20] Schabas (n 7 above) 551.

the 'international justice' community: the assemblage of 'global' human rights NGOS, scholars, activists and other actors.[21] Finally, these concerns have come to pass, in many instances, not as a result of the provisions and principles of the Rome Statute but *in spite of them*; perhaps none more than those underpinning the regime of complementarity.

3 Complementarity (in)ction

Complementarity has repeatedly been described as the 'cornerstone' of the Rome Statute, which was both pivotal in obtaining the requisite ratifications for the Rome Statute to become operational,[22] and in principle it governs whether the ICC acts (or does not act) in any situation or case. During the negotiations to the Rome Statute, the question of whether the ICC would have 'primary' jurisdiction became a sticking point. European states and civil society advocated for an international court with primary jurisdiction to ensure accountability for human rights violations.[23] African states on the other hand insisted that the ICC should be an effective complement to national criminal justice systems; this stemmed from the fear of an overzealous, sovereignty-usurping international court, which fear was motivated by the reasons outlined above. As a result, there were significant safeguards included in the Rome Statute to address this concern.

During the drafting of the Rome Statute the International Law Commission (ILC) sought to limit the jurisdiction of the ICC by making it complementary to national jurisdictions with the Court only exercising jurisdiction where domestic prosecutions would be 'unavailable or ineffective'.[24] Reporting on its work, the ILC insisted that '[a]bove all… the

[21] McAuliffe (n 4 above) 265 (arguing that 'scholars, activists, actors and judges within or surrounding the Court' share a 'progressive cosmopolitanism').

[22] J Spilman 'Complementarity or Competition: The Effect of the ICC's Admissibility Decision in Kenya on Complementarity and the Article 17 (1) Inquiry' (2013) *Richmond Journal of Global Law and Business Online* 5.

[23] F Megret 'In Search of the "Vertical": Towards an Institutional Theory of International Criminal Justice's Core' (n 4 above); McAuliffe (n 4 above) 273.

[24] United Nations General Assembly *Report of the International Law Commission on the work of its Forty-Sixth Session, Draft Statute for an International Criminal Court* UN Doc/A/49/335, Preamble, para 3. For a detailed overview of the drafting process of the Rome Statute see M El Zeidy *The principle of complementarity in international criminal law: origin, development and practice* (2008) 109–132.

Draft Statute must provide further assurances that the proposed Court would be complementary to national courts and that the new system would not undermine existing law enforcement efforts'.[25] This decision to grant domestic prosecutions *primacy* over 'international' prosecutions was a deliberate choice at Rome to reverse the hierarchy that applied between the ad hoc Tribunals and domestic courts, where the former had primacy over the latter.[26]

This is not to say that the 'principle of complementarity' (as it became known) was altogether without risk; there was still a possibility of 'structures of inequality'[27] emerging in the application of the principle, particularly insofar as the unable exception to its application was concerned, which was more likely to apply to 'weaker' states. Nevertheless, at least as far as the text was concerned, it codified a clear preference for domestic over international prosecutions. It did not take long for the consensus to begin to unravel.[28] There were signs of slippage from the outset, when the OTP solicited its first situation by way of a 'self-referral' from the DRC in 2004, notwithstanding the presumption that domestic proceedings were supposed to be the norm. An inference can be drawn that the Prosecutor actually extorted the self-referral (perhaps *extorted* is more appropriate, given that the Prosecutor threatened to open his own *proprio motu* investigation if the DRC did not refer the situation).[29] This

[25] United Nations General Assembly *Report of the International Law Commission on the work of its Forty-Sixth Session: 1994* U.N.Doc. A/CN.4/464/Add.1 (22 February 1995) para 7.

[26] Article 9 Statute of the International Criminal Tribunal for the former Yugoslavia; Article 8 Statute of the International Tribunal for Rwanda. In the *Tadic* case the ICTY's Appeals Chamber held that the tribunal's primacy of jurisdiction was justified as article 2(7) of the UN Charter provides for UN mandates to take precedence over state sovereignty. *Prosecutor v Tadic,* Decision on the Defence Motion for Interlocutory Appeal on Jurisdiction IT-94-1-AR72 paras 55–60.

[27] KM Clarke, AS Knotterus & E de Volder 'Africa and the ICC: An Introduction' in KM Clarke, AS Knotterus & E de Volder (eds) *Africa and the ICC: Perceptions of Justice* (2016) 11.

[28] F Megret & M Samson, 'Holding the Line on Complementarity in Libya: The Case for Tolerating Flawed Domestic Trials' (2013) 11 *Journal of International Criminal Justice* 571–572.

[29] P Gaeta, 'The International Criminal Court and Complementarity: From Theory to Practice' (2004) 2 *Journal of International Criminal Justice* 949.

was followed by two more situations by way of 'self-referral' under similar conditions, i.e. Uganda and the Central African Republic.[30]

Underlying these early 'self-referrals' was the OTP's theory of 'uncontested admissibility', in terms of which 'the complementarity test is satisfied by inactivity, rather than by an overt manifestation of a State's unwillingness or inability to proceed'.[31] Whether or not this practice violated the letter of the 'complementarity' principle (we would suggest it did), it certainly ran afoul of its spirit and raised a number of policy concerns.[32] For those hoping to ensure that existing power imbalances in the international order did not make their way into the work of the ICC, including African states, the OTP's approach to complementarity raised particular concerns.

As noted above, there was already a structural bias built into the inability aspect of the complementarity regime, which would more likely effect weaker or poorer states whose 'national judicial system' would more likely be found to be have 'collapse[d]' or become unavailable.[33] In fact, at the time of the Rome Statute's drafting, Louise Arbour—the former Chief Prosecutor of the ad hoc Tribunals—reportedly argued 'the regime would work in favour of rich, developed countries and against poor countries'; as while the 'Prosecutor might easily make the claims that a justice system in an underdeveloped country was ineffective and therefore "unable" to proceed,... the difficulties involved in challenging a State with a sophisticated and functional justice system would be virtually insurmountable'.[34] In 1998, such concerns were somewhat mitigated by the revision of the draft Statute at Rome whereby the 'collapse' of the domestic system contemplated in article 17(3) was amended so as to be 'total or substantial collapse', not merely a 'partial' one.

[30] CK Hall, 'Positive Complementarity in Action' in C Stahn & M El Zeidy (eds) *The International Criminal Court and Complementarity: From Theory to Practice* (2014) 1014–1051, 1018.

[31] W Schabas & M El Zeidy 'Article 17: Issues of Admissibility' in O Triffterer & K Ambos (eds) *The Rome Statute of the International Criminal Court: A Commentary* (2016) 797.

[32] See McAuliffe (n 4 above) 281–285.

[33] See Article 17(3) Rome Statute.

[34] As recounted in W Schabas *An Introduction to the International Criminal Court* (2017) 178.

Under the 'uncontested admissibility' theory, however, the OTP empowered itself to negotiate (or extort) a concession from individual states that they were not necessarily unwilling or unable, but that their judicial systems were, and would remain, 'inactive'; without the OTP having to conclude that formally or convince a Court thereof. Inevitably, this new-found power on the part of the OTP would be more easily exercised in respect of weaker states, as the first three situations that came before the ICC would confirm. As discussed below, this 'inactivity' test, and the power appropriated by the OTP to apply it, would come to replace the 'inability' test altogether in the recent Iraq admissibility determination.

If the first situations on the Court's docket arrived on the basis that the states concerned were willing, but not quite willing enough, to prosecute them; its supporters soon turned to ensuring that the next set of cases stayed on the Court's docket on the basis that the states were *too willing* to do so. Following the UN Security Council's referral of the situation in Libya to the ICC in February 2011, the post-Gaddafi Libyan authorities invoked complementarity to challenge the admissibility of the cases of Saif Al-Islam Gaddafi and Abdullah Al-Senussi.[35] Some ICC supporters, however, argued that the Libya authorities were, in essence, too willing to prosecute these cases domestically—at the expense of the rights of the accused persons—and that these cases should therefore remain with the ICC.[36] In terms of this due process thesis, 'states who wish to retain control over cases must ensure that trials adhere to international standards

[35] See *Application on behalf of the Government of Libya pursuant to Article 19 of the ICC Statute*, ICC-01/11-01/11-130-Conf; *Application on behalf of the Government of Libya relating to Abdullah Al-Senussi pursuant to Article 19 of the ICC Statute*, ICC-01/11-01/11-307-Conf-Exp.

[36] R Teitel 'Local Injustice: Why We Shouldn't Forget about Saif Gaddafi' *I-CONnect Blog of the International Journal of Constitutional Law and Constitution Making* 16 October 2012 http://www.iconnectblog.com/2012/10/local-injustice-why-we-shouldnt-forget-about-saif-gaddafi/ (accessed on 24 May 2021); J O'Donohue & S. Rigney 'The ICC Must Consider Fair Trial Concerns in Determining Libya's Application to Prosecute Saif al-Islam Gaddafi Nationally' *EJIL.Talk! Blog of the European Journal of International Law* 8 June 2012 https://www.ejiltalk.org/the-icc-must-consider-fair-trial-concerns-in-determining-libyas-application-to-prosecute-saif-al-islam-gaddafi-nationally/ (accessed on 24 May 2021); and C Stahn 'Libya, the International Criminal Court and Complementarity: A Test for Shared Responsibility' (2012) 10 *Journal of International Criminal Justice* 325.

of due process … as found in international human rights instruments'.[37] 'Due process' was proposed in the course of the investigations into Libya as an *additional* requirement to be met before domestic proceedings could displace the ICC under the principle of complementarity and is not part of the text of the Rome Statute[38]. While the ICC Appeals Chamber appears to have rejected this argument,[39] it highlighted the risks of further structural biases in the application of the complementarity regime as a result of a focus on the substance of domestic procedures, and the up ending of the balance struck at Rome between domestic and international proceedings.

McAuliffe argues that the Prosecutor's strategy of soliciting self-referrals and efforts of the Court's supporters to 're-work' complementarity form part of a broader strategy to move away from the 'horizontal framework' contained in the Rome Statute rooted in State consent and deferential to the State's primacy of action regarding criminal prosecutions in favour of a 'vertical framework'. With the vertical framework 'the Court enjoys priority over the national jurisdiction, incorporating notions of superior supranationality as an international body and implying a relationship of authority by intervening in the domain of domestic affairs'.[40]According to McAuliffe, since 1998 the ICC's gradual shift towards a vertical construction of its relationship to states represented a 'conscious choice' by the Court and its supporters to move away

[37] Megret & Sampson (n 28 above) 574.

[38] See K Heller 'The Shadow Side of Complementarity: The Effect of Article 17 of the Rome Statute on National Due Process' (2006)17 *Criminal Law Forum* 260–270.

[39] *Prosecutor v. Saif Al-Islam Gaddafi and Abdullah Al-Senussi,* ICC01/11-01/11-565, Judgment on the Appeal of Mr Abdullah Al-Senussi against the Decision of Pre-Trial Chamber I of 11 October 2013 Entitled 'Decision on the Admissibility of the Case against Abdullah Al-Senussi', Appeals Chamber, 24 July 2014, paras 2–3. The Court held: 'Taking into account the text, context and object and purpose of the provision, this determination is nto one that involves an assessment of whether the due process rights of a suspect have been breached per se. …However, there *may be circumstances*…whereby violations of the rights of the suspect are so egregious that the proceedings can no longer be regarded as being capable of providing any genuine form of justice to the suspect so that they should be *deemed…to be* "inconsistent with an intent to bring the person to justice."'

[40] McAuliffe (n 4 above) 259–260.

from the delicate balance struck at Rome between traditional statism and cosmopolitan supranationalism.[41]

The reworking of 'complementarity' into so-called *positive* complementarity was central to this shift.[42] According to Stahn, by 2008, the 'classical vision of complementarity' (as 'an instrument to overcome sovereignty fears' of states and to 'remedy shortcomings or failures of domestic jurisdiction') had already been replaced by the 'positive' version, in terms of which 'complementarity is not only an instrument to monitor state action, but also a forum for managerial interaction between the Court and States'.[43] According to McAuliffe, such arguments represent 'the tendency of scholars, activists, judges and lawyers in international criminal law to infer verticality or supranationality from the pure idea of international criminal justice on the basis of good faith but partial interpretations of texts agreed earlier by sovereignty-conscious States who would prefer a more horizontal relationship'.[44]

It stands to reason that the shift towards 'verticality or supranationality' would have been more difficult had its effects been felt by 'stronger states' (historically, politically and economically). In this regard, it is telling that some ICC judges have recently begun to rein in the OTP just as its investigations have begun to have such effects, not on the basis of complementarity, but on the terms often associated with it. Reasons advanced by the judges include that 'the Court is not meant – or equipped – to address any and all ... international crimes', has limited 'financial and human resources', and must manage 'victims' expectations'.[45] Beyond weak and strong states, the gradual shift that empowers a global, largely Western elite consisting not just of Court functionaries, but also of academics and NGO representatives to oversee and manage the domestic proceedings (overwhelmingly in African states), has unnerving colonial parallels and more recent ones in respect of the ICTR, as discussed below. The same

[41] McAuliffe (n 4 above) 273.

[42] See, for example, C Stahn 'Complementarity: A Tale of Two Notions', (2008)19 *Criminal Law Forum* 87–113.

[43] Stahn (n 42 above) 88.

[44] McAuliffe (n 4 above) 265.

[45] ICC *Decision Pursuant to Article 15 of the Rome Statute on the Authorisation of an Investigation into the Situation in the Islamic Republic of Afghanistan* (12 April 2019) paras. 90 & 95–96.

is true of the over-emphasis on African states when it comes to interventions in the name of 'positive complementarity'—a secondary effect of this shift—such as 'capacity-building' and criminal law reform.[46]

4 A Double Standard?

As African states had expressed their clear preference for a 'horizontal framework', they had reasons for growing concern regarding these shifts in the understanding of the principle of complementarity, arising not only from the potential application of a *higher* standard to domestic proceedings than they had agreed to at Rome, but the application of a *double standard* when compared to their Western counterparts. A prime example was the experience of Rwanda with the ICTR, where that Tribunal transferred cases to France and the Netherlands without stringent due process guarantees or assessments but took five years to transfer its first case to Rwanda (and only after Rwanda had created a special due process law applying solely to Article 11*bis* transferees, abolished the death penalty and built a state-of-the-art prison).[47] Another example was the OTP's 2006 Iraq decision, which avoided considering complementarity in any detail, but satisfied itself—in a sentence—that 'national proceedings had been initiated with respect to each of the relevant incidents', and concluded that 'effectively functioning national legal systems are in principle the most appropriate and effective forum for addressing allegations of crimes of this nature'.[48]

Until such time as there was a 'complementarity assessment' in respect of a situation *outside of Africa* these particular 'double-standard' concerns remained somewhat speculative, however, as there was nothing against which to compare the standard adopted in complementarity assessment of African states. Notably, this was partly due to the OTP's inconsistent approach to the question of admissibility, insofar as whether to consider 'complementarity' before 'gravity', or the other way around. For example, the OTP managed to avoid applying the complementarity regime to the allegations of crimes by UK soldiers in 2006 and the Israeli Defence Force

[46] See further C Gevers, 'Back to the Future?: Civil Society, the 'Turn to Complementarity' in Africa and Some Critical Concerns' (2016) *Acta Juridica* 95.

[47] See Gevers (n 46 above) 124–125.

[48] ICC Office of the Prosecutor *Letter to Senders re Iraq* (9 February 2006) 9.

in 2014[49] by focussing on gravity, for reasons unknown but not beyond speculation.[50]

In December 2020, almost two decades after the ICC came into operation, and 15 years after it was first asked to investigate crimes by UK forces in Iraq, the OTP subjected a non-African state to a substantive 'complementarity assessment'.[51] In determining that the numerous international crimes that it found were likely to have been committed by UK forces in Iraq were inadmissible on the grounds of complementarity, the OTP completely abandoned its vertical approach to complementarity, in favour of a return to the 'horizontal framework, rooted in State consent and deferential to the State's primacy of action regarding criminal prosecutions'.[52] The decision both in terms of its conclusion and the lengths the OTP went to reach it leaves little doubt that there is a double standard when it comes to complementarity assessments, between African states and non-African states, or at least between African states and powerful Western states. For these reasons, it is worth considering the OTP's UK admissibility determination in some detail, not least of all because it cannot be appealed and so is less likely to receive the critical attention it deserves.

The OTP began its 184-page decision by noting that 'more than ten year long domestic process, involving the examination of thousands of allegations, has resulted in *not one single case being submitted for prosecution*: a result that has deprived the victims of justice'.[53] The

[49] See ICC Office of the Prosecutor *Situation on Registered Vessels of Comoros, Greece and Cambodia: Article 53(1) Report* (6 November 2014).

[50] We now know that that decision in respect of alleged UK crimes in Iraq was singularly significant; as, had it considered complementarity in 2006, the OTP would presumably have found the UK's domestic proceedings both 'unwilling' and neither impartial nor independent.

[51] In its 2015 Request to open an investigation into crimes committed in Georgia under article 15, the OTP briefly considered the domestic proceedings in Georgia and Russia, concluding that the relevant cases were partly admissible, on that basis that domestic proceedings in the former had become 'inactive' and that those in the latter did 'not appear vitiated at this stage by a lack of willingness or inability'. ICC Office of the Prosecutor *Corrected Version of "Request for authorisation of an investigation pursuant to article 15"* (16 October 2015) ICC-01/15-5-Corr para. 323.

[52] McAuliffe (n 4 above) 261.

[53] *Situation in Iraq* (n 5 above) para. 6. The OTP Report ended with the same observation (see para 496).

casual observer might conclude that the OTP should have ended its complementarity assessment there, however, it proceeded to explain[54]:

> This outcome might trigger apprehension that either the claims submitted were frivolous and vexatious, or, conversely, that the UK process was not genuine and was designed to intentionally shield alleged perpetrators from criminal responsibility. Unpacking these issues has proven more complex than might immediately be expected.

The devil was in the detail, sort of. In truth, the first 'apprehension' mentioned by the OTP did not require much 'unpacking', as it swiftly confirmed its 2017 finding that there was a reasonable basis to believe that members of UK armed forces committed numerous war crimes in Iraq between March 2003 and July 2009. A contradiction of the OTP's 2006 Iraq Decision, without consequence.[55] Ultimately, it was the second 'apprehension'—namely, that the UK process was not 'genuine'—that required 'unpacking' by the OTP.

Before setting out how the OTP reached its benign conclusion from such a damning opening, it is worth noting some of the adverse findings that the OTP made regarding the UK's domestic proceedings along the way (euphemistically called 'areas of concern').[56] We limit ourselves to seven examples: First, that the UK Government and the Ministry of Defence had been 'reluctant, if not at times hostile, partners to pursuing claims of criminal responsibility' for past abuses, and there were 'indications of unwillingness on [their] part…to genuinely investigate and prosecute past abuses committed by British personnel in Iraq'.[57] Second, that the 'initial measures' taken by the British army to investigate and prosecute the alleged crimes 'fell short of the standards set out in…the Statute, both in terms of inaction and unwillingness to genuinely carry out the relevant investigations'.[58] Third, that the domestic institutional mechanism established to address these 'initial failings' (following

[54] As above.

[55] *Situation in Iraq* (n 5 above) paras 7, 493.

[56] *Situation in Iraq* (n 5 above) para 152.

[57] *Situation in Iraq* (n 5 above) para 461, 480.

[58] *Situation in Iraq* (n 5 above) para 494 (see further para 5).

the intervention of UK courts)[59]—the 'Iraq Historic Allegations Team (IHAT)—was placed under immense political pressure and eventually closed down ahead of schedule in 2017 based on 'political considerations in the form of a publicly stated commitment to protect the UK armed forces'.[60] Fourth, that IHAT and its replacement (the 'Service Police Legacy Investigations') received more than 3600 allegations (possibly substantially more)[61] and the 'vast majority' of which (over 70%) were 'sifted out and never reached full investigation as a result, while of cases submitted to full investigation only a handful were referred for prosecution'.[62] As noted, not one was prosecuted. Fifth, the OTP identified multiple 'concerns' with this 'sifting' process, including that a large number of allegations were 'dismiss[ed]...without further investigation' on the basis of 'proportionality', but the UK refused to say how many or disclose the relevant factors (but included the 'particularly problematic' consideration of 'passage of time' resulting from 'their own past failings').[63] Sixth, the OTP independently verified and found credible, 'balanced' and consistent public allegations by former British investigators and prosecutors of a 'cover-up' by UK authorities (including 'intentional disregarding, falsification, and/or destruction of evidence as well as the impeding or prevention of certain investigative inquiries and the premature termination of cases').[64] Seventh, that, as a result of the Iraq investigations, the UK government was in the process of passing legislation providing a statutory presumption *against* prosecution of current or former UK service members for offences committed outside the UK in course of duty.

Despite these findings, however, the OTP ultimately concluded that the UK was neither inactive nor unwilling in its investigation and (non)prosecution of these allegations, and therefore 'the potential cases

[59] *Situation in Iraq* (n 5 above) para 160–163.

[60] *Situation in Iraq* (n 5 above) para 457 (see further para 182).

[61] *Situation in Iraq* (n 5 above) para 180.

[62] *Situation in Iraq* (n 5 above) para 305. According to the Report, of the more than 3600 allegations received, '2,367 (or 65%) were ultimately closed', of which '1,667 were dismissed at the initial assessment stage, 661 were dismissed following pre-investigation case assessment, and 39 were discontinued at the investigation stage'.

[63] *Situation in Iraq* (n 5 above) para 160.

[64] *Situation in Iraq* (n 5 above) para 408.

arising from the situation currently appear to be inadmissible in view of complementarity'.[65]

The OTP concluded that the UK was not 'inactive' on the basis that '[t]he information available indicates that the UK authorities … have initiated a number of criminal proceedings (involving pre-investigative assessment of claims, investigations, *and a more limited number of prosecutions*)'.[66] This determination by the OTP relied on a re-characterisation and a mischaracterisation (at best). The re-characterisation was the inclusion of the UK authorities' decision not to investigate over 70% of the allegations (or 'filter' or 'sift', to use the preferred euphemisms of the OTP and UK),[67] as a form of 'activity' (action by inaction, perhaps). The mischaracterisation was the repeated claim by the OTP that these criminal proceedings had involved 'a *more limited* number of prosecutions', despite recognising elsewhere that they had resulted in exactly zero prosecutions (or, straightforward inaction): *at best* a mischaracterisation, if not an outright falsehood.

This approach to 'inactivity' stands in stark contrast to that of the OTP in the Kenya admissibility challenges[68]; where the government argued that the constitutional and judicial reforms it had implemented (including the adoption of a new constitution in August 2010 and the pending appointment of a new Chief Justice and High Court judges pursuant to the newly enacted Judicial Services Act)[69] paved the way for the domestic prosecution of the accused, and that it had already initiated investigations into some of the 'Ocampo six' and promised to regularly update the Court as to the progress of these.[70] In response, the OTP argued that the commitment by Kenya to initiate investigations

[65] *Situation in Iraq* (n 5 above) para 489.

[66] *Situation in Iraq* (n 5 above) para 275.

[67] *Situation in Iraq* (n 5 above) paras 8, 170, 188, 196, 276, 304, 305, 308, 312, 330, 346, 349, 363, 431, 482, 498; David Calvert-Smith, *Review of the Iraq Historic Allegations Team,* available at https://www.gov.uk/government/publications/review-of-iraq-historic-allegations-team (accessed on 24 May 2021).

[68] *Prosecutor v. William Ruto & Others* (ICC-01/09-01/11) and *Prosecutor v. Francis Muthaura & Others* (ICC-01/09-02/11) Application on behalf of the Government of the Republic of Kenya Pursuant to article 19(2)(b) of the ICC Statute (Pre-Trial Chamber II).

[69] *Prosecutor v. William Ruto & Others* (n 68 above) paras 48–50 & 52–55.

[70] *Prosecutor v. William Ruto & Others* (n 68 above) para 14.

was not sufficient to satisfy the admissibility requirements[71]; as although the reforms implemented by Kenya indeed paved the way for investigations into the 2007 post-election violence in question, the investigations remained hypothetical.[72] The Pre-Trial Chamber agreed, finding that the 'inactivity' on the part of the government of Kenya made it unnecessary to rule on the inability or unwillingness test.[73] The government of Kenya appealed this decision,[74] and the Appeals Chamber upheld the ruling.[75] As Spilman noted at the time, the Kenyan admissibility decisions seemed to place a higher burden on States to maintain or retrieve jurisdiction through requiring sufficient probative evidence to prove that an investigation is ongoing, and shift the burden of proving admissibility from the Prosecutor to the State challenging admissibility.[76] Prior to the Kenya admissibility decisions, scholars had interpreted article 17 to mean that the burden of proof in admissibility challenges would fall upon the prosecutor; by shifting of the burden of proof from to States' challenging admissibility this interpretation risked heightening the structural biases arising from the political and economic disparities between states in the West, which have the human, infrastructural and financial resources to meet the requirements set out by the Court; and politically and economically weaker states lacking such resources.[77]

[71] *Prosecutor v William Ruto & Others* (ICC-01/09-01/11) Prosecution Response to ' Application on behalf of the Government of Kenya Pursuant to article 19 of the ICC Statute (Pre-Trial Chamber II) para 20.

[72] *Prosecutor v. William Ruto & Others* (n 72 above) para 25–26.

[73] *Prosecutor v. William Ruto & Others* Admissibility Challenge Decision para 70; *Prosecutor v. Francis Muthaura & Others* case, Admissibility Challenge Decision para 66.

[74] *Prosecutor v. William Ruto & Others* (ICC-01/09-01/11) and *Prosecutor v. Francis Muthaura & Others* (ICC-01/09-02/11) Document in Support of the ' Appeal of the Government of Kenya Challenging the Admissibility of the Case Pursuant to Article 19 (2) (b) of the Statute' (Appeals Chamber).

[75] ICC Judgment on the appeal of the Republic of Kenya against the decision of Pre-Trial Chamber II of 30 May 2011 entitled ' Decision on the Application by the Government of Kenya Challenging the Admissibility of the Case Pursuant to article 19 (2) (b) of the Statute (Appeals Chamber)'.

[76] Spilman (n 22 above) 17–19, 20.

[77] Spilman (n 22 above) 13–15. See also Max du Plessis and Christopher Gevers 'South Africa's Foreign Policy and the International Criminal Court: on African Lessons, Security Council Reform and Possibilities for an Improved ICC' in T Shaw & J Warner

In any event, the OTP's finding on the first 'step' of the 'admissibility assessment' (i.e. *activity*) appeared to paint it into a corner in respect of the second step (i.e. *genuineness*).[78] Simply put: if a domestic criminal justice system 'acts' on 'thousands of complaints', when there are reasonable grounds to believe that numerous war crimes have been, but *cannot bring a single case to prosecution,* what conclusion can one reach other than that domestic system is either (clearly) unwilling or (chronically) unable to prosecute these crimes? Nevertheless, the OTP was able to conclude that the UK's domestic proceedings were not *not* genuine through a combination of (1) the parsing of the evidence of problems, (2) the 'narrow' construction of the 'unwilling' criterion under article 17 and (3) a conservative, pre-emptive and self-defeating approach to the applicable evidential burden.

First, the OTP parsed the evidence of 'areas of concern' in respect of the UK's domestic proceedings in such a way as to disarm its impact. For example, instead of considering the UK government's conduct as a whole, the OTP distinguished between the conduct of 'different national institutions', and their successive office bearers,[79] and then offset or excused one against the other.[80] Most productively, the OTP drew a distinction between (and a line under) the 'repeatedly acknowledged…critical failings' of 'initial criminal investigations' which, it concluded, demonstrated *both* inaction and unwillingness,[81] and the 'subsequent steps taken by the UK authorities…to *re-examine historical allegations*' (i.e. the IHAT and SPLI investigations). This distinction between the 'initial' (or 'historical') domestic proceedings was then put to considerable work, not only to absolve the latter of the sins of the former (despite both being the actions of the, similarly absolved, UK State), but also to go so far as to justify

(eds) *African Foreign Policies in International Institutions, Contemporary African Political Economy* (2018) 207–208.

[78] *Situation in Iraq* (n 5 above) para 154.

[79] *Situation in Iraq* (n 5 above) para 460.

[80] See *Situation in Iraq* (n 5 above) para 480.

[81] *Situation in Iraq* (n 5 above) para 494.

the sins of the latter in terms of 'effectiveness and pace'[82] as the unavoidable baggage of those of the former.[83] It also set in motion a progress narrative from these initial failings to the subsequent re-examinations.[84]

This approach to the evidence resulted in, or produced, a 'mixed picture'[85] of domestic proceedings, and created the appearance of reasonable conduct and genuine efforts, or, as the OTP confidently declares at one point: of conduct that is 'not so unreasonable or deficient as to constitute evidence of unwillingness to carry out relevant investigations or prosecutions genuinely'.[86] However, it defies logic that while multiple civil cases have been settled by the UK government,[87] there has been no prosecutions. This is why, ultimately, the OTP could get no further than concluding that the UK was not unwilling; a conclusion that it could only reach through a narrow construction of the legal test(s) applicable to the 'second step of the complementarity assessment'[88]: *genuineness*.

The OTP began its genuineness enquiry by casting aside the question whether the UK was '*unable* to undertake *genuine proceedings*' (one it had set itself at the outset),[89] focussing solely on the question of it's possible '*unwillingness* to carry them out genuinely'.[90] It then further narrowed down the 'tests under article 17(2)(a) - (c)' concerning 'unwillingness genuinely to proceed', making all three dependent on a positive finding of an intent on the part of the UK authorities to 'shield the person[s] concerned from criminal responsibility for crimes within the jurisdiction of the Court' (i.e. article 17(2)*(a)*). Even on this limited standard the OTP might have found the UK 'unwilling' based on the outcome of their activity, or lack thereof, following the construction of

82 *Situation in Iraq* (n 5 above) para 500.

83 *Situation in Iraq* (n 5 above) para 361.

84 *Situation in Iraq* (n 5 above) para 500.

85 *Situation in Iraq* (n 5 above) para 481.

86 *Situation in Iraq* (n 5 above) para 350.

87 As the OTP noted, civil cases 'continue to be settled, and for those cases not settled, litigation before the [UK] High Court has established that the underlying facts did constitute ill-treatment', which suggested that 'the bulk of claims meet the threshold for objective attribution to the UK armed forces'. *Situation in Iraq* (n 5 above) para 483.

88 *Situation in Iraq* (n 5 above) para 279.

89 *Situation in Iraq* (n 5 above) para 9.

90 *Situation in Iraq* (n 5 above) para 280.

article 17(2)(a) proposed by Schabas and El Zeidy (which the OTP itself cited). In terms of this construction, 17(2)(a) is 'a test for discerning the bad faith of a State by way of *checking the effectiveness of national proceedings*' (based on 'any intentional deficiency or serious negligence....that lead to negative results').[91] The failure to bring a single prosecution following a 'more than ten year long domestic process' would appear to qualify as a negative result, or at least not a very effective one, by most standards. The OTP explicitly sidestepped a result-based assessment, however, by drawing on human rights jurisprudence on the right to effective remedy to conclude that '[t]his is not an obligation of result, but of means'.[92]

In assessing the *means* adopted by UK investigators and prosecutors to the allegations in question, the OTP adopted two standards, that ran in parallel. The first was a reasonableness standard, drawn from human rights jurisprudence and its notion of a 'margin of appreciation'[93] which asked whether the actions 'appear reasonable' (or at least 'do not appear *unreasonable*').[94] The second, and more important, was inference-based, and asked 'whether the facts, on their face, demonstrate an intent to shield persons from criminal responsibility'.[95] In the event that the means adopted by investigators and prosecutors failed the first standard, then the second (lower) standard invariably came to the UK's assistance. Applying these standards, the OTP found that various problematic aspects of the UK's proceedings either 'appear[ed] reasonable',[96] or in any event 'not so unreasonable or deficient as to constitute evidence of unwillingness to carry out relevant investigations or prosecutions genuinely, in the sense of showing an intent to shield perpetrators from criminal justice'.[97] This finding was applied to (i) the 'filtering criteria' by which 'around 70

[91] See *Situation in Iraq* (n 5 above) note 504 (citing W Schabas & M El Zeidy 'Article 17: Issues of Admissibility' in Triffterer & Ambos (n 31 above) 819.

[92] *Situation in Iraq* (n 5 above) para 297.

[93] *Situation in Iraq* (n 5 above) para 362.

[94] *Situation in Iraq* (n 5 above) para 361.

[95] *Situation in Iraq* (n 5 above) para 347.

[96] *Situation in Iraq* (n 5 above) para 312.

[97] *Situation in Iraq* (n 5 above) para 350.

percent of the allegations were sifted out and never reached full investigation'[98]; (ii) the decision to dismiss 'a significant amount of claims' as contaminated by 'vexatious litigation'—even though they were substantiated independently elsewhere[99]; (iii) the decision to close a considerable number[100] of allegations of ill-treatment based on an opaque 'proportionality assessment; and (iv) the 'paucity of cases concerning command responsibility that … resulted in referrals for prosecution, and the subsequent fate of those cases'.[101] More difficult to dismiss under article 17(2)(a) were the direct and specific allegations of cover-up made by former investigators and soldiers.[102] Rather than make a finding on the allegations which it indicated were credible, 'balanced' and consistent,[103] the OTP resorted to the evidential burden: concluding that the '[v]erification of these allegations could have established a basis to seek the opening of an investigation', but the OTP could not substantiate them 'with evidence *that it could rely upon in court*'.[104]

The OTP then applied the same approach to the other two 'unwilling' tests—concerning 'unjustified delay' (article 17(2)(b)) and 'independence and impartiality' (article 17(2)(b))—which it interpreted narrowly and applied selectively to the facts. Going against its own 2013 policy, the OTP interpreted that phrase 'an unjustified delay…which in the circumstances is inconsistent with an intent to bring the persons concerned to justice' as requiring specifically establishing 'the intention not 'to bring the person concerned to justice'.[105] Not only did the OTP conclude that

[98] *Situation in Iraq* (n 5 above) para 305.

[99] *Situation in Iraq* (n 5 above) paras 322, 338.

[100] The OTP noted that 'it is difficult to gauge the exact number of cases which were closed on proportionality grounds', but 'it appears to be significant'. *Situation in Iraq* (n 5 above) para 351. When the OTP tried to 'close these information gaps', the UK refused to provide the necessary information. See *Situation in Iraq* (n 5 above) para 359.

[101] *Situation in Iraq* (n 5 above) para 371.

[102] *Situation in Iraq* (n 5 above) paras 372–3.

[103] *Situation in Iraq* (n 5 above) para 408.

[104] *Situation in Iraq* (n 5 above) paras 407–409.

[105] *Situation in Iraq* (n 5 above) paras 413–4. According to the OTP's *Policy Paper on Preliminary Examinations* (2013): 'Unjustified delay in the proceedings at hand may be assessed in light of indicators such as … whether there *is evidence of a lack of intent* to bring the person(s) concerned to justice' (para. 52). The OTP cited this passage, in fact. See *Situation in Iraq* (n 5 above) para 415.

it could not find evidence of 'intentionality' in respect of the delay,[106] it found that the 'past failings' of UK authorities actually *justified* the inability of IHAT and SPLI to 'subsequently carry out effective investigations' at the appropriate 'pace'[107]; claiming to concur with a British court's 2016 observation that 'the occurrence of past delay makes yet further delay more legitimate'.[108] Aside from the fact that the judge in question actually said *precisely the opposite*,[109] there are at least two problems with this reasoning. First, it disaggregated the 'State' and applied the test selectively to its constituent institutions, letting one benefit from the 'past failings' of another, rather than judging the domestic proceedings as a whole. Second, the evidence does not support the claim that things had improved under the IHAT and SPLI, as there has still been unjustified delays,[110] no prosecutions and the domestic political climate appears to be getting even more hostile (as evidenced by the early closure of IHAT).

It is important to briefly point out the speciousness of this approach to delays in domestic proceedings more generally, which amounts to condoning a state not investigating properly and causing a delay, then later investigating properly but being justifiably unable to proceed 'practically' on account of the 'passage of time' caused by it own delay. It is, in effect, a recipe for slow-walking cases into oblivion (to paraphrase Heller), albeit one that relies on an accomplice in the OTP willing to allow the State to 'run up the clock' during the initial phase of 'inaction and unwillingness' (in this case on the basis of 'gravity').[111] The risibility

[106] The OTP concluded that despite the 'various issues of concern on the issue of delay, it could not attribute them to a lack of willingness to carry out the proceedings genuinely'. *Situation in Iraq* (n 5 above) para 500 (see further para 433).

[107] *Situation in Iraq* (n 5 above) para 500.

[108] *Situation in Iraq* (n 5 above) para 432.

[109] The passage in question comes from *Al-Saadoon & Ors v Secretary of State for Defence* (Rev 1) [2016] EWHC 773 (Admin) (07 April 2016), where Justice Leggatt observed: 'One of the essential attributes of an effective investigation is that it should be carried out promptly. That has not on any view been achieved in this case when the death occurred more than a decade ago. *But I do not consider that the occurrence of past delay makes yet further delay more legitimate*' (para 33). From the context of the passage, it appears that the OTP may have meant to 'concur' with what Justice Leggatt actually said, but the error is telling as the misquoted formulation better reflects the OTP's overall argument regarding the effect of 'past delays'.

[110] *Situation in Iraq* (n 5 above) para 425.

[111] *Situation in Iraq* (n 5 above) para 494.

of this approach is only outpaced by the fact that this recipe for slow-walking might equally be used to describe the OTP's own approach to the investigation in Iraq (and the Pre-Trial Chamber's reasoning in the Afghanistan): refusing to investigate in 2006 for lack of evidence, then declining to investigate in 2020 in large part for reasons arising from the 'passage of time'.

The OTP approached the third 'unwilling' test (concerning 'independence and impartiality') in the same fashion: adopting an unduly onerous 'requirement of intentionality' and then distinguishing between the 'early steps taken by the UK authorities' (which it found to be 'marred by a lack of independence and impartiality')[112] and the 'subsequent historical investigations'[113] by IHAT and SPLI. In addition, the OTP effected a distinction between 'the [UK] State' and its different 'national institutions',[114] in order to isolate and minimise the effects 'strong government and parliamentary pressure' to protect the UK armed forces (which it later described as showing 'indications of unwillingness').[115] The OTP noted that this pressure[116]:

> [C]ould be a relevant consideration for assessing whether *'the State'* was acting with an intent to shield persons from criminal responsibility within the meaning of article 17. However, in situations where ***different national institutions*** may demonstrate varying and inconsistent degrees of willingness/unwillingness, ***primary consideration should be given to the conduct of the competent authorities responsible for carrying out the proceedings in question.***

As it had with the specific cover-up allegations, when it came to assessing the broader political pressure the OTP once again resorted (or retreated) to the question of evidence.[117]

[112] *Situation in Iraq* (n 5 above) para 446.

[113] *Situation in Iraq* (n 5 above) para 447.

[114] A distinction that runs counter to the text of article 17 of the Rome Statute, as well as the OTP's own conclusion later on in the Report. See *Situation in Iraq* (n 5 above) para 485.

[115] *Situation in Iraq* (n 5 above) para 480.

[116] *Situation in Iraq* (n 5 above) para 457.

[117] *Situation in Iraq* (n 5 above) para 458.

In fact, throughout its assessment the OTP adopted a conservative, pre-emptive and self-defeating approach to the applicable evidential burden. While the OTP did not articulate the standard it applied, beyond noting that it was 'a high threshold',[118] it was clearly higher than the standard that ordinarily applies to preliminary investigations (i.e. a reasonable basis to proceed). The reason for the OTP applying this higher standard was pre-emptive, it assumed that the UK (or Iraq) would challenge its admissibility based on article 18 of the Statute,[119] anticipating both the kind of 'evidence it could rely upon in court',[120] and the 'required level of proof before the Court'. In effect, the OTP jumped ahead two steps in the process and applied a conservative interpretation of what the evidential standard *at that stage* might be.[121] Moreover, even if one accepts that this conservative, pre-emptive approach was a reasonable one, to be taken seriously it needs to be applied consistently. If the OTP anticipated its evidence being tested in Court under an article 18 challenge, it should have anticipated that the UK would have to close the 'information gaps'[122] regarding domestic proceedings, gaps that the UK had explicitly refused to close, despite the OTP's polite requests.[123] These included basic and fundamental evidence regarding the domestic proceedings, including an 'overall paucity of…information'[124] regarding the grounds on which UK investigators had terminated an unknown,[125]

[118] *Situation in Iraq* (n 5 above) paras 283 & 484.

[119] *Situation in Iraq* (n 5 above) para 501.

[120] *Situation in Iraq* (n 5 above) paras 412, 409.

[121] See K Heller 'The Nine Worlds that (Wrongly) Doomed the Iraq Investigation' *OpinioJuris.org* 10 December 2020 https://opiniojuris.org/2020/12/10/the-nine-words-that-wrongly-doomed-the-iraq-investigation/ (accessed on 24 May 2021).

[122] *Situation in Iraq* (n 5 above) para 359.

[123] When it asked the UK government for more 'detailed information…, including individual data on each allegation', it simply refused to give it. *Situation in Iraq* (n 5 above) para 359. The OTP buried its outrage in a footnote, see *Situation in Iraq* (n 5 above) note 583.

[124] *Situation in Iraq* (n 5 above) para 362.

[125] The report blithely noted that '[w]hile it is difficult to gauge the exact number of cases which were closed on proportionality grounds, *it appears to be significant*: for example, in August 2018, the SPLI informed the office that 457 of the 1667 allegations it had closed were on the basis of proportionality'. *Situation in Iraq* (n 5 above) para 351.

but overwhelming majority,[126] of complaints without fully investigating them[127]; and the very question of whether there had in fact been any prosecutions.[128]

Perhaps the most significant aspect of the OTP's approach—particularly in the longer term—was the conflation of the assessment of 'inability' with mere 'activity', thereby making it a purely *qualitative* measure and entrenching the structural bias in favour of better-resourced states, a risk that was possible but not inevitable in the design of the complementarity regime in 1998. Following this approach, a State that does *something* will pass the inability test, despite that fact that it is possible for states to undertake multiple procedural actions, and establish multiple institutions, and achieve nothing in terms of prosecutions (as the present matter shows). Notably, at the outset of its assessment the OTP did in fact separate the preliminary question of inactivity from the subsequent questions of whether the State is either unwilling or 'unable to undertake genuine proceedings'.[129] Had the OTP followed through and considered whether the UK was '*unable* to undertake genuine proceedings', it would have been a lot harder to find the situation inadmissible on account of complementarity. This is because it would not have been impossible to avoid two (related) approaches to assessing the UK proceedings: (i) a result-based approach and (ii) systemic approach. If one considers either the number of convictions (none, as far as the OTP could tell), or the effectiveness of the domestic proceedings as a whole (bearing in mind the substantial number of substantiated claims (many settled civilly) and the level of activity by UK authorities), it is difficult to avoid the conclusion that the UK is 'unable to undertake genuine proceedings'. This conclusion is further reinforced by the UK's track record historically of being unable to prosecute international crimes committed by its armed forces or in its name.[130]

[126] *Situation in Iraq* (n 5 above) para 351.

[127] See, in particular, *Situation in Iraq* (n 5 above) paras 351–363.

[128] In its conclusion on 'genuineness', the OTP states that 'none of the cases resulting from completed IHAT or SPLI investigations and referred for further action *appear to have resulted in any prosecution in court*'. *Situation in Iraq* (n 5 above) para 481.

[129] *Situation in Iraq* (n 5 above) para 9 (see further para 154).

[130] See further C Gevers 'Prosecuting the Crime Against Humanity of Apartheid: Never, Again' (2018) 1 *African Yearbook of International Humanitarian Law* 25; and

In all these respects the OTP's approach to the UK's domestic proceedings represents a complete about-turn in its approach to complementarity. Following two decades of a gradual shift towards 'verticality' or 'supranationality', in a single and significant decision the OTP has reverted back to the horizontal framework envisioned at Rome in 1998, one 'rooted in State consent and deferential to the State's primacy of action regarding criminal prosecutions'.[131] This reversion to Rome is one that, in theory, African states should welcome for the reasons set out above, except that they have good reason to believe that it is not the standard that will apply to them in future. Rather, what emerges from the OTP's Iraq decision, the first detailed assessment of complementarity outside of Africa—and in respect of a powerful, Western state—is a clear double-standard when it comes to complementarity.

What is more, the legal mechanics of how this double-standard operated in the Iraq decision are closely connected to the practice of 'slow-walking' investigations, as the OTP would not have been able, both practically and legally, to reach this conclusion had it considered the question in 2006, when UK crimes in Iraq were first brought to its attention. As noted above, this practice is already evident in the OTP's approach to other situations concerning powerful, Western states and their allies: Afghanistan and Palestine. In this respect, the reason the OTP took such a charitable view of the UK's remarkably unsuccessful attempt to prosecute the most recent crimes committed in the name of the West might be that it very closely mirrors its own record; just as the abysmal track record of the UK more generally in this regard mirrors that of International Criminal Law as a whole, where there has not been a single prosecution of the crimes committed by the West or in its name, be it during colonialism, decolonisation or apartheid.[132]

5 Concluding Remarks

The AU began its controversial 2017 ICC 'Withdrawal Strategy' by setting out the reasons that African states had supported the 'the rule of

C Gevers 'Africa and International Criminal Law' in Heller, Megret, Nouwen, Ohlin & Robinson (n 6 above) 154.

[131] McAuliffe (n 4 above) 259–260.

[132] See further Gevers (n 130).

law movement' in 1998 and envisioned the proposed ICC 'as a beacon of emancipation [and] a solution for their continent's injustices', reasons which had as much to do with 'Africa's emancipatory future' as its violent past.[133]Not only the recent past of the Rwanda genocide, but also 'the injustices of South African apartheid, and the results of the long anti-colonial struggles against European imperialism'.[134] Two decades prior (in 1998), the OAU delegate at Rome had cited the same longer history as the reason why 'Africa had a particular interest in the establishment of the Court'.[135] While, just over fifty years ago (in 1966), newly independent African states were threatening to boycott another International Court that 'African countries [had]... lost faith in',[136] for behaving in a manner that was 'transparent with racism and the old regime of colonialism'.[137]

In 1966 it was the International Court of Justice (ICJ) that drew the ire of African states at the UN General Assembly, after the 'scandalous and wicked judgement'[138] in respect of *South West Africa* case—brought by Liberia and Ethiopia on behalf of all African states—which had 'deeply shaken [their] faith in the rule of law'[139] and 'placed in question the very existence of the Court'.[140] Notably, in 1966, African states effectively

[133] African Union *Withdrawal Strategy Document: Draft 2* (12 January 2017) para. 1.

[134] As above.

[135] As reported in Rome Proceedings 104.

[136] United Nations General Assembly 21st Session (1433rd Plenary Meeting 1433) para. 59.

[137] United Nations General Assembly 21st Session (1414th Plenary Meeting) para. 68. As the Algerian delegate put it: 'The Court, conceived at a time when colonial law was a part of international morality, no longer corresponds to the needs of an era when the concepts of liberation of peoples have become fundamental principles of international law. The Judgement of 18 July 1966 is inspired more by the philosophy of the nineteenth century than by the ideals which led our Assembly to adopt the resolutions on decolonization. The gap between the evolution of the world and stagnation of institutions is a serious contradiction which must be remedied'. United Nations General Assembly 21st Session (1447th Plenary Meeting) para. 130.

[138] United Nations General Assembly 21st Session (1432nd Plenary Meeting) para. 113.

[139] United Nations General Assembly 21st Session (1414th Plenary Meeting) para. 24.

[140] United Nations General Assembly 21st Session (1439th Plenary Meeting) para. 1.

accused the ICJ of 'slow-walking' the decision,[141] and then 'tak[ing] refuge in technicalities',[142] 'specious arguments and legalistic terms'.[143] The fall-out dominated the 1966 General Assembly[144] and led to the dropping of any reference to the ICJ from the two International Human Rights Covenants.[145] It would also have a marked but largely overlooked impact on International Criminal Law. In the aftermath of the ICJ's 1966 decision African states pushed for the inclusion of the crime of apartheid in the 1968 Convention on the Non-Applicability of Statutory Limitations to War Crimes and Crimes Against Humanity (the New York Convention), and for the drafting and adoption of the 1973 Convention on the Suppression and Punishment of the Crimes of Apartheid. The 1973 Convention not only criminalised apartheid and envisioned unprecedented powers for its prosecution by domestic courts,[146] it also led to a study being commissioned by the UN in 1980 for an 'International Criminal Court' to prosecute apartheid and other international crimes.[147] The author of that study, Cherif Bassiouni, would later claim that it was the blueprint for the Rome Statute.[148]

There is another lineage from 1966 to the present: during the drafting of the African Charter of Human and Peoples' Rights in the 1980s,

[141] The delegate from Burkina Faso (then Upper Volta) put it in more clinical terms, asking: 'Was it necessary to spend 336 h on order to pronounce judgement on procedure alone? Were 3,756 pages of evidence required to state that Ethiopia and Liberia had not established any interest in the case? Lastly, did the Court need 112 sittings to accept a system - I refer to apartheid - which had been rejected by the United Nations as contrary to its Charter? Was so much time, so much evidence, really needed in order to put us off with such a fallacious excuse?'. United Nations General Assembly 21st Session (1425th Plenary Meeting) para. 50.

[142] United Nations General Assembly 21st Session (1419th Plenary Meeting) para. 13.

[143] United Nations General Assembly 21st Session (1433rd Plenary Meeting) para. 74.

[144] On the opening day of the 21st UN General Assembly delegates voted to 'continue every morning with the general debate and *every afternoon with the discussion of the question of South West Africa*'. See United Nations General Assembly 21st Session (1419th Plenary Meeting) para. 233.

[145] United Nations General Assembly 21st Session (1495th Plenary Meeting) para 76.

[146] See further Gevers (n 131 above).

[147] See *Implementation of the International Convention on the Suppression and Punishment of the Crime of Apartheid: Resolution 12 (XXXVI)* 36th Session of the Commission on Human Rights (26 February 1980).

[148] C Bassiouni & W Schabas (eds) *The Legislative History of the International Criminal Court Vol. I* (2016), 36, 39–40.

consideration was given to including a provision establishing an African Court to prosecute international crimes (including apartheid), but the proposal was abandoned because of the ongoing efforts by the UN to establish 'an international court to repress crime against mankind'.[149] In 2014 African states took the first step towards establishing such a court by way of the 'Malabo Protocol',[150] and the AU's Withdrawal Strategy not only called for 'a robust strategy to enhance [it's] ratification' but also included a proposed amendment to the Rome Statute that would make the ICC 'complementary to national and *regional* criminal jurisdictions'.[151]

What these resonances between 1966 and the present illustrate is that the problems African states have raised with respect to the ICC and 'international justice' are not novel, and neither are its proposed solutions. Following the 1966 decision, African states resorted to strengthening *domestic* justice avenues (i.e. through the 1968 New York Convention and the 1973 Apartheid Convention) and (almost) establishing a new regional Court to prosecute international crimes. Today, African states are proposing 'continental and country level ownership of …international criminal justice through the strengthening [of] national and regional judicial systems'.[152] In the 1980s the 'regionalization of international criminal law'[153] was put on hold on account of efforts at the UN that ultimately led to the Rome Statute; however, despite the 'revolutionary' nature of the ICC African states find themselves back in 1966 in many respects.

Unless the ICC and its supporters finally take the concerns of African states seriously—the longstanding ones expressed in 1998 and those that have 'crept' in since then—and try to address them in earnest, African states and the Court are likely to drift further apart. Perhaps for good this time. This would undoubtedly be to the detriment of both an 'effective' ICC and noble ideal of the 'highest standards of international justice'.

[149] Organisation of African Unity *Rapporteur's Report of the Ministerial Meeting in Banjul, The Gambia* OAU Doc. CAB/LEG/67Draft Rapt. Rpt (II) Rev. 4 para. 13.

[150] *Protocol on Amendments to the Protocol on the Statute of the African Court of Justice and Human Rights.*

[151] Paras. 27 & 30. Notably, the proposed amendment was to the Preambular paragraph and not article 17.

[152] *Withdrawal Strategy Document* (n 133 above) para 27.

[153] *Withdrawal Strategy Document* (n 133 above) para 8.

References

Al-Saadoon & Ors v Secretary of State for Defence (Rev 1) [2016] EWHC 773 (Admin) (07 April 2016).

Bassiouni, C & Schabas, W (eds) *The Legislative History of the International Criminal Court Vol. I* (Brill: Leiden 2016).

Brown, B 'Primacy or Complementarity: Reconciling the Jurisdiction of National Courts and International Criminal Tribunals', (1998) 23 *Yale Journal of International Law* 383.

Calvert-Smith, D *Review of the Iraq Historic Allegations Team*, available at https://www.gov.uk/government/publications/review-of-iraq-historic-allegations-team (accessed on 14 April 2021).

Dugard, J 'Palestine and the ICC: Institutional Failure or Bias?' (2013) 11(3) *Journal of International Criminal Justice* 563.

du Plessis, M & Gevers, C 'South Africa's Foreign Policy and the International Criminal Court: on African Lessons, Security Council Reform and Possibilities for an Improved ICC' in Shaw, T & Warner, J (eds) *African Foreign Policies in International Institutions, Contemporary African Political Economy* (Palgrave Macmillan: New York 2018).

du Plessis, M & Gevers, C 'The Role of the International Criminal Court in Africa: The Epic Fails?' in Sarkin, J & Siang'andu, E (eds.) *Africa's Role and Contribution to International Criminal Justice* (Intersentia: Cambridge 2020).

El Zeidy, M *The principle of complementarity in international criminal law: origin, development and practice* (Brill: Leiden 2008).

Gaeta, P 'The International Criminal Court and Complementarity: From Theory to Practice' (2004) 2 *Journal of International Criminal Justice* 949.

Gevers, C 'Back to the Future?: Civil Society, the 'Turn to Complementarity' in Africa and Some Critical Concerns', (2016) *Acta Juridica* 95.

Gevers, C 'Prosecuting the Crime Against Humanity of Apartheid: Never, Again' (2018) 1 *African Yearbook of International Humanitarian Law* 25.

Gevers, C 'Africa and International Criminal Law' in Heller, Megret, Nouwen, Ohlin & Robinson (eds) *The Oxford Handbook of International Criminal Law* (Oxford University Press: Oxford 2020).

Hall C 'Positive Complementarity in Action' in Stahn, C & El Zeidy, M (eds) *The International Criminal Court and Complementarity: From Theory to Practice* (Cambridge University Press: Cambridge 2014).

Heller, K 'The ICC in Palestine: Be Careful What You Wish For', *Justice in Conflict*, 2 April 2015, available at: https://justiceinconflict.org/2015/04/02/the-icc-in-palestine-be-careful-what-you-wish-for.

Heller, K 'The Nine Worlds that (Wrongly) Doomed the Iraq Investigation' *OpinioJuris.org* 10 December 2020.

Clarke, KM, Knotterus, AS & de Volder, E 'Africa and the ICC: An Introduction' in Clarke, KM, Knotterus, AS & de Volder, E (eds) *Africa and the ICC: Perceptions of Justice* (Cambridge University Press: Cambridge 2016).

McAuliffe, P 'From Watchdog to Workhorse: Explaining the Emergence of the ICC's Burden-Sharing Policy as an Example of Creeping Cosmopolitanism' (2014) 13 *Chinese Journal of International Law* 259.

Megret, F 'In Search of the "Vertical': Towards an Institutional Theory of International Criminal Justice's Core' in Carsten, S & van den Herik, L (eds) *Future Perspectives of International Criminal Justice* (Springer: New York 2010).

Megret, F & Samson, M 'Holding the Line on Complementarity in Libya: The Case for Tolerating Flawed Domestic Trials' (2013) 11 *Journal of International Criminal Justice* 571.

O'Donohue, J & Rigney, S 'The ICC Must Consider Fair Trial Concerns in Determining Libya's Application to Prosecute Saif al-Islam Gaddafi Nationally', *EJIL.Talk! Blog of the European Journal of International Law*, 8 June 2012, https://www.ejiltalk.org/the-icc-must-consider-fair-trial-concerns-in-determining-libyas-application-to-prosecute-saif-al-islam-gaddafi-nationally/ (accessed on 14 April 2021).

Schabas, W *Introduction to the International Criminal Court* (Cambridge University Press: Cambridge 2017).

Schabas, W 'The Banality of International Justice', (2013) 11 *Journal of International Criminal Justice* 545.

Schabas, W, Triffterer, O & Ambos, K (eds.) *Commentary on the Rome Statute*.

Schabas, W & El Zeidy, M 'Article 17: Issues of Admissibility' in Triffterer, O & Ambos, K (eds) *The Rome Statute of the International Criminal Court: A Commentary* (Hart: London 2016).

Spilman, J 'Complementarity or Competition: The Effect of the ICC's Admissibility Decision in Kenya on Complementarity and the Article 17 (1) Inquiry' (2013) *Richmond Journal of Global Law and Business Online* 1.

Stahn, C 'Complementarity: A Tale of Two Notions' (2008)19 *Criminal Law Forum* 87–113.

Stahn, C 'Libya, the International Criminal Court and Complementarity: A Test for Shared Responsibility' (2012)10 *JICJ* 325–349.

Teitel, R 'Local Injustice: Why We Shouldn't Forget about Saif Gaddafi', *I-CONnect Blog of the International Journal of Constitutional Law and Constitution Making*, 16 October 2012, http://www.iconnectblog.com/2012/10/local-injustice-why-we-shouldnt-forget-about-saif-gaddafi/ (accessed on 14 April 2021).

Appraising the Regime of Cooperation Under the Malabo Protocol

Suzgo Lungu

1 Introduction

The establishment of an African regional court with criminal jurisdiction has an ambitious history. For decades, the African Union (AU) mulled over this idea without success.[1] However, three events accelerated the AU's decision to conclude the Protocol on Amendments to the Protocol on the Statute of the African Court of Justice and Human Rights ('Malabo Protocol') which establishes a regional court clothed with criminal jurisdiction, namely,

> [...] the indictment of or arrest warrants issued by certain European states against senior African state officials under charges of crimes under international law; the indictment and issuance of an ICC arrest warrant against

[1] Amnesty International *Malabo Protocol: Legal and Institutional Implications of the Merged and Expanded African Court,* January 2016, p 9, https://www.amnesty.org/download/Documents/AFR0130632016ENGLISH.PDF (accessed on 4 November 2020).

S. Lungu (✉)
Southern Africa Litigation Centre (SALC), Johannesburg, South Africa

E. C. Lubaale and N. Dyani-Mhango (eds.), *National Accountability for International Crimes in Africa*,
https://doi.org/10.1007/978-3-030-88044-6_3

President Al-Bashir of Sudan; and the indictment and trial before the ICC of President Uhuru Kenyatta of Kenya, and his deputy, William Ruto.[2]

It is the timing of the commencement of the negotiations and speed at which the Malabo Protocol was adopted by the Assembly of Heads of State and Government ('Assembly') that attracted criticism. Commentators have argued that the establishment of the African Court of Justice and Human Rights ('African Court') is political as it was set up 'to settle scores with the International Criminal Court [so that it] would be used as a strategic mechanism to shield senior officials from prosecution through diplomatic immunity'.[3] Supporters of the African Court have argued that the African Court's expansive jurisdiction fittingly responds to the needs of Africans' resolving their own problems.[4] It has been further argued that the African Court is an important mechanism that can be used to respond to the rising cases of gross human rights violations emanating from unending armed conflicts and other instabilities. Some parts of Africa have seen a surge in horrific crimes that are committed by both governments and rebel groups, yet very few have been held accountable.[5] Proponents of the African Court, therefore, support the adoption of the Malabo Protocol as a response to the fight against impunity and international crimes thereby complementing the work of the International Criminal Court ('ICC').[6] The Malabo Protocol intends to replace the Protocol to the African Charter on Human and Peoples' Rights on the Establishment of an African Court on Human and Peoples' Rights

[2] Amnesty International as above.

[3] O Malima 'The Malabo Protocol: The legal muscle tackle crimes of dignity in Africa' *Africa Matters,* 11 February, 2018 online at https://www.africamattersinitiative.com/post/2018/02/11/the-malabo-protocol-the-legal-muscle-to-tackle-crimes-of-dignity-in-africa (accessed on 29 November 2020).

[4] S Ford 'Between Hope and Doubt: The Malabo Protocol and the Resource Requirements of an African Criminal Court,' in CC Jalloh, KM Clarke and VO Nmehielle (eds) *The African Court of Justice and Human and Peoples' Rights in Context*, (Chicago: Cambridge University press 2019), https://doi.org/10.1017/9781108525343.039, online (accessed on 25 April 2021).

[5] Amnesty International (n 1 above) 5.

[6] TB Bouweknegt 'African Solutions' to African Problems at the Extraordinary African Chambers and 'Distant Justice' at the International Criminal Court' (2019) 17(5) *Journal of International Criminal Justice*, 981–1004.

('AfCHPR')[7] and the Protocol of the Court of Justice of the African Union ('ACJ').[8] In the Malabo Protocol, the list of crimes[9] has been expanded as compared to the ICC.

The establishment of an international criminal tribunal practically raises procedural and substantive issues on cooperation. Like any international criminal tribunal, the African Court needs the support of both contracting and non-contracting states for cooperation. Cooperation may take several forms including identifying and locating persons,[10] arresting, detaining or extraditing persons to the African Court,[11] and surrendering or transferring accused persons to the court'.[12] This raises the issue of the strength of the African Court's regime on cooperation in fighting international crimes and the scourge of impunity. This chapter critically analyses the Malabo Protocol's provisions on cooperation and offers recommendations for strengthening it. A majority of the recommendations are drawn from the jurisprudence that has developed at the International Criminal Court ('ICC') relating to the subject of state cooperation. The chapter highlights the provisions on cooperation and, where necessary, offers suggestions on enabling it to operate effectively with the yet to be established court. This chapter offers insights into a possible new framework of cooperation.

[7] Protocol to the African Charter on Human and Peoples' Rights on the Establishment of an African Court on Human and Peoples' Rights, adopted on June 10, 1998.

[8] Protocol of the Court of Justice of the African Union, adopted on 1 July, 2003.

[9] D Seda, "The African Court," *Development and Cooperation Newsletter* (accessed on 20 November 2016), https://www.dandc.eu/en/article/african-union-plans-extend-jurisdiction-african-court-justice-and-human-rights, (accessed on 30 November 2020); Foundations for Human Rights "Understanding the Malabo Protocol: The Potentials, the pitfalls, and the way forward for international justice in Africa- "Africa's Evolving Continental Court Structures", available online at http://www.fhr-mirror.org.za/index.php/latest_news/understanding-malabo-protocol/ (accessed on 4 November 2020).

[10] Art 46L(2)(a) of the Malabo Protocol.

[11] Art 46L(2)(d) of the Malabo Protocol.

[12] Art 46L(2)(e) of the Malabo Protocol. See, also, Z Wenqi 'On co-operation by states not party to the International Criminal Court' (2006) 861(88) *International Review of the Red Cross*, 88.

2 Malabo Protocol's Regime of Cooperation

The general provision on cooperation and judicial assistance under the Malabo Protocol is enshrined in only one provision, namely Article 46L. According to this provision contracting states must 'cooperate with the Court in the investigation and prosecution of persons accused of committing the crimes defined by this Statute'. The Malabo Protocol may extend the obligation to cooperate with the African Court to 'regional or international courts, non-States Parties or cooperating partners of the African Union'.[13] The Malabo Protocol's provision of cooperation focuses strongly on contracting states. Regional or international courts, non-state parties or cooperating partners of the African Union may also cooperate with the African Court through Agreements concluded on an ad hoc basis.[14] The focus on contracting states and non-contracting states for cooperation through ad hoc arrangements mirrors the ICC framework on cooperation as enshrined under Article 86 of the Rome Statute.

Article 86 of the Rome Statute provides for the general obligations of contracting states to 'cooperate fully with the Court in its investigation and prosecution of crimes within the jurisdiction of the Court'. Article 87 of the Rome Statute provides the comprehensive procedural steps to be taken by the ICC in terms of the requesting states. The distinction in the cooperation obligations for contracting and non-contracting states' under the Malabo Protocol is consistent with most international judicial institutions. For contracting states, the cooperation obligation is mandatory as compared to non-contracting states whose responsibility is usually voluntary.[15] Non-contracting states' cooperate with the African Court through 'ad hoc arrangements' as is the case with ICC.[16]

However, the African Court's framework on cooperation, unlike the ICC, does not have a provision for the cooperation of non-contracting states with the African Court based on other grounds. As held by the Pre-Trial Chamber of the ICC (PTC) in *the Prosecutor v Omar Hassan Ahmad Al-Bashir (Decision on the Cooperation of the Democratic Republic of the Congo regarding Omar Al Bashir's Arrest and Surrender to the ICC,*

[13] Art 46L(3) of the Malabo Protocol; Wenqi (n 12 above) 88.

[14] Art 46L(3) of the Malabo Protocol.

[15] Wenqi (n 12 above) 89.

[16] Art 12(3) of the Rome Statute as read with Article 87(5) of the Rome Statute.

the Prosecutor v Al Bashir) (the DRC cooperation cases)[17] and others[18] the obligation of states to cooperate with the ICC may be imposed by the United Nations Security Council ('UNSC') acting under the United Nations ('UN') Chapter VII powers. Where a case is referred to the ICC by the UNSC, Article 13(b) of the Rome Statute[19] as read with Article 25 of the UN Charter[20] obliges both contracting and non-contracting states to cooperate with the ICC.[21] Cooperation in this regard is imposed on all states by the UNSC in exercise of the powers enshrined in Chapter VII of the UN Charter as a means of maintaining international peace and security.[22] Any state that fails to cooperate with the ICC following a UNSC Chapter VII resolution threatens international peace and security and must, therefore, be sanctioned by the UNSC.[23] According to Article

[17] *Prosecutor v Omar Hassan Ahmad Al-Bashir (Decision on the Cooperation of the Democratic Republic of the Congo regarding Omar Al Bashir's Arrest and Surrender to the ICC, the Prosecutor v Al Bashir),* ICC-02/05-01/09, Pre-Trial Chamber I, 9 April 2014.

[18] *Prosecutor v Omar Hassan Ahmad Al-Bashir (Decision on the Cooperation of the Republic of Malawi regarding Omar Al Bashir's Arrest and Surrender to the ICC, the Prosecutor v Al Bashir),* ICC-01/05-01/09, Pre-Trial Chamber I, 12 December 2011; *Prosecutor v Omar Hassan Ahmad Al-Bashir (Decision on the Cooperation of the Republic of Chad regarding Omar Al Bashir's Arrest and Surrender to the ICC, the Prosecutor v Al Bashir),* ICC-02/05-01/09, Pre-Trial Chamber I, 13 December 2011; *Prosecutor v Omar Hassan Ahmad Al Bashir (Decision under article 87(7) of the Rome Statute on the non-applicability by South Africa with the request by the Court for the arrest and surrender of Omar Al-Bashir),* ICC-02/05-01/09, para 5–16; see also *transcripts of the Consultation meeting* at ICC-02/05-01/09-243-Anx2; ICC-02/05-01/09-240; ICC-02/05-01/09-239-Conf-Anx1; *Prosecutor v Saif Al-Islam Gadaffi,* (*Decision on the non-compliance by Libya with requests for cooperation by the Court and referring the matter to the United Nations Security Council*), 10 December 2014, ICC-01/11-01/11-577.

[19] Under art 13(b) of the Rome Statute, the ICC may exercise jurisdiction with respect to a crime where a situation was referred 'to the Prosecutor by the Security Council acting under Chapter VII of the Charter of the United Nations'.

[20] By virtue of Art 25 of the UN Charter, all decisions made by the UN Security Council are binding upon all UN member states.

[21] UNSC Res. 1593 (2005), (31 March 2005), UN Doc. S/RES/1593 (2005).

[22] Wenqi (n 12 above) 89–92.

[23] S Lungu and N Dyani-Mhango 'Surrender Suspects: Reflecting on the Role of the Security Council through the Lens of the Responsibility to Protect (R2P)' (2018) *African yearbook on International Humanitarian Law* 119.

25 of the UN Charter, a UNSC resolution binds all UN member states, mainly where the UNSC is acting according to its Chapter VII powers.[24]

It is argued that the Malabo Protocol must similarly allow the Peace and Security Council of the African Union to impose obligations on non-contracting states. The latter must cooperate with decisions of the African Court, where a state's failure threatens regional peace and security. The power to impose obligations on non-contracting states will be drawn from the provisions of the Protocol Relating to the Establishment of the Peace and Security Council of the African Union ('Peace and Security Protocol').[25] Since the Peace and Security Council of the AU is already supposed to 'work closely with the United Nations Security Council',[26] the Malabo Protocol can similarly empower the Peace and Security Council to impose cooperation obligations on non-contracting states as a means of maintaining regional peace and security.

The difficulty with delegating enforcement powers to the Peace and Security Council of the AU is that the African Court is likely going to face similar challenges as those faced by the ICC where non-cooperating states have not been sanctioned by the political organs mandated to enforce cooperation under the Rome Statute.

The foregoing also attest to the fact that any international judicial institution can seek state cooperation with decisions of international criminal tribunals from both contracting and non-contracting states depending on the circumstances of the case. Any regime of cooperation must accordingly and systematically separate the general obligations for contracting and non-contracting states. That is why the Rome Statute's provisions on cooperation are systematically divided into those containing general obligations and those dealing with particular obligations. Article 86 of the Rome Statute of the ICC ('Rome Statute') provides for the general obligation of contracting states to cooperate and render judicial assistance 'in accordance with the provisions of the State' and 'within the jurisdiction of the Court'.[27] Article 87(5) of the Rome Statute provides for cooperation obligations for non-contracting states. The separation of cooperation

[24] D Bowett 'The Impact of Security Council Decisions on Dispute Settlement Procedures,' (1994) (5) *European Journal of International Law*, 89–101, 93.

[25] Arts 3 and 7 of the Protocol Relating to the Establishment of the Peace and Security Council of the African Union.

[26] Art 17 of the Peace and Security Council Protocol.

[27] Art 86 of the Rome Statute; Wenqi (n 12 above) 89.

obligations also assists in the development of a robust vertical regime of cooperation like the one that was established under the International Criminal Tribunal for the former Yugoslavia (ICTY) and the International Criminal Tribunal for Rwanda (ICTR).[28]

Unlike the Rome Statute where the obligation of non-contracting states is well codified, the provisions on cooperation under the Malabo Protocol lack clarity on the exact nature and scope of the obligations of non-contracting states' to cooperate with the African Court. The Malabo Protocol also lacks clarity on whether non-contracting states may have a similar obligation as contracting states in certain circumstances.

The Malabo Protocol's regime of cooperation as enshrined in Article 46L is, therefore, not comprehensive enough and is weak. Sluiter can trace the difference between the ICC's 'less vertical'[29] approach to cooperation to the diplomatic conference where its negotiators were reluctant 'to emphasise [on] problems and conflicts that may arise in the cooperation relationship between States Parties and the Court'.[30] The reluctance led to the framers of the Rome Statute to develop a 'harmony approach' towards cooperation and Judicial Assistance.[31] One would make similar arguments for the Malabo Protocol that its framers drafted the cooperation framework with less emphasis on 'problems and conflicts that may arise in the cooperation relationship between States Parties and the Court'[32] as was the case with the ICC. The explanation for the weakness of the Malabo Protocol can be to its negotiating history. Its framers (member states to the AU) invested more in provisions that protected their interests like the immunity clause as compared to provisions that entrench a robust regime of cooperation across the board.[33] The emphasis on selected provisions that favoured negotiators led to the adoption of an instrument that had weak provisions on state cooperation.

[28] S/RES/827, (25 May 1993), Paragraph 4.

See S/RES/955 (1994) (8 November, 1994), full text available online at https://documents-dds-ny.un.org/doc/UNDOC/GEN/N95/140/97/PDF/N9514097.pdf?OpenElement (accessed on 30 November 2020).

[29] G Sluiter, 'Enforcing Cooperation: Did the Drafters Approach It the wrong way?'(2018) (16) *Journal of International Criminal Justice p* 383–402, 384.

[30] Sluiter (n above 29) 384.

[31] 'as above'.

[32] Sluiter (n 29 above) 384.

[33] Amnesty International (n 1 above).

The lack of legal certainty on the model of cooperation especially created for the Malabo Protocol is, therefore, relevant for the African Court and AU's member states.

3 The Need for a Relational Clarity Between the ICC and the African Court Under the Malabo Protocol

The relational connection between the ICC and the Malabo Protocol is another area worth exploring. Article 46H of the Malabo Protocol stipulates that the jurisdiction of the African Court is 'complementary to that of *National Courts* and *to the Courts of the Regional Economic Communities* where specifically provided for by the Communities'.[34] From the above provision, one observes that the yet to be established African Court is not complementary to the work of the ICC. Yet the two courts have similar objectives of fighting international crimes and ending impunity. The Malabo Protocol does not clarify whether the African Court has a cooperation relationship with the ICC and domestic courts. As Durdevic observed, 'the concept of the ICC jurisdiction as an extension of national jurisdiction will be realised only when domestic courts become the ICC enforcement mechanisms'.

Similarly, the African Court could consider the necessity of concluding a cooperation relationship with the ICC. While the African Court need not be turned into an extension of the ICC, it can consider being the latter's regional enforcement mechanism. Not only does the Malabo Protocol distort the cooperation model (-viz- whether it is vertical or horizontal) between state parties and the African Court especially for those that are also contracting parties to the ICC, it also seriously weakens the ICC's campaign on improving state cooperation. Consequently, the relationship between the two courts needs to be clarified because the establishment of a new regional criminal tribunal is supposed to complement the work of the ICC in the fight against international crimes and ending impunity. The relational clarity between the African Court and the ICC is necessary considering that state parties to the Malabo Protocol

[34] Emphasis added.

would still be required to resolve conflicting obligations arising from their membership to the Rome Statute.[35]

4 Towards a Strengthened Regime of Cooperation Under the Malabo Protocol

Several issues relevant to the conversation on state cooperation under international criminal law are missing from the Malabo Protocol, including under Article 46L. Article 46L of the Malabo Protocol fails to stipulate the procedural steps that states need to take when cooperating with the African Court. The provision also fails to specify the procedure for states' consultation with the African Court; the nature of the duty to cooperate; the details on the remedies available to the African Court to impose against states' failure to cooperate as earlier observed.

A closer perusal of Article 46L shows that its framers assumed that state cooperation under the Malabo Protocol would be straight forward. Article 46L is 'strongly rooted in the assumption of a good-faith partnership between the [African] court and States Parties, something which [...] is not always the case'.[36] However, as the ICC realised when it dealt with the issue of the failure by both contracting and non-contracting states to cooperate in the arrest and surrender of President Al Bashir and others, states cooperation with decisions of an international criminal tribunal is full of challenges. It is, therefore, vital that any international criminal tribunal must invest heavily in the establishment of a robust regime of cooperation. The procedural and substantive aspects of the law on cooperation under the Malabo Protocol must be articulated towards enabling states to fight international crimes and impunity collectively.

4.1 Procedural and Substantive Elements of the Duty to Cooperate Under the Malabo Protocol

The design of any legal framework on cooperation must show a causal link or interrelationship between the domestic legal processes and those of the international tribunal. This distinction is essential as any request for cooperation commences at the international tribunal which requires

[35] See art 98 of the Rome Statute.

[36] Sluiter (n 29 above) 385.

an activation by domestic mechanism before compliance can be achieved. Some of the procedures that are crucial for a successful cooperation regime in the custodial state include the procedure on executing warrants for arrest[37]; summoning of suspects[38]; communication and service of requests for cooperation[39]; and the elements required for surrendering a suspect to the international tribunal.

Concerning the duty to arrest and surrender a suspected offender, the custodial state's domestic criminal procedure is the first place to handle the request. Article 58 of the Rome Statute provides for several elements which must be satisfied on reasonable grounds before an arrest is conducted. These include the following: the requested state assessing whether the suspect committed the offence within the jurisdiction before an arrest is authorised or executed.[40] The African Court should also satisfy itself that the suspect's arrest is necessary to ensure his attendance at trial and that he 'does not obstruct or endanger the investigation or the court proceedings'.[41] The cooperation framework of the Malabo Protocol must also identify administrative figures responsible for the transmission of the African Court's request for the arrest and surrender of a suspect. Most International Criminal Tribunals entrustes the responsibility for managing administrative measures in the hands of the Registrar of the Court.[42]

Article 59 of the Rome Statute provides for the general obligations of contracting states when arresting suspects and Article 89 deals with the surrender of a suspect to the ICC. These provisions are deliberately separated to deal with the issue of arrest at domestic level (where a suspect will first be indicted) and his or her surrender to the international tribunal, which is after he or her has appeared before the latter court. A comprehensive African Court's regime of cooperation must be alive to these distinctions. It must provide for procedures on how a state will handle

[37] Art 58 of the Rome Statute.

[38] Art 58(7) of the Rome Statute.

[39] See *Prosecutor v Omar Hassan Ahmad Al-Bashir (Decision Regarding Omar Al Bashir's Potential Travel to the United States of America*, Pre-Trial Chamber II, 18 September, 2013, ICC-02/05-01/09, para 3.

[40] Art 58(a) of the Rome Statute.

[41] Art 58(1)(b)(i)(ii)(iii) of the Rome Statute.

[42] *Prosecutor v Omar Hassan Ahmad Al-Bashir (Decision regarding Omar Al-Bashir's potential travel to the United States of America,* Pre-Trial Chamber, 18 September 2013, ICC-02/05-01/09, para 3.

a request from the African Court in both the custodial state, which is where the request is first processed and the African Court, which will be the one to issue a warrant for arrest. When executing the request for arrest and surrender, any legal framework on cooperation must adhere to fair trial standards.[43]

It is also possible for suspected offenders to challenge the issuance of a warrant for their arrest on various grounds. Consequently, the law on cooperation must provide for grounds that permits indicted suspects to challenge requests for cooperation for their arrest and surrender as this fortifies the principle of a fair trial in criminal matters.[44]

Under the Rome Statute, for example, a suspect may object to his or her surrender on several grounds including the failure to comply with the *ne bis in idem rule*,[45] fair trial grounds,[46] and immunity,[47] among others. Ultimately, the ICC is responsible for determining whether the request for surrender must be complied with or not.[48] Although there is

[43] Article 55 of the Rome Statute; G Conway, '*Ne Bis in Idem* in international law' (2003) (3) *International Law Review*, 217–244; M Phua 'The Principle of *Ne Bis in Idem* in International Law: European Inspiration?' *iLawyer, 4* August4, 2015, online https://ilawyerblog.com/principle-ne-bis-idem-international-law-european-inspiration/, (accessed on 21 November 2020); JK Stewart 'Fair trial Rights under the Rome Statute from a Prosecution Perspective ICTR Symposium' *Symposium Paper presented in Arusha, Tanzania, 7 November 2014*, online at https://unictr.irmct.org/sites/unictr.org/files/publications/compendium-documents/i-fair-trial-rights-rome-statute-prosecution-perspective-stewart.pdf, (accessed on 23 November 2020).

[44] Judge Patrick Robinson, 'The Right to a Fair Trial in International Law, with Specific Reference to Work of the ICTY', online at https://bjil.typepad.com/Robinson_macro.pdf, (accessed on 28 November 2020); International Committee of the Red Cross, 'Practice relating to Rule 100: Fair trial Guidelines'*IHL Database*, online at https://ihl-databases.icrc.org/customary-ihl/eng/docs/v2_cha_chapter32_rule100, (accessed on 28 November 2020).

[45] Art 89 of the Rome Statute.

[46] Art 59(2) of the Rome Statute; also 69(4) of the Rome Statute.

[47] Art 98(2) of the Rome Statute.

[48] *Prosecutor v Omar Hassan Ahmad Al-Bashir (Decision under article 87(7) of the Rome Statute on the non-compliance by South Africa with the request by the Court for the arrest and surrender of Omar Al-Bashir)*, Pre-Trial Chamber II, 6 July, 2017; *Decision Following the Prosecutor's request for an order further clarifying that the Republic of South Africa is under obligation to immediately arrest and surrender Omar Al Bashir, The Prosecutor v Omar Hassan Ahmad Al Bashir*, (ICC-02/05-01/09), Pre-Trial Chamber II, 13 June 2015.

debate as to whether the principle of *ne bis in idem rule* has crystallised into a customary international law principle, it is, nevertheless, a general principle of law recognised by several legal systems.[49] The preservation of this principle is cardinal to the regime of cooperation under the Malabo Protocol.

On guaranteeing fair trial standards, one could draw lessons from the Rome Statute's Article 59(2) which obliges contracting states to respect suspects' fair trial rights including the obligation to take suspects promptly before national courts following their arrest.[50] It also entails assessing whether their arrest is lawful before the domestic court commences the process of surrendering the suspect to the African Court.[51] The reason why a suspect's arrest in the custodial state is provisional is that the latter court is required first, to examine whether the arrest is lawful or not before they authorise surrender.[52]

The arrest of a suspect who enjoys immunity *ratione Materiae* and immunity *ratione personae* always causes challenges. Immunity *ratione personae* attach to a distinctive but limited group of individuals, namely Heads of State,[53] Head of Government[54] and diplomats[55] and 'state officials on a special mission abroad'.[56] Another category of individuals includes 'a serving Minister of Foreign Affairs'[57] even though this is

[49] Conway (n 43 above) 217–244.

[50] JK Stewart 'Fair trial Rights under the Rome Statute from a Prosecution Perspective ICTR Symposium' Symposium PaperArusha, Tanzania, 7 November, 2014, online https://unictr.irmct.org/sites/unictr.org/files/publications/compendium-documents/i-fair-trial-rights-rome-statute-prosecution-perspective-stewart.pdf (accessed 23 November 2020).

[51] JK Cogan 'International Criminal Courts and Fair Trials: Difficulties and Prospects' (27) (2002) *Yale Journal of International Law* 116–119.

[52] Article 59(1) of the Rome Statute.

[53] *Case concerning Certain Questions of Mutual Assistance in Criminal Matters (Djibouti v France), ICJ Judgment of 4 June 2008,* para 190.

[54] *Case Concerning the Arrest Warrant of 11 April 2000 (the Democratic Republic of the Congo v Belgium)* International Court of Justice, February 14, 2002. ICJ Reports 2002para 51, online at https://www.icj-cij.org/en/case/121/judgments (accessed on 25 April 2021).

[55] Arts 29 and 31 of the Vienna Convention on Diplomatic Relations.

[56] D Akande and S Shah 'Immunity of State Officials, International Crimes and Foreign Domestic Courts' (2011) 21(4), *European Journal of International Law* 815–852, 817.

[57] *Case Concerning the Arrest Warrant* (n 54 above) para 53.

disputed as not being supported by state practice.[58] Immunity *ratione personae* are enjoyed by individuals so long as they are in office.

The other category of immunity, *ratione materiae*, 'attaches to acts performed by state officials in the exercise of their functions'.[59] Immunity *ratione materiae* accords immunity from prosecution to officials in 'the jurisdiction of other states in relation to acts performed in their official capacity'.[60] This category of immunity may 'be relied upon by persons or bodies that are not state officials or entities but have acted on behalf of the state'.[61] It can also be relied upon by officials even after they have stopped serving in office.

When it comes to cooperating with the arrest and surrender of a person who enjoys immunity, one must distinguish between entitlement to immunity and the obligation of states to cooperate with the international tribunal. It is one thing to assert that an individual enjoys immunities under international law, and quite another to say that states can lawfully disregard a request for cooperation from an international criminal tribunal for his/her arrest and surrender if so indicted.[62]

Consequently, a legal framework on cooperation must legislate on how states will deal with these competing obligations-viz respecting the inviolability of those who are entitled to immunities, on the one hand, and cooperating with the international tribunal, on the other. Clarifying on how states will deal with the competing obligations enhances state cooperation as it assists in resolving them quickly when faced with such dilemma.[63] As an example, Article 98 of the Rome Statute obliges the ICC to proceed with a request for the arrest and surrender of a person who enjoys immunities *only if* the requested state does not violate international law by cooperating with the court.[64] A request for the arrest

[58] As above 820.

[59] Akande and Shah (n 56 above) 817.

[60] As above 825.

[61] As above.

[62] P Gaeta 'Does President Al Bashir Enjoy Immunity from Arrest' (2009)(7) *Journal of International Criminal Justice* 315–332;

[63] J Foakes 'Immunity for International Crimes? Developments in the law on Prosecuting Heads of State in Foreign Court' (2011) no *02 Briefing Paper, International Law Programme, IL BP*; D Tladi 'The ICC Decisions on Chad and Malawi: On Cooperation, Immunities and Article 98' (2013) (11) *Journal of International Criminal Justice* 199.

[64] Art 98 of the Rome Statute; See also, Gaeta (n 62 above).

and surrender of a person who enjoys immunities may be possible where a waiver is obtained from the third state, which is the non-contracting state to the ICC.[65] Although the Rome Statute allows states to resolve competing obligations involving persons that enjoy immunities, challenges on state cooperation with ICC requests to arrest and surrender such suspects still remain.[66] A regime of cooperation must, therefore, resolve these issues to defray fears that the ICC faced when it came to the request for the arrest and surrender of President Al Bashir.[67]

Although the Rome Statute permits states to refuse or object to a request for cooperation in certain circumstances, the ultimate decision on whether the state may proceed to do so rests with the ICC. Article 97 of the Rome Statute allows the requested state to consult with the ICC where 'it identifies problems which may impede or prevent the execution of the request'. The requested state may cite several factors including the insufficiency of information presented by the ICC to execute the request[68]; the failure to locate the person being wanted or that investigations have disclosed that 'the person in the requested State is not the person named in the warrant'[69]; and that 'the execution of the request

[65] Art 98(2) of the Rome Statute; Gaeta as above.

[66] D Jacobs 'A Sad homage to Antonio Cassese: The ICC's confused pronouncements on State Compliance and Head of State Immunity', 15 December, 2011, online athttps://dovjacobs.com/2011/12/15/a-sad-hommage-to-antonio-cassese-the-iccs-confused-pronouncements-on-state-compliance-and-head-of-state-immunity/ (accessed on 23 November 2020); E de Wet 'The Implications of President Al Bashir's visit to South Africa for International and Domestic law' (2015) 13(5) *Journal of International Criminal Justice*,1049–1071.

[67] *Prosecutor v Omar Hassan Ahmad Al-Bashir (Decision on the Cooperation of the Republic of Malawi regarding Omar Al Bashir's Arrest and Surrender to the ICC, the Prosecutor v Al Bashir)*, ICC-01/05-01/09, Pre-Trial Chamber I, 12 December 2011; *Prosecutor v Omar Hassan Ahmad Al-Bashir (Decision on the Cooperation of the Democratic Republic of the Congo regarding Omar Al Bashir's Arrest and Surrender to the ICC, the Prosecutor v Al Bashir)*, ICC-02/05-01/09, Pre-Trial Chamber I, 9 April 2014; *Prosecutor v Omar Hassan Ahmad Al-Bashir (Decision on the Cooperation of the Republic of Chad regarding Omar Al Bashir's Arrest and Surrender to the ICC, the Prosecutor v Al Bashir)*, ICC-02/05-01/09, Pre-Trial Chamber I, 13 December 2011; *Prosecutor v Omar Hassan Ahmad Al Bashir (Decision following the Prosecutor's request for an order further clarifying that the Republic of South Africa is under obligation to immediately arrest and surrender Omar Al Bashir.*

[68] Art 97(a) of the Rome Statute.

[69] Art 97(b) of the Rome Statute.

in its current form would require the requested State to breach a pre-existing treaty obligation undertaken with respect to another State'.[70] In *Prosecutor v Omar Hassan Ahmad Al-Bashir (Decision under Article 87(7) of the Rome Statute on the non-compliance by South Africa with the request by the court for the arrest and surrender of Omar Al-Bashir)*,[71] the Pre-Trial Chamber II of the ICC held that a state could not refuse to cooperate with the ICC or postpone the execution of its request to arrest and surrender a suspect.[72] It may qualify or suspend the request because the responsibility of rejecting the request rests with the ICC. The requested state may only consult with the African Court when it has reasons for refusing or objecting the surrender of a suspect.

4.2 Consultation with the African Court

Article 97 of the Rome Statute, on which the right to consult is based, has been heavily criticised. Kress and Prost contend that this provision 'signals a cooperative approach to the resolution of problems [under the Rome Statute] and presumes good faith efforts on the part of the Court and the State'.[73] It unnecessarily gives room for states to 'legitimately raise all kind of problems in the execution of cooperation requests'.[74] The cooperative nature of this provision 'does not favour a result-oriented and vertical cooperation'[75] model required in a healthy and effective cooperation regime. To the contrary, the above provision gave states an opportunity to raise all sorts of excuses against cooperation. Sluiter observes that the reference to 'consultations between the State Party and the Court' under Article 97 of the Rome Statute evidences a 'harmony approach'

[70] Art 97(c) of the Rome Statute.

[71] *Prosecutor v Omar Hassan Ahmad Al-Bashir (Decision under Article 87(7) of the Rome Statute on the non-compliance by South Africa with the request by the Court for the arrest and surrender of Omar Al-Bashir)*, Pre-Trial chamber II, 6 July 2017.

[72] Ibid para 104.

[73] C Kress and K Prost, 'Article 97' in O. Triffterer (ed.) *Commentary on the Rome Statute of the International Criminal Court-Observers' Notes, Article by Article* (2nd edn.) (2008), 1599–1601, 1599.

[74] Sluiter (n 29 above) p 385.

[75] 'As above 386.

to cooperation,[76] which weakens the cooperation regime of the Rome Statute.

If the African Court were to draw lessons from the experience of the ICC on the subject of consultation, it must assess whether they should permit states to consult with the court before cooperating. Member States to the Malabo Protocol ought to decide whether they should adopt the harmony approach, as argued by Sluiter, or set down a more vertical and strong regime of cooperation which leaves no room for doubt that the ultimate decision-maker on whether a state may refuse or object to a request for cooperation is the African Court. This is important because it enables the African Court to continue being in charge of all cooperation processes at all stages.

The legal framework on cooperation must also elaborate on the consequences for states or individuals' failure to cooperate with the African Court. It should also elaborate on which organ(s) of the AU will be entrusted with the responsibility of enforcing the African Court's decisions. It must also clarify the procedure that will be followed in cases of non-compliance. Writing with respect to the Rome Statute, Sluiter argued that the logical sequence of events to be followed in determining whether a state has failed to comply with a decision of the ICC is as follows: there must be 'a problem in the execution of a request'[77] followed by 'consultations, a judicial finding of non-compliance and enforcement action by the ASP or the UNSC'[78] in that order.

The ICC's powers to enforce cooperation under the Rome Statute are provided for in Article 87(7). In terms of the procedure, the provision sets down a 'two-stage analysis'[79] for enforcing non-cooperation.

[76] As above.

[77] Sluiter (n 29 above) 387.

[78] As above.

[79] *Prosecutor v Uhuru Muigai Kenyatta, (Decision on prosecution's application for a finding of non-compliance under Article 87 (7) of the Statute),* I *Trial Chamber V (B),* Judgment of 19 August 2015, ICC-01/09-02/11 OA 5, (hereinafter referred to as 'the Kenyatta Judgment'); C/f *Prosecutor v Saif Al-Islam Gadaffi,* (Decision on the non-compliance by Libya with requests for cooperation by the Court and referring the matter to the United Nations Security Council), 10 December 2014, ICC-01/11-01/11-577, paras 24–25, 33–34; See also *Prosecutor v Omar Al Hassan Ahmad Bashir, (Decision on the Prosecutor's Request for a Finding of Non-Compliance Against the Republic of the Sudan*), 9 March 2015, ICC-02/05-01/09-227, paras 18–19; See also *Prosecutor v Omar Hassan Ahmad Al Bashir, (Decision on the Cooperation of the Democratic Republic of the*

The first step is the establishment of whether a state has failed to cooperate with the ICC. The second step is the determination of whether the non-complying state can be referred to the Assembly of States Parties or the UNSC, two bodies entrusted with the responsibility of supervising non-compliance with decisions of the ICC.[80] According to the Appeals Chamber in *Prosecutor v Omar Hassan Ahmad Al-Bashir (in the Jordan Referral re Al-Bashir Appeal),*[81]

> [...] it is only when the Chamber has established that *both* conditions are met that it may proceed to consider whether to refer the State to the Assembly of States Parties or the UN Security Council or both, following a finding of non-compliance.[82]

The other issue worth considering pertains to a finding of failure to comply with decisions of the African Court, for purposes of determining states' non-compliance. The International Criminal Tribunal for the former Yugoslavia (ICTY) in *the Blaskic Subpoena Judgment*, in its determination, held that a state would be held liable for failing to comply with the decision of the tribunal and not political organs established for enforcing cooperation.[83] Any new regime of cooperation must not deviate from this[84] principle and should ensure that a state's failure to cooperate with the court will only be established if it pertains to a failure to cooperate with the order or request of a tribunal and not political organs established to supervise states' compliance with its decisions. A

Congo Regarding Omar Al Bashir Bashir's Arrest and Surrender to the Court), 9 April 2014, ICC-02/05-01/09-195, para 34.

[80] Art 87(7) of the Rome Statute.

[81] *Prosecutor v Omar Hassan Ahmad Al-Bashir (Jordan Referral re Al-Bashir Appeal)*, para 8, Judgment of 6 May 2019, ICC-02/05-01/09 OA2, available online at https://www.icc-cpi.int/CourtRecords/CR2019_02856.PDF, (accessed on 24 November 2020).

[82] *Jordan Referral re Al-Bashir Appeal* (n 81 above) para 8.

[83] The judgment was delivered in the context of Article 29 of the ICTY Statute, *Prosecutor v Blaskic*, Case IT-95-14/2/, (*Judgment on the Request of the Republic of Croatia for Review of the Decision of Trial Chamber II of 18 July 1997*), Appeals Chamber, 29 Oct. 1997, para 35, available online at http://www.icty.org/x/cases/blaskic/acdec/en/71029JT3.html (accessed on 14 November 2020).

[84] (Otto Triffierer & Kai Ambos (eds), n 73 above) 2036.

state should only focus on complying with a decision that is a product of a judicial activity proper'.[85]

4.3 Proposed Organs for Enforcing State Cooperation Under the Malabo Protocol

The foregoing discussion raises another critical issue on states cooperation, namely, which organs will be responsible for enforcing state non-cooperation under the Malabo Protocol? Any regime of cooperation must identify an organ that will be responsible for enforcing states compliance with decisions of the regional court. Under the Inter-American Court of Human Rights ('IActHR'), for example, the IActHR supervises states compliance with its judgement.[86] However, it notifies the General Assembly of the Organisation of American States ('OAS') through reports which are presented annually.[87]

Under the European Court on Human Rights ('ECtHR'), the Committee of Ministers (CoM) assisted by the Secretariat's Department for the Execution of Judgments supervises state compliance.[88] For the

[85] *Prosecutor v Blaskic* (n 83 above) para 36.

[86] See *Case of Baena-Ricardo* et al. *v. Panama, (Competence), (Sr. C) No. 104, Judgment of November 28, 2003,* paras 58, 59 and 60.

[87] *Baena-Ricardo* (n 86 above) p 538, paras 110- 116 of the Judgment. *Case of Cantos v Argentina, (Monitoring Compliance with Judgment),* (Ser. C, NO. 21), (26 *August, 2010),* para 5, online at http://www.corteidh.or.cr/docs/supervisiones/cantos_26_08_10_ing.pdf (accessed on 13 February 2019); See also footnote 4 of the Order which cites the OAS GA's resolution AG/RES. 2292 (XXXVII-O/07) Order of the General Assembly of the OAS passed on the fourth plenary session, celebrated on June 5, 2007, titled *Observations and Recommendations to the Annual Report of the Inter-American Court of Human Rights,* operative paragraph fourth; OAS GA's resolution AG/RES. 2408 (XXXVIII-O/08) Order of the General Assembly of the OAS passed on the fourth plenary session, celebrated on June 3, 2008, titled *Observations and Recommendations to the Annual Report of the Inter-American Court of Human Rights,* operative paragraph fourth; and OAS GA resolution AG/RES.2500 (XXXIX-O/09) Order of the General Assembly of the OAS passed on the fourth plenary session, celebrated on June 4, 2009, titled *Observations and Recommendations to the Annual Report of the Inter-American Court of Human Rights,* operative paragraph fourth.

[88] For a comprehensive overview of this departments work see Council of Europe, Department for the Execution of Judgments of the European Court of Human Rights, Committee of Ministers' Human Rights Meetings, online at https://www.coe.int/en/web/execution/committee-of-ministers-human-rights-meetings (accessed on 12 November 2017); B Cali and N Bruch, *Monitoring The Implementation of Judgments of*

AfCHPR, the Executive Council acting on behalf of the Assembly of the African Union is responsible for monitoring compliance.[89] However, the system for monitoring compliance with decisions of the AfCHPR is yet to be operational. Recently the AfCHPR adopted a Draft Framework for Reporting and Monitoring Execution of Judgments and other Decisions of the African Court ('Draft Framework') following a resolution of the Executive Council authorising it to propose 'a concrete reporting mechanism'[90] for monitoring compliance with its judgements. Although the Draft Framework was not presented to the Assembly through the Permanent Representative Committee ('PRC') of the AU,[91] it has already been criticised for its 'over-reliance of non-judicial institutions in the enforcement of the African Court's judgments'.[92]

As for the Rome Statute, this responsibility is left in the hands of the UNSC and Assembly of States Parties (ASP).[93] A matter is referred to the UNSC 'where the Security Council referred [it] to the Court'.[94] Similarly, the African Court may consider identifying organs that will be responsible for enforcing its decisions.

The above examples, which are certainly not exhaustive, illustrate the weakness of the Malabo Protocol's regime of cooperation. The Malabo Protocol left out several crucial issues relevant to any discussion on state cooperation under international criminal law. In the future, the African Court must re-assess the relevance of Article 46L to the fight

the European Court of Human Rights: A Handbook for Non-Governmental Organisation, (University College London, Baoak al and Nicola Brunch, 2011): 12–13.

89 See Rule 64(2) of the Rules of the African Court on Human and Peoples' rights; Article 29(2) of the protocol. See also Art 1 read with Arts 10–13 of the Constitutive Act.

90 EX.CL/Dec.1013(XXXIII) *Decision on the Activity Report of the African Court on Human and Peoples' Rights (AfCHPR) (2018)*, para 4; See also M. Plagis, 'Implementation of the Judgments of the African Court on Human and Peoples Rights' 6 August, 2019, available online at http://www.acthprmonitor.org/implementation-of-the-judgments-of-the-african-court-on-human-and-peoples-rights/ (accessed on 10 August 2020).

91 EX.CL/1126(XXXIV)Annex 1, Activity Report of the African Court on Human and Peoples' Rights (2018).

92 S Lungu 'An appraisal of the Draft Framework for Reporting and Monitoring Execution of Judgments of the African Court on Human and Peoples' Rights' (2020) 4 *African Human Rights Yearbook* 144, 152.

93 Art 87(7) of the Rome Statute.

94 As above.

against international crimes and impunity. The Malabo Protocol can draw lessons from the ICC, particularly on its experience in dealing with non-cooperation cases. As the Malabo Protocol has not yet entered into force and the criminal tribunal yet to start operating, one can acknowledge that problematic scenarios for the African Court have not arisen. The court should use this period to strengthen its regime of cooperation under the Malabo Protocol.

5 Towards a New Framework on Cooperation for the Malabo Protocol

The experience drawn from ICC cases on the situation of Sudan teaches every proponent of international criminal justice that having a robust legal framework on cooperation is a recipe for a successful fight against impunity and international crimes. In that regard, any steps towards enhancing the regime of cooperation under the Malabo Protocol must make the African Court an important pioneer in this fight. It must centrally position itself on all issues related to cooperation. The Malabo Protocol must clarify on a number of issues concerning cooperation including the nature and scope of the obligation of non-contracting states; its relationship with the ICC; the procedural aspects pertaining to arrest and surrender; its central role during state consultations; and the duty to arrest and surrender. The Malabo Protocol must identify organs that will assist in monitoring state cooperation. However, where independent organ(s) have been established, it must not overreach its powers and interfere with the work of those organs.[95] Instead, the organs must be empowered to adopt measures, including sanctions against the non-cooperating state. Some of the sanctions may include suspension from

[95] *Prosecutor v Uhuru Muigai Kenyatta, (Decision on prosecution's application for a finding of non-compliance under Article 87 (7) of the Statute),* I *Trial Chamber V (B),* Judgment of 19 August 2015, ICC-01/09-02/11 OA 5, (hereinafter referred to as 'the Kenyatta Judgment'); C/f *Prosecutor v Saif Al-Islam Gadaffi,* (Decision on the non-compliance by Libya with requests for cooperation by the Court and referring the matter to the United Nations Security Council), 10 December 2014, ICC-01/11-01/11-577, paras 24–25, 33–34; See also *Prosecutor v Omar Al Hassan Ahmad Bashir, (Decision on the Prosecutor's Request for a Finding of Non-Compliance Against the Republic of the Sudan*), 9 March 2015, ICC-02/05-01/09-227, paras 18–19; See also *Prosecutor v Omar Hassan Ahmad Al Bashir, (Decision on the Cooperation of the Democratic Republic of the Congo Regarding Omar Al Bashir Bashir's Arrest and Surrender to the Court)*, 9 April 2014, ICC-02/05-01/09-195, para 34; *Prosecutor v Omar Hassan Ahmad Al-Bashir*

membership of the AU in accordance with Article 23(2) of the Constitutive Act of the AU. However, the scope and extent of measures to be imposed must be guided by the circumstances of each case.

6 Conclusion

This article was about responding to the growing concerns on the adoption of the Malabo Protocol. The growing indignation to the adoption of the Malabo Protocol focused on selected topics including the expanded jurisdiction of the court on the nature of crimes, the prohibition in prosecuting those that enjoy immunity, and the apparent lack of resources to finance the yet to be established court. Some of these concerns have already come to pass as six years down the line the Malabo Protocol has not received enough ratification for its entry into force.

This article has demonstrated that in addition to the foregoing concerns, the Malabo Protocol lacks a strong regime of cooperation. The chapter has highlighted the areas that would strengthen the regime of cooperation for the yet to be established African Court. The proposals advanced in the chapter may not be new and unprecedented steps under international criminal law; they are, however, a necessary departure from the current status of the regime of cooperation under the Malabo Protocol. Only if the Protocol's regime of cooperation is enhanced, will the authority and effective functioning of the yet to be established African Court be materialised.

Bibliography

Books

Kress, C. and Prost, K. 'Article 97' in O. Triffterer (ed.) *Commentary on the Rome Statute of the International Criminal Court-Observers' Notes, Article by Article* (2nd edn.) (2008), 1599–1601, 1599.

Ford, S. 'Between Hope and Doubt: The Malabo Protocol and the Resource Requirements of an African Criminal Court,' in C.C. Jalloh, K.M. Clarke and V. O. Nmehielle (eds) *The African Court of Justice and Human and Peoples'*

(in the Jordan Referral re Al-Bashir Appeal), para 8, Judgment of 6 May 2019, ICC-02/05-01/09 OA2, available online at https://www.icc-cpi.int/CourtRecords/CR2019_02856.PDF, (last accessed on 21 September 2019).

Rights in Context, (2019), online at DOI: https://doi.org/10.1017/9781108525343.039, (accessed 25 April, 2021).

Journals

Akande, D. and Shah, S., 'Immunity of State Officials, International Crimes and Foreign Domestic Courts' (2011) 21(4), *European Journal of International Law*, 815–852.

Bouweknegt, T.B 'African Solutions' to African Problems at the Extraordinary African Chambers and 'Distant Justice' at the International Criminal Court', (2019), 17 (5), *Journal of International Criminal Justice*, 981–1004.

Bowett, D., 'The Impact of Security Council Decisions on Dispute Settlement Procedures,' (1994) 5 *European Journal of International Law*, 89–101.

Cogan, J. K., 'International Criminal Courts and Fair Trials: Difficulties and Prospects' (2002) 27 *Yale Journal of International Law*, 116–119.

Conway, G., '*Ne Bis in Idem* in international law' (2003) 3 *International Law Review*, 217–244.

De Wet, Erika, 'The Implications of President Al Bashir's visit to South Africa for International and Domestic law' (2015) 13(5) *Journal of International Criminal Justice*,1049–1071.

Gaeta, P., 'Does President Al Bashir Enjoy Immunity from Arrest' (2009) 7, *Journal of International Criminal Justice*, 315–332.

Lungu, S and Dyani-Mhango, N., 'Surrender Suspects: Reflecting on the Role of the Security Council through the Lens of the Responsibility to Protect (R2P)' (2018) *African yearbook on International Humanitarian Law,* 119.

Lungu, S., 'An appraisal of the Draft Framework for Reporting and Monitoring Execution of Judgments of the African Court on Human and Peoples' Rights' (2020) 4 *African Human Rights Yearbook*, 144–164, 152.

Sluiter, G., 'Enforcing Cooperation: Did the Drafters Approach It the wrong way?'(2018) 16 *Journal of International Criminal Justice* 383–402, 384.

Tladi, D., 'The ICC Decisions on Chad and Malawi: On Cooperation, Immunities and Articles 98', (2013) 11, *Journal of International Criminal Justice*, 199.

Wenqi, Z. 'On co-operation by states not party to the International Criminal Court,' (2006) 861(88) *International Review of the Red Cross*, 88.

Online Publications

Amnesty International, 'Malabo Protocol: Legal and Institutional Implications of the Merged and Expanded African Court' 2 May 2017. p 9, https://www.amnesty.org/download/Documents/AFR0130632016ENGLISH.PDF (4 accessed on November 2020).

Cali B. and Bruch, N., *Monitoring The Implementation of Judgments of the European Court of Human Rights: A Handbook for Non-Governmental Organisation*, (2011): 12–13.

Council of Europe, Department for the Execution of Judgments of the European Court of Human Rights, Committee of Ministers' Human Rights Meetings, online at https://www.coe.int/en/web/execution/committee-of-ministers-human-rights-meetings, last accessed on 12 November, 2017.

Foakes, J., 'Immunity for International Crimes? Developments in the law on Prosecuting Heads of State in Foreign Court' (2011) no. *02 Briefing Paper, International Law Programme, IL BP*.

Foundations for Human Rights, "Understanding the Malabo Protocol: The Potentials, the pitfalls, and the way forward for international justice in Africa- "Africa's Evolving Continental Court Structures", A Communique released on 7–8 November, 2016 online at http://www.fhr-mirror.org.za/index.php/latest_news/understanding-malabo-protocol/ (accessed on 4 November 2020) .

International Committee of the Red Cross, 'Practice relating to Rule 100: Fair trial Guidelines' *IHL Database*, online at https://ihl-databases.icrc.org/customary-ihl/eng/docs/v2_cha_chapter32_rule100 (accessed on 28 November 2020).

Jacobs, D., 'A Sad homage to Antonio Cassese: The ICC's confused pronouncements on State Compliance and Head of State Immunity', 15 December, 2011, online at https://dovjacobs.com/2011/12/15/a-sad-hommage-to-antonio-cassese-the-iccs-confused-pronouncements-on-state-compliance-and-head-of-state-immunity/ (accessed on 23 November 2020).

Malima, O. 'The Malabo Protocol: The legal muscle tackle crimes of dignity in Africa' *Africa Matters,* 11 February, 2018 online at https://www.africamattersinitiative.com/post/2018/02/11/the-malabo-protocol-the-legal-muscle-to-tackle-crimes-of-dignity-in-africa (accessed on 29 November 2020).

Phua, M., 'The Principle of *Ne Bis in Idem* in International Law: European Inspiration?' *iLawyer, 4* August4, 2015, online at https://ilawyerblog.com/principle-ne-bis-idem-international-law-european-inspiration/.

Plagis, M. , 'Implementation of the Judgments of the African Court on Human and Peoples Rights' 6 August, 2019, available online at http://www.acthprmonitor.org/implementation-of-the-judgments-of-the-african-court-on-human-and-peoples-rights/ (accessed on 10 August 2020).

Robinson, P. 'The Right to a Fair Trial in International Law, with Specific Reference to Work of the ICTY', online at https://bjil.typepad.com/Robinson_macro.pdf (accessed on 28 November 2020).

Seda, D., "The African Court," *Development and Cooperation Newsletter*, 20 November, 2016, online at https://www.dandc.eu/en/article/african-union-plans-extend-jurisdiction-african-court-justice-and-human-rights (accessed on 30 November 2020).

Stewart, J.K 'Fair trial Rights under the Rome Statute from a Prosecution Perspective ICTR Symposium' *Symposium Paper presented in Arusha, Tanzania, 7 November 2014,* online at https://unictr.irmct.org/sites/unictr.org/files/publications/compendium-documents/i-fair-trial-rights-rome-statute-prosecution-perspective-stewart.pdf (accessed on 23 November 2020).

Resolutions

African Union

Activity Report of the African Court on Human and Peoples' Rights, African Court on Human and Peoples' Rights AU Doc. EX.CL/1126(XXXIV)Annex 1 (2018).

Decision on the Activity Report of the African Court on Human and Peoples' Rights (AfCHPR). AU Doc. EX.CL/Dec.1013(XXXIII) (2018).

United Nations

United Nations Security Council Resolution S/RES/955 (1994) (8 November, 1994), online at https://documents-dds-ny.un.org/doc/UNDOC/GEN/N95/140/97/PDF/N9514097.pdf?OpenElement (accessed on 30 November 2020).

Organisation of American States

Order of the General Assembly of the OAS passed on the fourth plenary session, celebrated on June 5, 2007, titled *Observations and Recommendations to the Annual Report of the Inter-American Court of Human Rights,* operative paragraph fourth OAS GA's resolution AG/RES. 2292 (XXXVII-O/07).

Order of the General Assembly of the OAS passed on the fourth plenary session, celebrated on June 3, 2008, titled *Observations and Recommendations to the Annual Report of the Inter-American Court of Human Rights,* operative paragraph fourth; OAS GA's resolution AG/RES. 2408 (XXXVIII-O/08).

Order of the General Assembly of the OAS passed on the fourth plenary session, celebrated on June 4, 2009, titled *Observations and Recommendations to the Annual Report of the Inter-American Court of Human Rights,* operative paragraph fourth. OAS GA resolution AG/RES.2500 (XXXIX-O/09).

Treaties

Protocol to the African Charter on Human and Peoples' Rights on the Establishment of an African Court on Human and Peoples' Rights, adopted on June 10, 1998.

Protocol on Statute of the Court of Justice of the African Union, adopted on 1 July, 2003.

Universal Jurisdiction as a Tool in Promoting Accountability for International Crimes in Africa: Exploring the Significance of Hissene Habre's Conviction

Innocent Mung'omba

1 Introduction

The dawn of independence on the African continent brought with it renewed hope for peace and the erasure of the horrific and agonising memories of the colonial era. Given the exhilarating atmosphere characterised by the Pan-African spirit obtaining at the time of independence, a prediction that the perpetration of international crimes would take centre stage in Africa would have been unfathomable. Notwithstanding the global human rights protection machinery spearheaded by the United Nations, Africa has witnessed the orchestration of international crimes including genocide, war crimes and crimes against humanity, with victims left yearning for justice. Cases involving the commission of international crimes on the African continent have largely been pursued by the International Criminal Court, a situation that illuminates doubts about the ability

I. Mung'omba (✉)
Africa Legal Network, Musa Dudhia & Co., Lusaka, Zambia

E. C. Lubaale and N. Dyani-Mhango (eds.), *National Accountability for International Crimes in Africa*,
https://doi.org/10.1007/978-3-030-88044-6_4

of African national courts to prosecute international crimes committed on African soil.

Universal jurisdiction has always been an option available to African states in the dispensation of international criminal justice. Under universal jurisdiction, each State has a right to prosecute individuals alleged to have committed international crimes regardless of the nationality of the offender or where the offence was committed. However, African states have not been keen to apply the principle of universal jurisdiction. This appears to be predicated on the notion that the invocation of the principle of universal jurisdiction would run counter to the principle of non-intervention in the affairs of a sovereign State. This notwithstanding, in what could be described as an intriguing and stunning achievement, Africa in 2016 recorded its first-ever conviction on the basis of universal jurisdiction. This was the conviction of Hissene Habre, the former President of Chad, by a Court in Senegal for international crimes committed on Chadian soil.

Hissene Habre came to power in 1982. While at the helm of power, Habre masterminded an atrocious campaign against his own people through the Documentation and Security Directorate, a security agency later known as "the instrument of terror". Through this security agency, Habre suppressed ethnic groups such as the Sara and the Hedjarai in the south and the Zaghawa in the northeast of Chad.[1] During his reign from 1982 to 1990, Habre is said to have spearheaded acts of torture, murder, rape and crimes against humanity.[2] In 1990, Habre's regime was toppled by Idriss Deby forcing Habre to flee to Senegal.

In 1992, a Commission of inquiry set up by the new government accused Habre's regime of orchestrating 40,000 politically motivated murders and systematic torture.[3] In January 2000, a complaint against Habre was filed in Senegal by Habre's victims. Soon after, Habre was charged by Senegalese authorities for crimes allegedly committed on Chadian territory. This initial drive to prosecute Habre suffered a setback

[1] K Seelinger 'Rape and the President: The Remarkable Trial and (Partial) Acquittal of Hissène Habré' (2017) 34 *World Policy Journal* 17.

[2] Reed Brody 'Victims Bring a Dictator to Justice: The Case of Hissene Habre' June 2017 https://www.brot-fuer-die-welt.de/fileadmin/mediapool/2_Downloads/Fachinformationen/Analyse/Analysis70-The_Habre_Case.pdf (accessed 3 June 2021).

[3] Trial International 'Hissene Habre' https://trialinternational.org/latest-post/hissene-habre/ (accessed 3 June 2021).

when the Court of Appeal of Dakar ruled that Senegalese tribunals had no jurisdiction to preside over acts of torture committed by a foreign national outside Senegal.[4] Meanwhile, before the initial attempts to prosecute Habre had finally come to a halt, another attempt had been set in motion in the Belgian capital, Brussels. The institution of legal proceedings in Brussels was done on the basis of Belgium's universal jurisdiction law.[5] Belgium proceeded to request for Habre's extradition in 2005. This extradition request was rejected.[6]

In 2012, Senegal and the African Union reached an agreement to establish the Extraordinary African Chambers (hereinafter referred to as the "EAC") in the Senegalese court system to try offences committed during Habre's rule in Chad.[7] The Chambers' jurisdiction was based on the principle of universal jurisdiction. The statute establishing the EAC provided for jurisdiction to try the offence of genocide, crimes against humanity, war crimes and torture.[8] In 2016, the EAC found Habre guilty of crimes against humanity, war crimes, torture and rape.[9] With the exception of rape, this conviction was upheld in 2017 by the Appeals Chamber of the EAC. This marked the first-ever African conviction employing the principle of universal jurisdiction. The fact that this was the first-ever African conviction on the basis of universal jurisdiction raises important implications regarding the dispensation of international criminal justice in Africa. Consequently, this chapter seeks to unpack the significance of the Habre conviction in the application of universal jurisdiction as a tool in fostering national accountability for international crimes in Africa.

[4] https://www.asser.nl/upload/documents/20121105T030720-Cour%20dappel%20Dakar%2004-07-2000.pdf (accessed 3 June 2021).

[5] International Crimes Database 'Hissène Habré' http://www.internationalcrimesdatabase.org/Case/762 (accessed 3 June 2021).

[6] G Musila 'African Union and the Evolution of International Criminal Justice in Africa: Challenges, Controversies and Opportunities' http://www.academia.edu (accessed 1 June 2021).

[7] Brody (n 2 above).

[8] Article 4 of the Statute of the Extraordinary African Chambers within the Senegalese Judicial System for the Prosecution of International Crimes Committed on the Territory of the Republic of Chad during the period from 7 June 1982 to 1 December 1990.

[9] *Ministère Public v Hissein Habré* EAC (30 May 2016) (Habre case).

The concept of universal jurisdiction has had a fair share of literature. Kamminga[10] argued that under customary international law, it is an entitlement for nations to apply universal jurisdiction in respect of genocide, crimes against humanity, war crimes and torture. This means that universal jurisdiction is a right possessed by each nation. This chapter goes a step further as it examines Senegal's exercise of the right to universal jurisdiction when it tried Hissene Habre and whether this amounted to interference in the internal affairs of Chad. Hogestol[11] argued that Habre's conviction is set to become a significant precedent for international criminal justice in the region. Here, the author meant that Habre's conviction was set to have a positive impact on the application of universal jurisdiction in Africa. However, this chapter will argue that the possibility of Habre's conviction having a positive impact on the application of universal jurisdiction in Africa, depends on African states being able to achieve a delicate balance between a state's right to non-intervention and the right of other states to exercise universal jurisdiction. Yee[12] argued that universal jurisdiction could be a useful instrument in the protection of human rights. Clearly, the crimes that are subject to universal jurisdiction constitute a violation of fundamental human rights. For example, genocide constitutes a violation of the right to life. This chapter considers how universal jurisdiction was utilised as a tool to bring Habre to account for the human rights violations committed in Chad.

2 Understanding Universal Jurisdiction

Under customary international law, universal jurisdiction is a right possessed by every state.[13] This essentially entails that the courts of any nation are entitled to try international crimes such as piracy, genocide, crimes against humanity and torture committed anywhere in the world. Generally, for a state to exercise jurisdiction over crimes, there must be a link between the state exercising jurisdiction and the crime. This

[10] M Kamminga 'Lessons Learned from the Exercise of Universal Jurisdiction in Respect of Gross Human Rights Offences'(2001) 23 *Human Rights Quarterly* 965.

[11] S Hogestol 'The Habre Judgment at the Extraordinary African Chambers: A Singular Victory in the Fight Against Impunity' (2016) 34 *Nordic Journal of Human Rights* 156.

[12] S Yee 'Universal Jurisdiction: Concept, Logic, and Reality' (2011) 10 *Chinese Journal of International Law* 529 530.

[13] Kamminga (n 10 above) 965.

link can be established by showing that the crimes were committed in the territory of the State claiming jurisdiction (territoriality principle) or that the accused is a national of the State claiming jurisdiction (nationality principle).[14] Under the protective principle, the jurisdictional link is established by showing that the alleged crimes threaten the interests of the state claiming jurisdiction.[15] Here, reference to the territoriality, nationality and protective principle of jurisdiction is made to illustrate the uniqueness of universal jurisdiction as a principle of criminal jurisdiction.

The principle of universal jurisdiction stands out from the other three principles of jurisdiction explained above because under universal jurisdiction, there is no requirement for a link between the state exercising criminal jurisdiction and the crime.[16] This means that a state exercising universal jurisdiction does not need to show that the crimes were committed on its territory or that the offender is its national. It also does not need to show that the alleged crimes are a threat to its interests. Therefore, in the circumstances of Habre's trial in Senegal, the fact that Habre was not a national of Senegal and that the crimes were not committed in Senegal could not bar Senegal from prosecuting Habre. This is because universal jurisdiction requires no link between the state claiming jurisdiction and the alleged crime.

Despite the fact that universal jurisdiction requires no jurisdictional link, the application of universal jurisdiction is not without a condition. It is widely accepted under international law that for a state to exercise universal jurisdiction, the alleged offender must be present on the territory of the state intending to apply universal jurisdiction.[17] This position is also affirmed by Principle 1(2) of the Princeton Principles on Universal Jurisdiction which makes the presence of the accused before the judicial body of the prosecuting state, a condition for the application of universal jurisdiction. The Princeton Principles on Universal Jurisdiction are principles that leading jurists from around the world and legal experts came up

[14] Palestinian Centre for Human Rights 'The Principle and Practice of Universal Jurisdiction: PCHR's Work in the Occupied Palestinian Territory' https://www.fidh.org/IMG/pdf/PCHR_Work_Report_Web.pdf (accessed 2 June 2021).

[15] Palestinian Centre for Human Rights (n 14 above) 15.

[16] Palestinian Centre for Human Rights (n 14) 15.

[17] A Dube 'The AU Model Law on Universal Jurisdiction: An African Response to Western Prosecutions Based on the Universality Principle' (2015) 18 *PER/PELJ* 462.

with to guide the application of universal jurisdiction.[18] In the circumstances of Habre's case, the requirement of the accused's presence on the territory of the prosecuting state was met as Habre was present on Senegalese territory.

2.1 Nature of Offences Subject to Universal Jurisdiction Under Customary International Law

A consideration of the nature of offences that are subject to universal jurisdiction under customary international law is relevant in understanding the principle of universal jurisdiction because not all offences are subject to universal jurisdiction. Offences that are subject to universal jurisdiction under customary international law are linked to the concept of *jus cogens* or peremptory norms of general international law.[19] A peremptory norm of general international law has been defined as "a norm accepted and recognised by the international community of states as a whole as a norm from which no derogation is permitted and which can be modified only by a subsequent norm of general international law having the same character".[20] It therefore means that crimes that are subject to universal jurisdiction under customary international law go against norms which are universally recognised and accepted as norms from which no derogation is permitted.

For anything to qualify as part of customary international law, it must have the elements of state practice and *opinio juris*.[21] *Opinio juris* denotes a subjective belief by a state that it is bound by a certain law.[22] This means that crimes regarded as subject to universal jurisdiction are to be regarded as so because states have the subjective belief that universal jurisdiction ought to be exercised over such crimes as a matter of law. According to

[18] Global Policy Forum 'Princeton Principles on Universal Jurisdiction: Princeton Project on Universal Jurisdiction' https://www.globalpolicy.org/component/content/article/163/29391.html (2 June 2021).

[19] N Kazemi 'Justifications for Universal Jurisdiction: Shocking the Conscience Is Not Enough' (2013) 49 *Tulsa Law Review* 5.

[20] Article 53 of the Vienna Convention on the Law of Treaties, 1969.

[21] J Paust 'Customary International Law: Its Nature, Sources and Status as Law of the United States' (1990) 12 *Michigan Journal of International Law* 61.

[22] Legal Information Institute 'Opinio Juris (International Law)' https://www.law.cornell.edu/wex/opinio_juris (accessed 2 June 2021).

Addis,[23] under customary international law, piracy, slave trade, genocide, crimes against humanity, war crimes and torture constitute the crimes that are subject to universal jurisdiction.

An analysis of Habre's trial before the EAC reveals that the question of what crimes are subject to universal jurisdiction can be a contentious one. Initially, the EAC convicted Habre for personally raping one woman among other offences.[24] The Appeals Chamber of the EAC while upholding the conviction for other crimes quashed the conviction for personally raping one woman.[25] It held that the charge for personal commission of rape had not been included as part of the charges that framed the trial.[26] Despite the reasoning of the Appeals Chamber, it must be noted that the EAC had initially erred by trying Habre for personally raping one woman as this offence does not constitute a crime that is subject to universal jurisdiction under customary international law.

Furthermore, in Article 6 of the Statute creating the EAC,[27] rape constituted a crime against humanity if it was "committed as part of a wide spread or systematic attack directed against any civilian population". In Habre's case, however, the rape of one woman by Habre did not qualify as a crime against humanity because it was committed against one person as opposed to a civilian population as defined in Article 6 of the statute creating the EAC.

2.2 *Offences Subject to Universal Jurisdiction Under Treaty Law*

A consideration of what offences are subject to universal jurisdiction under treaty law is relevant in understanding the nature of universal jurisdiction because a state may choose to rely on treaty law in the application of universal jurisdiction. Treaty law has codified what is under customary international law with respect to offences that are subject to universal

[23] A Addis 'Imagining the International Community: The Constitutive Dimension of Universal Jurisdiction' (2009) 31 *Human Rights Quarterly* 136.

[24] The Habre case.

[25] Le Procureur General v Habre EAC (Appeals Chamber Judgment, 27 April 2017) (Habre Appeal case).

[26] *(The Habre Appeal case).*

[27] Statute of the Extraordinary African Chambers within the Senegalese Judicial System for the Prosecution of International Crimes Committed on the Territory of the Republic of Chad during the period from 7 June 1982 to 1 December 1990.

jurisdiction. Article VI of the Convention on the Prevention and Punishment of the Crime of Genocide 1948 (hereinafter referred to as "the Genocide Convention") provides that persons charged with the offence of genocide may be tried "by such international penal tribunal as may have jurisdiction with respect to those contracting parties which shall have accepted its jurisdiction". This grant of jurisdiction to an international penal tribunal in relation to genocide under Article VI of the Genocide Convention is cited as codifying genocide, as an offence subject to universal jurisdiction.[28]

The offence of torture is also codified under the Convention against Torture and Other Cruel, Inhuman or Degrading Treatment or Punishment, 1984 (hereinafter referred to as "the Convention against Torture"). This is by virtue of Article 5(2) of this Convention which mandates each state party to take steps to establish its jurisdiction over torture-related offences in situations where the accused is present in any territory under its jurisdiction. Therefore, a state party to this convention can rely on Article 5(2) as a basis for exercising universal jurisdiction.

In addition to codifying crimes that are already considered as subject to universal jurisdiction under customary international law, treaty law has also included other crimes not covered under customary international law. One such treaty is the United Nations Convention against Illicit Traffic in Narcotic Drugs and Psychotropic Substances, 1988. Under Article 4 (2) (b) of this Convention, any state party may establish its jurisdiction over offences such as the importation of any narcotic drug contrary to the 1961 Single Convention on Narcotic Drugs, provided the accused is present on its territory and is not extradited to another state party. Thus, this Convention adds drug trafficking as a crime subject to universal jurisdiction. This addition of other crimes by treaty law is important as it extends the arm of justice to other crimes.

As already noted, the accused must be present on the territory of the state intending to exercise universal jurisdiction. Where the alleged offender is not present on the territory of the state intending to apply universal jurisdiction, certain treaties make the crimes that are subject to universal jurisdiction extraditable offences. This means that if an accused

[28] T Maluwa 'The Principle of Universal Jurisdiction and Its Application in Africa: Reconciling Conceptual Logic with Political Reality' https://www.eamja.org/10th%2520EAMJA%2520conference%2520held2520in2520 (accessed 2 June 2021).

is in another country, the country intending to exercise universal jurisdiction can ask the country in which the accused is present to hand over the accused to it for purposes of prosecution. For example, Article 8(1) of the Convention against Torture provides that torture-related offences "shall be deemed to be included as extraditable offences in any extradition treaty existing between state parties". Therefore, treaty law by providing for extradition makes the exercise of universal jurisdiction easier in instances where the accused is not present in the territory of the state intending to exercise universal jurisdiction.

2.3 *The Rationale for Universal Jurisdiction*

The widely stated rationale for universal jurisdiction is that certain crimes such as genocide, war crimes and crimes against humanity offend humanity as a whole and thus concern all states.[29] The crimes that are subject to universal jurisdiction are regarded as so heinous that they affect the entire world. It is on this basis that states can prosecute foreign individuals for certain crimes committed in other states. Nevertheless, the adequacy of this rationale has been doubted. Reliance on the heinousness of crimes as the rationale for the application of universal jurisdiction has shortcomings because other heinous crimes such as extra-judicial killings and forced disappearances are not considered as subject to universal jurisdiction.[30]

One key explanation as to why certain crimes such as extra-judicial killings are not considered as being subject to universal jurisdiction could be the lack of state practice and *opinio juris* on such crimes. This is because state practice and *opinio juris* are essential in the determination of what crimes are subject to universal jurisdiction under customary international law.

Another view put forward is that the key rationale for the application of universal jurisdiction is justice and not deterrence.[31] This assertion is true to the extent that universal jurisdiction does not serve to deter the commission of international crimes in reality but in theory only. This

[29] M Morris 'Universal Jurisdiction in a Divided World: Conference Remarks' (2001) 35 *New England Law Review* 337.

[30] Addis (n 23 above) 138–139.

[31] Kamminga (n 10 above) 944.

is because there is evidence that shows that the commission of international crimes has continued despite the initiation of prosecutions based on universal jurisdiction. For example, some of the grave crimes during the Bosnian conflict in former Yugoslavia, including the disappearance and likely execution of thousands of people were committed at a time when the issuance of indictments based on universal jurisdiction by the International Tribunal had already begun.[32] Equally, at a time when the International Tribunal had already begun investigating abuses in Kosovo on the basis of universal jurisdiction, hundreds of people were massacred in Kosovo.[33] This is a demonstration that to a larger extent, universal jurisdiction does not serve to deter the commission of crimes in reality.

Particularly on the African continent, it is too early to ascertain whether prosecutions based on universal jurisdiction deter the commission of international crimes. This is because Africa has only had one successful prosecution (Habre's prosecution) on the basis of universal jurisdiction. As Habre's conviction only came recently in 2016, the deterrent effect of this conviction on the African continent remains to be seen.

2.4 Universal Jurisdiction and the Principle of Non-intervention

European states such as Belgium have regarded universal jurisdiction as a legal weapon in the fight against international crimes. This was evident when a Belgium court tried 4 Rwandese nationals among them two Benedictine nuns, Sisters Maria Kisito and Gertrude, for their role in the 1994 Rwanda genocide.[34] This was on the basis of universal jurisdiction as the nuns were neither Belgian nationals nor was the alleged crime committed on Belgian soil. In stunning contrast, African states have not been keen in invoking universal jurisdiction as a tool in the delivery of international criminal justice. The reluctance by some countries to invoke universal jurisdiction could perhaps be attributed to the difficulty in reconciling

[32] International Council on Human Rights Policy 'Hard Cases: Bringing Human Rights Violators to Justice Abroad' https://reliefweb.int/sites/reliefweb.int/files/resources/F8D2DF85C8AE339EC125742B0039BD54 (accessed 2 June 2021).

[33] International Council on Human Rights Policy (n 32) 12.

[34] L Keller 'Belgian Jury to Decide Case Concerning Rwandan Genocide' American Society of International Law, volume 6 Issue 13, 25 May 2001 https://www.asil.org/insights/volume/6/issue/13/belgian-jury-decide-case-concerning-rwandan-genocide (accessed 2 June 2021).

the principle of non-intervention in the internal affairs of other states and universal jurisdiction as a tool of international criminal justice. This difficulty was acknowledged by the Israeli Supreme Court in landmark case of *Attorney General v Eichmann*[35] when it stated that the application of universal jurisdiction with respect to international offences (with the exception of piracy) was generally resisted for the reason that it was likely to involve "excessive interference with the competence of the State in which the offence was committed".

In *Nicaragua v United States*,[36] the principle of non-intervention was held to mean that every sovereign state has the right to conduct its affairs without external interference. This means that other states must take a "hands off" approach and leave a sovereign state to freely decide its own political, social, economic and legal affairs. Accordingly, it may appear legally sound to assert that the Courts of a State in whose territory an offence was committed should be the right Courts to exercise jurisdiction over the offence and not the Courts of a foreign state.

Senegal's initial refusal to prosecute Habré in Senegalese national courts or in the alternative, to extradite Habre to Belgium for trial was anchored on the principle of state sovereignty.[37] To elaborate, Senegal's understanding appeared to be that prosecuting Habre, a Chadian citizen, in Senegal was a violation of Chad's state sovereignty. In the words of Tunkin, state sovereignty denotes "the inherent supremacy of the State in its territory and independence in international relations".[38] Accordingly, state sovereignty excludes interference in the internal affairs of a state as the state has supremacy in its territory. Understood in this way, Senegal's contention was that prosecuting Habre who was not Senegalese for crimes committed outside Senegal would amount to interference in the internal affairs of Chad, thereby violating Chad's state sovereignty. Hence, the legal challenge at this point was whether the application of universal jurisdiction violates the principle of non-intervention in the affairs of a sovereign state.

35 Criminal Case No. 40/61 (1968) 36 ILR 5.

36 *(1986) ICJ Reports 202.*

37 G Gillenwater 'Chad/Senegal: Former Chad Dictator Hissène Habré Prosecuted' https://www.loc.gov/law/foreign-news/article/chadsenegal-former-chad-dictator-hissne-habr-prosecuted/ (accessed 2 June 2021).

38 K Gevorgyan, 'Concept of State Sovereignty: Modern Attitudes' http://www.ysu.am/files/Karen_Gevorgyan.pdf (accessed 2 June 2021).

This legal question as to whether the application of universal jurisdiction violates the principle of non-intervention in the affairs of a sovereign state has been long standing in international criminal law discourse. The view that universal jurisdiction violated the principle of non-intervention in the affairs of a state was not only evident in Africa but also in a section of society in the United States. In the United States, this was evident when the Universal Jurisdiction Rejection Bill was introduced in the United States House of Representatives. The preamble of the Bill affirmed that universal jurisdiction was "an assault on the internationally accepted concept of state sovereignty".[39] Although the Bill was not passed, its introduction to the US House of Representatives was testament that there was a view by some sections of society that universal jurisdiction was in conflict with the principle of non-intervention which is corollary to state sovereignty.

Was Senegal therefore correct to have initially asserted that it could not try Habre under the principle of universal jurisdiction because such would impinge upon the state sovereignty of the Republic of Chad? Certainly Not! Universal jurisdiction is a well-established principle of international law and can thus not be excluded. For example, Article 5(2) of the Convention against Torture mandates each state party to take steps to establish its jurisdiction over torture-related offences in situations where the accused is present in any territory under its jurisdiction. Therefore, a state party to this convention can rely on Article 5(2) as a basis for exercising universal jurisdiction. As both the principle of non-intervention and universal jurisdiction are well-established principles of law, neither principle should exclude the application of the other. Hence, this chapter advocates for the striking of a delicate balance between the two seemingly conflicting principles of international law.

2.4.1 Striking a Balance

Striking a balance between the principle of non-intervention and universal jurisdiction must begin with the recognition that the right of a state to non-intervention is not absolute. Anthony Sammons observes that there has been a recognition by international law that intervention in a nation's

[39] Universal Jurisdiction Rejection Act of 2003 https://www.govtrack.us/congress/bills/108/hr2050 (accessed 2 June 2021).

domestic jurisdiction is permissible in some circumstances.[40] Sammons notes that Article 39 of the Charter of the United Nations permits intervention in instances where a state commits a "breach of the peace" or an "act of aggression" which threatens "international peace and security".[41] Under Article 39 of the Charter of the United Nations, the determination of the existence of any threat to the peace, breach of the peace or an act of aggression is made by the Security Council.

At the African level, intervention in a state's affairs is contemplated under Article 4(h) of the Constitutive Act of the African Union, 2000. Article 4(h) of the Constitutive Act of the African Union as amended by Article 4 of the Protocol on Amendments to the Constitutive Act of the African Union 2003 recognises:

> The right of the Union to intervene in a member state pursuant to a decision of the Assembly in respect of grave circumstances, namely: war crimes, genocide and crimes against humanity as well as a serious threat to legitimate order to restore peace and stability to the Member State of the Union upon the recommendation of the peace and security council.

The implication of the above-cited provision is that where war crimes, genocide or crimes against humanity are being committed in a member state, that member state cannot invoke the principle of non-intervention in a bid to avoid intervention by the African Union. Equally, where there is a serious threat to legitimate order, the African Union is entitled to intervene. The decision to include the right of intervention in the Constitutive Act of the African Union arose from concerns about the African Union's failure to intervene in Africa's catastrophic human rights violations such as the 1994 Rwanda genocide.[42] Hence, since intervention in the affairs of other states in certain instances is recognised under the Charter of the United Nations and the Constitutive Act of the African Union, it follows that intervention through universal jurisdiction as a means of prosecuting international crimes such as genocide is legally

[40] A Sammons 'The Under-Theorization of Universal Jurisdiction: Implications for Legitimacy on Trials of War Criminals by National Courts (berkeley.edu)' https://lawcat.berkeley.edu/record/1118658 (accessed 2 June 2021).

[41] Sammons (n 40 above) 119–120.

[42] B Kioko 'The Right of Intervention Under the African Union's Constitutive Act: From Non-Interference to Non-intervention' (2003) 85 *IRRC* 852.

permissible. Accordingly, the right of a state to non-intervention in its affairs or its state sovereignty should not operate to bar the application of universal jurisdiction.

Notwithstanding the legal entitlement that nations have to intervene through universal jurisdiction, it is cardinal to ascertain the exact point at which other states can intervene through universal jurisdiction. This is fundamental in achieving a balance between a state's right to non-intervention and the right of other states to exercise universal jurisdiction. Drawing from Kratochwil's[43] work, Sammons[44] proposed three controlling conditions that needed to be satisfied before other states could intervene. Firstly, other states can only intervene if a government is going against clearly established international obligations, for instance committing genocide. Secondly, the situation should be so serious to the extent that a less intrusive option is unavailable. Thirdly, the intervention should possess collective legitimacy from the international community. This chapter adopts the three controlling conditions as suggested by Sammons and argues that before a state can invoke universal jurisdiction, the three controlling conditions must be met.

In the case of Hissene Habre, a consideration of the facts surrounding Habre's trial and conviction reveals that the three controlling conditions as suggested by Sammons were met. In relation to the first controlling condition, it cannot be put in doubt that the atrocious acts carried out by Habre's regime constituted an abrogation of clearly established international obligations. This is because offences such as crimes against humanity which Habre allegedly committed go against the peremptory norms of international law.[45] Since Habre's regime had violated clearly established international obligations, the first controlling condition for a state to intervene as explained by Sammons was met.

With respect to the second controlling condition, the situation in Chad was serious because approximately 40,000 people were killed, with many

[43] Friedrich Kratochwil, "Sovereignty as Dominium: Is there a Right of Humanitarian Intervention?" in Beyond Westphalia?: State Sovereignty and International Intervention' (ed) GM Lyons & M Mastanduno (Baltimore: Johns Hopkins University Press, 1995) 39–40.

[44] Sammons (n 40 above) 121.

[45] United Nations 'Crimes against Humanity' https://www.un.org/en/genocideprevention/crimes-against-humanity.shtml (accessed 2 June 2021).

more kidnapped, tortured or raped during Habre's rule.[46] The report by the commission of inquiry with respect to the crimes committed during Habre's rule revealed that family members of those arrested during Habre's regime were evicted from their homes and women and children were thrown into the streets.[47] According to this report, "nothing was immune to this murderous madness, and the entire country was in a state of terror".[48] Apart from prosecuting Habre through universal jurisdiction, no other less intrusive option was available to Senegal in bringing Habre to justice because Habre was on Senegalese territory. Moreover, Chad, Habre's home country where the offences were committed did not oppose the prosecution of Habre abroad as it waived his immunity from prosecution abroad.[49]

With respect to the third condition, the intervention by Senegal through universal jurisdiction possessed collective legitimacy from the international community. This is because Habre's prosecution in Senegal was the outcome of a sustained international effort to bring Habre to justice.[50] This collective legitimacy was expressed by the support rendered by the international community in prosecuting Habre. For instance, the creation of the EAC that tried Habre was funded by the international community.[51] In sum, all the three controlling conditions as advanced by Sammons were satisfied before Senegal intervened through universal jurisdiction.

In addition to the three controlling conditions stated above, this chapter adopts the African perspective expressed under Article 4(b) of the African Union Model National Law on Universal Jurisdiction over

[46] British Broadcasting Corporation 'Hissene Habre: Chad's Ex-President Seeks to Overturn Verdict' https://www.bbc.com/news/world-africa-38555035 (accessed 2 June 2021).

[47] Report of the Commission of Inquiry into the Crimes and Misappropriations committed by Ex-President Habre, His Accomplices and/or accessories (7 May 1992).

[48] The Report (n 47 above) 79.

[49] Human Rights Watch 'Chad Lifts Immunity of Ex-Dictator' https://www.hrw.org/news/2002/12/05/chad-lifts-immunity-ex-dictator (3 June 2021).

[50] Open Society Foundations 'Talking Justice: The Long Road to the Extraordinary African Chambers' https://www.opensocietyfoundations.org/podcasts/talking-justice-the-long-road-to-the-extraordinary-african-chambers (3 June 2021).

[51] Sofia Christensen 'Court Rejects Former Chad President's Appeal' https://www.voanews.com/africa/court-rejects-former-chad-presidents-appeal (3 June 2021).

International Crimes (hereinafter referred to as "the AU Model Law on Universal Jurisdiction"). This Article prescribes that before universal jurisdiction can be exercised, an opportunity to try the matter must be given to the court of the state in which the offences were allegedly committed, provided that the state in question is willing and able to prosecute. This provision is crucial in striking a balance between a state's right to non-intervention on the one hand and the right of other states to exercise universal jurisdiction on the other. This is because by giving an opportunity to judicial institutions in the state in which the offences were committed to try the offences, that state's right to non-intervention is respected. At the same time, the right of other states to exercise universal jurisdiction is guaranteed in the event that the state in whose territory the offences were committed is unwilling and unable to try the offences.

Ultimately, the possibility of Habre's conviction being a legal breakthrough to the future application of universal jurisdiction in Africa depends on African states being able to achieve a balance between a state's right to non-intervention and universal jurisdiction. If this balance is not achieved, oppressive regimes on the African continent will be resisting universal jurisdiction on the basis that universal jurisdiction amounts to interference in the internal affairs of other states.

3 How Universal Jurisdiction Was Employed as a Tool to Achieve Justice in the Habre Case

The circumstances prevailing at the time rendered it difficult albeit not impossible to try Habre and bring him to account for his crimes in his home country of Chad which had the primarily obligation to prosecute him. Firstly, Habre was not present on Chadian territory and Chad never requested his extradition from Senegal.[52] Secondly, there were serious concerns as to whether Habre would be fairly tried in Chad.[53] Senegal had backtracked on its decision to expel Habre to Chad after concerns were raised over the risk that Habre would be mistreated or even killed in Chad. Thus, these factors in addition to the fact that Habre was within

[52] Human Rights Watch 'The Case of Hissène Habré Before the Extraordinary African Chambers in Senegal' https://www.hrw.org/sites/default/files/news_attachments/qa_eng_april_16.pdf (accessed 3 June 2021).

[53] Human Rights Watch (n 52 above) 11.

Senegalese territorial jurisdiction placed Senegal in a better position to try Habre.

However, Senegal could not assert ordinary jurisdiction to try Habre because Habre was neither a Senegalese citizen nor where the crimes committed on Senegalese Soil. This left universal jurisdiction as a plausible mechanism under which Senegal could legally bring Habre to account for the crimes committed against the Chadian people. This is because there is no nexus required between the state exerting jurisdiction and the crimes committed for a state to exert jurisdiction under the principle of universal jurisdiction.

Under the auspices of the African Union, a tribunal was set up within the Senegalese Court system to try Habre under the principle of universal jurisdiction. During the trial of Habre, the primary applicable law was not Senegalese law but the Statute establishing the EAC.[54] As the Statute was a result of an agreement between the African Union and Senegal, it constituted international law. Senegalese law was only to be resorted to where the Statute establishing the EAC was silent.[55] This means that the EAC was a hybrid tribunal mandated to apply both Senegalese national law and international law. At the conclusion of the trial, Habre was found guilty on charges of torture, crimes against humanity and war crimes.[56] On appeal, the Appeals Chamber of the EAC while upholding the conviction for other crimes quashed the conviction for personally raping one woman.[57] It held that the charge for personal commission of rape had not been included as part of the charges that framed the trial.

From the foregoing, it can be appreciated that universal jurisdiction enabled Senegal to hold Habre accountable despite the fact that Habre was not a Senegalese national and the fact that the alleged crimes were not committed in Senegal. Through universal jurisdiction, justice was

[54] Article 16 (1) of the Statute of the Extraordinary African Chambers within the Senegalese Judicial System for the Prosecution of International Crimes Committed on the Territory of the Republic of Chad during the period from 7 June 1982 to 1 December 1990.

[55] Article 16 (2) of the Statute of the Extraordinary African Chambers within the Senegalese Judicial System for the Prosecution of International Crimes Committed on the Territory of the Republic of Chad during the period from 7 June 1982 to 1 December 1990.

[56] The Habre case.

[57] The Habre Appeal case.

achieved for Habre's victims. The successful conviction of Habre proved that universal jurisdiction can be an effective tool in bringing perpetrators of international crime to account for their crimes in situations where a country in whose territory the crimes were committed is unable to bring the perpetrator of international crimes to justice.

4 Significance and Legacy of Habre's Conviction with Respect to Universal Jurisdiction

The Human Rights Watch observed that Habre's case demonstrated that "universal jurisdiction is an important safety net to ensure that suspects of atrocities do not enjoy impunity in a third state when they cannot be prosecuted before the courts of the country where the crimes were allegedly committed or before an international court".[58] The fact that Habre was tried in Senegal is of special significance to the African continent given that most of the international crimes committed on the continent have been tried by the International Criminal Court. The success of Senegal in prosecuting Habre on the basis of universal jurisdiction indicated that African states are capable of exercising universal jurisdiction and that it was possible to have an African driven international criminal justice system which can effectively bring perpetrators of international crime to account for their crimes.

The Human Rights Watch however pointed out that the "Habré trial does not negate the importance of the ICC and the use of universal jurisdiction by non-African states, including European courts, for crimes committed in Africa".[59] While this claim by the Human Rights Watch could be legitimate considering the fact that Habre's case was only the first universal jurisdiction case undertaken in Africa, the fact that Habre's successful prosecution in Senegal was a clear demonstration that African states have the ability and can take the leading role in the prosecution of international crimes committed on the African Continent cannot be down played.

However, if African states are going to successfully build on the legacy of the successful prosecution of Habre in Senegal, there must

[58] Human Rights Watch 'Q&A: The Case of Hissène Habré before the Extraordinary African Chambers in Senegal' https://www.hrw.org/news/2016/05/03/qa-case-hissene-habre-extraordinary-african-chambers-senegal#25 (accessed 3 June 2021).

[59] Human Rights Watch (n 58 above). Para. 26.

be strong political will by African governments. As Reed Brody, a renowned human rights lawyer who was instrumental in bringing Habre to justice observed, political will by the Senegalese government was pivotal in Habre's successful prosecution.[60] Habre's successful prosecution sent an inspiring message of hope across the African continent that an African led international criminal justice system was possible but the lack of political will by some African states to use universal jurisdiction in prosecuting perpetrators of international crimes threatens that message of hope. A perfect example is that of Equatorial Guinea and its failure to bring former Gambian President, Yahya Jammeh to account for his alleged crimes. Yahya Jammeh ruled The Gambia from 1996 to 2017. His regime is accused of widespread human rights abuses such as torture, enforced disappearances, extra-judicial killings and arbitrary detention.[61] He fled The Gambia to Equatorial Guinea after his defeat in the presidential election. Despite mounting calls for Jammeh's prosecution, Equatorial Guinea has not taken any concrete steps to bring Habre to Justice using universal jurisdiction as Senegal did, with the President of Equatorial Guinea pledging to protect Jammeh.[62] This signals that if universal jurisdiction is to be a successful tool in promoting accountability for international crimes, there must be strong political will by African governments.

Additionally, to build on the success of Habre's conviction in Senegal, African states must readily embrace the principle of universal jurisdiction and enshrine it in their domestic legislation. To this end, the African Union has provided for the AU Model Law on Universal Jurisdiction which would assist the African continent in the fight against international crimes if incorporated in the domestic legislation of various African countries. As the name suggests, it is a model law meant to provide a template to members of the African Union, to be used in formulating their domestic national legislation on the application of universal jurisdiction.

[60] Human Rights Watch https://www.hrw.org/news/2021/04/01/interview-reed-brody-jammeh2justice-campaign (accessed 3 June 2021).

[61] Trial International 'Universal Jurisdiction Review 2021' http://cja.org/wp-content/uploads/2021/04/Trial-International_UJAR_DIGITAL.pdf (accessed 3 June 2021) 56.

[62] *The Guardian* 'Equatorial Guinea Says It Will Protect Former Gambian Leader' 27 January 2018 https://www.theguardian.com/world/2018/jan/27/equatorial-guinea-says-it-will-protect-yahya-jammeh-former-gambian-leader (accessed 3 June 2021).

Article 4(a) of the AU Model Law on Universal Jurisdiction asserts that:

> The Court shall have jurisdiction to try any person alleged to have committed any crime under this law, regardless of whether such a crime is alleged to have been committed in the territory of the State or abroad and irrespective of the nationality of the victim, provided that such a person shall be within the territory of the State.

As used in the above provision, "the court" means the highest court in a nation with original jurisdiction.[63] The provision cited above restates the position that under universal jurisdiction, a domestic court of a state can try any person for certain crimes despite the crimes being committed abroad and against foreign nationals.

5 Conclusion and Recommendations

The success of Senegal in prosecuting Habre on the basis of universal jurisdiction indicated that African states are capable of exercising universal jurisdiction. Further, Habre's trial showed that universal jurisdiction can be a powerful tool in bringing perpetrators of international crimes to justice. African states must therefore draw inspiration from Habre's conviction and prosecute other individuals suspected of having committed international crimes on the continent. In order to build on the success of Habre's conviction, African states need to achieve a balance between a state's right to non-intervention and the right of other states to intervene through universal jurisdiction. In achieving this balance, African states must adopt in their respective domestic legislation, the position under Article 4(b) of the AU Model Law on Universal Jurisdiction. This Article states that before universal jurisdiction can be exercised, an opportunity to try the matter must be given to the court of the State in which the offences were allegedly committed, provided that the state in question is willing and able to prosecute. By giving an opportunity to courts in the state in which the offences were committed to try the offences, a state's right to non-intervention is respected. Equally, the right of other states to exercise universal jurisdiction is guaranteed in the event that the State in whose territory the offences were committed is unwilling and unable

[63] Article 2 of the AU Model Law on Universal Jurisdiction.

to try the offences. The prospect of Habre's conviction being a breakthrough in the application of universal jurisdiction in Africa also depends on the political will by African governments. Through the application of universal jurisdiction, African states can take the leading role in the prosecution of international crimes on the continent.

Bibliography

Books

Kratochwil, F 'Sovereignty as Dominium: Is There a Right of Humanitarian Intervention?' in *Beyond Westphalia?: State Sovereignty and International Intervention* (ed) GM Lyons & M Mastanduno (Johns Hopkins University Press: Baltimore, 1995).

Journal Articles

Addis A 'Imagining the International Community: The Constitutive Dimension of Universal Jurisdiction' (2009) 31 *Human Rights Quarterly* 136.

Dube A 'The AU Model Law on Universal Jurisdiction: An African Response to Western Prosecutions Based on the Universality Principle' (2015) 18 *PER/PELJ* 462.

Hogestol S 'The Habre Judgment at the Extraordinary African Chambers: A Singular Victory in the fight Against Impunity' (2016) 34 *Nordic Journal of Human Rights* 156.

Kamminga M 'Lessons Learned from the Exercise of Universal Jurisdiction in Respect of Gross Human Rights Offences' (2001) 23 *Human Rights Quarterly* 965.

Kazemi N 'Justifications for Universal Jurisdiction: Shocking the Conscience Is Not Enough' (2013) 49 *Tulsa Law Review* 5.

Kioko B 'The Right of Intervention Under the African Union's Constitutive Act: From Non-interference to Non-intervention' (2003) 85 *IRRC* 852.

Morris M 'Universal Jurisdiction in a Divided World: Conference Remarks' (2001) 35 *New England Law Review* 337.

Paust J 'Customary International Law: Its Nature, Sources and Status as Law of the United States' (1990) 12 *Michigan Journal of International Law* 61.

Seelinger K 'Rape and the President: The Remarkable Trial and (Partial) Acquittal of Hissène Habré' (2017) 34 *World Policy Journal* 17.

Yee S 'Universal Jurisdiction: Concept, Logic, and Reality' (2011) 10 *Chinese Journal of International Law* 529–530.

Statutes

The African Union Model Law on Universal Jurisdiction.

The Statute of the Extraordinary African Chambers within the Senegalese Judicial System for the Prosecution of International Crimes Committed on the Territory of the Republic of Chad during the period from 7 June 1982 to 1 December 1990.

The Vienna Convention on the Law of Treaties, 1969.

Reports

Report of the Commission of Inquiry into the Crimes and Misappropriations committed by Ex-President Habre, His Accomplices and/or accessories (May 7, 1992).

Internet Sources

British Broadcasting Corporation 'Hissene Habre: Chad's Ex-President Seeks to Overturn Verdict' https://www.bbc.com/news/world-africa-38555035 (accessed 2 June 2021).

Gevorgyan, K 'Concept of State Sovereignty: Modern Attitudes' http://www.ysu.am/files/Karen_Gevorgyan.pdf (accessed 2 June 2021).

Gillenwater 'Chad/Senegal: Former Chad Dictator Hissène Habré Prosecuted' https://www.loc.gov/law/foreign-news/article/chadsenegal-former-chad-dictator-hissne-habr-prosecuted/ (accessed 2 June 2021).

Global Policy Forum 'Princeton Principles on Universal Jurisdiction: Princeton Project on Universal Jurisdiction' https://www.globalpolicy.org/component/content/article/163/29391.html (accessed 2 June 2021).

Human Rights Watch 'Chad Lifts Immunity of Ex-Dictator' https://www.hrw.org/news/2002/12/05/chad-lifts-immunity-ex-dictator (3 June 2021).

Human Rights Watch 'The Case of Hissène Habré Before the Extraordinary African Chambers in Senegal' https://www.hrw.org/sites/default/files/news_attachments/qa_eng_april_16.pdf (accessed 3 June 2021).

Human Rights Watch 'Q&A: The Case of Hissène Habré Before the Extraordinary African Chambers in Senegal' https://www.hrw.org/news/2016/05/03/qa-case-hissene-habre-extraordinary-african-chambers-senegal#25 (accessed 3 June 2021).

Human Rights Watch https://www.hrw.org/news/2021/04/01/interview-reed-brody-jammeh2justice-campaign (accessed 3 June 2021).

https://www.asil.org/insights/volume/6/issue/13/belgian-jury-decide-case-concerning-rwandan-genocide (accessed 2 June 2021).

International Crimes Database 'Hissène Habré' http://www.internationalcrimesdatabase.org/Case/762 (accessed 3 June 2021).

International Council on Human Rights Policy 'Hard Cases: Bringing Human Rights Violators to Justice Abroad' https://reliefweb.int/sites/reliefweb.int/files/resources/F8D2DF85C8AE339EC125742B0039BD54 (accessed 2 June 2021).

Keller L 'Belgian Jury to Decide Case Concerning Rwandan Genocide' *American Society of International Law*, volume 6 Issue 13, 25 May 2001 https://www.asil.org/insights/volume/6/issue/13/belgian-jury-decide-case-concerning-rwandan-genocide (accessed 2 June 2021).

Legal Information Institute 'Opinio Juris (International Law)' https://www.law.cornell.edu/wex/opinio_juris (accessed 2 June 2021).

Maluwa T 'The Principle of Universal Jurisdiction and Its Application in Africa: Reconciling Conceptual Logic with Political Reality' https://www.eamja.org/10th%2520EAMJA%2520conference%2520held2520in2520 (accessed 2 June 2021).

Musila G 'African Union and the Evolution of International Criminal Justice in Africa: Challenges, Controversies and Opportunities' http://www.academia.edu (accessed 1 June 2021).

Open Society Foundations 'Talking Justice: The Long Road to the Extraordinary African Chambers' https://www.opensocietyfoundations.org/podcasts/talking-justice-the-long-road-to-the-extraordinary-african-chambers (accessed 3 June 2021).

Palestinian Centre for Human Rights 'The Principle and Practice of Universal Jurisdiction: PCHR's Work in the Occupied Palestinian Territory' https://www.fidh.org/IMG/pdf/PCHR_Work_Report_Web.pdf (accessed 2 June 2021).

Reed Brody 'Victims Bring a Dictator to Justice: The Case of Hissene Habre', June 2017 https://www.brot-fuer-die-welt.de/fileadmin/mediapool/2_Downloads/Fachinformationen/Analyse/Analysis70-The_Habre_Case.pdf (accessed 2 June 2021).

République du Sénégal, Cour d'appel de Dakar, Chambre d'accusation, https://www.asser.nl/upload/documents/20121105T030720-Cour%20dappel%20Dakar%2004-07-2000.pdf (accessed 3 June 2021).

Sammons A 'The Under-Theorization of Universal Jurisdiction: Implications for Legitimacy on Trials of War Criminals by National Courts (berkeley.edu)' https://lawcat.berkeley.edu/record/1118658 (accessed 2 June 2021).

Sofia Christensen 'Court Rejects Former Chad President's Appeal' https://www.voanews.com/africa/court-rejects-former-chad-presidents-appeal (3 June 2021).

The Guardian 'Equatorial Guinea Says It Will Protect Former Gambian Leader', 27 January 2018 https://www.theguardian.com/world/2018/jan/27/

equatorial-guinea-says-it-will-protect-yahya-jammeh-former-gambian-leader (accessed 3 June 2021).

Trial International 'Hissene Habre' https://trialinternational.org/latest-post/hissene-habre/ (accessed 3 June 2021).

Trial International 'Universal Jurisdiction Review 2021' http://cja.org/wp-content/uploads/2021/04/Trial-International_UJAR_DIGITAL.pdf (accessed 3 June 2021) 56.

Universal Jurisdiction Rejection Act of 2003 https://www.govtrack.us/congress/bills/108/hr2050 (accessed 2 June 2021).

United Nations 'Crimes Against Humanity' https://www.un.org/en/genocideprevention/crimes-against-humanity.shtml (accessed 2 June 2021).

Case Law

Ministère Public v Hissein Habré EAC (30 May 2016).

Attorney General v Eichmann Criminal Case No. 40/61 (1968) 36 ILR 5.

Nicaragua v United States (1986) ICJ Reports 202.

Le Procureur General v Habre EAC (Appeals Chamber Judgment, 27 April 2017).

Complementarity and Criminal Liability of Companies in Africa: Missing the Mark?

Charmika Samaradiwakera-Wijesundara

1 Introduction

In this chapter I seek to explore the idea of accountability for international crimes in national courts in the context of Africa, pivoting from South Africa, with specific focus on the corporation as a juristic person. In so doing I will ask the question whether in undertaking this exercise, debates about direct versus indirect liability and which platforms are best suited, we may be missing the mark. Here I am referring to a mark as both a point/goal and as a person.[1] In other words I will contend with whether the debate on corporate criminal accountability for international crimes and the reforms being advocated for have identified the correct person to hold accountable.

[1] *Merriam-Webster* https://www.merriam-webster.com/dictionary/mark (accessed 31 May 2021).

C. Samaradiwakera-Wijesundara (✉)
School of Law, University of the Witwatersrand, Johannesburg, South Africa
e-mail: charmika.wijesundara@wits.ac.za

International Institute of Social Studies, The Hague, Netherlands

E. C. Lubaale and N. Dyani-Mhango (eds.), *National Accountability for International Crimes in Africa*,
https://doi.org/10.1007/978-3-030-88044-6_5

In part I, I will situate the significance for accountability in a brief historical foregrounding of the relationship between the state and corporation in the founding South Africa, drawing parallels to Nigeria, the implications of continuing corporate harm and the relationship between the state and the corporation as juristic persons. In so doing I aim to provide a brief critical historicism of the object of analysis: the juristic person of the corporation and problematise its nature.[2]

In part II, I will attempt to systematically unpack the meanings of the core concepts employed in this exercise: international crimes and accountability. I will consider both what they tend to mean currently in mainstream international criminal law discourse and what they have the potential to mean in the light of arguments for a more substantive systematic approach.

In part III, I will use a similar model, consideration of both 'is' (current position) and 'ought to be' (arguments for reform), to outline the current accountability mechanisms for international crimes across international and domestic platforms and their limitations. I will proceed to a consideration of the regional mechanisms, as collective power to support increased domestic control the parameters of juristic personality, that emerge as a possible solution to navigate the challenges that both international and domestic levels present. Having established a sense of what is meant by accountability and the mechanisms that exist to secure it I will attempt to zoom the lens of analysis outwards in order to interrogate the unstated assumptions that dominate debates about corporate accountability. The intention is to understand the existing regime of corporate criminal liability for international crimes, arguments for its reform and articulate the way in which this falls short of a systemic intervention into the root causes of harms facilitated by the corporation. Thus, attempting to reveal how the focus on the corporation as a person and the consequences of its conduct elides the more fundamental issue of the authorisation of the corporation as a person and the parameters in which it is permitted to operate.

[2] See A Sekyi-Otu 'Fanon and the Possibility of Postcolonial Critical Imagination' in Gibson N (ed), *Living Fanon—Global Perspectives* (2011) Palgrave Macmillan, New York 46, as employed in S Sibanda '"Not Yet Uhuru"—The Usurpation of the Liberation Aspirations of South Africa's Masses by a Commitment to Liberal Constitutional Democracy' unpublished PhD Thesis, University of the Witwatersrand, 2018 33–35 on history as more than mere context, but the challenge of colonial narratives of knowledge and purported universal truths.

I will conclude with a critical consideration of the paradox of the existing liberal paradigm that utilises an abstract individualism to justify corporate accountability for harm while simultaneously entrenching the corporate power that enables the harm to be systemically perpetuated in the first instance, and whether accountability could be better achieved with an African philosophy paradigm that centres the human being-becoming beyond atomistic conceptions of accountability and human relations broadly; a paradigm that is arguably already implicit in the regional mechanisms.

2 Part I: Historicising the Corporation and Interrogating Its Nature

2.1 *Foregrounding the Relationship Between the Corporation, the State in the Formation of African States*

Before unpacking the concept of accountability, it would be useful to consider both the harm, the perpetrators of that harm and the persons who endured the harm for which accountability is contemplated. Indeed, at face value the need for accountability arises from the perpetration of international crimes by corporations. This can be construed as accountability for the harm caused by the excesses of corporate power. However, in order to appreciate the systemic nature of the problem of power, harm and accountability it is useful to consider the workings of corporations at some significant moments in history. Rather than to provide a comprehensive account, which would be beyond the scope of this chapter, I hope to simply ground these otherwise abstract conceptions. In so doing I endeavour to demonstrate the tenuous (if not fictitious) delimitations of public and private power in the context of juristic personality (as state and corporation) in Africa.

While in the interests of expediency this analysis is anchored in South Africa, it is important to recognise that this phenomenon was not exclusive to it. For example though Nigeria and South Africa are on opposite ends of the continent, they have more in common than meets the eye. They both have been described as 'economic giants of Africa' and they have been reported as having the highest amounts of illicit capital flight in the world.[3] Fundamentally both states were precipitated by colonial corporations. These corporations served as vessels to exploit the vast natural resources in the territories to the exclusion, exploitation and mass decimation of the people indigenous to those territories.

I have argued that the Dutch East India Company (DEIC) illustrates how the corporation is an instrument of coloniality.[4] Spearheaded by Jan van Riebeck in 1652, the DEIC set out to establish a refreshment station at the Cape, and later established a colony of which van Riebeck also served as governor.[5] Despite reliance on trade with indigenous peoples, as their commercial strength grew, the DEIC started expanding inward territorially.[6] Wars were instigated to remove perceived threats to their domination; eventually enabling the DEIC to tax the indigenous Khoi communities in cattle and eventually force them into a monetary economy of the DEIC's design.[7,8] This is reported to have precipitated the collapse of the economic and socio-political existence of the indigenous communities, transforming their relationship from free traders with agency to captive labour.[9] The Roman Dutch common law, imposed by the DEIC, formed the foundations of mercantile law and labour relations in South

[3] K Dev & D Cartwright- 'Illicit Financial Flows from Developing Countries: 2004–2013' (Global Financial Integrity 2015) 8 http://www.gfintegrity.org/wp-content/uploads/2015/12/IFF-Update_2015-Final-1.pdf (accessed 31 May 2021); B Meyersfeld 'Committing the Crime of Poverty: The Next Phase of the Business and Human Rights Debate' 160–172 in C Rodriguez-Garavito (ed) *Business and Human Rights Beyond the End of the Beginning* (2017) 178.

[4] C Samaradiwakera-Wijesundara 'Interrogating Recognition of the Legal Personality of the Company: Is the Company an Instrument of Coloniality?' unpublished LLM Thesis, University of the Witwatersrand, 2018 58–66; C Samaradiwakera-Wijesundara 'The Fiction of the Juristic Person: Reassessing Personhood in Relation to People' in Melissa Steyn & William Mpofu (eds) *Decolonising the Human: Reflections from Africa on Difference and Oppression* (2021) Wits University Press 186 at 194–196.

[5] Geen *The Making of the Union of South Africa* (1946) 7.

[6] Lucas *An Archaeology of Colonial Identity: Power and Material Culture in the Dwars Valley, South Africa* (2004) 72.

[7] As above.

[8] As above.

[9] As above.

Africa while the epistemicidaly substituting and perversely misconstruing indigenous law and governance systems.[10]

A similar pattern unfolds in 1878 in the Niger Delta. George Goldie formed the United Africa Company (UAC) made in the image of the East India Company (EIC) and obtained control of the Niger Delta's and its next main export, after it was established as the Slave Coast, palm oil.[11] This control secured the territory for Brittan from other European interests at the Berlin Conference and changed the UAC, later The National Africa Company, through a royal charter of incorporation with authority to administer the Niger Delta and surrounds into the Royal Niger Company (RNC).[12] Despite verbal agreements with the indigenous Kings, Goldie is reported to have moved inland and instituted treaties granting the RNC monopoly to the exclusion of the local communities who had been selling palm oil competitively to Europe.[13] Attempts to sell outside of the monopoly were met with charges of 'obstructing commerce' followed by exile and mysterious deaths such as was the case with Jaja of Opobo.[14] This is said to have set the tone for Kings in the area to view trade agreements with Europeans with greater circumspection and culminated in King Koko Mingi VIII, after unsuccessful attempts to break the monopoly, succeeding in an attack on the RNC headquarters.[15] The attack was successful. Nonetheless, British recalcitrance to negotiate and later retaliation resulted in King Koko being outlawed.[16] This happened after he refused a settlement from the British Parliamentary Committee.[17] He then committed suicide in exile in 1898.[18] The circumstances are said to have lost RNC publicity in Britain and resulted in the sale of Nigeria

[10] MB Ramose 'In Memoriam: Sovereignty and the "New" South Africa' *Griffith Law Review* 16, no. 2 (2007) 314.

[11] C Nwanze 'Who Sold Nigeria to the British for £865k in 1899?' https://africasacountry.com/2014/04/historyclass-who-sold-nigeria-to-the-british-for-865k-in-1899 (accessed 28 May 2021).

[12] As above.

[13] As above.

[14] As above.

[15] As above.

[16] As above.

[17] As above.

[18] As above.

to the British Crown.[19] The RNC carries on as an early predecessor of Unilever after having been acquired by the joint efforts of the British Lever Brothers and Dutch Jurgens' and Van der Bergh's.[20] Now still in operation, Unilever lives on.

The pattern is chillingly similar—down to the white male figurehead of the sovereign-corporation.[21] The ideological golden thread of domination and appropriation of labour and land runs through the history of encounters with the corporation.[22] This process often elides the relationship between political and commercial interests and the symbiotic relationship between the state and the corporation.[23] As Grovogui has noted, international law provided the framework for erasing the subjectivity of colonised peoples and denying their/our humanity.[24] International law treatises were utilised in this context to legally permit genocide, slavery and large-scale appropriation of land and other resources.[25] Anghie reflects on how positivism was used to develop a vocabulary that objectified and dehumanised in order to legitimise heinous violence in the name of the divine right to conquest and later the civilising mission.[26] Systemic dehumanisation and the installation of conditions of poverty and inequality were perpetrated through the corporation thus embedding the irony of corporations having personhood over human beings deprived of theirs.[27] The contemporary connection to Unilever reminds us that this is not behaviour that can be relegated to the past as a mere relic of

[19] As above.

[20] BS Yamey 'The History of Unilever. By Charles Wilson' *The Economic Journal* 66, no. 264 (December 1956) 730.

[21] C Samaradiwakera-Wijesundara (n 4 above) 40–41.

[22] As above.

[23] V Rao "*A Brief History of the Corporation 1600–2100*" 2011 http://www.ribbonfarm.com/2011/06/08/a-brief-history-of-the-corporation-1600-to-2100/ (accessed 05 August 2020); Callinicos *Imperialism and Global Political Economy* (2009) 136.

[24] S Grovogui *Sovereigns, Quasi Sovereigns and Africans: Race and Self-Determination in International Law* (1996) 55.

[25] KB Nunn 'Law as a Eurocentric Enterprise' *Law and Inequality: A Journal of Theory and Practice* 15, no. 2 (1997) 362.

[26] A Anghie *Imperialism, Sovereignty and the Making of International Law* (2005) 38.

[27] Samaradiwakera-Wijesundara (note 4 above).

colonialism, but lives on in the very design and purpose of the corporation. Again, we can turn to South Africa and Nigeria for contemporary examples.

In August of 2012, 34 human beings occupied as miners were killed extra-judicially, by South African Police Services personnel, in the course of demanding a living wage on Lonmin's Marikana Mine.[28] This was purportedly reprisal by the Mine precipitated by growing discontent with the impact of the strike action gaining traction across the country on its bottom line.[29] This massacre is one instance of the broader state of repression and resistance in the context of the exploitative conditions faced by mineworkers and affected communities in South Africa long established in colonial-apartheid.[30] Terblanche comments on how unfree black labour '...has been a permanent feature of South Africa's economic history since 1652 and is destined to remain a defining characteristic of the South Africa landscape for decades to come'.[31] 'The reality is that mining operations often result in worse conditions after the conclusion of the operations, than existed before mining began'.[32] The context has and continues to be exploitative by design and as such corporations do not only contribute to creating poverty but actively 'bank on it'.[33] While a commission of inquiry was led—the scope focused on state accountability.[34]

In a similar turn of events, the devastation faced by the Ogoni peoples in the Niger Delta can be traced to the Shell Petroleum Development Corporation (SPDC), a joint venture between British Shell (Shell) and

[28] T Madlingozi 'Social Justice in a Time of Neo-Apartheid Constitutionalism: Critiquing the Anti-Black Economy of Recognition, Incorporation and Distribution.' *Stellenbosch Law Review* 1 (2016) 138–139; N Ndlovu Morgan Ndlovu 'Living in the Marikana World: The State, Capital and Society' *International Journal of African Renaissance Studies* 8, no. 1 (2013) 47–48.

[29] As above.

[30] As above.

[31] S Terreblanche *Lost in Transformation: South Africa's Search for a New Future Since 1986* (2012) 4.

[32] B Meyersfeld 'Empty Promises and the Myth of Mining: Does Mining Lead to Pro-Poor Development?' *Business and Human Rights Journal* 2, no. 1 (January 2017) 33 and 50.

[33] As above.

[34] Marikana Commission of Inquiry: Report (2015) https://www.sahrc.org.za/home/21/files/marikana-report-1.pdf.

Royal Dutch-Petroleum (RDP), for the extraction and production of oil formed in 1956.[35] The SPDC later formed a joint venture with parastatal Nigerian Petroleum Company (NPC).[36] Rather than benefit, this resulted in great harm to the Ogoni Peoples including severe air, soil and water pollution resulting in toxic contamination of air, soil and water supplies.[37] In 1990 the Movement for the Survival of the Ogoni People (MOSOP), which was formed to defend the human rights of the Ogoni Peoples, was met with violent repression and reprisal by the Nigerian military after requests for intervention by Shell and RDP.[38] This intervention precipitated atrocities against the Ogoni Peoples including 'widespread' and 'systemic', extra-judicial executions, arbitrary killings and extended detention, and torture.[39] In addition to the provision of resources Shell and RDP is alleged to have invested in the extra-judicial and judicial murders of Ogoni activists.[40] Attempts at holding the corporations liable in foreign courts were unsuccessful.[41] What is relevant is that the accountability of the Nigerian government was established by the quasi-judicial regional African Commission (AC).[42] The new Nigerian government admitted in a verbal note in the Ogoni case that there were and still are human rights violations perpetrated by oil corporations in Nigeria.[43] As was the case in the Marikana Massacre it appears that, while the states received some

[35] M Jain & B Meyersfeld, 'Lessons from Kiobel v Royal Dutch Petroleum Company: Developing Homegrown Lawyering Strategies Around Corporate Accountability' *South African Journal on Human Rights* 30, no. 3 (2014) 430.

[36] F Coomans 'The Ogoni Case Before the African Commission on Human and Peoples' Rights' *The International and Comparative Law Quarterly* 52, no. 3 (July 2003) 749.

[37] Jain & Meyersfeld (n 35 above) 430.

[38] As above.

[39] Jain & Meyersfeld (n 35 above) 433.

[40] As above 430.

[41] *Kiobel v Royal Dutch Petroleum Co* 2013 133 s Ct 1659 (No 10 1491).

[42] Communication 155/96, The Social and Economic Rights Action Center and the Center Economic, and Social Rights/Nigeria; http://www.cesr.org/ESCR/africancommission.htm. It was communicated to the parties on 27 May 2002 (Ogoni case).

[43] N Verbale 127/2000 submitted by the Nigerian government at the 28th session of the Commission in Oct 2000 (Verbal note Ogoni case).

censure, the corporations at the centre, with their roots in the same countries that perpetuated colonial conquest of the same territories, evaded liability and 'business as usual' continues.

It is clear from this that the corporation has been instrumental in establishing the legal systems that circularly justify their own operations in the jurisdictions that they continue to cause systemic harm in—and thus there appears no break from the colonial interests and orientation that first propelled them. Given this far reaching and ongoing harm, both spectacular and systemic, the contemplation of accountability requires the identification of the actor/s to be held to account. This raises the question of who or what the corporation actually is.

2.2 *Who or What Is a Corporation?*

In the broad sense the pragmatic question of what the object of analysis is becomes immediately complicated in the case of the corporation as a juristic person. Is it in fact an object or a subject? Domestically the corporation as we know it today is a construct of the law granted as a concession of state power to enable a juristic person to come into being thereby limiting the liability of the natural persons that animate it to their financial investment and efforts.[44] This is not to suggest that corporations are homogenous, however does point out the ideological golden thread and fundamental characteristics that make a corporation.[45] Core to the corporation as we know it is this juristic personality that renders it a distinct person. Ultimately a '[p]erson' signifies what the law makes it signify'.[46] This grants the corporation characteristic perpetual/immortal ownership of property and attendant rights of personhood while shielding the actual human beings who animate and benefit from it through the device of 'limited liability'.[47] According to Boberg '[t]he importance of being a person in the eyes of the law, both public and private, lies in the

[44] O Gierke *Political Theories of the Middle Age* (1900) 68.

[45] Samaradiwakera-Wijesundara (note 4 above).

[46] J Dewey "The Historic Background of Corporate Legal Personality" *The Yale Law Journal* 35, no. 6 (1926) 655; for a critical history of the nature and purpose of the corporation see C Samaradiwakera-Wijesundara 'The Fiction of the Juristic Person: Reassessing Personhood in Relation to People' in Melissa Steyn & William Mpofu (note 4) 194–196.

[47] R Penington 'Origin of Corporations' *Corporate Practice Review* 3 (1931) 33–37.

fact that only a person can have rights and duties'.[48] As a juristic person it is technically a subject in domestic law being a rights bearer.

In Africa the colonially founded nation state and corporation have been conspicuously co-constitutive. The development of the nation state and corporation are parallel.[49] The argument for the need for human rights to protect against an excess of state power logically extends to the excess of corporate power as the juristic person serves in both cases to concentrate power and enable such excesses.[50] Notwithstanding this, corporations are not recognised as subjects in international law even though they, like states, are juristic persons. Pahuja and Saunders account for this as First World States having secured a discursive shift away from critical consideration of the role of corporations and the authority of Developing and Third World countries to exercise their sovereignty in determining their powers within their territory—to one that entrenched the idea that the corporation was necessarily beneficial for development and inherently a private entities which should be allowed to travel across domestic jurisdictions, but be outside the purview of international regulation but to ensure the fair treatment of these private entities.[51] The focus of international law has been justified as concerning public actors and thus states excluding private actors (which corporations are regarded to be). In this way the corporation mirrors the nation state yet avoids public-scrutiny through evoking the public–private binary.[52]

Pahuja situates this shift in the racialised global world order that reveals that newly independent states in the late 1970s unsuccessfully challenged on an international institutional level.[53] Third World states grappling to reimagine and reconstruct international law as a tool to

[48] PQR Boberg *Law of Persons and The Family* 2 ed (1999) 3.

[49] RC Slye 'Corporations, Veils, and International Criminal Liability.' *Brooklyn Journal of International Law* 33, no. 3 (2008) 956 and 961.

[50] As above 961.

[51] S Pahuja & A Saunders 'Rival Worlds and the Place of the Corporation in International Law' in Dann and Von Bernstorff (eds), *Decolonisation and the Battle for International Law* (2018) 172.

[52] Slye (n 49 above) 956.

[53] S Pahuja 'Corporations, Universalism and the Domestication of Race in International Law' (29 January 2018). Forthcoming in Duncan Bell (ed) *Empire, Race and Global Justice* (Cambridge University Press), Available at SSRN: https://ssrn.com/abstract=3324846.

secure control over property and conduct of actors in their jurisdictions was met with the perverse entrenchment of private property even illicitly gained through colonisation and protection of the continued activities of putatively private actors.[54] As such this juristic person is neither authentically a subject nor an object, and its continued recognition is not an inevitable fact but rather the product of political, economic and social power. Fundamentally it is persons acting through and benefitting from the instrument that need to be held accountable for the harm it causes.

3 Part II: Unpacking the Content of 'International Crimes' and 'Accountability'

3.1 Spectacular Aberrations or Systemic Harm? Understanding Poverty and Inequality as Crimes Against Humanity

3.1.1 Expanding Our Understanding of International Crimes Under the RS

I contend that we should favour a purposive approach that focuses on the substance of accountability being sought, over form, namely the technical aspects of how accountability is sought. As such when navigating structures for corporate accountability we should consider a lens that accurately captures the range of harm for which accountability is sought rather than one that obfuscates it. In this instance it would mean not only seeing how corporations can be held criminally liable for international crimes, but how our understanding of international crimes can and should be expanded to account for harm caused by corporations. In this way we transcend liability as simply attribution of blameworthiness for harm towards accountability as taking responsibility for that harm and its consequences.

According to the Rome Statute (RS), which sets up the International Criminal Court (ICC) as the flagship of international criminal law, international crimes are crimes against humanity, genocide war crimes and aggression (international crimes).[55] The ICC only has jurisdiction over natural persons for crimes committed after its enactment and provides liability for punishment on the basis of individual responsibility.[56] This

[54] As above.

[55] Article 5 RS.

[56] Article 25(2) RS.

definition focuses on the instant of spectacular aberrations that cause large-scale harm. This may be situated in the mainstream liberal conception of the individual as an abstract agent at the centre of affairs and thus, in terms of the critique of liberalism, does not account for the systemic operation of powers that co-constitute the individual and collectives as both actors and those acted upon.[57] As such, within this paradigm poverty is often reduced to material lack or scarcity of basic amenities needed for survival and is often presented as acontextual and inevitable.[58] Pogge, while operating within a liberal paradigm committed to universal morality and non-racial equality, recognises that colonialism, slavery and genocide have shaped global poverty and inequality, but prescribes to teleology that suggests this shaping ends at political liberation.[59] Blunt argues that Pogge's evocation of global poverty as a crime against humanity may expand our conception of international crimes.[60] This departs from the premise that global poverty is a human rights violation and that extreme and widespread poverty is a crime against humanity.[61] Blunt recognises that this assessment needn't be pegged against the RS's conception of crimes against humanity, but that this provides an entry point to evaluate the plausibility of this notion within the operational international criminal law framework.[62] While attempting to capture the institutional operation of poverty that expands the consideration beyond individual relations, this argument doesn't account for its relationship to continued global racialised and gendered inequality. Despite being accepted as a problem it is not generally situated within the dynamics of colonial and imperial power disparities.[63]

Still, Pogge's account of human rights as institutional goes some way in linking atomistic individual relations with institutional dynamics of

[57] R Abbey *The Return of Feminist Liberalism* (2011) 15.

[58] S Fredman "The Potential and Limits of an Equal Rights Paradigm in Addressing Poverty" *Stellenbosch Law Review* 22, no. 3 (2011) 566.

[59] T Pogge, 'Recognized and Violated by International Law: The Human Rights of the Global Poor' *Leiden Journal of International La* 18 (2005) 723.

[60] T Pogge *World Poverty and Human Rights* 2000 176 in GD Blunt 'Is Global Poverty a Crime Against Humanity?' *International Theory* 7, no. 3 (2015) 541.

[61] Blunt (n 60 above) 540.

[62] As above.

[63] As above.

power with colonial and imperial origins.[64] Especially to the extent that it presents how global poverty and inequality operates within a coercive international state-based system with asymmetries in power that grant poor states no alternative.[65] This coercive international system makes poverty 'foreseeable and avoidable'.[66] This is on the basis that privileges are granted to states (including control over territorial resources and borrowing powers to indebt the people of the state) regardless of how states came to power, and that powerful states disproportionately determine the rules of the global economy.[67] This provides no incentive for poorer states to secure human rights over the interests of corporations.[68] The poverty that results is not an accident, but the product of a refusal to change the system by those empowered to do so.[69] Human rights instruments such as the Universal Declaration of Human Rights (UNDHR) already recognise the right to a living standard sufficient for 'health and well-being' and the entitlement to a 'social order in which' these rights can be 'fully realised'.[70]

In terms of Article 7(1)(k) the RS allows for acts comparable to listed crimes against humanity which amount to 'causing great suffering, or serious injury to body or to mental or physical health' to be included among them.[71] This suggests that global poverty would be classifiable as a crime against humanity if it meets the definitional criteria or if it resembles acts specifically named as crimes against humanity. Blunt suggests that it does both.[72] According to article 7(1) of the RS a crime against humanity

[64] Pogge also suggests that individual human beings have a 'negative duty to not support coercively imposed social institutions that "foreseeably and avoidably" leave people without secure access to the content of their human rights; Pogge (n 60 above) 176 in Blunt (n 60 above) 542.

[65] Pogge (n 60 above) 41–42 in Blunt (n 60 above) 542–545.

[66] As above.

[67] As above.

[68] Pogge (n 60 above) 120 in Blunt (n 60 above) 545; B Meyersfeld 'Committing the Crime of Poverty: The Next Phase of the Business and Human Rights Debate' 160–172 in C Rodriguez-Garavito (n 3 above) 178.

[69] Pogge (n 60 above) 41–42 in Blunt (n 60 above) 542–545.

[70] The United Nations Declaration of Human Rights 1948 (UNDHR) Articles 25(1) and 28; Blunt (n 60 above) 542.

[71] Blunt (n 60 above) 540.

[72] As above.

is 'any of the [listed acts] when committed as part of a widespread or systematic attack directed against any civilian population, with knowledge of the attack'. Blunt draws out the acts of enslavement (Article 7(2)(c)) and the crime of apartheid (Article 7(2)(j)) as parallel to global poverty as they deprive human beings of the ability to live a life with agency and pursue their own definitions a meaningful life.[73] Slavery, apartheid and global poverty operate through dehumanisation and domination which grants absolute power over humans who are subsequently robbed of their agency to pursue their own conceptions of lives of meaning.[74] Extreme poverty is intertwined with slavery as the global system erodes states stability and abilities to protect their citizens/inhabitants rendering them vulnerable to exploitation in order to survive.[75] Blunt argues that there is an observable causal nexus between institutions that cause global poverty and contemporary forms of slavery.[76] Domination and exploitation persist under dangerous working conditions, indentured labour and wage-slavery.[77]

Furthermore an attack does not have to amount to physical/explicit violence according to the ICTR case of *Akayesu*.[78] Implicit violence or the threat of violence is inherent in slavery—yet it is not an explicit form of violence alone that makes slavery reprehensible—it is the deprivation of agency of another human being.[79] Article 7(2)(a) of the RS encompasses an attack 'pursuant to or in furtherance of a State or organizational policy to commit such attack'. This provision is meant to cover militias and actors that operate at a distance from the state.[80] Blunt argues if organisational capacity serves as ground for liability then it would logically follow that an organisation such as the WTO is capable of such organisational responsibility given how it sets economic policy that impacts the

[73] As above.

[74] As above.

[75] As above 561.

[76] As above.

[77] As above 561–562.

[78] Judgement, Akayesu (ICTR-96-4-T), Chamber I, 2 September 1998, par. 581 (*Akayesu*); Blunt (n 60 above) 552.

[79] Blunt (n 60 above) 552.

[80] As above 553.

lives of billions.[81] The requirement that the attack be widespread and systematic connects otherwise disparate acts.[82] In *Akayesu* 'attack' has been described as large-scale action carried out against multiple victims in an organised pattern reliant on common policy which draws on public or private resources.[83] The global aspect of poverty together with global economic policy and trade instruments that are the workings of certain actors suggests it is systemic and widespread.[84] Knowledge of the attack to establish *mens rea* may be argued on the basis of *dolus eventualis* in respect of reasonable awareness of the likely consequences of conduct.[85] This is consistent with the burden of proof in respect of 'command responsibility' and 'common purpose'.[86] Blunt argues that an international system that deliberately creates and perpetuates extreme poverty certainly suggests knowledge or at least reasonable foreseeability of the outcome of extreme poverty.[87] This results in large-scale preventable death.[88]

The 'churchillian' position that 'the poor will always be with us' and that the international economic system, albeit imperfect, is the best we have is exposed as a delusion comparable to others used to propagate crimes against humanity throughout history.[89] This understanding ought to alert us to the moral urgency of the problem and incite us to action.[90] The question persists: Why hasn't it? Before turning to the question of accountability it is useful to point out the conspicuous absence of consideration of the gendered and racialised nature of poverty and its relationship to inequality. This can be superficially attributed to the widely recognised situation of human rights, in its current lexicography, in liberal

[81] As above 554.

[82] As above.

[83] *Akayesu*; Blunt (n 60 above) 555.

[84] As above 554.

[85] As above 554–555.

[86] As above.

[87] As above 557–558.

[88] As above.

[89] As above.

[90] As above.

ideology.[91] Stahn reflects on Critical Race Theory Scholars and Third World Approaches to International Law's long-standing critiques on the framing of international crimes around atrocity violence and the tendency to obfuscate the underlying socio-economic (and political) causes of varying forms of violence.[92] This observation is astute, but must go further.

3.1.2 Racialised and Gendered Poverty and Inequality as Violence

When global poverty and inequality are considered two historical aspects are often either underplayed or omitted in favour of a liberal non-racial and apolitical narrative of incremental legal progressivism.[93] One the one hand, is how a hierarchical conception of race and gender was both crystallised by and circularly used to justify colonial and imperial domination in the interests of a co-constitutive capitalist, patriarchal white supremacist global world order.[94] On the other hand, is that political independence of the colonies did not automatically transform the colonial ideology and supporting infrastructure upon which they were established; nor provide liberation from subordination by settler-colonial, colonial and imperial power.[95] Therefore mainstream discourse tends to elide the systemic installation of poverty and inequality, and it's racialised and gendered operation.[96]

[91] MW Mutua 'Savages, Victims, and Saviors: The Metaphor of Human Rights' *Harvard International Law Journal* 42, no. 1 (2001) 221.

[92] C Stahn 'Liberals vs Romantics: Challenges of an Emerging Corporate International Criminal Law' *Case Western Reserve Journal of International Law* 50 (2018) 98.

[93] ER George 'The Enterprise of Empire: Evolving the Understandings of Corporate Identity and Responsibility' 19 50 in Martin & Bravo (eds) *The Business and Human Rights Landscape: Moving Forward, Looking Back* (2015) 50.

[94] JM Modiri 'Towards a "(Post-)apartheid" Critical Race Jurisprudence: "Divining Our Racial Themes"' *SAPL* 27 (2012) 265; A Quijano 'Coloniality of Power, Eurocentrism, and Latin *America*' *Nepantla: Views from South* 1, no. 3 (2000) 543.

[95] S Sibanda 'Not Purpose-Made! Transformative Constitutionalism, Post-Independence Constitutionalism and the Struggle to Eradicate Poverty' *Stellenbosch Law Review* 22, no. 3 (2011) 495–497; Madlingozi (n 28 above) 124.

[96] JM Modiri 'Law's Poverty' *Potchefstroom Electronic Law Journal* 18, no. 2 (2015) 228–231; C Albertyn 'Gendered Transformation in South African Jurisprudence: Poor Women and the Constitutional Court' *Stellenbosch Law Review* 3 (2011) 592.

It is not simply that global poverty is an accident, nor is a historical fact; it is an ongoing function of racialised and gendered oppression.[97] Modiri causes us to recognise that this oppression is not to be understood as resulting from a single force, but rather a vector of 'cultural, social, economic and political forces' that continue with the momentum of the global colonial-imperial system.[98] This poverty and inequality is, in this way systemic, not only in the material sense but in the psycho-social sense that implicates our being in the world.[99] Thus ending poverty is more than a distributive question, but one of ontology.[100] This sanitising tendency of liberalism elides the manner in which concepts such as the corporation operate charged with ideology instrumental to maintaining poverty and inequality.[101] For example the suggestion that the 'the business of business is business' justifies the prioritisation of profit as legitimate and inherently harmless[102]; as opposed to pathological and inherently dangerous.[103] Meyersfeld reflects on how international law was not 'designed' to achieve accountability for human rights violations of corporations that could travel across jurisdictions across inconsistently empowered regulatory systems.[104] It certainly wasn't, but it has been established that this was not an accident either—to the contrary Nigeria and South Africa provide evidence of how it was designed to facilitate impunity not accountability.[105] The liberal lens through which the

[97] Modiri (n 96) 225 and 246.

[98] As above 230.

[99] As above.

[100] As above.

[101] Samaradiwakera-Wijesundara Played by the Rules The Problem with Business—And Human Rights (forthcoming for Corporate Accountability, Business and Human Rights: an African Perspective project hosted by CALS in collaboration with the Open Society Initiative for Southern Africa and Southern African Research Watch).

[102] DG Baird & MT Henderson. 'Other People's Money' *Stanford Law Review* 60, no. 1 (2008) 1323–1324; M Friedman *Capitalism and Freedom* 1962 112; Hahlo *South African Company Law Through the Cases* 6 ed 1999 4.

[103] J Bakan *The Corporation: The Pathological Pursuit of Profit and Power* 2 and 158.

[104] B Meyersfeld 'The South African Constitution and the Human-Rights Obligations of Juristic Persons' *South African Law Journal* 137, no. 3 (2020) 456.

[105] Anghie (n 26 above) 38; Grovogui (n 24) 55; Ndlovu-Gatsheni & Makoni 'The Globaility of the Local? A Decolonial Perspective on Local Economic Development in South Africa' *Local Economy* 29 no. 4 (2014) 512.

world is viewed distorts the picture of a global system of power designed to flourish off poverty and inequality and the relative vulnerability and disempowerment of the Global South.[106]

In this way we may understand the instrumentality of the company in perpetuating racialised and gendered poverty and inequality amounts to systemic violence. In addition to this, Baron et al. provoke thinking about violence through phenomenological terms and suggest that outside direct violence (physical world), indirect violence (in the world of thoughts and ideas) there is the underexplored violence of pacification (in the ontological and existential world-making).[107] That violence is not only an object but a structure within which people operate that influences our intersubjective relations.[108] This allows recognition of the ways in which violence is normalised and made invisible through domination and how liberalism both elides and produces this violence.[109] Baron et al. reflect on how Romans understood *pax* not only as peace, but as submission to Rome (with parallels to *pax* Britannia and Americana).[110] 'Liberal imagination blinkers itself to the ways pacification functions as violence in our world order'.[111] This is reflected in the sentiment of the liberal philosopher Mill 'What [the natives] require is not a government of force, but one of guidance. Being, however, in too low a state to yield to the guidance of any but those to whom they look up as the possessors of force, the sort of government fittest for them is one [that] possesses force, but seldom uses it'.[112] This is a liberal endorsement of pacification as violence as the most effective instrument of domination (couched in terms of curatorship). It is not surprising then that under this paradigm slavery is growing in the

[106] This may warrant a healthy dose of circumspection when considering 'reforms' championed by those in power who not only benefit from poverty and inequality as status quo but have been instrumental in orchestrating it; see Madlingozi (n 28 above) 128–129.

[107] IZ Baron, J Havercroft, I Kamola, J Koomen, J Murphy, & A Prichard 'Liberal Pacification and the Phenomenology of Violence' *International Studies Quarterly* 63 (2019) 203.

[108] Baron et al. (n 107 above) 203–204.

[109] As above.

[110] As above 204.

[111] As above.

[112] JS Mill *Considerations on Representative Government* 1998 232–233 in Baron et al. (n 107 above) 206.

form of indentured labour, forced labour and contract slavery.[113] As such violent outbursts, in the context of colonialism and neoliberal capitalism, are simply breakdowns of pacification as opposed to breaks in peace.[114]

This accounts for the realm outside of humanity to which black peoples have been relegated in justification and production of global domination characterised by violence and marginality.[115] The deprivation of subjectivity normalised arbitrary death in its practices and social conventions.[116] Gordon contends that any attempt to change this state amounts to an act of violence since change requires visibility and visibility is violent when you are meant to be invisible through erasure.[117] This recalls the argument that eruptions amount to a breakdown of pacification which operates as a violence of subjugation.[118] Modiri references state sanctioned violence against through extra-judicial killings, torture and assault that is meted out to subdue service delivery protests, wage protests, evictions and demolitions.[119] Relating this back to the corporation we may,

> consider that personhood at the time that the legal personality of the company was first recognised had a particular profile. This is the profile of authority being the white man.[120] It is evident that the first companies were not owned or controlled by women or black people; did not carry on activities aimed at benefiting women or black people; were not sanctioned by the authority of women or black people; and status as a legal person at the time was not attributable to women or black people. The recognition of the legal personality of the company therefore, implies that the company could not be characterised as either a woman or black person.

[113] JA Gordon 'Theorizing Contemporary Practices of Slavery: A Portrait of the Old in the New' Paper presented at *American Political Science Association Annual Meeting* New Orleans 2012 in Baron et al. (n 107 above) 206.

[114] Baron et al. (n 107 above) 204.

[115] LR Gordon 'Through the Hellish Zone of Nonbeing: Thinking Through Fanon, Disaster, and the Damned of the Earth' *Human Architecture: Journal of the Sociology of Self-knowledge* 5, no. 12 (2007) 11.

[116] As above.

[117] As above.

[118] Baron et al. (n 107 above) 206.

[119] Modiri (n 96 above) 238.

[120] As above.

> Attribution of personhood meant attribution of the status of the white man. Therefore, within this colonial frame of reference the person that the legal person of the company is equated to is the white man. The company therefore entered the system of world power as a colonizer.[121]

Corporations have not only been complicit but have been directly instrumentalised to perpetrate racialised and gendered violence of varying forms. Even in the absence of visible armed warfare, poverty and inequality are violence and the perpetrators must be held accountable in order for justice to prevail. Therefore, when we conceptualise international crimes, we should account for the fact that the corporation does not operate in a vacuum. In the light of this conception of international crimes, I turn to considering what is contemplated by accountability.

3.2 How May We Understand Accountability Substantively? The Peace Versus Justice Debate as a Question of Immunity and Impunity

Having understood the corporation's instrumentality in perpetuating spectacular violence as well as the systemic violence of poverty and inequality as seen in the historicisation of the corporation in South Africa and Nigeria, we may turn to consider what accountability could entail in respect of corporate accountability for international crimes. In undertaking this exercise, we would benefit from a consciousness of what is framed as accountability but is substantively not. In other words, how can we understand accountability substantively?

In international criminal law the 'peace versus justice' debate has come to euphemise situations where realpolitik and pacification is favoured over justice for human beings. Bassiouni draws the parallel between 'peace' used in this context and realpolitik and parallels 'justice' to accountability.[122] Realpolitik can be described as the aim of political settlement without regard for moral and ethical outcomes.[123] Accountability on the other hand envisions conflict resolution through accounting for the

[121] Samaradiwakera-Wijesundara (note 4 above) 39–40.

[122] MC Bassiouni 'Justice and Peace: The Importance of Choosing Accountability Over Realpolitik' *Case Western Reserve Journal of International Law* 35, no. 2 (Spring 2003) 191.

[123] As above.

truth, imposing sanctions against perpetrators, and providing redress to victims in a manner that encompasses both redistributive and retributive justice.[124] 'The pursuit of realpolitik may settle more immediate problems of a conflict, but, as history reveals, its achievements are frequently at the expense of long-term peace, stability and reconciliation'.[125] Bassiouni reveals that the resolution to adopt realpolitik strategies tends to take place during clandestine discussions or through deliberately complicated formalities and processes that are designed to manipulate the narrative and public perceptions.[126] In this way formalities are deliberately deployed to elide the realpolitik in operation and render norms, principles and institutions unenforceable due to opacity; or through designing deliberate administrative, logistic or monetary barriers to accessing institutions mandated to provide justice to reduce or nullify their efficacy.[127] The human rights movement that followed World War II (WWII) has crystallised the opposition between realpolitik and justice.[128]

'The advocates of realpolitik demand justice... as, at worst, a nuisance and, at best, a tool to achieve their goals'.[129] For example, realpolitik was at play in the international community's treatment of the Armenian genocide.[130] The preamble to the Hague Statute was used to attempt to frame the systematic killing of a civilian population as a violation of 'the laws of humanity' orchestrated by Turkish officials.[131] However it was rejected by the United States of America (US) and Japan as a violation of legal positivism, which was also the reason for the rejection of 1910 Treaty of Sevres which would have provided for the prosecution of Turkish troops (several of whom were already in British custody at the time).[132] However, it was the Treaty of Lausanne that was ratified instead, which carried an unpublished protocol granting amnesty to those that

[124] As above.

[125] As above.

[126] As above 192.

[127] As above.

[128] As above.

[129] As above 194.

[130] As above.

[131] As above.

[132] As above 195.

would have been prosecuted had the Treaty of Sevres been ratified.[133] This amnesty can be traced to the desire to secure Turkey's cooperation as a strategic ally against the communist Soviet Union.[134] Political interests trumped justice for the Armenians and, as Bassiouni reminds us, Hitler posed the question, '[w]ho now remembers the Armenians?' in 1939 serves as a reminder of the chilling consequences of realpolitik.[135]

While Nuremberg and Tokyo broke new ground '...the guiding vision for these prosecutions was political strategy'.[136] The ICTY also saw the prioritisation of realpolitik which resulted in a truce more than peace and may account for the massacres that followed in later years.[137] In questioning whether it is naïve to argue for accountability rather than realpolitik, Bassiouni notes, '... the complex truth of political violence, its harsh reality, has a way of resurfacing long after half-truths and misrepresentations encouraged by realpolitik have been voiced and officially accepted'.[138] As such we may regard the ICTY as having only partially secured accountability; having reshaped psychological, political and legal frames of reference for international criminal justice.[139] The ICTR did not prosecute persons associated with the incumbent government party (RPF).[140] The reservations have been attributed to dependence on government cooperation for operations.[141] Bassiouni warns,

> [n]ow that the advocates of realpolitik have realized that they can no longer eliminate justice from the political settlement equation, as was the case after World War I and II and so many cases thereafter, the danger is that justice will be co-opted, subverted, and used as a fig leaf to achieve accommodation. Even so, the efforts of advocates of realpolitik to barter and compromise justice go on, and impunity is the carrot that they offer

[133] As above.

[134] As above.

[135] As above.

[136] As above 197.

[137] As above 198–199.

[138] As above 200.

[139] As above.

[140] M Sirleaf 'The African Justice Cascade and the Malabo Protocol' *International Journal of Transitional Justice* 11 (2017) 83.

[141] As above.

> to leaders of conflicts who have committed terrible crimes, as a way of securing a political settlement.[142]

As such he contends that we should see the ICC not as something that will prevent injustice but rather as one means of striving for accountability.[143]

It may be argued that liberalism has been deployed as this fig-leaf to co-opt the values underpinning human rights into an institutional system of realpolitik that would render any meaningful realisation or accountability defunct. This is exacerbated by perceptions that the ICC is excessively immersed in domestic politics in Africa, and the focus on individual as opposed to systemic interventions create the impression that violations occur in a vacuum and absolve other contributors, such as corporate actors, of liability.[144] As such the concern is that reliance on the ICC may compromise Africa's efforts to develop independent and sustainable solutions to its challenges.[145] Gathii has highlighted how the preoccupation with the human rights corpus had shifted the Global South agenda from more pertinent questions of self-determination.[146] Propelled by this argument I have argued that recent the framing of Business and Human Rights (BHR) interventions play into states being 'played by the rules' to the extent that 'Third World states must submit to the authority and rules of the game, with the West as a rule-maker and player, in the aspirations of replicating the West as the universal ideal - thereby legitimating its superiority and authority while simultaneously delegitimizing its own'.[147]

On this issue of the implications of realpolitik on sovereignty of African states, Dyani-Mhango provokes us to consider the nuances of (head of state personal) immunity by considering the rationale being the equality of states preventing one state from claiming judicial authority over another, and safeguarding the sovereignty of a state by preventing

[142] Bassiouni (note 122 above) 204.

[143] As above.

[144] Sirleaf (n 140 above) 84.

[145] WM Matasi & J Brohmer 'Proposed International Criminal Chamber Section of the African Court of Justice and Human Rights: A Legal Analysis.' *South African Yearbook of International Law* 37 (2012) 252.

[146] JT Gathii '*International Law and Eurocentricity*' *European Journal of International Law* 9 (1998) 191.

[147] Gathii (n 146 above) 187; Samaradiwakera-Wijesundara (note 101 above).

interference under the guise of personal indictments of heads of state.[148] This nuance is especially valuable in the context of the apparent disproportionate focus on African heads of states for ICC intervention, falling short of targeting on the basis of consensual jurisdiction, but being conspicuous enough to warrant notice.[149] This becomes even more of a contention, as Dyani-Mhango points out, in the context of ambiguity on the part of the United Nations Security Council (SC) on the obligations of a party-state of the RS to surrender a non-party state serving leader.[150] In the context of the dynamics of the Global North and South it may even be argued that there is a degree of overreach on the part of the ICC given that three of the permanent members of the SC (US, China and Russia), and their allies, are beyond the reach of the ICC due to veto powers and non-ratification of the RS.[151]

While the *Al Bashir* case[152] raised much consternation about the issue of immunity the lingering question is not about who is being indicted, but who is not.[153] The corporation can be conceived as granting the natural persons behind the juristic personality de facto immunity by rendering the pursuit of profit banal.[154] Furthermore, it facilitates smoke-and-mirror evasion of accountability through allowing risk to be legally hedged through insurance, shell/liability vehicles in corporate structures and exponential networks of ownership through the proliferation of company groups across jurisdictions with infinite and compounded numbers of shareholders. Limited liability can in fact be argued to be a synonym for

[148] N Dyani-Mhango 'South Africa's Dilemma: Immunity Laws, International Obligations, and the Visit by Sudan's President Omar Al Bashir' *Washington International Law Journal* 26, no. 3 (2017) 544–545.

[149] As above 542.

[150] As above 543.

[151] Sirleaf (n 140 above) 83.

[152] *Southern Africa Litigation Centre v. Minister of Justice and Constitutional Development* 2015 (5) SA 1 (GP) see Dyani-Mhango (n 148 above) 543.

[153] The targets of international law have been African Heads of State rather than the corporations that finance and enable them for example in the case of Charles Taylor's diamond and timber corporate relations in Liberia; see B Meyersfeld 'Committing the Crime of Poverty: The Next Phase of the Business and Human Rights Debate' 160–172 in C Rodriguez-Garavito (n 3 above) 178.

[154] B Stephens 'The Amorality of Profit: Transnational Corporations and Human Rights' *Berkeley Journal of International Law* 20, no. 3 (2002) 46.

impunity especially in the context of realpolitik operating to bar meaningful piercing of the veil to systemically intervene in the harm that corporations cause, as well as serving to obfuscate lines of authority and accountability. On what basis is this immunity that grants impunity justified? Not only is this immunity provided but it is sanitised of immorality through the instrument of the corporation as activities done in the putatively legitimate endeavour to maximise profits.[155] This operates in the context of colonial conquest having been exacted through the corporation as seen in the cases of South Africa and Nigeria.

Bassiouni reflects on the three interlocking dimensions of meaningful international justice being ideas (norms and morality), instruments (legal and institutional) and enforcement.[156] This is useful as it not only emphasises that justice is not possible without enforcement, but reminds us that ideas influence both instruments and their use. It appears that the discussions around corporate accountability all too often focus on the instrumentalisation of law without really confronting the norms and political will that supports the conception of the corporation as we know it now. These guidelines may assist in navigating the relationship between international criminal justice and self-determination.[157] Furthermore it provides a framework for what accountability that is meaningful and sustainable must entail.

4 Part III Considering the Available Mechanisms for Accountability for International Crimes

4.1 *International Context: Corporate Accountability in the ICC*

4.1.1 *The Current Position*

International precedent for corporate criminal liability is putatively attributed to the Military Tribunals at Nuremberg post World War II.[158]

[155] Samaradiwakera-Wijesundara (n 101 above).

[156] Bassiouni (note 122 above) 202.

[157] Bassiouni (note 122 above) 202; Gathii (note 146 above) 191.

[158] TJ Fokwa Jean 'In Search of or Direct Corporate Responsibility for Human Rights Violations in Africa: Which Way Forward?' unpublished PhD Thesis, University of Pretoria 2004 37; T van Deventer 'Criminal Prosecution of Corporates for Human Rights Violations.' *Without Prejudice* (December 2012) 9; German conglomerate and chemical firm IG Farben, as a producer of poisonous gas and facilitator of Germany's ability to wage

This has been criticised as no corporation was declared criminally liable during the trials and the RS does not extend jurisdiction directly over juristic persons.[159] The RS decision to exclude direct corporate criminal liability can be attributed to corporate conduct being reducible to individual human conduct.[160] It is argued that the aim of international criminal law is to hold individuals accountable for injustice and remove the devices, such as rank and office, which facilitate impunity and realpolitik.[161] In this sense Nuremberg is precedent for piercing the veil of sovereignty of the state too.[162] The choice to apportion liability individually was therefore deliberate and has the de facto effect of precluding business people from escaping criminal liability behind the veil of juristic personality.[163]

In addition to this barrier to direct liability is the traditional understanding of criminal law that provides that only human beings capable of criminal wrongdoing on the basis of capacity for *mens rea* (criminal state of mind).[164] The argument is that an abstract entity is incapable of *mens rea*. This also speaks to the Germanic origins of guilt derived from

war despite resource sanctions, appeared as a corporate defendant through its directors. Of twenty three defendants fourteen were found guilty and sentenced to imprisonment. They, unlike the others, were unable to raise the defence of necessity on the basis of having acted on their own volition in constructing an operation adjacent to a concentration camp for the purposes of drawing slave labour from it.

[159] MSA Wattad 'Natural Persons, Legal Entities, and Corporate Criminal Liability Under the Rome Statute.' *UCLA Journal of International Law and Foreign Affairs* 20, no. 2 (Fall 2016) 394 and 413.

[160] Since the aim of the RS was to secure human culpability, at the time many state parties did not recognise corporate criminal liability domestically, and buy-in to the RS may also have been jeopardised by insisting on a novel and underdeveloped extension of liability see Wattad (n 159 above) 415.

[161] Wattad (n 159 above) 394.

[162] Slye (n 49 above) 957.

[163] van Deventer (n 158 above) See Justice Robert H. Jackson, Chief U.S. prosecutor at the Nuremberg Trials, Opening Statement before the International Military Tribunal (21 November 1945), https://www.roberthjackson.org/collection/speeches/ (last visited: 21 November 2015) [https://perma.cc/LDZ2-B5MB] in Wattad (n 159 above) 392.

[164] Wattad (n 159 above) 393.

the condemnation of severely antisocial behaviour that warrants punishment in the interests of justice.[165] The logic of holding the individual behind the action liable rather than let a fiction/construct absorb the liability thereby shielding wrongdoers from the consequences of their conduct is sound. The limitation of this logic is the systemic operation of corporations that are not heterogeneous and often employ deliberately nebulous control and liability structures. That behaviour and mental state are co-constituted by and towards what Bakan describes at the pathological pursuit of profit.[166] To this end individual wrongdoers in a corporation could be identified and removed despite gains made by the corporation and this could have no impact on the operations of the corporation—because that's just what corporations do.[167]

A further limitation to consider is that individuals could be deliberately scapegoated, and expendable, attracted to the position by compensation designed to offset the risk attached. That said—it is true that direct (corporation as a person) and indirect (individuals in the corporation) liability is not mutually exclusive. The complexities of the nature of the corporation warrant careful consideration of what conduct and interests of the shareholders are sanitised by the very existence of the juristic person despite the consequences contributing to international crimes.[168] The corporation presents as a person that '... has neither a body to be kicked nor [a] soul to be damned'.[169] This supports the observation that the corporation is by design permitted to be pathologically

[165] M Kremnitzer 'A Possible Case for Imposing Criminal Liability on Corporations in International Criminal Law.' *Journal of International Criminal Justice* 8 (2010) 910; Wattad (n 159 above) 398.

[166] Bakan (n 103 above) 158.

[167] As above.

[168] Consider the absence of liability of all the other stakeholders in the corporations present at Nuremberg and those that facilitated heinous activities.

[169] According to Cassim this expression often cited to demonstrate the fictive nature of the corporate person cannot be traced to a primary source but has been widely quoted and credited to Lord Chancellor Baron Thurlow in the late 18th see Farouk HI Cassim 'Introduction to the New Companies Act: General overview of the Act' in Farouk HI Cassim (ed) *Contemporary Company Law* 2nd ed. (2012) 31; *Century in Commissioner Inland Revenue v Richmond Estates (Pty) Ltd* 1956 (1) SA 602 (A) 606; *Manong and Associates (Pty) Ltd v Minister of Public Works* 2010 (2) SA 167 (SCA) para. 4; see also Wattad (n 159 above) 400.

antisocial.[170] Nonetheless, the absence of direct liability does not necessarily translate to corporate impunity. The indirect liability may extend to shareholders who either personally commit the crime,[171] or facilitate its commission through aiding and abetting or providing resources such as fuel, weapons, finance, private security, and intelligence towards criminal activity.[172] Stahn describes aiding and abetting as controversial on account of the difficulties of separating regular corporate activities from criminal activities.[173] This further supports circumspection in the very design of the corporation. Nonetheless, the RS contemplates contribution or attempted contribution in any other way by a group of persons acting for a common purpose.[174] As such indirect corporate criminal liability is possible in respect of international crimes.

A practical challenge to this route, however, is that a corporation is not simply a group of people and that the central common profit making purpose is presented as innocuous. The requirement of 'intent and knowledge' needed to be proven in respect of international crimes may be difficult to establish in respect of individuals operating within a broader collective.[175] It is argued that 'organ liability' (directors, shareholders, etc.) or vicarious liability may be used to establish the state of mind of the corporation—but this becomes circular logic since individual liability would already have to have been established.[176]

4.1.2 Arguments for Reform

There are circumstances where the corporate veil is pierced in order to expose individuals to personal liability.[177] While these circumstances vary across jurisdictions this remedy tends to be regarded as exceptional which is not surprising since it undermines the fundamental premise of the corporation which is its distinct legal personality. The insistence of holding individuals rather than the corporation criminally liable appears

[170] Bakan (n 103 above) 158.

[171] Slye (n 49 above) 961.

[172] Art 25(3)(c) of RS; van Deventer (n 158 above); Wattad (n 159 above) 412.

[173] Stahn (n 92 above) 112–113.

[174] Art 25(3)(d) of RS; van Deventer (n 158 above).

[175] Wattad (n 159 above) 420.

[176] As above.

[177] Wattad (n 159 above) 398.

to be dissipating and several jurisdictions recognise corporate criminal liability in the twentieth century.[178] The drive towards recognition of direct criminal liability for corporations has been attributed towards anti-impunity human-rights movements and development of international criminal law.[179]

There are several arguments presented for direct corporate criminal liability. These include that corporations have financial resources that could provide for more meaningful reparations[180]; criminal liability enables greater moral and legal injunctions[181]; since corporations enjoy privileges on account of juristic personality, such as capacity to contract, they should enjoy corollary burdens such as capacity for *mens rea*[182]; corporate action has a greater potential harm[183]; systemic punishment is more effective for systemic conduct that results in harm[184]; the absence of recognition of direct corporate criminal liability allows corporations to contract with states for services that facilitate to perform criminal activity while simultaneously securing immunity from prosecution[185]; corporations' criminal conduct occurs across jurisdictions and thus requires coordinated state intervention in order to achieve enforceable redress, punishment and prevention[186]; corporations are easier to identify for criminal prosecution than individuals within a corporate structure[187] since individuals may die or be difficult to locate,[188] the accumulation of conduct of natural people may result in criminal conduct in a way that individual conduct does not,[189] and this kind of liability incentivises

[178] Stahn (n 92 above) 97.

[179] As above.

[180] Wattad (n 159 above) 398; Stahn (n 92 above) 120.

[181] RS Article 6; Wattad (n 159 above) 417.

[182] Wattad (n 159 above) 398.

[183] Slye (n 49 above) 960.

[184] As above.

[185] Wattad (n 159 above) 412.

[186] As above 416; Stahn (n 92 above) 120.

[187] Wattad (n 159 above) 398.

[188] As above.

[189] Slye (n 49 above) 960.

shareholders to exercise greater discernment when appointing directors (and determining corporate culture).[190]

Wattad suggests equivalent criminal sanctions for corporations who commit international crimes can be deployed in order to reach corporate property.[191] The equivalent of the death penalty or life imprisonment could be liquidation or asset forfeiture; social isolation could be reflected in prohibition of participation in public tenders/procurement.[192] The argument extends, since the right to human dignity is not directly implicated, that the onus for criminal liability may be lower than with natural persons.[193] Furthermore since the RS provides for forfeiture of assets derived directly or indirectly from a crime the existing infrastructure for this liability exists already.[194]

The idea of equivalent penalties on corporate assets, parallel to individual liability, is compelling however is not as straightforward as it may seem. There is often a complex nexus of legal and natural persons holding assets in a corporate structure—again often deliberately designed to funnel resources out of liability's way and concentrate risk in avoidance of liability. Consideration of how to disentangle these structures, potentially across continents, needs to be given. Furthermore competing claims on assets and unintended consequences of actions like liquidation are relevant. The most vulnerable in the corporate food chain are most likely to suffer in the case of liquidation—while fines may be passed down to consumers through price increases and employees through retrenchment. Those who actually benefited from the criminal corporate conduct may go entirely unscathed.

Stahn regards it a weakness in international criminal justice that corporate malfeasance has not been investigated and prosecuted on a wide scale given the profiteering from and financing of atrocities.[195] Modern corporate criminal liability remains focused on individuals and how systemic

[190] Wattad (n 159 above) 398.

[191] Wattad (n 159 above) 395. Part VII of the RS provides for forfeiture of assets derived directly or indirectly from a crime.

[192] Wattad (n 159 above) 400.

[193] Kremnitzer (n 165 above) 915; Wattad (n 159 above).

[194] Part VII of the RS; Wattad (n 159 above) 395.

[195] Stahn (n 92 above) 123.

injustice can be addressed is still unresolved.[196] The role of the ICC is likely to remain minimal in this pursuit.[197] To this end direct corporate accountability may have the effect of increasing impunity rather than accountability, especially to the extent that liability (as in a finding of responsibility or guilt) does not necessarily translate to accountability (as elaborated upon in Part II). This presents a tension between atomised responsibility that vests in individuals and systemic accountability. What is important to note is that direct corporate liability does not translate into a systemic intervention. Thus amending the RS to extend to corporate criminal liability is not a solution to the problem of corporate impunity.[198] There is arguably no need to do so as corporations may be held liable through individuals and through domestic legislation. Wattad asserts that there is no fundamental difference between holding a corporation criminally liable at international and domestic levels.[199] I agree with this for reasons detailed below. There are also good reasons to exclude direct corporate liability, while direct and indirect liability is not mutually exclusive, the convenience of the former may give way to further realpolitik rather than accountability.

4.2 *Corporate Accountability in the Domestic Context*

4.2.1 *The Current Position in Foreign Domestic Courts (National Courts Outside of Africa)*

In understanding the available remedies for corporate accountability in domestic courts we may again depart from the pivot of South Africa and be informed by similar experiences in Nigeria. Jain and Meyersfeld make the point that there is something to be learnt from failed attempts at corporate accountability.[200] *Kiobel v Royal Dutch Petroleum Company* (*Kiobel*) concerns liability of the SPDC for aiding and abetting the Nigerian government in committing crimes against the Ogoni Peoples of the Niger Delta by providing resources including vehicles and finance.[201] It

[196] As above.

[197] As above.

[198] Wattad (n 159 above) 416.

[199] As above 417.

[200] Jain & Meyersfeld (n 35 above) 430 and 433.

[201] As above 430.

was brought in terms of the Alien Tort Claims Statute (ATCS) by Nigerian Nationals with political asylum in the US precluded from a fair trial in Nigeria due to the incumbent government's implication.[202] While not speaking to criminal liability the case provides important context on the operation of realpolitik in international justice manifesting in domestic courts. The claim was brought on the grounds of aiding and abetting the violation of the law of the nations by inter alia committing crimes against humanity. The ATCS carves out jurisdiction for delict/tort claims to be brought by non-US citizens for violations by the US of its obligations in terms of the law of the nations or agreements.[203] Despite the range of issues before the court being concerned with the law of the nations it elected to 'avoid making decisions which would offend the sovereignty of a nation or be inconsistent with US foreign policy relations'.[204] This is reminiscent of what the South African government submitted in respect of the *Khulumani* ATCS litigation, which I return to below, and begs the question of what that foreign policy is if it is admittedly potentially consistent with atrocities.[205] The court essentially took a formalistic and antiquated approach in the interpretation of the ATCS, even ignoring some of its own precedent in the process, to hold that it doesn't have jurisdiction over conduct in another territory in these circumstances.[206]

While judgement does not preclude corporate accountability in future, Jain and Meyersfeld ask the question of whether it is logical to seek 'economic justice' from those who regard the conduct of corporations as 'business as usual' (where the corporations activities are viewed as legitimate if not valued), have incentive not to hold corporations to account (and rather benefit from exploitation and weak regulation) and actively participate in concentrating power and resources in the Global North?[207] *Kiobel* is not exceptional. US courts dismissed ATS claims against Rio-Tinto, an Anglo-Australian mining corporation, for human rights abuses in the South Pacific and Khulumani's claims against corporations that aided and abetted apartheid atrocities; while United Kingdom (UK)

[202] As above.

[203] As above.

[204] As above 434.

[205] *Khulumani v Barclays National Bank Ltd* 2007 504 F 3d 254 (2d Cir 2007).

[206] Jain & Meyersfeld (n 35 above) 438.

[207] As above 443.

courts dismissed claims by South African mineworkers against UK-based mining companies for human rights violation is South Africa.[208] Despite the absence of accountability for historical (let alone ongoing) atrocities, countries like South Africa continue to look to these same jurisdictions for direction on how to frame its corporate law and even interventions designed at achieving corporate accountability.[209] This does not make it unsurprising given the colonial and imperial reach of Western hegemony and the infrastructure it entrenches.[210]

Mutua's 'savages-victims-saviours' metaphor to represent the international narrative about African states, their citizens as victims (of the state, tradition and culture) and saviours as the human rights corpus itself (represented by NGOs and the enlightened West) is used to expose the fronting as saviours for the propagation of liberal thought and philosophy towards normalising and institutionalising subordination.[211] In this way they serve as instruments of violence.[212] As such the '[ATCS] claims…reinforce the image of the US courts as a beacon of global human rights'.[213] This beacon may share more in common with a jailhouse floodlight.

While *Khulumani* can be reflexive of the limitations of seeking justice outside of South Africa, it also evidences that the interests of the state are not always aligned with those of its peoples. At the time of the *Khulumani* litigation in the US the then Minister of Constitutional Development and Justice, Penuell Maduna, lodged an ex parte application as an amicus curiae advocating for the dismissal of the case on the basis that the TRC had already addressed this political issue; and that failure to dismiss the case would have adverse consequences for foreign direct investment into South Africa.[214] Prior to this, the then President of South Africa Thabo

[208] As above 449.

[209] T Mongalo 'South Africanizing Company Law for a Modern Competitive Economy' *South African Law Journal* 121, no. 1 (2004) 115–116; JP Ongeso 'Corporate Accountability in South Africa: Sharpening the Role of Criminal Law' *South African Journal of Criminal Justice* 29, no. 3 (2016) 243.

[210] Sibanda (n 95 above) 495–497.

[211] Mutua (n 11 above) 204; Jain & Meyersfeld (note 35 above) 445.

[212] Baron (n 107 above) 206.

[213] Jain & Meyersfeld (n 35 above) 446.

[214] N Bohler-Muller 'Against Forgetting: Reconciliation and Reparation After the Truth and Reconciliation Commission' *STELL LR* 3 (2008) 466 474–475; *In re*

Mbeki is reported to have opposed the litigation on the basis that it interferes with South Africa's sovereign entitlement to deal with the legacy of apartheid in accordance with internal politics and constitutional arrangements.[215] Davis notes how the South African government's insistence that the case be dismissed lest economic relations with the US be jeopardised gives the impression of neo-imperialism.[216] This would explain why, rather than simply supporting the litigation in favour a possible compensatory award to South Africans who have suffered under apartheid, the government could allow itself to be positioned in opposition to those interests in the interests of maintaining good favour with the economic powers that prevail.[217]

4.2.2 *The Current Position in Domestic Courts (Courts Within South Africa)*

The RS has been domesticated into South African Law.[218] This means the South African government has an obligation to investigate and prosecute international crimes.[219] In addition to this South Africa recognises international law, both agreements and customary international law, as the law of the land.[220] There is also a peremptory obligation to consider international law when interpreting the Constitution of the Republic of South Africa, 1996 (Constitution) and to favour interpretations that are consistent with international law.[221] Precedent suggests that this may extend to private actors as well.[222]

South African Apartheid Litigation, 346 F Supp 2 d 538, 542 (SDNY, 2004); Samaradiwakera-Wijesundara (note 4 above).

[215] R Davis 'General Motors concedes to Khulumani in apartheid reparations case' https://www.dailymaverick.co.za/article/2012-03-01-general-motors-concedes-to-khulumani-in-apartheid-reparations-case/#.WoVii4Nua01.

[216] As above.

[217] Samaradiwakera-Wijesundara (note 4 above).

[218] The Implementation of the Rome Statute of the International Criminal Court Act 27 of 2002 (ICC Act).

[219] Dyani-Mhango (n 148 above) 561.

[220] Sections 231 and 232 of the Constitution.

[221] Section 39 of the Constitution.

[222] *National Commissioner of the South African Police Service v Southern African Human Rights Litigation Centre and Another* (CCT 02/14) [2014] ZACC 30; 2015 (1) SA 315 (CC); 2015 (1) SACR 255 (CC); 2014 (12) BCLR 1428 (CC) (30 October

How far the domestic accountability can go depends on political will, which becomes murky ground given the economic, political and social power corporations wield.[223] As we have seen, states, including South Africa, generally have been reluctant to extend criminal liability over corporations even when domestic law enables this in order to protect economic and political interests.[224] On that basis states have more incentive to protect or even collaborate with corporations over protecting the human rights interests of affected people even as citizens.[225] Policy plans in the Global South are not always aligned with poverty eradication and that corporations are not in the habit of channelling profit into, rather than out of, impoverished countries.[226] This is part of the problem with the proposed Business and Human Rights (BHR) model that places the obligation on states to protect human rights while corporations only have voluntary obligations.[227] Even on paper this appears to be a contradiction in terms given that an obligation traditionally denotes mandatory rather than voluntary conduct.

George recognises that international and foreign law would reasonably be apprehended with circumspection if not disavowed as a product of colonialism by African states but reflects on how South Africa has both embraced it and innovated '...international law through reconciling indigenous and international normative concepts in revolutionary ways that advance human dignity'.[228] This is an approving reference to the Constitutional Court's Ubuntu jurisprudence. The question of why reconciliation is desirable or necessary is not often interrogated. While seemingly innocuous it may carry within it, if uncritically resorted to,

2014); Jain & Meyersfeld (n 35 above) 453 concerning allegations of torture having taken place in Zimbabwe, with no indication of action by the Zimbabwe authorities, resulting in an obligation on the South African Police Service to investigate and prosecute on the basis of the ICC Act and Constitutional obligations.

[223] Wattad (n 159 above) 413. Stahn (n 92 above) 107.

[224] Wattad (n 159 above) 413.

[225] As above.

[226] B Meyersfeld 'Committing the Crime of Poverty: The Next Phase of the Business and Human Rights Debate' 160–172 in C Rodriguez-Garavito (n 3 above) 178.

[227] As above.

[228] ER George 'International Law and African Judiciaries: The Example of South Africa.' *American Society of International Law Proceedings* 104 (2010) 329.

dilution, assimilation and pacification—a kind of realpolitik.[229] It's this impulse to reconcile rather than evaluate against. That is to say to centre indigenous knowledge systems and filter out that which is incompatible. I will return to how regional mechanisms may have been more successful at achieving this than South Africa's domestic courts. For now, I will proceed to consider the technical framework for corporate accountability.

Juristic persons including the state and corporations are bound by the Bill of Rights.[230] The Criminal Procedure Act (CPA) provides that liability can follow a director or servant of a company in terms of law or at common law, for an act, with or without intent instructions or permission, express or implied, given by a director or servant of that corporate body, or any omission with or without particular intent in respect of an act that ought to have been performed by or on his instructions given by a director or servant of that corporate body in exercise of his powers or performance of his duties or in furthering the interests of the corporation.[231] Knowledge is not a requirement on the part of the corporation.[232] Farisani points out that this creates a reverse onus to the extent that the director or servant involved is deemed to have committed a crime which potentially violates the presumption of innocence.[233] While this is perfectly sound logic in the abstract, placed in context, this would entail protecting the accused and generating an easy avenue for reasonable doubt in the nebulous nexus of organisational and group conduct. If it were true that this reverse onus provision were also inconsistent with the Constitution and invalid it would essentially render defunct statutory vicarious criminal liability for corporations. Unless followed by a move to lower the standard of proof in respect of corporate misconduct. Farisani does not address the implications of the corporation in this assessment.

[229] Madlingozi (n 28 above) 124; Baron (n 107 above) 206.

[230] Section 8(2) of the Constitution of the Republic of South Africa, 1996 (Constitution).

[231] Section 332(1) of the Criminal Procedure Act 51 of 1977 (CPA).

[232] Ongeso (n 209 above) 234.

[233] Section 332(7) CPA; DM Farisani 'Corporate Criminal Liability in South Africa: What Does History Tell Us About the Reverse Onus Provision?' *Fundamina* 23, no. 1 (2017) 17; *S v Coetzee* 1997 SACR 379 CC where the court held that s 332(5) of the CPA was unconstitutional and invalid to the extent that the reverse onus violated the presumption of innocence in terms of Section 35(3)(h) of the Constitution.

This begs the question of whether this is a move towards greater corporate impunity—what about the victims of corporate crime?[234]

4.2.3 Arguments for Reform in Domestic Courts (Within South Africa)

The fact that the RS does not extend jurisdiction over direct corporate criminal liability does not mean that domestic courts cannot.[235] Ongeso advocates for direct liability as it accounts for the complexity of the corporate structure translating to actions being the compounded efforts of groups of individuals.[236] He identifies a gap in the statutory regime in that holding and subsidiary corporations are not addressed.[237] Since these are each independent juristic persons the implications are that they are not liable for the actions or related corporations unless there are grounds for piercing the corporate veil in terms of the Companies Act, 2008 or Common Law.[238] A further gap that I must point out is that shareholders are not covered in terms of the CPA's statutory criminal liability. The implications of this are also far reaching since it is often the shareholders that appoint and influence if not control the board of directors, and whose interests form the bulk of what is regarded as the best interests of the company, which interests the directors have a fiduciary obligation to honour.[239] Ongeso suggests that a direct model of corporate criminal liability for South Africa would harness the state's duty to protect people against human rights violations and that criminal law would be an effective instrument for enforcement.[240] He further suggests

[234] The fact a parallel is drawn between the callous apartheid reverse onus provision without consideration of the historical power position of the corporation and the need for accountability, as well as the benefits that directors and shareholders draw from corporate actions including maleficence, again runs the risk of missing the mark.

[235] Wattad (n 159 above) 412.

[236] Ongeso (n 209 above) 231.

[237] As above 234.

[238] Section 20(9) of the Companies Act allows for piercing the corporate veil where there has been 'gross abuse of the juristic person' and does not preclude common law piercing of the veil.

[239] FHI Cassim 'Introduction to the New Companies Act: General Overview of the Act' in FHI Cassim (ed) *Contemporary Company Law* 2nd ed. (2012) 31.

[240] Ongeso (n 209 above) 243.

taking guidance from jurisdictions that provide for direct corporate criminal liability including Australia's assessment of 'corporate culture' which includes policy, conduct and practice to deduce whether the corporate culture facilitates criminality,[241] and the UK's standard of the 'reasonable company' measured to include oversight by senior members over junior members.[242]

Other than the argument that criminal liability packs more of a punch and that direct liability allows for consideration of collated collective action there is no decisive case for direct criminal liability being a necessary tool for corporate accountability. More particularly the matter of evasion of liability by human actors is not addressed. While it may be appreciated that this is not mutually exclusive—attention to this detail is important to not trade one form of impunity for another—especially accounting for the convenience that only pursuing the corporation will provide legal practitioners. Furthermore, neither the existing nor proposed regime accounts for the systemic actors and their interests in maintaining poverty and inequality.[243] As far as the regulatory framework of South Africa goes despite mention of social responsibility and human rights vocabulary permeating the traditionally 'private law' space—without an intervention in business as usual—it remains short of a systemic intervention.

[241] As above.

[242] As above 244.

[243] Jain & Meyersfeld have given us the counter-argument to logic in the global context - why approach those who benefit from the status quo to change it? (Jain & Meyersfeld [n 35 above] 443) The same question may be asked in the domestic context. The Constitution as it stands represents a political commitment and is not divorced from political will but is co-constitutive of it (see Sibanda [n 95 above] 495–497 and S Sibianda 'When do you call time on a compromise? South Africa's discourse on transformation and the future of transformative constitutionalism' *Law, Democracy & Development* 24 [2020]); The question in this context is why Section 8(2) or any other domestic legal instrument would be used to dismantle the privileges of corporate extraction upon which South Africa was built? (see Terreblanche [N 31 above] 63–71) and MP More, More 'Fanon and the Land Question in (Post) Apartheid South Africa' in Nigel C Gibson (ed) Living Fanon: Global Perspectives [2011] 170).

4.3 Regional Context: The ACJHPR After the Malabo Protocol

4.3.1 The Current Regional Position

Any instrument is dependent on the will of the person with the power wielding it—this requires a paradigm shift that may begin with the question of whether a juristic person should be a person at all or whether the human beings that animate it should be held to account for their conduct. This would require a reconsideration and imagination of business relations, in a superficial sense that may recognise human beings' positive obligations towards each other individually and as collectives, and that harmony in society cannot be achieved till poverty and inequality is urgently addressed. This places the impetus on us as human beings to craft instruments that serve society and human welfare, not carve out of the blood, sweat and sorrow of fellow human beings towards the unsustainable and environmentally catastrophic putative prosperity of a few. The same ideological currents that prevent corporate accountability at an international level appear to persist at the domestic level; and this can be situated within the colonial paradigm of global power relations. Therefore, even for states to reimagine the parameters and content of juristic personality and accountability of persons—there appears to be a need for a value driven collective shift.

A starting point to this may be present at the regional level.[244] The infrastructure for regional cooperation already exists such as the African Court of Justice and Human and Peoples Rights (ACJHPR) in terms of the African Charter on Human and Peoples Rights (African Charter), and sub-regional bodies such as the Court for the Economic Community of West African States (ECOWAS) and South African Development Community (SADC).[245] Article 21 of the African Charter provides 'All **peoples shall freely dispose of their wealth and natural resources**. This right shall be exercised in the **exclusive interests of the people**. In no case shall people be deprived of it'. Regional coalitions and NGOs also have capacity to weigh on accountability such as the African Coalition for Corporate Accountability (my emphasis).[246] The Treaty of the SADC (SADC Treaty) explicitly includes objectives to, in terms of Article 5,

[244] Jain & Meyersfeld (n 35 above) 452.

[245] As above.

[246] As above.

> (a) promote sustainable and equitable economic growth and socio-economic development that will **ensure poverty alleviation with the ultimate objective of its eradication, enhance the standard and quality of life** of the people of Southern Africa and **support the socially disadvantaged through regional integration**; (b) **promote common** political values, systems and other shared **values which are transmitted through institutions which are democratic, legitimate and effective**;... (d) **promote self-sustaining development** on the basis of **collective self-reliance, and the interdependence** of Member States; (e) achieve complementarity between national and regional strategies and programmes; (f) promote and **maximise productive employment and utilisation of resources** of the Region; (g) achieve sustainable utilisation of natural resources and effective protection of the environment; (h) **strengthen and consolidate the long standing historical, social and cultural affinities** and links among the people of the Region. (my emphasis)

A commitment to accountability for corporate actions is evidenced in the AC's decision on the communication on the *Ogoni* case[247] alleging that the military government of Nigeria condoned and facilitated violation of human rights of the Ogoni peoples in its practices and policies in aid of the joint efforts of the NPC and SPDC.[248] Noteworthy in the case is the absence of hierarchy or categorical application of the various civil, political, economic, social and cultural as well as collective rights in the African Charter—where there is no provision for progressive realisation of rights.[249] Thus the African Charter advocates for an urgent rather than incremental approach to the realisation of rights that places a positive obligation on states to act. Conduct of private parties or parties that cannot be identified can be imputed to the state for failure to act with the requisite care to prevent or address a violation of rights.[250] The Commission also recognised a minimum core that can be described as an 'obligation...not to destroy or contaminate food sources; not to allow private parties to destroy or contaminate food sources; and not to prevent people's efforts

[247] Communication 155/96, The Social and Economic Rights Action Center and the Center Economic, and Social Rights/Nigeria; http://www.cesr.org/ESCR/africancommission.htm. It was communicated to the parties on 27 May 2002.

[248] Coomans (n 36 above) 749.

[249] As above 750–751.

[250] As above 755.

to feed themselves'.[251] Although there was decisive condemnation of the Nigerian government for its conduct, a lacuna on the accountability of the corporations involved since the African Commission's jurisdiction did not extend to them.[252] However, the Malabo Protocol, which provides *inter alia* for the ACJHPR to extend to corporate criminal liability, has far-reaching implications on the direction taken by the AC.[253]

4.3.2 Arguments for Reform/pending Reforms in the Region

Sirleaf suggests that the Malabo Protocol presents an important alternative regional vision of criminal justice that seeks to address the circumspection around biases in the prevailing international criminal justice system.[254] The prevailing credibility issues arise from the concerns that 'political considerations predominate over criminal ones..' and the ACJHPR is less likely to reproduce the geopolitical hierarchies that the ICC does and does not carry the taint of neo-colonial power dynamics.[255] The ACJHPR would also theoretically be in a position to navigate between the extremes of the removed and geopolitically influenced international courts and the overfamiliarity and susceptibility to elite influence of domestic courts.[256] This could avoid the custodial power relations of the international courts that replicate the colonial realpolitik and such transformations in the global order have amounted to reconfigurations rather than radical paradigm shifts[257]; as well as the concern that states themselves have not transcended colonial infrastructure and attendant dynamics of power.[258]

The Malabo Protocol envisages three sections of the ACJHPR that encompasses general affairs, human rights and international criminal

[251] As above 757.

[252] As above 759–760.

[253] Malabo Protocol African Court of Justice and Human Rights, *Protocol on Amendments to the Protocol on the Statute of the African Court of Justice and Human Rights* (11 June 2000)/Protocol on Amendments to the Protocol on the Statute of the African Court of Justice and Human Rights (Malabo Protocol).

[254] Sirleaf (note 140 above) 71.

[255] As above 74.

[256] As above.

[257] Madlingozi (n 28 above) 124.

[258] As above.

law.[259] It is innovative on many levels including the provision for forcible intervention in the case of serious human rights violations and the positive duty on states to respect and protect human rights.[260] The extension of jurisdiction of the crimes covered '...recognises that massive violations do not exist in a vacuum, but instead are embedded in systems of criminality...' and through regional integration provides a means to navigate colonial borders that have precipitated conflict and instability in the region.[261] The jurisdiction of the court would extend to the currently recognised international crimes as well as '...crimes of unconstitutional change of government, piracy, terrorism, mercenarism, corruption, money laundering, trafficking in people, trafficking in drugs, trafficking in hazardous waste and illicit exploitation of resources'.[262] Furthermore, forms of responsibility extend to '...initiating, instigating, organising, directing, facilitating, financing, counselling or participating as principal, co-principal, agent or accomplice'.[263] It challenges corporate immunity by providing for corporate liability while granting serving heads of state immunity.[264] The Malabo Protocol provides for complementary jurisdiction with national courts.[265] The provision for 'hybrid courts' that incorporate international and national judges and staff and synthesise national and international law may provide for more efficacious interventions that are received as more familiar and credible—and potentially pose less of a threat to sovereignty.[266] The Malabo Protocol is also able to leverage the mutually reinforcing potential of regional stability and compliance.[267] A further innovation is the obligation to act positively to prevent the commission of international crimes.[268] This has the potential to allow for both recognising the systemic nature of harm perpetrated

[259] Article 6A Malabo Protocol; Matasi & Brohmer (note 145 above) 254.

[260] Sirleaf (note 140 above) 73.

[261] As above 76.

[262] Article 28A; Matasi & Brohmer (note 145 above) 254.

[263] Sirleaf (note 140 above) 76.

[264] Article 46C and Article 46A of the Malabo Protocol; Matasi & Brohmer (note 145 above) 254.

[265] Matasi & Brohmer (note 145 above) 262.

[266] Sirleaf (note 140 above) 81; Matasi & Brohmer (note 145 above) 267.

[267] Sirleaf (note 140 above) 87.

[268] Article 4(h); Sirleaf (note 140 above) 76.

by corporations, in addition to the spectacular instances of harm, and allowing for corporate criminal accountability that emphasises redress.

The ACJHPR seems to be responsive to an international criminal system that, at best, has served Africa to a limited extent, and at worst has inhibited its independence. It is not clear how the ACJHPR would relate to the ICC, but it does seem that *pacta sunt servanda* would bind state parties to their obligations in terms of the RS yet withdrawal from the RS would only be a partial solution to concerns around infringement of sovereignty since non-party states would be able to be reached through the SC.[269] It is possible that Lorde's provocation that 'the masters' tools will never dismantle the masters' house' is being adopted on the one hand, with reduced reliance on the ICC,[270] and altered on the other hand to the extent that the tools attributed to the master may very well dismantle his house if they are not in his hands pursuing the works that he envisages. Nonetheless, the challenge of enforceability looms large as does the caution against allowing direct criminal liability of corporations to translate into greater impunity for individuals who operate behind the veil of the juristic person. The fundamental and significant difference between proposed direct liability at international and domestic levels considered thus far, and the Malabo protocol is the latter's contextualisation of criminal liability operating systemically as opposed to in isolation—while recognising that individuals have obligations to safeguard the well-being of others. Despite the potential that the ACJHPR has to be an accountability mechanism towards justice—it will at best be a curative treatment or balm to the broader problem of corporate harm.

4.4 Prevention Is Better Than Cure: African Philosophy on Personhood

Returning to our understanding of substantive accountability in Part II, requiring ideas (norms and morality), instruments (legal and institutional) and enforcement, as per Bassiouni,[271] we may observe that much focus has been placed on the instruments and enforcement, but not very much on the ideas that inform them—especially towards securing

[269] Matasi & Brohmer (note 145 above) 264.

[270] A Lorde *Sister Outsider:Essays and Speeches by Audrey Lorde* 1984 110–111.

[271] Bassiouni (note 122 above) 202.

systemic redress. This can be seen to be attributable from the tendency of liberal conceptions of the legal framework's individualistic ahistorical conception accountability that elides the norms and morality premised on colonial and imperial interests that make poverty and inequality not only a consequence of the world order, but a necessary condition for it.

The paradigm upon which the regional mechanisms cited above operate may provide a hint of the paradigmatic shift fermenting that may assist in achieving substantive accountability of corporations through the interrogation of the legitimacy of juristic personality and the re-imagination of the corporation in its entirety. This paradigm centres collective efforts and accountability to well-being over atomistic individualism and the pathological pursuit of profit. This may be attributed to the ethical influence of African philosophy. While being careful to avoid creating the impression that either 'African' or 'African philosophy' is homogenous or conflating the nuances, I draw here on what has been identified as a unifying thread within these bodies of knowledge.[272] That thread is the centrality of character. On the one hand, generally rejecting the idea that personhood is an essentialist, absolute and static category.[273] On the other hand, recognising that is attained in the process of living in community with other persons and determined through conduct (as obligations to other persons rather than absolute entitlements of oneself).[274]

I shall refer to *Ubuntu* to encapsulate the adage ***umuntu ngumuntu ngabantu*** that iterates across the continent conveying, non-exhaustively on account of limits of English to capture the bounds of its meaning, 'to be a human be-ing is to affirm one's humanity by recognising the humanity of others and, on that basis, establish humane relations with them'.[275] As such,

[272] C Ngwena *What Is Africaness?:Contesting Nativism in Race, Culture and Sexualities* (2018) 17.

[273] IA Menkiti. 'Person and Community in African Traditional Thought.' In *African Philosophy, an Introduction* 1984 176; K Gyeke 'African Ethics' https://plato.stanford.edu/entries/african-ethics/.

[274] As above.

[275] MB Ramose *African Philosophy Through Ubuntu* 1999 52; This has been paralleled to ***mutunchi***, ***iwa*** and ***agwa*** in the context of Nigeria see V Mabvurira 'Hunhu/ Ubuntu Philosophy as a Guide for Ethical Decision Making in Social Work.' *African Journal of Social Work* 10, no. 1 (2020) 73.

> Umuntu must be the embodiment of Ubuntu because the fundamental ethical, social and legal judgement of human dignity and conduct is based upon Ubuntu. Ubuntu is the principle that we act humanely and with respect towards others as a way of demanding the same from them. Similarly, law to be worth its name and to command respect must evince Ubuntu.[276]

This does not translate to a crude utilitarianism which dissolves the individual as, notwithstanding the concern with collective well-being, kindness and humanness features in the centrality of the maintenance of justice and harmony.[277] This does not advocate for superficial politeness and denial of conflict but rather, '[j]ustice as the restoration of equilibrium…'[278] Discharging our ethical behaviour as persons, in relation to ourselves and others, makes us a person in an ongoing process and journey through life. The corollary is that when a human being displays '…conduct very often appears cruel, wicked, selfish, ungenerous or unsympathetic…' they would be described as 'not a person' (e.g. in Akan '*onnye onipa*' or in Sotho 'gase motho').[279]

Even this admittedly over-simplified account of *Ubuntu* carries far-reaching implications for law and the societies that it constitutes.[280] For the purposes of this chapter we can draw the following. Regional instruments call on us to be attentive to our positive obligations to the welfare of fellow human beings as an urgent commitment, that we do not operate in silos but are interconnected and that justice has retributive, reparative and restorative dimensions that must be addressed in order to achieve equilibrium. Therefore, the harm perpetrated by corporations cannot be justified by the pursuit of profit or eventual hope of development—but immediate interventions are required to interrupt the harm that began through colonial enterprising and continues through the instrument of the corporation. Rather than justify the corporation based on perceived

[276] MB Ramose 'An African perspective on justice and race' 2001 https://them.polylog.org/3/frm-en.htm, para. 8.

[277] Molema *The Bantu: Past and Present* 1920 116 in Gyeke (n 273 above).

[278] Ramose (n 276 above) para. 4.

[279] Gyeke (n 273 above); Ramose (n 275 above) 53.

[280] Referring here to Sibanda's call to consider the Constitution as an act of constituting and think about the implications of what it means to constitute a society (see Sibanda [n above 243]).

good, overlooking the embedded harm, is the option to innovate ways beyond the corporation that do not derogate from personhood.

If we read this together with the adage '*Kgosi ke Kgosi Ka Batho*' that can be understood to mean that 'the source and justification of royal power is the people'.[281] We can extrapolate that sovereign power is derived from the people and that there is an obligation on states to ensure justice. This includes through the accountability of persons for the use of their power and, if needs be, curtailment of the parameters of that power. That is to say—these are grounds to interrogate whether the recognition of the personhood of the corporation is justified given how this has allowed ultimately people to conduct themselves in an inherently antisocial manner, and allowed past violations to go without redress. A detailed engagement with the implications of this is beyond the scope of this chapter, but what is important to illustrate is the possibility and importance of a paradigm shift that enables us to think beyond regulating the corporation within the existing paradigm to reimagining the corporation within a paradigm that centres human being-becoming that would not justify a pathological pursuit of profit at the expense of human well-being nor dare call such pursuit amoral given the injustices facilitated by this approach.

In summation the consequences of this shift, cursorily, under the current legal paradigm the juristic person cannot simply be a person by incorporation but must become one through its conduct. The implication is that it would lose this entitlement if it caused harm to other persons (especially if it were committed to its own profit over well-being). The furthermore fundamental implications are that juristic personhood of an abstract entity would not be permissible at all—since it removes from people that animate it the accountability for their conduct—and an entire restricting of economic relations would be in order.

5 Concluding Thoughts

The recurrent challenges around securing corporate accountability crystallises into the question: Why strive to hold corporations accountable for abusing their power when it is available, if not incumbent, on authorities to curtail the parameters of their power at the outset? Rather than

[281] Ramose (n 275 above) 52–53.

departing from the premise that corporations and juristic personality as we know it is legitimate and absolute/perennial/inevitable why not reverse the onus, given that corporate power is a concession and that concession has been used for nefarious purposes, to require that corporations must comply with obligations and provide details of the nexus of accountability? This may force corporations to keep their operations small enough to manage and thereby also allow for greater competition and distribution of work. If the rejoinder is that this is not pragmatic because corporations must be incentivised to operate in a jurisdiction (i.e. we need them more than they need us) then we must concede that we are trapped in a race to the bottom and accountability, inimical to distinct personality and its attendant limited liability, is a farce since people controlling corporations will continue to dictate the terms that are most conducive to their interests. All countries are susceptible to this—including economic giants in Africa as precedent has shown. A further possibility is revising limited liability all together and simply not granting distinct personality to the corporation.[282] This would avoid the displacement of liability onto vulnerable people and ensure accountability.

In this paper I have contended that the meaning of international crimes extends to global poverty and inequality and that substantive accountability must be sought over realpolitik when establishing corporate criminal liability. I have also made the observation that the trend towards direct corporate liability may increase rather than decrease impunity. This is especially so if it is applied in a manner that is uncritical of the instrumentalisation of corporate juristic personality for the precise purposes of sanitising the evasion liability by human actors and beneficiaries. In other words the systemic harm must be accounted for.

Regional mechanisms may prove more effective for these purposes than international or domestic platforms given the power of concerted and collective action, underpinned by shared values, to counter the operations of realpolitik and pervasive colonial and imperial dynamics of power. Furthermore, that these mechanisms gesture towards an entirely different ethical paradigm—that of African philosophy—provides the prerogative to rethink the parameters of juristic personality that enables the concentration of power in the corporation and ultimately immunises human beings from accountability.

[282] P Ireland 'Limited Liability, Shareholder Rights and the Problem of Corporate Irresponsibility' *Cambridge Journal of Economics* 34 (2010) 839.

Justice does not exist in a vacuum. Like eating and breathing to sustain the body of a person—justice sustains the being. As much as we cannot put off eating and breathing, we cannot put off justice. The notion that there should be 'African solutions to African problems' read in this context disavows accusations of parochialism in favour of revealing the emancipatory and harmonising potential of African knowledge systems and the values systems embedded therein. This is a challenge to liberate ourselves from taking for granted the neutrality of instruments, such as the corporation, in order to interrogate the underlying norms and ideology against the value systems we wish to inculcate and objectives of personhood and human well-being we wish to nurture.

References

Books

Abbey, R *The Return of Feminist Liberalism* (McGill-Queen's University Press: Montreal 2011).

Anghie, A *Imperialism, Sovereignty and the Making of International Law* (Cambridge University Press: Cambridge 2005).

Bakan, J *The Corporation: The Pathological Pursuit of Profit and Power* (Free Press New York: New York 2004).

Boberg, PQR *Law of Persons and The Family* 2 ed (Juta & Co: Kenwyn 1999).

Callinicos, A *Imperialism and Global Political Economy* (Polity Press: Cambridge 2009).

Geen, MS *The Making of the Union of South Africa* (Longmans, Green and Co. of Paternoster Row: London 1946).

Grovogui, S *Sovereigns, Quasi Sovereigns and Africans: Race and Self-Determination in International Law* (University of Minnesota Press: Minneapolis 1996).

Hahlo *South African Company Law Through the Cases* 6 ed (Juta & Co: Kenwyn 1999).

Lorde, A *Sister Outsider: Essays and Speeches by Audrey Lorde* (Crossing Press: Trumansburg 1984).

Lucas, G *An Archaeology of Colonial Identity: Power and Material Culture in the Dwars Valley, South Africa* (Kluwer Academic/Plenum Publishers: New York 2004).

Mill, JS 'Considerations on Representative Government' in John Gray (ed) *On Liberty and Other Essays* (Oxford University Press: Oxford 1998).

Friedman, M *Capitalism and Freedom* (The University of Chicago Press: London 1962).

Ngwena, C *What Is Africaness?: Contesting Nativism in Race, Culture and Sexualities* (Pretoria University Press: Pretoria 2018).

Pogge, T *World Poverty and Human Rights: Cosmopolitan Responsibilities and Reforms* 2nd ed. (Polity: Cambridge 2008).

Pogge, T *Politics as Usual: What Lies Behind the Pro-Poor Rhetoric* (Polity: Cambridge 2010).

Ramose, MB *African Philosophy Through Ubuntu* (Mond Books: Harare 1999).

Robinson, CJ *Black Marxism: The Making of the Black Radical Tradition* (Zed: London 1983).

Terreblanche, S *Lost in Transformation: South Africa's Search for a New Future Since* (KMM Review Publishing: Johannesburg 1986).

Book Chapters

Cassim, FHI 'Introduction to the New Companies Act: General Overview of the Act' in Cassim, FHI (ed) *Contemporary Company Law* 2nd ed. (Juta & Co: Kenwyn 2012).

George, ER 'The Enterprise of Empire: Evolving the Understandings of Corporate Identity and Responsibility' 19–50 in Martin & Bravo (eds) *The Business and Human Rights Landscape: Moving Forward, Looking Back* (New York: Cambridge University Press 2015).

Menkiti, IA 'Person and Community in African Traditional Thought.' in Wright, R (ed) *African Philosophy, an Introduction* (University Press of America: Lanham 1984).

Meyersfeld, B 'Committing the Crime of Poverty: The Next Phase of the Business and Human Rights Debate' in Rodriguez-Garavito, C (ed) *Business and Human Rights Beyond the End of the Beginning* (Cambridge University Press: Cambridge 2017).

More, MP 'Fanon and the Land Question in (Post) Apartheid South Africa' in Gibson, NC (ed) *Living Fanon: Global Perspectives* (Palgrave Macmillan: New York 2011).

Pahuja, S & Saunders, A 'Rival Worlds and the Place of the Corporation in International Law' in von Bernstorff, J & Dann, P (eds) *The Battle for International Law: South-North Perspectives on the Decolonization Era* (Published to Oxford Scholarship Online 2019).

Samaradiwakera-Wijesundara, C 'The Fiction of the Juristic Person: Reassessing Personhood in Relation to People' in Steyn, M & Mpofu, W (eds) *Decolonising the Human: Reflections from Africa on Difference and Oppression* (Wits University Press: Johannesburg 2021).

Wolpe, H 'Capitalism and Cheap Labour Power in South Africa: From Segregation to Apartheid' in Beinart, W & Dubow, S (eds) *Segregation and Apartheid in Twentieth-Century South Africa* (Routledge: London 1995).

Forthcoming

Samaradiwakera-Wijesundara, C 'Played by the Rules: The Coloniality of Business—And Human Rights' in Meyersfeld, B (ed) *Corporate Accountability, Business and Human Rights: An African Perspective* a CALS and OSISA initiative (forthcoming).

Articles

Albertyn, C 'Gendered Transformation in South African Jurisprudence: Poor Women and the Constitutional Court' (2011) 3 *Stellenbosch Law Review* 591.

Baird, DG & Henderson, MT 'Other People's Money' (2008) no. 1 *Stanford Law Review* 60, 1309.

Baron, IZ, Havercroft, J, Kamola, I, Koomen, J, Murphy, J & Prichard, A 'Liberal Pacification and the Phenomenology of Violence' (2019) 63 *International Studies Quarterly* 199.

Bassiouni, MC 'Justice and Peace: The Importance of Choosing Accountability Over Realpolitik' (2003) 35, no. 2 Spring *Case Western Reserve Journal of International Law* 191.

Blunt, GD 'Is Global Poverty a Crime Against Humanity?' (2015) 7, no. 3 *International Theory* 539.

Bohler-Muller, N 'Against Forgetting: Reconciliation and Reparation After the Truth and Reconciliation Commission' (2008) 3 *STELL LR* 466.

Coomans, F 'The Ogoni Case Before the African Commission on Human and Peoples' Rights' (2003) 52, no. 3 July *The International and Comparative Law Quarterly* 749.

Dewey, J 'The Historic Background of Corporate Legal Personality' (1926) 35, no. 6 *The Yale Law Journal* 655.

Dyani-Mhango, N 'South Africa's Dilemma: Immunity Laws, International Obligations, and the Visit by Sudan's President Omar Al Bashir' (2017) 26 no. 3 *Washington International Law Journal* 535.

Farisani, DM 'Corporate Criminal Liability in South Africa: What Does History Tell Us About the Reverse Onus Provision?' (2017) 23, no. 1 *Fundamina* 1.

Fredman, S 'The Potential and Limits of an Equal Rights Paradigm in Addressing Poverty' (2011) 22, no. 3 *Stellenbosch Law Review* 566.

Gathii, JT '*International Law and Eurocentricity*' (1998) 9 *European Journal of International law* 184.

George, ER 'International Law and African Judiciaries: The Example of South Africa' (2010) 104 *American Society of International Law Proceedings* 329.

Gordon, LR 'Through the Hellish Zone of Nonbeing: Thinking Through Fanon, Disaster, and the Damned of the Earth' (2007) 5, no. 12 *Human Architecture: Journal of the Sociology of Self-knowledge* 5.

Ireland, P 'Limited Liability, Shareholder Rights and the Problem of Corporate Irresponsibility' (2010) 34 *Cambridge Journal of Economics* 837.

Jain, M & Meyersfeld, B 'Royal Dutch Petroleum Company: Developing Home-grown Lawyering Strategies Around Corporate Accountability' (2014) 30, no. 3 *South African Journal on Human Rights* 430.

Kremnitzer, M 'A Possible Case for Imposing Criminal Liability on Corporations in International Criminal Law' (2010) 8 *Journal of International Criminal Justice* 909.

Mabvurira, V 'Hunhu/ Ubuntu Philosophy as a Guide for Ethical Decision Making in Social Work' (2020) 10, no. 1 *African Journal of Social Work* 73.

Madlingozi, T 'Social Justice in a Time of Neo-Apartheid Constitutionalism: Critiquing the Anti-Black Economy of Recognition, Incorporation and Distribution' (2016) 1 *Stellenbosch Law Review* 123.

Matasi, WM & Brohmer, J 'Proposed International Criminal Chamber Section of the African Court of Justice and Human Rights: A Legal Analysis' (2012) 37 *South African Yearbook of International Law* 248.

Meyersfeld, B 'Empty Promises and the Myth of Mining: Does Mining Lead to Pro-Poor Development?' (2017) 2, no. 1 January *Business and Human Rights Journal* 31.

Meyersfeld, B 'The South African Constitution and the Human-Rights Obligations of Juristic Persons' (2020) 137, no. 3 *South African Law Journal* 439.

Modiri, JM. 'Law's Poverty' (2015) 18, no. 2 *Potchefstroom Electronic Law Journal* 224.

Modiri, JM 'Towards a "(Post-)apartheid" Critical Race Jurisprudence: "Divining our Racial Themes"' (2012) 27 *South African Public Law* 231.

Mongalo, T 'South Africanizing Company Law for a Modern Competitive Economy' (2004) 121, no. 1 *South African Law Journal* 93.

Morgan N 'Living in the Marikana World: The State, Capital and Society' (2013) 8, no. 1 *International Journal of African Renaissance Studies* 46.

Mutua, MW 'Savages, Victims, and Saviors: The Metaphor of Human Right' (2001) 42, no. 1 *Harvard International Law Journal* 201.

Nattrass, N 'The Truth and Reconciliation Commission on Business and Apartheid: A Critical Evaluation' (1999) 98, no. 392 July *African Affairs* 373.

Ndlovu, M & Makoni, EN 'The Globaility of the Local? A Decolonial Perspective on Local Economic Development in South Africa' (2014) 29, no. 4 *Local Economy* 505.

Nunn, KB 'Law as a Eurocentric Enterprise' (1997) 15, no. 2 *Law and Inequality: A Journal of Theory and Practice* 323.

Ongeso, JP 'Corporate Accountability in South Africa: Sharpening the Role of Criminal Law' (2016) 29, no. 3 *South African Journal of Criminal Justice* 225.

Penington, R 'Origin of Corporations' (1931) 3 *Corporate Practice Review* 33.

Quijano, A 'Coloniality of Power, Eurocentrism, and Latin America' (2000) 1, no. 3 *Nepantla: Views from South* 533.

Ramose, MB 'In Memoriam: Sovereignty and the "New" South Africa' (2007) 16, no. 2 *Griffith Law Review* 310.

Scheffer, D 'Corporate Liability Under the Rome Statute' (2016) 57, Spring *Harvard International Law Journal* 35.

Sibanda, S 'Not Purpose-Made! Transformative Constitutionalism, Post-Independence Constitutionalism and the Struggle to Eradicate Poverty' (2011) 22, no. 3 *Stellenbosch Law Review* 482.

Sibanda, S 'When Do You Call Time on a Compromise? South Africa's Discourse on Transformation and the Future of Transformative Constitutionalism' (2020) 24 *Law, Democracy &Development* 384.

Singer, P 'Famine, Affluence and Morality' (1972) 1, no. 3 *Philosophy and Public Affairs* 229.

Sirleaf, M 'The African Justice Cascade and the Malabo Protocol' (2017) 11 *International Journal of Transitional Justice* 71.

Slye, RC 'Corporations, Veils, and International Criminal Liability' (2008) 33, no. 3 *Brooklyn Journal of International Law* 955.

Stahn, C 'Liberals vs Romantics: Challenges of an Emerging Corporate International Criminal Law' (2018) 50 *Case Western Reserve Journal of International Law* 91.

Stephens, B 'The Amorality of Profit: Transnational Corporations and Human Rights' (2002) 20, no. 3 *Berkeley Journal of International Law* 45.

Tully, J 'Modern Constitutional Democracy and Imperialism' (2008) 46 *Osgoode Hall Law Journal* 461.

van Deventer, T 'Criminal Prosecution of Corporates for Human Rights Violations' (2012) *Without Prejudice* December 9.

Wattad, MS-A 'Natural Persons, Legal Entities, and Corporate Criminal Liability Under the Rome Statute' (2016) 20, no. 2 Fall *UCLA Journal of International Law and Foreign Affairs* 391.

Yamey, BS 'The History of Unilever. By Charles Wilson' (1956) 66, no. 264 December *The Economic Journal* 730.

Internet Articles and Encyclopedias

https://www.dailymaverick.co.za/article/2012-03-01-general-motors-concedes-to-khulumani-in-apartheid-reparations-case/#.WoVii4Nua01 Davis, R 'General Motors Concedes to Khulumani in Apartheid Reparations Case' (accessed 28 July 2020).

https://plato.stanford.edu/archives/fall2011/entries/african-ethics/ Gyekye, Kwame, "African Ethics", *The Stanford Encyclopedia of Philosophy* (Fall 2011 Edition), Edward N. Zalta (ed) (accessed 28 July 2020).

https://africasacountry.com/2014/04/historyclass-who-sold-nigeria-to-the-british-for-865k-in-1899#:~:text=The%20Royal%20Niger%20Company%20and,Sir%20George%20Goldie Nwanze, C 'Who Sold Nigeria to the British for £865k in 1899? The Royal Niger Company and the Founding of What Became Nigeria' *Africa Is a Country* 28 April 2014 (accessed 27 May 2021).

https://ssrn.com/abstract=3324846 Pahuja, S 'Corporations, Universalism and the Domestication of Race in International Law' (29 January 2018). Forthcoming in Duncan Bell (ed) *Empire, Race and Global Justice* (Cambridge University Press) (accessed 28 July 2020).

https://them.polylog.org/3/frm-en.htm Ramose, MB 'An African Perspective on Justice and Race' 2001 (accessed 28 July 2020).

http://www.ribbonfarm.com/2011/06/08/a-brief-history-of-the-corporation-1600-to-2100/ Rao, V. '*A Brief History of the Corporation 1600–2100*' 2011 (accessed 28 July 2020).

Statute, Treaties and Protocols

N Verbale 127/2000 submitted by the Nigerian government at the 28th session of the Commission in Oct 2000 (Verbal note Ogoni case).

Malabo Protocol African Court of Justice and Human Rights, *Protocol on Amendments to the Protocol on the Statute of the African Court of Justice and Human Rights* (11 June 2000)/Protocol on Amendments to the Protocol on the Statute of the African Court of Justice and Human Rights (Malabo Protocol).

Rome Statute of the International Criminal Court, art. 25, 17 July 1998, 2187 U.N.T.S. 90. (RS).

Universal Declaration of Human Rights (The United Nations 1948) (UNDHR).

Reports and Reviews

Gordon, JA 'Theorizing Contemporary Practices of Slavery: A Portrait of the Old in the New' (2012) Paper presented at *American Political Science Association Annual Meeting* New Orleans.

K Dev & D Cartwright- 'Illicit Financial Flows from Developing Countries: 2004–2013' (Global Financial Integrity 2015) 8 http://www.gfintegrity.org/wp-content/uploads/2015/12/IFF-Update_2015-Final-1.pdf (accessed 31 May 2021).

Marikana Commission of Inquiry: Report on Matters of Public, National and International Concern Arising out of the Tragic Incidents at the Lonmin Mine in Marikana, In the North West Province (2015) https://www.sahrc.org.za/home/21/files/marikana-report-1.pdf

U.N. Doc. A/HRC/7/7 30 ("Promotion and Protection of all Human Rights, Civil, Political, Economic, Social and Cultural Rights, Including the Right to Development: Report on the Working Group on the Use of Mercenaries as Means of Violating Human Rights and Impeding the Exercise of the Right of People to Self-Determination").

National Cases

Mankayi v AngloGold Ashanti Ltd 2011 (3) SA 237 (CC) (*Mankayi*).

National Commissioner of the South African Police Service v. Southern African Human Rights Litigation Centre and Another 2014 (1) SA 30 (CC) (*Zimbabwe*).

Southern Africa Litigation Centre v. Minister of Justice and Constitutional Development 2015 (5) SA 1 (GP) para. 2 (*Al Bashir* HC).

Tribunals

Prosecutor v. Germain Katanga, Judgment Pursuant to Article 74 of the Statute, ICC-01/04-01/07-3436-tENG, 07 March 2014, paras. 1404–1410.

Prosecutor v. Kristic, Case No. IT-98-33-T, Judgment, at ¶ 638 (Int' Crim. Trib. For the Former Yugoslavia 2 August 2001) http://www.icty.org/x/cases/krstic/tjug/en/krs-tj010802e.pdf.

Prosecutor v. Musema, Case No. ICTR-96-13-A, Judgment and Sentence (27 January 2000), http://unictr.unmict.org/sites/unictr.org/files/case-documents/ictr-96-13/trial-judgements/en/000127.pdf.

The Flick Trial, Case No. 48, 9 L. Rep. Trials War Crim. 1 [US Mil.Trib., Nuremberg] (April 20 December 22, 949).

Prosecutor v. Perišić, Case No. IT-04-81-A, Appeals Judgment of Judge Meron, ¶ 73 (Int'l Crim. Trib. for the Former Yugoslavia 28 February 2013) http://www.icty.org/x/cases/perisic/acjug/en/130228judgement.pdf [https://perma.cc/MH8Z-V9DK].

Prosecutor v. Šainović, Case No. IT-05-87-A, Appeals Judgment of Judge Daqun ¶ 1649–1650 (Int'l Crim. Trib. for the Former Yugoslavia

23 January 2014) http://www.icty.org/x/cases/milutinovic/acjug/en/140123.pdf [perma.cc/UT7Q-NBE5].

Judgement, Akayesu (ICTR-96-4-T), Chamber I, 2 September 1998, par. 581 (hereinafter Akayesu).

Prosecutor v. Aleksovski, IT-95-14/1-T, Judgment, 15 June 1999, para. 78.

Prosecutor v. Thomas Lubanga Dyilo, ICC-01/04-01/06, Decision on the Confirmation of Charges, ¶ 920 (29 January 2007), https://www.icccpi.int/CourtRecords/CR2012_03942.PDF.

Prosecutor v Mbarushimana, ICC-01/04-01/10. Decision on the Confirmation of Charges, 16 December 2011, para. 285.

Prosecutor v. Al Khayat, Case No. STL-14-05/PT/AP/AR26.1, Decision on Interlocutory Appeal Concerning Personal Jurisdiction in Contempt Proceedings, T 27 (Special Trib. For Lebanon 2 October 2014) (discussing the decision of the Al-Jadeed case).

Prosecutor v. Taylor, Case No. SCSL-03-01-A, Appeals Judgment of Judge King ¶ 474 (Special Ct. for the Sierra Leone 26 September 2013) http://www.rscsl.org/Documents/Decisions/Taylor/Appeal/1389/SCSL-03-01-A-1389.pdf [perma.cc/BSN4-UPHT].

Dissertations

Fokwa, TJ 'In Search of or Direct Corporate Responsibility for Human Rights Violations in Africa: Which Way Forward?' unpublished PhD Thesis, University of Pretoria 2004 URI: http://hdl.handle.net/2263/1082.

Samaradiwakera-Wijesundara, C 'Is the Company an Instrument of Coloniality?: Interrogating the Recognition of the Legal Personality of the Company' unpublished LLM Thesis, University of the Witwatersrand, Johannesburg http://wiredspace.wits.ac.za/bitstream/handle/10539/27017/Samaradiwakera-Wijesundara%20(Final%20LLM%20Dissertation).pdf?sequence=1.

S Sibanda '"Not Yet Uhuru" - The Usurpation of the Liberation Aspirations of South Africa's Masses by a Commitment to Liberal Constitutional Democracy' unpublished PhD Thesis, University of the Witwatersrand http://wiredspace.wits.ac.za/bitstream/handle/10539/29657/Sanele%20Sibanda%20-%20Not%20Yet%20Uhuru%20-%20Final%20Final%20Submission.pdf?sequence=1.

Dictionary

Merriam-Webster's *Collegiate Dictionary*. 10th ed. Springfield, MA: Merriam Webster, 1993. https://www.merriam-webster.com/dictionary/mark (accessed 31 May 2021).

PART II

The Complementarity Principle and Prospectives

Expanding the Scope of Complementarity? Towards Institutionalised Complementarity Between the International Criminal Court and National Criminal Justice Systems in Africa

Evelyne Owiye Asaala

1 Introduction

The fact that the only heads of states indicted by the International Criminal Court (ICC) come from the continent of Africa is a key factor that has contributed to anti-ICC sentiments within the region. This fact when juxtaposed with the reality that African states comprise the majority state parties to the Rome Statute, coupled with the enthusiasm they displayed

E. O. Asaala (✉)
University of Nairobi, Nairobi, Kenya

E. C. Lubaale and N. Dyani-Mhango (eds.), *National Accountability for International Crimes in Africa*,
https://doi.org/10.1007/978-3-030-88044-6_6

in the negotiation, adoption, signature, ratification of the Statute[1] and self-referrals underscore the viewpoint that African states do not support impunity for international crimes. Yet, the sour relationship between the ICC and African states continue to hamper the war against impunity on the continent, with African states having over time, and fuelled by the African Union's (AU) non-cooperation and calls for withdrawal, become reluctant to cooperate with the ICC in the arrest and surrender of specific indicted individuals, al-Bashir being the most recent example. This paper urges the ICC to reconsider its relationship with African states and the AU at large in the war against impunity for international crimes. It implores for a change of tact in implementing the concept of complementarity as one way through which the adverse impact of this stand-off can be mitigated. The ICC together with African states and in conjunction with the AU through the Assembly of State Parties to the Rome Statute (ASP) should, thus, work towards institutionalising the concept of complementarity in a manner that provides for a sustained interaction between national criminal justice systems and the ICC.

This institutionalised complementarity will make significant contribution in not only advancing the development of the principle but also it will easily win over local legitimacy and political will in subsequent prosecutions of international crimes. In fact, it will provide overall coordination of the governance structure in prosecuting international crimes in national courts. Yet, this does not imply that local legitimacy, absence of political will and governance are the only challenges that compromise the realisation of the principle of complementarity in national criminal justice systems. This contribution acknowledges the diversity of reasons that underly the failure by domestic courts to play their part in complementarity. These reasons frame from governance, political, technical, financial, *et cetera*.[2] The chapter does not assume that institutionalised interactions

[1] Thirty-four African states are parties to the Rome Statute. In comparison with other continents, Africa has the largest membership of the Court. M du Plessis 'The International Criminal Court and its work in Africa: Confronting the myths' ISS Monograph No. 173 (2008) on the general involvement by African states and regional blocs in the various processes leading to the adoption of the Rome Statute; M du Plessis 'The International Criminal Court that Africa wants' ISS Monograph No. 172 (2010).

[2] *Report on the Proceedings of the 2010 Kampala Review Conference.* The report documents a wide range of challenges key among them including lack of a social infrastructure, weak economies, lack of judicial infrastructure, et cetera.

between the ICC and national courts are likely to solve all possible challenges. However, it argues that a pre-existing good governance structure in national criminal justice systems that enjoys local legitimacy and political will is central in realising effective complementarity, especially given the constant presence of the ICC factor. In fact, although all the self-referrals targeted rebels or non-state actors, this chapter acknowledges that the absence of well governed and independent national criminal justice systems greatly influenced the five self-referrals from the continent.[3] As such, a standing interaction between the ICC and national criminal justice systems will positively impact the practice of complementarity in a fundamental way. Not only does it ensure local legitimacy for prosecution of international crimes, it also guarantees effective procedural aspects relating to prosecuting international crimes. This supportive structure of the ICC is embedded within its potential threat to seize the matter where circumstances allow. This kind of a framework is likely to gel the concept of complementarity within already existing structures of national criminal justice systems. Currently, the ideology that underlies the theory and practice of complementarity is one that prompts a relationship between the ICC and national courts in the aftermath of conflict.[4] This chapter will therefore seek to introduce a mind shift in the interpretation and application of the theory and principle of complementarity. Instead of a restrictive theoretical interpretation, which limits the principle to a responsive approach to international crimes in post-conflict states, it advocates for a broad interpretation that favours institutionalised practice of complementarity. Yet, it does not pigeon-hole complementarity to criminal prosecutions alone. Rather, it advocates for a multi-dimensional understanding of the concept in a manner that accommodates diversity of principles. It therefore, inter alia, endorses the creation and sustenance of national political will in prosecuting international crimes, appropriate physical infrastructure, judicial dialogue, capacity building, strengthening

[3] For African cases referred to the ICC and their respective trigger mechanisms, see International Criminal Court, 'Situations Under Investigation', https://www.icc-cpi.int/pages/situations.aspx (accessed 12 November 2020).

[4] C Bassiouni 'Introduction to International Criminal Law' in C Bassiouni (ed) *Post-Conflict Justice, International and Comparative Law Series* (2002) 58; ICC-OTP, 'Policy Paper on Preliminary Examination' (November 2013) para 102, https://www.icc-cpi.int/iccdocs/otp/OTP-Policy_Paper_Preliminary_Examinations_2013-ENG.pdf (accessed 2 May 2020); See generally (n 6).

of governance structures of national criminal justice systems, recognition of African approaches to justice, among others, through a sustained and structured interaction between the ICC and national criminal justice systems. Hopefully this will help entrench easy application of the principle of complementarity within national criminal justice systems. This contribution does not advocate for the ICC to renege on its central judicial role, rather it encourages for a change of tact in its judicial role. Instead of emphasising on self exercise of the judicial role, the ICC should focus much attention to helping nation states in executing their primary mandate of prosecuting international crimes and only seize the matter in the most deserving cases. This is particularly so with respect to states that are willing to exercise this mandate but unable because of a myriad of reasons.

This chapter makes the central assumption that a national criminal justice system that is well governed, equipped and enjoys local legitimacy and political will, offers a great opportunity for effective complementarity and thus a potential solution to the challenges imposed by the souring relationship between African states and the ICC.[5] It therefore sets out to discuss these issues in four parts. First, the paper introduces the study. Second, it provides a theoretical framework of the concept of complementarity. Third, it lays down the frameworks of good governance in national criminal justice systems and their co-relation with the principle of complementarity. This discussion will also clearly bring out the challenges facing African national criminal justice systems particularly in their attempt to complement the ICC in holding accountable the perpetrators of international crimes. Fourth, the chapter explores a framework of institutionalising complementarity between the ICC and national criminal justice systems. Drawing from the previous discussion, this section identifies the key aspects of an effective complementarity system as the possible areas necessitating continuous cooperation between the ICC and national criminal justice systems. Finally, the paper draws some conclusions.

[5] On withdrawal from the Rome Statute and the need for an African solution, see AU Assembly 'Decision on the International Criminal Court (ICC)', Assembly/AU/Dec.622(XXVIII), Doc. Doc. EX.CL/1006(XXX), 28th Ordinary Session, 30–31 January 2017, para 8; AU 'Withdrawal Strategy Document' (Version 12.01.2017) para 8, available at https://www.hrw.org/sites/default/files/supporting_resources/icc_withdrawal_strategy_jan._2017.pdf (accessed 30 April 2021).

2 Complementarity in Theory

The principle of complementarity has been defined in multiple ways.[6] Central in these definitions, is the aspect of distributing jurisdictional mandate over international crimes between the ICC and national criminal justice systems. In particular, it is the emphasis of the primary role bestowed upon national criminal justice systems in prosecuting international crimes. In its preamble, the Rome Statute acknowledges the primary role of national criminal justice mechanisms to ensure prosecution of the most serious crimes of concern to the international community.[7] Article 1 of the Rome Statute is also peppered with provisions that underscore the primacy of national criminal justice systems in prosecuting international crimes. It provides in mandatory terms that the ICC '...shall be complementary to national criminal jurisdictions'.

Complementarity has also been theorised in numerous antagonisms. Key to this chapter are the notions of 'positive or negative' as well as 'vertical or horizontal' complementarity. Complementarity is positive when the national courts effectively exercise their jurisdiction to hold the perpetrators of international crimes accountable through prosecution.[8] Complementarity is termed as negative when national courts fail to genuinely hold accountable the perpetrators of human rights violations.[9] This general understanding of complementarity, where international

[6] See generally *Review Conference of the Rome Statute Draft Resolution on Complementarity* ICCASP/8/Res.9 Annex VII 8 June 2010; WW Burke-White 'Proactive Complementarity: The International Criminal Courts in the Rome System of International Justice' (2008) (1) *Harvard International Law Journal* 53; C Stahn 'Taking Complementarity Seriously: On the Sense and Sensibility of "Classical", "Positive" and "Negative" Complementarity' in C Stahn and M Zeidy (eds) *The International Criminal Court and Complementarity: from Theory to Practice* Vol. 2 (2011) 233–282; EO Asaala 'The International Criminal Court Factor on Transitional Justice in Kenya' in K Ambos and OA Maunganidze (eds) *Power and Prosecutions: Challenges and Opportunities for International Criminal Justice in Sub-Saharan Africa* (2010) 124, for an analysis of various schools of thought's analysis of the principle.

[7] Para 4.

[8] W Colish 'The International Criminal Court in Guinea: A Case Study of Complementarity' (2013) 26 (2) *Revue Québécoise de Droit International* 23, 37–39; Burke-White 'Proactive Complementarity: The International Criminal Court and National Courts in the Rome System of International Justice' (n 6) 54.

[9] Stahn 'Taking Complementarity Seriously: On the Sense and Sensibility of "Classical", "Positive" and "Negative" Complementarity' in Stahn and El Zeidy (eds) *International Criminal Court and Complementarity: From Theory to Practice* (n 6 above) 260.

courts operate higher in the hierarchy than the domestic courts is what Cedric Ryngaert calls vertical complementarity.[10] This can be contrasted with horizontal complementarity, where an international Court enjoys the same jurisdictional space with another.[11] A new version of positive complementarity has been described as 'hybrid complementarity'—where an international tribunal extends support and mutual assistance to its member states in undertaking national prosecution of international crimes and at the same time uses threats to compel the relevant state to execute its mandate.[12]

In practice, all these theories are reactive and ad hoc in the sense that they perceive the relational mandate between the ICC and national courts in prosecuting international crimes to come into play in the aftermath of international crimes. Indeed, whenever international crimes occur, the dictates of international criminal law underscore the need to implement the complementarity principle. The ICC, other international institutions as well as the civil society movement then push for and support initiatives towards implementing this principle since underlying this principle is the need to strengthen and allow national criminal justice systems to assume the primary responsibility to prosecute international crimes.

3 National Criminal Justice Systems and Their Role in Prosecuting International Crimes in Africa

That complementarity denotes the 'entirety of norms governing the complementary relationship between the International Criminal Court and national jurisdictions',[13] is testament to the obvious role of national jurisdictions in prosecuting international crimes. The notion 'entirety of norms' embodies multiple substantive and procedural aspects central in the dispensation of criminal justice at the national level. Yet, a full account

[10] C Ryngaert 'Horizontal Complementarity' in Stahn and El Zeidy (eds) *International Criminal Court and Complementarity: from Theory to Practice* (n 6) 855.

[11] As above.

[12] Colish 'The International Criminal Court in Guinea: A Case Study of Complementarity' (n 8 above) 34.

[13] See generally M Benzing 'The Complementarity Regime of the International Criminal Court' (2003) 7 *Max Planck Yearbook of United Nations Law* 592.

of the notion of complementarity in this context must give an appraisal of its practice by African states. This practice, in the context of the main question posed in this chapter, serves three functions. First, it offers an analysis of the structure of national governance systems in implementing complementarity. Second, it exposes the numerous challenges that bedevil effective implementation of complementarity. Third, it provides indicators on how to possibly anchor an institutionalised complementarity between the ICC and national criminal justice systems.

3.1 The Governance Structure of National Criminal Justice Systems

The governance structure in national criminal justice systems in Africa comprises institutions, substantive laws and procedural aspects. At the institutional level, it is generally the police, the Office of the Director of Public Prosecution and the judiciary that play a key role in national criminal justice systems. While the police effect arrests and conduct investigations in almost all national criminal justice systems in Africa, in some jurisdictions, the police also carry out prosecution of the case while other states have a separate independent body designated for prosecution: the Office of the Director of Public Prosecution. The role of adjudication is usually conducted by the judiciary. Another notable institution that adjudicates over crimes in national jurisdictions in Africa are traditional or customary law courts. A majority of African countries use traditional mechanisms for ordinary crimes, albeit in a limited sense.[14] An AU report has for instance noted traditional courts as a main stay in South Sudan's criminal justice system as it handles over 90% of all the cases.[15]

Substantive law is another central component of the governance structure for prosecuting international crimes. It is through the law

[14] Most commonwealth African countries have statutory provisions allowing the use of customary law, albeit to a limited degree. For example, Section 8 of the Judicature Act of Kenya lists customary law as a source of law in the country. Moreover, although they are not recognised by the law, Kenya still has traditional *barazas* which are used in villages by local chief as traditional courts to solve disputes among villagers; Section 211(3) of the Constitution of the Republic of South Africa, 1996 calls on South African courts to apply customary law 'when that law is applicable, subject to the Constitution and any legislation that specifically deals with customary law'.

[15] *Report of the African Union Commission of Inquiry on South Sudan* 1 15 October 2014, para 286 http://www.peaceau.org/uploads/auciss.final.report.pdf (accessed 22 November 2020).

that national courts are conferred with jurisdiction over international crimes; the law also spells out certain procedural guarantees as well as human rights entitlements for accused persons, the victims and witnesses. Although a majority of African states are state parties to the Rome Statute, the philosophy that a country ascribes to, whether dualist or monist, in applying international law in domestic courts has a direct impact in the determination of which laws apply in prosecuting international crimes. Any deficiency in the legal framework aligning itself to the appropriate rules for either of these philosophies is likely to compromise prosecuting international crimes. This challenge was experienced in Kenya in relation to prosecuting the actual perpetrators, those who did not bear the highest responsibility, of international crimes in the 2007/2008 Post Election Violence.[16] Although Kenya had ratified the Rome Statute on 15 March 2005, the law domesticating the Rome Statute came into force on 1 January 2009 way after its Post-Election Violence.[17] As such national courts were left with the only option of prosecuting ordinary municipal crimes instead of international crimes such as crimes against humanity for those not singled out by the ICC.[18]

External factors too play a fundamental role in national criminal justice systems. The absence of political will, political interference with the judiciary, the role of the civil society, financial and technical aspects are some of the external factors that influence the effectiveness of national criminal justice systems.[19] In most cases, post-conflict states are fraught with challenges ranging from lack of facilities to bias caused by the preceding conflict, weak or non-existent institutional structures, suspicion among the political class and an eroded economy. If not cushioned, these factors can easily work together to undermine any national prosecution of alleged perpetrators of international crimes.

[16] EO Asaala 'Prosecuting the 2007 Post Election Violence-Related International Crimes in Kenyan Courts: Exposing the Real Challenges' in M Mbondenyi, E Asaala, T Kabau and A Waris (Eds) *Human Rights and Democratic Governance in Kenya: A Post-2007 Appraisal* (2015) 345.

[17] https://asp.icc-cpi.int/en_menus/asp/states%20parties/african%20states/Pages/kenya.aspx (accessed 17 May 2021).

[18] Asaala 'Prosecuting the 2007 Post Election Violence-Related International Crimes in Kenyan Courts: Exposing the Real Challenges' (n 16).

[19] As above.

3.2 *The Practice of Prosecuting International Crimes in National Courts in Africa*

Post-conflict African countries have had several attempts at implementing the principle of complementarity. A preliminary survey of the continent reveals several efforts exerted towards these ends albeit in varied levels. While some post-conflict African countries can be said to have gotten hold of the principle, others fit the description of running after it while a majority seem to be crawling on their knees as they struggle to implement the principle. Yet, there are those that are indifferent with the principle altogether.

Uganda, the Democratic Republic of the Congo (DRC) and Senegal (via the Extraordinary African Chambers) are the only regional states with practices that demonstrate visible effort in seeking the prosecution of international crimes and in a manner that complements the ICC.

Uganda established an International Crimes Division (ICD) of the High Court in 2008.[20] It was anticipated that the ICD would improve national prosecution of international crimes, particularly so with regard to the Lord's Resistance Army (LRA)-related cases. Once it was fully operationalised, its first trial was against Thomas Kwoyela,[21] a former LRA commander arrested in the DRC in 2008. Kwoyela was charged with war crimes and 53 alternative charges alleging kidnap with intent to murder, aggravated robberies, offences under the Geneva Conventions *et cetera*.[22] He was arraigned in court in September 2010 and his trial began only in July 2011 after several delays. These delays, according to Sharon Nakandha, were due to the numerous challenges the ICD faces as a result of its budgetary constraints. In addition, were some legal questions raised by Kwoyela's defence team.[23] Chief among these was the legal question

[20] This was redesignated in 2011 through Legal Notice No. 10 of 2011, The High Court (International Crimes Division) Practice Directions 2011 clause 3. This was initially called the War Crimes Division.

[21] *Uganda v. Thomas Kwoyelo alias Latoni*, HCT-00-ICD-Case No. 02/10.

[22] JLOS Annual Report, 72.

[23] Constitutional Court Ruling, *Thomas Kwoyelo alias Latoni v. Uganda* (Constitutional Petition No. 036 of 2011. Among other questions, his legal team questioned the criminal liability of a victim turned perpetrator as he was conscripted by the LRA as a child soldier, his alleged torture, the applicability of the Amnesty Act et cetera.

on the applicability and constitutionality of the Amnesty Act.[24] Other key problems included administrative challenges of lack of key internal structures such as a victims and witness unit and an outreach unit.[25] The latter is what, according to Nakandha, compelled the Court to postpone Kwoyela's trial by months. Although the government offered the use of its media to reach out to affected communities, it was important for the court to reach out physically to Northern Uganda, which may not have been possible due to constrained resources. Another serious administrative challenge bedevilling Uganda's ICD is the lack of adequate human resources. Appeals from the ICD are subject to the ordinary Appeal Courts, which handle numerous other civil and criminal matters,[26] but the human resources of these courts have not been bolstered.[27]There is fear that this will likely lead to adjournments of many cases due to lack of forum, as has been the situation with ordinary cases.[28]In a constitutional petition in November 2011, Kwoyela challenged his prosecution on the basis of an Amnesty Act before the Constitutional Court. Not only was the amnesty law declared constitutional, but the court also ordered the ICD to cease Kwoyela's trial.[29] This decision was overturned by the Supreme Court of Uganda and ICD ordered to subject Kwoyela to trial again.[30] Political pressure and the intricacies of donor funding remain

[24] S Oola 'In the Shadow of Kwoyelo's Trial: The ICC and Complementarity in Uganda' in C de Vos, S Kendall and C Stahn (eds) *Contested Justice: The Politics and Practice of International Criminal Court Interventions* (2015) 163.

[25] S Nakandha 'The Kwoyelo Case at the ICD: The Realities of Complementarity in Practice' https://www.ijmonitor.org/2016/05/the-kwoyelo-case-at-the-icd-the-realities-of-complementarity-in-practice/ (accessed 3 March 2020).

[26] P Acirokop, *Accountability for Mass Atrocities: The LRA Conflict in Uganda*, LLD Thesis, University of Pretoria (2013), Chapter 5, https://repository.up.ac.za/bitstream/handle/2263/23898/06chapter6.pdf?sequence=7 (accessed 3 June 2020).

[27] As above.

[28] As above.

[29] *Thomas Kwoyelo Alias Latoni v Uganda* Constitutional Petition No. 036/11 [Arising Out of HCT-00-ICD-Case No. 2/10] Ruling of the Court of 22 September 2011 (Constitutional Court of Uganda) at para 625.

[30] See Supreme Court Ruling, Constitutional Appeal No. 1 of 2012, *Uganda v. Thomas Kwoyelo*, 8 April 2015; S. Nakandha, 'Supreme Court of Uganda Rules on the Application of the Amnesty Act' (16 April 2015), www.ijmonitor.org/2015/04/supreme-court-ofu ganda-rules-on-the-application-of-the-amnesty-act/ (accessed 6 July 2020).

major factors that influence both the trial process as well as the outcome of judicial announcements.[31]

As regards the DRC, following its ratification of the Rome Statute in 2002, the Military Penal Code was passed in the same year. This formed the basis upon which the military tribunals were initially the only tribunals prosecuting international crimes. The International Centre for Transitional Justice (ICTJ) has, however, raised concern that some of the provisions of this legislation fall short of the Rome Statute standards. For example, its mode of responsibility falls short of the command responsibility under article 28 of the Rome Statute; its definition of war crimes and crimes against humanity falls short of the Rome Statute definitions; and it omits penalties for war crimes and also provides for the death penalty.[32] To remedy this situation, judges have referred directly to Rome Statute provisions since the DRC is a monist state.[33] In April 2013, Parliament passed the Law on the Organization, Functioning and Jurisdiction of the Courts (LOCJ), granting civilian courts (particularly, Courts of Appeals) jurisdiction over the prosecution of core international crimes.[34]

A study conducted by the ICTJ found that 'between January 2009 and December 2014, judicial authorities in the DRC had opened 39 cases related to events that had occurred between 2002 and 2014 in eastern DRC (Ituri, North Kivu, and South Kivu)'.[35] This is a very small number compared to the mass atrocities committed during the period under investigation.[36] Political pressure where special interests are at stake, coupled with lack of political will, especially from the neighbouring Rwandan government, in relation to proceedings against foreign

[31] Oola 'In the Shadow of Kwoyelo's Trial: the ICC And Complementarity in Uganda' (n 24 above) 165.

[32] ICTJ 'The Accountability Landscape in Eastern DRC: Analysis of the National Legislative and Judicial Response to International Crimes (2009–2014)' https://www.ictj.org/sites/default/files/ICTJ-Briefing-DRC-Prosecutions-2015_1.pdf (accessed 5 October 2020).

[33] Sources (1) judges referring directly to the Rome Statute, and (2) the position that the DRC is a monist state.

[34] Projet de loi modi ant et complétant la loi organique No. 13/011-B of April 11, 2013 portant organisation, fonctionnement, et compétences des juridictions de l'ordre judiciaire en matière de répression des crimes de génocide, des crimes contre l'humanité et des crimes de guerres, April 2014.

[35] As above.

[36] As above.

armed groups, have been cited as the major challenges contributing to the low levels of investigation.[37] In addition, due to limited access to areas where serious crimes have been committed, the DRC judicial system relies on information from external partners such as the United Nations Organization Stabilization Mission in the Democratic Republic of the Congo (MONUSCO), UN agencies, and NGOs.[38] As a result, 'whenever crimes occur outside of the realm of an international partner's area of intervention, little or no information is gathered and no investigations or prosecutions are initiated'.[39] Given these challenges, it is impossible to argue that the DRC judicial system provides an effective positive complementarity mechanism in the fight against impunity for international crimes.

In the third instance, the Extraordinary African Chambers (EAC) in Senegal was established as an internationalised court under the auspices of the AU to prosecute international crimes committed in Chad between 7 June 1982 and 1 December 1990.[40] This period corresponds to Hissèn Habrè's rule in Chad. On 30 May 2016, the EAC convicted Habrè for war crimes, crimes against humanity and torture.[41] This conviction is significant for a number of reasons.

First, the history preceding Habrè's prosecution is so riddled with uncertainties that one would have expected a different verdict from the Senegalese courts. In January 2000, Senegal commenced criminal

[37] As above.

[38] As above.

[39] As above.

[40] *Statut des Chambres africaines extraordinaires au sein des juridictions sénégalaises pour la poursuite des crimes internationaux commis au Tchad durant la période du 7 juin* 1982 *au 1er décembre* 1990.

[41] *Ministère Public v Hissene Habré*, Judgment of 30 May 2016, Chambre Africaine Extraiordinaire d'Assises, avalble at http://www.chambresafricaines.org/pdf/Jugement_complet.pdf (accessed 11 November 2020). For further reading on the judgment, see S A E Høgestøl, 'The Habré Judgment at the Extraordinary African Chambers: A Singular Victory in the Fight Against Impunity' (2016) 34 (3) *Nordic Journal of Human Rights* 147–156. Habré is, however, appealing his conviction ('Communiqué de presse: Démarrage des audiences du procès en appel', 29 December 2016, http://www.chambresafricaines.org/index.php/le-coin-des-medias/communiqu%C3%A9-de-presse/649-communiqu%C3%A9-de-presse-d%C3%A9marrage-des-audiences-du-proc%C3%A8s-en-appel.html (accessed 11 June 2020); BBC News 'Chad's Hissen Habré Removed from Senegal Court' 20 July 2015, www.bbc.com/news/world-africa-33592142 (accessed 6 September 2020).

proceedings against Hissen Habré, a former president of Chad who was exiled in Senegal, for crimes against humanity and torture. Senegal's appeal court held that it had no jurisdiction to prosecute Habré for the alleged crimes since Senegal had not enacted legislation implementing the Convention against Torture and Other Cruel, Inhuman or Degrading Treatment and Punishment of 1984 (UN Convention against Torture) and that Habré was a non-Senegalese and the alleged crimes had been committed outside of Senegal.[42] Senegal's highest court, the Cour de Cassation, later upheld this decision.[43]

Belgium sought the extradition of Habré to Belgium to stand trial for the alleged crimes. Senegal's rejection of the extradition was applauded by the AU, which called upon Senegal to ensure his prosecution.[44] The AU mandated 'the Republic of Senegal to prosecute and ensure that Hissen Habré is tried, on behalf of Africa, by a competent Senegalese court with guarantees for fair trial'.[45] This was never done. Hence, in February 2009, Belgium instituted proceedings against Senegal before the International Court of Justice (ICJ), claiming Senegal was in breach of its international treaty and customary law obligations. The ICJ duly found Senegal in breach of its international conventional obligation to expedite investigations and subsequent prosecution of Habré.[46] The Court observed that article 27 of the Vienna Convention on the Law of Treaties, which reflects customary international law, could not allow Senegal to rely on its internal law to defeat its international law obligation.[47]

In July 2015, Habré's trial recommenced before a Senegalese court and led to his conviction, which gives renewed hope that an African court can convict a former sitting head of state for international crimes.

[42] *Questions relating to the obligation to prosecute or extradite (Belgium v Senegal)* Judgement, [2012] ICJ Reports 422, para 76 (referring to Court of Appeal (Dakar), *Chambre d'accusation, Public Prosecutor's Office and François Diouf* v. *Hissène Habré,* Judgment No. 135, 4 July 2000).

[43] Ibid. (also referring to Court of Cassation, *première chambre statuant en matière pénale, Souleymane Guengueng et al.* v *Hissène Habré,* Judgment No. 14, 20 March 2001).

[44] AU Assembly 'Decision on the Hissen Habré Case and the African Union' Assembly/AU/Dec.127 (VII), Doc. Assembly/AU/3 (VII), 7th Ordinary Session, 1–2 July 2006.

[45] As above, para 5(iii).

[46] *Belgium v Senegal* (n) para 70.

[47] As above, para 113.

Arguably, since the establishment of the court under the auspices of the AU involved other African states, the conviction confirms that African states have resolved to allow zero tolerance of impunity for international crimes.

Yet, despite these positive efforts, the trend established in the examples above is testament to the ailing governance structures inherent in most African national criminal justice systems. Worse still, it is evident that to fully incorporate the key aspects of an effective complementarity framework at the national level, one requires coordination of numerous functions ordinarily fragmented among different government agencies as complementarity involves several players like the legislative arm, the judiciary, the police, several ministries and or departments as well as the victims. The lack of an overall body charged with the responsibility to coordinate the various activities, supervise and follow-up on all these entities is, thus, counterproductive to the very objective of complementarity. As such, there lacks coherence in implementing the principle of complementarity as all these agencies deal with a host of other issues and for some of them investigations and or prosecution may not be their sole priority. In five instances, African countries have preferred self-referral of situations within their countries to the ICC due to their inability to effectively prosecute the alleged perpetrators. However, the reality that most of these self-referrals use the ICC as the bull dog to fix their problems with rebels or eliminate their political opponents cannot be ignored. Thus, while this contribution advocates for an expansion of the concept of complementarity as one way of overcoming some of these challenges and also to restore concerted efforts between the ICC and African states in the fight against impunity for international crimes, it is mindful of creating national mechanism that have capacity to hold accountable individual from the ruling class or senior government officials as well as their opponents. It is argued that institutionalised complementarity has the potential to resolve a majority of these challenges and thus prepare national criminal justice systems for prosecution of international crimes.

Other than prosecution efforts in national courts, post-conflict African state practice suggests the incorporation of traditional justice concepts and systems within the broad ambit of complementarity. Traditional procedures of *gacaca* and *mato oput* are the only mechanisms that have either been proposed or used by post-conflict African states in holding perpetrators accountable for international crimes. As such, they provide this chapter with a sound basis for establishing the suitability of African traditional approaches within the institutionalised concept of complementarity. For example, the utilisation of African approaches like *gacaca* in Rwanda and proposals for using *mato oput* for ICC indictees in Uganda have all been anchored on the need for accountability for past atrocities,[48] thus raising questions on their complementarity nature to the ICC.

However, several flaws inherent in these African approaches have been pointed out as undermining the principle of complementarity. For example, on overall *gacaca* has been disapproved for compromising due process, thus denying accused persons their right to fair trial. Although *gacaca* courts held competences similar to ordinary courts,[49] some of their procedural aspects came under scrutiny for allegedly affecting the justice these institutions dispensed. First, *gacaca* has been criticised for having lay judges presiding over the crimes of genocide and crimes against humanity. These judges, entirely unfamiliar with methods of legal interpretation, were bound to face difficulties, particularly given the complex nature of international crimes. It can been argued that this incompetency denies an accused person the right to fair trial in the sense that the presiding judges are unlikely to appreciate the nature of the crimes within the context of international criminal law as well as enforce international human rights standards.

But this kind of criticism is based on a misunderstanding of the true *gacaca* process. Not only did these lay judges possess what Timothy Longman calls 'contextual competence',[50] but, as pointed out above, *gacaca* was only used for low-level and less complex cases. As such, there was no need for these laymen to possess the complex knowledge of the due process required by international standards. Besides, having a

[48] It should be noted that these mechanisms have been used before for accountability of non-ICC offences.

[49] Article 39, Organic Law No. 16/2004 Establishing the organisation, competence and functioning of *gacaca* courts charged with prosecuting and trying the perpetrators of the crime of, genocide and other, crimes against humanity, committed between 1 October 1990 and 31 December 1994. This is with regard to investigation, prosecution and judgment.

[50] T Longman 'Justice at the Grassroots? Gacaca Trials in Rwanda' in N Roht-Arriaza and J Mariezcurrena (eds) *Transitional Justice in the Twenty-First Century: Beyond Truth Versus Justice* (2006) 219; S Thomson and R Nagy 'Law, Power and Justice: What Legalist Fails to Address in the Functioning of Rwanda's *Gacaca* Courts' (2011) 5 *The International Journal of Transitional Justice* 18.

fully trained judge preside over *gacaca* would effectively change *gacaca* court into an ordinary court, thus depriving it of its traditional character. Indeed, the existence of *gacaca* courts of this nature would be irrelevant and counterproductive as they completely negate the traditional justice model inherent in the *gacaca*.

Secondly, it has been argued that the right to legal representation was not recognised under *gacaca's* procedures.[51] This effectively compromises the right of an accused to legal representation. Notably, however, the traditional manner in which *gacaca* was conducted did not necessitate a legal representative. The entire community was given the right to participate either for or against an accused person, a community that had directly experienced crimes allegedly committed by an accused. Their evidence—whether in defence or accusation—of the accused person was based on actual facts of their experiences and not legalese. A decision by the bench, based on these presentations, was therefore regarded as direct justice to the victims as opposed to legal arguments. Moreover, given the fact that the presiding judges were lay persons it would have been counterproductive to have a trained legal representative. Phil Clark views the exclusion of legal representatives as fair since most accused persons could not afford them; by excluding them, *gacaca* became more participatory.[52]

Thirdly, it is also argued that the lack of documentary evidence in *gacaca* trials was highly compromising to due process.[53] This not only undermined evidentiary rules, but also weakened the outcome of *gacaca* courts. Apart from the lack of use of physical evidence,[54] *gacaca* trials had no police and judicial investigations.[55] Yet, the trials were discursive in nature. They relied entirely on testimony given by perpetrators, victims

[51] Article 64, Organic Law No. 16/2004.

[52] P Clark 'Hybridity, Holism and "Traditional" Justice: The Case of Gacaca Courts in Post-Genocide Rwanda' (2007) 39 (4) *George Washington International Law Review* 765–837.

[53] A Corey and SF Joireman 'Retributive Justice: The *Gacaca* Courts in Rwanda' (2004) 85 *African Affairs* 83.

[54] Ibid.

[55] Corey and Joireman 'Retributive Justice' (n 53); B Ingelaere '"Does the Truth Pass Across the Fire Without Burning?" Locating the Short Circuit in Rwanda's *Gacaca* Courts' (2009) 47 (4) *Journal of Modern African Studies* 516.

and bystanders.[56] Verbal testimony was sufficient to sustain a verdict.[57] One may argue, however, that the process left accused persons with no protection against misrepresentation of facts. This anomaly seems to have been cured by the requirement to corroborate the evidence adduced during the public participation processes.

Fourthly, it is argued that *gacaca* courts further lacked credibility in that some of its judges had been implicated and potential witnesses threatened.[58] Threats against witnesses indicate the weaknesses in the witness protection programme as well as the security of *gacaca* judges. Christopher Le Mon, for example, documents a chilling account of numerous witnesses in *gacaca* courts who were killed across the country in a brutal manner, including the president of a *gacaca* court in Gisanza.[59] These incidents raised fears among the public and largely contributed to a decline in public participation.[60] Yet not even the Western court system has water-tight witness protection. The ICC Office of the Prosecutor (OTP) has previously acknowledged that her reasons for her withdrawal of Kenyatta's case was due to deaths of 'several people who may have provided important evidence regarding Mr. Kenyatta's actions ... while others were too terrified to testify for the Prosecution'.[61]

Fierens further argues that the genocide effectiveness was such that perpetrators, co-perpetrators and accomplices could simply establish *gacaca* courts among themselves.[62] Several other commentators have acknowledged the sustained criticism that *gacaca* court was manipulated

[56] Ingelaere 'Does the Truth Pass Across the Fire Without Burning?' Locating the Short Circuit in Rwanda's *Gacaca* Courts' (n 55) 516.

[57] Ibid.

[58] J Fierens '*Gacaca* Courts: Between Fantasy and Reality' (2005) *Journal of International Criminal Justice* 12.

[59] CJ Le Mon 'Rwanda's Troubled *Gacaca* Courts' (2007) 14 (2) *Human Rights Brief* 17–18.

[60] Ibid.

[61] *Prosecutor v Uhuru Muigai Kenyatta* (Notice of withdrawal of the charges against Uhuru Muigai Kenyatta) ICC-01/09-02/11-983 (5 December 2014) Trial Chamber V(B); OTP 'Statement of the Prosecutor of the International Criminal Court, Fatou Bensouda, on the withdrawal of charges against Mr. Uhuru Muigai Kenyatta' (5 December 2014), https://www.icc-cpi.int/Pages/item.aspx?name=otp-statement-05-12-2014-2 (accessed 21 November 2020).

[62] Fierens '*Gacaca* Courts' (n 58 above) 12.

for political ends.[63] This has been termed the Tutsi version of victor's justice or revenge trials.[64] This already creates a perception of partiality, which undermines an accused's right to fair trial. Yet this criticism is not entirely true. *Gacaca* courts were not created arbitrarily. There was a proper legal framework for its incorporation in the transitional period as a traditional mechanism. It is therefore not entirely true that perpetrators would simply team up with co-perpetrators and accomplices and set up a *gacaca* court. An assertation of this kind only fuels widespread misconceptions about Africa's traditional mechanisms of justice.

Similarly, translated into 'drinking the herb of the Oput tree, blinding-bitter' in the Acholi language, *mato oput* is a traditional justice mechanism commonly practised among the Acholi people of Northern Uganda.[65] Unlike gacaca, this mechanism has never been used in the context of accountability for international crimes, as was the case with *gacaca*. This is merely a proposal by the Acholi community, the LRA leaders, the President of Uganda, academic debate among scholars, and civil society. The process is usually undertaken when misfortunes have befallen the offending clan, thus leading to social pressure on the perpetrator or his or her family to seek reconciliation.[66]

One major criticism of the *mato oput* process is the absence of the modern sense of punishment of the perpetrators. Yet, within the *mato oput* traditional process, punishment is first carried out by the spirits, as opposed to leaving the entire aspect to those overseeing the process. It is the spiritual punishment that prompts a process which is more reconciliatory. Nonetheless, the modern sense of punishment of the perpetrator is greatly downgraded in this process.

[63] MA Drumbl *Atrocity, Punishment and International Law* (2007) 193; Corey and Joireman 'Retributive Justice: The *Gacaca* Courts in Rwanda' (n 53); J Sarkin 'The Tension Between Justice and Reconciliation in Rwanda: Politics Human Rights, Due Process and the Role of the *Gacaca* Courts in Dealing with the Genocide' (2001) 45 (2) *Journal of African Law* 149; L Haberstock 'An Analysis of the Effectiveness of the *Gacaca* Court System in Post-Genocide Rwanda' (2014) 8 (4) *Global Tides* 10.

[64] As above.

[65] GS Gordon 'Complementarity and Alternative Justice' (2009) 88 (3) *Oregon Law Review* 247. It should be noted that *mato oput* is a mechanism used among one clan or tribe of the Acholi as a community and not throughout the entirety of northern Uganda, which has other tribes with different traditions.

[66] As above.

This chapter therefore holds the view that African mechanisms like the *gacaca* may have some weaknesses but that these are not sufficient to write off these mechanisms as accountability measures for international crimes. As alternative accountability mechanisms, traditional African approaches remain relevant in the war against impunity for international crimes and should be incorporated within national systems as recommended below.

4 A Framework for Institutionalising Complementarity Between the ICC and National Criminal Justice Systems in Africa

The practice of the ICC as well as numerous scholars have penned down frameworks necessary for effective implementation of positive complementarity. Key for these frameworks are the aspects of partnership, assistance, cooperation, vigilance, burden-sharing *et cetera*. Yet, all these frameworks put the action of the state at the fore and the ICC support only comes in later when required. This contribution envisages an understanding of positive complementarity to be one where both the ICC and states reinforce each other's efforts before, during and after criminal prosecution of international crimes. Thus, this contribution seeks to propose a framework of complementarity that not only institutionalises criminal prosecutions but also takes into account political, technical, economic aspects as well as African approaches to accountability.

Upon the operationalisation of the ICC, a group of experts was established in the year 2003 to reflect on the legal, policy and management issues likely to challenge the OTP as a result of the complementarity regime under the Rome Statute.[67] The framework advocated by this group of experts in one of partnership, cooperation and vigilance.[68] This framework was further underscored during the 2010 Kampala Review

[67] See generally, 'Paper on Some Policy Issues Before the Office of the Prosecutor, September 2003' http://icc-cpi.int/library/asp/LMO_20040906_En.pdf (accessed 30 March 2021).

[68] Office of the Prosecutor 'Informal Expert Paper: The Principle of Complementarity in Practice' ICC-OTP 2003 at 8–14 https://www.icc-cpi.int/RelatedRecords/CR2009_02250.PDF (accessed 30 March 2020).

Conference.[69] Scholars too echo a similar framework.[70] Essentially, while the ICC has to partner with states in ensuring accountability for international crimes, it ought to remain vigilant over the execution processes and to ensure that the investigations and subsequent prosecutions are genuine. Failure to meet this threshold the matter becomes admissible in accordance with the admissibility criteria established under article 17. Indeed, the OTP has since reiterated its observance of this framework in practice.[71]

At a policy level, the OTP also adopts positive complementarity which entails the prosecutor encouraging, and even assisting, national jurisdictions in prosecuting these crimes. This approach, nonetheless, has got its own limitations. The OTP acknowledges that its efforts in encouraging national prosecutions and working with national jurisdictions proceed only to the extent that they do not compromise any future admissibility proceedings.[72] The OTP notes that its interactions with national jurisdictions may extend to any of the following:

> monitoring activities, send in-country missions, request information on proceedings, hold consultations with national authorities as well as with intergovernmental and non-governmental organisations, participate in awareness-raising activities on the ICC, exchange lessons learned and best practices to support domestic investigative and prosecutorial strategies, and assist relevant stakeholders to identify pending impunity gaps and the scope for possible remedial measures.[73]

Although at policy level the prosecutor has adopted positive complementarity, at a practical level the prosecutor has, however, adopted an expanded form of positive complementarity. While the prosecutor encourages national prosecution, the prosecutor makes it clear that failure of

[69] Review Conference of the Rome Statute, Complementarity, Resolution RC/Res 6 8 June 2010.

[70] See generally, (n 5 & 6).

[71] ICC-OTP, 'Policy Paper on Preliminary Examination' (November 2013) para 102, https://www.icc-cpi.int/iccdocs/otp/OTP-Policy_Paper_Preliminary_Examinations_2013-ENG.pdf (accessed 2 May 2020).

[72] ICC-OTP, 'Policy Paper on Preliminary Examination' (November 2013) para 102, https://www.icc-cpi.int/iccdocs/otp/OTP-Policy_Paper_Preliminary_Examinations_2013-ENG.pdf (accessed 2 May 2020).

[73] As above.

national prosecutions would mean that either he/she will exercise *proprio motu* powers to investigate.[74] This version of positive complementarity is what Will Colish describes as 'hybrid complementarity—a mixture of incentives and threats, on the one hand, and support and mutual assistance on the other'.[75] This section nuances further this concept of a hybrid complementarity in a manner that broadens its scope and also institutionalises it.

This chapter broadens complementarity to include African approaches to justice in transitional societies. In its report, the AU acknowledged that 'in many developing and post-conflict societies where formal justice lacks capacity and does not have legitimacy among the people, various forms of customary courts step into the gap to deliver justice'.[76] This, coupled with the practice where states have experimented with traditional justice mechanisms, necessitates a consideration on how to incorporate traditional mechanisms within the institutionalised complementarity.

Concerning institutionalisation, the experts report urges the ICC and the Assembly of State Parties to develop an action plan for effective complementarity.[77] Such an action plan would act as a basis for institutionalised complementarity. In order to ensure that national criminal justice systems are enabled and ready for positive complementarity this contribution proposes a framework that institutionalises both substantive and procedural aspects of complementarity. Technical assistance, enactment of legislations, capacity building, physical infrastructure, definition of roles for various stakeholders like the civil society, regional entities, the donor community are key aspects for effective complementarity.[78] Local

[74] Statement by the ICC prosecutor on the Situation in Guinea, 15 September 2010 https://www.icc-cpi.int/NR/rdonlyres/2F445DAF-DC4D-4D0C-9160-04634AED23EA/282481/TranslationofGuineaStatementREVIEWEDENG.pdf (accessed 6 September 2020).

[75] W Colish 'The International Criminal Court in Guinea: A Case Study of Complementarity' 26 (2) *Revue Québécoise de Droit International*, Colish 'The International Criminal Court in Guinea: A Case Study of Complementarity' (2013) 34.

[76] *Report of the African Union Commission of Inquiry on South Sudan* para 292.

[77] Office of the Prosecutor 'Informal Expert Paper: The Principle of Complementarity in Practice' ICC-OTP 2003 at 8–14 https://www.icc-cpi.int/RelatedRecords/CR2009_02250.PDF page 22.

[78] See generally Proceedings of the Kampala Review Conference on the Rome Statute, by the Focal points (Denmark and South Africa) RC/ST/CM/INF.2 30 May 2010.

legitimacy and the establishment of a conducive political environment too are essential factors to effective complementarity.

The overall structure of complementarity must be anchored in the law. First and foremost, every African state must ensure ratification of the Rome Statute and its domestication in accordance to their respective rules that govern the application of international law in national courts. It is here that the Assembly of State Parties, the AU and the civil society have a crucial role to lobby states and create awareness on this aspect. Second, every African state should enact its national implementing legislation on complementarity. A national legal framework is necessary in laying down the institutional infrastructure and the rules and regulations necessary for effective complementarity. Noting that complementarity entails cooperation of several actors like other states, the donor community, regional entities, the respective government and civil society, the law must lay down the mode of engagement of these players. It must also provide for the role of the various institutions like witness protection system or the victim protection unit in fulfilling the key aspects of complementarity. For example, it can make provision on economic requirements, infrastructure, capacity building and various forms of assistance. For example, it may provide for the role of the state in establishing the infrastructure of national courts, investigatory facilities such as forensic laboratories and their personnel, physical infrastructure for prosecuting officers set apart for international crimes or prison facilities. While this may not require the ICC to fund the projects, it may foster collaborative efforts among states, regional entities, the international donor community and civil society to ensure their realisation. Provision of technical assistance and capacity building as applicable to the investigatory departments, the prosecution department and the judicial organ, including the defence counsels and the council for victims are equally of importance. The Kampala Review Conference report envisage this kind of assistance to include trainings of the police.[79] It is also significant that states involve civil society in capacity building.[80]

https://asp.icc-cpi.int/en_menus/asp/complementarity/Documents/RC-ST-CM-INF.2-ENG.pdf (accessed 15 May 2021).

[79] Report of the Bureau at Eighth Resumed Session, para 17.

[80] Human Rights Watch 'Civil Society Declaration on Africa and the Review Conference of the Rome Statute of the International Criminal Court' 24

States whose justice system utilise traditional mechanisms should also provide for a formal link between national criminal mechanisms and traditional approaches or procedures. States will, therefore, have to undertake three important roles in this regard. To begin with, they will have to ensure they harmonise all traditional approaches within their respective jurisdictions. This is because, in most countries, there are diverse communities with varied traditional approaches. Furthermore, traditional approaches should undergo some limited formalisation to enable their formal recognition. For example, there should be a linkage between national justice systems and the traditional mechanisms. This linkage could assume, for instance, the three forms suggested by Gregory Gordon.[81] First, the traditional mechanisms can rely on national courts for enforcement of their orders.[82] Secondly, the national judicial system could be the ultimate appeal body for perpetrators aggrieved by decisions made by traditional mechanisms.[83] In this regard, every accused person will be expected to first pass through the traditional mechanism as a prerequisite of exhausting local remedies. This kind of linkage must be carefully crafted. Due consideration must be given to the nature of international crimes whose perpetrators and victims are likely to spread beyond a particular community or country, thus involving persons who do not necessarily ascribe to some of these traditional approaches. Thirdly, the traditional mechanisms could be integrated within the national judicial system, as was the case with *gacaca*.[84] Some general guidelines in this regard can be adopted at the AU level. Furthermore, states will have to undertake a general documentation of the harmonised traditional approaches. As the anthropologist Tim Allen notes, there is a lack of systematic documentation of *mato oput* despite the variations in its practices and ceremonies even among the Acholi community

May 2010 https://www.hrw.org/news/2010/05/24/civil-society-declaration-africa-and-review-conference-romestatute-international (accessed 12 April 2021).

[81] GS Gordon 'Complementarity and Alternative Justice' (2009) 88 (3) *Oregon Law Review*, 677.

[82] As above.

[83] As above.

[84] As above.

itself.[85] Documentation would not only create certainty of procedures and substantive content of the practice, but also enable an easy linkage between the traditional mechanisms and any other formal criminal mechanisms, whether national or international. Documentation would also enable a precise articulation of the specificities that certain traditional concepts of justice entail, thereby ensuring consistency and transparency in their adjudication. As Metz suggests, it may also call for a refashioning of this concept in order to ensure that its ideals are construed in the light of current situations.[86] In doing the documentations, states may need to consult the respective communities in order to guard against false information. Thus, traditional justice procedures can be incorporated within national criminal justice systems in so far as accountability for international crimes is concerned.

However, this contribution argues that the various African traditional procedures should be limited to resolving post-conflict disputes involving the second or third tier of perpetrators of international crimes within the African region. These should include those perpetrators whose level of involvement precludes them from prosecution as bearing the highest responsibility and subjects them to alternative national mechanisms. This would assuage any fears surrounding the challenge of treating all traditional approaches as monolithic and with the ability to complement the ICC. Every state is, therefore, allowed to legislate on the manner in which their respective traditional approaches inter-relates with its national criminal justice system with respect to second- and third-tier perpetrators of international crimes. Those bearing most responsibility should, however, not be dealt with through these traditional mechanisms. The question as to how these traditional approaches relate to the ICC will therefore not arise. This is because their target group will be very different. It is therefore the role of the respective states to ensure that it adopts appropriate rules and regulations that offer substantive guidance on the criteria to be used in identifying individuals who are subject to these traditional approaches. This could involve, for instance, categorising the offences,

[85] T Allen 'War and Justice in Northern-Uganda: An Assessment of the International Criminal Court's Intervention' (2005), https://www.files.ethz.ch/isn/56421/2005-02_AllenICCReport.pdf (accessed 16 January 2017).

[86] T Metz 'Ubuntu as a Moral Theory and Human Rights in South Africa' (2011) 11 *African Human Rights Law Journal* 536.

then allocating minor offences or misdemeanours to these traditional mechanisms.

By ratifying international treaties, states bind themselves to diligently carry out their responsibilities under these treaties in good faith.[87] This implies that, with respect to fulfilling the Rome Statute principle of complementarity, a state must ensure that its municipal criminal mechanisms adhere to the required standards. This would require, for instance, the local traditional mechanisms to have investigatory powers as well as follow established rules of due process. Local traditional mechanisms that lack these aspects cannot therefore complement the ICC or a similar international tribunal. Nonetheless, it is important that national criminal justice systems adopt a comprehensive definition of justice—and not just limit it to ICC-approach of justice but also extend it to traditional African approaches to justice.

National legislation must also address the difficult question of conditional amnesty. Most traditional procedures grant amnesty or pardon as a prerequisite for reconciliation. Every state must make it clear whether conditional amnesty should be allowed, and if so, the conditions upon which it is to be granted. By enacting the Amnesty Act of 2000, Uganda, for example, extended amnesty to all those individuals who had engaged in combat since 1986.[88] This was meant to facilitate cessation of violence and reintegration and resettlement of former combatants into society. The Act encouraged reconciliation and 'any other function that is associated or connected with the execution of the functions stipulated in [the] Act'.[89] It is in keeping with this provision that, according to Cecily Rose, the Ugandan Amnesty Commission encouraged traditional cleansing ceremonies, thus promoting reconciliation.[90]

The legislations institutionalising complementarity could offer further guidance on the question of conditional amnesty, particularly with respect to second- and third-level perpetrators of international crimes. Although

[87] Article 26, Vienna Convention on the Law of Treaties, 1969.

[88] C Rose 'Looking Beyond Amnesty and Traditional Justice and Reconciliation Mechanisms in Northern Uganda: A Proposal for Truth-Telling and Reparations' (2008) 28 (2) *Boston College Third World Law Journal*.

[89] Sections 9 (c)–(e), Amnesty Act of Uganda of 2000.

[90] Rose 'Looking Beyond Amnesty and Traditional Justice and Reconciliation Mechanisms in Northern Uganda' (n 88) 359.

this study recognises that a state has an obligation to prosecute international crimes, it argues that this is not an absolute responsibility. Moreover, some writers have argued that there is a customary international law obligation, or at least an emerging one, on the duty to prosecute international crimes.[91] It is argued here, though, that this does not represent the true position in international law. Save in the case of Genocide,[92] the duty to prosecute does not exclude other measures of accountability. While the prohibition of some international crimes is a customary law and, in some instances, even *jus cogens* norms, it does not mean that prosecution of these crimes is the only accountability measure and that the requirement to prosecute is either customary international law norm or *jus cogens*. Thus, accountability measures could take other forms in order to dispense different forms of justice to the victims. Justice does not always imply prosecution, and it does not bar those involved from facing alternative accountability measures. Adam Branch strongly supports this reasoning, stating as follows in relation to the ICC's intervention in Uganda:

> The decision, on the one hand, to seek justice through punishment or, on the other, to forgo punishment in favour of justice through reconciliation, is a decision that must be made by the concrete community that is the victim of the crimes and that will have to live with the consequences of the decision. "Humanity" is too thin a community upon which to base a universal right to punish... If local injustice is the price to be paid for the kind of international justice that results from ICC prosecution, then we must abandon the Court and imagine new modes of building a truly global rule of law.[93]

[91] R Memari 'The Duty to Prosecute Crimes Against Humanity Under Universal Jurisdiction, Customary International Law, and Conventional International Law' (2012) 31 *International Proceedings of Economics Development and Research* 131.

[92] In *Reservations to the Convention on Genocide, Advisory Opinion [1951] ICJ Reports 8*, the ICJ acknowledged the customary international law nature of the Genocide Convention. However, the Genocide Convention limits the absolute duty to prosecute to the offence of genocide alone.

[93] A Branch 'International Justice, Local Injustice: The International Criminal Court in Northern Uganda' (2004) *Dissent* 5; T Allen 'War and Justice in Northern-Uganda: An Assessment of the International Criminal Court's Intervention' (2005) 65, https://www.files.ethz.ch/isn/56421/2005-02_AllenICCReport.pdf (accessed 16 January 2021).

Thus, accountability through traditional mechanisms suffices in certain exceptional circumstances, particularly in relation to those who do not bear the highest responsibility for international crimes. This is important especially at the grass-roots level in order to end the vicious circle of conflict and unending victimhood. In the event that states are willing to grant amnesty to low-level perpetrators, those granted amnesty could also be subjected to traditional mechanisms for purposes of reconciliation and restoration.

National legislation institutionalising complementarity should therefore recognise African traditional procedures. A study can be conducted at the regional level to develop a general framework that should further guide states on the applicability of traditional approaches within the context of international crimes. In particular, the rules should offer guidance on the relationship between these mechanism and national prosecution mechanism; the criteria applicable when deciding the levels of perpetrators to face the traditional mechanisms or national prosecution as well as those to face prosecution in an international forum in the event of failure of national mechanism and the applicability of amnesties or pardons in these traditional approaches.

The current policy and practice of complementarity portray the role of the ICC to be that of advocacy and nothing more. This study advocates for the need to adopt the necessary legislative rules and regulations in which a clear institutional structure is established to implement positive complementarity between the ICC and states. Again, within the OTP, an office mandated to monitor positive complementarity should be established. This office can act as an early warning sign with respect to states inability to effect complementarity and thus prompting the need to strengthen efforts towards partnership or cooperation with such states in instituting mechanisms that guarantee effective cooperation. This may not necessarily require the ICC to directly carryout all the necessary assistance required. As the Kampala Review Conference correctly notes,[94] the ICC may act as a catalyst in initiating the efforts towards effective complementarity through collaborative efforts of international actors, the donor community, other states, regional organisations, the civil society *et cetera*.

[94] See generally Review Conference of the Rome Statute Draft Resolution on Complementarity ICCASP/8/Res.9 Annex VII 8 June 2010; MO Owuor 'The International Criminal Court and Positive Complementarity: Legal and Institutional Framework' LLD Thesis, University of Pretoria (2017) 173.

This will neither detract the ICC from its core functions nor will it have a huge budgetary implication.

Besides, there lacks coordination of the application of complementarity on the continent. The practice is fragmented and lacks coherence among African states. The ICC in conjunction with African states must establish national focal points within every country's criminal justice system for coordination and monitoring of complementarity at the national level. It is this office that should constantly liaise with the ICC monitoring body on aspects of inability to implement complementarity and therefore the different forms of assistance, government initiatives in this regard and their deficiencies.

Political good will and political interference with the judiciary are also essential factors that undermine effective complementarity. History has shown that the ICC easily enjoy political goodwill of heads of states and senior state officials whenever any prospective indictees originate from political opponents.[95] The contrary is true where investigations are launched against state officials. A report has noted the need for states to adopt a wide range of measures such as reinforcing judicial independence, strengthening capacity and independence as well as political support.[96] Where the sitting political elites are a potential target, the ICC may seek to have the AU through the ASP exert the relevant political pressure in order to ensure accountability. This argument presupposes that the ICC will have to ensure existing collaborative efforts with the AU in order to enjoy its support in such crisis.

5 Concluding Remarks

The tension between the ICC and African states has compromised the fight against impunity for international crimes in Africa. One way to surmount this challenge is through expanding the scope of the principle and practice of complementarity. Rather than a restrictive approach in the interpretation and the practice of this principle, which puts the actions of

[95] See for example the case of Uganda in W Schabas 'The International Criminal Court at Ten' (2011) *Criminal Law Forum* 503.

[96] See generally International Centre for Transitional Justice synthesis report 'Supporting Complementarity At the National Level: from Theory to Practice' Greentree Estate, Manhasset New York 25–26 October 2012 para 6 available at http://www.ictj.org/sites/default/files/ICTJ-Report-Greentree-III-Synthesis-ENG-2012.pdf.

states at the fore and only in the aftermath of conflict, this contribution has advocated for a mind shift in a manner that expands the scope and institutionalises the principle of complementarity. As such, both the ICC and African states have to reinforce each other's efforts towards national prosecution of international crimes through a well-established structure of institutionalised complementarity. This structure should embody all the normative and practical aspects of complementarity and will involve several players including regional entities like the AU, the ASP, the donor community, the ICC OTP, the civil society and the states themselves. National legislation will specify the roles and mode of engagement for each of these players. This structure should neither perceive the ICC to be a donor nor compromise its judicial role as established under the Rome Statute. Rather, it should perceive the ICC as an overall observer who acts as a catalyst to prompt certain actions in order to ensure that the criminal justice system of every state is ready to prosecute international crimes whenever they occur.

Bibliography

Book Chapters

Asaala EO 'Prosecuting the 2007 Post Election Violence-Related International Crimes in Kenyan Courts: Exposing the real challenges' in Mbondenyi M, Asaala E, Kabau T and Waris A (eds) *Human Rights and Democratic Governance in Kenya: A Post-2007 Appraisal* (2015).

Asaala EO 'The International Criminal Court Factor on Transitional Justice in Kenya' in Ambos K and Maunganidze AO (eds) *Power and Prosecutions: Challenges and Opportunities for International Criminal Justice in Sub-Saharan Africa* (2010).

Bassiouni C 'Introduction to International Criminal Law' in Bassiouni C (ed) *Post-Conflict Justice, International and Comparative Law Series* (2002).

Benzing M 'The Complementarity Regime of the International Criminal Court' (2003) 7 *Max Planck Yearbook of United Nations Law.*

Drumbl MA *Atrocity, Punishment and International Law* (2007).

Longman T 'Justice at the Grassroots? Gacaca Trials in Rwanda' in Roht-Arriaza N and Mariezcurrena J (eds) *Transitional Justice in the Twenty-First Century: Beyond Truth Versus Justice* (2006).

Oola S 'In the Shadow of Kwoyelo's Trial: The ICC and Complementarity in Uganda' in de Vos C, Kendall S and Stahn C (eds) *Contested Justice: The Politics and Practice of International Criminal Court Interventions* (2015).

Ryngaert C 'Horizontal Complementarity' in Stahn C and Zeidy M (eds) *The International Criminal Court and Complementarity: From Theory to Practice* Vol. 2 (2011).

Stahn C 'Taking Complementarity Seriously: On the Sense and Sensibility of "Classical", "Positive" and "Negative" Complementarity' in Stahn C and Zeidy M (eds) *The International Criminal Court and Complementarity: From Theory to Practice* Vol. 2 (2011).

Journal Articles

Branch A 'International Justice, Local Injustice: The International Criminal Court in Northern Uganda' (2004) *Dissent*.

Burke-White WW 'Proactive Complementarity: The International Criminal Courts in the Rome System of International Justice' (2008) (1) *Harvard International Law Journal*.

Clark P 'Hybridity, Holism and "Traditional" Justice: The Case of Gacaca Courts in Post-Genocide Rwanda' (2007) 39 (4) *George Washington International Law Review*.

Colish W 'The International Criminal Court in Guinea: A Case Study of Complementarity' (2013) 26 (2) *Revue Québécoise de Droit International*

Corey A and Joireman SF 'Retributive Justice: The *Gacaca* Courts in Rwanda' (2004) 85 *African Affairs* 83.

Fierens J '*Gacaca* Courts: Between Fantasy and Reality' (2005) *Journal of International Criminal Justice* 12.

Gordon GS 'Complementarity and Alternative Justice' (2009) 88 (3) *Oregon Law Review*.

Haberstock L 'An Analysis of the Effectiveness of the *Gacaca* Court System in Post-Genocide Rwanda' (2014) 8 (4) *Global Tides*.

Høgestøl SAE 'The Habré Judgment at the Extraordinary African Chambers: A Singular Victory in the Fight Against Impunity' (2016) 34 (3) *Nordic Journal of Human Rights*.

Ingelaere B '"Does the Truth Pass Across the Fire Without Burning?" Locating the Short Circuit in Rwanda's *Gacaca* Courts' (2009) 47 (4) *Journal of Modern African Studies*.

Le Mon CJ 'Rwanda's Troubled *Gacaca* Courts' (2007) 14 (2) *Human Rights Brief*.

Memari R 'The Duty to Prosecute Crimes Against Humanity Under Universal Jurisdiction, Customary International Law, and Conventional International Law' (2012) 31 *International Proceedings of Economics Development and Research*.

Metz T 'Ubuntu as a Moral Theory and Human Rights in South Africa' (2011) 11 *African Human Rights Law Journal*.

Rose C 'Looking Beyond Amnesty and Traditional Justice and Reconciliation Mechanisms in Northern Uganda: A Proposal for Truth-Telling and Reparations' (2008) 28 (2) *Boston College Third World Law Journal*.

Sarkin J 'The Tension Between Justice and Reconciliation in Rwanda: Politics Human Rights, Due Process and the Role of the *Gacaca* Courts in Dealing with the Genocide' (2001) 45 (2) *Journal of African Law*.

Schabas W 'The International Criminal Court at Ten' (2011) *Criminal Law Forum*.

Thomson S and Nagy R 'Law, Power and Justice: What Legalist Fails to Address in the Functioning of Rwanda's *Gacaca* Courts' (2011) 5 *The International Journal of Transitional Justice*.

Policy Papers

Du Plessis M 'The International Criminal Court and Its Work in Africa: Confronting the Myths' ISS Monograph No. 173 (2008).

Du Plessis M 'The International Criminal Court That Africa Wants' ISS Monograph No. 172 (2010).

AU Assembly 'Decision on the International Criminal Court (ICC)' Assembly/AU/Dec.622(XXVIII).

Doc. EX.CL/1006(XXX), 28th Ordinary Session, 30–31 January 2017.

Review Conference of the Rome Statute, Complementarity, Resolution RC/Res 6 8 June 2010.

ICC-OTP, 'Policy Paper on Preliminary Examination' (November 2013) para 102, https://www.icc-cpi.int/iccdocs/otp/OTP-Policy_Paper_Preliminary_Examinations_2013-ENG.pdf.

Reports

Report on the Proceedings of the 2010 Kampala Review Conference.

Review Conference of the Rome Statute Draft Resolution on Complementarity ICCASP/8/Res.9 Annex VII 8 June 2010.

Report of the African Union Commission of Inquiry on South Sudan.

Proceedings of the Kampala Review Conference on the Rome Statute, by the Focal points (Denmark and South Africa) RC/ST/CM/INF.2 30 May 2010.

Case Law

Uganda v. Thomas Kwoyelo alias Latoni, HCT-00-ICD-Case No. 02/10.

Thomas Kwoyelo Alias Latoni v Uganda Constitutional Petition No. 036/11 [Arising Out of HCT-00-ICD-Case No. 2/10] Ruling of the Court of 22 September 2011 (Constitutional Court of Uganda).

Ministère Public v Hissene Habré, Judgment of 30 May 2016, Chambre Africaine Extraiordinaire d'Assises, available at http://www.chambresafricaines.org/pdf/Jugement_complet.pdf.

Court of Cassation, *première chambre statuant en matière pénale, Souleymane Guengueng et al.* v *Hissène Habré,* Judgment No. 14, 20 March 2001.

Prosecutor v Uhuru Muigai Kenyatta (Notice of withdrawal of the charges against Uhuru Muigai Kenyatta) ICC-01/09–02/11–983 (5 December 2014) Trial Chamber V(B).

In *Reservations to the Convention on Genocide, Advisory Opinion [1951) ICJ Reports 8.*

Thesis

Acirokop P *Accountability for Mass Atrocities: The LRA Conflict in Uganda*, LLD Thesis, University of Pretoria (2013), Chapter 5, https://repository.up.ac.za/bitstream/handle/2263/23898/06chapter6.pdf?sequence=7.

Owuor MO 'The International Criminal Court and Positive Complementarity: Legal and Institutional Framework' LLD Thesis, University of Pretoria (2017).

Internet Sources

Allen T 'War and Justice in Northern-Uganda: An Assessment of the International Criminal Court's Intervention' (2005), https://www.files.ethz.ch/isn/56421/2005-02_AllenICCReport.pdf.

AU 'Withdrawal Strategy Document' (Version 12.01.2017) para 8, available at https://www.hrw.org/sites/default/files/supporting_resources/icc_withdrawal_strategy_jan._2017.pdf.

BBC News 'Chad's Hissen Habré Removed from Senegal Court' (20 July 2015), www.bbc.com/news/world-africa-33592142.

Communiqué de presse: Démarrage des audiences du procès en appel' (29 December 2016), http://www.chambresafricaines.org/index.php/le-coin-des-medias/communiqu%C3%A9-de-presse/649-communiqu%C3%A9-de-presse-d%C3%A9marrage-des-audiences-du-proc%C3%A8s-en-appel.html.

https://asp.icc-cpi.int/en_menus/asp/complementarity/Documents/RC-ST-CM-INF.2-ENG.pdf (accessed 15 May 2021).

Human Rights Watch 'Civil Society Declaration on Africa and the Review Conference of the Rome Statute of the International Criminal Court'

(24 May 2010), https://www.hrw.org/news/2010/05/24/civil-society-declaration-africa-and-review-conference-romestatute-international.
ICTJ 'The Accountability landscape in Eastern DRC: Analysis of the National Legislative and Judicial Response to International Crimes (2009–2014)', https://www.ictj.org/sites/default/files/ICTJ-Briefing-DRC-Prosecutions-2015_1.pdf.
International Criminal Court, 'Situations Under Investigation', https://www.icc-cpi.int/pages/situations.aspx (Accessed 12 November 2020).
International Centre for Transitional Justice synthesis report 'Supporting Complementarity at the National Level: From Theory to Practice' Greentree Estate, Manhasset New York (25–26 October 2012) available at http://www.ictj.org/sites/default/files/ICTJ-Report-Greentree-III-Synthesis-ENG-2012.pdf.
Nakandha S 'The Kwoyelo Case at the ICD: The Realities of Complementarity in Practice', https://www.ijmonitor.org/2016/05/the-kwoyelo-case-at-the-icd-the-realities-of-complementarity-in-practice/.
Nakandha S 'Supreme Court of Uganda Rules on the Application of the Amnesty Act' (16 April 2015), www.ijmonitor.org/2015/04/supreme-court-ofuganda-rules-on-the-application-of-the-amnesty-act/.
Office of the Prosecutor 'Informal Expert Paper: The Principle of Complementarity in Practice' ICC-OTP 2003 at 8–14, www.icc-cpi.int_iccdocs_doc_doc654724.pdf.
OTP 'Statement of the Prosecutor of the International Criminal Court, Fatou Bensouda, on the Withdrawal of Charges Against Mr. Uhuru Muigai Kenyatta' (5 December 2014), https://www.icc-cpi.int/Pages/item.aspx?name=otp-statement-05-12-2014-2.
Paper on Some Policy Issues Before the Office of the Prosecutor (September 2003), http://icc-cpi.int/library/asp/LMO_20040906_En.pdf.
Report of the African Union Commission of Inquiry on South Sudan 1 (15 October 2014), http://www.peaceau.org/uploads/auciss.final.report.pdf.
Statement by the ICC prosecutor on the Situation in Guinea (15 September 2010), https://www.icc-cpi.int/NR/rdonlyres/2F445DAF-DC4D-4D0C-9160-04634AED23EA/282481/TranslationofGuineaStatementREVIEWED ENG.pdf.

African Restorative Justice Approaches as Complementarity: The Case of Libya

Emma Charlene Lubaale and James Carkeek

1 Introduction

Complementary is at the heart of the international criminal justice regime under the Rome Statute of the International Criminal Court (ICC). In terms of this notion, national justice systems are to play a central role in fostering accountability for international crimes, with the ICC being a court of last resort. The Rome Statute makes it explicit that the ICC is complementary to "national criminal jurisdictions"[1] and in breathing life to the notion of complementarity, most African states have focused on

[1] United Nations General Assembly, Rome Statute of the International Criminal Court, adopted on 17 July 1998 and came into force in 2002. Article 1 and Preamble (Hereinafter, Rome Statute).

E. C. Lubaale (✉)
Faculty of Law, Rhodes University, Eastern Cape, South Africa
e-mail: e.lubaale@ru.ac.za

J. Carkeek
Pupil Member of the Pretoria Society of Advocates, Pretoria, South Africa
e-mail: james@npnauto.co.za

E. C. Lubaale and N. Dyani-Mhango (eds.), *National Accountability for International Crimes in Africa*,
https://doi.org/10.1007/978-3-030-88044-6_7

criminal prosecution rather than restorative justice.[2] But while emphasis has generally been placed on the punitive approach to justice, post-conflict African states have multiple competing needs, over and above the punishment of those responsible for the crimes committed. Among these are: reconciliation, peace, rebuilding of the economy, reparations, addressing the root causes of conflict and healing.

Libya, a non-state party to the Rome Statute, is one of the states grappling with these competing needs. The situation in Libya, currently before the ICC, pertains to the atrocities committed during and after the reign of Muamar Gadhafi, the former president of Libya.[3] War crimes and crimes against humanity were allegedly committed and warrants of arrest have been issued by the ICC against various suspects including Saif Gadhafi (the son of late Muamar Gadhafi).[4] At the national level, criminal proceedings have been ongoing. However, aside from undermining various human rights guarantees, they have been one-sided (i.e. targeting the former Gadhafi regime) and as a result, caused further divisiveness among Libyans. Hardly any efforts have been made to address the root causes of the conflict, or, the much-needed healing, reparation and reconciliation to ensure that Libya moves past the disastrous effects of the conflict. An approach that effectively blends criminal prosecution and restorative justice approaches could go a long way in ensuring that Libya's post-conflict justice mechanisms deliver on the competing needs of this country. Moreover, like many African states, Libya already has traditional justice mechanisms presided over by tribal leaders which could provide a solid framework for invoking a blended approach to post-conflict justice in Libya. However, would an approach that places traditional justice mechanisms at the centre of accountability be on par with Libya's obligations under the Rome Statute which, among others, refers to "investigations" or "prosecution"?

[2] See generally the strategies invoked in post-conflict states in Africa including Uganda, Libya, Sudan, Kenya, the Democratic Republic of the Congo, Mali, the Central African Republic and Cote d Ivoire.

[3] C Yakinthou, C Buff, and L Clifford, *Advancing Transitional Justice in Conflict-Affected Contexts: A Case Study for Libya* (2016) 1–19.

[4] *The Prosecutor v Saif Al-Islam Gadhafi*, https://www.icc-cpi.int/libya/gaddafi, accessed 20 May 2021.

Much has been written on the subject of criminal prosecution, its limits and the prospects of restorative approaches in Africa. Minow[5] engages with the question of the compatibility alternative justice mechanisms with the Rome Statute framework. The author draws on African countries including Rwanda, South Africa and Uganda. However, the complexities peculiar to Libya are not explored. Libya presents a unique situation. Not only does it have unique restorative justice approaches that have potential to respond to the volatile environment in Libya, it is also not a state party to the Rome Statute. From the perspective of treaty law obligations, Libya is not under obligation to align itself with ICC-inclined approaches such as its emphasis on criminal prosecutions to the exclusion of other justice approaches. How is it then that Libya still struggles to invoke a justice approach that accords due regard to the already operational restorative justice approaches in Libya? The discussion in this chapter also moves away from an approach that "others" African restorative approaches. Minow, in her work, still views African traditional approaches as "alternatives," an approach that still entrenches the view that criminal prosecutions are the ideal or acceptable form of justice. Elsewhere, Lubaale[6] has engaged with the subject of alternative justice mechanisms in Africa. Drawing on situations in states including Uganda and Rwanda, the author has used the lens of legal pluralism to demonstrate the role of traditional justice mechanisms in international criminal justice. The author, however, fails to grapple with the issue of the practicality of this lens in a state which is not under obligations to invoke a punitive approach such as Libya.

Cryer,[7] in a 2010 publication, engaged with a subject similar to some of the key issues raised in this chapter. The author engaged with approaches that can complement or serve as alternatives to criminal prosecutions. None of the mechanisms discussed in Cyer's work does so within

[5] M Minow, 'Do Alternative Justice Mechanisms Deserve Recognition in International Criminal Law?: Truth Commissions, Amnesties, and Complementarity at the International Criminal Court' (2019)60 *Harvard International Law Journal* 1–45.

[6] EC Lubaale, 'Legal Pluralism as a Lens Through Which to Understand the Role and Place of TJMS in International Criminal Justice' (2020) *Journal of Legal Pluralism and Unofficial Law* 180–202.

[7] R Cryer, 'Alternatives and Complements to Criminal Prosecution' in R Cryer et al. (eds) *An Introduction to International Criminal Law and Procedure* (Cambridge University Press 2012) 561–578.

the unique context of Libya. Moreover, Cryer's work couldn't have been in position to engage in such a discussion because the Libya issue was only referred to the ICC in 2011, a year after the publication. Akhavan[8] confronts the old-age peace versus justice debate which he describes as some form of "judicial romantism." He demonstrates that the interventions by the ICC in Africa have not necessarily impeded peace. Rather, such interventions are more likely to help prevent atrocities. Adopting a slightly different perspective, the discussion in this chapter does not dismiss criminal prosecution. Rather, it underscores the role and place of African restorative justice approaches where such need arises. Effectively, the issue is not whether or not the ICC should intervene through criminal prosecution. Rather, it is that where African restorative justice mechanisms have the potential to deliver on post-conflict justice, the ICC should be prepared to give way to these approaches without necessarily labelling them barbaric or not good enough to deliver on justice. Sarkin[9] grapples with the issue of "how conditional amnesties can assist transitional societies in delivering on the right to the truth." The discussion in this chapter draws on the viewpoints advanced by this author and goes on to demonstrate their practicality in the context of Libya. In this chapter, we also demonstrate how traditional justice mechanisms can help breath life to the views of authors like Sarkin. All the relevant literature closely related to the subject under discussion in this chapter cannot be exhausted. What is indisputable, however, is the fact no work has thus far engaged with restorative justice as a form of complementarity in a non-state party to the Rome Statute, i.e. Libya.

Based on the above scholarly gap, the purpose of this chapter is to underscore the role and place of African restorative approaches in post-conflict states such as Libya and to debunk narratives of the non-suitedness of traditional justice mechanisms for international crimes. At the heart of the discussion is the emphasis that African restorative justice approaches should be recognised as justice approaches in their own right and not alternatives. The chapter goes on to demonstrate that while previous attempts to invoke traditional justice mechanisms in international criminal justice have been met with resistance and dubbed inadequate to

[8] P Akhavan, 'Are International Criminal Tribunals a Disincentive to Peace? Reconciling Judicial Romanticism with Political Realism' (2009)31 *Human Rights Quarterly* 624–654.

[9] JJ Sarkin, 'How Conditional Amnesties Can Assist Transitional Societies in Delivering on the Right to the Truth' (2017)6 *International Human rights Law Review* 143–175.

address international crimes, placing them at the centre of international criminal justice would not undermine Libya's obligations. The chapter is divided into six sections including the introduction. Section two engages with the United Nations Security Council's (UNSC's) referral of the situation of Libya to the ICC. It demonstrates how, despite not being a party to the Rome Stature, Libya is having to be bound by the Rome Statute regime of complementarity as well as the interpretation that has been accorded to this regime. This section also addresses the issue of intrusion into one of the core concepts of the international order—that of consent of parties to international treaties. The third section discusses the crisis of post-conflict justice in Libya by underscoring the limits of the various post-conflict approaches that have been invoked thus far to breathe life to the notion of complementarity. Having pointed out the limitations of the mechanisms already in place in Libya, section four engages with the prospects of traditional justice mechanisms, in particular, the potential of the tenets of these mechanisms to speak to the post-conflict needs of Libya. The fifth section assesses African traditional justice mechanisms in the light of the Rome Statute complementarity regime and arrives at the conclusion that the Rome Statute places no obligation on states to prosecute, let alone, to invoke punitive approaches to the exclusion of all other approaches in post-conflict justice. The sixth section draws a conclusion and makes appropriate recommendations.

2 UNSC Council Referrals and Treaty Law: How Did Libya Become Subject to the Complementarity Regime?

International law is comprised of many sources. Treaties, custom and judicial decisions remain the predominant ones among them. Like any legal system, these sources are often in conflict with each other. This is increasingly evident in a globalised world where international agreements play a larger role on a daily basis. This conflict is not simply between one type of source, say treaty law, and another, say custom, but often between existing treaties. One need only look at the debate around Head of State immunities and the obligation to arrest Omar Al-Bashir to see how these conflicts play out. In fact, it is to be expected from a treaty such as the Rome Statute[10] that it will upset the existing legal order.

The pluralistic nature of the sources of international law is one of its biggest strengths, however, it also becomes a weakness and a stumbling block for its development. International law can develop either through the organic development of custom or through treaty law, specifically those treaties known as "law-making treaties."[11] These are treaties in which obligations that are general norms are created. They are not single event obligations where a single compliance will discharge the obligation. Rather, they create a system of norms and rules to govern the parties. The Vienna Convention on the Law of Treaties[12] can quite easily be seen as being a law-making treaty. However, the consequence of the increased use of treaty law is that where those treaties incorporate customary law, the treaty puts a freeze on the development of that custom. The treaty takes that custom and then sets that as the standard that cannot continue to grow and develop organically but rather, amended when the treaty is amended, if ever.[13]

2.1 Pushing the Boundaries of International Law

In creating the first permanent international criminal court, the Rome Statute had to make intrusions into the existing order. However, the one in question in this chapter is the intrusion into one of the core concepts of the international order: that of consent. Parties that have not consented to the Rome Statute are none the less subject to its provisions under certain circumstances. These intrusions come in two primary forms: Article 12(2)(a) and Article 13(b). The former is fairly uncontroversial, in that it states that the court has jurisdiction if the crimes were committed in the territory of, or onboard a vessel or aircraft of the state party. It does not state that the offender has to be a national of a state party. What matters is that the offence happened in the jurisdiction of a state party. As

[10] Rome Statute, footnote 1 above.

[11] J Crawford, *Brownlie's Principles of Public International Law* (8th Edition, Oxford University Press 2012) 31.

[12] United Nations, *Vienna Convention on the Law of Treaties*, 23 May 1969, United Nations, Treaty Series, volume 1155, 331, https://www.refworld.org/docid/3ae6b3a10.html, accessed 3 May 2021.

[13] Crawford, footnote 11 above, 31.

such nationals of non-state parties to the Rome Statute are bound by the terms of the Rome Statute. This is a fairly simple concept. If one travels as a tourist to a foreign land, they are bound by the laws of that land. Naturally, the same would apply if you are a soldier trying to commit, or not commit war crimes. The result of this change is that nations such as the United States of America have passed laws[14] and signed agreements[15] with allies, to prevent extradition of their soldiers should they ever be indicted by the ICC.

The more controversial of the two intrusions into the concept of consent comes from Article 13(b). This article states:

> The Court may exercise its jurisdiction with respect to a crime referred to in article 5 in accordance with the provisions of this Statute if:
>
> (b) A situation in which one or more of such crimes appears to have been committed is referred to the Prosecutor by the Security Council acting under Chapter VII of the Charter of the United Nations; ...

This article grants extremely broad powers to the UNSC. There is no jurisdictional limit imposed on the UNSC. It may simply refer a matter to the Prosecutor for investigation. The referred matter does not have to come from a state party to the Rome Statute and it does not have to include a state party at all. In practice, the UNSC has accepted that it is not bound by jurisdictional limits and has only referred non-state parties to the Prosecutor for investigation.[16] But the question remains: How is this done? Neither Sudan nor Libya, consented to Article 13(b) in any manner. Article 34 of the Vienna Convention of the Law of Treaties is expressly clear: no treaty may bind a third party without its consent. So how then does the UNSC have the power to bind these non-state parties?

[14] American Service-Members Protection Act (ASPA, Title 2 of Pub.L. 107-206).

[15] These come in the form of Bilateral Immunity Agreements, which are based on Article 98 of the Rome Statute which prohibits the member state from acting inconsistently with its obligations under international law.

[16] To date this comes in the form of Sudan under Resolution 1593 and Libya under Resolution 1970.

2.2 Powers of the Security Council:

The UNSC has the power to create international criminal tribunals. Article 39 of the United Nations Charter[17] (hereafter UNC) empowers the UNSC to determine breaches to peace and to maintain peace and security. This is a very broad power. However, it is still constrained by law. The UNC expressly limits the powers available to the UNSC to be in line with the principles of the Charter. The Charter, therefore, speaks of specific powers and not absolute *fiat* of the UNSC.[18] Thus, in order to take direct action, the UNSC has to determine a threat to peace. What counts as a threat to peace may come in many forms and is a highly complex question. The International Criminal Tribunal of the Yugoslavia (ICTY), when looking at whether the situation in the Former Yugoslavia counted as a threat to peace held that the history of action by the UNSC showed a clear outline as to what it considered to be a threat to peace. Action taken by the UNSC showed that it considered both International Armed Conflicts (IACs) as well as Non-International Armed Conflicts (NIACs) to be threats to peace.[19] The Special Tribunal of Lebanon (STL) on the other hand refused to entertain the question on reviewing the classification of a threat to peace. Here they held that there was no standard required by the UNC for there to be a threat to peace. As such, and because the matter is so highly complex, and ultimately political, decision on this should be left with the UNSC and the UNSC alone.[20]

In order to create a tribunal, the UNSC will have to employ its extraordinary powers under Chapter VII. No precise article in Chapter VII confers the power to establish a judicial body. However, in *Tadic* the ICTY found that Article 41 was worded in such a way that it allowed for any action that did not include the use of force. The court held that the examples listed in Article 41 were merely illustrative of the kinds of

[17] United Nations, *Charter of the United Nations*, 24 October 1945, 1 UNTS XVI, https://treaties.un.org/doc/publication/ctc/uncharter.pdf, accessed 4 May 2021.

[18] UNC Article 24(2) and *The Prosecutor v Tadic* (IT-94-1) Decision on the Defence Motion for Interlocutory Appeal on Jurisdiction 2 October 1995, paragraph 28.

[19] *Tadic*, paragraph 30.

[20] *The Prosocutor v Ayyesh* (STL-11-01) Decision on the Defence Appeal Against the Trial Chamber's "Decision on the Defence Challenge to the Jurisdiction and Legality of the Tribunal" 24 October 2012, paragraph 51.

measures that could be employed by the UNSC.[21] The court went on to hold that though the UNSC does not have judicial powers, it may still establish a judicial body because this body serves the primary function of the UNSC, namely the maintenance of peace and security.[22] To support this claim the court points to the fact that the General Assembly does not have military or police powers but may still create emergency forces to respond to a crisis. As such, the UNSC has the discretion to create a judicial body where it will serve the interests of the maintenance of peace, it is not the delegation of powers that it does not have. If this were so it would have rendered the creation of the court *ultra vires* as the Rule of Law requires that no action be taken without an empowering provision. Rather it is one of the many measures that could be employed individually or in concert with others, to bring about the goal of peace and security. The ICTY, however, refused to comment on the appropriateness of the decision to create the court. Holding that it was a decision best left to the UNSC as it was beyond the scope of their powers.

The STL, in contrast, stated that they do not have the power to review the decision of the UNSC, both to determine a threat to peace (as discussed above) as well as whether the response by the UNSC to such a determination is appropriate.[23] The STL rejected the power to review the UNSC on three grounds. Firstly, they held that nowhere in their founding Statute is there authority to make such a review.[24] Secondly, there is nothing in the UNC that allows for general reviews of the UNSC.[25] The ICJ rejected the view that it has this power as part of its inherent jurisdiction. It is clear that such power is not part of the charter. In fact, an express inclusion of such power was rejected by the parties to the UNC at the time of drafting. The STL argued that if the ICJ does not have this power, then the STL, an independent body with a narrower jurisdiction than the ICJ, would not have this power.

What makes the ICC unique compared to the ad hoc courts is that the court retains a far more nuanced control over its own jurisdiction. By no means should it be thought that the Court can review a resolution of the

21 *Tadic*, paragraph 35.

22 *Tadic*, paragraph 38.

23 *Ayyesh*, paragraph 35.

24 *Ayyesh*, paragraph 36.

25 *Ayyesh*, paragraph 39.

UNSC in terms of whether or not a breach of peace in terms of Article 39 has occurred. Rather, what it does retain are the limitations imposed by the principle of complementarity. These questions of inadmissibility can be raised either by the defence, the Court on its own initiative.[26] What this means is that the court can, in certain circumstances, legitimately decline to hear a case despite the UNSC referral based on jurisdictional limitations. This option was not present for the ad hoc tribunals. As seen above, they were granted their jurisdiction and told to investigate. The only limiting factor was subject matter. Further, this principle of complementarity is included in every referral. It cannot be divorced from the operation of the court. The UNSC will make a referral to the ICC and from that point on the Rome Statute applies in its entirety. The Statute is an all or nothing document as shown by the inclusion of Article 120 which prohibits any reservations to any part of the Statute. This position that the statute applies in its entirety was stated by Pre-Trial Chamber II in its 11 December 2017 decision regarding the non-compliance of the Hashemite Kingdom of Jordan.[27] Here the court held that "the effect of a Security Council resolution triggering the Court's jurisdiction under article 13(b) of the Statute is that the legal framework of the Statute applies in its entirety with respect to the situation referred."[28] The PTC went on to state that the terms of cooperation as required by the UNSC are set out in the Rome Statute.[29]

But this still leaves the question of *how* the UNSC has these powers to impose obligations on non-states party to the Rome Statute. The answer is that these obligations are not rooted in the Rome Statute, instead they are obligations owed to the UNSC by virtue of those member states being members of the United Nations. What happens is that in making a referral to the ICC, the UNSC creates a situation in which the referred nation is now in an analogous position to that of a state party, but is in fact not

[26] L Arbour and M Bergsmo, 'Conspicuous Absence of Jurisdictional Overreach' (1999) 1 *International Law Forum Du Droit International* 14.

[27] *The Prosecutor v Omar Hassan Ahmad Al Bashir* (Situation in Darfurm, Sudan) Pre-Trial Chamber II, Decision under Article 87(7) of the Rome Statute on the non-compliance of Jordan with the request by the Court for the arrest and surrender of Omar Al-Bashir, Case No ICC-02/05-01/09, 11 December 2017.

[28] As above, paragraph 37.

[29] As above.

one.[30] When the UNSC refers a matter to the ICC. The UNSC is not binding the non-state party in terms of the Rome Statute. Instead the UNSC is invoking a combination of authorities conferred on it. Firstly, in terms of Article 25 of the UNC all member states of the UN are required by law to comply with decision of the UNSC acting in terms of its own authority. As we have seen, it is well established that the UNSC can create judicial bodies in pursuit of the maintenance of Peace. Coupled with this is the supremacy clause of Article 103 of the UNC. This article states that obligations incurred under the UNC take precedence over all other obligations under international law should there be a conflict between those obligations. Thus, the legal position is that the UNSC creates obligations in terms of its Chapter VII powers that member states are obliged to comply with, and those UNSC obligations then take precedence over all other possible conflicting obligations that nation may have at the international level.

The reason the UNSC can do this is because it is taking advantage of Article 13(b) of the Rome Statute. As stated above, 13(b) allows for the UNSC to extend the court's jurisdiction to situations in non-states party. The UNSC is well aware that the ICC can only act in accordance with its statute and only its statute. It knows this as it is contained clearly in Article 1 of the Rome Statute that the court, its functions and jurisdiction are governed by the statute. This means that when the UNSC takes a resolution to extend the jurisdiction of the court to a non-states party, it knows that the jurisdiction of the court necessitates the rest of the legal framework of the court being applied.[31] The conferral of jurisdiction is thus conferred in accordance with the Rome Statute and thus all states, not simply states parties to the Rome Statute will be required to accept that the Court can act in accordance with its Statute.[32]

[30] J Iyi, 'Re-thinking the Authority of the UN Security Council to Refer Nationals of Non-party States to the ICC' (2019)66 *Netherlands International Law Review* 399. See also the recent decision in the case of the ICC Appeals Chamber in the case of Jordan, the Court has made it clear that Sudan is under obligations to cooperate because it is now in a position analogous to that of a state party to the Rome Statute by virtue of the wording of the UNSC Resolution, Judgment in the Jordan Referral re Al-Bashir Appeal, 06 May 2019, ICC-02/05-01/09-397-Corr., paragraph 140.

[31] D Akande, 'The Legal Nature of Security Council Referrals to the ICC and Its Impact on Al Bashir's Immunities' (2009)7 *Journal of International Criminal Justice* 340.

[32] As above at 341.

When the UNSC passes a resolution such as 1593 and 1970 the rest of the UN is legally bound to accept the new jurisdiction of the Court. By simply extending the jurisdiction in this manner, the UNSC does not require the UN member states to do anything with that jurisdiction unless the UNSC also requires cooperation from the UN member states.[33] This conferral of jurisdiction, when read with Art 25 and 103 of the UNC means that member states of the UN are estopped from denying both the expanded jurisdiction and, as stated above, that the court acts in accordance with the Rome Statute as a whole.[34] Finally by requiring that the state, in which jurisdiction has been extended, complies fully with the court, this state is now bound by the content of the Rome Statute. The Court and its functioning only happen in terms of the Rome Statute and so anyone wishing to comply and cooperate with the Court must do so in terms of said Statute. These states are, thus, in an analogous position to states party to the Statute. It is in this fashion that the UNSC can make the Rome Statute binding on non-state parties without directly imposing the obligations of the Rome Statute on states who have not consented to the Rome Statute.

With the UNSC's referral of the situation in Libya to the ICC, Libya became indirectly bound by the Rome Statute, including its regime of complementarity so much so that that its national accountability mechanisms have to a large extent leaned towards a punitive approach to the exclusion of workable African restorative approaches. Libya has also for some time now invoked a range of approaches to breathe life to the notion of complementarity. However, to what extent is it delivering on the justice needs of post-conflict Libya?

3 The Crisis of Post-conflict Justice in Libya

Libya's approach to post-conflict justice has entailed a number of mechanisms ranging from criminal prosecution, amnesties, to lustration laws. But as will be demonstrated in this section, all these post-conflict mechanisms have neither been successful in fostering accountability, nor, ensured peace-building, transition to democracy, accountability and the

33 As above.

34 As above.

much-desired reconciliation, all of which remain critical in addressing the post-conflict needs of Libyans.

3.1 Criminal Prosecution: Flaws in the Accountability Framework and the Targeting of Gadhafi Loyalists

In challenging the admissibility of the case against Al-Sennusi, Libya submitted, among others, that it had a functional justice system to prosecute those responsible for the atrocities committed during and after the Gadhafi regime.[35] In demonstrating its commitment to accountability for international crimes, Libya was open to the ICC's seizure of the matter were it to fail to foster criminal accountability in its national courts.[36]

Despite Libya's commitment to prosecuting those responsible for international crimes, gaps in the accountability framework are identifiable including the absence of a clear legislative framework to define the crimes allegedly committed such as torture and other ill-treatment, enforced disappearance, extrajudicial, arbitrary and summary executions, rape and other forms of sexual and gender-based violence and slavery.[37] The system also recognises a number of defences which make it hard for criminal accountability to be fostered. Notable is the defence of superior orders and the non-recognition of command responsibility.[38] The criminal justice system of Libya also leaves a lot to be desired in as far as the trial rights of those accused of crimes are concerned. Notable rights at stake include the right to be promptly informed of the charges, the right to be brought promptly before a judge, the right to habeas corpus, the right to legal counsel and the right not to be compelled to incriminate oneself.[39] Aside from the gaps in the criminal accountability framework, strife and social divisions remain rife. Close to a decade since Gadhafi's overthrow, Libyans' hope for a transition to democracy, peace-building

[35] *Prosecutor v Saif AL-Islam Gadhafi and Abdullah Al-Senussi*, Decision on the admissibility of the case against Abdullah Al-Senussi ICC-01/11-01/11-466-Red, 11 October 2013 | Pre-Trial Chamber I, paragraph 214.

[36] As above, paragraph 312.

[37] International Commission of Jurists, *Accountability for Serious Crimes Under International Law in Libya: An Assessment of the Criminal Justice System* (2019)1–102: International Commission of Jurists: Switzerland.

[38] As above.

[39] As above.

and reconciliation continue to be shuttered as Libya continues to be characterised by human rights violations comprising of extrajudicial killings, arbitrary arrests and detention, slavery, torture, among others.[40]

In terms of actual national proceedings, criminal prosecutions are tantamount to victor's justice. Officials under the Gadhafi regime have been the main targets of criminal proceedings at the national level despite the anti-Gadhafi revolutionaries equally being responsible for some of the atrocities committed.[41] Just like the Gadhafi loyalists, reports indicate that anti-Gadhafi revolutionaries were directly involved in the commission of several atrocities including unlawful killings, torture, arbitrary detentions and abductions.[42] However, because these militants took on a revolutionary stance against Gadhafi, they have been labelled "liberators" by some sections of society despite their criminal responsibility. On the other hand, Gadhafi loyalists have suffered the brunt of the harsh post-conflict legal regime. Several Gadhafi loyalists and officials under the Gadhafi regime have been sentenced to death while hundreds have been arbitrarily arrested and detained without trial.[43]

3.2 Lustration Laws and the Alienation of Gadhafi Loyalists

In 2013, the Political Isolation Law was passed.[44] This law had the effect of alienating sections of Libyans and further causing division, grievances and conflict. In terms of this law, Gadhafi loyalists and those who served under the Gadhafi regime were not to hold any political or official positions in Libya during Libya's transition. At the heart of the law was lustration which places a demand on anyone holding public office in a new political regime to be vetted with a view of assessing their link and loyalty to the previous political regime. While this approach sought to avoid

[40] E Soad, *Assessing the Impact of Transitional Justice Mechanisms in Post-conflict Societies: Lessons Drawn for Libya* (2019) 1–327, PhD Thesis, University of Sheffield; Amnesty International, 'The Battle for Libya: Killings, Disappearances and Torture' (2011) 1–109, https://www.amnesty.org/download/Documents/32000/mde190252011en.pdf, accessed 20 May 2021.

[41] CK Lamont, 'Contested Governance: Understanding Justice Interventions in Post-Qadhafi Libya' (2016)10 *Journal of Intervention and State building* 382–399.

[42] Soad, footnote 40 above, 78, 268.

[43] As above.

[44] Political Isolation Law of Libya, 2013.

the infiltration of post-conflict governance with the same old problematic doctrines that most probably led to conflict, the motivation behind the law has largely been vengeance and a tool for advancing a one-sided form of justice.[45] For the militants who had for some time fought against the Gadhafi regime, the law served to alienate them.

Especially ironic about the lustration laws is the fact that most of the militants who played a role in the anti-Gadhafi revolutionaries were defectors from the Muammar Gadhafi regime. Notable are Mustafa Abdel-Jalil who was Gadhafi's justice minister, Mahmoud Jibril, Gadhafi's head of planning and economic development and Mohammed Magarief, an ambassador under the Gadhafi regime.[46] All three of these officials defected from the Gadhafi regime and subsequently played leading roles in boosting the revolution's and the rebels' political legitimacy. Despite switching camp to support the rebel groups against Gadhafi, their ideologies were at some point pro-Gadhafi and if anything, the lustration laws ought to have applied to them too. However, the lustration laws were not applicable to them despite their previous commitment to the Gadhafi regime. This state of affairs demonstrates the divisiveness of these laws. More than anything, these post-conflict approaches are more politically motivated and geared towards a one-sided form of justice rather than fostering transitional justice.[47] Reports suggest that they have caused more division, conflict and grievance among Libyans than foster justice.[48] Although the laws were ultimately revoked following criticisms from various corners including rights groups,[49] they left a mark and are still informally applied.

[45] M Kersten, 'Libya's Political Isolation Law: Politics and Justice or the Politics of Justice?', 5 February 2014, https://www.mei.edu/publications/libyas-political-isolation-law-politics-and-justice-or-politics-justice, accessed 20 May 2021.

[46] As above.

[47] As above.

[48] Human Rights Watch Report, 'Libya, Reject Political Isolation Law': Provisions for Exclusion Too Vague, Sweeping', 4 May 2013, https://www.hrw.org/news/2013/05/04/libya-reject-political-isolation-law, accessed 20 May 2021.

[49] As above, BBC News, 'Libya Revokes Bill Which Banned Gadhafi-Era Officials from Office', 2 February 2015, https://www.bbc.com/news/world-latin-america-31104099, accessed 20 May 2021.

3.3 Amnesty Laws and the Exclusion of Gadhafi Loyalists

Various amnesty laws have been enacted since 2011 to foster transition. Notable is Law 38 which was passed in 2012.[50] This law grants blanket amnesty to all anti-Gadhafi revolutionaries who revolted against the Gadhafi regime. The amnesty law covers all atrocities committed in the course of protests against the Gadhafi regime. The law has had the effect of branding anti-Gadhafi revolutionaries as national heroes despite the atrocities they committed against Libyans.[51] By elevating themselves above criminal justice using this law, a sense of privilege has been created and ultimately, contempt has arisen from Gadhafi loyalists who now question the true essence of post-conflict criminal justice. The one-sided nature of criminal justice has fuelled violence, conflict and resentment, with the Gadhafi loyalists feeling sidelined by process.

The Law No. 6 is also commonly referred to as Tobruk Amnesty Law.[52] It grants general amnesty to all those who committed atrocities between 2011 to the date of its passing. However, certain crimes including murder, terrorism, torture and kidnap do not fall within the ambit of this law. Unlike Law 38, Law 6 applies to all including Gadhafi loyalists and officials who served under his regime. Moreover, for one to benefit from amnesty under this law, they must commit to reconciling with their victims. Relying on this law, Saif Gadhafi (currently awaiting trial before the ICC) was granted amnesty following a conviction and sentence of death.[53] The Libya's Attorney General, however, submitted that the amnesty granted was not effective as there were procedural irregularities that were not adhered to in the application of Law No. 6 of 2015 to Saif Gadhafi.[54] Among others, the law did not cover serious crimes

[50] Law No. 38 of 2012.

[51] Soad, footnote 40 above, 272; F Gaub, 'A Libyan Recipe for Disaster' (2014)56 *Survival, Global Politics and Strategy* 101–120; International Crisis Group, 'Trial by Error: Justice in Post-Qadhafi Libya. Middle East/North Africa Report No.140' (2013) 1–47, http://www.operationspaix.net/DATA/DOCUMENT/7904~v~Trial_By_Error__Justice_in_Post-Qadhafi_Libya__Middle_East_North_Africa_Reports_no_140_.pdf, accessed 20 May 2021.

[52] Law No. 6 of 2015 of Libya on general amnesty.

[53] Situation in Libya in the case of *The Prosecutor v Saif Al-Islam Gadhafi*, Pre-Trial Chamber I, ICC-01/11-01/11, 15 November 2018, paragraph 42.

[54] As above, paragraph 8.

such as crimes against humanity for which Saif was implicated. Furthermore, Saif did not engage in the reconciliatory process with his victims as prescribed by the law. Therefore, the case against him remained admissible before the ICC.

Law No. 6 has for some time been the subject of adjudication in proceedings before the ICC. More recently (2020), in the Gadhafi admissibility case, the Appeals Chamber of the ICC arrived at its final decision on the admissibility of the Gadhafi case, with this law featuring prominently in its judgement.[55] Saif had challenged the admissibility of the case against him on two grounds. First, that Article 20(3) of the Rome Statute barred the ICC from trying him again as he had already been tried, convicted and sentenced by a Court in Libya. Secondly, that he benefited from the amnesty law which led to his release from prison following his death sentence. But re-echoing the ruling of the Pre-trial Chamber, the Appeal Chamber found Gadhafi's case admissible before the ICC.[56] The decision of the Appeals Chamber is particularly critical on account of its engagement with the issue of the amnesty laws in Libya.

Suffice it to note that the compatibility of amnesties with international law has been and continues to be a subject of scholarly debate.[57] While there is no customary international law rule prohibiting the grant of amnesties for serious crimes, generally, blanket amnesties are frowned

[55] Situation in Libya in the case of *The Prosecutor v Saif Al-Islam Gadhafi*, Judgment on the appeal of Mr Saif Al-Islam Gadhafi against the decision of Pre-Trial Chamber I entitled 'Decision on the "Admissibility Challenge by Dr. Saif AlIslam Gadhafi pursuant to Articles 17(1)(c), 19 and 20(3) of the Rome Statute"' of 5 April 2019, Appeal Chamber judgment delivered on 9 March 2020.

[56] As above, paragraph 2, page 1.

[57] See e.g. A Garcia, 'Transitional (In)Justice: An Exploration of Blanket Amnesties and the Remaining Controversies Around the Spanish Transition to Democracy' (2015)43 *International Journal of Legal Information* 75–135; JC Portilla, 'Amnesty: Evolving 21st Century Constrains under International Law' (2014)38 *Fletcher Forum of World Affairs* 169; K McNamara, 'Seeking Justice in Ugandan Courts: Amnesty and the Case of Thomas Kwoyelo' (2013)12 *Washington University Global Studies Law Review* 653; M Jackson, 'Amnesties in Strasbourg' (2018)38 *Oxford Journal of Legal Studies* 451.

upon under international law.[58] In any case, an approach that unconditionally exonerates perpetrators from accountability would not pass international law muster as it may be impossible to grant blanket amnesties and at the same time honour international obligations. Bassiouni's view of blanket amnesties is that they constitute a breach of "social contract." He adds that:

> if the right of punishment originally belonged to the victim and the international legal community exercises it on behalf of the victim, it cannot be traded in for blanket amnesties … Political negotiators acting on behalf of major powers have compromised the victim's right and breached the "social contract" for international criminal justice by bartering accountability for political settlements … Granting pardon without justification clearly hinders the pursuit of justice because it destroys all beliefs of fairness, equality of application of the law … it also eradicates hopes of deterring similar crimes from being committed in the future.[59]

Various decisions at the regional level have also demonstrated the undesirability blanket amnesties where gross human rights violations are committed. In *Barrios Altos v Peru*, the Inter-American Court of Human Rights, for the first time, pronounced that "all amnesty provisions … are inadmissible, because they are intended to prevent the investigation and punishment of those responsible for serious human rights violations such as torture, extrajudicial, summary or arbitrary execution and forced disappearance, all of them prohibited because they violate non-derogable rights recognized by international human rights law."[60] The United Nations has also taken a firm stance against amnesties and in a 2004 report made

[58] The United Nations High Commissioner for Human Rights defines a blanket amnesty as one that 'exempts broad categories of perpetrators from prosecution without requiring any application on the part of the beneficiary or an inquiry into the facts of each situation.' See United Nations High Commissioner for Human Rights, 'Rule of Law Tools for Post-conflict States' (2009) UN Doc HR/Pub/09/1.

[59] C Bassiouni, *Introduction to International Criminal Law* (Brill Nijhoff 2013) 973–974.

[60] *Barrios Altos v Peru*, Inter-American Court of Human Rights Series C No 75, 14 March 2001, paragraph 41.

it clear that all endorsement of amnesty for war crimes, crimes against humanity and genocide must be rejected.[61]

While for some time, amnesties have generally been frowned upon especially when international crimes are in issue, their total exclusion has in recent times been the subject of scrutiny, with some commentators contending that such viewpoints are unfounded.[62] Not surprisingly, in a 2014 decision of the European Court of Human Rights in *Marguš v Croatia*, the Grand Chamber took the position that despite the view that amnesties are a no-go where gross human rights violations are in issue, their total exclusion is unfounded especially where they are part of reconciliation, compensation and reparation processes for victims and involve some form of accountability.[63] The Extraordinary Chambers in the Courts of Cambodia, in a 2011 decision, decided that: "certain conditional amnesties such as those providing for some form of accountability have also met widespread approval."[64] More recently, the International Law Commission's Special Rapporteur on Crimes Against Humanity has indicated hesitancy to embrace total exclusions of amnesties for crimes against humanity and rather advised that each national law should be assessed within its context and in accordance with the treaty laws binding on those states.[65] Moreover, while rights groups have largely criticised states for failing to foster accountability for international crimes, their criticism has largely been attributed to the blanket amnesties handed down

[61] United Nations Security Council, 'The rule of law and transitional justice in conflict and post-conflict societies', Report of the Secretary General, 23 August 2004, UN Doc S/2004/616, paragraph 64(c).

[62] K McEvoy and L Mallinder, 'Amnesties in Transition: Punishment, Restoration, and the Governance of Mercy' (2012)39 *Journal of Law and Society* 410–440.

[63] *Marguš v Croatia* [GC] ECHR 2014-III, paragraph 139. See also *Thomas Kwoyelo v Uganda* ACHPR Communication 431/12 (17 October 2018). Specifically, see the African Commission on Human and Peoples' Rights *obiter dicta* comments on amnesties in paragraphs 283–293.

[64] Decision on Ieng Sary's Rule 89 Preliminary Objections (Ne bis in idem and amnesty and pardon) [2011] Extraordinary Chambers in the Courts of Cambodia Trial Chamber (Extraordinary Chambers in the Courts of Cambodia Trial Chamber). On the same viewpoint, see also G Fiddler, 'Using a Conditional Amnesty and Truth and Reconciliation Commission as a Transitional Justice Mechanism in Syria' (2015) 47 *The George Washington Institute of International Law Review* 901.

[65] United Nations General Assembly International Law Commission, Third report on crimes against humanity by SD Murphy, Special Rapporteur (23 January 2017) UN Doc A/CN.4/704, paragraph 296.

rather than amnesties accompanied by some form of accountability.[66] More recently, some commentators are also convinced that the fact that the Rome Statute is silent on the issue of amnesties, by implication, recourse to them, subject to some form of accountability, remains an option for states desirous of having recourse to amnesties in addressing post-conflict challenges.[67]

In regard to the amnesty granted to Saif, the Appeals Chamber did not explicitly reject the grant of amnesty. It, however, emphasised that amnesty received by Saif was not binding on the ICC because the amnesty law of Libya excluded perpetrators of crimes against humanity from benefiting from the law.[68] In addition, Saif did not go through the reconciliatory process with the victims of crimes as envisaged by the amnesty law.[69] The Appeals Chamber steered clear of engaging with the issue of whether the ICC regime makes room for amnesty and instead addressed the matter on procedural technicalities relating to the national amnesty law. The move by the ICC to steer clear of this debate could either be tactical—to avoid being entangled in the controversial debate of amnesties under international law, or, because of the seemingly settled nature of the Rome Statute on the matter. But all considered, Saif Gadhafi's case remains admissible before the ICC, with prospects of securing him for trial still far from practical after a decade since this case started unfolding.

The various mechanisms invoked in Libya, as can be gleaned from the narrative in this section, have largely been unsuccessful in fostering both criminal accountability and the post-conflict needs of Libya. While the culture of divisiveness was existent during the Gadhafi regime, the transitional justice mechanisms in the country have entrenched this challenge

[66] See e.g. Amnesty International, 'South Sudan: Crippled Justice System and Blanket Amnesties Fueling Impunity for War Crimes' (2019), https://www.amnesty.org/en/latest/news/2019/10/south-sudan-crippled-justice-system-and-blanket-amnesties-fuelling-impunity-for-war-crimes/, accessed 20 May 2021.

[67] See generally, M Freedman, *Necessary Evils: Amnesties and the Search for Justice* (Cambridge: Cambridge University Press 2010); C Bell, 'Negotiating Human Rights' in John Darby and Roger MacGinty (eds) *The Management of Peace Processes* (Macmillan Press 2000) 210–229; C Bell, *Peace Agreements and Human Rights* (UK: Oxford University Press 2000); L Mallinder, 'Can Amnesties and International Justice Be Reconciled?' (2007)1 *The International Journal of Transitional Justice* 208–230.

[68] Admissibility Challenge by Dr. Saif AlIslam Gadhafi, footnote 35 above, paragraphs 66, 85 and 96.

[69] As above, paragraph 82.

further. Libya remains fragile and divisions between Gadhafi loyalists and anti-Gadhafi revolutionaries remain rife. This has further fuelled conflict, violence and grievance among Libyans. The ideal of democracy, reconciliation, restoration and peace-building that Libyans have long yearned for remain a far-reaching goal. In this regard, Soad observes that "the deep wounds inflicted on society need time and help to heal, but the weak state and its fragile legal system cannot provide that assistance."[70] In fact, the situation in Libya since 2011 has steadily descended into a civil war because the root causes of the violence and conflict have hardly been addressed. The mechanisms that Libya has considered have further caused division and grievances thus dividing the nation further and shuttering all prospects of transitioning to democracy. In the words of Najla, "local and international reconciliation initiatives have failed to break the violence, whose roots extend deep into Libyan society and reach back into the colonial period."[71] She adds that:

> the number of conflicts that need to be transformed in Libya and the number of parties that need to be reconciled are each depressingly large. The gloom is all the darker because efforts at reconciliation launched since the revolution have so far failed. In most cases, failure springs from the same set of reasons: persistent divisions in society, the political isolation of former Gadhafi supporters, and an abiding desire for revenge.[72]

4 Traditional Justice Mechanisms: A Ray of Hope?

Africa is rich in tradition and traditional justice mechanisms are not a new phenomenon. Traditionally, conflict in all African traditional societies was subject to the conflict resolution mechanism of the respective societies. With the advent of formal justice systems, these mechanisms still continued to play a role in conflict resolution. Literature abounds on their potential to effectively respond to and address the needs and realities of those affected by crime, promote peace and reconciliation, foster a

[70] Soad, footnote 40 above, 131.

[71] E Najla, 'Customary Practice and Restorative Justice in Libya: A Hybrid Approach' (2015) *Special Report* 2.

[72] As above, 5.

bottom-up approach to conflict resolution rather than a top-down imposition of uniform approaches often alien to a population, ensure accessibility to justice for the affected population and promote restorative responses to conflict in society.[73]

The potential of traditional justice mechanisms has been evident in a number of post-conflict states including Rwanda, Uganda, Mozambique and Burundi.[74] The Gacaca process in Rwanda, a customary justice process, provided a ray of hope in a situation where the formal justice framework taking the form of the International Criminal Tribunal of Rwanda (ICTR) was incapable of addressing the ethnic tensions that characterised the conflict in Rwanda.[75] The crimes committed were innumerable and under no circumstance could the Rwandan prisons have been in position to accommodate the convicts were a strictly punitive approach to be invoked. The Rwanda Genocide left over one million people dead, thus, pursuing punitive justice for this nature of atrocities was far from realistic.[76] Moreover, the formal criminal justice processes were incapable of addressing the tribal tensions between the Hutu and Tutsi people which were at the heart of the Rwanda genocide. The Gacaca Process was community-based and restorative in nature. It aimed at reconciling, repairing harm, communal healing, rebuilding and restoring of broken relations across conflicting parties.[77] While the process had its fair share of challenges including gaps in addressing cases of sexual violence,[78] it helped address the pressing needs of the communities, ensuring that these communities moved and healed after the conflict.

Beyond Rwanda, mention can be made of the *Mato Oput* traditional justice mechanisms in Uganda. This traditional justice process

[73] T Longman, 'An Assessment of Rwanda's Gacaca Courts' (2009)21 *Peace Review* 304–312; V Igreja et al., 'Gamba Spirits, Gender Relations, and Healing in Post-Civil War Gorongosa, Mozambique' (2008)14 *Journal of the Royal Anthropological Institute* 353–371; Lubaale, footnote 6 above, 180–202.

[74] Lubaale, footnote 6 above, 180–202.

[75] As above.

[76] S Tamale, *Decolonisation and Afro-Feminist* (Daraja Press 2020) 156–159.

[77] As above.

[78] BA Olwine, 'One Step Forward, But Two Steps Back: Why Gacaca in Rwanda Is Jeopardizing the Good Effect of Akayesu on Women's Rights s Rights' (2011)17 *Willian and Mary Journal of Race, Gender and Social Justice* 639–663.

featured prominently in the transitional justice mechanisms in post-conflict Northern Uganda. The *Mato Oput*, like most other traditional mechanisms, is mediational in nature and the approaches invoked are derived from the indigenous communities of Northern Uganda. The process entails acknowledgement of wrongdoing as opposed to punishment, it seeks to heal and restore broken relations that results from the commission of crimes.[79] Reparation also constitutes a major feature of the *Mato Oput* process.[80] This traditional justice mechanism has played a key role in dealing with crimes committed in Northern Uganda.[81] While some of the alleged perpetrators of the atrocities in Northern Uganda including Dominic Ongwen have been indicted by the ICC, the *Mato Oput* has still been playing a role in fostering post-conflict justice in the Northern Uganda communities. This process has particularly played a key role in reintegrating and reconciling child soldiers with the communities against which these children committed atrocities.[82] Despite the process being criticised by some as inadequate to deal with serious crimes,[83] it garnered support from the Northern Uganda communities. Heeding to the voices of the Northern Ugandan population, the president of Uganda, Yoweri Kaguta Museveni had this to say: "what we have agreed with our people is that they should face traditional justice, which is more compensatory than a retributive system."[84] He added: "if that's what the community wants, then why would we insist" on a trial by the ICC?[85]

While Colombia's approach to post-conflict justice cannot be categorised as an African traditional justice mechanism, it embodies features

[79] As above, 159–161.

[80] As above.

[81] Among Hope, 'The Application of Traditional Justice Mechanisms to the Atrocities Committed by Child Soldiers in Uganda: A Practical Restorative Justice Approach' (2013)13 *African Human Rights Law Journal* 441–463.

[82] As above.

[83] See e.g. See e.g. A Branch, 'Exploring the Roots of LRA Violence: Political Crisis and Ethnic Politics in Acholiland' in T Allen and K Vlassenroot (eds) *The Lord's Resistance Army Myth and Reality* (Zed Books 2010) 22–44; A Branch, *Displacing Human Rights War and Intervention in Northern Uganda* (Oxford University Press 2011).

[84] AK Bangura, 'The Politics of the Struggle to Resolve the Conflict in Uganda: Westerners Pushing Their Legal Approach Versus Ugandans Insisting on Their Mato Oput' (2008)2 *The Journal of Pan African Studies* 142–178.

[85] As above.

of restorative justice which are at the heart of African traditional justice mechanisms. The situation in Colombia is currently under preliminary investigations by the ICC. It is alleged that atrocities taking the form of war crimes and crimes against humanity have been committed by both the government security forces of Colombia and the various rebel groups.[86] The counts canvassed in these investigations include murder, forcible transfer of population, imprisonment and other severe deprivation of physical liberty, sexual violence, torture, rape, intentional attacks against civilians, cruel treatment, outrages on personal dignity, taking of hostages and using children to participate in hostilities.[87] The preliminary investigations by the ICC seek, among others, to assess whether the national proceedings in Colombia are capable of barring the ICC from admitting the situation in Colombia before the ICC.

With the signing of the *Agreement for the Termination of the Conflict and Construction of a Stable and Lasting Peace* between the government of Colombia and the rebel groups, Colombia has set in motion various mechanisms to foster post-conflict justice.[88] Three mechanisms are envisaged and these include: Truth, Coexistence and Non-Repetition Commission (CEV); Search Unit for Persons Presumed Disappeared in the context and because of the armed conflict (UBDP) and the Special Jurisdiction for Peace (JEP).[89] The JEP seeks to criminally prosecute those responsible for the most atrocious crimes committed during the conflict. The three-prong mechanism by Colombia illustrates the country's commitment to not only hold to account those responsible for the atrocities committed, but also, to foster reconciliation, healing and restoration after decades of protracted conflict. Critical to note, the JEP has invoked a mixed approach to justice in the sense that it combines aspects of punitive and restorative justice. Through this approach, offenders and victims of crime are to engage in dialogue geared towards reintegration and reconciliation between offenders and victims in

[86] Agreement for the Termination of the Conflict and Construction of a Stable and Lasting Peace (2016) 1–37, https://www.peaceagreements.org/wgenerateAgreementPDF/1845, accessed 20 May 2021.

[87] As above.

[88] As above.

[89] As above.

a community.[90] Crime is understood not just as an attack on the individual but on the community as a whole. The Agreement makes it clear that while sanctions may be imposed by the courts, these sanctions should be restorative in nature, seeking to repair the damage and satisfy victims' needs rather than punish the offender.[91] Alternatives to punitive sanctions are therefore encouraged.

In Libya, despite invoking punitive mechanisms in its post-conflict justice processes, recourse to approaches that foster restoration, healing and reparation is not alien to this country. Traditional justice mechanisms that embody these elements have been a major feature in Libya's system. These mechanisms became even more visible and functional with the advent of the *bedouinization* culture during the Gadhafi era.[92] The culture of *bedouinization* gave tribal identity a significant status in the Libyan society. Even with the demise of the Gadhafi regime, the role of traditional justice mechanisms in Libya remains alive and well.[93] This system of justice is run by tribal leaders who remain the custodians of Libya's long-standing and oldest societal institutions.[94] They have a major influence not just on the leadership of Libya but also its peace and security on account of the loyalty and allegiance they garner from Libyans. These leaders rely largely on customary law to resolve conflict.[95] The system has particularly been functional because it is accessible to the majority of Libyans, many of whom prefer it to the formal system of justice. These traditional justice mechanisms remain a recognised system of conflict resolution in Libya. Najla offers a vivid practical case of how this approach to crime has played out in Libya:

> Ahmad, a businessman from a well-known family in Benghazi, was stabbed by two men while walking at night; he received minor injuries. At the time, no one recognized the offenders, but Ahmad's father went to the police station to report the crime. A week later, two strangers knocked

[90] As above.

[91] As above.

[92] P Cole and F Mangan, 'Tribe, Security, Justice, and Peace in Libya Today' (2016) 1–48, https://www.usip.org/sites/default/files/PW118-Tribe-Security-Justice-and-Peace-in-Libya-Today.pdf, accessed 30 May 2021.

[93] As above.

[94] As above.

[95] As above.

> at the door of the home of the tribal leader of Ahmad's family. The two men represented the offenders' tribal leaders; they were inquiring about Ahmad's health. A week after that, they visited again, this time asking Ahmad's family to waive their right to go to court and, instead, to settle the matter privately because the two attackers were minors, acting under the influence of alcohol, and were not expected to cause trouble again. Ahmad's father agreed to renounce his personal right but did not drop the right of the state. The issue was eventually resolved during an official meeting between the traditional leaders from both sides. The leaders made the decision on behalf of the two families: The offenders were jailed for a short time.[96]

The Ahmed case demonstrates the potential of traditional justice mechanisms to foster accountability on the one hand and reconciliation, reparation, restoration and healing on the other. The Gacaca process, *Mato Oput* and the Libyan traditional justice framework are testament to the fact that the rich traditions of African communities provide a framework for post-conflict justice in countries seeking sustainable solutions to post-conflict challenges. These mechanisms embody features of restorative justice as are currently being invoked in states like Colombia. The potential of these mechanisms in fostering national accountability for international crimes lies in their suitability to address pressing issues in post-conflict states such as racial, tribal and social tensions that are often deeply entrenched in post-conflict societies. The critical issue, however, is whether such an approach would be on par with the Rome Statute which, among others, mandates states to "investigate" or "prosecute"?

5 African Traditional Justice Mechanisms and Complementarity

As consistently alluded to, the notion of complementarity is at the heart of the ICC regime of international criminal justice. This principle finds force in several provisions of the Rome Statute. Both the preamble and Article 1 of the Rome Statute consider the ICC as a court "complementary to national criminal jurisdictions." As a court that is merely complementary to national criminal justice jurisdictions, the ICC can only admit cases falling under its jurisdiction under the exceptional circumstances. In terms

96 Najla, footnote 71 above, 6.

of Article 17 of the Rome Statute, cases are inadmissible before the ICC where:

a. The case is being investigated or prosecuted by a State which has jurisdiction over it, unless the State is unwilling or unable genuinely to carry out the investigation or prosecution;
b. The case has been investigated by a State which has jurisdiction over it and the State has decided not to prosecute the person concerned, unless the decision resulted from the unwillingness or inability of the State genuinely to prosecute;
c. The person concerned has already been tried for conduct which is the subject of the complaint, and a trial by the Court is not permitted under Article 20, paragraph 3;
d. The case is not of sufficient gravity to justify further action by the Court.

As a starting point, a critical reading of the Rome Statute suggests that there is no binding obligation on states to exercise jurisdiction, criminalise and prosecute international crimes at the national level. Not surprisingly, some authors argue that this is a gap in the Rome Statute that should have been foreseen in the light of the fact that national prosecutions are at the heart of the international criminal justice regime under the Rome Statute.[97] In addition, while Article 17 (cited above) refers to the notions of "investigation" and "prosecution," the Rome Statute offers no explicit definitions for these terms. Nowhere in the Rome Statute is it indicated that the notion "investigation" or "prosecution" as referred to in Article 17 is for purposes of retributive justice or mechanisms geared towards punishment and sentences commensurate with the gravity of international crimes committed. Strictly speaking therefore, Article 17 does not mandate states to invoke retributive justice or punitive approaches. Effectively then, traditional justice mechanisms, truth commissions, etc., which as consistently alluded to embody features of restorative justice, can be interpreted to fall within the ambit of the two notions of "investigation" and "prosecution" for purposes of Article 17 provided they are sufficiently genuine.

[97] D Tladi, 'Complementarity and Cooperation in International Criminal Justice Assessing Initiatives to Fill the Impunity Gap' (2014) Institute of Security Studies 1–14, https://www.files.ethz.ch/isn/185933/Paper277.pdf, accessed 20 May 2021.

In its interpretation of Article 17(1)(a) of the Rome Statute, the ICC has observed that for a case to be inadmissible before the ICC, a state must demonstrate that "a) the person subject to the domestic proceedings is the same person against whom the proceedings before the Court are being conducted; and b) the conduct that is subject to the national investigation is substantially the same conduct that is alleged in the proceedings before the Court."[98] It should follow therefore that if traditional justice mechanisms being invoked at the national level involve the same person and for the same conduct, the national traditional justice proceedings should suffice to bar the ICC from admitting such a case. Keller has in this regard observed that while traditional justice mechanisms may not generally fall within the ambit of "investigation" or "prosecution," there is room for the ICC to broadly interpret the Rome Statute to encompass traditional justice mechanisms.[99]

It is, however, notable that despite the absence of obligation to criminalise, prosecute and invoke punitive approaches, various organs of the ICC, commentators and even national courts have assumed that such an obligation exists, and this assumption continues to be ossified. For example, the Office of the Prosecutor has averred that states' commitment to the Rome Statute brings with it a "responsibility" to criminally prosecute.[100] While the notion "responsibility" does not carry the weight of binding obligations, San-Hyun, the President of the ICC as he then was, suggested that such obligation exists when he noted that "states parties to the Rome Statute have an obligation to ensure that their national justice systems are capable of conducting proceedings into alleged crimes of this kind."[101] In its report on the preliminary investigations in Iraq/United Kingdom, the Office of the Prosecutor of the ICC suggested that the type of justice envisaged by Article 17 is criminal prosecution giving rise

[98] Pre-Trial Chamber I, Decision on the admissibility of the case against Saif Al-Islam Gadhafi, 31 May 2013, ICC-Ol/ll-Ol/ll-344-Red (hereinafter, Gadhafi Admissibility Decision), paragraphs 61, 74 and 76–77.

[99] LM Keller, 'Achieving Peace with Justice: The International Criminal Court and Ugandan Alternative Justice Mechanisms' (2009)23 *Connecticut Journal of International Law* 209–279, 256.

[100] F Bensouda, 'The Rome Statute Ten Years On: Where to from Here for the ICC?', Lecture at Melbourne University Law School, 17 February 2011.

[101] Sang-Hyun Song, 'The International Criminal Court: A Global Commitment to End Impunity', Presentation at Istanbul Bilgi University, 22 May 2013.

to retributive justice. The report noted that: "in principle, only national investigations that are designed to result in criminal prosecutions can trigger the application of article 17(a)-(c). As such, the Office has examined the findings of other mechanisms only in so far as they may be relevant to possible criminal proceedings."[102]

The posture that these organs have taken on the exact nature of accountability at the national level has seemingly informed the interpretation and meaning that Africa's national jurisdictions have given to the term "accountability" or complementarity in general. For example, the North Gauteng High Court of South Africa held that South Africa was under obligation "imposed both in terms of international law and South African law" to investigate and prosecute those alleged to have committed international crimes.[103] This is despite the fact that no such obligation exists under international law. In addition, the steps taken (including establishment of criminal courts and enacting criminal legislation) by some African states (including Uganda, Libya and Kenya) to address post-conflict violence is testament to the misconception that there is an obligation to criminally prosecute and to adopt a punitive approach to international crimes.[104]

The two notions "investigation" and "prosecution" as referred to in Article 17 have also been skewed towards criminal prosecution and punishment. This has been affirmed by commentators like Nouwen and Werner who submit that "complementarity in the legal sense thus creates space for alternative forum of criminal jurisdiction to that of the ICC, but not to an alternative conception of justice."[105] They add that within the confines of the ICC regime, dialogues on alternative forms of justice "are accepted only if they live up to the apparently de-localised modern

[102] Office of the Prosecutor, 'Situation in Iraq/UK: Final Report', 9 December 2020, page 92, https://www.icc-cpi.int/itemsDocuments/201209-otp-final-report-iraq-uk-eng.pdf, accessed 20 May 2021.

[103] *South African Litigation Centre and Another v National Director of Public Prosecutions and Others*, 2012 (10) BCLR 109 (GNP), paragraph 15.

[104] In terms of applicable framework, all these countries have generally invoked a punitive approach to post-conflict justice, with traditional justice mechanisms hardly featuring in the justice process.

[105] S Nouwen and W Werner, 'Monopolizing Global Justice: International Criminal Law as Challenge to Human Diversity' (2015)13 *Journal of International Criminal Justice* 157–176.

and most of all higher standard of global justice applied by the ICC."[106] A problematic assumption therefore continues to be buttressed to the effect that proceedings at the national level can only bar the ICC from intervening or prosecuting a case if the said proceedings are retributive or punitive in nature.

The few African governments which have sought to rely on traditional justice mechanisms have received scathing criticism based on the assumption that international criminal justice entails the punishment of those responsible for "the most serious crimes of concern to the international community."[107] When Uganda tried to invoke the traditional justice mechanism of *Mato Oput* in respect of the international crimes committed during the Northern Uganda conflict, the former Prosecutor of the ICTR and the International Criminal Tribunal for the former Yugoslavia (ICTY), Richard Goldstone, labelled Uganda's attempt a violation of international standards. He condemned the Ugandan President (Yoweri Museveni), stating: "Museveni is acting in contravention of international law."[108] He added: "His government signed the 1998 Rome Statute, and offers of amnesty violate the letter of the law."[109]

And while traditional justice mechanisms have potential to address the complex post-conflict challenges in Libya, such an approach unveils a complex justice structure that would seemingly disturb the current trend on what national accountability should entail. Traditional justice mechanisms generally recognise the limits of punitive justice, with options such as reconciliation, pardon and apologies being a major feature of these justice approaches. Embracing these mechanisms in post-conflict justice potentially alters our understanding of international criminal justice. More than anything, to invoke traditional justice mechanisms, despite their potential in addressing the post-conflict needs of African states, could be criticised as an affront to international criminal law which aims to ensure that perpetrators of the "most serious crimes of concern to the international community" are punished.

[106] As above.

[107] Preamble to the Rome Statute.

[108] Goldstone in K Glassborrow, 'Peace Versus Justice in Uganda' (2010), https://iwpr.net/global-voices/peace-versus-justice-uganda, accessed 20 May 2021.

[109] As above.

Traditional justice mechanisms, like retributive justice, restorative justice, etc., are all forms of justice in their own right. However, the literature has reduced traditional justice mechanisms to "alternatives" to retributive justice.[110] Retributive justice is perceived as the main and ideal form of justice. Whenever mention is made of traditional justice mechanisms in post-conflict justice, scholars often get trapped into the debate of "peace versus justice"[111]—suggesting that justice is sacrificed at the altar of peace when traditional justice mechanisms are invoked. Traditional justice mechanisms are therefore generally presented as approaches that do not advance justice because justice has been confined to retributive justice. These mechanisms, however, constitute forms of justice in their own right and in addition to delivering on justice, they may also be able to deliver on other post-conflict challenges such as peace if genuinely and effectively implemented.

In addition, use of the term "alternative" makes these mechanisms to be a departure from the ideal or acceptable norm—the acceptable norm being retributive justice. The exaltation of retributive justice has served to "other" African traditional justice mechanisms and presented them as everything that is contrary to international standards.[112] Commentators have often described traditional justice mechanisms as conduits for "impunity" and a loophole via which those responsible for international crimes "escape international criminal justice."[113] These narratives have rendered traditional justice mechanisms "inferior" and consequently, placed them on the fringes of workable approaches to post-conflict justice.

The tendency to alienate traditional justice mechanisms with no clear foundation in the Rome Statute brings sharply into perspective the colonial history of alienation of customary law in Africa. The colonial era saw the institutionalisation of Western laws and as Tamale observes:

[110] See e.g. conceptualisation by A Greenawalt, 'Complementarity in Crisis: Uganda, Alternative Justice, and the International Criminal Court' (2009)50 *Virginia Journal of International Law* 108–162.

[111] Glassborrow, footnote 108 above.

[112] On such "othering", Young agrees, contending that: "To experience cultural imperialism means to experience how the dominant meanings of a society render the particular perspective of one's own group invisible at the same time as they stereotype one's group and mark it out as Other." IM Young, *Justice and the Politics of Difference* (Princeton: Princeton University Press 1990) 58–59.

[113] Glassborrow, footnote 108 above.

> when colonialists introduced written laws, new legal professionals and an 'independent' court system, they touted them as more 'civilized' than the old legal order. The new legalities promised to overcome the 'whims' of the 'primitive' pre-colonial legal system. But the fact is that the historical roots of the un-professionalized justice system that the majority of Africans (*wananchi*) use for dispute resolution run deep in their traditional cultures. Hierarchies of norms were introduced with those of the colonialists always sitting on top. Filtered through the Eurocentric prism of dualities, the tendency is to view the modern against the traditional and the formal against the customary.[114]

Claassens and Mnisi, however, warn that such problematic dichotomies "obscure the cross-cutting reality of the lived experiences of people."[115]

The current international criminal justice regime continues to alienate traditional justice mechanisms in the international criminal justice framework despite there being no explicit provision in the Rome Statute barring their application. Both Africa and the rest of the international community have been made to believe that traditional justice mechanisms condone impunity, are not good enough to foster international criminal justice, are inferior and to invoke them would be to violate international law. But African traditional justice mechanisms have long been vouched for in addressing conflict in African societies and they can still play a role in fostering a restorative approach to post-conflict violence. There is therefore a need to increasingly have recourse to African restorative approaches and all other workable forms of restorative justice approaches not just in Libya but Africa as a whole.

6 Conclusion

The ICC seeks to punish those most responsible for the "most serious crimes of concern to the international community." By its very nature, the goals of the ICC are always going to be smaller than the goals of the nation in which those crimes were committed. Even if one restricts the comparison to merely the question of justice, and leaves out rebuilding the nation, the economy, the society as a whole, the ICC will still have

114 Tamale, footnote 76 above, 134.

115 A Claassens and S Mnisi, 'Rural Women Redefining Land Rights in the Context of Living Customary Law' (2009)25 *South African Journal on Human Rights* 493.

goals that are significantly narrower than that of the nation in question. Holding to account those most responsible for the international crimes has little to do with holding responsible the people with whom the victims lived that one day turned on them. The layers and types of perpetration that happen in the crimes of interest to the ICC mean that even if the likes of Saif Gadhafi or Omar Al Bashir are ever put on trial, the requirements of holding "those most responsible" to account mean that the individual soldiers or militia members who are directly responsible for crimes, never will be. In these cases, therefore, the ICC does not bring justice in the eyes of the victims because their direct perpetrator is still walking free. For example, arresting and putting Bashir on trial does not bring justice to the person living in Arawala (in Sudan) who still has to see the man who shot their mother and burnt their house down.[116] As such, the tensions between the ICC and the victims, the public, and the nation as a whole, exist right from the outset.

It is, therefore, vital that when the ICC does take an interest in a situation that it is aware of the broader considerations of the people in whose name it is seeking to bring justice. The very western, and sometimes alien, approach of the ICC's limited retributive justice needs to embrace the spirt of complementarity more deeply than simply asking if a trial before a judge in a courtroom has happened. The value that restorative justice approaches have goes beyond seeing a handful of persons in prison. They go to rebuilding communities, rebuilding trust between people and allowing nations to heal in a way that a small number of criminal trials cannot achieve. One need only look to the results of the Gacaca process to see this.

This brings us back to the point of a state being unwilling or unable to prosecute a matter, and the question of amnesties. The ICC avoided the question of the validity of amnesties in general in the Saif Gadhafi case, but at the same time, was directly involved in the process in Colombia that led to the peace deal, and possible amnesty deals for various combatants in that ongoing conflict. It is commendable to the Prosecutor in this instance for this involvement in recognising that justice is more than a trial in The Hague. By being involved in this process the Prosecutor and

[116] International Criminal Court, 'Alleged Crimes [in Sudan] (Non-exhaustive List)' 2021, https://www.icc-cpi.int/darfur/harunkushayb/pages/alleged-crimes.aspx, accessed 13 June 2021. The town of Arawala is one of the many towns in Sudan that suffered the brunt of the atrocities committed during the Al-Bashir regime.

the ICC ensured that their obligations under the Rome Statute were met, but at the same time recognised that complementarity is a much broader question than a check box enquiry into if a trial and conviction have taken place. It is our hope that this awareness and recognition will carry over to more situations and will be transferred over with the change in leadership at the court that is to come. In fact, this is essential in ensuring that the court no longer alienates member states from Africa. The expansion of nations under investigation is a start to repairing the reputational damage done to the court by only targeting African situations but if the court truly wants to not be seen as another tool of imperialism designed to subjugate Africa, then the court needs to allow itself to be guided and developed by African practices, thoughts and understandings of justice. Africa must have an equal say in what it means to enforce justice within the international order or else African states will constantly be viewed as subjects of justice rather than fellow citizens.

Acknowledgements I acknowledge funding from the National Research Foundation (Funding to EC Lubaale, Grant No: 127504) towards the funding of writing retreats that informed the conceptual development of my contributions to this book. Support from the Rhodes University Research Committee Grant is also acknowledged.

Bibliography

Agreement for the Termination of the Conflict and Construction of a Stable and Lasting Peace (2016), https://www.peaceagreements.org/wgenerateAgreementPDF/1845 (accessed 20 May 2021).

Akande, D 'The Legal Nature of Security Council Referrals to the ICC and Its Impact on Al Bashir's Immunities' (2009)7 *Journal of International Criminal Justice* 333.

Akhavan, P 'Are International Criminal Tribunals a Disincentive to Peace? Reconciling Judicial Romanticism with Political Realism' (2009)31 *Human Rights Quarterly* 624.

American Service-Members Protection Act (ASPA, Title 2 of Pub.L. 107-206).

American Service-Members Protection Act 2002.

Amnesty International, 'South Sudan: Crippled Justice System and Blanket Amnesties Fueling Impunity for War Crimes' (2019), https://www.amnesty.org/en/latest/news/2019/10/south-sudan-crippled-justice-system-and-blanket-amnesties-fuelling-impunity-for-war-crimes/ (accessed 20 May 2021).

Amnesty International, 'The Battle for Libya: Killings, Disappearances and Torture' (2011) 1–109, https://www.amnesty.org/download/Documents/32000/mde190252011en.pdf (accessed 20 May 2021).

Among, H 'The Application of Traditional Justice Mechanisms to the Atrocities Committed by Child Soldiers in Uganda: A Practical Restorative Justice Approach' (2013)13 *African Human Rights Law Journal* 441.

Arbour, L and Bergsmo, M 'Conspicuous Absence of Jurisdictional Overreach' (1999)1 *International Law Forum Du Droit International* 13.

Bangura, AK 'The Politics of the Struggle to Resolve the Conflict in Uganda: Westerners Pushing Their Legal Approach Versus Ugandans Insisting on Their Mato Oput' (2008)2 *The Journal of Pan African Studies* 142.

Barrios Altos v Peru, Inter-American Court of Human Rights Series C No 75, 14 March 2001.

Bassiouni, C *Introduction to International Criminal Law* (Brill Nijhoff 2013).

BBC News, 'Libya Revokes Bill Which Banned Gadhafi-Era Officials from Office', 2 February 2015, https://www.bbc.com/news/world-latin-america-31104099 (accessed 20 May 2021).

Bell, C 'Negotiating Human Rights' in J Darby and R MacGinty (eds), *The Management of Peace Processes*, 210–229 (UK: Macmillan Press 2000).

Bell, C *Peace Agreements and Human Rights* (Oxford University Press 2000).

Bensouda, F 'The Rome Statute Ten Years On: Where to from Here for the ICC?' Lecture at Melbourne University Law School, 17 February 2011.

Branch, A 'Exploring the Roots of LRA Violence: Political Crisis and Ethnic Politics in Acholiland' in Allen, T and K Vlassenroot (eds), *The Lord's Resistance Army Myth and Reality* (Zed Books 2010).

Branch, A *Displacing Human Rights War and Intervention in Northern Uganda* (Oxford University Press 2011).

Claassens, A and Mnisi, S 'Rural Women Redefining Land Rights in the Context of Living Customary Law' (2009)25 *South African Journal on Human Rights* 491.

Cole, P and Mangan, F 'Tribe, Security, Justice, and Peace in Libya Today' (2016), https://www.usip.org/sites/default/files/PW118-Tribe-Security-Justice-and-Peace-in-Libya-Today.pdf (accessed 20 May 2021).

Crawford, J *Brownlie's Principles of Public International Law* (8th Edition, Oxford University Press 2012).

Cryer, R 'Alternatives and Complements to Criminal Prosecution' in R Cryer et al. (eds), *An Introduction to International Criminal Law and Procedure* (Cambridge University Press 2012).

Decision on Ieng Sary's Rule 89 Preliminary Objections (Ne bis in idem and amnesty and pardon) [2011] Extraordinary Chambers in the Courts of Cambodia Trial Chamber (Extraordinary Chambers in the Courts of Cambodia Trial Chamber).

Fiddler, G 'Using a Conditional Amnesty and Truth and Reconciliation Commission as a Transitional Justice Mechanism in Syria' (2015) 47 *The George Washington Institute of International Law Review* 893.

Freedman, M *Necessary Evils: Amnesties and the Search for Justice* (Cambridge University Press 2010).

Garcia, A 'Transitional (In)Justice: An Exploration of Blanket Amnesties and the Remaining Controversies Around the Spanish Transition to Democracy' (2015)43 *International Journal of Legal Information* 75.

Gaub, F 'A Libyan Recipe for Disaster' (2014)56 *Survival, Global Politics and Strategy* 101.

Glassborrow, K 'Peace Versus Justice in Uganda' (2010), https://iwpr.net/global-voices/peace-versus-justice-uganda (accessed 20 May 2021).

Greenawalt, A 'Complementarity in Crisis: Uganda, Alternative Justice, and the International Criminal Court' (2009)50 *Virginia Journal of International Law* 108.

Human Rights Watch Report, 'Libya, Reject Political Isolation Law': Provisions for Exclusion Too Vague, Sweeping', 4 May 2013, https://www.hrw.org/news/2013/05/04/libya-reject-political-isolation-law (accessed 20 May 2021).

Igreja, V et al. 'Gamba Spirits, Gender Relations, and Healing in Post-Civil War Gorongosa, Mozambique' (2008)14 *Journal of the Royal Anthropological Institute* 353–371.

International Commission of Jurists *Accountability for Serious Crimes Under International Law in Libya: An Assessment of the Criminal Justice System* (International Commission of Jurists 2019).

International Crisis Group, 'Trial by Error: Justice in Post-Qadhafi Libya. Middle East/North Africa Report No.140' (2013), http://www.operationspaix.net/DATA/DOCUMENT/7904~v~Trial_By_Error__Justice_in_Post-Qadhafi_Libya__Middle_East_North_Africa_Reports_no_140_.pdf (accessed 20 May 2021).

Iyi, J 'Re-thinking the Authority of the UN Security Council to Refer Nationals of Non-party States to the ICC' (2019)66 *Netherlands International Law Review* 391.

Jackson, M 'Amnesties in Strasbourg' (2018)38 *Oxford Journal of Legal Studies* 451.

Keller, LM 'Achieving Peace with Justice: The International Criminal Court and Ugandan Alternative Justice Mechanisms' (2009)23 *Connecticut Journal of International Law* 209.

Kersten, M 'Libya's Political Isolation Law: Politics and Justice or the Politics of Justice?', 5 February 2014, https://www.mei.edu/publications/libyas-political-isolation-law-politics-and-justice-or-politics-justice (accessed 20 May 2021).

Lamont, CK 'Contested Governance: Understanding Justice Interventions in Post-Qadhafi Libya' (2016)10 *Journal of Intervention and State building* 382.

Law No. 6 of 2015 of Libya.

Law No. 38 of 2012, Libya.

Longman, T 'An Assessment of Rwanda's Gacaca Courts' (2009)21 *Peace Review* 304.

Lubaale, EC 'Legal Pluralism as a Lens Through Which to Understand the Role and Place of TJMS in International Criminal Justice' (2020) *Journal of Legal Pluralism and Unofficial Law*.

Mallinder, L 'Can Amnesties and International Justice Be Reconciled?' (2007)1 *The International Journal of Transitional Justice* 208.

Marguš v Croatia [GC] ECHR 2014-III.

McEvoy, K and Mallinder, L 'Amnesties in Transition: Punishment, Restoration, and the Governance of Mercy' (2012)39 *Journal of Law and Society* 410.

McNamara, K 'Seeking Justice in Ugandan Courts: Amnesty and the Case of Thomas Kwoyelo' (2013)12 *Washington University Global Studies Law Review* 653.

Minow, M 'Do Alternative Justice Mechanisms Deserve Recognition in International Criminal Law?: Truth Commissions, Amnesties, and Complementarity at the International Criminal Court' (2019)60 *Harvard International Law Journal* 1.

Najla, E 'Customary Practice and Restorative Justice in Libya: A Hybrid Approach' (2015) *Special Report* 1.

Nouwen, S and Werner, W 'Monopolizing Global Justice: International Criminal Law as Challenge to Human Diversity' (2015)13 *Journal of International Criminal Justice* 157.

Office of the Prosecutor, 'Situation in Iraq/UK: Final Report', 9 December 2020, https://www.icc-cpi.int/itemsDocuments/201209-otp-final-report-iraq-uk-eng.pdf (accessed 20 May 2021).

Olwine, BA 'One Step Forward, But Two Steps Back: Why Gacaca in Rwanda Is Jeopardizing the Good Effect of Akayesu on Women's Rights s Rights' (2011)17 *Willian and Mary Journal of Race, Gender and Social Justice* 639.

Political Isolation Law of Libya, 2013.

Portilla, JC 'Amnesty: Evolving 21st Century Constrains Under International Law' (2014)38 *Fletcher Forum of World Affairs* 169.

Pre-Trial Chamber I, Decision on the Admissibility of the Case Against Saif Al-Islam Gadhafi, 31 May 2013, ICC-Ol/ll-Ol/ll-344-Red (hereinafter, Gadhafi Admissibility Decision).

Sang-Hyun, S, The International Criminal Court: A Global Commitment to End Impunity, Presentation at Istanbul Bilgi University, 22 May 2013.

Sarkin, JJ 'How Conditional Amnesties Can Assist Transitional Societies in Delivering on the Right to the Truth' (2017)6 *International Human rights Law Review* 143.

Situation in Libya in the case of *The Prosecutor v Saif Al-Islam Gadhafi*, Pre-Trial Chamber I, ICC-01/11-01/11, 15 November 2018.

Situation in Libya in the Case of *The Prosecutor v Saif Al-Islam Gadhafi*, Judgment on the appeal of Mr Saif Al-Islam Gadhafi against the decision of Pre-Trial Chamber I entitled 'Decision on the "Admissibility Challenge by Dr. Saif AlIslam Gadhafi pursuant to Articles 17(1)(c), 19 and 20(3) of the Rome Statute"' of 5 April 2019, Appeal Chamber judgment delivered on 9 March 2020.

Soad, E *Assessing the Impact of Transitional Justice Mechanisms in Post-conflict Societies: Lessons Drawn for Libya* (PhD Thesis, University of Sheffield 2019).

South African Litigation Centre and Another v National Director of Public Prosecutions and Others, 2012 (10) BCLR 109 (GNP).

Tamale, S *Decolonisation and Afro-Feminist* (Daraja Press 2020).

The Prosocutor v Ayyesh (STL-11-01) Decision on the Defence Appeal Against the Trial Chamber's "Decision on the Defence Challenge to the Jurisdiction and Legality of the Tribunal", 24 October 2012.

The Prosecutor v Omar Hassan Ahmad Al Bashir (Situation in Darfurm, Sudan) Pre-Trial Chamber II, Decision under Article 87(7) of the Rome Statute on the non-compliance of Jordan with the request by the Court for the arrest and surrender of Omar Al-Bashir, Case No ICC-02/05-01/09, 11 December 2017.

The Prosecutor v Saif AL-Islam Gadhafi and Abdullah Al-Senussi, Decision on the admissibility of the case against Abdullah Al-Senussi ICC-01/11-01/11-466-Red, 11 October 2013 | Pre-Trial Chamber I.

The Prosecutor v Saif Al-Islam Gadhafi, https://www.icc-cpi.int/libya/gaddafi (accessed 20 May 2021).

The Prosecutor v Tadic (IT-94-1) Decision on the Defence Motion for Interlocutory Appeal on Jurisdiction 2 October 1995.

Thomas Kwoyelo v Uganda ACHPR Communication 431/12 (17 October 2018).

Tladi, D 'Complementarity and Cooperation in International Criminal Justice Assessing Initiatives to Fill the Impunity Gap' (2014) Institute of Security Studies 1–14, https://www.files.ethz.ch/isn/185933/Paper277.pdf (accessed 20 May 2021).

United Nations, *Charter of the United Nations*, 24 October 1945, 1 UNTS XVI, https://treaties.un.org/doc/publication/ctc/uncharter.pdf (accessed 4 May 2021).

United Nations General Assembly, Rome Statute of the International Criminal Court, 17 July 1998 Article 1 and Preamble.

United Nations General Assembly International Law Commission, Third Report on Crimes Against Humanity by SD Murphy, Special Rapporteur (23 January 2017) UN Doc A/CN.4/704.

United Nations High Commissioner for Human Rights, 'Rule of Law Tools for Post-conflict States' (2009) UN Doc HR/Pub/09/1.

United Nations, *Vienna Convention on the Law of Treaties*, 23 May 1969, United Nations, Treaty Series, vol. 1155, p. 331, https://www.refworld.org/docid/3ae6b3a10.html (accessed 3 May 2021).

United Nations Security Council, 'The Rule of Law and Transitional Justice in Conflict and Post-conflict Societies', Report of the Secretary General, 23 August 2004, UN Doc S/2004/616.

Yakinthou, C et al. *Advancing Transitional Justice in Conflict-Affected Contexts: A Case Study for Libya* (2016).

Young, IM *Justice and the Politics of Difference* (Princeton: Princeton University Press 1990).

Now Available but Still Not Accessible to the ICC: Bashir and Africa's Politics

Emma Charlene Lubaale

1 Background

The commission of atrocities, some of which constitute gross human rights violations, has been and continues to be a major occurrence across states. African states have not been an exception in as far as these disquieting occurrences are concerned. Some of the atrocities committed have shocked the conscious of humanity that they have fallen squarely within the ambit of international crimes. The attacks on humanity have left the international community with no option but to devise means of response. International criminal justice has stood out as one of the approaches relevant to putting an end to the impunity by perpetrators of these crimes. Mention of international criminal justice in this age brings sharply into focus the role and mandate of the International Criminal Court (ICC)—a Court whose statutory framework is anchored in the Rome Statute of the International Criminal Court (Rome Statute). In enacting the Rome Statute, states affirmed 'that the most serious crimes of concern to the

E. C. Lubaale (✉)
Faculty of Law, Rhodes University, Eastern Cape, South Africa
e-mail: e.lubaale@ru.ac.za

E. C. Lubaale and N. Dyani-Mhango (eds.), *National Accountability for International Crimes in Africa*,
https://doi.org/10.1007/978-3-030-88044-6_8

international community as a whole must not go unpunished and that their effective prosecution must be ensured by taking measures at the national level and by enhancing international cooperation.'[1]

The ICC is a Court 'complementary to national jurisdictions.'[2] Effectively, national courts are to have the first bite on the apple in as far as criminal accountability for international crimes is concerned. Interventions by the ICC are therefore a measure of last resort. The implication of this is that both the ICC and national courts can exercise jurisdiction over international crimes. The jurisdictions of national courts over all crimes, including international crimes, are subject to the national laws of the state in issue while the ICC's jurisdiction is clearly mapped out in the Rome Statute.[3] In terms of Article 13 of the Rome Statute, the jurisdiction of the ICC can be triggered through a state's own referral, a referral by the United Nations Security Council (UNSC) acting on in terms of Chapter VII of the United Nations Charter and by the ICC Prosecutor on his/her own initiative.[4] All the foregoing means of triggering the jurisdiction of the ICC have thus far played out in proceedings before the ICC in the situations of Uganda, Sudan and Kenya, respectively.[5] Regardless of the manner in which the jurisdiction of the ICC is triggered, state cooperation remains essential in ensuring that those accused are brought to justice before the ICC.

The cooperation of states in securing those accused is particularly pivotal because the ICC does not have Police structures of its own to execute this task. The drafters of the Rome Statute envisaged the critical need for state cooperation in the investigation and prosecution of cases before the ICC, going as far as making it explicit that state parties should cooperate fully with the ICC in its investigation and prosecution of international crimes under its jurisdiction.[6] Securing those accused of

[1] Preamble of the Rome Statute of the International Criminal Court, 17 July 1998, 2187 U.N.T.S. 90 (entered into force on 1 July 2002) (Rome Statute).

[2] Preamble and Article 1 of the Rome Statute.

[3] Article 13 of the Rome Statute.

[4] As above.

[5] See generally ICC, *Situations Under Investigation*, available at https://www.icc-cpi.int/pages/situation.aspx (accessed 22 November 2020).

[6] Article 86 of the Rome Statute.

international crimes to face trial before the ICC has not always been an easy task especially when it involves sitting presidents who are in possession of power. When wielded, this power has ensured that they escape arrest. Nowhere has this challenge been more evident than in the case against the former president of Sudan, Omar al-Bashir, who currently faces charges before the ICC. Al-Bashir has been charged with several counts of crimes against humanity, war crimes and genocide.[7] Despite the first warrant to arrest him being issued in 2009, al-Bashir continued to travel across several African and Asian states without being arrested by any of them for purposes of prosecution before the ICC. The failure by various states including South Africa, Chad and Malawi to arrest al-Bashir triggered tensions between the ICC and African states, with some states such as South Africa going as far as threatening and even acting on the threat to withdraw from the Rome Statute.[8] These tensions also rejuvenated discussions on the need for African states to have an African Court designated to prosecute international crimes—citing, amongst others, the witch-hunting tendencies of the ICC against African states.[9]

[7] ICC, *Situation in Darfur, Sudan* ICC-02/05, available at https://www.icc-cpi.int/darfur (accessed 22 May 2021).

[8] P Fabricius, 'South Africa Confirms Withdrawal from ICC', Daily Maverick, 7 December 2017, available at https://www.dailymaverick.co.za/article/2017-12-07-south-africa-confirms-withdrawal-from-icc/ (accessed 22 November 2020). For a discussion on this and other threats to withdraw, see R Chipaike et al., 'African Move to Withdraw from the ICC: Assessment of Issues and Implications' (2019)75 *India Quarterly: A Journal of International Affairs* 334–350; EY Omorogbe, 'The Crisis of International Criminal Law in Africa: A Regional Regime in Response?' (2019)66 *Netherlands International Law Review* 287–311. On Malawi, Chad and South Africa's failure to arrest Al-Bashir, see generally ICC decisions in Situation in Darfur, Sudan in the Case of *The Prosecutor v Omar Hassan Ahmad Al-Bashir*, Decision under Article 87(7) of the Rome Statute on the non-compliance by South Africa with the request by the Court for the arrest and surrender of Omar Al-Bashir, 6 July 2017; Situation in Darfur, Sudan, In the case of the *Prosecutor v Omar Hassan Ahmad Al Bashir*, Decision pursuant to Article 87(7) of the Rome Statute on the refusal of the Republic of Chad to comply with the cooperation requests issued by the Court with respect to the arrest and surrender of Omar Hassan Ahmad Al Bashir, Pre-Trial Chamber I, 13 December 2011; Situation in Darfur, Sudan, In the case of the *Prosecutor v Omar Hassan Ahmad Al Bashir,* Decision Pursuant to Article 87(7) of the Rome Statute on the Failure by the Republic of Malawi to Comply with the Cooperation Requests Issued by the Court with Respect to the Arrest and Surrender of Omar Hassan Ahmad Al Bashir, Pre-Trial Chamber I, 13 December 2011.

[9] African Union, 'Withdrawal Strategy Document' (2017), https://www.hrw.org/sites/default/files/supporting_resources/icc_withdrawal_strategy_jan._2017.pdf, accessed 15 June 2021; *The Guardian*, 'African Leaders Plan Mass Withdrawal from International

In April 2019, al-Bashir was ousted from presidency, effectively bringing an end to his 30-year reign as president of Sudan. Over a decade since the first warrant of arrest was issued against him, it seemed reasonable to assume that al-Bashir was finally in close reach of the ICC for purposes of commencing the long-awaited ICC trial in respect of the charges brought against him. Such an assumption would be reasonable in the light of the fact that al-Bashir no longer enjoyed the privileges associated with his former position as president. Over a year since his ousting, al-Bashir is yet to face trial for the charges against him before the ICC as he has not been surrendered to the ICC by the current Sudanese government. The current Sudanese government has, as recently as February 2020, affirmed its commitment to cooperate with the ICC in ensuring that al-Bashir is prosecuted for the international crimes he allegedly committed.[10] However, no guarantee exists for such commitment. The failure to arrest and surrender al-Bashir, despite the seemingly conducive environment that the Sudanese government currently finds itself, raises issues on whether there is real commitment by the current government to advance or cooperate in the advancement of international criminal justice in respect of the international crimes committed in Darfur.

The purpose of this chapter is to provide an understanding of how the events in Sudan since the ousting of al-Bashir have posed a challenge to the surrender of al-Bashir to the ICC. It also demonstrates how, despite making commitments to ensure that al-Bashir is surrendered, the al-Bashir case could be used by the current leadership as a tool to settle Sudan's internal political conflicts. This purpose is accomplished by engaging with a number of critical questions and these are: What is the composition of the government committing to cooperate with the ICC in bringing al-Bashir to justice? Has the possibility of some of the members of this government being implicated in the commission of international crimes been considered? Put differently, is it probable that some members of the current Sudanese government are implicated in the same atrocities

Criminal Court', 31 January 2017, available at https://www.theguardian.com/law/2017/jan/31/african-leaders-plan-mass-withdrawal-from-international-criminal-court (accessed 22 November 2020).

[10] Human Rights Watch Report, 'Sudan Opens Door for ICC Prosecutions: Ex-President Bashir May Finally Face Trial for Alleged Darfur Crimes', 12 February 2020, available at https://www.hrw.org/news/2020/02/12/sudan-opens-door-icc-prosecutions (accessed 22 November 2020).

that al-Bashir is wanted for by the ICC? What then is the implication of this state of affairs for the effective cooperation of Sudan with the ICC in as far as accountability for crimes allegedly committed by al-Bashir is concerned? Suffice it to state that this state of affairs is not unique to Sudan. The ICC appears to have walked down a similar path before in respect of the Ugandan situation which is currently before the ICC. What cautionary tale does Uganda offer the ICC in dealing with Sudan in as far as the tendency of states using the ICC for national political gain is concerned? In engaging with these issues, the chapter is divided into the following subsections: an examination of the Sudan situation before the ICC with focus on al-Bashir; the 2020 renewed commitments by Sudan to cooperate with the ICC amidst an al-Bashir infiltrated leadership; the politics surrounding the referral of the situation in Uganda and lessons it offers; a possible replay of the Ugandan movie in Sudan; and conclusion.

2 Understanding the Sudan Situation Before the ICC and al-Bashir

The warrants of arrest against al-Bashir relate to a war in Darfur that dates back to the early years of 2000.[11] In 2003, the renowned Sudanese Liberation Movement (SLM) and the Justice and Equality Movement (JEM), both rebel groups, waged war against the Sudanese government, accusing it of oppressing the non-Arab population in Darfur.[12] The government of Sudan, under the leadership of al-Bashir, responded to these rebel attacks by engaging various armed forces including the Sudanese Military, the Police and Militia such as the Janjaweed.[13] This conflict led to the commission of multiple atrocities by both the rebel groups and the Sudanese government-sanctioned forces.[14] Amongst the strategies invoked by the government to respond to these attacks was ethnic cleansing which was geared towards elimination of the non-Arab

[11] The first warrant for arrest for Omar Hassan Ahmad Al Bashir was issued on 4 March 2009, the second on 12 July 2010. AL Bashir is still not yet before the ICC.

[12] Human Rights Watch Report, 'Human Rights Benchmarks for Sudan', 3 May 2017, available at https://www.hrw.org/news/2017/05/03/human-rights-benchmarks-sudan (accessed 22 November 2020).

[13] As above.

[14] As above.

population.[15] This approach saw the death of hundreds of thousands of civilians.[16] Reports also suggest that the government of Sudan, through its forces, engaged in the forceful eviction and displacement of the non-Arab civilian population in Darfur.[17] Displacement was effected through massive and indiscriminate bombing of the Darfur region, effectively displacing civilians from their homes.[18] Reports also document a wide range of atrocities committed by both the government and rebel groups including sexual violence against women and girls; abduction of children to serve as child soldiers; looting of civilian property including crops, cattle and other forms of property; burning of thousands of villages; and destruction of infrastructure and water resources, making it possible for the displaced civilians to return to their homes.[19]

Although Sudan is not a party to the ICC, the jurisdiction of the ICC in respect of the atrocities alleged in Darfur was triggered by the UNSC Referral of the situation in Darfur to the ICC in terms of Article 13(b) of the Rome Statute. According to the UNSC, the atrocities allegedly committed in Darfur constitute a threat to international peace and security thus warranting the exercise of the UNSC Chapter VII powers.[20] The ICC's investigations in the situation in Darfur commenced in June 2005 and in accordance with these investigations, those implicated include the Janjaweed Militia, Sudanese Government officials and leaders of the Resistance Front.[21] The charges against those implicated entail the following crimes:

[15] Situation in Darfur, footnote 7 above.

[16] Human Rights Watch Report, footnote 12 above.

[17] Human Rights Watch Report, 'Darfur in the Shadows: The Sudanese Government's Ongoing Attacks on Civilians and Human Rights', 5 June 2011, available at https://www.hrw.org/report/2011/06/05/darfur-shadows/sudanese-governments-ongoing-attacks-civilians-and-human-rights (accessed 22 November 2020).

[18] As above.

[19] As above.

[20] United Nations Security Council, Resolution 1593 Adopted by the Security Council at its 5158th Meeting on 31 March 2005, available at https://www.icc-cpi.int/NR/rdonlyres/85FEBD1A-29F8-4EC4-9566-48EDF55CC587/283244/N0529273.pdf (accessed 22 November 2020).

[21] Situation in Darfur, footnote 7 above.

- Genocide: genocide by killing; genocide by causing serious bodily or mental harm; and genocide by deliberately inflicting on each target group conditions of life calculated to bring about the group's physical destruction;
- War crimes: murder; attacks against the civilian population; destruction of property; rape; pillaging; and outrage upon personal dignity; violence to life and person; intentionally directing attacks against personnel, installations, material, units or vehicles involved in a peacekeeping mission; and
- Crimes against humanity: murder; persecution; forcible transfer of population; rape; inhumane acts; imprisonment or severe deprivation of liberty; torture; extermination; and torture.[22]

Al-Bashir, one of those implicated in accordance with these investigations, faces five counts of crimes against humanity, three counts of genocide and two counts of war crimes in respect of atrocities committed between 2003 and 2008.[23] These counts relate to allegations of torture, murder, pillage, extermination and intentional attacks on the civilian population.[24] What stands out clearly from the conflict in Darfur is that government forces were at the centre of the atrocities committed and not surprisingly, charges were preferred against various government officials at the time including al-Bashir. Until April 2019, al-Bashir was still the head of state of Sudan and as such, enjoyed the privileges that come with such a position. It could then be understood why Sudan's cooperation with the ICC was futile. Would the dynamics change after al-Bashir's overthrow, or, the status quo in terms of power would be maintained?

As already alluded to, following his ousting, al-Bashir was charged and prosecuted for crimes relating to financial irregularity and corruption.[25] Though sentenced to 2 years of imprisonment in 2019, al-Bashir, now 76 years of age, was sent to a reform centre on account of his

[22] As above.

[23] As above.

[24] As above.

[25] *The Guardian*, 'Ex-Sudan Leader Omar al-Bashir Sentenced to Two Years for Corruption', 14 December 2020, available at https://www.theguardian.com/world/2019/dec/14/sudanese-court-sentences-omar-al-bashir-to-2-years-in-prison (accessed 22 November 2020).

age.[26] However, even though al-Bashir was convicted and sentenced by Sudan's national criminal justice system, the case against him remains admissible before the ICC. The systematic interpretation of the Rome Statute suggests that under the ICC regime, emphasis is on the conduct and not legal characterisation.[27] In terms of Article 17 (1)(a) of the Rome Statute, 'a case is inadmissible where the case is being investigated or prosecuted by a state which has jurisdiction over it, unless the state is unwilling or unable genuinely to carry out the investigation or prosecution.' The ICC's notion of a case in accordance with the foregoing provision pertains to the same person and the same conduct.[28] Thus, since emphasis is on the conduct and not the crime, states can prosecute on the basis of

[26] As above.

[27] Article 17 and Article 20(3) of the ICC Statute give states the option to prosecute international crimes by relying on ordinary crimes. For commentaries on this see, e.g., F Ward, *Direct Application of International Criminal Law in National Courts* (Asser Press 2005) 30–32; SMH Nouwen, *Complementarity in the Line of Fire: The Catalysing Effect of the International Criminal Court in Uganda and Sudan* (Cambridge University Press 2013) 40–41; R Bellelli, *International Criminal Justice: From the Rome Statute to Its Review* (Ashgate Publishing 2010) 176; G Conway, 'Ne Bis in Idem and the International Criminal Tribunals' (2003)14 *Criminal Law Forum* 358; JB Terracino, 'National implementation of ICC Crimes: Impact on National Jurisdictions and the ICC' (2007)5 *Journal of International Criminal Justice* 421–440; J Kleffner, 'The Impact of Complementarity on National Implementation of Substantive International Criminal Law' (2003) *Journal of International Criminal Justice* 86–96; K Ambos, *Treatise on International Criminal Law* (Oxford University Press 2013) 405; C Stahn, 'Libya, the International Criminal Court and complementarity: A Test for 'Shared responsibility' (2012)10 *Journal of International Criminal Justice* 337–338; M Bergsmo et al., 'Complementarity After Kampala: Capacity Building and the ICC's Legal Tools' (2010)2 *Goettingen Journal of International Law* 798; KJ Heller, 'A Sentence-Based Theory of Complementarity' (2011)53 *Harvard International Law Journal* 202.

[28] Decision on the admissibility of the case against Saif Al-Islam Gaddafi (ICC-01/11-01/11), Pre-Trial.

Chamber I, 31 May 2013, paragraph 86. However, some scholars contend that even with this test, states are hardly left with any discretion except to mirror the proceedings of the ICC. On this see, e.g., MA Newton, 'The Quest for Constructive Complementarity' in C Stahn and M El Zeidy (eds) *The International Criminal Court and Complementarity: From Theory to Practice* (Cambridge University Press 2011) 321–322; F Mégret, 'Too Much of a Good Thing? Implementation and the Uses of Complementarity' in C Stahn and M El Zeidy (eds) *The International Criminal Court and Complementarity: From Theory to Practice* (Cambridge University Press 2011) 361.

ordinary crimes.[29] Although recourse can be made to ordinary crimes to advance accountability for international crimes, the ordinary crimes for which al-Bashir was charged with and ultimately convicted of in Sudan do not relate to the conduct he is charged with at the ICC. Before the ICC, he faces charges for conduct relating to war crimes, crimes against humanity and genocide. It is against this backdrop that the case against him at the ICC remains admissible.

3 Renewed Commitment to Cooperate with the ICC by an al-Bashir-Infiltrated Leadership

In 2014, the prosecutor of the ICC, Fatou Bensouda, took a decision to shelf the case against al-Bashir for lack of cooperation from states which failed to ensure that he is arrested and brought to trial.[30] With the ousting of al-Bashir from presidency in April 2019, hopes for him facing trial before the ICC seemed to come alive. Additionally, with the national trial for financial irregularity and corruption now out of the picture, it could be presumed that focus would now be placed on cooperating with the ICC. Fatou Bensouda, the ICC Prosecutor, seems to see a glimmer of hope. In December 2019, she informed the UNSC that she had been 'emboldened by the positive political changes' in Sudan and accordingly hopes that 'Sudan will honor its commitment to deliver justice.'[31] Her hopes seem to be met by commitments from the current Sudanese leadership which has indicated its preparedness to cooperate with the ICC to ensure that al-Bashir faces justice. In February 2020, Mohammed Hassan al-Taishi, a civilian member of Sudan's top leadership (the Sovereign Council), indicated that: 'We agreed that everyone who had arrest warrants issued

[29] *Prosecutor v Thomas Lubanga Dyilo* (Decision on the Prosecutor's Application for a Warrant of Arrest, Article 58, ICC-01/04-01/06-8, Pre-Trial Chamber I, 10 February 2006, paragraphs 30–38).

[30] *The Prosecutor v Omar Hassan Ahmad Al Bashir*, Case No. ICC-02/05-01/09, ICC Website, 'Al Bashir Case', https://www.icc-cpi.int/darfur/albashir, accessed 14 June 2021; see also BBC News, 'ICC Prosecutor Shelves Darfur War Crimes Inquiries', 12 December 2014, available at https://www.bbc.com/news/world-africa-30458347 (accessed 22 November 2020).

[31] United Nations News, 'Deliver Justice' for Atrocity Crimes in Darfur, Top Court Prosecutor Tells Security Council', 18 December 2019, available at https://news.un.org/en/story/2019/12/1053991 (accessed 22 November 2020).

against them will appear before the ICC. I am saying this very clearly.'[32] Al-Taishi added: 'We can only achieve justice if we heal the wounds with justice itself.'[33] Adding voice to this commitment is General Abel Fattah al-Burhan, the chairperson of the Sudanese Sovereign Council, who has, as recently as February 2020, made it known to Human Rights Watch that: 'We [the Sovereign Council] agreed no one is above the law, and that people will be brought to justice, be it in Sudan or outside Sudan with the help of the ICC.'[34] He added, 'We will fully cooperate with the ICC.'[35] Abdallah Hamdok, the current Prime Minister of Sudan, has also expressed similar sentiments in as far as cooperation with the ICC is concerned.[36] The issue that needs to be resolved, however, is whether these commitments bear prospects in the light of the current composition of Sudanese leadership. The discussion below resolves this issue.

In April 2019, amidst months-long protests from various factions of the civilian population, it became increasingly clear that the civilian population was not about to back down. Sooner or later, the Sudanese government, under the leadership of al-Bashir, would be ousted. This ousting would have major implications for members of the military, many of whom directly or indirectly played a role in the commission of the atrocities in Darfur. Effectively, the Sudanese defence minister at the time, Abdel Raheem Hussein, and Vice president of Sudan at the time, Ibn Auf, both military personnel, announced the military's overthrow and arrest of al-Bashir.[37] Upon ousting al-Bashir, a Transitional Military Council (TMC), comprising of seven military generals was set up to take charge of the country while it transitioned to civilian governance.[38] The TMC was mandated to oversee the transition period of Sudan which was to last no more than two years. In terms of leadership, Lieutenant General Abdel Fattah al-Burhan and General Mohammed Hamadan Dagalo were

[32] Human Rights Watch Report, footnote 12 above.

[33] As above.

[34] As above.

[35] As above.

[36] As above.

[37] BBC News, 'Sudan Coup: Why Omar al-Bashir Was Overthrown', 15 April 2019, available at https://www.bbc.com/news/world-africa-47852496 (accessed 22 November 2020).

[38] BBC News, 'Sudan Crisis: What You Need to Know', 16 August 2019, available at https://www.bbc.com/news/world-africa-48511226 (accessed 22 November 2020).

appointed as chairperson and deputy chairperson of the TMC, respectively.[39] But who are these two individuals and what implication would their leadership have for their cooperation with the ICC in the al-Bashir case?

The head and deputy head of the TMC were leaders in Sudan's military force during al-Bashir's reign. Lieutenant general Burhan, the Chairperson of the TMC (as it were then), has been accused of committing atrocities during military operations against non-Arab civilians in Darfur in 2003 when he was chief of ground forces.[40] Furthermore, at the time Dagalo was sworn in as deputy head of the TMC, he was the commander of the paramilitary unit Rapid Support Forces (RSF).[41] The RSF is comprised of Arab militias who fought on the side of government forces in the Darfur war during al-Bashir's reign as president.[42] The RSF is implicated in the commission of a number of atrocities in Darfur.[43] Members of the RSF have also been implicated in the alleged human rights violation committed after the ousting of al-Bashir from presidency.[44] It is alleged that the RSF responded to civilian protests through indiscriminate killings and detention of civilians without trial.[45] Reports of rights groups, including Amnesty International and Human Rights Watch, document that since April 2019, Sudanese government forces, including the RSF, have committed serious human rights violations that

[39] As above.

[40] M Amin, 'Profile: Members of Sudan's Sovereign Council Sudan Unveiled 11-Member Council That Will Run Country During 3-Year Transitional Period', 21 August 2019, available at https://www.aa.com.tr/en/africa/profile-members-of-sudans-sovereign-council/1561302 (accessed 22 November 2020).

[41] As above.

[42] As above.

[43] Human Rights Watch Report, 'Men with No Mercy: Rapid Support Forces Attacks Against Civilians in Darfur, Sudan', 9 September 2015, available at https://www.hrw.org/report/2015/09/09/men-no-mercy/rapid-support-forces-attacks-against-civilians-darfur-sudan (accessed 22 November 2020).

[44] Human Rights Watch Report, 'They Were Shouting 'Kill Them': Sudan's Violent Crackdown on Protesters in Khartoum', 17 November 2019, available at https://www.hrw.org/report/2019/11/17/they-were-houting-kill-them/sudans-violent-crackdown-protesters-khartoum (accessed 22 November 2020).

[45] As above.

could be characterised as war crimes and crimes against humanity.[46] These violations include the unlawful killing of civilians, destruction of villages, sexual violence, forced displacement and looting. Dagalo is allegedly linked to these violations.[47] With the leadership of these two generals, chances for surrender of al-Bashir would arguably be slim.

Worthy to note, after the establishment of the TMC, civilian protestors did not back down on their protests; they continued to demonstrate on the streets of Khartoum demanding for the establishment of a civilian-led government. The Sudanese Professional Association, one of the groups at the forefront of these protests, took to the streets, demanding that al-Bashir be held to account, and for a civilian presidential governance with the defence minister being the only representative from the military.[48] Leaders of these protests considered the ousting of al-Bashir by the military a staged coup aimed at depriving civilian protesters of their hard-earned victory over al-Bashir. One commentator was on record for observing as follows: 'what is happening now is a big trick; this is the same regime of al-Bashir and so they want to cheat us in order to maintain the interests of the ruling party seniors, the security organs and the entire regime.'[49] Some members of the Sudanese Professionals Association equally called into question the TMC, observing that it was a reincarnation of the old al-Bashir regime.[50]

Following the relentless protests from the civilian population, a power-sharing agreement was concluded between civilian representatives and the military. In August 2019, the two sides reached an agreement on a number of issues including power-sharing for 39 months; conducting of elections after the 39 months; formation of a Sovereign Council, a cabinet and a legislature; and appointment of a military general to

[46] As above; Amnesty International Report, 'Sudan 2019', available at https://www.amnesty.org/en/countries/africa/sudan/report-sudan/ (accessed 22 November 2020).

[47] As above; Amin, footnote 40 above.

[48] Aljazeera News, 'Sudan's Military Removes al-Bashir: All the Latest Updates', 20 April 2019, available at https://www.aljazeera.com/news/2019/04/sudan-army-removes-bashir-latest-updates-190411125048555.html (visited 22 November 2020).

[49] As above.

[50] As above.

lead the Sovereign Council which would oversee the transition.[51] The Sovereign Council would have the effect of replacing the TMC and it would have 11 members: five of these being civilians, the five others being members of the military and 1 of the members to be agreed upon by consensus. In terms of this agreement, the cabinet would be headed by a prime minister who would be elected by the civilian pro-democracy movement. The Sovereign Council of Sudan has since been constituted, comprising of six civilians and five members of the military.[52] Lieutenant General Burhan, the former head of the TMC, was appointed to head the Sovereign Council. Other military members appointed to form part of this council include General Mohammed Hamadan Dagalo, Lieutenant Generals Yasser Atta, Ibrahim Gaber and Shams al-Din Kabashi. From the civilian section, appointees include Mohammed Sheikh Idris, Al-Siddiq Tawer Kafi, Mohammed Osman Hassan al-Taishi, Mohamed al-Fakeeh, Aisha Moussa al-Saeed, Rajaa Nicola and Al-Siddig Dawer. In terms of profiles of the military members of the Sovereign Council: Shams al-Din Kabashi is the former spokesperson of the defunct TMC; Lieutenant General Yasser is the former chief of staff of the defunct TMC and former consul-general to Djibouti under al-Bashir; General Ibrahim Jaber was a naval commander under al-Bashir's reign and was a member of the defunct TMC; General Dagalo as already noted is widely known to have profound influence over Sudan's military during and after al-Bashir's reign and also implicated in the atrocities committed in Darfur.[53] The implication of this composition for the Sovereign Council's cooperation with the ICC in handing over al-Bashir to the ICC cannot be overstated. Again, just like the TMC, the infiltration of Sudan's leadership with military weakened calls for surrender of al-Bashir to the ICC.

It is notable that the Sovereign Council is at the helm of Sudan's current leadership and transition to democracy. This Council has since appointed Abdalla Hamdok to serve as prime minister during this period.

[51] Sudan Constitutional Declaration, 'Draft Constitutional Charter for the 2019 Transitional Period' (2019) 1–21, https://constitutionnet.org/sites/default/files/2019-08/Sudan%20Constitutional%20Declaration%20%28English%29.pdf (accessed 22 May 2021).

[52] As above. See also Aljazeera News, 'Sudan Forms 11-Member Sovereign Council, Headed by al-Burhan', 20 August 2019, available at https://www.aljazeera.com/news/2019/08/sudan-forms-11-member-sovereign-council-headed-al-burhan-190820204821614.html (accessed 22 November 2020).

[53] As above, Amin, footnote 40 above.

In this capacity, Hamdok heads Sudan's cabinet. Despite the existence of other structures including the cabinet and legislature, the Sovereign Council still constitutes the top leadership of Sudan. Therefore, it can be gathered that despite the ousting of al-Bashir, his footprints remain evident in the current leadership of Sudan. It is worth emphasising that part of the leadership of Sudan's Sovereign Council served under al-Bashir's reign. Reports do suggest that some of them directly or indirectly took part in the military campaigns that resulted in the numerous atrocities committed in Darfur.[54] The military system's continued infiltration of the current Sudanese leadership is testament to the fact that al-Bashir's 30-year rule enabled him to construct an intricate web within the military; so complex that dismantling one part of it exposes many other members of the military to criminal accountability. A thorough investigation of these military members' dealings under the al-Bashir regime could probably render them candidates for indictment before the ICC. Incidentally, it is this same leadership that Fatou Bensouda has to count on to surrender al-Bashir for trial before the ICC. Could this then explain the wavering commitment by Sudan's current leadership to cooperate with the ICC? Perhaps yes. As already alluded to, in February 2020, in his statement to Human Rights Watch, al-Burhan, the head of the Sovereign Council, indicated Sudan's commitment to cooperate with the ICC. However, as of 2019, al-Burhan was opposed to transferring al-Bashir to The Hague. In fact, three days after the February 2020 announcement to Human Rights Watch, al-Burhan made it clear that cooperation with the ICC did not necessarily mean that Bashir would be handed over to the ICC. He categorically pointed out that 'the word 'appearance' doesn't mean that the wanted persons would be sent to The Hague.'[55] Al-Burhan is clearly non-committal in as far as surrender of al-Bashir to the ICC is concerned. Note is to also be taken of the fact that soon after the overthrow of al-Bashir, Omar Zein Abideen, one of the military leaders of the defunct TMC, indicated that al-Bashir would not be handed over to

[54] See Amin, footnote 40 above on profiles of members of the military of the Sovereign Council.

[55] M Amin, 'Suspect Still at Large': Why Sudan Hasn't handed Omar Bashir over to the ICC', 12 March 2020, available at https://www.middleeasteye.net/news/sudan-why-omar-bashir-icc-international-criminal-court (accessed 22 November 2020).

the ICC for trial; rather, he would be tried in Sudan.[56] This posture is quite problematic considering the obligation of states to cooperate with the ICC. Of course, Sudan is not a party to the Rome Statute. One could therefore argue that such an obligation does not exist regarding the Al-Bashir case. Contrary to such possible argument, the obligation of Sudan is not rooted in the Rome Statute. Article 13(b) of the Rome Statute allows for the UNSC to extend the ICC's jurisdiction to situations in non-state parties. Certainly, the UNSC is well aware that to exercise such jurisdiction, the ICC would have to invoke the Rome Statute. Therefore, whereas theoretically Sudan only owes the UNSC allegiance by virtue of being a member of the United Nations, the UNSC creates a situation in which the referred nation, in this case Sudan, is now in a situation similar to that of state parties to the Rome Statute despite not being a party itself.[57] It is, however, submitted that non-state parties including Sudan owe no treaty obligations to the ICC because they are not party to the Rome Statute. From a treaty law perspective, it could be argued that Sudan is not in violation of its international law obligations by not cooperating with the ICC in as far as the Al-Bashir case is concerned. However, in the recent decision in the case of the ICC Appeals Chamber in the case of Jordan, the Court has made it clear that Sudan is under obligations to cooperate because it is now in a position analogous to that of a state party to the Rome Statute by virtue of the wording of the UNSC Resolution.[58]

Pertinent to note, the renewed commitments to cooperate with the ICC as announced by the various individuals in Sudan's current leadership arose from a peace talk session between Sudan's current leadership and the rebel groups in Darfur.[59] These talks saw Sudan's government negotiate and sign an initial peace deal with the rebel group.[60] These

[56] J Kirby, 'Sudan's Military Says It Won't Extradite Omar al-Bashir to Face War Crimes Charges', 12 April 2019, https://www.vox.com/world/2019/4/12/18307649/sudan-omar-al-bashir-war-crimes-icc-military (accessed 22 May 2020).

[57] For a detailed discussion on this, see J Iyi, 'Re-thinking the Authority of the UN Security Council to Refer Nationals of Non-party States to the ICC' (2019)66 *Netherlands International Law Review* 399.

[58] See Judgment in the Jordan Referral re Al-Bashir Appeal, 06 May 2019, ICC-02/05-01/09-397-Corr., paragraph 140.

[59] Aljazeera News, 'Sudan's Government Signs Initial Peace Deal with Rebel Group', 25 January 2020, available at https://www.aljazeera.com/news/2020/01/sudans-government-signs-peace-deal-rebels-200125062016599.html (accessed 22 November 2020).

[60] As above.

talks, which remain ongoing, seek to negotiate a deal between the current leadership and the rebel groups in Darfur.[61] It is hoped that these negotiations will bring an end to the long-standing conflict in Darfur which is currently characterised by sporadic attacks from these rebels. At the heart of the rebel group's demands in these negotiations is the need to ensure that the current leadership surrenders al-Bashir for trial before the ICC.[62] In fact, the announcement by al-Taishi in February 2020, indicating Sudan's commitment to cooperate with the ICC, came during the peace negotiations in Juba between the rebel groups and the Sovereign Council. Note cautiously, however, that even with the rebel groups' demands to have al-Bashir surrendered, some members of the rebel groups are also implicated in the commission of atrocities in Darfur. These negotiations continue to evolve and concessions continue to be made. Thus, depending on the outcome, the negotiations have potential to shape Sudan's posture on cooperation with the ICC. It can therefore be deduced from this state of affairs that commitments by Sudan to cooperate with the ICC have wavered and continue to waver, causing one to wonder whether Sudan is genuinely committed to international criminal justice.

Sudan's current leadership would not be the first to express support and commitment to cooperating with the ICC is ensuring the arrest and surrender of the al-Bashir. In 2009, one of Sudanese rebel groups signified similar support and commitment. When the first warrant of arrest was issued against al-Bashir in 2009, chief Khalil Ibrahim the leader of the JEM, a major militant group against the then al-Bashir governance, expressed his support as follows: 'We are admiring the ICC, we are fully supporting the ICC. We are ready to go to ICC including myself and we are ready to work as tool [for the] ICC to capture anybody.'[63] He was optimistic that the issuance of an arrest warrant against al-Bashir would

[61] As above.

[62] Aljazeera News, 'Sudan Agrees Those Wanted by ICC Should Appear Before Court', 11 February 2020, available at https://www.aljazeera.com/news/2020/02/sudan-darfur-rebels-agree-prosecution-wanted-icc-200211135956815.html (accessed 22 November 2020); BBC News, 'Omar al-Bashir: Sudan Agrees Ex-president Must Face ICC', 11 February 2020, available at https://www.bbc.com/news/world-africa-51462613 (accessed 7 June 2021).

[63] 'Darfur Rebels Vow Full ICC Cooperation Ahead of Ruling on Bashir Case', Sudan Tribune, 2 March 2009, available at https://www.sudantribune.com/spip.php?article30331 (visited on 22 November 2020).

be 'an end of his legitimacy to be president of Sudan.'[64] The JEM leader promised that his military group would 'work hard to bring [al-Bashir] down.'[65] He added that should al-Bashir fail to cooperate with the ICC 'the war will intensify.'[66] Nouwen and Werner comment on the actions of these rebel groups as follows:

> Rather than looking to the Court for accountability, these leaders' interest in the ICC lies in the fact that it brands their opponents as international criminals while they, by paying lip-service to fashionable international concepts, can gain international legitimacy. But as soon as rebel movements are in a militarily and politically weaker position and see the ICC as ineffective in changing the Sudanese government, they easily forget about the importance of 'justice'.[67]

As sure as night follows day, when JEM could no more guarantee support from Chad in 2010, the leadership of JEM was very quick to sign an agreement with the Sudanese al-Bashir government.[68] This agreement would have had the effect of granting amnesty to JEM members who were implicated in the perpetration of crimes. For these rebels, commitment to international criminal justice, all of sudden, flew out of the window. Across all these wavering commitments, be it the current government leadership or the rebel groups, is the tendency to play the card of international criminal justice when it suits a warring party's political agenda.

All considered, one gathers that the leadership structure that the ICC is counting on to secure al-Bashir for trial before the ICC is itself allegedly implicated in the commission of the international crimes that al-Bashir should be facing before the ICC. Indeed, in terms of spirit of the Rome Statute, the ICC would expect that states cooperate fully with it in its

[64] As above.

[65] As above.

[66] As above.

[67] SMH Nouwen and WG Werner, 'Doing Justice to the Political: The International Criminal Court in Uganda and Sudan' (2011)21 *European Journal of International Law* 957.

[68] 'Framework Agreement to Resolve the Conflict in Darfur Between the Government of Sudan and the Justice and Equality Movement', Doha, 23 February 2020.

investigation and prosecution of crimes within its jurisdiction. The situation in Sudan, however, presents complex challenges in that expecting the leadership to cooperate with the ICC is as good as incriminating some members of this government. Is it therefore less of a surprise that Sudan is seemingly non-committal in as far as cooperation with the ICC is concerned. Indeed, there was a national trial that saw Sudan's court prosecute al-Bashir for financial crimes and corruption. However, a two-year sentence that ultimately turned into rehabilitation in a reform centre is far from commitment to criminal accountability for the atrocities committed by al-Bashir. The true intentions of the Sudanese government can hardly be discerned; nonetheless, it seems plausible that recourse to these national proceedings is a strategy geared towards convincing the international community that some action is being taken whereas there is no real intention of ensuring that al-Bashir faces justice for the more serious atrocities he allegedly committed. It has been reported that al-Bashir remains under investigations for the 1989 coup.[69] Even assuming these investigations commence, what are the odds that this 76-year-old frail former president will live to be punished for the crimes he is accused of?

Worthy to note, the ICC seems to have walked down a similar path before, with the past conduct of states like Uganda being testament to this reality. The next section discusses the manner in which the Ugandan government played the card of commitment to international criminal justice for national political leverage. The discussion in this section seeks to highlight the cautionary tale that Uganda offers the ICC regarding Sudan in as far as manipulation of international criminal justice to settle national political challenges is concerned.

4 The Politics Surrounding the Referral of the Situation in Uganda to the ICC: Lessons in Dealing with Sudan

There is an inclination towards assuming that politics has no place in discussions of international criminal justice. Moreno Ocampo, the former

[69] 'Sudan Prosecutors Question Bashir Over 1989 Coup That Brought Him to Power', 11 December 2019, available at https://www.middleeastmonitor.com/20191211-sudan-prosecutors-question-bashir-over-1989-coup-that-brought-him-to-power/ (visited on 22 November 2020).

ICC Prosecutor, in trying to separate politics from international criminal justice, is on record for noting that: 'my duty is to apply the law without other factors to adjust to the law.'[70] While sentiments such as these may seem ideal, the reality on ground is that various actors in international criminal justice will often be entangled in politics. Nowhere has politics been rife than in states' cooperation with the ICC. Situations before the ICC such as the Ugandan situation are testament to the opportunistic practice of political leaders to use international criminal justice as a tool for settling national political scores. This should, however, be less of a surprise as commentators have long observed that international criminal justice platforms such as the ICC can be susceptible to political manipulation. In this regard, Beigbeder submits that despite national leaders' commitment to cooperating with the ICC in executing its task of accountability for international crimes, they can be manipulative, going as far as using international criminal justice to politically cover up their role in the commission of international crimes.[71] Muwereza adds that in almost all conflicts where government security forces have responded to attacks by rebel groups, these forces have actively played a role in the perpetration of international crimes.[72] Sadly, because these sitting governments are often directly or indirectly implicated in the commission of these crimes, they are most likely to use their political power and connections to evade justice and to shield government security forces.[73]

Simmons and Danner add that some states will even proceed to request for the involvement of strong international institutions like the ICC, hoping that the power that these institutions wield will be an asset in their military campaign against rebel groups.[74] For these states therefore, cooperation with the ICC remains relevant as long as the ICC's involvement

[70] 'Keynote address Mr. Luis Moreno-Ocampo, Prosecutor of the International Criminal Court, Council on Foreign Relations', Washington DC, 4 February 2010.

[71] Y Beigbeder, *Judging Criminal Leaders. The Slow Erosion of Impunity* (Martinus Nijhoff 2002) cited in N Muwereza, 'Who and Where to Punish in a Criminally Loaded Conflict of Northern Uganda: A Dilemmatic Juxtaposition of Forms of Justice in the Northern Uganda Conflict' (2010)5 *African Journal of Criminology and Justice Studies* 109–118.

[72] Muwereza, footnote 71 above, at 109.

[73] As above.

[74] A Beth Simmons and A Danner, 'Credible Commitments and the International Criminal Court' (2010)64 *International Organisation* 234.

delivers on weakening rebel groups' power over sitting governments. Simmons and Danner have used the notion of 'credible commitments' to provide an explanation on why states, despite their weak national frameworks, make commitments to the ICC through ratification of the Rome Statute.[75] They are of the opinion that these states stand to gain from such commitment. Despite some of these states lacking sound national structures to make good their commitments, they commit, only to subsequently delegate the enforcement power to the ICC which is then left to carry the burden of holding perpetrators of international crimes to account. Nouwen and Werner concur, submitting that 'international criminal justice has become a weapon in political struggles.'[76] The authors contend that warring parties, be it government-sanctioned forces or rebel groups, often use the ICC to label their opponents enemies to human kind and present themselves as friends of the ICC and as such, prepared to cooperate with the ICC to bring the enemies to justice.[77] With the ICC falling prey to this enemy/friends dichotomy, those proclaiming to be friends may fall through the cracks of accountability. The authors also allude to the fact that commitments to cooperation by the various warring parties often shift depending on the extent to which such cooperation offers them political leverage.

Nouwen and Werner submit that 'there is nothing wrong with attempts to protect the Court from political interference.'[78] They, however, aptly submit that failure to critically analyse and engage with these realities blinds international criminal justice players and actors to the politics of both states and the ICC itself. McDonald concurs with Nouwen and Werner and in this regard observes that the failure to confront this reality has caused the interventions of the ICC in countries like Uganda to backfire, with gaps in criminal accountability existing in respect of the international crimes committed by both national security forces and rebel groups.[79] From the views of commentators on the nexus

[75] As above.

[76] Nouwen and Werner, footnote 67 above, at 962.

[77] As above.

[78] As above, at 943.

[79] A Macdonald, 'In the Interests of Justice? The International Criminal Court, Peace Talks and the Failed Quest for War Crimes Accountability in Northern Uganda' (2017)11 *Journal of Eastern African Studies* 628.

between politics and international criminal justice, one gathers that in one way or the other, the issues raised have in fact played out in the ICC's involvement in some cases. With the current state of affairs in Sudan, a replay remains imminent if caution is not taken by the relevant actors in international criminal justice. Uganda, however, offers caution from multiple dimensions.

Uganda is one of the countries with a situation at the ICC.[80] The situation relates to a conflict that arose from rebel groups' dissatisfaction with the ruling Ugandan government. This conflict, which lasted for over twenty years, erupted in 1986 when the Lord's Resistance Army (LRA) resorted to war against the Ugandan government for its alleged exclusion of the Northern Uganda people from the political, social and economic affairs of the country.[81] The government of Uganda, through government-sanctioned defence forces, retaliated, with this retaliation resulting in the commission of human rights violations so serious to constitute war crimes and crimes against humanity. Both the LRA and the Ugandan government defence force have been implicated in the commission of these serious violations.[82] Reports also suggest that other government security forces including Police officers, prison officers and the Local Defence Forces were time and again involved in the violations

[80] 'Situation in Uganda ICC-02/04', available at https://www.icc-cpi.int/uganda (accessed 22 November 2020).

[81] The Resolve, 'The Kony Crossroads: Can the LRA Outlast Obama's Presidency', available at http://www.theresolve.org/ (accessed 10 May 2021); Report by Uganda Human Rights Commission & United Nations High Commissioner for Human Rights, 'The Dust Has Not Yet Settled' (2011) 1–99, available at http://www.ohchr.org/Documents/Press/WebStories/DustHasNotYetSettled.pdf (accessed 10 May 2021); S Opinia and F Bubenzer, 'Gender Justice and Reconciliation in Northern Uganda', 2011, available at http://www.ijr.org.za/publications/pdfs/JRP%20IJR%20Policy%20Brief%20Gender%20Justice.pdf (accessed 10 May 2021); V Ladisch, 'From Rejection to Redress Overcoming Legacies of Conflict-Related Sexual Violence in Northern Uganda', 2015, available at https://www.ictj.org/sites/default/files/ICTJ-Report-Uganda-Children-2015.pdf (accessed 10 May 2021); Human Rights Watch Report, 'Uprooted and Forgotten: Impunity and Human Rights Abuses in Northern Uganda', September 2005, Volume 17, available at https://www.hrw.org/reports/2005/uganda0905/ (accessed 10 May 2021); T Allen, *Trial Justice, the International Criminal Court and the Lord's Resistance Army* (Zed Books 2006) 59.

[82] Human Rights Watch, footnote 81 above.

recorded in Northern Uganda.[83] In 2003, Uganda referred the situation in Northern Uganda to the ICC.[84] This would be the first case in which a state party to the Rome Statute invoked Articles 13(a) and 14 of the Rome Statute to trigger the ICC's jurisdiction. Subsequent to initial investigations, the ICC issued warrants for the arrest of some of the leaders of the LRA including Dominic Ongwen, Rasa Lukiwaya, Okot Odhiambo, Joseph Kony and Vincent Otti.[85] Judgement against Ongwen for war crimes and crimes against humanity was handed down on 4 February 2021.[86]

Prior to Uganda's ratification of the Rome Statute and referral of the situation in Uganda to the ICC, the government of Uganda, under the leadership of Museveni, had explored various approaches to weakening the LRA rebels. These approaches range from peace talks, granting of amnesty to leaders of the LRA, to military actions. The Ugandan government's first attempt to peace talks with the LRA leaders was between 1992 and 1994.[87] The failed peace talks saw both the LRA and Ugandan government forces revert to military action. The trend of unsuccessful peace talks would manifest years later during the Juba peace process between 2006 and 2008.[88] Amnesty also constituted a major feature in attempts to end the Northern Uganda war. This strategy saw the enactment of Uganda's Amnesty Act of 2000 which provided blanket amnesty to anyone who had taken part in rebellion against the government of Uganda since 1986.[89] Such a person must have agreed to denounce rebellion and military action against the government and surrendered his/her weapons to the government of Uganda. The blanket amnesty was hardly a success in that aside from being criticised for being a threat to international criminal justice, it failed to attract the necessary response from the

[83] As above.

[84] Situation in Uganda, footnote 80 above.

[85] As above.

[86] See *Prosecutor v Dominic Ongwen*, Situation in Uganda, Trial Chamber IX, Trial Judgment, ICC-02/04-01/15, 4 February 2021.

[87] JM Royo, 'War and Peace Scenarios in Northern Uganda' (2008)6 *Quaderns De Construcció De Pau* 1–18.

[88] As above.

[89] As above.

target groups—the LRA rebel leaders. None of the senior LRA commanders took up the amnesty offer. Such rejection saw the LRA continue in its military action against the Ugandan government between 2000 and 2003. The Ugandan defence forces retaliated and again, this resulted in the commission of atrocities by both the rebel groups and government forces.

The government of Uganda took multiple actions, all of which are beyond the scope of this discussion. Apparent in all these actions, however, is the fact that the approaches invoked time and again drifted between reconciliatory approaches and military action. Both approaches, however, remained unsuccessful in bringing the conflict to an end. Uganda ratified the Rome Statute in 2002 after numerous failed attempts to containing this conflict. Now bound by the Rome Statute, the ICC's intervention became an option for Uganda to resolve its national challenges. In referring the situation of Uganda to the ICC, the reasoning behind such referral was as follows:

> Having exhausted every other means of bringing an end to this terrible suffering, the Republic of Uganda now turns to the newly established ICC and its promise of global justice. Uganda pledges its full cooperation to the Prosecutor in the investigation and prosecution of LRA crimes, achievement of which is vital not only for the future progress of the nation, but also for the suppression of the most serious crimes of concern to the international community as a whole.[90]

The wording of Uganda's referral does suggest that Uganda was desperate to bring the perpetrators of the international crimes committed during this conflict to justice. While the referral, on the face of it, was well-intentioned, the manner in which it played out and ultimately, the outcomes it has yielded do suggest that in many respects, the Ugandan government used the ICC as a tool to settle Uganda's national political woes. Commitment to advancement international criminal justice was the least of Uganda's priorities. The political manipulation of this referral process can be gleaned from a number of dynamics, all of which cannot be exhausted. A few shall, however, suffice. Noticeable, for example, is the fact that, as per the above referral, the said quest for accountability

[90] Government of Uganda, 'Referral of the Situation Concerning the Lord's Resistance Army', Kampala, December 2003, paragraph 6.

focusses on LRA crimes to the exclusion of the crimes committed by government security forces. By focussing on the LRA crimes to the exclusion of the crimes by government forces, the ICC successfully offered the Ugandan government international backing after decades of failed attempts to weaken the LRA rebels. The manner in which the ICC prosecutor intervened in the Ugandan situation, i.e. targeting the LRA, would suggest that the ICC implemented Uganda's wish to have LRA rebels prosecuted to the exclusion of government-backed security forces. Effectively, the referral succeeded in giving the Ugandan government leverage in its decade-long struggle to weaken the LRA.

It is also notable that the Ugandan government referred this situation to the ICC at a time when it was desperate for support and approval from the Ugandan electorate. This period was characterised by endless protests from random civilians, civil society organisations and political opposition parties headed by opposition leaders such as Kizza Besigye (Museveni's major political opponent at the time).[91] The government was condescendingly criticised for failing to bring the Northern Uganda war to end.[92] Museveni's referral of the Northern Uganda situation to the ICC allowed him to re-invent himself as a leader fully committed to bringing this conflict to an end. Effectively, the referral tactfully worked in the government's favour. Sections of the Ugandan electorate, especially from Northern Uganda, were once again reminded that the Ugandan government, under the leadership of Museveni, had their best interests at heart.

Despite Museveni's exploration of peace processes in resolving this conflict, he time and again had recourse to military action. His recourse to military action always had always been the subject of criticism. His leadership had severally been criticised for its unjustified expenditure on the military and firearms. This, commentators submitted, was to the detriment of the funding of other socio-economic sectors including health, social security and education.[93] With the issuance of arrest warrants against LRA leaders, efforts to follow through with the peace processes at the time aborted. The LRA, which felt betrayed by the issuance

[91] A Branch, 'Uganda's Civil War and the Politics of ICC Intervention' (2007)21 *Ethics and International Affairs* 185.

[92] As above.

[93] As above.

these warrants, reverted to military action. With this move by the LRA, Museveni now felt justified to have recourse to military action to quell the attacks advanced by the LRA. With the national and international attention that the referral of the Ugandan situation to the ICC brought to the Northern Uganda conflict, there was renewed justification for the government's expenditure on the military. Effectively, another national political score was settled.

The referral also delivered on restoration of Uganda's international relations. Prior to the referral, Sudan not only provided a military base for the LRA rebels; it also gave military support to the LRA.[94] This gave the LRA leverage over the Ugandan government forces for years. With the referral of Uganda's situation to the ICC, Sudan became wary of being in the limelight as an enabler of a rebel group which faced charges for international crimes before the ICC. There was therefore a change in posture by Sudan soon after the referral. Sudan effected this by withdrawing its support from the LRA. In addition, for the first time, after years of Uganda's struggle to launch attacks against the LRA, Sudan allowed Uganda's forces to extend their operations against the LRA's military bases in Sudan.[95] All these actions had the overall effect of weakening the LRA and effectively helped Uganda to not only settle its national political scores, but also restore its relations with Sudan. These relations appear to be alive and well to date. As recently as 2020, when engaged on whether Uganda would consider granting al-Bashir asylum, Uganda's minister of foreign affairs, Okello Oryem, responded that 'if Uganda is approached to grant asylum to Bashir it is an issue that can be considered at the highest level of our leadership.'[96] While the minister's statement is in no way a guarantee that such asylum would be granted, it is an indication of the ongoing relations between Sudan and Uganda and

[94] Human Rights Watch Report, 'Northern Uganda And Sudan's Support for the Lord's Resistance Army', 29 July 1998, available at https://www.hrw.org/legacy/campaigns/sudan98/testim/house-07.htm (accessed 22 May 2021); Human Rights Watch Report, 'Sudan: Regional Government Pays Ugandan Rebels Not to Attack', 2 June 2006, available at https://www.hrw.org/news/2006/06/02/sudan-regional-government-pays-ugandan-rebels-not-attack (accessed 22 May 2021).

[95] G Maina and J Ahere, 'The Never-Ending Pursuit of the Lord's Resistance Army', Accord Policy and Practice Brief, March 2002; M Schomerus, 'They Forget What They Came For': Uganda's Army in Sudan' (2012)6 *Journal of East African Studies* 124–153.

[96] Aljazeera, footnote 48 above.

the openness of African leaders to protect each other's back, even after they are ousted from leadership.

Uganda's ulterior motives in referring this situation to the ICC would be seen to later influence the decision of the ICC on who prosecute in respect of this conflict. The cases before the ICC and indeed the arrest warrants issued thereafter targeted members of the LRA to the exclusion of the Ugandan government-backed security forces. In justifying of the ICC's focus on the LRA rebels, Moreno Ocampo explained that:

> The criteria for selection of the first case was gravity. We analyzed the gravity of all crimes in northern Uganda committed by the LRA and Ugandan forces. Crimes committed by the LRA were much more numerous and of much higher gravity than alleged crimes committed by the UPDF. We therefore started with an investigation of the LRA. At the same time, we also collected information on other groups from a variety of sources. We collected documents and conducted interviews. We will continue to collect information on allegations concerning all other groups, to determine whether the Statute thresholds are met and the policy of focusing on the persons most responsible is satisfied.[97]

This explanation would, however, be questionable given the well-documented atrocities allegedly committed by government-backed forces. The glaring impartiality on the part of the ICC regarding who to prosecute was on par with Uganda's aim to have the ICC investigation and prosecution focus on members of the LRA. Effectively, the Ugandan government appears to have succeeded in influencing and directing the course of international criminal justice regarding who faces trial at the ICC. Ocampo's explanation above suggests that he had the option to investigate and prosecute members of Uganda's national defence force, but for the issue of gravity. But even assuming these atrocities met the gravity threshold and accordingly, the ICC proceeded to indict members of Uganda's defence force (who would by implication include Museveni in his capacity as the commander in chief of Uganda's defence force), practically speaking, this could have marked the beginning of the slow death of Uganda's situation at the ICC as its highly improbable Museveni

[97] International Criminal Court, 'Statement of the Chief Prosecutor on the Uganda Arrest Warrants', The Hague, 14 October 2005, available at https://www.icc-cpi.int/nr/rdonlyres/3255817D-fd00-4072-9F58-fdb869F9B7cf/143834/lmo_20051014_English1.pdf (accessed 22 May 2021).

would cooperate with the ICC in prosecuting both members of the LRA and government defence forces. Focussing on members of the LRA was a safe bet for the ICC given Uganda's lack of real commitment to international criminal justice.

With the referral of the Ugandan situation to the ICC, one would have expected unwavering cooperation from the Ugandan government in as far as prosecution of the LRA leaders was concerned. This, however, was not the case. The Ugandan government went back and forth between criminal accountability and peace processes. There was, however, no real commitment to any of these approaches. It was always about what worked in favour of the government leadership. Not surprisingly, even after referring the situation to the ICC, Museveni still called the LRA rebels for peace negotiations knowing full well that these negotiations, if successful, could have closed the door to criminal accountability before the ICC.[98] The Ugandan government seemed more committed to addressing the national political challenges that came with this conflict rather than international criminal justice. Not coincidentally, even though it is the Ugandan government, which on its own volition referred this situation to the ICC, it time and again threatened to withdraw the situation, purportedly to advance peace.[99]

Uganda's lack of commitment to international criminal justice can also be gleaned from the slow pace at which national prosecutions have proceeded. After the referral of this situation to the ICC, Uganda demonstrated its commitment to national accountability for the international crimes perpetrated in Northern Uganda. Uganda established a national framework for accountability of those responsible for international crimes—the International Crimes Division of the High Court of Uganda.[100] Thus far, one LRA former rebel, Thomas Kwoyelo, has been indicted. The case against Kwoyelo, which commenced in 2011,

[98] See the results of these talks by way of the: Agreement on Accountability and Reconciliation between the Government of Uganda and the Lord's Resistance Army/Movement (Juba Peace Agreement) 29 June 2007, available at http://www.amicc.org/docs/Agreement_on_Accountability_and_Reconciliation.pdf (accessed 22 May 2021).

[99] S Malo, 'Withdrawing the Case of Uganda from the Jurisdiction of the International Criminal Court' (2009)3 Cornell *International Affairs Review* 1–2.

[100] The International Crimes Division (ICD), previously referred to as the War Crimes Division, was established in 2008. In 2011, the WCD was reconstituted as the ICD in accordance with Clause 6 of the High Court (International Crimes Division) Practice Direction, 2011, Legal Notice No. 10 of 2011.

has hardly gone past preliminary objections.[101] His trial has been characterised by innumerable adjournments, and to date, it is far from clear when, let alone whether, it will be concluded.[102] Suffice it to state that no member of the national defence forces has been indicted by the International Crimes Division in respect of the atrocities committed in the Northern Uganda conflict. All considered, despite the establishment of a national framework for accountability, the entire process appears to be some form of window-dressing as not even the proceedings against former LRA members have registered progress. A deceptive picture is therefore created, with the international community assuming that action is being taken at the national level whereas no real progress has been made. The lack of progress in proceedings before the international crimes division and the failure to indict members of the national defence forces is testament to the fact that there is no real commitment to advance international criminal justice by the Ugandan government.

What is indisputable amidst all these pranks is the fact that the entire referral process has aided the Ugandan government in settling its political woes. As Muwereza submits, 'the referral process alone has been calculated into political formulae.'[103] In any case, Uganda's judiciary was capable of prosecuting the LRA rebels at the time it referred this situation to the ICC. Even so, the Ugandan government took a decision to refer it and effectively, succeeded in not only surrendering the prosecutorial burden of its decade-long enemy (the LRA) to the ICC, but also, attaining international legitimation for every action taken to address its national political challenges. Therefore, international criminal justice became a weapon to settle national political struggles without real commitment to fostering accountability for international crimes.

5 Back to Sudan: A Possible Replay of the Ugandan Movie?

The situation in Uganda may not be identical to Sudan's; nonetheless, some features cut across both situations. Firstly, in both, there

[101] O Nyeko, 'A Test Case for Justice in Uganda: Government Should Signal More Commitment to Uganda's International Crimes Division' (2018) *Human Rights Watch*.

[102] As above.

[103] Muwereza, footnote 71 above, at 116.

are national efforts to bring perpetrators of the atrocities committed to justice. However, these efforts are falling short of holding perpetrators to account for the international crimes allegedly committed. In Sudan, there is no denying that some form of prosecution has taken place against al-Bashir. These proceedings, however, fall short of holding al-Bashir to account for the international crimes he allegedly committed. Secondly, in both, the organs expected to foster accountability for the alleged international crimes are themselves implicated in these crimes. As pointed out, some members of Sudan's leadership are very much caught up in the atrocities al-Bashir is wanted for at the ICC. In the case of Uganda, the fact that national defence forces were implicated in the atrocities committed in the Northern Uganda conflict has resulted in the total absence of trial in both national courts and the ICC. The literature has demonstrated that accountability for international crimes is an uphill task where those in leadership are equally implicated and the situation is not any different in Sudan.[104]

Thirdly, just like Uganda, Sudan's commitment to cooperate with the ICC in the prosecution of al-Bashir before the ICC keeps wavering. In the case of Sudan, since the ousting of al-Bashir in 2019, the new leadership has shifted goal posts—in some cases committing to cooperating and in some cases, having nothing to do with discussion of surrendering al-Bashir to the ICC. In as far Uganda is concerned, the wavering support can be gleaned from Uganda's threats to withdraw its situation from the ICC despite the self-referral. The wavering commitment demonstrates a lack of genuine commitment of international criminal justice. Instead, states are making certain promises to find a place within the international social circle. Ba attributes this behaviour to the socialisation theory.[105] Towns explains this further by observing that many states make such commitments because of pressure from rights groups and the incentives that come with such commitment.[106]

[104] EC Lubaale, 'Military Courts and Prosecution of Offences by National Defense Forces in the Dawn of the Complementarity Regime: The Case of Uganda' (2017) *Criminal Law Forum* 709–746; EC Lubaale, 'The Dominant Role of Commanders in the Sudanese Military Justice System and Accountability for International Crimes' (2018) 26 *African Journal of International and Comparative Law* 391–406.

[105] Omar Ba, *States of Justice: The Politics of the International Criminal Court* (Cambridge University Press 2020) 91.

[106] See generally A Towns, *Women and States: Norms and Hierarchies in International Relations* (Cambridge: Cambridge University Press 2010).

Worthy to note, Uganda's cooperation with the ICC over the years has mainly rested on the ICC's exclusion of government security forces from prosecution. As already alluded to, literature abounds on the selectiveness of prosecution, with government forces resting comfortably while the opponents of the Ugandan government face justice both nationally and at the ICC.[107] It remains to be seen whether the same cooperation can be expected from Sudan where some of those at the helm of leadership are also implicated in the commission of international crimes. This perhaps explains Sudan's posture, with wavering promises being made to surrender al-Bashir but no real commitment to foster accountability for international crimes.

As in the Ugandan case at the time of referral, there is so much going on in Sudan for it to guarantee cooperation with the ICC. The rebel groups in Darfur refuse to back down in the commission of atrocities,[108] thus causing continued instability in Sudan even after the ousting of al-Bashir. The Sovereign Council continues to engage in the middle of peace talks with the rebel groups from Darfur.[109] With the unstable nature of Sudan's current government, the need to address national political challenges is seemingly far more critical to these players than cooperation with the ICC because there is a lot at stake for all of them. Peace processes and other means of ending the continuing instability in Sudan remain on the government's agenda. Throughout these negotiations, concessions can be made and will continue to be made. Amidst these concessions, it is to be expected that every actor is in it for a deal that best protects them. Those in need of protection include members of the Sovereign Council some of whom have been implicated in the alleged commission of international crimes. The rebel groups indeed insist on surrender of al-Bashir to the ICC. However, they too are susceptible to being black-mailed because they also had their fair share of responsibility in the atrocities committed in Darfur. Thus, despite the Sovereign Council's commitment to cooperating with the ICC, there is no guarantee that Sudan will deliver on these commitments under the current leadership as such cooperation rests

[107] Lubaale, 'Military Courts', footnote 104 above; Lubaale, 'The Dominant Role', footnote 104 above.

[108] Human Rights Watch Report, 'Word Report 2020: South Sudan Events of 2019', available at https://www.hrw.org/world-report/2020/country-chapters/south-sudan (accessed 22 May 2021).

[109] Aljazeera, footnote 59 above.

heavily on the political environment current in Sudan. In the light of these circumstances, the ICC could very well constitute one of Sudan's many weapons in addressing its internal political struggles. Promises on cooperation can continue to be made but without real commitment to international criminal justice.

The above state of affairs brings sharply into focus the old peace versus justice debate. Scholars have long been divided on this subject. Some have argued and in fact justified the need for states to prioritise peace because of the adverse effects of continued violence.[110] Sseda, for example, submits that 'in peaceful times, peace and justice co-exist, and their relationship seems uncomplicated. After a conflict, however, it becomes estranged. Demands for criminal accountability can then be an obstacle to peace.'[111] Other scholars, however, have attacked this viewpoint, contending that states cannot flirt with perpetrators of gross human rights violations in the name of peace.[112] From this point of view, there cannot be peace without justice. And of course, at the heart of the ICC is the mission to end impunity by holding perpetrators of these crimes criminally responsible. While some scholars have vouched for a balance between international justice, reconciliation and peace,[113] and others referred to the peace versus justice debate a false dichotomy,[114] the practicality of striking the balance has often been an uphill task. Often, states recovering from conflict are clamouring for peace. Despite the criticism levelled against an approach that places peace ahead of justice, states are

[110] See, e.g., P Clark, 'The International Criminal Court's Impact on Peacebuilding in Africa' in T McNamee and M Muyangwa (eds) *The State of Peacebuilding in Africa* (Switzerland: Palgrave Macmillan 2020) 235–256.

[111] D Sseda, 'Revisiting the Peace Versus Justice Debate' (2020) *Development and Cooperation*, https://www.dandc.eu/en/article/demands-criminal-accountability-can-be-obstacle-peace (accessed 6 June 2021).

[112] See, e.g., D Pankhurst, 'Issues of Justice and Reconciliation in Complex Political Emergencies: Conceptualising Reconciliation, Justice and Peace' (1999)20 *Third World Quarterly* 239–256.

[113] CC Jalloh, 'International Justice, Reconciliation and Peace in Africa' (2015) *CODESRIA Policy Briefs* 1–12; B Krzan, 'International Criminal Court Facing the Peace vs. Justice Dilemma' (2016)2 *International Comparative Jurisprudence* 81–88.

[114] K Mansour and L Riches, *Peace Versus Justice: A False Dichotomy Contemporary Issues in Conflict Resolution* (2017) 1–16, https://www.sciencespo.fr/psia/sites/sciencespo.fr.psia/files/Peace_versus_Justice-A_False_Dichotomy.pdf (accessed 6 June 2021).

often prepared to enter into peace deals with those accused of committing these atrocities just so that peace reigns. Fostering stability in these states may even mean sacrificing the commitment to cooperation with the ICC at the altar of negotiation with rebel groups. Thus, even with the criticism levelled against the peace approach, the reality on ground is that states are still open to invoking that option because there is often so much at stake in these volatile environments. Effectively therefore, promises on cooperation can continue to be made by these states but without real commitment to international criminal justice. It is circumstances such as these that the ICC has to be strategic in dealing with states coming of conflict.

6 Conclusion

The aim of this chapter was to address two issues: the first related to the nature of cooperation the ICC can expect from a government which is implicated in the alleged commission of international crimes and the second was with regard to lessons that states like Uganda offer the ICC regarding Sudan. The discussion has demonstrated that some members of Sudan's current interim government allegedly cooperated with al-Bashir in the commission of the atrocities he is wanted for by the ICC. This state of affairs has major implication for Sudan's cooperation with the ICC. Precisely put, cooperation can hardly be guaranteed. Thus, while al-Bashir's overthrow seemingly created a conducive environment for him to be surrendered to the ICC, he remains inaccessible to the ICC because of the political dynamics current in Sudan. Indeed, the situation in Sudan is still unfolding and a lot is bound to change. This makes conclusions on how the al-Bashir issue will play out speculative. Undeniable, however, is the fact that countries like Uganda have, in circumstances similar to what Sudan is currently facing, previously used international criminal justice as a weapon to settle national political struggles. In the case of Uganda, the ICC played along, with this game going as far as totally excluding government security forces from accountability. This state of affairs underscores the need for a thorough acknowledgement and evaluation of the political dimensions in states that the ICC is involved with to avoid falling in the trap of uninformed interventions. It is possible that the actions by Sudan's interim government including its wavering commitments to cooperating with the ICC as well as the national proceedings against al-Bashir, are just a reinvention of the age-old practice by states to manipulate international criminal justice to settle national political struggles. It is therefore imperative for the various actors in international criminal justice including the ICC to tread carefully.

In conclusion, the challenge of holding sitting presidents to account may not be as simplistic as stripping them of the presidential office. Some of these dictatorial regimes have been in existence for decades and the power they wield does not automatically vanish after they have been ousted. Like al-Bashir, many are at the centre of complex national structures; so complex that their ousting cannot automatically strip them of the power they wield. Again, this state of affairs underscores the need for a thorough acknowledgement and evaluation of the political dimensions in states that the ICC is involved with.

Acknowledgements I acknowledge funding from the National Research Foundation (Funding to EC Lubaale, Grant No: 127504) towards the funding of writing retreats that informed the conceptual development of my contributions to this book. Support from the Rhodes University Research Committee Grant is also acknowledged.

References

Books, Book Chapters and Journal Articles

Allen, T *Trial Justice, the International Criminal Court and the Lord's Resistance Army* (Zed Books 2006).

Ambos, K *Treatise on International Criminal Law* (Oxford University Press 2013).

Ba, O *States of Justice: The Politics of the International Criminal Court* (Cambridge University press 2020).

Beigbeder, Y *Judging Criminal leaders. The Slow Erosion of Impunity* (Martinus Nijhoff 2002).

Bellelli, R *International Criminal Justice: From the Rome Statute to Its Review* (Ashgate Publishing 2010).

Bergsmo, M et al. 'Complementarity After Kampala: Capacity Building and the ICC's Legal Tools' (2010)2 *Goettingen Journal of International Law* 791.

Beth AS and Danner A, 'Credible Commitments and the International Criminal Court' (2010)64 *International Organisation* 225.

Branch, A 'Uganda's Civil War and the Politics of ICC Intervention' (2007)21 *Ethics and International Affairs* 179.

Chipaike, R et al. 'African Move to Withdraw from the ICC: Assessment of Issues and Implications' (2019)75 *India Quarterly: A Journal of International Affairs* 334.

Clark, P 'The International Criminal Court's Impact on Peacebuilding in Africa' in T McNamee and M Muyangwa (eds) *The State of Peacebuilding in Africa* (Switzerland: Palgrave Macmillan 2020).

Conway, G 'Ne Bis in Idem and the International Criminal Tribunals' (2003)14 *Criminal Law Forum* 351.

Heller, KJ 'A Sentence-Based Theory of Complementarity' (2011)53 *Harvard International Law Journal* 593.

Iyi, M 'Re-thinking the Authority of the UN Security Council to Refer Nationals of Non-party States to the ICC' (2019)66 *Netherlands International Law Review* 391.

Jalloh, CC 'International Justice, Reconciliation and Peace in Africa' (2015) *CODESRIA Policy Briefs* 1.

Kleffner, J 'The Impact of Complementarity on National Implementation of Substantive International Criminal Law' (2003) *Journal of International Criminal Justice* 86.

Krzan, B 'International Criminal Court Facing the Peace vs. Justice Dilemma' (2016)2 *International Comparative Jurisprudence* 81.

Lubaale, EC 'Military Courts and Prosecution of Offences by National Defense Forces in the Dawn of the Complementarity Regime: The Case of Uganda' (2017) *Criminal Law Forum* 709.

Lubaale, EC 'The Dominant Role of Commanders in the Sudanese Military Justice System and Accountability for International Crimes' (2018)26 *African Journal of International and Comparative Law* 391.

Macdonald, A 'In the Interests of Justice? The International Criminal Court, Peace Talks and the Failed Quest for War Crimes Accountability in Northern Uganda' (2017)11 *Journal of Eastern African Studies* 628.

Maina, G and Ahere, J 'The Never-Ending Pursuit of the Lord's Resistance Army' Accord Policy and Practice Brief, March 2002.

Malo, S 'Withdrawing the Case of Uganda from the Jurisdiction of the International Criminal Court' (2009)3 *Cornell International Affairs Review* 1.

Mégret, F 'Too Much of a Good Thing? Implementation and the Uses of Complementarity' in C Stahn and M El Zeidy (eds) *The International Criminal Court and Complementarity: From Theory to Practice* (Cambridge University Press 2011).

Muwereza, N 'Who and Where to Punish in a Criminally Loaded Conflict of Northern Uganda: A Dilemmatic Juxtaposition of Forms of Justice in the Northern Uganda Conflict' (2010)5 *African Journal of Criminology and Justice Studies* 109.

Newton, MA 'The Quest for Constructive Complementarity' in C Stahn and M El Zeidy (eds) *The International Criminal Court and Complementarity: From Theory to Practice* (Cambridge University Press 2011).

Nouwen, SMH *Complementarity in the Line of Fire: The Catalysing Effect of the International Criminal Court in Uganda and Sudan* (Cambridge University Press 2013).

Nouwen, SMH and Werner, WG 'Doing Justice to the Political: The International Criminal Court in Uganda and Sudan' (2011)21 *European Journal of International Law* 941.

Nyeko, O 'A Test Case for Justice in Uganda: Government Should Signal More Commitment to Uganda's International Crimes Division' (2018) *Human Rights Watch*.

Omorogbe, EY 'The Crisis of International Criminal Law in Africa: A Regional Regime in Response?' (2019)66 *Netherlands International Law Review* 287.

Pankhurst, D 'Issues of Justice and Reconciliation in Complex Political Emergencies: Conceptualising Reconciliation, Justice and Peace' (1999)20 *Third World Quarterly* 239.

Rome Statute of the International Criminal Court, 17 July 1998, 2187 U.N.T.S. 90 (entered into force on 1 July 2002).

Royo, JM 'War and Peace Scenarios in Northern Uganda' (2008)6 *Quaderns De Construcció De Pau* 1.

Schomerus M "They Forget What They Came For': Uganda's Army in Sudan' (2012)6 *Journal of East African Studies* 124.

Sseda, D 'Revisiting the Peace Versus Justice Debate' (2020) *Development and Cooperation*, https://www.dandc.eu/en/article/demands-criminal-accountability-can-be-obstacle-peace (accessed 6 June 2021).

Stahn, C 'Libya, the International Criminal Court and Complementarity: A Test for 'Shared Responsibility'' (2012)10 *Journal of International Criminal Justice* 337.

Terracino, JB 'National Implementation of ICC Crimes: Impact on National Jurisdictions and the ICC' (2007)5 *Journal of International Criminal Justice* 421.

Towns, A *Women and States: Norms and Hierarchies in International Relations* (Cambridge University Press 2010).

Ward, F *Direct Application of International Criminal Law in National Courts* (Asser Press 2005).

Cases

Decision on the Admissibility of the Case Against Saif Al-Islam Gaddafi (ICC-01/11-01/11), Pre-Trial Chamber I, 31 May 2013.

Judgment in the Jordan Referral re Al-Bashir Appeal, 06 May 2019, ICC-02/05-01/09-397-Corr.

Prosecutor v Thomas Lubanga Dyilo (Decision on the Prosecutor's Application for a Warrant of Arrest, Article 58, ICC-01/04-01/06-8, Pre-Trial Chamber I, 10 February 2006).

Prosecutor v Omar Hassan Ahmad Al Bashir, Case No. ICC-02/05-01/09.

Situation in Darfur, Sudan in the Case of *The Prosecutor v Omar Hassan Ahmad Al-Bashir*, Decision Under Article 87(7) of the Rome Statute on the Non-compliance by South Africa with the Request by the Court for the Arrest and Surrender of Omar Al-Bashir, 6 July 2017.

Situation in Darfur, Sudan, In the Case of the *Prosecutor v Omar Hassan Ahmad Al Bashir*, Decision Pursuant to Article 87(7) of the Rome Statute on the refusal of the Republic of Chad to Comply with the Cooperation Requests Issued by the Court with Respect to the Arrest and Surrender of Omar Hassan Ahmad Al Bashir, Pre-Trial Chamber I, 13 December 2011.

Situation in Darfur, Sudan, In the Case of the *Prosecutor v Omar Hassan Ahmad Al Bashir*, Decision Pursuant to Article 87(7) of the Rome Statute on the Failure by the Republic of Malawi to Comply with the Cooperation Requests Issued by the Court with Respect to the Arrest and Surrender of Omar Hassan Ahmad Al Bashir, Pre-Trial Chamber I, 13 December 2011.

Websites, Reports, Resolutions and Internet Sources

Agreement on Accountability and Reconciliation Between the Government of Uganda and the Lord's Resistance Army/Movement (Juba Peace Agreement) 29 June 2007, http://www.amicc.org/docs/Agreement_on_Accountability_and_Reconciliation.pdf (accessed 22 May 2021).

African Union, 'Withdrawal Strategy Document' (2017), https://www.hrw.org/sites/default/files/supporting_resources/icc_withdrawal_strategy_jan._2017.pdf, (accessed 15 June 2021).

Aljazeera News, 'Sudan's Military Removes al-Bashir: All the Latest Updates', 20 April 2019, https://www.aljazeera.com/news/2019/04/sudan-army-removes-bashir-latest-updates-190411125048555.html (accessed 22 November 2020).

Aljazeera News, 'Sudan Forms 11-Member Sovereign Council, Headed by al-Burhan', 20 August 2019, https://www.aljazeera.com/news/2019/08/sudan-forms-11-member-sovereign-council-headed-al-burhan-190820204821614.html (accessed 22 November 2020).

Aljazeera News, 'Sudan's Government Signs Initial Peace Deal with Rebel Group', 25 January 2020, https://www.aljazeera.com/news/2020/01/sudans-government-signs-peace-deal-rebels-200125062016599.html (accessed 22 November 2020).

Aljazeera News, 'Sudan Agrees Those Wanted by ICC Should Appear Before Court', 11 February 2020, https://www.aljazeera.com/news/2020/02/sudan-darfur-rebels-agree-prosecution-wanted-icc-200211135956815.html (accessed 22 November 2020).

Amin, M 'Profile: Members of Sudan's Sovereign Council Sudan Unveiled 11-Member Council That Will Run Country During 3-Year Transitional Period', 21 August 2019, https://www.aa.com.tr/en/africa/profile-members-of-sudans-sovereign-council/1561302 (accessed 22 November 2020).

Amin, M 'Suspect Still at Large': Why Sudan Hasn't Handed Omar Bashir Over to the ICC', 12 March 2020, https://www.middleeasteye.net/news/sudan-why-omar-bashir-icc-international-criminal-court (accessed 22 November 2020).

Amnesty International Report, 'Sudan 2019', https://www.amnesty.org/en/countries/africa/sudan/report-sudan/ (accessed 22 November 2020).

BBC News, 'ICC Prosecutor Shelves Darfur War Crimes Inquiries', 12 December 2014, https://www.bbc.com/news/world-africa-30458347 (accessed 22 November 2020).

BBC News, 'Sudan Coup: Why Omar al-Bashir Was Overthrown', 15 April 2019, https://www.bbc.com/news/world-africa-47852496 (accessed 22 November 2020).

BBC News, 'Sudan Crisis: What You Need to Know', 16 August 2019, https://www.bbc.com/news/world-africa-48511226 (accessed 22 November 2020).

BBC News, 'Omar al-Bashir: Sudan Agrees Ex-president Must Face ICC', 11 February 2020, https://www.bbc.com/news/world-africa-51462613 (accessed 7 June 2021).

'Darfur Rebels Vow Full ICC Cooperation Ahead of Ruling on Bashir Case', Sudan Tribune, 2 March 2009, https://www.sudantribune.com/spip.php?article30331 (visited on 22 November 2020).

Fabricius, P 'South Africa Confirms Withdrawal from ICC', Daily Maverick, 7 December 2017, https://www.dailymaverick.co.za/article/2017-12-07-south-africa-confirms-withdrawal-from-icc/ (accessed 22 November 2020).

'Framework Agreement to Resolve the Conflict in Darfur Between the Government of Sudan and the Justice and Equality Movement', Doha, 23 February 2020.

Government of Uganda, 'Referral of the Situation Concerning the Lord's Resistance Army', Kampala, December 2003.

High Court (International Crimes Division) Practice Direction, 2011, Legal Notice No. 10 of 2011.

Human Rights Watch Report, 'Northern Uganda and Sudan's Support for the Lord's Resistance Army', 29 July 1998, https://www.hrw.org/legacy/campaigns/sudan98/testim/house-07.htm (accessed 22 May 2021).

Human Rights Watch Report, 'Uprooted and Forgotten: Impunity and Human Rights Abuses in Northern Uganda', September 2005, Volume 17, https://www.hrw.org/reports/2005/uganda0905/ (accessed 10 May 2021).
Human Rights Watch Report 'Sudan: Regional Government Pays Ugandan Rebels Not to Attack', 2 June 2006, https://www.hrw.org/news/2006/06/02/sudan-regional-government-pays-ugandan-rebels-not-attack (accessed 22 May 2021).
Human Rights Watch Report, 'Darfur in the Shadows: The Sudanese Government's Ongoing Attacks on Civilians and Human Rights', 5 June 2011, https://www.hrw.org/report/2011/06/05/darfur-shadows/sudanese-governments-ongoing-attacks-civilians-and-human-rights (accessed 22 November 2020).
Human Rights Watch Report, 'Men with No Mercy: Rapid Support Forces Attacks Against Civilians in Darfur, Sudan', 9 September 2015, https://www.hrw.org/report/2015/09/09/men-no-mercy/rapid-support-forces-attacks-against-civilians-darfur-sudan (accessed 22 November 2020).
Human Rights Watch Report, 'Human Rights Benchmarks for Sudan', 3 May 2017, https://www.hrw.org/news/2017/05/03/human-rights-benchmarks-sudan (accessed 22 November 2020).
Human Rights Watch Report, 'They Were Shouting 'Kill Them': Sudan's Violent Crackdown on Protesters in Khartoum', 17 November 2019, https://www.hrw.org/report/2019/11/17/they-were-houting-kill-them/sudans-violent-crackdown-protesters-khartoum (accessed 22 November 2020).
Human Rights Watch Report, 'Sudan Opens Door for ICC Prosecutions: Ex-president Bashir May Finally Face Trial for Alleged Darfur Crimes', 12 February 2020, https://www.hrw.org/news/2020/02/12/sudan-opens-door-icc-prosecutions (accessed 22 November 2020).
Human Rights Watch Report, 'Word Report 2020: South Sudan Events of 2019', https://www.hrw.org/world-report/2020/country-chapters/south-sudan (accessed 22 May 2021).
International Criminal Court Website, 'Situations Under Investigation', https://www.icc-cpi.int/pages/situation.aspx (accessed 22 November 2020).
ICC Website, 'Al Bashir Case', https://www.icc-cpi.int/darfur/albashir (accessed 14 June 2021).
International Criminal Court, 'Statement of the Chief Prosecutor on the Uganda Arrest Warrants', The Hague, 14 October 2005, https://www.icc-cpi.int/nr/rdonlyres/3255817D-fd00-4072-9F58-fdb869F9B7cf/143834/lmo_20051014_English1.pdf (accessed 22 May 2021).
'Keynote Address Mr. Luis Moreno-Ocampo, Prosecutor of the International Criminal Court, Council on Foreign Relations', Washington DC, 4 February 2010.

Kirby, 'J Sudan's Military Says It Won't Extradite Omar al-Bashir to Face War Crimes Charges', 12 April 2019, https://www.vox.com/world/2019/4/12/18307649/sudan-omar-al-bashir-war-crimes-icc-military (accessed 22 May 2020).

Ladisch, V 'From Rejection to Redress Overcoming Legacies of Conflict-Related Sexual Violence in Northern Uganda', 2015, https://www.ictj.org/sites/default/files/ICTJ-Report-Uganda-Children-2015.pdf (accessed 10 May 2021).

Mansour, K and Riches, L *Peace Versus Justice: A False Dichotomy Contemporary Issues in Conflict Resolution* (2017) 1–16, https://www.sciencespo.fr/psia/sites/sciencespo.fr.psia/files/Peace_versus_Justice-A_False_Dichotomy.pdf (accessed 6 June 2021).

Opinia, S and Bubenzer, F 'Gender Justice and Reconciliation in Northern Uganda', 2011, http://www.ijr.org.za/publications/pdfs/JRP%20IJR%20Policy%20Brief%20Gender%20Justice.pdf (accessed 10 May 2021).

Report by Uganda Human Rights Commission & United Nations High Commissioner for Human Rights, 'The Dust Has Not Yet Settled' (2011) 1–99, http://www.ohchr.org/Documents/Press/WebStories/DustHasNotYetSettled.pdf (accessed 10 May 2021).

Sudan Constitutional Declaration, 'Draft Constitutional Charter for the 2019 Transitional Period' (2019) 1–21, https://constitutionnet.org/sites/default/files/2019-08/Sudan%20Constitutional%20Declaration%20%28English%29.pdf (accessed 22 May 2021).

'Sudan Prosecutors Question Bashir over 1989 Coup That Brought Him to Power', 11 December 2019, https://www.middleeastmonitor.com/20191211-sudan-prosecutors-question-bashir-over-1989-coup-that-brought-him-to-power/ (accessed 22 May 2021)

'Situation in Uganda ICC-02/04', https://www.icc-cpi.int/uganda (accessed 22 May 2021).

The Guardian, 'African Leaders Plan Mass Withdrawal from International Criminal Court', 31 January 2017, https://www.theguardian.com/law/2017/jan/31/african-leaders-plan-mass-withdrawal-from-international-criminal-court (accessed 22 May 2021).

The Guardian, 'Ex-Sudan Leader Omar al-Bashir Sentenced to Two Years for Corruption', 14 December 2020, https://www.theguardian.com/world/2019/dec/14/sudanese-court-sentences-omar-al-bashir-to-2-years-in-prison (accessed 22 May 2021).

The Resolve, 'The Kony Crossroads: Can the LRA Outlast Obama's Presidency', http://www.theresolve.org/ (accessed 10 May 2021).

United Nations Security Council, Resolution 1593 Adopted by the Security Council at its 5158th Meeting on 31 March 2005, https://www.icc-cpi.int/NR/rdonlyres/85FEBD1A-29F8-4EC4-9566-48EDF55CC587/283244/N0529273.pdf (accessed 22 November 2020).

PART III

Ongoing Prospectives and Challenges of National Accountability for International Crimes in Africa

Complementarity and Federalism: Prosecuting International Crimes Under the Rome Statute Complementarity Principle in Nigeria as a Federal State

Muyiwa Adigun

1 Introduction

On 1 July 2002, the Rome Statute of the International Criminal Court[1] (hereafter the Rome Statute or Statute) came into force. As of April 2021, 123 states had ratified the Statute[2] and 33 of them are from Africa.[3] Article 1 of the Rome Statute provides that the ICC 'shall be complementary to national criminal jurisdictions'. Article 17 requires state parties to the Statute to investigate and prosecute international crimes

[1] Rome Statute of the International Criminal Court (Rome Statute) (adopted 17 July 1998, entered into force 1 July 2002) 2187 UNTS 3.

[2] International Criminal Court, 'The states parties to the Rome Statute' https://asp.icc-cpi.int/en_menus/asp/states%20parties/Pages/the%20states%20parties%20to%20the%20rome%20statute.aspx (accessed 25 April 2021).

[3] Footnote 2 above.

M. Adigun (✉)
Faculty of Law, University of Ibadan, Ibadan, Nigeria

E. C. Lubaale and N. Dyani-Mhango (eds.), *National Accountability for International Crimes in Africa*,
https://doi.org/10.1007/978-3-030-88044-6_9

over which they have jurisdiction and that it is when they are 'unwilling' or 'unable' that the ICC will intervene and take over from them. The principle embodied in articles 1 and 17 of the Rome Statute is known as the principle of complementarity. Although article 17 is not couched in a positive obligatory term but only considers crimes recognised under the Rome Statute as being suitable for investigation and prosecution domestically,[4] nonetheless it emphasises 'policy prescriptions in favour of national action'[5] by state parties. The fundamental tenet of the ICC is that it operates on a principle of complementarity: this means that the ICC shall not supersede domestic criminal courts, but rather complement them in cases where there is a conspicuous unwillingness or inability to investigate and prosecute. That means that the autonomy, as well as legislative/prescriptive and judicial sovereignties of states are not impugned or compromised but rather reinforced by this international court—making it not a court of first instance but rather one that seeks to close any potential gaps in order to quell the possibility of impunity for serious crimes in international law.

A number of challenges in domestic prosecution of the crimes recognised under the Rome Statute have been identified. Some of these challenges are obsolete criminal justice systems, failure to take cognizance of traditional conception of justice, immunity of heads of state and lack of political will among others.[6] The litany of challenges mentioned herein

[4] The only obligation imposed in the Rome Statute is that states should facilitate cooperation with the ICC: article 88. For the argument that art 17 of the Rome Statute does not really impose obligation to prosecute see D Robinson 'The inaction controversy: Neglected words and new opportunities' in C Stahn & MM El Zeidy (eds) *The International Criminal Court and complementarity: From theory to practice* vol I (2011) 495–496 and R Radstan 'Situation and case: Defining the parameters' in C Stahn & MM El Zeidy (eds) *The International Criminal Court and complementarity: From theory to practice* vol I (2011) 449–450.

[5] Robinson (footnote 4 above) 496–498.

[6] N Dyani-Mhango 'Reflecting on South Africa's attempt to withdraw from the Rome statute in favour of immunities for sitting heads of state: An analysis of the International Crimes Bill 2017' (2020) 28(2) *African Journal of International and Comparative Law* 319–351; M Adigun *The International Criminal Court and Nigeria: Implementing the complementarity principle of the Rome statute* (2018); N Dyani 'Is the International Criminal Court targeting Africa? Reflections on the enforcement of international criminal law in Africa' in VO Nmehielle *Africa and the future of international criminal justice* (2012) 196–214; Due Process of Law Foundation *Digest of Latin American jurisprudence on international crimes* (2010).

speak to the inability or unwillingness of the state party to deal with such crimes. However, the challenge that federalism may pose has not been seriously addressed. On the surface, federalism may be challenging if one considers the decision of the Judicial Committee of the Privy Council in *Attorney-General for Canada v Attorney-General for Ontario*.[7] In this case, the Privy Council held that treaty making is radically different from treaty implementation where implementation requires amending domestic laws or enacting a new law and that while treaty making is the exclusive preserve of the executive, treaty implementation is the exclusive preserve of the legislature. The Privy Council further held that the legislative function in respect of treaty implementation is shared by both the Federal Government and the Provincial Governments and where the subject matter of the treaty falls within the legislative competence of the Provincial Governments; it is the Provincial Governments that will carry out the implementation by way of statutory enactment. This implies that if the implementation of the principle of complementarity requires action on the part of the federating units and they fail to act as required, implementation will be stalled and the federal state as a party to the treaty will be in violation of its international obligations at the international plane. This is because domestic constitutional arrangement cannot be offered as an excuse for failing to fulfil an international obligation.[8]

Although, the challenge posed by federalism has not been seriously addressed, nonetheless it is worth mentioning *The International Criminal Court and Nigeria: Implementing the Complementarity Principle of the Rome Statute*.[9] This work is relevant for two reasons. First, it specifically addresses the implementation of the principle of complementarity in Nigeria. Secondly, while the work addresses various statutory models for Nigeria, it takes cognisance of the question of federalism. Thus, it is argued that the relevant part of the Rome Statute may be attached to an implementing Act, but the Federal Government and federating States would jointly enact the Act.[10] On the other hand, it is also suggested

[7] (1937) AC 326.

[8] *LaGrand (FRG v US)*, 2001 ICJ 104 (June 27), 40 ILM 1069; *Soering v United Kingdom* (1989) 11 EHRR 439.

[9] M Adigun *The International Criminal Court and Nigeria: Implementing the complementarity principle of the Rome statute* (2018).

[10] Footnote 9 above, 57–71.

that crimes recognised under the Rome Statute may be enacted as ordinary crimes without referring to the Rome Statute. With this approach, the Federal Government and federating units would each enact its own statute.[11] It is also suggested that the crimes under the Rome Statute can be enacted into law as gross violations of human rights. In this approach, the Federal Governments and State Governments would have to enact their respective laws since they are all competent to legislate on human rights under the Nigerian Constitution 1999.[12] Lastly, it is argued that the Nigerian Constitution 1999 may be amended while the relevant provisions of the Rome Statute are made part of the Constitution. With this approach, the challenge of federalism is completely averted.[13]

What this study seeks to do differently is twofold. First, it is argued that there is a conceptual similarity, though not completely identical, between the principle of complementarity and the concept of federalism. In the principle of complementarity, there are two levels of criminal jurisdiction: one is international while the other is domestic. In the concept of federalism, there are two levels of governance: one is central while the other is provincial. Secondly, it is argued that while the principle of complementarity regulates the relationship between an international tribunal and a domestic court, it can also operate between the central government and the federating units in a federal system. Despite this difference with the previous work, what is common between the two of them is that federalism can be somewhat challenging. With respect to the principle of complementarity, the challenging nature of federalism can be likened with the occasional tension between an international tribunal and states in closing impunity gap.[14]

This study is divided into six section. The first section introduces the study. The second section examines the principle of complementarity. The third section examines the concept of federalism. The fourth section explores how the principle of complementarity may find expression in federalism and the challenge that the nature of federalism may pose.

[11] Footnote 9 above, 71–73.

[12] Footnote 9 above, 73–76.

[13] Footnote 9 above, 76–81.

[14] On the occasional tension between an international tribunal and states, see M Adigun 'The principle of complementarity: A reflection on its meaning, origin and types in international criminal law' (2021) 29(1) *African Journal of International and Comparative Law* 82–94, 91.

The fifth section examines how the principle of complementarity may be implemented within the framework of the Nigerian federalism and how the nature of Nigerian federalism may hinder the implementation of the Rome Statute complementarity in Nigeria. The sixth section concludes the study.

2 The Principle of Complementarity

The principle of complementarity presupposes the existence of two tribunals. Of these two tribunals, one is domestic while the other is international. Each of them is required to compensate for any deficiency found in the other. Some of the deficiencies found at the domestic level includes provisions on immunity, amnesty, pardon, parole, lack of witness protection regime, lack of independence of the prosecuting authority and lack of independence of the judiciary.[15] At the international plane, an international tribunal depends on the cooperation of states for its effectiveness and is limited in terms of financial and material means.[16] There have been five formulations on the principle of complementarity.[17] The first one is the 1937 League of Nations complementarity. Under this formulation, states had primacy and the sole prerogative to determine the case that an international tribunal would adjudicate upon. In 1934, France suffered from the waves of terrorist attacks from the Balkans, Central and Southern Europe.[18] These events made France to call for the establishment of an International Criminal Court. This Court was expected to exercise jurisdiction on terrorism. What eventually emerged was the 1937 League of Nations Convention. Under this Convention, states would be the ones to decide to prosecute before their domestic courts or send the defendant to the International Criminal Court. The state involved would be the one

[15] See footnote 9 above.

[16] Decision Pursuant to Art 15 of the Rome Statute on the Authorization of an Investigation into the situation in the Republic of Kenya Pre-Trial Chamber II ICC-01/09-19. 31 March 2010, dissenting judgment of Judge Hans-Peter Kaul, para 10. See also M Adigun 'The Rome statute complementarity principle and the creation of the African Court of Justice and Human and Peoples' Rights' (2018) 4(1–2) *African Journal of International Criminal Justice* 1, 16.

[17] Adigun 'A reflection' (footnote 14 above).

[18] MD Dublin *International terrorism: Two League of Nations Conventions 1934–1937* (1991) 7–11.

to determine whether it was capable to prosecute the defendant and even if it was not capable it could still decide not to send the defendant to the International Criminal Court for prosecution.[19]

The second formulation is the complementarity principle of the International Military Tribunal (IMT). Under this formulation, there is a division of labour between an international tribunal and a domestic court. When the Second World War was coming to an end, there were preparations to punish those who committed war crimes. In the Moscow Declaration of 1943, it was stated that 'the major criminals, whose offences have no particular geographical localisation'[20] would be prosecuted 'by joint decision of the Governments of the Allies'.[21] This Declaration formed the basis of the establishment of the IMT through the London Agreement of 8 August 1945.[22] Those criminals whose offences could be located within the territory of a particular country would 'be sent back to the Countries in which their abominable deeds were done in order that they may be judged and punished according to the laws of these liberated countries and of free governments'.[23] To punish those criminals whose crimes were location bound, the Allied Control Council, which was acting as the legislative body for Germany enacted Law No. 10 in December 1945. The law was geared towards punishing international crimes committed in Germany and it was to be implemented by

[19] Convention for the Creation of an International Criminal Court, opened for signature at Geneva, 16 November 1937, art 2 reprinted in M Hudson *International legislation* vol VII (1941) 880; MM El Zeidy 'The genesis of complementarity' in C Stahn & MM El Zeidy (eds) *The International Criminal Court and complementarity: From theory to practice* vol I (2011) 99; JG Starke 'The Convention for the Creation of an International Criminal Court' (1938) 19 *British Yearbook of International Law* 216.

[20] The Tripartite Conference at Moscow October 19–30 1943 reprinted in International Conciliation No 395 (1943) 599–605 (Moscow Declaration).

[21] Footnote 20 above.

[22] Agreement for the Prosecution and Punishment of the Major War Criminals of the European Axis, and Charter of the International Military Tribunal, London, 8 August 1945, UNTS No 251 (1951) 280.

[23] Footnote 20 above.

each commander in his zone.[24] Thus, a division of labour was established between the IMT, and the Tribunal established under the Control Council Law with each complementing the other.

In the same vein, the International Military Tribunal for the Far East (IMTFE) was established. It was meant to punish the major Japanese war criminals. These criminals were selected 'on the basis of their position rather than direct evidence of culpability'.[25] They were those who took 'advantage of their power and their official positions and their own personal prestige and influence'.[26] Those who did not have 'leadership background' were not prosecuted before the IMTFE. Instead, they were to be prosecuted separately by each of the 'occupied or colonised territories'.[27] Thus, like the IMT, the IMTFE was also to complement Tribunals set up domestically in Japan. The difference was that leadership was the criterion to determine the cases to be prosecuted by the IMTFE and the tribunals established in the 'occupied or colonised territories'.

The third formulation is that of the 1994 International Law Commission (ILC) complementarity principle. Under this formulation, what was intended was that even if a state ratifies the Draft Statute, the fact of the state's ratification does not automatically confer the exercise of compulsory jurisdiction on the international tribunal. Each case would still be referred to the court before it could compulsorily assume jurisdiction. After the Nuremberg trials, the General Assembly wanted the principles developed from the trials to be more or less codified and thus directed the ILC to prepare a 'Draft Code of Offences against the Peace and Security of Mankind'.[28] On 9 December 1948, prior to the time the directive

[24] Allied Control Council Law No 10, Punishment of Persons Guilty of War Crimes, Crimes against Peace and Crimes against Humanity, 20 December 1945, Official Gazette of the Control Council for Germany, No 3, Berlin, 31 January 1946.

[25] N Boister & R Cryer *The Tokyo International Military Tribunal: A reappraisal* (2008) 50–69.

[26] International Military Tribunal for the Far East (Indictment) https://www.trumanlibrary.gov/library/research-files/indictment-international-military-tribunal-far-east (accessed 25 April 2021).

[27] N Bernaz & R Prouvèze 'International and domestic prosecutions' in MC Bassiouni (ed) *The Pursuit of international criminal justice: A world study on conflicts, victimization, and post-conflict justice* vol I (2010) 280.

[28] GA Res, 177 (II), 2nd Session, 123rd Plenary Meeting, 21 November 1947.

was issued, the General Assembly adopted the Convention on the Prevention and Punishment of the Crime of Genocide (Genocide Convention)[29] but the relationship between international tribunal and domestic courts could not be resolved during the period the Convention was being negotiated.[30] Thus, the General Assembly also mandated the ILC to consider establishing an international tribunal that would be competent to enforce the Code.

In 1950, the ILC submitted its report to the General Assembly, but it was not until 1983 that the ILC had the opportunity to consider the issue of the relationship between domestic courts and international tribunal again.[31] Between 1983 and 1989, the views of the members of the ILC were divergent and could not be reconciled. Thus, the General Assembly had to pass three resolutions requesting the ILC to come up with a more concrete proposal on the issue of international criminal jurisdiction.[32] This focused on the imposition of responsibility, the crimes over which it would have jurisdiction and their definitions. Between 1990 and 1994, the ILC deliberated extensively on the request of the General Assembly and came up with a Draft Statute in 1994.[33] Under the Draft Statute, the international criminal court was to 'supplement, rather than replace, existing national criminal jurisdictions'.[34] It was 'intended to be complementary to national criminal justice systems in cases where such trial procedures may not be available or may be ineffective'.[35] With this, the court could not act if 'States concerned were willing and able to exercise their own jurisdiction over the offence'.[36] What makes this formulation

[29] GA Res, 260 (III), 3rd Session, 179th Plenary Meeting, 9 December 1948, 174–177.

[30] See Convention on the Prevention and Punishment of the Crime of Genocide (adopted 9 December 1948, entered into force 12 January 1951) 78 UNTS 277, art 6.

[31] Summary Records of the Meetings of the Thirty-Fifth Session (3 May–22 July 1983), 1983 Yearbook of International Law Commission, vol 1.

[32] GA Res 43/164 (1988), 76th Plenary Meeting; GA Res 44/32 (1989), 72nd Plenary Meeting; GA Res 44/39 (1989), 72nd Plenary Meeting.

[33] MM El Zeidy 'The genesis of complementarity' (footnote 19 above) 115–116.

[34] 1994 Yearbook of International Law Commission, vol I, 9 and 191.

[35] 1994 International Law Commission Draft Statute in 1994 International Law Commission Report 37, preamble, para 3.

[36] 1994 Yearbook of International Law Commission, vol I, 23.

different from that of the 1937 League of Nations Convention is that there are conditions to be met by the state to be able to exercise jurisdiction unlike the 1937 formulation which did not stipulate any criterion. Nonetheless, the International Criminal Court would not have compulsory jurisdiction in respect of international crimes upon which a state party could exercise jurisdiction until a particular case is referred to the court. This implies that being a party to the Draft Statute does not automatically confer jurisdiction on the Court and that each case would still have to be referred to it.

The fourth formulation is the primacy of the ad hoc tribunals. This is a complete opposite of the 1937 formulation. In this instance, it is the international tribunals that determine if domestic court of the state will have any case to adjudicate upon. After the Balkan massacre of 1991, the United Nations Security Council (UNSC) established the International Criminal Tribunal for Yugoslavia (ICTY) as a means of restoring peace.[37] Similarly, the UNSC established the International Criminal Tribunal for Rwanda (ICTR) because of the genocide committed in that country in 1994.[38] Article 9 of the ICTY Statute stipulates that 'the International Tribunal and national courts shall have concurrent jurisdiction'[39] and that 'the International Tribunal shall have primacy over national courts'[40] which may 'at any stage of the procedure...formally request national courts to defer to...[its] competence...'[41] Article 10 adds that the ICTY may prosecute a person already tried by national courts if 'the act for which he or she was tried was characterised as an ordinary crime'[42] or 'the national court proceedings were not impartial or independent, were

[37] Statute of the International Tribunal for the Prosecution of Persons Responsible for Serious Violations of International Humanitarian Law Committed in the Territory of the Former Yugoslavia Since 1991, SC Res 827, UN SCOR, 48th Sess, Annex, 3417th mtg., UN Doc S/Res/827 (1993) (ICTY Statute).

[38] Statute of the International Tribunal for the Prosecution of Persons Responsible for Serious Violations of International Humanitarian Law Committed in Rwanda, SC Res 955, UN SCOR, 49th Sess, Annex, 3453rd mtg., UN Doc S/Res/955 (1993) (ICTR Statute).

[39] Article 9(1).

[40] Article 9(2).

[41] Footnote 40 above.

[42] Article 10(2)(b).

designed to shield the accused from international criminal responsibility, or the case was not diligently prosecuted'.[43]

The Statute of the ICTR was more forcefully couched. Article 8 stipulates that 'the International Tribunal for Rwanda and national courts shall have concurrent jurisdiction'[44] and that 'the International Tribunal for Rwanda shall have primacy over the national courts of all States'[45] which may 'at any stage of the procedure…formally request national courts to defer to its competence'.[46] Like the ICTY, the Statute of the ICTR also contains article 10. It can be stated that the reason for article 10 was to avoid the temptation or risk of sham trials, political influence and mass prosecutions given the fact that many people were involved in their commission.

When the ICTY and the ICTR were to be closed, the UNSC adopted 'completion strategies'.[47] Because of this, the Rules of Procedure and Evidence (RPE) of the two tribunals had to be amended. Under Rule 11*bis* of the ICTY,[48] the tribunal had the competence to refer a case 'after an indictment has been confirmed and prior to the commencement of trial'[49] to the state where the crime was committed, or where the accused was arrested or 'having jurisdiction and being willing and adequately prepared to accept such a case'.[50] Before the Tribunal could refer a case, it shall 'consider the gravity of the crimes charged and the level of responsibility of the accused'[51] and give 'the State authorities concerned the opportunity to be heard, revoke the order [of referral] and make a formal request for deferral'[52] 'before the accused is found

[43] Footnote 42 above.

[44] Article 9(1).

[45] Article 9(2).

[46] Footnote 45 above.

[47] See SC Res 1503 (2003) UN Doc S/Res/1503 and SC Res 1534 (2004) UN Doc S/Res/1534.

[48] ICTY Rules of Evidence and Procedure (RPE) IT/32/Rev 47, 28 August 2012 as amended.

[49] Footnote 48 above, 11bis(A).

[50] Footnote 48 above, 11bis(A)(iii).

[51] Footnote 48 above, 11bis(C).

[52] Footnote 48 above, 11bis(F).

guilty or acquitted by a national court'.[53] The ICTR[54] Rule 11 *bis* was couched in a way similar to that of the ICTY. However, the ICTR was not required to consider the gravity of the offence and the criminal culpability of the defendant although in practice, these were often considered by the Court.[55] The primacy of the ICTY and the ICTR was also meant to complement the judicial system in Yugoslavia and Rwanda although the states were in a subordinate position with the Tribunals since they alone had the competence to determine cases that could be tried by these states.

The fifth formulation is the Rome Statute complementarity principle. Under this formulation, the International Criminal Court has both compulsory and optional jurisdiction.[56] When a state ratifies the Rome Statute, the International Criminal Court automatically has compulsory jurisdiction which can be exercised upon the fulfilment of certain conditions.[57] The optional jurisdiction is in respect of self-referral.[58] Certain conditions, or pre-conditions, however, have to be met before the jurisdiction of the ICC can be triggered. Thus, the Court can only exercise compulsory jurisdiction if the state concerned is 'unwilling' and/or 'unable' to investigate and prosecute when it has jurisdiction. On 9 December 1994, the General Assembly established an Ad hoc Committee[59] with the mandate to critically re-examine the 'major substantive and administrative issues' generated by the 1994 draft.[60] The Ad hoc Committee dedicated its effort towards refining the criteria for

[53] Footnote 52 above.

[54] ICTR Rules of Evidence and Procedure 1 October 2009 as amended.

[55] E Møse 'Main achievements of the ICTR' (2005) 3 *Journal of International Criminal Justice* 920, 932; MM El Zeidy 'From primacy to complementarity and backwards: (Re)-visiting rule 11 bis of the ad hoc tribunals' (2008) 57 *International & Comparative Law Quarterly* 403, 410.

[56] El Zeidy 'The genesis of complementarity' (footnote 19 above) 134–137.

[57] Rome Statute, art 17 provides that the 'Court shall determine that a case is inadmissible where…'

[58] *Prosecutor v Thomas Lubanga Dyilo, Decision on the Prosecutor's Application for a Warrant of Arrest* ICC-01/04-01/06-8-Corr, Pre-Trial Chamber 1, 10 February 2006, para 18.

[59] GA Res 49/53, 9 December 1994.

[60] Report of the Ad hoc Committee on the Establishment of an International Criminal Court UN GAOR, 50th Sess, Supp No 22, UN Doc A/50/22 (1995), para 154.

the functioning of the principle of complementarity in the 1994 ILC Draft Statute.[61] The terms 'available' and 'ineffective' in the Preamble to the 1994 ILC Draft Statute were severely criticised and were considered vague by several delegations.[62]

In 1995, the Preparatory Committee replaced the Ad hoc Committee. The issue of the vagueness of the terms adopted in the Preamble of the 1994 ILC Draft Statute resurfaced.[63] While some delegations favoured a definition with more clarity, others preferred the terms deleted completely.[64] In August 1997, John Holmes, the head of the Canadian delegation, presented a draft provision (article 35) on complementarity during the session of the Preparatory Committee. The draft provision was approved at the end of the session.[65] In addition, the terms 'unwilling' and 'unable' which had earlier found expression in the report of the 1992 Working Group were adopted by the draft provision with more detailed and thorough criteria for assessment.[66] This eventually formed part of the Draft Final Act.[67] Deliberations on complementarity continued in Rome especially during the plenary meetings.[68] The final outcome of deliberations was embodied in article 17 of the Rome Statute.[69]

If one considers the evolution of the principle of complementarity, it appears that under the 1937 League of Nations Convention, states appear

[61] El Zeidy 'The genesis of complementarity' (footnote 19) 130.

[62] Report of the Ad hoc Committee 1995 (footnote 60 above) para 41.

[63] Report of the Preparatory Committee on the Establishment of an International Criminal Court UN GAOR, 51st Sess, vol 1, Supp No 22, UN Doc A/51/22 (1995), paras 154 and 161.

[64] Footnote 63 above, para 161.

[65] Decisions Taken by the Preparatory Committee at its Session Held 4 to 15 August 1997, UN GAOR, 52 mtg, UN Doc A/AC.249/1997/L.8/Rev.1 (1997).

[66] Footnote 65 above, 10–12.

[67] Report of the Preparatory Committee on the Establishment of an International Criminal Court, Draft Statute and Draft Final Act, UN Doc A/Conf. 183/2/Add.1 (1998), art 15.

[68] Report of the Preparatory Committee on the Establishment of an International Criminal Court, UN Doc A/Conf. 183/2 (14 April 1998), art 15; UN Doc A/Conf. 183/SR.2, para 70; UN Doc A/Conf. 183/SR.3, paras 48 and 88; UN Doc A/Conf. 183/SR.4, paras 27 and 42; UN Doc A/Conf. 183/SR.5, paras 21 and 39; UN Doc A/Conf. 183/SR.6, paras 31 and 100; UN Doc A/Conf. 183/SR.7, para 101; UN Doc A/Conf. 183/SR.8, paras 1 and 77.

[69] Rome Statute, art 17.

to maintain a more dominant position whereas under the ICTY and the ICTR complementarity principle, international tribunals appear to maintain a more dominant position. This can be said to be a kind of paradigm shift. The rationale behind this can be said to be the way the international court or tribunal is created. The 1937 League of Nations Convention was a product of treaty at the time when the concept of sovereignty was much potent whereas the ICTY and the ICTR were created by the Security Council whose definite stipulations prescribing a course of conduct could be said to be a sort of legislation or decree for the whole world. Under the Rome Statute complementarity principle, there appears to be a balance between rabid sovereignty and outright legislation due to the combination of optional and compulsory jurisdiction in the Rome Statute.

Nonetheless, it is noteworthy that the practical working of the principle of complementarity is flexible and one formulation of the principle of complementarity may operate like any other forms of complementarity.[70] Thus, the 1937 League of Nations complementarity model may operate like that of the IMT where a division of labour exists between the International Criminal Court and its domestic counterparts. Similarly, the ad hoc tribunals primacy model may operate like that of its 1937 League of Nations opposite model if the international tribunal allows all the prosecutions to be carried out before domestic courts. Also, the complementarity model of the Rome Statute may operate like that of the IMT model where the ICC decides to prosecute the 'major leaders' or those who bear the greatest responsibility and leaves domestic courts to carry out the prosecution of subordinate suspects. As it will be demonstrated later in this study, this flexibility is important for the working of complementarity principle within a federal state. This is because it will be possible for the central government and each of the federating units to cooperatively close the impunity gap.

3 The Concept of Federalism

Federalism as a concept presupposes the existence of two levels of governance where power is shared between them. One level of governance is that of the central government while the other level is that

[70] MM El Zeidy *The principle of complementarity in international criminal law: Origin, development and practice* (2008) 7.

of the governments of the constituent units.[71] The power is shared in line with the principles of centralisation and non-centralisation together with other checks and balances.[72] With the principle of centralisation and non-centralisation, certain powers necessarily belong to the central government and cannot be taken from it; and at the same time certain powers necessarily belong to the constituent units and cannot be taken from them. The principle of decentralisation is different from that of centralisation and non-centralisation. What the principle of decentralisation implies is that there is an absolute authority which devolves power as it chooses and could decide to take it back. This is different from federalism where neither the central government nor the constituent units is absolute.[73] Federalism is considered the most pragmatic approach to

[71] On federalism, see generally KC Wheare *Federal government* 4th ed (1967); A Menon & MA Schain (eds) *Comparative federalism: The European Union and the United States in comparative perspective* (2006); S Dosenrode 'Federalism' in S Dosenrode (ed) *Approaching the EUropean federation?* (2007) 7–37.

[72] EE Osaghae 'What man has joined together: Ethnicity, federalism and state politics' An Inaugural Lecture delivered at the University of Ibadan, Thursday 22 August 2019, 11.

[73] EE Osaghae 'A reassessment of federalism as a degree of decentralization' (1990) 20(1) *Publius: The Journal of Federalism* 83–90; RL Watts 'Federalism, federal systems, and federations' (1998) *Annual Review of Political Science* 117–137; B Theret 'Regionalism and federalism: A comparative analysis of the regulation of economic tensions between regions by Canadian and American federal intergovernmental transfer programmes' (1999) 23(3) *International Journal of Urban and Regional Research* 479–512; X Song 'Thinking federal: The relevance of federalism to China' (2000) 10(3) *Regional and Federal Studies* 107–128; M Escobar-Lemmon 'Fiscal decentralization and federalism in Latin America' (2001) 31(4) *Publius: The Journal of Federalism* 23–41; EK Yeoh & E Devadason (eds) *Emerging trading nation in an integrating world: Global impacts and domestic challenges of China's economic reform* (2007) 235; P Graefe & A Bourns 'The gradual defederalization of Canadian health policy' (2009) 39(1) *Publius: The Journal of Federalism* 187–209; K Barkey & FC Godart 'Empires, federated arrangements, and kingdoms: Using political models of governance to understand firms' creative performance' (2013) 34(1) *Organization Studies* 79.

issues of diversity[74] be they ethnic,[75] cultural,[76] religious, territorial[77] or economic.[78]

Federalism can be conceived in two ways. It may be conceived as a system of government or as a solution. As a system of government, the principles of power sharing are to a large extent stated clearly in a written constitution[79] whereas in federalism as a solution, the emphasis is on pragmatism and problem solving where the peculiar situation of a community is taken cognizance of.[80] Federalism as a solution is not tied to a fixed set of constitutional principles or textbook rules and may manifest as consociationalism, proportionality, decentralisation, devolution, regionalisation, local autonomy and other forms of arrangement to redress what is considered wrong.[81] Federalism practised by the Anglo-Saxons and the Europeans is more of a system of government while federalism practised in Africa and Asia is more of a solution type.[82]

Federalism may come into existence through either of two processes. These processes are aggregation and dis-aggregation.[83] In aggregation, the constituent units come together to discuss the principle of power sharing in terms of what to be centralised and non-centralised.[84] The United States of America is a good example of an outcome of aggregation when thirteen constituent units came together, likewise Canada, Germany

[74] Osaghae 'What man has joined together' (footnote 72 above) 11.

[75] See MG Breen 'The origins of holding-together federalism: Nepal, Myanmar, and Sri Lanka' (2018) 48(1) *Publius: The Journal of Federalism* 26–50; K Adeney *Federalism and ethnic conflict regulation in India and Pakistan* (2007); YT Fessha *Ethic diversity and federalism: Constitution making in South Africa and Ethiopia* (2010) 25–61.

[76] W Norman *Negotiating nationalism: Nation-building, federalism, and secession in the multinational state* (2006) 73–92.

[77] See W Swenden, 'Governing diversity in South Asia: Explaining divergent pathways in India and Pakistan' (2018) 48(1) *Publius: The Journal of Federalism* 102–133.

[78] R Simeon 'Constitutional design and change in federal systems: Issues and questions' (2009) 39(2) *Publius: The Journal of Federalism* 241–261, 242.

[79] Osaghae 'What man has joined together' (footnote 72) 11.

[80] Footnote 79 above.

[81] EE Osaghae 'Federalism and the management of diversity in Africa' (2004) 5 *Identity, Culture and Politics* 162, 168.

[82] Osaghae 'What man has joined together' (footnote 72 above) 11.

[83] CJ Friedrich *Trends of federalism in theory and practice* (1968) 9.

[84] Footnote 83 above.

and Switzerland. In dis-aggregation, a previously unitary community divides itself into constituent units.[85] Ethiopia, Nigeria, Tanzania and India exemplify the process of dis-aggregation. Federalism is often established for a purpose irrespective of the process.[86] The purpose for which it is established is not fixed in time as it keeps changing as the circumstances of the constituent units are changing. This implies that federalism requires constant restructuring and re-working to respond to the changing circumstances of the constituent units.[87]

Federalism created by the process of aggregation where the constituent units had already formed and consolidated is likely to be more relatively stable.[88] Examples are the United States, Canada, Germany and Switzerland. On the other hand, federalism created by the process of dis-aggregation may have its constituent units already formed and consolidated like Ethiopia, Tanzania and Comoros; or may have the constituent units forming like Nigeria and India. Where the constituent units are forming, such federalism may be more relatively unstable.[89] However, this is not to suggest that such federalism will automatically fail. What it implies is that the process of restructuring will be more intense and will require a higher level of political skills and visionary leadership.

4 The Principle of Complementarity in Federalism

As previously noted, the principle of complementarity presupposes the existence of two criminal jurisdictions where one is international, and the other is domestic. To the extent that the central government and the constituent units can exercise criminal jurisdiction in certain instances in

[85] Footnote 83 above.

[86] WH Riker *Federalism: Origin, operation, significance* (1964) ch 2; WH Riker 'Federalism' in FI Greenstein & NW Polsby (eds) *Handbook of political science: Governmental institutions and processes* (1975) 93–172; WS Livingston 'A note on the nature of federalism' (1952) 67(1) *Political Science Quarterly* 81–95.

[87] WS Livingston 'A note on the nature of federalism' (1952) 67(1) *Political Science Quarterly* 81–95 93; Osaghae 'What man has joined together' (footnote 72 above) 18–19.

[88] Osaghae 'What man has joined together' (footnote 72 above) 25.

[89] Footnote 88 above, 26.

federalism, the two levels of governance in federalism can yield the principle of complementarity. Since the principle of complementarity has the goal of ending impunity, federalism may also have this as one of its goals.

In the preceding analysis, there are been five formulations of the principle of complementarity, each of these formulations may find expression in solution-type federalism between the central government and the constituent units. Thus, like the 1937 League of Nations Convention model in which states alone determined the case they wanted the international tribunal to adjudicate upon, the constituent units in their exercise of criminal jurisdiction may determine the case that the central government may adjudicate upon. Similarly, like the complementarity principle of the IMT in which there was division of labour between domestic court and an international tribunal, there may also be a division of labour between the central government and the constituent units. Thus, international crimes whose commission extends beyond the territory of a constituent units may be taken up by the central government while those crimes whose commission is limited to the territory of a constituent unit may be adjudicated upon by the constituent unit in question.

In addition, like the primacy expressed in the jurisprudence of the ICTY and the ICTR, which is a reversal of the 1937 League of Nations Convention model, it may be possible to have an arrangement where the central government determines the case that constituent units can adjudicate upon. In the same vein, it may be possible to have an arrangement reflective of the 1994 International Law Commission complementarity model where the central government cannot assume compulsory jurisdiction and each case would be negotiated between the central government and the constituent units. Lastly, it may be possible to have an arrangement similar to the Rome Statute complementarity model where the central government can exercise compulsory jurisdiction if the constituent unit is unwilling or unable or admits that it cannot prosecute and is considered to have indirectly referred itself.

With the above, can federalism be hindering or enhancing to the goal of complementarity principle? Federalism can indeed be enhancing or hindering. With respect to any arrangement other than that of the 1937 League of Nations model, federalism is enhancing. With respect to an arrangement similar to that of the League of Nations, federalism may be hindering because the federating units alone determine the case that the central government can adjudicate upon with its intervention capable of being foreclosed where the federating units decide not to refer any case to it.

5 Implementing the Rome Statute Complementarity Principle in Nigeria as a Federal State

Before discussing the implementation of the Rome Statute complementarity principle in Nigeria as a federal state, the nature of the Nigerian federalism will be discussed first. The Constitution of the Federal Republic of Nigeria 1999 (Nigerian Constitution 1999) is the operative constitution in Nigeria. It declares itself supreme and binding on all authorities and persons in Nigeria.[90] It prevails over any other law in Nigeria and any law inconsistent with it is void to the extent of its inconsistency.[91] It also stipulates that Nigeria is 'a Federation consisting of States and a Federal Capital Territory'.[92] It is made up of 36 States.[93]

In the Nigerian Constitution 1999, powers are divided into legislative, executive and judicial powers.[94] At the federal level, legislative power is vested in a 'National Assembly for the Federation'.[95] The National Assembly consists of 'a Senate and a House of Representatives'.[96] The National Assembly has the power to make laws for the 'peace, order and good government of the Federation or any part thereof...'[97] The National Assembly can legislate on the Exclusive Legislative List[98] and the Concurrent Legislative List.[99] If any 'Law' enacted by the legislative organ in the State is inconsistent with any 'law' made by the National

[90] Constitution of the Federal Republic of Nigeria, 1999, sec 1(1).

[91] Nigerian Constitution 1999, sec 1(3).

[92] Nigerian Constitution 1999, sec 2(2).

[93] Nigerian Constitution 1999, sec 3(1).

[94] Nigerian Constitution 1999, secs 4, 5 and 6.

[95] Nigerian Constitution 1999, sec 4(1).

[96] Footnote 95 above.

[97] Nigerian Constitution 1999, sec 4(2).

[98] Nigerian Constitution 1999, second schedule, part I.

[99] Nigerian Constitution 1999, sec 4(4)(a) and second schedule, part II.

Assembly, the 'law' made by the National Assembly shall prevail and that other 'Law' shall to the extent of its inconsistency be void.[100]

At the State level, the legislative power of a State of the Federation is vested in the 'House of Assembly of the State'.[101] The House of Assembly of a State is empowered 'to make laws for the peace, order and good government of the State or any part thereof...'[102] The House of Assembly of a State is empowered to make laws on matters within the Concurrent Legislative List[103] and on those matters that are residual.[104] Thus, States share legislative powers with the Federal Government in respect of matters in the Concurrent Legislative List. Residual matters are matters which are not listed in both the Exclusive Legislative List and the Concurrent Legislative List excluding the Fundamental Objectives and Directive Principles of State Policy and Fundamental Rights.[105] Criminal matters are essentially residual. However, the National Assembly can legislate on federal offence which is defined as 'an offence contrary to the provisions of an Act of the National Assembly or any law having effect as if so enacted'.[106]

The executive power of the Federation is vested in the President and that power may be exercised by him either directly or through the Vice-President and Ministers of the Government of the Federation or officers in the public service of the Federation.[107] The executive power of the Federation extends to the execution and maintenance of the Nigerian Constitution 1999, all laws made by the National Assembly and to all matters with respect to which the National Assembly has, for the time being, power to make laws.[108] With respect to the prosecution of federal offences, only the Attorney-General of the Federation is empowered.[109] While federal offences are infractions of an Act of National Assembly with

[100] Nigerian Constitution 1999, sec 4(5).

[101] Nigerian Constitution 1999, sec 4(6).

[102] Nigerian Constitution 1999, sec 4(7).

[103] Nigerian Constitution 1999, sec 4(4)(a) and second schedule, part II.

[104] Nigerian Constitution 1999, sec 4(7).

[105] Footnote 104 above.

[106] Nigerian Constitution 1999, sec 286(3).

[107] Nigerian Constitution 1999, sec 5(1)(a).

[108] Nigerian Constitution 1999, sec 5(1)(b).

[109] Nigerian Constitution 1999, sec 174(1)(a).

penal consequences, they can be prosecuted in a State. The most important consideration is if the tenor of the Act is to the effect that the crime is to be prosecuted in any State. Therefore, 'the State High Court [can] be used as a venue for the prosecution of cases'[110] and the Attorney-General of the Federation cannot be 'prevented from exercising his functions on the grounds that his jurisdiction does not extend to any particular State in Nigeria'.[111] The Attorney-General of the Federation may however delegate his or her power to prosecute to the Attorney-General of the State[112] and the power so delegated may be exercised by that Attorney-General of the State or any officer in his or her department or Ministry.[113]

At the State level, the executive power of a State is vested in the Governor of that State and it may be exercised by him either directly or through the Deputy Governor and Commissioners of the Government of that State or officers in the public service of the State.[114] The executive power of the State extends to the execution and maintenance of the Nigerian Constitution 1999, all laws made by the House of Assembly of the State and to all matters with respect to which the House of Assembly has, for the time being, power to make laws.[115] The executive power of the State shall not be exercised to impede or prejudice the exercise of the executive power of the Federation,[116] endanger any asset or investment of the Government of the Federation in that State,[117] or endanger the continuance of a Federal Government in Nigeria.[118] With respect to criminal prosecution at the State level, it is the Attorney-General of the State that is empowered to do it.[119]

[110] *Attorney General Ondo v Attorney General Federation* [2002] FWLR (Pt. 111) 1972, 2210–2211, paras E–A.

[111] Footnote 110 above, 2167 paras D–E.

[112] Administration of Criminal Justice Act 2015, sec 268(4).

[113] Nigerian Constitution 1999, sec 268(5).

[114] Nigerian Constitution 1999, sec 5(2)(a).

[115] Nigerian Constitution 1999, sec 5(2)(b).

[116] Nigerian Constitution 1999, sec 5(3)(a).

[117] Nigerian Constitution 1999, sec 5(3)(b).

[118] Nigerian Constitution 1999, sec 5(3)(c).

[119] Nigerian Constitution 1999, sec 211(1)(a).

The judicial power of the Federation is vested in the courts established for the Federation.[120] The courts established for the Federation which are relevant here are the Supreme Court of Nigeria,[121] the Court of Appeal,[122] the Federal High Court[123] and the High Court of the Federal Capital Territory, Abuja.[124] Each of these courts has 'all the powers of a superior court of record'.[125] With respect to criminal matters, the High Court of the Federal Capital Territory has unlimited jurisdiction on all crimes committed in Abuja[126] while the Federal High Court can only exercise jurisdiction in respect of 'treason, treasonable felony and allied offences'.[127] Appeals from these courts go to the Court of Appeal[128] and the Supreme Court[129] which do not have original jurisdiction on crime.

The judicial power of a State is vested in the courts established for a State. The court established for a State which is relevant here is the High Court of a State.[130] This court also has 'all the powers of a superior court of record'.[131] The judicial power extends to 'government or authority and to any persons in Nigeria'.[132] With respect to crime, it has unlimited jurisdiction in respect of crimes committed in the territory of a State.[133] While federalism applies to the legislature and the executive, it does not apply to the judiciary. The reason is that appeal lies from all courts established for the States to the Court of Appeal and the Supreme Court which are

[120] Nigerian Constitution 1999, sec 6(1).

[121] Nigerian Constitution 1999, sec 6(5)(a).

[122] Nigerian Constitution 1999, sec 6(5)(b).

[123] Nigerian Constitution 1999, sec 6(5)(c).

[124] Nigerian Constitution 1999, sec 6(5)(d).

[125] Nigerian Constitution 1999, sec 6(3).

[126] Nigerian Constitution 1999, sec 257(1).

[127] Nigerian Constitution 1999, sec 251(2).

[128] Nigerian Constitution 1999, sec 241(1)(a).

[129] Nigerian Constitution 1999, sec 232(2).

[130] Nigerian Constitution 1999, sec 270.

[131] Nigerian Constitution 1999, sec 6(3).

[132] Nigerian Constitution 1999, sec 6(6)(a).

[133] Nigerian Constitution 1999, sec 272(1).

courts established for the Federation[134] and whose decisions are binding on them.[135]

Having discussed the Nigerian federalism, the implementation of the Rome Statute complementarity principle in Nigeria as a federal state will now be examined. It is noteworthy that Nigeria ratified the Rome Statute of the International Criminal Court on 27 September 2001.[136] Thus, it is required to implement the principle of complementarity by investigating and prosecuting the crimes recognised under the Statute. In implementing the complementarity principle, section 12 of the Nigerian Constitution 1999 becomes apposite. Section 12 provides that

> (2) The National Assembly may make laws for the Federation or any part thereof with respect to matters not included in the Exclusive Legislative List for the purpose of implementing a treaty.
>
> (3) A bill for an Act of the National Assembly passed pursuant to the provisions of subsection (2) of this section shall not be presented to the President for assent, and shall not be enacted unless it is ratified by a majority of all the Houses of Assembly in the Federation.

The implication of the above provision is that while only the federal government can negotiate a treaty, its implementation may be done by the National Assembly alone or by the National Assembly and each of the House of Assembly of the 36 States.[137] Where the subject matter of the treaty is within the Exclusive Legislative List, only the National Assembly will implement the treaty by enacting it into law.[138] Where the subject matter of the treaty is within the Concurrent Legislative List or where it falls within residual matters, it is the National Assembly and each House of Assembly of the federating States that will implement it by enacting it into law.[139] The enactment will be an Act of the National Assembly.[140]

In implementing the complementarity principle in Nigeria, provisions will be made in an Act of the National Assembly for the prosecution of the

[134] Nigerian Constitution 1999, secs 233(1) and 240.

[135] Footnote 134 above.

[136] International Criminal Court (footnote 2 above).

[137] Adigun *The ICC and Nigeria* (footnote 9 above), 66–67.

[138] Footnote 137 above.

[139] Footnote 137 above.

[140] Nigerian Constitution 1999, sec 12(3).

crimes recognised under the Rome Statute in Nigeria. These crimes are war crimes, crimes against humanity and genocide. Aggression appears to be excluded from domestic investigation and prosecution because of the 'understanding' that it should be excluded[141] although there is nothing that precludes a state party from prosecuting aggression as treason domestically.[142] Once these crimes are enacted into law, they will become federal offences. Since crime is a residual matter under the Nigerian Constitution 1999, the implication is that the National Assembly and each House of Assembly of the 36 States in Nigeria will participate in the enactment process.

Section 12 of the Nigerian Constitution 1999 can accommodate various complementarity models between the Federal Republic of Nigeria and the federating States. Since section 12 is written in the Nigerian Constitution, it can be argued that federalism of a constitutional type makes this arrangement possible. From another perspective, it can be argued that the arrangement between the Federal Government and the federating States reflects federalism of a solution type. A more plausible argument is that solution-type federalism is embedded in constitutional federalism by virtue of section 12 of the Nigerian Constitution 1999.

As previously noted, the operation of the principle of complementarity is flexible. With this, the National Assembly and the House of Assembly of each State can jointly enact an Act to achieve any or a combination of the complementarity models previously discussed in the process of implementing the Rome Statute complementarity principle. Thus, they can have an arrangement where there will be a division of labour between the Federal Government and each of the federating States like the IMT complementarity model where there is division of labour between an international tribunal and a domestic court. In this respect, international crimes whose commission transcends the boundaries of a single State can be prosecuted by the Federal Government while those ones whose commission is within the State can be prosecuted by the State concerned.

[141] International Criminal Court, *Understandings regarding the amendments to the Rome Statute of the International Criminal Court on the Crime of Aggression*. RC/10/Add.1. 11 June 2010. Paragraph 5 is headed: 'Domestic jurisdiction over the crime of aggression' and it is stated as follows: 'It is understood that the amendments shall not be interpreted as creating the right or obligation to exercise domestic jurisdiction with respect to an act of aggression committed by another State.'

[142] S Sayapin *The crime of aggression in international criminal law: Historical development, comparative analysis and present state* (2014) 217–222.

They can also have an arrangement like that of the ICTY and the ICTR complementarity model. In this respect, just as international tribunals determine the cases that domestic courts will prosecute, the Federal Government can also be able to determine the cases that the federating States will prosecute. The Federal Government and the federating States can also agree to have an arrangement reflective of the 1994 ILC complementarity model. Thus, the Federal Government will not have the capacity to assume compulsory jurisdiction and its jurisdiction will have to be negotiated in respect of each case. It may also be possible for the Federal Government to have an arrangement like the Rome Statute complementarity model with the federating States. In this respect, the federating States will have the power to prosecute but if they are unwilling or unable, or admits that they cannot prosecute, the Federal Government will take it over. However, the 1937 League of Nations model must be avoided because the Federal Republic of Nigeria will not be able to investigate and prosecute the crimes under the Rome Statute. As previously noted, under this model, states alone have the competence to determine the cases that international tribunals can adjudicate upon. In this respect, federating States alone will be able to determine the cases that the Federal Government can adjudicate upon.

But it can be questioned if the situation reminiscent of the 1937 League of Nations model can be produced in Nigeria. Are the constituent States not expected to act and operationalise the domestication of the Rome Statute? Can the constituent States act in a manner inconsistent with Nigeria's obligation under the Rome Statute? While the constituent States in Nigeria are not expected to act in a manner inconsistent with Nigeria's obligation under international law including the Rome Statute, the legal position is that they are not obligated to act in line with Nigeria's commitment at the international plane.[143] As a matter of fact, some States in Nigeria have even acted in a manner contrary to Nigeria's obligation under international law. A typical case in point is the implementation

[143] See TS Braimah 'Child marriage in Northern Nigeria: Section 61 of part 1 the 1999 Constitution and the protection of children against child marriage' (2014) 14 *African Human Rights Law Journal* 475; ES Uwauche 'Child marriage in Nigeria: (Il)legal and (un)constitutional?' (2015) 5 *African Human Rights Law Journal* 421.

of the Convention on the Rights of the Child in Nigeria.[144] Nigeria enacted the Convention into law through the Child's Rights Act 2003.[145] However, while some States in Nigeria adopted the Act by enacting their own respective Child's Rights Laws, some States decided not to, while some States adopted some parts of the Act. Jigawa State, one of the federating States in Nigeria exemplified a State that adopted some parts. While the Child's Rights Act defines a child as a person below the age of eighteen years,[146] Jigawa State Child's Rights Law 2006 defines a child as any person below the age of puberty.[147] The implication is that since the two enactments prohibit child marriage,[148] a person below the age of eighteen years can get married in Jigawa if the person has reached the age of puberty whereas the person cannot get married under the Child Rights Act. Of course, it can be argued that Jigawa did not act contrary to Nigeria's obligation under the Convention on the Rights of the Child since article 2 of the Convention defines a child as a person below eighteen unless under the law that applies to the child, majority is attained earlier. Nonetheless, it shows what federating States in Nigeria can do. In any event, those States that have refused to adopt the Act can be said to be acting contrary to Nigeria's obligation under the Convention.[149]

Having established that section 12 of the Nigerian Constitution 1999 can accommodate various complementarity models, the issue which becomes apposite to be addressed is how Nigeria will report its activities in terms of investigation and prosecution of any of the crimes recognised under the Rome Statute to the ICC to avoid being taken over

[144] Adopted and opened for signature, ratification and accession by General Assembly Resolution 44/25 of 20 November 1989, entered into force 2 September 1990, 1577 UNTS 3.

[145] Cap C50 Laws of the Federation of Nigeria (LFN) 2004.

[146] Section 277.

[147] Section 2(1).

[148] Child's Rights Law (Jigawa), sec 15(1); Child's Rights Act 2003, secs 21, 22 and 23.

[149] However, see M Adigun, 'The implementation of the Convention on the Rights of the Child in Nigeria' (2019) (3) July *Public Law* 476–494 where it is argued that the Child Rights Act 2003 is binding on the States and that it is superfluous or wasteful for those States that adopted it while those States that have refused to adopt the Act are belatedly misguided.

by the Court on the ground of unwillingness and inability.[150] It can be argued that where it is the State within the Nigerian federation that is investigating or prosecuting any of the crimes recognised under the Rome Statute, Nigeria will indicate steps taken by that State. This point underscores the reason why the 1937 League of Nations complementarity model must be avoided. This is because once the federating State concerned decides not to investigate and prosecute, the Federal Government is helpless, and its helplessness will produce the consequence of unwillingness and inability which may necessitate the intervention of the ICC.

It has been suggested that 'the duty to exercise criminal jurisdiction' within the context of complementarity should not be construed strictly and that it should rather be considered an obligation 'to ensure that a genuine investigation be undertaken'.[151] Therefore, in the light of the relationship between the principle of complementarity and the concept of federalism, it can be argued that Nigeria is still the one doing the investigation or prosecution since the State is a unit within the Nigerian federation.

If complementarity should not be construed strictly, it should also be possible for a State within the Nigerian federation to delegate its criminal jurisdiction to another. If Nigeria gives its report, it will indicate the steps taken by the State to which the criminal jurisdiction has been delegated. Again, Nigeria is still the one doing the investigation or prosecution since the delegated State is a unit within its territory.

It is noteworthy that in international law, a state can delegate its criminal jurisdiction to another.[152] In the light of the relationship between the

[150] Rome Statute, art 17.

[151] C Kress "'Self-referrals' and 'waivers of complementarity': Some considerations in law and policy' (2004) 2 *Journal of International Criminal Justice* 944, 946.

[152] See The Tokyo Convention on Offences and Certain other Acts Committed on Board Aircraft (signed 14 December 1963, entered into force 4 December 1969) 704 UNTS 220; the Hague Convention for the Suppression of Unlawful Seizure of Aircraft (signed 16 December 1970, entered into force 14 October 1971) 860 UNTS 105; Montreal Convention for the Suppression of Unlawful Acts against the Safety of Civil Aviation (signed 23 September 1971, entered into force 26 January 1973) 974 UNTS 178; the Convention on the Prevention and Punishment of Crimes against Internationally Protected Persons including Diplomatic Agents (adopted 14 December 1973, entered into force 20 February 1977) 1035 UNTS 167; the New York Convention against the taking of Hostages (adopted 17 December 1979, entered into force 3 June 1983) 1316 UNTS

principle of complementarity and the concept of federalism, such delegation between States in Nigeria is not out of place. However, it can be countered that delegation in the context of international law cannot be transposed to Nigerian federalism most especially when it was created by a process of dis-aggregation with the Nigerian Constitution creating the federating units and not the other way round. In other words, while delegation can be understood in a federalism formed by a process of aggregation where the constituent units jointly formed a constitutional pact, this cannot apply in a federalism formed by dis-aggregation since the constitution created the constituent units.

While this argument is persuasive, nonetheless it can be adequately met. In Nigeria, the general power to legislate on crime under the Nigerian Constitution 1999 is a residual matter within the sole competence of the federating States. Therefore, delegation is a necessary consequence of this constitutional provision even though Nigerian federalism is a product of dis-aggregation. Therefore, at a broader level of abstraction, it is not the process that matters but the provision of the constitution.

205; Convention against Torture and other Cruel, Inhuman and Degrading Treatment (adopted 10 December 1984, entered into force 26 June 1987) 1465 UNTS 85; the Rome Convention for the Suppression of Unlawful Acts against the Safety of Maritime Navigation (signed 10 March 1988, entered into force 1 March 1992) 1678 UNTS 222; UN Convention against Illicit Traffic in Narcotic Drugs and Psychotropic Substances (adopted 20 December 1988, entered into force 11 November 1990) 1582 UNTS 95; the Convention on the Safety of United Nations and Associated Personnel (adopted 9 December 1994, entered into force 15 January 1999) 2051 UNTS 363; the International Convention for the Suppression of Terrorist Bombings (adopted 15 December 1997, entered into force 23 May 2001) 2149 UNTS 256; the International Convention for the Suppression of the Financing of Terrorism (adopted 9 December 1999, entered into force 10 April 2002) 2178 UNTS 197; Council Framework Decision of 13 June 2002 on Combating Terrorism (2002/475/JHA), *Official Journal of the European Communities* I.164/3-7, 22.6.2002, art 9(1); European Convention on the Transfer of Proceedings in Criminal Matters (signed 15 May 1972, entered into force 30 March 1978) ETS No 73, art 3; Agreement between Member States of the European Communities on the Transfer of Proceedings in Criminal Matters 1990 (2009/C 219/03), *Official Journal of the European Communities* C219.7, 22.9.2009; The Treaty on Mutual Legal Assistance in Criminal Matters between the Government of the Federal Republic of Nigeria and the Government of the Republic of South Africa (Ratification and Enforcement) Act Cap T24 Revised Laws of the Federation of Nigeria (LFN) 2004. For an analysis of some of these treaties within the paradigm of 'extradite or prosecute' see L Reydams, *Universal jurisdiction: International and municipal legal perspectives* (2003) ch 3. See also D Akande 'The jurisdiction of the International Criminal Court over nationals of non-Parties: Legal basis and limits' (2003) 1 *Journal of International Criminal Justice* 618, 622.

6 Conclusion

This study examines the relationship between the principle of complementarity and the concept of federalism and the challenge that federalism may pose. It finds that in the principle of complementarity, there are two criminal jurisdictions with one being international while the other is domestic and that the two of them complements each other to close impunity gap. With respect to the concept of federalism, there are two levels of governance with one being the central government while the other is that of the federating units and that while each is distinct from the other, the two are interdependent. Against the backdrop of these findings, it is argued that there are five models of the principle of complementarity, that while each of these models is distinct, their operation in practical terms may manifest like any of the others and that they may find expression between a central government and federating units in a federal state. Having argued thus, the study examines section 12 of the Nigerian Constitution 1999 on treaty implementation and submits that the section can accommodate various complementarity models between the Federal Republic of Nigeria and any of the States within the Nigerian Federation in the process of implementing the Rome Statute complementarity model but that the 1937 League of Nations model may be hindering and pose a challenge and should be avoided. Since Nigeria may have to report to the ICC under the Rome Statute, it suffices once Nigeria gives account of what the relevant federating State does. Therefore, Nigeria may consider this in its effort to implement the Rome Statute which may prevent its criminal justice system from being overwhelmed in a situation of mass atrocity.

References

Books

Adeney K *Federalism and ethnic conflict regulation in India and Pakistan* (New York: Palgrave Macmillan 2007)

Adigun M *The International Criminal Court and Nigeria: Implementing the complementarity principle of the Rome statute* (Abingdon: Routledge 2018)

Boister N & Cryer R *The Tokyo International Military Tribunal: A reappraisal* (Oxford: Oxford University Press 2008)

Dublin MD *International terrorism: Two League of Nations Conventions 1934–1937* (Millwood, NY: Kraus Microform 1991)

Due Process of Law Foundation *Digest of Latin American jurisprudence on international crimes* (Washington, DC: Due Process of Law Foundation 2010)

El Zeidy MM *The principle of complementarity in international criminal law: Origin, development and practice* (Leiden: Martinus Nijhoff Publishers 2008).

Fessha YT *Ethic diversity and federalism: Constitution making in South Africa and Ethiopia* (Surrey: Ashgate Publishing Ltd 2010).

Friedrich CJ *Trends of federalism in theory and practice* (New York: Frederick A Praeger Publishers 1968).

Menon A & Schain MA (eds) *Comparative federalism: The European Union and the United States in comparative perspective* (Oxford: Oxford University Press 2006).

Norman W *Negotiating nationalism: Nation-building, federalism, and secession in the multinational state* (Oxford: Oxford University Press 2006).

Reydams L *Universal jurisdiction: International and municipal legal perspectives* (Oxford: Oxford University Press 2003).

Riker WH *Federalism: Origin, operation, significance* (Boston: Little, Brown 1964).

Sayapin S *The crime of aggression in international criminal law: Historical development, comparative analysis and present state* (The Hague: TMC Asser Press 2014).

Wheare KC *Federal government* 4th ed (London: Oxford University Press 1967).

Yeoh EK & Devadason E (eds) *Emerging trading nation in an integrating world: Global impacts and domestic challenges of China's economic reform* (Kuala Lumpur: Institute of Chinese Studies, University of Malaya 2007).

Chapters in Books

Bernaz N & Prouvèze R 'International and domestic prosecutions' in MC Bassiouni (ed) *The Pursuit of international criminal justice: A world study on conflicts, victimization, and post-conflict justice* vol I (Antwerpen: Intersentia 2010).

Dosenrode S 'Federalism' in Dosenrode S (ed) *Approaching the EUropean federation?* (Hampshire: Ashgate Publishing Ltd 2007).

Dyani N 'Is the International Criminal Court targeting Africa? Reflections on the enforcement of international criminal law in Africa' in Nmehielle VO *Africa and the future of international criminal justice* (The Hague: Eleven International Publishing 2012).

El Zeidy MM 'The genesis of complementarity' in C Stahn & MM El Zeidy (eds) *The International Criminal Court and complementarity: From theory to practice* vol I (Cambridge: Cambridge University Press 2011).

Radstan R 'Situation and case: Defining the parameters' in Stahn C & El Zeidy MM (eds) *The International Criminal Court and complementarity: From theory to practice* vol I (Cambridge: Cambridge University Press 2011).

Riker WH 'Federalism' in FI Greenstein & NW Polsby (eds) *Handbook of political science: Governmental institutions and processes* (Reading MA: Addison-Wesley1975).

Robinson D 'The inaction controversy: Neglected words and new opportunities' in Stahn C & El Zeidy MM (eds) *The International Criminal Court and complementarity: From theory to practice* vol I (Cambridge: Cambridge University Press 2011).

Articles

Adigun M 'The implementation of the Convention on the Rights of the Child in Nigeria' (2019) (3) July *Public Law* 476.

Adigun M 'The principle of complementarity: A reflection on its meaning, origin and types in international criminal law' (2021) 29(1) *African Journal of International and Comparative Law* 82.

Adigun M 'The Rome statute complementarity principle and the creation of the African Court of Justice and Human and Peoples' Rights' (2018) 4(1–2) *African Journal of International Criminal Justice* 1.

Akande D 'The jurisdiction of the International Criminal Court over nationals of non-Parties: Legal basis and limits' (2003) 1 *Journal of International Criminal Justice* 618.

Barkey K & Godart FC 'Empires, federated arrangements, and kingdoms: Using political models of governance to understand firms' creative performance' (2013) 34(1) *Organization Studies* 79.

Braimah TS 'Child marriage in Northern Nigeria: Section 61 of part 1 the 1999 Constitution and the protection of children against child marriage' (2014) 14 *African Human Rights Law Journal* 475.

Breen MG 'The origins of holding-together federalism: Nepal, Myanmar, and Sri Lanka' (2018) 48(1) *Publius: The Journal of Federalism* 26.

Dyani-Mhango N 'Reflecting on South Africa's attempt to withdraw from the Rome statute in favour of immunities for sitting heads of state: An analysis of the International Crimes Bill 2017' (2020) 28(2) *African Journal of International and Comparative Law* 319.

El Zeidy MM 'From primacy to complementarity and backwards: (Re)-visiting rule 11 bis of the ad hoc tribunals' (2008) 57 *International & Comparative Law Quarterly* 403.

Escobar-Lemmon M 'Fiscal decentralization and federalism in Latin America' (2001) 31(4) *Publius: The Journal of Federalism* 23.

Graefe P & Bourns A 'The gradual defederalization of Canadian health policy' (2009) 39(1) *Publius: The Journal of Federalism* 187.

Kress C "Self-referrals' and 'waivers of complementarity': Some considerations in law and policy' (2004) 2 *Journal of International Criminal Justice* 944.

Livingston WS 'A note on the nature of federalism' (1952) 67(1) *Political Science Quarterly* 81.

Møse E 'Main achievements of the ICTR' (2005) 3 *Journal of International Criminal Justice* 920.

Osaghae EE 'A reassessment of federalism as a degree of decentralization' (1990) 20(1) *Publius: The Journal of Federalism* 83.

Osaghae EE 'Federalism and the management of diversity in Africa' (2004) 5 *Identity, Culture and Politics* 162.

Osaghae EE 'What man has joined together: Ethnicity, federalism and state politics' An Inaugural Lecture delivered at the University of Ibadan, Thursday 22 August 2019.

Simeon R 'Constitutional design and change in federal systems: Issues and questions' (2009) 39(2) *Publius: The Journal of Federalism* 241–261.

Song X 'Thinking federal: The relevance of federalism to China' (2000) 10(3) *Regional and Federal Studies* 107.

Starke JG 'The Convention for the Creation of an International Criminal Court' (1938) 19 *British Yearbook of International Law* 216.

Swenden W 'Governing diversity in South Asia: Explaining divergent pathways in India and Pakistan' (2018) 48(1) *Publius: The Journal of Federalism* 102.

Theret B 'Regionalism and federalism: A comparative analysis of the regulation of economic tensions between regions by Canadian and American federal intergovernmental transfer programmes' (1999) 23(3) *International Journal of Urban and Regional Research* 479.

Uwauche ES 'Child marriage in Nigeria: (Il)legal and (un)constitutional? (2015) 5 *African Human Rights Law Journal* 421.

Watts RL 'Federalism, federal systems, and federations' (1998) *Annual Review of Political Science* 117.

Statutes

Allied Control Council Law No 10, Punishment of Persons Guilty of War Crimes, Crimes against Peace and Crimes against Humanity, 20 December 1945, Official Gazette of the Control Council for Germany, No 3, Berlin, 31 January 1946.

Child's Rights Act 2003 Cap C50 Laws of the Federation of Nigeria (LFN) 2004.

Child's Rights Law (Jigawa).

Constitution of the Federal Republic of Nigeria 1999.

The Treaty on Mutual Legal Assistance in Criminal Matters between the Government of the Federal Republic of Nigeria and the Government of the Republic of South Africa (Ratification and Enforcement) Act Cap T24 Revised Laws of the Federation of Nigeria (LFN) 2004.

Cases

Attorney General Ondo v Attorney General Federation [2002] FWLR (Pt. 111) 1972.

Attorney-General for Canada v Attorney-General for Ontario (1937) AC 326.

Decision Pursuant to Art 15 of the Rome Statute on the Authorization of an Investigation into the situation in the Republic of Kenya Pre-Trial Chamber II ICC-01/09-19. 31 March 2010, dissenting judgment of Judge Hans-Peter Kaul.

LaGrand (FRG v US), 2001 ICJ 104 (June 27), 40 ILM 1069.

Prosecutor v Thomas Lubanga Dyilo, Decision on the Prosecutor's Application for a Warrant of Arrest ICC-01/04-01/06-8-Corr, Pre-Trial Chamber 1, 10 February 2006

Soering v United Kingdom (1989) 11 EHRR 439.

Treaties

Agreement between Member States of the European Communities on the Transfer of Proceedings in Criminal Matters 1990 (2009/C 219/03), *Official Journal of the European Communities* C219.7, 22.9.2009.

Agreement for the Prosecution and Punishment of the Major War Criminals of the European Axis, and Charter of the International Military Tribunal, London, 8 August 1945, UNTS No 251 (1951) 280.

Convention against Torture and other Cruel, Inhuman and Degrading Treatment (adopted 10 December 1984, entered into force 26 June 1987) 1465 UNTS 85.

Convention for the Creation of an International Criminal Court, opened for signature at Geneva, 16 November 1937, art 2 reprinted in M Hudson *International legislation* vol VII (1941) 880.

Convention on the Prevention and Punishment of Crimes against Internationally Protected Persons including Diplomatic Agents (adopted 14 December 1973, entered into force 20 February 1977) 1035 UNTS 167.

Convention on the Prevention and Punishment of the Crime of Genocide (adopted 9 December 1948, entered into force 12 January 1951) 78 UNTS 277.

Convention on the Rights of the Child (adopted and opened for signature, ratification, and accession by General Assembly Resolution 44/25 of 20 November 1989, entered into force 2 September 1990) 1577 UNTS 3.

Convention on the Safety of United Nations and Associated Personnel (adopted 9 December 1994, entered into force 15 January 1999) 2051 UNTS 363.

European Convention on the Transfer of Proceedings in Criminal Matters (signed 15 May 1972, entered into force 30 March 1978) ETS No 73.

International Convention for the Suppression of Terrorist Bombings (adopted 15 December 1997, entered into force 23 May 2001) 2149 UNTS 256.

International Convention for the Suppression of the Financing of Terrorism (adopted 9 December 1999, entered into force 10 April 2002) 2178 UNTS 197.

Montreal Convention for the Suppression of Unlawful Acts against the Safety of Civil Aviation (signed 23 September 1971, entered into force 26 January 1973) 974 UNTS 178.

New York Convention against the taking of Hostages (adopted 17 December 1979, entered into force 3 June 1983) 1316 UNTS 205.

Rome Convention for the Suppression of Unlawful Acts against the Safety of Maritime Navigation (signed 10 March 1988, entered into force 1 March 1992) 1678 UNTS 222.

Rome Statute of the International Criminal Court (Rome Statute) (adopted 17 July 1998, entered into force 1 July 2002) 2187 UNTS 3.

The Hague Convention for the Suppression of Unlawful Seizure of Aircraft (signed 16 December 1970, entered into force 14 October 1971) 860 UNTS 105.

Tokyo Convention on Offences and Certain other Acts Committed on Board Aircraft (signed 14 December 1963, entered into force 4 December 1969) 704 UNTS 220.

UN Convention against Illicit Traffic in Narcotic Drugs and Psychotropic Substances (adopted 20 December 1988, entered into force 11 November 1990) 1582 UNTS 95.

International Instruments

1994 International Law Commission Report 37.

1994 Yearbook of International Law Commission vol I.

Council Framework Decision of 13 June 2002 on Combating Terrorism (2002/475/JHA), *Official Journal of the European Communities* I.164/3-7, 22.6.2002.

Decisions Taken by the Preparatory Committee at its Session Held 4 to 15 August 1997, UN GAOR, 52 mtg, UN Doc A/AC.249/1997/L.8/Rev.1 (1997).

Draft Code of Offences against the Peace and Security of Mankind GA Res, 177 (II), 2nd Session, 123rd Plenary Meeting, 21 November 1947.
GA Res 43/164 (1988), 76th Plenary Meeting.
GA Res 44/32 (1989), 72nd Plenary Meeting.
GA Res 44/39 (1989), 72nd Plenary Meeting.
GA Res, 260 (III), 3rd Session, 179th Plenary Meeting, 9 December 1948.
ICTR Rules of Evidence and Procedure 1 October 2009.
ICTY Rules of Evidence and Procedure (RPE) IT/32/Rev 47, 28 August 2012.
International Criminal Court, *Understandings regarding the amendments to the Rome Statute of the International Criminal Court on the Crime of Aggression*. RC/10/Add.1. 11 June 2010.
Report of the Ad hoc Committee on the Establishment of an International Criminal Court UN GAOR, 50th Sess, Supp No 22, UN Doc A/50/22 (1995).
Report of the Preparatory Committee on the Establishment of an International Criminal Court UN GAOR, 51st Sess, vol 1, Supp No 22, UN Doc A/51/22 (1995).
Report of the Preparatory Committee on the Establishment of an International Criminal Court, Draft Statute and Draft Final Act, UN Doc A/Conf. 183/2/Add.1 (1998).
Report of the Preparatory Committee on the Establishment of an International Criminal Court, UN Doc A/Conf. 183/2 (14 April 1998).
SC Res 1503 (2003) UN Doc S/Res/1503.
SC Res 1534 (2004) UN Doc S/Res/1534.
Statute of the International Tribunal for the Prosecution of Persons Responsible for Serious Violations of International Humanitarian Law Committed in the Territory of the Former Yugoslavia Since 1991, SC Res 827, UN SCOR, 48th Sess, Annex, 3417th mtg., UN Doc S/Res/827.
Statute of the International Tribunal for the Prosecution of Persons Responsible for Serious Violations of International Humanitarian Law Committed in Rwanda, SC Res 955, UN SCOR, 49th Sess, Annex, 3453rd mtg., UN Doc S/Res/955 (1993).
Summary Records of the Meetings of the Thirty-Fifth Session (3 May–22 July 1983), 1983 Yearbook of International Law Commission, vol 1.
The Tripartite Conference at Moscow October 19–30, 1943, reprinted in International Conciliation No 395 (1943) 599–605.

Internet Sources

International Criminal Court, 'The states parties to the Rome Statute' https://asp.icc-cpi.int/en_menus/asp/states%20parties/Pages/the%20states%20parties%20to%20the%20rome%20statute.aspx (accessed 25 April 2021).

International Military Tribunal for the Far East (Indictment) https://www.trumanlibrary.gov/library/research-files/indictment-international-military-tribunal-far-east (accessed 25 April 2021).

Accountability for Violations Against Internally Displaced Persons in Nigeria: Finding a Nexus Between International Criminal Justice and Human Rights Violations

Azubike Chinwuba Onuora-Oguno, Oluwabunmi Niyi-Gafar, and Ikebundu Francis Ekene

1 Introduction

The creation of the International Criminal Court (ICC) represented the culmination of a long journey in what has been called the Struggle Against Impunity.[1] In a report to the United Nations Commission on Human

[1] See 'Rome Statute of the International Criminal Court: Overview', https://legal.un.org/icc/general/overview.htm (accessed 20 January 2021).

A. C. Onuora-Oguno (✉)
Department of Jurisprudence and International Law, Faculty of Law, University of Ilorin, Ilorin, Nigeria
e-mail: onuoraoguno.ac@unilorin.edu.ng

International Institute of Social Studies, Hague, The Netherlands

O. Niyi-Gafar
Faculty of Law, University of Ilorin, Ilorin, Nigeria

E. C. Lubaale and N. Dyani-Mhango (eds.), *National Accountability for International Crimes in Africa*,
https://doi.org/10.1007/978-3-030-88044-6_10

Rights in 1997, Louis Joinet highlighted four phases of the struggle from the 1970s through the end of the millennium.[2] The first phase which largely took place in Latin America was driven by civil society organizations which sought to guarantee the rights of political prisoners suffering at the hands of repressive regimes. The second phase took place in the 1980s, when states began granting sweeping amnesties to prevent prosecutions. However, victims' organizations became increasingly organized and vocal in response to this move. The third phase emerged as a result of peace deals and democratization processes triggered by the end of the Cold War, where questions of impunity played an important part in debates on accountability. The fourth phase came with the maturity of regional human rights courts and international systems of human rights protection and a series of decisions outlawing amnesty provisions and insisting on serious crimes being prosecuted.

Crimes committed as a result of violation of the human rights of IDPs could be regarded as crimes against humanity if they meet the definitional elements of crimes against humanity. The discussion in this chapter, however, does not engage in a detailed analysis of the issue of whether or not these violations amount to crimes against humanity. What is indisputable, however, is that these violations undermine several rights guaranteed under both Nigerian law and the various international treaties to which Nigeria is party. Most of these violations are perpetrated by the security personnel who are supposed to protect these displaced persons.

Human rights are those rights which every human being enjoys as a result of being human. These rights are contained in the different international human rights treaties and conventions such as the Universal Declaration on Human Rights and the African Convention on Human and People's Rights. These rights are also guaranteed under the Nigerian Constitution and are regarded as fundamental, with every citizen is

I. F. Ekene
University of Ilorin, Ilorin, Nigeria

[2] Cited in P Seils, An Introduction to the Role of National Courts and the ICC in Prosecuting International Crimes (Handbook on Complementarity: An Introduction to the Role of National Courts and the ICC in Prosecuting International Crimes) 3.

entitled to enjoy them.[3] Violation of guaranteed rights under the Constitution is actionable under the law. Thus, IDPs in the north-east of Nigeria are very much entitled to these rights and the protection conferred on them either by national legislation or the international human rights treaties which Nigeria has domesticated and ratified.[4]

This chapter discusses the various human rights violations experienced by the IDPs in the north-eastern part of Nigeria, the effects of these violations, and the challenges in protecting the human rights of these IDPs. Whilst Boko Haram rebels are largely implicated in these atrocities, government security agents who are in charge of protecting the IDPs are also on record for the gross violation of human rights against IDPs. With the well-documented attack on the rights of IDPs in this region, this chapter assesses the ability and willingness of Nigeria to ensure that perpetrators of these atrocities are held to account. It is also notable that the link between human rights violations and international crimes is settled, with literature illustrating that some violations are so gross that they meet the threshold of serious crimes such as war crimes and crimes against humanity.[5] Against this backdrop, the chapter also investigates the roles and powers of the ICC to intervene in human rights protection of IDPs, particularly where the state seems not to be forthcoming at the national level.

[3] Chapter 4 of the Constitution of the Federal Republic of Nigeria (CFRN) 1999 as amended.

[4] YA Fabur 'Benchmarking The Rights of Internally Displaced Persons in the Fight Against Boko-Haram Insurgency in Nigeria' (2016) 6 *Nigerian National Human Rights Commission Journal* 20.

[5] J Pablo 'The Close Relationship Between Serious Human Rights Violations and Crimes Against Humanity: International Criminalization of Serious Abuses' (2017) 17 *Anuario Mexicano de Derecho Internacional* 146. See also EC Lubaale and AO Jegede, 'Gross Human Rights Violations in the Context of Armed Conflict: The Cautionary Tale That Uganda Offers Nigeria' in R Adeola and AO Jegede (eds), *Governance in Nigeria post-1999: Revisiting the Democratic 'New Dawn' of the Fourth Republic* (2019) 231–246.

2 Human Rights Violation and International Criminal Justice: Establishing the Nexus

The situation in the north-eastern region of Nigeria remains one of the largest humanitarian crisis in Africa.[6] As already noted, IDPs continue to suffer the brunt of this crisis, with violation against them by both Boko Haram rebels and government security forces being well-documented.[7] In his report on the human rights of internally displaced persons in Nigeria, the Special Rapporteur on the human rights of internally displaced persons reported that 'evidence of widespread human rights violations in the north-east by non-State armed groups and State actors means that the situation must also be recognized as a human rights crisis'.[8] The Special Rapporteur called for urgent action to be taken to address the ongoing epidemic of abuse and exploitation against IDPs.[9]

Whilst all the violations against IDPs in Nigerian may not necessarily meet the threshold of international crimes, the overlap between the gross human rights violations against them and international crimes such as crimes against humanity may not be ruled out. Recalling this nexus, Schabas recognized that the growth of the international human rights movement laid the foundation for the work of the ICC, with the Rome Statute 'replete with language derived from sources of human rights

[6] United Nations High Commissioner for Human Rights Report, 'Nigeria Emergency' (2021), https://www.unhcr.org/nigeria-emergency.html (accessed 12 July 2021).

[7] On past and ongoing human rights violation against IDPs by both Boko Haram rebels and government security forces, see Human Rights Watch Report, 'Nigeria: Officials Abusing Displaced Women: Girls Displaced by Boko Haram and Victims Twice Over' 31 October 2016, https://www.hrw.org/news/2016/10/31/nigeria-officials-abusing-displaced-women-girls (accessed 11 July 2021); Report of the United Nations High Commissioner for Human Rights, 'Violations and Abuses Committed by Boko Haram and the Impact on Human Rights in the Countries Affected' Human Rights Council Thirtieth session, Agenda item 2, Annual report of the United Nations High Commissioner for Human Rights and reports of the Office of the High Commissioner and the Secretary-General, 9 December 2015, A/HRC/30/67; A Surajo, Displaced Persons in North-Eastern Nigeria: Causes, Effects and the Role of Social Workers' (2020) 8 *Sociology and Anthropology* 57–65.

[8] Report of the Special Rapporteur on the human rights of internally displaced persons on his mission to Nigeria (A/HRC/35/27/Add.1) 2017.

[9] As above.

law'.[10] Theodor Meron, the former President of the International Criminal Tribunal of the Yugoslavia also confirmed the nexus between human rights violations and international crimes by observing that crimes against humanity 'overlap with some violations of fundamental human rights (such torture, rape or enslavement), which thus become criminalized under a multilateral treaty'.[11]

The United Nations Security Council (UNSC) has also taken cognizance of this nexus. In its referral of the situation of Sudan to the ICC, the UNSC noted that:

> Taking note of the report of the International Commission of Inquiry on violations of international humanitarian law and human rights law in Darfur (S/2005/60), [...] encourages the Court, as appropriate and in accordance with the Rome Statute, to support international cooperation with domestic efforts to promote the rule of law, protect human rights and combat impunity in Darfur.[12]

The wording of the UNSC Resolution referring to situation of Libya to the ICC in 2011 uses similar human rights language. In its Preamble and paragraph 4, the UNSC noted that:

> Deploring the gross and systematic violation of human rights, including the repression of peaceful demonstrators, expressing deep concern at the deaths of civilians, and rejecting unequivocally the incitement to hostility and violence against the civilian population made from the highest level of the Libyan government [...] decides to refer the situation in the Libyan Arab Jamahiriya since 15 February 2011 to the Prosecutor of the International Criminal Court.[13]

From the language of the Resolutions referring these situations to the ICC, one gathers that a major motivation for both referrals was the seriousness of the human rights violations in both Darfur and Libya.

[10] W Schabas, *The International Criminal Court: A Commentary on the Rome Statute* (2010) 7.

[11] Cited in Pablo (n 5 above) 152.

[12] Resolution 1593 (2005), Adopted by the Security Council at its 5158th meeting, on 31 March 2005, S/RES/1593 (2005).

[13] United Nations Security Council Resolution (2011 [1970]), Resolution Adopted by the Security Council at its 6491st meeting, on 26 February 2011, S/RES/1970 (2011).

The UNSC clearly perceived the link between international criminal responsibility and human rights violations, thus, calling the ICC to intervene.

The ICC has also on occasion demonstrated the link between human rights and international crimes in his its judgments. In *Prosecutor v Germain Katanga and Mathieu Ngudjolo Chui*, in concluding that inhuman acts in terms of article 7(1)(k) of the Rome Statute were crimes against humanity, the ICC drew on human rights, going on to rule that:

> in accordance with article 7(l)(k) of the Statute and the principle of *nullum crimen sine lege* pursuant to article 22 of the Statute, inhumane acts are to be considered as serious violations of international customary law and the basic rights pertaining to human beings, drawn from the norms of international human rights law, which are of a similar nature and gravity to the acts referred to in article 7(1) of the Statute.[14]

One gathers from the ICC's ruling above that crimes against humanity, in several ways, amount to criminalization of serious human rights violations. Where these violations meet the objective and subjective elements as defined by the ICC Elements of Crimes document, for example, they can be properly categorized as crimes against humanity.

[14] *The Prosecutor v Germain Katanga and Mathieu Ngudjolo Chui*, Situation in The Democratic Republic of The Congo, ICC-01/04-01/07, 30 September 2008, Decision on the confirmation of charges, para 448. On the nexus between gross human rights violations and individual criminal responsibility by other criminal tribunals, see also the Extraordinary Chambers in the Courts of Cambodia. This Court was established to prosecute international crimes and other serious national crimes committed during the reign of Khmer Rouge between 1975 and 1979. In *Case 001* (Appeal Judgment, Supreme Court Chamber, 3 February 2012, para 261), the ECCC exercised jurisdiction over persecutory acts despite their not falling within the ambit of international crimes as envisaged by the ECCC. In favoring prosecution, the ECCC ruled that although these acts did constitute international crimes per se, they resulted in 'breaches of fundamental human rights under treaty or customary international law in order to rise to the requisite level of gravity and severity'. Similarly, the International Criminal Tribunal of the Yugoslavia, also mandated to prosecute international crimes committed in the former Yugoslavia during the Balkan war, ruled in *Prosecutor v Kupreskic* (IT-95-16-T, Judgment, Trial Chamber, 14 January 2000, para 563) that 'other inhumane acts' can instead be identified in international standards on human rights such as those laid down in the Universal Declaration on Human Rights of 1948 and the two United Nations Conventions on Human Rights of 1966. Drawing upon the various provisions of these texts, it is possible to identify asset of basic rights appertaining to human beings, the infringement of which may amount, de-pending on the accompanying circumstances, to a crime against humanity.

All considered, the link between the gross human rights violations against IDPs in North-Eastern Nigeria on the one hand and the mandate on Nigeria to prosecute perpetrators of these atrocities to account for crimes against humanity or any related violations would not be far-fetched. And as Pablo has rightly captured it, 'the international norm which triggers international (criminal) individual liability has an impact on the principle of respect for fundamental rights. All of this reflects an increasing interaction between international human rights law and international criminal law'.[15] Given the nexus between human rights and international criminal justice, it is argued in this chapter that the atrocities committed against IDPs in North-East Nigeria warrant accountability by Nigeria's criminal jurisdiction. Failure to foster accountability by Nigeria's national courts suggests that the ICC's intervention is warranted. For the ICC to intervene and for the principle of complementarity to find application to these atrocities, it is important to understand the mandate of the ICC. For this purpose, the next section discusses this aspect.

3 An Overview of the International Criminal Court

3.1 Establishment

The ICC, which is governed by the Rome Statute of 1998, is a permanent treaty-based independent international court established for the purpose of making sure that perpetrators of serious crimes of concern to the international community do not go unpunished.[16] The ICC prosecutes individual perpetrators of international crimes such as crimes against humanity, war crimes, genocide and the crime of aggression,[17] with the aim of contributing to the prevention of grave crimes that threaten the peace, security and well-being of the world.[18] Prior to the establishment

[15] Pablo (n 5 above) 159.

[16] See International Criminal Court, 'The ICC at a Glance' https://www.icc-cpi.int/Publications/ICCAtAGlanceENG.pdf (accessed 21 June 2021).

[17] MO Brein 'International Criminal Court (ICC): The Encyclopedia of Crime and Punishment' 2016, available at https://www.researchgate.net/publication/309486379 (accessed 21 January 2021).

[18] See the Preamble to the Rome Statute which established the International Criminal Court.

of the ICC, there have been ad hoc tribunals set up to prosecute perpetrators of such international crimes over the years at the particular time the crimes were committed.[19] However, these tribunals had limited jurisdiction in the sense that they could only try crimes committed within a specific time-frame and during a specific conflict, thus, it was realized that there is a need for a permanent and independent international criminal court which is more practical and wide reaching.[20]

3.2 *Jurisdiction*

The focus of the ICC is to prosecute individuals, and not states, who have committed one or more of the offences stated above (as defined in the Rome Statute) whenever the conditions for the court's exercise of jurisdiction over the accused person is satisfied.[21] Save for situations where a case is referred to it by the United Nations Security Council whose resolution binds all United Nations member states,[22] the Court only has jurisdiction to prosecute such international crimes committed within the territory of a state party,[23] or anywhere in the world provided the perpetrators are nationals of a state party to the Rome Statute.[24] It is important to note at this juncture that the ICC was not established to replace or take charge of, but rather to complement national criminal justice systems, thus, it can prosecute cases only if national justice systems do not carry out proceedings either as a result of unwillingness or inability[25] This is a fundamental principle known as the principle of complementarity which will be examined in detail in the subsequent section of this chapter.

[19] O Melanie, 'International Criminal Court' in WG Jennings (ed), *The Encyclopedia of Crime and Punishment* (Wiley 2015) 1.

[20] As above.

[21] See International Criminal Court, 'Understanding the International Criminal Court', https://www.icc-cpi.int/iccdocs/pids/publications/uicceng.pdf (accessed 21 June 2021).

[22] See art 13 (b) Rome Statute. This has happened on two occasions: in 2005 when the UNSC referred the situation in Darfur, Sudan (SC Res 1593); and in 2011, with the referral of the situation in Libya (SC Res 1970), both non-state parties.

[23] Art 12(1) (a) Rome Statute of the International Criminal Court, 17 July 1998, 2187 U.N.T.S. 90 (entered into force on 1 July 2002) (Rome Statute).

[24] Art 12(2) (b) Rome Statute.

[25] ICC, n 16 above.

Also, there is what could be referred to as durational jurisdiction of the ICC which is to the effect that the court's power to try cases is limited to crimes committed on or after July 1, 2002 when the ICC was fully established or to crimes committed at a subsequent time depending on the date a state ratifies the statute.[26] Furthermore, whether the ICC will be able to assume jurisdiction on a matter depends on certain other factors relating to the substance of the offence committed. First, the Court cannot even commence investigation not to talk of try a matter until it has been established that the concerned state party is unwilling or unable to prosecute the perpetrator of the offence.[27] No wonder the Court is regarded as a court of last resort. In determining unwillingness or inability, the Court will consider whether the state has taken measures to shield the suspect from criminal responsibility, or, whether it has impartially and independently conducted the proceeding, or whether the state is able to arrest the accused and obtain necessary evidences to carry out the proceeding.[28] Secondly, there are some sections in the Rome Statute which relate to the level of seriousness of a crime that can be prosecuted by the ICC. The Statute provides that the Court shall determine a case to be inadmissible where the case is not of sufficient gravity to justify further action by the Court.[29] It also provides that the prosecutor of the ICC may conclude that there is no sufficient basis for a prosecution for failure to meet admissibility criteria under Article 17 or because the prosecution is not in the interest of justice, taking into account all the surrounding circumstances.[30]

3.3 Structure

The ICC is basically composed of three organs: the Office of the Prosecutor, the Office of the Registrar and the Chambers.[31]

[26] Melanie, n 19 above, 2.

[27] See 'The International Criminal Court: How Non-Governmental Organizations Can Contribute to the Prosecution of War Criminals' September, 2004, *Human Rights Watch*, 8.

[28] n 9 above.

[29] Art 17(1) (d) Rome Statute.

[30] Art 53(2) Rome Statute.

[31] Human Rights Watch, n 27 above, 10.

The office of the prosecutor, which acts as an independent organ from the Court, is saddled with the responsibility of gathering information about crimes and present evidence against an accused person before the court.[32] The office is headed by the Prosecutor and assisted by the Deputy Prosecutor both elected by the assembly of state parties to receive and examine referrals and communications in order to determine whether there exists a reasonable cause of action to investigate and prosecute persons responsible for the crimes within the powers of the court.[33] In order to duly carry out its functions, the office of the prosecutor is divided into three sections. The Investigation Section is responsible for gathering and examining evidences as well as questioning accused persons, victims and witnesses.[34] The Prosecution Section is responsible for litigating accused persons before the court.[35] The last section which is the Jurisdiction, Complementarity and Cooperation Section is responsible for assessing information received and situations referred to the Court with the aim of determining their admissibility.[36]

The Registry is a neutral organ of the ICC headed by the registrar.[37] The Registry's function is to run the administration and keep the records of the court as a whole.[38] The registry is also responsible for locating witnesses and victims and make sure they are well protected during their participation in the trial.[39] It also ensures that the Court is properly serviced and develops effective mechanism for assisting victims, witnesses and the defence in order to safeguard their rights under the Rome Statute and the rules of Procedure and Evidence.[40] Furthermore, the registry serves as the Court's official instrument of communication responsible for the court's public information and outreach activities.[41]

32 As above.

33 See ICC, n 16 above, 3.

34 ICC, n 21 above, 10.

35 As above.

36 As above.

37 See ICC, n 16 above, 3.

38 Human Rights Watch, n 27 above, 11.

39 As above.

40 See ICC, n 21 above, 11.

41 As above.

The Chambers which carry out the judicial functions of the Court consist of three chambers; the Pre-Trial Chamber which has seven judges, the Trial Chamber which has six judges and the Appeal Chamber which has five judges.[42] The Pre-Trial Chamber settles all issues that may arise before trial begins. It basically performs a supervisory role on how the Office of the Prosecutor carries out its functions in order to preserve the rights of suspects, witnesses and victims during investigation and to ensure the integrity of the proceedings.[43] The Pre-Trial Chamber also has to decide whether or not to issue warrants of arrest or summonses to anyone to appear before the Court upon the request of the Office of the Prosecutor.[44] In fact, it decides whether or not to confirm charges against a suspect and on the admissibility of cases and circumstances on the victim's participation at the pre-trial stage.[45] The Trial Chamber on the other hand hears cases and decides the guilt or otherwise of accused persons fairly and with respect for the rights of accused persons, whilst taking into account the protection and rights of witnesses and victims.[46] It also prescribes punishment and the extent of damages to be paid to victims in the different circumstances whenever a person has been found guilty of the charge.[47] Lastly, the Appeal Chamber, as the name implies, is the appellate section of the court. It receives any form of appeals coming from either the pre-trial or trial chamber, and after examining the grounds and weight of the appeal, it may uphold, reverse or amend the earlier decision on which the appeal is brought. In fact, the Appeal Chamber could order that a fresh trial be conducted on a matter before a different trial chamber.[48]

It is important to state that there is also, within the ICC, a division referred to as the Presidency. It consists of three judges (the president and two vice-presidents) elected by an absolute majority of the 18 judges

[42] See Human Rights Watch, n 27 above, 10.

[43] See ICC, n 21 above, 11.

[44] As above.

[45] As above.

[46] See Human Rights Watch, 10.

[47] As above.

[48] As above.

that make up the Court.[49] The presidency basically represents the Court to the outside world and helps organize the works of the judges.[50]

3.4 Crimes Within the Court's Jurisdiction

There are basically four crimes within the jurisdiction of the ICC as prescribed under the Rome Statute. The elements of these crimes as provided under a separate document adopted by the Assembly of States Parties to the Rome Statute—'Elements of Crime', help to define and expand the definition of each of them for a proper understanding of conduct that falls within the ambit of these crimes,[51] Namely, genocide,[52] crimes against humanity,[53] war crimes,[54] and crime of aggression.[55]

4 The Principle of Complementarity in International Criminal Justice

Since it was first introduced and included into the Rome Statute, the concept of complementarity has evolved very significantly because it presents a means for the ICC to maximize its impact in fostering accountability in both domestic courts and at the ICC.[56] This is as a result of proactive engagement with and assistance of domestic legal institutions

[49] See ICC, n 21 above, 9.

[50] As above.

[51] International Criminal Court, Elements of Crimes, 2011 reproduced from the Official Records of the Assembly of States Parties to the Rome Statute of the International Criminal Court, First session, New York, 3–10 September 2002 (United Nations publication, Sales No. E.03.V.2 and corrigendum), part II.B. The Elements of Crimes adopted at the 2010 Review Conference are replicated from the Official Records of the Review Conference of the Rome Statute of the International Criminal Court, Kampala, 31 May-11 June 2010 (International Criminal Court publication, RC/11).

[52] Art 6 of the Rome Statute.

[53] Art 7 of the Rome Statute.

[54] Art 8 of the Rome Statute.

[55] Art 5(2) of the Rome Statute.

[56] AM Katherine 'Prevention and Complementarity in the International Criminal Court: A Positive Approach' 1.

which have ultimately led to the ICC strengthening the rule of law in countries suffering from violent conflict and instability.[57]

The Rome Statute which establishes the ICC does not expressly define the term 'complementarity', but commentators have adapted the term to mean the totality of norms governing the relationship between national jurisdictions and the ICC.[58] The Statute in its preamble pointed out that the ICC hall be an international institution that is in a complimentary relationship with national criminal jurisdiction, such that it does not have primary jurisdiction over national authorities.[59] This means that the ICC only plays a subsidiary role and supplements national investigation and prosecution of the most serious crimes of international concern whenever domestic authorities fail to take necessary steps in investigation and prosecution of such crimes.[60] As such, a case is admissible in the ICC only when the state with original jurisdiction is unwilling or unable genuinely to investigate or prosecute perpetrators of such crimes.[61]

The principle of complementarity is very instrumental to differentiating the exercise of jurisdiction by the ICC from that of national authorities,[62] and as such may well prove to be one of the most controversial characteristics in the application of the Rome Statute. The principle has been described as a cornerstone of the ICC because it forms the basis of the entire functioning and structure of the Court.[63] It is a very crucial principle that must be taken into consideration at the earliest stage when the prosecutor considers initiating investigations. Whether or not he

[57] As above.

[58] M Benzing, 'The Complementarity Regime of the International Criminal Court: International Criminal Justice between State Sovereignty and the Fight against Impunity' 2003, 7, *Max Planck Yearbook of United Nations Law*, 592.

[59] As above.

[60] MA Newton 'Comparative Complementarity: Domestic Jurisdiction Consistent with the Rome Statute of the International Criminal Court' 2001, 167 *Mil. Law Review*, 20.

[61] Art 17 of the Rome Statute.

[62] See Cf. Report of the Preparatory Committee on the Establishment of International Criminal Court, GAOR 51st Sess., Suppl. No. 22, Doc. A/51/22, Para. 153.

[63] M Bergsmo 'Occasional Remarks on Certain State Concerns about the Jurisdictional Reach of International Criminal Court, and Their Possible Implications for the Relationship between the court and Security Council' (2000) 69 *Nord. Journal of International Law* 87.

would proceed with investigation and prosecution depends solely on the principle of complementarity.[64]

Article 17, subsection 1 of the statute provides thus:

Having Regard to Paragraph 10 of the Preamble and Article 1, the court shall determine that a case is inadmissible where:

> a. The case is being investigated or prosecuted by a State which has jurisdiction over it, unless the State is unwilling or unable genuinely to carry out the investigation or prosecution;
> b. The case has been investigated by a State which has jurisdiction over it and the State has decided not to prosecute the person concerned, unless the decision resulted from the unwillingness or inability of the State genuinely to prosecute;
> c. The person concerned has already been tried for conduct which is the subject of the complaint, and a trial by the court is not permitted under Article 20, Paragraph 3.

Subsection 2 further explains that in order to determine unwillingness in a particular case, the court shall consider, having regard to the principles of due process recognized by international law, whether one or more of the following exist, as applicable:

> a. The proceedings were or are being undertaken or the national decision was made for the purpose of shielding the person concerned from criminal responsibility for crimes within the jurisdiction of the court referred to in Article 5;
> b. There has been an unjustified delay in the proceedings which in the circumstances is inconsistent with an intent to bring the person concerned to justice;
> c. The proceedings were not or are not being conducted independently or impartially, and they were or are being conducted in a manner which, in the circumstances, is inconsistent with an intent to bring the person concerned to justice.

At its inception, the idea behind the principle of complementarity the need to balance the competing interests between those who clamour for a court with universal jurisdiction and those who prioritize state

[64] Art 53 (1) (b) of the Rome Statute and Rule 48 of the Rules of Procedure and Evidence.

sovereignty.[65] Therefore, sovereignty and efficiency are regarded as the most important rationales for the promulgation of the principle of complementarity.[66]

With regard to sovereignty, this notion anticipates a situation whereby states are to control the criminal law system in their own countries especially for serious crimes that have political consequences or context.[67] The Rome Statute is a voluntary treaty agreement entered into by state parties who also decide to what extent they are willing to give up their sovereign right to exercise criminal jurisdiction over their own territory and their own nationals regarding certain crimes.[68] This idea of states' criminal jurisdiction goes down to the notion of sovereign power of a state which is to the effect that states have monopoly of force evidenced in the power of the police to detain, arrest and investigate and that of the courts to try and punish.[69] It is clear that states would be reluctant to give out this power voluntarily; therefore, it is obvious that any agreement between them to set up a permanent international criminal court would only materialize if it would not confer on the court primacy of jurisdiction which is what the principle seeks to achieve.[70]

Moving on to the second rationale which is effectiveness, it could be said that this simply anticipates a situation whereby there would be an end to impunity, as well as deterrence of the future commission of such crimes.[71] Argument on this could be viewed from two angles; first, it was recognized that conducting trials of perpetrators of these crimes in the national courts may not be viable because of so many factors.[72]

[65] NS Benjamin *Building the International Criminal Court* (Cambridge University Press 2008) 73.

[66] P Seils 'An Introduction to the Role of National Courts and the ICC in Prosecuting International Crimes' *International Centre for Transitional Justice's Handbook on Complementarity* 6.

[67] As above This in fact distinguishes the ICC from the early tribunals that was set up by the international bodies to prosecute crimes of international concern. These early tribunals were more or less imposed on the states by the international bodies that set them up.

[68] As above, 7.

[69] As above.

[70] As above.

[71] See paragraph 4 and 5 of the Preamble to the Rome Statute.

[72] Seils, n 66 above, 8.

Secondly, arguments ensued from the experiences of initial tribunals over time as states began to feel that there were some inherent inefficiencies ranging from operating languages, distance from victims and crime scenes, witness protection and length of trials.[73] Overall, complementarity has, in one way or the other, helped to strike a balance state sovereignty and international criminal justice. In the context of Nigeria, an issue arises regarding whether, in light of the gross human rights violations against IDPs in North-Eastern Nigeria, there is commitment to holding those responsible for these atrocities to account in line with the principle of complementarity. The next sections resolve this issue.

5 The Situation of IDPS Viz a Viz Security Challenges and Human Rights Violations of IDPS in the North-East of Nigeria

The crisis in the north-eastern part of Nigeria remains one of the most severe in the world, with human rights violations continuing to be reported daily.[74] The Human Rights Writers Association of Nigeria (HURIWA) has described the neglect suffered by IDPs as the worst case of human rights violations.[75] In a report dated 29th of August 2018, Chaloka Beyani, a United Nations expert on internally displaced persons, described the situation in the country as displaying the hallmarks of the highest category of crises.[76] As a result of this, the worst forms of human rights violation are being suffered by these people who could be referred to as victims of circumstances.[77]

[73] As above.

[74] See A Report by the United Nations Office for the Coordination of Humanitarian Affairs (UNOCHA) in June 2018, https://www.unv.org/our-stories/improving-livig-conditions-internally-displaced-person-adamawa-north-east-nigeria (accessed 24 December 24 2018).

[75] See Saharareporters.com/2018/09/24/huriwa-neglect-suffered-idps-worst-case-human-rights-violations.

[76] See Nigeria: A Huge Displacement And Humanitarian Crisis Require Urgent Life-Saving and Protection Measures, https://www.ohchr.org/EN/NewsEvents/Pages/DisplayNews.aspx?NewsID=20428&LangID=E (accessed 24 February 2021).

[77] As above.

Firstly, the situation in Nigeria is that there is inadequate knowledge and understanding of the rights of the IDPs as provided for under international instruments[78] as well as the various local enactments. These rights include the right to life,[79] freedom of movement,[80] right to dignity of human person,[81] freedom of association,[82] right to personal liberty,[83] right to family and private life,[84] freedom from discrimination,[85] freedom of thought, conscience, and religion,[86] etc. IDPs have witnessed atrocities in addition to loosing families and succumbing to the insurgents' campaign of terror.[87] Out of fear of being pursued by the insurgents, IDPs are either perceived as supporters of insurgents or as informants to the authorities, thereby remaining silent and hidden.[88]

[78] E Alobo and S Obaji 'Internal Displacement in Nigeria and The Case for Human Rights Protection of Displaced Persons' (2016) 51 *Journal of Law, Policy and Globalization* 26.

[79] See Section 33 CFRN 1999 as amended; Article 7 of the African Charter on Human and People's rights (ratification and enforcement) act cap A9 Laws of the federation of Nigeria 2004.

[80] See Section 41 CFRN 1999 as amended; Article 12 of the African Charter on Human and People's rights (ratification and enforcement) act cap A9 Laws of the federation of Nigeria 2004.

[81] See Section 34 CFRN 1999 as amended; Article 5 of the African Charter on Human and People's rights (ratification and enforcement) act cap A9 Laws of the federation of Nigeria 2004.

[82] See Section 40 CFRN 1999 as amended; Article 11 of the African Charter on Human and People's rights (ratification and enforcement) act cap A9 Laws of the federation of Nigeria 2004.

[83] See Section 35 CFRN 1999 as amended; Article 6 of the African Charter on Human and People's rights (ratification and enforcement) act cap A9 Laws of the federation of Nigeria 2004.

[84] See Section 37 CFRN 1999 as amended; Article 9(1) of the African Charter on Human and People's rights (ratification and enforcement) act cap A9 Laws of the federation of Nigeria 2004.

[85] See Section 42 CFRN 1999 as amended; Article 3 of the African Charter on Human and People's rights (ratification and enforcement) act cap A9 Laws of the federation of Nigeria 2004.

[86] See Section 38 CFRN 1999 as amended; Article 8 of the African Charter on Human and People's rights (ratification and enforcement) act cap A9 Laws of the federation of Nigeria 2004.

[87] Alobo and Obaji, n 78 above, 30.

[88] As above.

Women and children remain the most susceptible to sexual and gender-based violence. There are several reports on instances of widespread rape, sexual harassment, forced marriage, child marriage and uncontrolled birth resulting into high rate of infant and maternal mortality in the IDP camps in Nigeria.[89] These violations fall within the ambit of crimes against humanity as provided in Article 7(1) (g) of the Rome Statute. Also, there is disregard for the needs of children in armed conflict situations. Children are been exposed to various forms of abuse. There are several cases of forceful conscription by the insurgents as child soldiers, suicide bombers and as sex slaves. As a result, many have been discontinued from schools.[90] According to the National Emergency Management Agency (NEMA), there are over 750 unaccompanied and separated children.[91]

Government officials have raped and sexually exploited internally displaced women and girls, and the government has not been doing enough to ensure that these people are protected and the abusers are prosecuted.[92] In late July 2016, Human Rights Watch documented sexual abuse, including rape and exploitation of 43 women and girls living in seven IDP camps in Maiduguri, the Borno state capital.[93] It is now much more disheartening that instead of getting the needed support for the horrific trauma suffered by these people, they are being abused and attacked by those who are supposed to protect them.[94] A situational assessment of IDPs in the North-East Nigeria in July 2016 reported that 66% of 400 displaced persons in Adamawa, Borno and Yobe states said that camp officials sexually abuse the displaced women and girls,[95] with some being drugged, raped and coerced into sex through false marriage promises or material/financial assistance. All of these atrocities meet the

[89] See 'IDP Protection Strategy 2015' www.humanitarianresponse.info/en/operatioons/nigeria/document/idp-protection strategy-2015 (accessed 22 February 2021).

[90] Alobo and S Obaji n 78 above, 31.

[91] See 'Humanitarian Need Overview' www.humanitarianresponse.info/en/operatioons/nigeria/document/idp-protection-strategy-2015 (accessed 22 February 2021).

[92] Nigeria: Officials abusing displaced women and girls (October 31, 2016), https://www.hrw.org/news/2016/10/31/nigeria-officials-abusing-displaced-women-girls (accessed 27 February 2021).

[93] As above.

[94] As above.

[95] As above.

threshold of crimes against humanity as provided for under Article 7 (1) of the statute.

Atrocities pertaining to sexual violence against women similar to those that IDP women in North-Eastern Nigeria would not be new to the ICC. The recent proceedings at the ICC against Dominic Ongwen, a former commander in the anti-government group Lord's Resistance Army in Uganda, paint a vivid picture of the ICC's commitment to holding perpetrators of acts of sexual violence against women to account.[96] On 4th February 2021, the ICC convicted Ongwen of 61 charges of war crimes and crimes against humanity, including a wide range of sexual crimes. Sexual and gender-based violence were at the heart of this case, and Ongwen was found guilty, amongst others, on the charges of rape as crime against humanity and war crime, sexual slavery as crime against humanity and war crime, forced pregnancy as crime against humanity and war crime, forced marriage as crime against humanity, enslavement as crime against humanity, torture as crime against humanity and war crime, and outrages upon personal dignity of women as war crime.[97]

Various forms of sexual violence against women have on several occasions been neglected by the international criminal justice despite obvious evidence of them being an affront to the fundamental rights of women. Women similar to IDP women in North-Eastern Nigeria often ended up without justice. On a positive note, the ICC cast the net wider to catch several human rights violations previously neglected by international criminal justice. Ongwen became the first person to be charged and convicted of the crime of forced marriage as a distinct crime under article 7(1)(k) of the Rome Statute. Forced pregnancy and forced marriage were also prosecuted for the first time as distinct punishable crimes before the ICC, with forced pregnancy being tried for the first time in international criminal law in general.

Thus, the Ongwen case, just like several other judgments that have gone ahead of it,[98] has demonstrated the practicality of fostering accountability for acts of violence against women that were previously condoned.

[96] *Prosecutor v Dominic Ongwen*, Situation in Uganda, Trial Chamber IX, Trial Judgment, ICC-02/04-01/15, 4 February 2021.

[97] As above.

[98] One such seminal decision is the International Criminal Tribunal for Rwanda decision in the case of *The Prosecutor v Jean-Paul Akayesu* (Appeal Judgment), ICTR-96-4-A, International Criminal Tribunal for Rwanda, 1 June 2001.

Moreover, victims of acts of violence including forced marriages have generally been victims of stigma and discrimination in their communities.[99] Affirming the criminality of these acts of violence against women is positive step towards recognition the seriousness of acts of violence against women. It also sends a message to perpetrators that such acts of violence against women will not go unpunished. In reading out the summary of the Ongwen judgment, Judge Schmitt, the Presiding Judge of ICC Trial Chamber IX, demonstrated the ICC's commitment to responding to the plight of victims of such atrocities by emphasizing that 'victims have a right not to be forgotten, and to be mentioned' in the ICC courtroom.[100] One would hasten to add that they should not be forgotten in national courts as the principle of complementarity envisages that women's first port of entry for accountability is national criminal jurisdictions.

Aside from sexual violence, most of the displaced persons live in IDP camps where their movement is extremely limited and some cases totally forbidden. For example, those living in Arabic Teachers' Village Camp reported that they are only allowed to move out of the camp for just about 8 hours daily whilst others in some other camps reported that their movement is highly restricted.[101] It is even worse when the IDPs were unable to get food at a particular point for one reason or the other. Even amidst these conditions, they were still denied the opportunity to go out to fend for themselves. Furthermore, displaced women from several communities told Human Rights Watch that the Nigerian army operated screening centres where they interrogate local people to determine how much involvement they had with militants. Whilst some were screened for a few days, others were interrogated daily for months before being released to camps. They are locked up whilst naked or in rags in these screening centres for the so-called interrogation exercise for several months.[102] These acts constitute crimes against humanity under

[99] See e.g. K Amone-P'Olak et al., 'Sexual Violence and General Functioning Among Formerly Abducted Girls in Northern Uganda: The Mediating Roles of Stigma and Community Relations—The WAYS Study' (2016) 16 *BMC Public Health* 64.

[100] International Criminal Court transcripts, available at https://www.icc-cpi.int/Transcripts/CR2021_01038.PDF (accessed 13 July 2021).

[101] As above.

[102] As above.

Article 7 (1) (e) which talks about imprisonment or other severe deprivation of physical liberty in violation of fundamental rules of international law.

6 Assessing Nigeria's Ability and Willingness to Address Violations Against IDPS Based on Its Current National Framework

Based on the discussion in the above section, the obligations of Nigeria with regard to protection of IDPs in the North-Eastern part of Nigeria are clear. In the past few years, Nigeria has recorded a large number of internal displacements compared to other countries in Africa,[103] with a very large number coming from the north-east.[104] With this incessant increase in the number of IDPs year in year out, a critical question is—has the Nigerian government been performing these obligations appropriately? This question is answered in this section.

As a result of the alarming rise in the number of IDPs in Nigeria, the federal government in 2003 set up a committee to draft a national policy on IDPs to assist in registration and issuance of identity cards, prevention and reduction of internal displacement, and allocation of responsibilities to agencies, organs of government, non-governmental and civil societies.[105] The policy, which is based on the Guiding Principles on Internal Displacement and the Kampala Convention, was prepared and presented to the government in 2011[106] and adopted in 2012. The policy aims at guiding the branches of government and humanitarian agencies in preventing displacement, protecting and assisting those displaced.[107] It also allocates responsibilities on appropriate government bodies for different aspects of short term, medium and long term response to internal displacement, with the existing National Commission for Refugees (NCFR) as the governmental focal point with the responsibility

[103] A Samade, 'Framework for the Care of IDPs' https://www.vanguardngr.com/2016/01/framework-for-the-care-of-idps-2/amp/ (accessed 7 March 2021).

[104] See www.internal-displacement.org/countries (accessed 7 March 2021).

[105] Ba Bukar 'Nigeria Needs to Take Responsibility for its IDPs' available at https://www.fmreview.org/young-and-out-of-place/bukar (accessed 7 March 2021).

[106] As above.

[107] As above.

of coordinating other agencies.[108] Furthermore, it empowers the NEMA, Human Rights Commission and the Institute of Peace and Conflict Resolution to support the activities of states and local governments in implementing the policy within their respective spheres of activities.[109] However, as beautiful as the policy is, its effectiveness is limited because of its non-binding nature, making it incapable of being enforced effectively by the government or the delegated actors.[110]

Also, even though there is no legal framework on the protection and assistance of IDPs in Nigeria, provision of assistance, protection, reintegration and resettlement for IDPs is undertaken by government agencies on an ad hoc and reactive basis.[111] However, this and a host of other approaches adopted by the Nigerian government in respect of its obligation towards IDPs shows weak commitment to meeting its obligations. The absence of robust measures has undermined efforts to respond to the plight of IDPs in North-Eastern Nigeria. For example, there are some IDP camps that are not even recognized by the government. The implication of this that there is no proper record and data analysis on the number of IDPs since the figures projected are limited to those camps organized and recognized by the government.[112]

In a report by Victor Mathias, a journalist of channels television, from his interaction with Ahmed Sajoh, the Adamawa State Commissioner for Information, governments are aware of the existence of new IDPs settlements but no step will be taken until the proper channel is taken to integrate them into the government's scheme.[113] This of course reveals the poor condition of the IDP settlement as well as the poor attitude of the government towards conforming to the obligations binding it with regard to IDPs.

The issue of security is majorly the responsibility of the federal government. There are several challenges facing the state in conforming to the obligation placed on it towards the protection and assistance of the IDPs.

[108] As above.

[109] As above.

[110] As above.

[111] As above.

[112] O Rotimi, 'IDPs in Nigeria and a Call for Urgent Intervention' (December 28, 2015) https://opinion.premiumtimesng.com/2015/12/28 (accessed 7 March 2021).

[113] As above.

Using Borno State as a case study, in a report on daily post, the chairman of Borno State Emergency Management Agency (SEMA), Alhaji Grema Terab, spoke on the challenges of the agency and how internally displaced persons in Borno have been managed, particularly with the renewed attack by the boko-haram and the rising influx of IDPs into different camps in the state.[114] He stated further that the state is trying its best but the federal allocation is no longer regular and this has resulted in a shift of responsibilities from the federal government to the state government.[115] In this report, it was made clear that it took a long whilst before the NEMA showed interest or concern in knowing the state of affairs of IDPs in the state.[116] Furthermore, it was stated that the issue of internal displacement especially in the state is beyond the capability of the state government due to the high increase in the number of persons faced with displacement and the incessant reduction in allocation from the federal government.[117]

The state government, though handicapped, tries its best to invite actors and partners in humanitarian services to take care of the IDPs such as United Nations Children's Emergency Fund (UNICEF) International Committee on Red Cross (ICRC). However, the inactiveness of the federal government has not been making it easy for the state government to conform to these obligations, and the state only hopes to have a better deal in times to come.[118]

7 The Adequacy of National Laws to Ensure Compliance

It is the responsibility of a state to ensure the full and equal enjoyment of human rights of all individuals under their territorial jurisdiction. This responsibility extends to all agents of the state such as the military, the police and other public authorities, whether at the federal, state or local

[114] M Maina, 'Borno: Our Major Challenge Now Is High Influx of IDPs—Grema Terab', https://dailypost.ng/2015/06/15/borno-our-major-challenge-now-is-high-influx-of-idps-grema-terab/ (accessed 21 June 2021).

[115] As above.

[116] As above.

[117] As above.

[118] As above.

level.[119] This responsibility is to the effect that the government and all its agents must act in compliance with human rights laws by refraining from any act which might interfere with or impair the exercise of rights.[120] Also, they must prevent and put a stop to any violation by a third party and such third party must be duly prosecuted and punished under the law and make sure that effective remedy is made available to the victims.[121] Also, in ensuring that individuals under its jurisdiction enjoy and exercise their human rights, a state is obliged to take all necessary and possible measures in respect to that. This will require that an adequate legal and administrative framework be put in place to build national capacity and support the implementation of rights.[122] For example, ensuring the right to fair hearing will require that an effective judicial system is put in place and ensuring the right to freedom from inhumane treatment requires an effective and well-trained security agency. Furthermore, many countries experiencing displacement have significant resource constraints[123] and Nigeria is not an exception. Human rights laws recognize that state with limited resources might not have the capacity to ensure the full realization of certain social and economic rights, although a state cannot use lack of resources as an excuse for not doing anything because it is obliged to take steps, to the maximum of its available resources, to achieve progressively the full realization of such rights.[124]

Nigeria as a nation does not have a specific *(or better still sufficient*[125]*)* local legislation that confers rights on or imposes duties on itself as a state for the protection and assistance of internally displaced persons.[126]

[119] See UNHCR; Handbook for the protection of internally displaced persons on https://www.unhcr.org (accessed 8 March 2021).

[120] As above.

[121] As above.

[122] As above.

[123] As above.

[124] See Art 2(1) United Nations General Assembly, International Covenant on Economic, Social and Cultural Rights, 16 December 1966, United Nations, Treaty Series, vol. 993.

[125] Words in italics mine. Of course, there are some acts in Nigeria whose provisions could be made applicable to the IDPs, example include the NEMA Act, The 2012 National Policy on Internal Displacement etc.

[126] Nigerian National Human Rights Commission Journal: A Publication of the National Human Rights Commission, 6, 9, December 2016.

A bill was presented by Martha Bodunrin (former MP House of Representatives) at the ICC Assembly of States Parties in December 2011 to implement the Rome Statute Crimes into Nigeria's national legal system based on the Revised Commonwealth Model Law.[127] The government then drafted a government Bill to implement it namely the 'Crimes against Humanity, Genocide and Related Offences Bill 2012'.[128] The effort led to the Bill passing the first reading in Senate. In May 2013, this Bill was further in the second reading in Senate but has not passed the House yet. In fact, the originators of the Bill wrote an open letter to the president of Nigeria calling for an end to impunity by *Boko Haram* but no response was received.[129] Also, Nigeria has not yet ratified the Amendments to the Rome Statute adopted by the 2010 Review Conference (Kampala Amendments) on the crime of aggression and on the use of certain weapons in armed conflict is not of an international character.[130]

Thus, the only instrument that confers peculiar rights on internally displaced persons as well as imposes duties on Nigeria to protect and assist these people is the African Union Convention for the Protection and Assistance of Internally Displaced Persons 2009, otherwise known as the Kampala Convention which Nigeria has ratified but is yet to domesticate.[131] The Kampala Convention is very comprehensive in terms of rights of internally displaced persons as well as the duties it has imposed on state parties to it including Nigeria.[132] The Convention provides for general obligation on state parties to it regarding IDPs, and that states are to undertake to ensure respect for the Convention.[133]

The 1999 Constitution of the Federal Republic of Nigeria (as amended) guarantees certain fundamental rights to all Nigerian citizens.[134] These rights, as the name implies, are fundamental to all Nigerian

[127] Parliamentarians for Global Action; Nigerian and the Rome Statute https://www.pgaction.org/ilhr/rome-statute/nigeria.html (accessed 24 June 2021).

[128] As above.

[129] As above.

[130] As above.

[131] National Human Rights Commission, n.126 above.

[132] As above.

[133] Art 3(1) African Union Convention for Protection and Assistance of Internally Displaced Persons 2009.

[134] See Chapter 4 CFRN 1999 as amended.

citizens and cannot be trampled upon by any person or authority except through due process excused under the law.[135] In other words, it is the obligation of the state to make sure that these fundamental rights as entrenched in the grund norm are enjoyed by every victim of internal displacement.

The task of addressing the issue of internal displacement is primarily the obligation of the government.[136] As discussed earlier in this paper, Nigeria does not have sufficient local legislation addressing issues of internal displacement.[137] However, there are certain provisions in certain acts of the national assembly that can be construed as putting obligations on the government for the betterment of the IDPs. An example of these Acts of the national assembly is the NEMA Act. This Act places certain obligation on the state to take care of and assist IDPs through distribution of emergency relief materials to victims and assistance in the rehabilitation of victims where necessary.[138] The state is also to liaise with state emergency management committees established under Section 8 of the Act to access and monitor, where necessary, the distribution of relief materials to disaster victims.[139] There is an equivalent of the NEMA Act at the state level in Nigeria. This is known as the State Emergency Management Agency (SEMA) law. This law is applicable in the various states in Nigeria,[140] thus, this has also put some obligations on state governments. These obligations include coordination of the activities of relevant agencies in prevention and management of disasters in the state,[141] responding promptly to any emergency at hand within the state, providing relief materials/financial assistance to victims of various disaster in the state, development of loss prevention programmes and

[135] YA Fobur, 'Balancing the Same Sex Marriage (Prohibition) Act, 2014 within Fundamental Human Rights in Nigeria' (2014) 4 *Journal of Nigerian National Human Rights Commission*.

[136] C Adeogun-Phillips, 'Do Internally Displaced People Have Right Under the Law?' www.vanguardngr.com/2015/10 (accessed 9 March 2021).

[137] See 'Nigerian National Human Rights Commission Journal' (December 2016) 6, *A Publication of the National Human Rights Commission* 9.

[138] Section 6 (j) NEMA Act.

[139] Section 6 (k) NEMA Act.

[140] Responsibilities: Lagos State Emergency Management Agency, https://lasema.lagosstate.gov.ng/responsibilities-2/ (accessed 9 March 2021).

[141] As above.

procurement of necessary technology to mitigate identified emergency situation.[142]

Another instrument enacted by the Nigerian legislator addressing the responsibilities of the state towards the protection and assistance of the IDPs is the National Policy on Internal Displacement 2012. This policy places certain obligations upon the state regarding the well-being of internally displaced persons.[143] Amongst those with explicit obligations under this Policy are the government, humanitarian agencies, host communities and armed. The state is specifically under the obligation to respect, protect and fulfil rights related to IDPs. As the primary duty-bearer in the realization of the rights of IDPs, the state is under obligation, amongstothers, to '[create] a legal framework for upholding the rights of internally displaced Persons'.[144] A progressive interpretation of this obligation suggests that the laws enacted should include channels of accountability to provide redress in instances when the rights of IDPs are undermined. But as can be gleaned from the discussion on the current legal framework on issues of IDPs in Nigeria, there is no single legislative enactment that provides foundation for the well-documented atrocities discussed in section 5 above to be prosecuted.

8 Conclusion

Crimes committed as a result of violation of the rights of IDPs could be regarded as crimes against humanity. The attitude of the Nigerian justice system, in making sure that the perpetrators of these evils are held to account constitutes either unwillingness or inability to prosecute. This state of affairs provides a foundational basis for the ICC to assume jurisdiction over cases arising from violation of IDPs especially from security agencies.

Nigeria is a signatory to the Rome Statute, and since the aim is to make sure perpetrators of these crimes do not go scot free, its national laws should be reformed in such a way as to provide considerable ease for the prosecution of such crimes. Furthermore, considering the alarming rate of these violations against the IDPs in Nigeria, government should be ready

[142] As above.

[143] Chapter 4 National Policy on Internal Displacement 2012.

[144] As above.

to work with civil and non-governmental organizations to make sure the ICC intervenes effectively in ensuring that offenders are punished.

References

Books, Book Chapters and Articles

Alobo, E and Obaji, S 'Internal Displacement in Nigeria and The Case for Human Rights Protection of Displaced Persons' (2016) 51 *Journal of Law, Policy and Globalization* 26.

Amone-P'Olak et al., 'Sexual Violence and General Functioning Among Formerly Abducted Girls in Northern Uganda: The Mediating Roles of Stigma and Community Relations—The WAYS Study' (2016) 16 *BMC Public Health* 64.

Bukar, BA 'Nigeria Needs to Take Responsibility for Its IDPs' available at https://www.fmreview.org/young-and-out-of-place/bukar (accessed 7 March 2021).

Benjamin, NS *Building the International Criminal Court* (Cambridge University Press 2008).

Benzing, M 'The Complementarity Regime of the International Criminal Court: International Criminal Justice Between State Sovereignty and the Fight Against Impunity' (2003) 7 *Max Planck Yearbook of United Nations Law* 592.

Bergsmo, M 'Occasional Remarks on Certain State Concerns about the Jurisdictional Reach of International Criminal Court, and Their Possible Implications for the Relationship Between the Court and Security Council' (2000) 69 *Nord. Journal of International Law* 87.

Brein, MO 'International Criminal Court (ICC): The Encyclopedia of Crime and Punishment' 2016, 1st Ed., 1.

Fabur, YA 'Benchmarking the Rights of Internally Displaced Persons in the Fight Against Boko-Haram Insurgency in Nigeria' (2016) 6 *Nigerian National Human Rights Commission Journal* 20.

Fobur, YA 'Balancing the Same Sex Marriage (Prohibition) Act, 2014 within Fundamental Human Rights in Nigeria' (2014) 4 *Journal of Nigerian National Human Rights Commission*.

Responsibilities: Lagos State Emergency Management Agency, https://lasema.lagosstate.gov.ng/responsibilities-2/ (accessed 9 March 2021).

https://www.google.com.ng/amp/dailypostng/2015/06/15 (accessed 8 March 2021).

'Humanitarian Need Overview' www.humanitarianresponse.info/en/operatioons/nigeria/document/idp-protection-strategy-2015 (accessed 22 February 2021).

ICC 'How Non-Governmental Organisations Can Contribute to the Prosecution of War Criminals' (September 2004), *Human Rights Watch* 8.

International Criminal Court 'Understanding the International Criminal Court' https://www.icc-cpi.int/iccdocs/pids/publications/uicceng.pdf (accessed 21 June 2021).

International Criminal Court 'The ICC at a Glance' https://www.icc-cpi.int/Publications/ICCAtAGlanceENG.pdf (accessed 21 June 2021).

'IDP Protection Strategy 2015' www.humanitarianresponse.info/en/operatioons/nigeria/document/idp-protection-strategy-2015 (accessed 22 February 2021).

Katherine, AM 'Prevention and Complementarity in the International Criminal Court: A Positive Approach' 1.

Lubaale, EC and Jegede, AO 'Gross Human Rights Violations in the Context of Armed Conflict: The Cautionary Tale That UGANDA Offers Nigeria' in R Adeola and AO Jegede (eds), *Governance in Nigeria Post-1999: Revisiting the Democratic 'New Dawn' of the Fourth Republic* (Pretoria University Law Press 2019) 231.

Melanie, O 'International Criminal Court' in WG Jennings (ed), *The Encyclopedia of Crime and Punishment* (Wiley 2015).

Maina, M 'Borno: Our Major Challenge Now Is High Influx of IDPs—Grema Terab', https://dailypost.ng/2015/06/15/borno-our-major-challenge-now-is-high-influx-of-idps-grema-terab/ (accessed 21 June 2021).

Newton, MA 'Comparative Complementarity: Domestic Jurisdiction Consistent with the Rome Statute of the International Criminal Court' (2001) 167 *Mil. Law Review* 20

Nigeria: A Huge Displacement and Humanitarian Crisis Require Urgent Life-Saving and Protection Measures, https://www.ohchr.org/EN/NewsEvents/Pages/DisplayNews.aspx?NewsID=20428&LangID=E (accessed 24 February 2021).

Nigeria: Officials Abusing Displaced Women and Girls (October 31, 2016), https://www.hrw.org/news/2016/10/31/nigeria-officials-abusing-displaced-women-girls (accessed 27 February 2021).

'Nigerian National Human Rights Commission Journal' (December 2016) 6 *A Publication of the National Human Rights Commission* 9.

Pablo, J 'The Close Relationship Between Serious Human Rights Violations and Crimes Against humanity: International Criminalisation of Serious Abuses' (2017) 17 *Anuario Mexicano de Derecho Internacional* 145.

Parliamentarians for Global Action; Nigerian and the Rome Statute https://www.pgaction.org/ilhr/rome-statute/nigeria.html (accessed 24 June 2021).

'Rome Statute of the International Criminal Court: Overview' https://legal.un.org/icc/general/overview.htm (accessed 20 January 2021).

Rotimi, O 'IDPs in Nigeria and a Call for Urgent Intervention' (December 28, 2015) https://opinion.premiumtimesng.com/2015/12/28 (accessed 7 March 2021).

Samade, A 'Framework for the Care of IDPs' https://www.vanguardngr.com/2016/01/framework-for-the-care-of-idps-2/amp/ (accessed 7 March 2021).

Schabas, W *The International Criminal Court: A Commentary on the Rome Statute* (Oxford University Press 2010).

Seils, P 'An Introduction to the Role of National Courts and the ICC in Prosecuting International Crimes' *International Centre for Transitional Justice's Handbook on Complementarity* 6.

Seils, P, An Introduction to the Role of National Courts and the ICC in Prosecuting International Crimes (Handbook on Complementarity An Introduction to the Role of National Courts and the ICC in Prosecuting International Crimes) 3.

Surajo, A 'Displaced Persons in North-Eastern Nigeria: Causes, Effects and the Role of Social Workers' (2020) 8 *Sociology and Anthropology* 57.

United Nations High Commissioner for Human Rights Report, 'Nigeria Emergency' (2021), https://www.unhcr.org/nigeria-emergency.html, accessed 12 July 2021.

UNHCR 'Handbook for the Protection of Internally Displaced Persons' https://www.unhcr.org (accessed 8 March 2021).

Treaties, Constitutions and Legislation

International Criminal Court, Elements of Crimes, 2011 reproduced from the Official Records of the Assembly of States Parties to the Rome Statute of the International Criminal Court, First session, New York, 3–10 September 2002 (United Nations publication, Sales No. E.03.V.2 and corrigendum), part II.B. The Elements of Crimes adopted at the 2010 Review Conference are replicated from the Official Records of the Review Conference of the Rome Statute of the International Criminal Court, Kampala, 31 May–11 June 2010 (International Criminal Court publication, RC/11).

International Criminal Court transcripts, available at https://www.icc-cpi.int/Transcripts/CR2021_01038.PDF (accessed 13 July 2021).

Rome Statute of the International Criminal Court, 17 July 1998, 2187 U.N.T.S. 90 (entered into force on 1 July 2002)

The Constitution of the Federal Republic of Nigeria, 1999 (as set out in chapter 4).

United Nations General Assembly, International Covenant on Economic, Social and Cultural Rights, 16 December 1966, United Nations, Treaty Series, vol. 993.

Cases

Case 001 (Appeal Judgment), Supreme Court Chamber, 3 February 2012.
Prosecutor v Dominic Ongwen, Situation in Uganda, Trial Chamber IX, Trial Judgment, ICC-02/04-01/15, 4 February 2021.
Prosecutor v Germain Katanga and Mathieu Ngudjolo Chui, Situation in The Democratic Republic of The Congo, ICC-01/04-01/07, 30 September 2008, Decision on the confirmation of charges.
Prosecutor v Jean-Paul Akayesu (Appeal Judgment), ICTR-96–4-A, International Criminal Tribunal for Rwanda, 1 June 2001.
Prosecutor v Kupreskic (IT-95-16-T, Judgment), Trial Chamber, 14 January 2000.

Reports and Resolutions

Cf. Report of the Preparatory Committee on the Establishment of International Criminal Court, GAOR 51st Sess., Suppl. No. 22, Doc. A/51/22, Para. 153.
Human Rights Watch Report, 'Nigeria: Officials Abusing Displaced Women: Girls Displaced by Boko Haram and Victims Twice Over' 31 October 2016, available at https://www.hrw.org/news/2016/10/31/nigeria-officials-abusing-displaced-women-girls (accessed 11 July 2021).
Report of the Special Rapporteur on the Human Rights of Internally Displaced Persons on His Mission to Nigeria (A/HRC/35/27/Add.1) 2017.
Report by the United Nations Office for the Coordination of Humanitarian Affairs (UNOCHA) in June 2018, https://www.unv.org/our-stories/improving-livig-conditions-internally-displaced-person-adamawa-north-east-nigeria (accessed 24 December 2018).
Report of the United Nations High Commissioner for Human Rights, 'Violations and Abuses Committed by Boko Haram and the Impact on Human Rights in the Countries Affected' Human Rights Council Thirtieth session, Agenda item 2, Annual report of the United Nations High Commissioner for Human Rights and reports of the Office of the High Commissioner and the Secretary-General, 9 December 2015, A/HRC/30/67.
Resolution 1593 (2005), Adopted by the Security Council at its 5158th meeting, on 31 March 2005, S/RES/1593 (2005).
United Nations Security Council Resolution 1970 (2011), Resolution Adopted by the Security Council at its 6491st meeting, on 26 February 2011, S/RES/1970 (2011).

The Establishment of the Hybrid Court for South Sudan and the Special Criminal Court for Central African Republic: Challenges and Prospects

Kasaija Phillip Apuuli

1 Introduction

'For countries emerging from destructive violence and massive human rights abuses, reckoning with the past remains the most challenging question'.[1] The classic response of societies to past egregious human rights violations has been criminal prosecutions undertaken at both national and international levels. Since December 2013, the Republic of South Sudan (RoSS) (hereinafter 'South Sudan') has been in a state of civil war in which crimes amounting to grave breaches of the Geneva Conventions, war crimes, crimes against humanity and possibly even genocide have been committed by the different sides in the conflict, mainly the

[1] M Goldstein-Bolocan 'Rwandan *Gacaca*: An Experiment in Transitional Justice' (2004) 2 *Journal of Dispute Resolution* 355, https://scholarship.law.missouri.edu/cgi/viewcontent.cgi?article=1471&context=jdr (accessed 21 April 2021).

K. P. Apuuli (✉)
Department of Political Science and Public Administration, Makerere University, Kampala, Uganda

E. C. Lubaale and N. Dyani-Mhango (eds.), *National Accountability for International Crimes in Africa*,
https://doi.org/10.1007/978-3-030-88044-6_11

Sudan People's Liberation Movement/Army-In Government (SPLM/A-IG) and the Sudan People's Liberation Movement/Army-In Opposition (SPLM/A-IO). South Sudan became an independent state in July 2011. On the other hand, since getting independence from France in 1960, the Central African Republic (CAR) has suffered from successive upheavals. After the dictatorships of Emperor Jean Bedel Bokassa and General Andre Kolingba, the country reverted back to democracy in 1993. However, the democratic experiment did not last long as by the year 2003, the democratically elected government of Ange Felix Patasse had been overthrown by General Francois Bozizé with the help of France and Libya. Subsequently, a civil war ensued culminating in the overthrow of the Bozizé government by the Séléka rebels in March 2013. The Séléka rule was characterized by widespread sectarian violence and human rights violations, which forced thousands of people to flee their homes in search of refuge. The emergence of the mainly Christian anti-Balaka comprising a collection of vigilante groups in resistance against the Séléka aggravated the human security situation.

This chapter discusses the attempts to address human rights violations committed in the civil wars in the RoSS and the CAR, through the establishment of hybrid courts. Both South Sudan and CAR are countries that are slowly emerging out of civil wars. In the case of the RoSS, the Agreement on the Resolution of the conflict in the Republic of South Sudan (ARCSS) that was signed in 2015 and revitalized in 2018 (hereinafter 'Revitalized Agreement') provides for inter alia the establishment of a Hybrid Court for South Sudan (HCSS) as part of the transitional justice and reconciliation arrangements. The court is mandated to investigate and prosecute individuals bearing responsibility for violations of international law and/or applicable South Sudanese law, committed from 15 December 2013 through the end of the Transitional Period. For the CAR, in June 2015, domestic legislation was adopted establishing the Special Criminal Court (SCC) with a mandate to investigate, prosecute and try serious violations of human rights and serious violations of international humanitarian law in particular the crime of genocide, crimes against humanity and war crimes. The chapter interrogates the reasons why hitherto the establishment of the HCSS has failed to materialize, and reviews the operations of the SCC in CAR. Unlike the political leadership of the Revitalized Transitional Government of National Unity (R-TGoNU) in

South Sudan that has been reluctant to establish the HCSS, the CAR transitional government has established the SCC. The chapter argues that holding individuals accountable for mass human rights violations that are normally committed due to politics may not necessarily end the violence in the two countries. Mass atrocity crimes are invariably caused by bad politics, and thus, the two countries could try to find solutions to this problem. Nevertheless, in both South Sudan and CAR, addressing the issue of accountability for human rights violations through individual prosecutions is just the first step towards ending impunity.

2 Conceptual Context

The decisions, since the early 1980s, of societies emerging from periods of gross abuses of human rights to examine their past, have kindled a significant dialogue among participants in the political processes over the importance of accountability.[2] In this regard, the debate has centred on issues of the level of local and international engagement in the accountability processes; the rules that should be applied in the process; the role of the victims; and the need for justice *vis-a-vis* the establishment of a true historical record of the past events. Accountability has a number of goals. Ratner and Abrams posit that 'the pursuit of accountability can be highly significant to the victims of atrocities-and their relatives and friends-by giving them a sense of justice and closure'.[3] Although such closure is neither guaranteed nor complete, '... the holding accountable of the perpetrator clearly has significance for victims'.[4]

Also, accountability forms a critical element for repairing the damage done to a society traumatized by massive human rights violations thus promoting national reconciliation. The process of reconciliation hinges on findings of *individual* guilt, creation of a historical record and initiation of a public dialogue over the events of the past and the path to the future. According to Arnould, prosecutions support reconciliation by ending impunity and setting a precedent for accountability through the enforcement of justice, thereby allowing societies to break from human

[2] SR Ratner & JS Abrams *Accountability for Human Rights Atrocities in International Law: Beyond the Nuremberg Legacy* (2nd edn.) (2001) 151.

[3] As above.

[4] As above.

rights abuses of the past by confronting those responsible.[5] Generally, accountability is central to reconciliation as a lack of it breeds feelings of injustice among the victims and hampers the creation of a human rights culture.[6]

However, it has also been cautioned that 'the compelling arguments in favor of accountability must be reconciled with the tensions that some forms of accountability may engender'.[7] There needs to be an assessment of the advantages and disadvantages of the prosecution forms of accountability against those of non-prosecution. In the context of ethnic-based strife (like in the case of the RoSS and CAR), criminal prosecutions might provide some closure for victims but fail to promote any long-term reconciliation for the society.[8] If prosecutions are determined as useful to advance the goals of the society, evidence shows that those held closest to the affected society, victim and perpetrators clearly advance the cause of accountability best.

Whilst Zalaquett has noted that 'punishment has a deterrence effect over the whole of society and … helps inhibit the commission of future crimes … [and particularly] those who are punished are deterred from committing crimes again',[9] Oduro avers that '[punishment] is the most forceful way to express moral outrage at the acts of perpetrators, and therefore states are legally obligated to punish … and only the threat of real sanctions will deer future abuse'.[10] Thus, the punishment option emphasizes that post-conflict retributive justice is necessary to heal the wounds and repair the private and public damage provoked by the human rights violators.

The prosecution of perpetrators of international crimes committed during a conflict is called for by the liberal-prosecution theorists who

[5] V Arnould 'Justice After Civil Wars: Truth Commissions' and War Crimes Tribunals' contribution to post-conflict reconciliation' (2006) LXI *Studia Diplomatica* 141.

[6] As above.

[7] Ratner & Abrams (n 2 above) 156.

[8] As above, 157.

[9] J Zalaquett 'Confronting Human Rights Violations Committed by Former Governments: Principles Applicable and Political Constraints' in NJ Kritz (ed) *Transitional Justice: How Emerging Democracies Reckon with Former Regimes* (vol. 1) (1995) 11.

[10] F Oduro 'Reconciling a Divided Nation Through a Non-Retributive Justice Approach: Ghana's National Reconciliation Initiative' (2005) 9 *International Journal of Human Rights* 330.

argue that prosecution is a must because 'when wrongdoers are not prosecuted, convicted and punished, a kind of impunity results'.[11] The lack of justice and accountability 'perpetrates a climate of impunity, which undermines the rule of law as well as exacerbates a sense of injustice and discrimination within communities'.[12] The argument in favour of the liberal-prosecutorial model is founded on moral and utilitarian grounds according to which justice in states recovering from human rights violations is seen as a moral duty arising from a liberal conception of human rights and of utilitarian benefit to both the transitional regime and the larger international order.[13] The common utilitarian arguments advanced for the adoption of the liberal-prosecutorial model include:

> [t]hat prosecution is necessary to assert the supremacy of democratic values and norms and to encourage the public to believe in them; prosecution is essential to establish the viability of the democratic system...; prosecution is necessary to establish the rule of law; prosecution is essential for deterrence-to prevent future atrocities elsewhere; that justice dissipates the call for revenge and militates against renewed fighting; that it is a fiction to think that a people can forget a crime against humanity, justice is required so that memory does not fester; that trials ... establish a historical record of a regime's atrocities so that the victims will live on in memory and future generations can understand their national past; that trials reduce tensions after a conflict by establishing individual responsibility over collective assignation of guilt-by demonstrating that individual men and not [whole communities] are murderers; and, that justice promotes reconciliation at both a personal and national levels.[14]

[11] L May *Crimes Against Humanity: A Normative Account* (2005) 227.

[12] JY Katshung 'Prosecution of Grave Violations of Human Rights in light of Challenges of national Courts and the ICC: The Congolese Dilemma' (2006) 7 *Human Rights Review* 21.

[13] PE Harrell *Rwanda's Gamble: Gacaca and A New Model of Transitional Justice* (2003) 43.

[14] As above 44. Also see S Landsman 'Alternative Responses to Serious Human Rights Abuses: Of Prosecution and Truth Commissions' (1996) 59 *Law & Contemporary Problems* 81–92; K Kindiki 'Prosecuting the Perpetrators of the 1994 Genocide in Rwanda: Its Basis in International Law and the Implication for the Protection of Human Rights in Africa' (2001) 1 *African Human Rights Law Journal* 64–77.

Generally, it has been argued that the failure to hold responsible, perpetrators of egregious crimes '… may vitiate the authority of the law itself'.[15] In effect, prosecutions strengthen the rule of law by teaching both the elites and the masses that the appropriate means of resolving conflict are through impartial justice.

Critics of the liberal-prosecution model such as Mamdani have strongly argued against prosecutions for what they consider as 'political crimes'.[16] They argue that mass violence and the resulting crimes are political in nature. Thus, the prosecution of individuals for such crimes would result in the further destabilization of the society. What is needed, they argue, is first to create conditions for the stabilization of the society before seeking criminal accountability. In this regard, Mamdani observes that '[whilst] criminal violence is the action of individual perpetrators … political violence requires a constituency and raises more difficult questions-among them, how to isolate the perpetrators … from their supporters'.[17] Criminal prosecutions would result in galvanizing support for the alleged perpetrators from their constituencies. Thus, in his separate opinion as a member of the African Union's Commission of Inquiry on South Sudan, Mamdani recommended that 'individual political accountability should follow collective political accountability, so as to give priority to the creation of a stable political order capable of withstanding the inevitable stress generated by the trial of prominent public officials'.[18] Mamdani seems to suggest that countries emerging out of mass violence should address the issue through community truth telling and reconciliation, before individualizing accountability. Nevertheless, truth and reconciliation also have its merits and demerits.

Truth and Reconciliation Commissions (also known as Truth Commissions) (TRC/TC) are bodies set up to investigate a past history of

[15] Harrell (n 13 above) 45; J Benomar 'Justice After Transitions' in NJ Kritz (ed.) *Transitional Justice: How Emerging Democracies Reckon with Former Regimes* (vol. 1) (1995) 32.

[16] M Mamdani, 'Who's to Blame in South Sudan?' *Boston Review*, 28 June 2018, http://bostonreview.net/world/mahmood-mamdani-south-sudan-failed-transition (accessed 22 April 2021).

[17] As above.

[18] M Mamdani 'A Separate Opinion, AU Commission of Inquiry on South Sudan' 20 October 2014, para. 196, https://www.peaceau.org/uploads/auciss.separate.opinion.pdf (accessed 22 April 2021).

violations of human rights in a particular country. Since 1974, there have been established more than twenty official commissions.[19] The primary characteristics of a TRC include: that it focuses on the past; does not focus on a particular event but attempts to paint the overall picture of human rights abuses or violations over a period of time usually temporarily and for a pre-defined period of time, ceasing to exist with the submission of a report of its findings; and is always with some sort of authority by way of its sponsor that allows it greater access to information, greater security or to dig into sensitive issues and create an impact with its report.[20] TRC's 'leave an honest account of the violence, prevents history from being lost or re-written, and allows a society to learn from its past in order to prevent a repetition of such violence in the future'.[21] Landsman strongly argues that TRC's 'help identify and hold up to social criticism prior violations of the rule of law, [thus] in this way, their work can reinforce respect for the law'.[22] The benefits of TRC's notwithstanding, they also suffer from drawbacks.

Firstly, there is disagreement among commentators whether the establishment of the truth actually helps to promote reconciliation. Hayner has argued that '[telling the truth] creates a deeper resentment and exacerbates old issues that have to be dug up a new'.[23] On the other hand, Landsman has noted that '[truth telling is] no panacea as [it cannot] as a general rule punish malefactors'.[24] Thus, he cautions that 'truth telling should only be sanctioned only when it ... can fully and effectively investigate prior wrongdoing ... and most importantly, does not seek to excuse the gravest sorts of crimes ...'.[25]

Secondly, there are doubts on public truth telling leading to both individual and national healing. Ridder argues that 'the assumption that truth

[19] L Olson 'Mechanisms Complementing Prosecution' (2002) 845 *International Review of the Red Cross* 176.

[20] PB Hayner 'Fifteen Truth Commissions-1974–1994: A Comparative Study' in NJ Kritz (ed.) *Transitional Justice: How Emerging Democracies Reckon with Former Regimes* (vol. 1) (1995) 225–226.

[21] As above 227.

[22] S Landsman 'Alternative Responses to Serious Human Rights Abuses: Of Prosecution and Truth Commissions' (1996) 59 *Law and Contemporary Problems* 88.

[23] Hayner (n 20 above) 229.

[24] Landsman (n 22 above) 92.

[25] As above.

telling provides the space for a cathartic release of emotions thus forming the basis for psychological healing for the individual and the society as a whole'[26] is a fallacy. In support of Ridder's view, Graybill and Lenegran have noted that 'nations do not have collective psyches which can be healed, nor do whole nations suffer post-traumatic stress disorder'.[27] Here, the example of South Africa is apt. Whilst the South African TRC was in session, an impression was created that wounds of the past were somehow being healed through the truth telling of those individuals who were appearing before it. However, it was found that the divide between the races was only mitigated and not eliminated.[28]

Lastly, truth telling raises the spectre of national reconciliation 'getting higher priority than justice and healing for individuals'.[29] A question has been posed: What sort of reconciliation is it that leaves many personal wounds untreated?[30] Truth telling gives the expression 'forgive and forget', a new and perhaps sinister meaning![31] Truth telling sometimes results in false national reconciliation as demonstrated by the example of Latin America. According to Ignaef, 'Latin American societies used [truth telling] to indulge in the illusion that they had put their pasts behind them. [However] it only allowed exactly the kind of false reconciliation with the past they had been expressly created to forestall'.[32]

In the end, both criminal prosecutions and truth telling and reconciliation after mass political violence have supporters and critics alike. The literature is divided and thus one has to adopt a pragmatic approach in applying the mechanisms entailed therein. In the case of South Sudan and

[26] Cited in CO Lerche III 'Truth Commissions and National Reconciliation: Some Reflections on Theory and Practice' (2000) 7 *Peace and Conflict Studies: A Journal of the Network of Peace and Conflict Studies* 6.

[27] L Graybill & K Lenegran 'Truth, Justice and Reconciliation in Africa: Issues and Cases' (2004) 8 *African Studies Quarterly* 4.

[28] As above (noting that political tolerance … remains scarce in South Africa's political culture). See also JA Vora & E Vora 'The Effectiveness of South Africa's Truth and Reconciliation Commission: Perceptions of Xhosa, Afrikaner and English South Africans' (2004) 34 *Journal of Black Studies* 301–302.

[29] Lerche III (n 26 above) 7.

[30] As above.

[31] As above.

[32] As above.

the CAR, one of the tools that have been picked up to hold accountable those allegedly responsible for egregious human rights violations is the institution of the hybrid tribunal. The hybrid tribunal is a genre of international justice, which combines international and local judicial elements. In these courts, international and local judges sit side by side, 'to try cases prosecuted and defended by teams of local lawyers working with those from other countries'.[33] The judges apply domestic law that has been reformed to accord with international standards.[34] The establishment of hybrid courts seeks to combine existing local enforcement capacity with international expertise.[35] According to Dickinson, 'the imperative of hybrid tribunals is made compelling because, purely domestic process[es are] impractical in light of the limited capacity of the indigenous legal system, while local distrust of the international processes, [vitiates the desire to establish purely international tribunals]'.[36] Thus, the tribunals 'provide a flexible mechanism for responding to the individual circumstances of a given case'.[37]

One of the strengths of the hybrid model is its perceived legitimacy both locally and internationally, as the sharing of responsibilities among international and local actors in the administration of justice, particularly with respect to accountability for serious human rights crimes, can help to establish the legitimacy of the process as well as strengthen the capacity of the local actors.[38] It is in the context especially of ensuring the legitimacy of the accountability and reconciliation processes in South Sudan and CAR that the hybrid court model of justice has been promoted.

In summary, there is a lack of a common approach by scholars on how to address mass human violations. Whilst some advocate for individual

[33] LA Dickinson 'The Promise of Hybrid Courts' (2003) 97 *American Journal of International Law* 295; R Cryer 'A Special Court for Sierra Leone?' (2001) 50 *International & Comparative Law Quarterly* 445.

[34] Dickinson (n 33 above) 295.

[35] J Cockayne 'The Fraying Shoestring: Rethinking Hybrid War Crimes Tribunals' (2005) 28 *Fordham International Law Journal* 616–680.

[36] Dickinson (n 33 above) 295.

[37] R Lipscomb 'Restructuring the ICC Framework to Advance Transitional Justice: A Search for a Permanent Solution in Sudan' (2005) 106 *Columbia Law Review* 205.

[38] LA Dickinson 'Transitional Justice in Afghanistan: The Promise of Mixed Tribunals' (2002) 31 *Denver Journal of International Law & Policy* 23–42, file:///C:/Users/USER/Downloads/SSRN-id1427509.pdf (accessed 22 April 2021).

criminal prosecutions, others favour truth and reconciliation. Based on these two stances, the chapter discusses the hybrid court processes in South Sudan and the CAR, and highlights the challenges facing them. It also questions whether individual prosecution is the best way forward for the two countries. The chapter's general conclusion is that the yet to be oprationalized HCSS and the SCC are just parts of the puzzle towards addressing mass atrocity crimes in South Sudan and the CAR. The chapter's overarching aim is to amplify on the literature on the two processes in particular and hybrid courts in general.

3 Conflicts in the RoSS and CAR

3.1 Republic of South Sudan

South Sudan descended into civil war in December 2013 following a power struggle in the ruling party the SPLM. The crisis spread to the national army the SPLA and fighting soon erupted pitting different factions and ethnic groups within the army. Whilst President Salva Kiir alleged that recently dismissed Vice President Riek Machar had attempted a *coup d'état*, the latter denied the charge. Subsequently, the fighting that had initially been confined to the capital city Juba spread to Bor (Jonglei), Malakal (Upper Nile) and Bentiu (Unity) states. The fighting, according to the African Union (AU) Commission of Inquiry on South Sudan,[39] was characterized by 'serious violations of human rights ... including murder, torture, rape and sexual violence, lootings and destruction of property, and recruitment and use of children in hostilities'.[40] Based on the collected evidence, it was generally the conclusion of the AU's

[39] The Commission was set up by the Chairperson of the AU Commission in consultations with the chairperson of the African Commission on Human and People's Rights and other relevant AU structures, following the AU PSC meeting in Banjul, Gambia on 30 December 2013. The Commission was inter alia tasked with 'investigating the human rights violations and other abuses committed during the conflict in South Sudan and to make recommendations on the best ways and means to ensure accountability, reconciliation, and healing among all South Sudanese communities'. The appointed Commission comprised the following: Olusegun Obasanjo (Nigeria) (Chairperson), and the members were Mahmood Mamdani (Uganda), Sophia Akuffo (Ghana), Bineta Diop (AU), and Pacifique Manirakiza (Burundi).

[40] AU '*Commission of Inquiry on South Sudan, Final Report of the African Union Commission of Inquiry on South Sudan*' (15 October 2014) para 1125.

Commission of Inquiry that serious violations of international humanitarian law (IHL) amounting to war crimes and crimes against humanity [had been] committed during the fighting.[41] However, no evidence of the commission of the crime of genocide was found. It was estimated in September 2018 that the civil war in South Sudan had resulted in the deaths of more than 400,000 persons.[42]

a. Central African Republic (CAR)

Successive crises have beset the CAR since its independence in 1960 marked by military coups and despotic rule.[43] The most recent crisis was precipitated by the removal from power of President François Bozizé by the northern-based Séléka rebel group in March 2013. Bozizé had earlier seized power from Ange-Félix Patassé and was first elected President in 2005 in elections recognized by the international community as being free and fair.[44] He subsequently embarked upon a process of national reconciliation but faced an uneasy tenure marked by incursions from the north following allegations of undue favour over his Gbaya ethnic group and the marginalization of others.[45] In 2011, Bozizé secured a second term in office in an election that was disputed by the opposition.[46] On 21 March 2013, the Séléka rebels launched an offensive and after three days of fighting seized Bangui. Bozizé fled to Cameroon and Michel Djotodia, the leader of one of the Séléka factions—the Union of Democratic Forces for Unity (UFDR)—declared himself President.[47]

[41] As above. See paras 1126 and 1133.

[42] LP Blanchard 'South Sudan's Civil War: Nearly 400,000 Estimated Dead' *CRS Insight* 28 September 2018, https://fas.org/sgp/crs/row/IN10975.pdf (accessed 23 April 2021); S Mednick 'Nearly 400,000 'Excess Deaths' Caused by South Sudan War' *AP News* 26 September 2018, https://apnews.com/4f5a8681027c4ee7894289c058805b3e/Nearly-400,000-'excess-deaths'-caused-by-South-Sudan-war (accessed 23 April 2021).

[43] V Arnould 'The Uncertain Promise of Hybrid Justice in the Central African Republic' *African Policy Brief no. 14* September 2015.

[44] Y Akpasom & JM Okeke 'From MISAB to MISCA: Protracted Conflicts and the Unending Regional Response to the Crises in Central African Republic' in FB Aboagye (ed.) *A Comprehensive Review of African Conflicts and Regional Interventions [CRACRI]* (2016) 182.

[45] As above.

[46] S Dersso *Annual Review of the African Union Peace and Security Council 2013/2014* (2014) 7.

[47] As above, 8.

The Séléka capture of Bangui worsened the already bad human rights situation. Even before coming to power, reports had emerged of alleged summary executions and targeted assaults, motivated by the victims' religious and ethnic identity.[48] Other alleged grave human violations included arbitrary arrest and detention (targeting, among others, family members and supporters of opposition parties), torture, recruitment of children, rape, disappearances, kidnapping and attacks on schools.[49] After the Séléka forces had taken power, hundreds of unidentified bodies were recovered from different parts of the capital, with the local Red Cross reporting at least 119 people being killed since the fall of the former government.[50] In addition, sexual violence, including rape, gang rape and sexual slavery of women and girls, was also reported. Meanwhile, during its capture of Bangui, the Séléka forces killed 13 South African soldiers[51] who had been deployed as part of the Libreville Peace Agreement of January 2013 between the government of the CAR and the Séléka Coalition.[52]

President Djotodia's rule was characterized by increased sectarian violence that saw the deliberate targeting of civilians along religious lines, which in turn led to massive human displacement.[53] There was also an acute increase in violence between Muslims and non-Muslims during this period as Djotodia was unable to effectively control his forces and ultimately stem the tide of violence that had swept the country.[54] The mainly Christian anti-Balaka vigilante groups emerged as a resistance movement against the Séléka in response to raids, kidnappings

[48] United Nations Security Council *Report of the Secretary General of the UN on the situation in Central African Republic, UN Doc. S/2013/261* (3 May 2013) para. 38, https://undocs.org/S/2013/261 (accessed 20 February 2021).

[49] As above.

[50] As above.

[51] BBC News 'Jacob Zuma: 13 South African Soldiers Killed in CAR' 25 March 2013, https://www.bbc.com/news/world-africa-21923624 (accessed 25 February 2021); N Gabara '13 SA Soldiers Confirmed Dead in CAR' *SA News* 25 March 2013, https://www.sanews.gov.za/africa/13-sa-soldiers-confirmed-dead-car (accessed 25 February 2021).

[52] A translated version of the agreement can be found at https://ucdpged.uu.se/peaceagreements/fulltext/CAR%2020130111eng_ceasefire.pdf (accessed 35 February 2021).

[53] Akpasom & Okeke (n 44 above) 183.

[54] As above.

and killings by the latter. According to the AU, clashes between anti-Balaka and Séléka resulted in serious violations of human rights, including killings, death threats and other acts of intimidation, arrests and abductions, as well as looting and destruction of property.[55] In the end, the 6th Extra Ordinary Summit of Heads of State and Government of the Economic Community of Central African States (ECCAS) held in N'djamena, Chad, on 10 January 2014 forced Djotodia to resign and retreat into exile. Subsequently, Alexander-Ferdinand Nguendet served briefly as acting President until the National Transitional Council (CNT) elected Catherine Samba-Panza as the new interim President from May 2013.

4 The Emergence of the HCSS and SCC

a. RoSS-HCSS

In January 2014, the regional organization—the Intergovernmental Authority on Development (IGAD)—commenced a mediation process to resolve the conflict in South Sudan. The mediation initially resulted in the conclusion by the parties of two landmark agreements: the Agreement on Cessation of Hostilities between the Government of South Sudan and the SPLM/A-IO, and the Agreement on the Status of Detainees between the Government of South Sudan and SPLM/A-IO.[56] The latter agreement specifically addressed the issue of political detainees who had been taken into custody by the government of Kiir on account that they had participated in the attempted *coup d'etat*. After protracted mediation by the IGAD, the parties to the conflict signed the Agreement in August 2015. Unfortunately, in July 2016, the implementation of the Agreement broke down, and the renewed fighting resulted in the commission a new round of human rights violations with the death toll being put at more than 300 persons including soldiers from both sides of the

[55] AU *Report of the Chairperson of the Commission on the situation in the Central African Republic and the activities of the African-led International Support Mission in the Central African Republic*, PSC/AHG/4(CDXVI) 29 January 2014, http://www.peaceau.org/uploads/auc.rpt.car.misca.activities.pdf (accessed 20 February 2021).

[56] KP Apuuli 'IGAD's Mediation in the Current South Sudan Conflict: Prospects and Challenges' (2015) 8 *African Security* 130.

SPLA and civilians.[57] Nevertheless, in the Agreement's preamble, the parties first 'acknowledged the social strife, disharmony between communities and mass violations of human rights in the country', and secondly, committed themselves to 'national reconciliation, accountability, healing and combatting impunity'.[58] This formed the background to Chapter V of the Agreement that was titled: Transitional Justice, Accountability, Reconciliation and Healing. In the Revitalized Agreement that was signed in September 2018,[59] Chapter V of the Agreement was adopted with slight variations. Under the Revitalized Agreement among the institutions envisaged to ensure transitional justice in South Sudan is the Hybrid Court with the other institutions being: the Commission for Truth, Reconciliation and Healing, and the Compensation and Reparation Authority. This chapter specifically addresses the institution of the Hybrid Court for South Sudan (HCSS).

The AU Commission is mandated to establish the HCSS to prosecute and investigate individuals bearing responsibility for violations of international law and/or applicable South Sudanese law committed from 15 December 2013 through the end of the transitional period.[60] The jurisdiction *ratione materiae* of the Court consists of serious crimes in international and national laws including genocide; crimes against humanity; war crimes; and other serious crimes under international law

[57] AFP 'At Least 300 Killed in Latest South Sudan Violence: UN' *Mail Online* 15 July 2016, http://www.dailymail.co.uk/wires/afp/article-3691844/At-300-killed-latest-South-Sudan-violence-UN.html (accessed 20 February 2021).

[58] See Agreement on the Resolution of the Conflict in the Republic of South Sudan Addis Ababa, 17 August 2015, https://unmiss.unmissions.org/sites/default/files/final_proposed_compromise_agreement_for_south_sudan_conflict.pdf (accessed 19 February 2021).

[59] In July 2016, the ARCSS broke down following renewed fighting between forces supporting President Kiir and First Vice President Machar in Juba. The latter fled Juba, and after trekking for more than forty days in the jungles of South Sudan and the Democratic Republic of the Congo (DRC), was evacuated from the DRC to Khartoum Sudan for medical treatment. The 31st Extraordinary Summit of IGAD Heads of State and Government held on 12 June 2017, called on "... all the parties [to the South Sudan conflict] to revitalize the full implementation of the ARCSS". Following intense mediation by the IGAD, the parties finally signed the Revitalized Agreement on 12 September 2018 available at https://www.dropbox.com/s/6dn3477q3f5472d/R-ARCSS.2018-i.pdf?dl=0 (accessed 15 February 2021).

[60] IGAD *Revitalized Agreement on the Resolution of the Conflict in the Republic of South Sudan (R-ARCSS)* (12 September 2018) para 5.3.1.1.

and other relevant laws of South Sudan including gender based crimes and sexual violence.[61] In order to ensure the independence of the Court from the Executive branch of the government, the HCSS is to operate outside the structures of the national judiciary and assume primacy over national courts of South Sudan.[62] The Court's independence is further enhanced by the majority of the judges (trial and appellate); prosecutors and defence counsels; and the registrar being drawn from African countries other than South Sudan, and its seat and composition being decided by the AU Commission.

In view of the continuing conflict in South Sudan and the recognition of the importance of protecting the victims and witnesses, the HCSS is tasked with implementing measures in line with applicable international laws, standards and practices.[63] Generally, the protection of victims and witnesses takes the form of personal physical safety, safety of family and friends, attention to their medical and psychological needs, and legal guarantees of confidentiality.[64] Witness protection in trials in South Sudan is very important because ordinary criminal investigation techniques such as search and seizure, finger printing and photographing cannot be effectively carried out due to ongoing conflict. As a result, trials will heavily rely on witness testimonies and statements.

The HCSS is obliged to ensure and respect due process rights of the accused in accordance with applicable laws, standards and practices.[65] The doctrine of due process constitutes the rules that seek to promote human rights in the criminal process and entails a number of things.[66] Firstly, legal procedures should be fair to the extent that they lead to or constitute fair treatment of the person(s) affected. Secondly, that within each type of

[61] As above, para 5.3.2.

[62] As above, para 5.3.2.2; JG Akech 'Rethinking Transitional Justice in South Sudan: Critical Perspectives on Justice and Reconciliation' (2020) *International Journal of Transitional Justice* 1–12.

[63] IGAD (n 60 above) para 5.3.4.1.

[64] FM Birhanu 'Balancing the Rights of the Accused with Measures for Protection of Victims and Witnesses in International Criminal Tribunals: The Case of the International Criminal Tribunal for Rwanda' unpublished LLM Dissertation, Makerere University, 2002 23.

[65] IGAD (n 60 above) para 5.3.4.2.

[66] DJ Galligan *Due Process and Fair Procedures: A Study of Administrative Procedures* (1996) 52.

legal process, there are authoritative standards based on the triers of values relevant to that process, which constitute the standards of fair treatment, so that a person treated in accordance with them is fairly treated. Lastly, that the basis for such treatment being fair treatment is the promise of society as a whole to each of its members that they will be treated in that way.

In order to individualize the crimes committed in South Sudan, the HCSS will individually hold accountable those who planned, instigated, ordered, committed, aided and abetted, conspired or participated in the planning, preparation and execution of crimes falling under its jurisdiction *rationae materiae*. The individualization of international crimes is important in order to counter dilemmas of 'collective punishment' or 'guilt by association'.[67] In the case South Sudan, there have been specific allegations that in the initial fighting, the Dinkas targeted the Nuer, and in turn the latter targeted the former during the fighting in Bor, Jonglei state.

Following the current trends in international law, no one will be exempted from criminal responsibility on account of their official capacity as government or elected officials, or claiming the defence of superior orders.[68] Moreover, the HCSS will not be impeded or constrained by statutes of limitations or the granting of pardons, immunities or amnesties. This latter aspect also conforms to the current trends in international law where amnesty/pardon/immunity is frowned upon for international crimes such as those that fall under the jurisdiction *rationae materiae* of the HCSS.[69]

Lastly, in terms of penalties, it is contemplated that the HCSS may order the forfeiture of property, proceeds and any assets acquired unlawfully or by criminal conduct.[70] It is also envisaged that the HCSS might also order the return of such forfeitures to their rightful owners or to the state of South Sudan.[71]

[67] Q Wright 'International Law and Guilt by Association' (1949) 43 *American Journal of International Law* 746–755.

[68] IGAD (n 60 above) para 5.3.5.5.

[69] MC Bassiouni 'Searching for Peace and Achieving Justice: The Need for Accountability' (1996) 59 *Law & Contemporary Problems* 17.

[70] IGAD (n 60 above) para 5.3.5.2.

[71] As above.

b. CAR-SCC

The establishment of the SCC in the CAR was prompted by the human rights violations that occurred as far back as 2003 when the *coup d'état* that brought General Bozizé to power gave rise to a pattern of human rights abuses.[72] However, the immediate trigger for the establishment of the SCC was 'the widespread violence [that] returned [to the country] in late 2012'.[73] In April 2014, as part of its conflict management agenda in the CAR, the UN Security Council established the United Nations Multidimensional Integrated Stabilization Mission in the Central African Republic (MINUSCA)[74] to succeed the AU's African-led International Support Mission in the Central African Republic (AFISM-CAR/MISCA) that had been established in June 2013.[75] In establishing MINUSCA, the UN Security Council specifically inter alia 'stressed the urgent and imperative need to end impunity in the CAR and to bring to justice perpetrators of violations of international humanitarian law and of abuses and violations of human rights'.[76] Owing to the collapse of CAR's central government, the UN Security Council gave MINUSCA exceptional powers to 'adopt urgent temporary measures (UTMs)' in order 'to maintain basic law and order and fight impunity'.[77] The UTMs mandate, therefore, 'allowed the UN troops to arrest and detain criminals'.[78]

[72] PI Labuda 'The Special Criminal Court in the Central African Republic-Failure or Vindication of Complementarity?' (2017) 15 *Journal of International Criminal Justice* 175–206.

[73] As above.

[74] UN Security Council *Resolution 2149 (2014) Adopted by the Security Council at its 7153rd meeting, on 10 April 2014, S/Res/2149 (2014)* (10 April 2014), https://undocs.org/S/RES/2149 (2014) (accessed 23 February 2021).

[75] AU *Communiqué of the 380th PSC meeting on the situation in the Central African Republic (CAR)* (17 June 2013), http://afcone.peaceau.org/en/article/communique-of-the-380th-psc-meeting-on-the-situation-in-the-central-african-republic-car (accessed 23 February 2021).

[76] UN (n 74 above).

[77] As above, para 40.

[78] PI Labuda 'UN Peace Operations: Tracking the Shift from Peacekeeping to Peace Enforcement and State Building' *EJIL: Talk!* 2 September 2015, https://www.ejiltalk.org/un-peace-operations-tracking-the-shift-from-peacekeeping-to-peace-enforcement-and-state-building/ (accessed 23 February 2021).

In August 2014, the UN signed a Memorandum of Intent (MoI) with the transitional government of CAR on the establishment of the SCC.[79] The MoI whilst setting out the powers and composition of the Court, laid the groundwork for negotiations on a temporary hybrid tribunal located within CAR's justice system.[80] Generally, the decision to establish the SCC was part of a broader UN effort to restore peace and security in the CAR.[81] Subsequently, on 24 April 2015, the CAR Transitional Parliament adopted an organic law establishing the SCC,[82]which was affirmed as constitutional in May 2015 by the Constitutional Court. The Court's establishment was accelerated by the national consultations known as the 'Bangui Forum' in which participants urged for the punishment of grave crimes in the CAR.[83] On 3 June 2015, the head of the transitional government Catherine Samba-Panza promulgated the SCC law in the *Journal Officiel*.[84] It is important to note that the SCC forms part of the CAR judicial order on par with other criminal tribunals, and thus, it is fully integrated into the CAR legal system.[85] The establishment of the institution experienced delays but eventually it started functioning in October 2018 by holding an inaugural session in Bangui. Whilst a discussion on the entire set up of the SCC is not possible within the contours of this chapter, I discuss three aspects of the institution,

[79] See Memorandum d'entente entre la Mission Multidimensionnelle intégré e des Nations Unies pour la stabilization en République centrafricaine et le Gouvernement de la République centrafricaine, signed 5 August, Ms. Isabelle Gaudeuille, Minister of Justice, 5 August 2014 and Mr. Babacar Gaye, Special Representative of Secretary General (7 August 2014), https://www.fidh.org/IMG/pdf/mou_minusca_-_rca_concernant_la_cps.pdf (accessed 20 February 2021).

[80] Labuda (n 72 above) 179.

[81] As above, 200.

[82] As above, 177.

[83] Human Rights Watch (HRW) '*"Looking for Justice"- The Special Criminal Court, a New Opportunity for Victims in the Central African Republic*' 17 May 2018, https://www.hrw.org/report/2018/05/17/looking-justice/special-criminal-court-new-opportunity-victims-central-african (accessed 21 February 2021).

[84] See Republique Centrafricaine, Loi organique portant creation, organization etfonctionnement de la Courpenale special, Loi no. 15/003 (3 June 2015), https://www.fidh.org/IMG/pdf/loi_organique_portant_cre_ation_organisation_et_fonctionnement_de_la_cps.pdf (*hereinafter* Loi. No. 15/003) (accessed 20 February 2021).

[85] Labuda (n 72 above) 182.

namely its jurisdiction *rationae materiae*; jurisdiction *rationae temporis* and composition.

i. Jurisdiction *rationae materiae* of the SCC

The SCC has jurisdiction over 'serious violations of human rights and international humanitarian law as defined by the Central African Penal Code and in accordance with the international obligations entered into by CAR in the area of international law, in particular genocide, crimes against humanity and war crimes'.[86] According to the prosecutorial strategy announced by the SCC's Special Prosecutor, Colonel Toussaint Muntazini, the Court focuses on the crimes of genocide, crimes against humanity and war crimes because 'it was created in the first place to [specifically] focus on those crimes'.[87] However, as Labuda has noted, 'serious violations of human rights is a generic term with no fixed content, and thus the SCC law suggests that sexual violence and crimes against children also form part of the Court's jurisdiction *rationae materiae*'.[88] Moreover, in choosing suspects to prosecute, the Special Prosecutor and the Investigative Judges consider elements such as 'the degree of responsibility', 'their actual role within armed groups or state institutions' and 'repeat offenders'.[89] The SCC does not focus on those most responsible for the commission of these crimes but rather applies the more general criterion of 'people who played a key role in committing crimes'.[90] The term 'key role' denotes perpetrators who exercised command and control over subordinates, planned and executed crimes, played a major role in directly or physically perpetrating crimes, committed especially odious crimes, and those who occupied command roles at national, regional or local level.[91]

[86] Article 3, Loi. No. 15/003.

[87] PI Labuda 'Open for Business': The Special Criminal Court launches investigations in the Central African Republic' *EJIL: Talk*! 8 February 2019, https://www.ejiltalk.org/open-for-business-the-special-criminal-court-launches-investigations-in-the-central-african-republic/ (accessed 20 February 2021).

[88] Labuda (n 72 above) 187.

[89] Labuda (n 87 above).

[90] As above.

[91] As above.

ii. Jurisdiction *rationae temporis* of the SCC

The SCC is mandated to prosecute crimes committed since January 2003.[92] This date was chosen to allow the institution to investigate crimes committed during the reign of Francois Bozizé, the President of CAR from 2003 to 2013.[93] It should also be noted that in 2013, a campaign of terror and violence was instituted as the Séléka rebels battled Bozizé forces for the control of Bangui. Thus, most of the egregious crimes were committed during this time, and therefore, the 2012–2015 conflict is expected to generate most of the SCC's caseload.[94] Moreover, the near total impunity enjoyed by the perpetrators made it imperative for the SCC to particularly focus on this period.

The law establishing the SCC also envisages that the institution would last for an initial period of five years from the time of its first operationalization and renewable in case of need.[95] However, it has been observed that 'it is highly unlikely that five years will be enough to build complex cases from the investigation to post-trial phases, let alone complete the SCC's ambitious mandate'.[96] Therefore, all focus is now on the institution to see how much it can achieve since its inaugural session in October 2018.

iii. Composition

The hybrid composition of the SCC is its most distinctive quality. The MoI between the UN and the CAR's Transitional Government affirmed the Court's mixed composition with a majority of international staff. However, the SCC law that was adopted later on by the CAR Transitional Parliament provides a majority of Central African magistrates and a minority of international staff, with detailed dispute resolution procedures

[92] HRW (n 83 above).

[93] PI Labuda 'The Special Criminal Court in the Central African Republic' (22 January 2018) 22 *ASIL Insights*, https://www.asil.org/insights/volume/22/issue/2/special-criminal-court-central-african-republic (accessed 19 February 2021).

[94] Labuda (n 72 above) 198.

[95] Article 70, Loi No. 15/003.

[96] Labuda (n 72 above) 190.

at each level.[97] The SCC law establishes four organs, namely the Court itself; the Registry; the Office of the Special Prosecutor; and a Special Unit of the Judicial Police.[98] The SCC's four chambers comprise: the Pre-Trial Investigation Chamber; the Special Indictment Chamber; the Trial Chamber; and the Appeals Chamber. Reflecting its status as a specialized jurisdiction integrated into the CAR's judiciary, the SCC is modelled on the French inquisitorial system where the prosecutor and judges have co-extensive powers to investigate crimes.[99] The SCC law also establishes a special unit of defence lawyers and provides for the possibility of legal aid for suspects, defendants and victims.[100] Between February 2017 and January 2018, most of the positions at the Court were filled.[101]

5 Observations

Whilst CAR's SCC is operational, the HCSS is yet to be established. Nevertheless, both institutions face nearly similar challenges including funding and ongoing conflicts in both South Sudan and CAR. Specifically, the HCSS faces the challenge of a political leadership that does not view prosecutions for international crimes as being a priority. In the case of the SCC, there is potential tension between the operations of the SCC and the ongoing International Criminal Court's (ICC) investigations in the CAR. I expound on these challenges among others in turn. I also discuss, in view of the ongoing conflicts in the two countries, whether individual prosecutions for mass crimes are the best way forward.

[97] As above, 184.

[98] Articles 7 and 8, Loi. No. 15/003.

[99] Labuda (n 72 above) 184.

[100] Articles 64 and 65, Loi. No. 15/003.

[101] For example, in addition to the International Chief Special Prosecutor who was appointed on 15 February 2015, Adelaide Dembele (Burkina Faso) and Emmanuelle Ducos (France) were appointed to serve as international investigating judges on 11 April 2017. On 5 May 2017, President Touadera appointed five national magistrates, Alain Ouaby-Bekai (Deputy National Special Prosecutor), Alain Tolmo (Substitute National Special Prosecutor), Patience Guerengbo and Michel Ngokpou (National Investigating Judges), and Jacob Sanny-Damili (National Judge). Dieudonne Detchou (Canada) was appointed Special International Prosecutor on 6 June 2017, and Koffi Kumelio A. Afande (Togo) and Beradette Houndekandji-Codjovi (Benin) were nominated to serve as International Judges in the Indictment Chamber.

a. Ongoing conflicts in the RoSS and CAR

The September 2018 signing of the Revitalized Agreement in Addis Ababa, Ethiopia, did not end the violence in the RoSS. The agreement, which provides for pre-transition and transition phases leading up to general elections, has been implemented in fits and starts. As at the beginning of September 2020, the UN was reporting 'the deterioration of the security situation at the sub-national level with complex conflicts emerging among ethnic groups operating along with increasingly fractious alliances and targeted security campaigns'.[102] It added that 'localised conflicts consumed multiple areas ... with multifaceted objectives involving civilian and uniformed combatants, along with varied levels of support from national stakeholders'.[103] The violence has partly been attributed to '[an] existing security vacuum occasioned by the continuous delay in the restructuring of State authorities'.[104] Generally, intercommunal violence has deepened throughout the country in particular in greater Jonglei, Lakes, Unity, Warrap and Western Bahr el-Ghazal states.[105]

The crimes that are being committed include: killings, abductions, sexual violence and the looting of civilian property, among other violations. The United Nations Mission in South Sudan (UNMISS) documented a total of 264 incidents, including arbitrary killings, abductions, conflict-related sexual violence, arbitrary arrests and detention (including proxy detention), torture and ill-treatment, forced military recruitment and the looting and destruction of civilian property.[106] The incidents resulted in at least 870 civilian casualties (529 persons killed and 341 wounded), including of at least 50 women and 34 children.[107] It is in this kind of environment that the HCSS is being established.

[102] UN Security Council *Situation in South Sudan-Report of the Secretary-General*, S/2020/890 (9 September 2020) para 19, https://undocs.org/S/2020/890 (accessed 15 February 2021).

[103] As above.

[104] ASK Njoroge *Report on the status of implementation of the Revitalized Agreement on the Resolution of the conflict in the Republic of South Sudan for the period 1 January to 31 March 2020, Report No. 006/20* (2020) para 13.

[105] UN Security Council (n 102 above) para 30.

[106] As above, para 53.

[107] As above.

With regard to the CAR, the election of Faustin-Archange Touadéra as President in March 2016 thus ending a two-year transition initially brought a lull in the fighting. However, it flared up again in 2017 and 2018, with armed groups (mainly the ex-Séléka factions and anti-Balaka militias) struggling for control of local economies, particularly taxation of trade, cattle and mining sites.[108] The ex-Séléka and anti-Balaka groups are responsible for atrocities against civilians, thousands of whom have lost their lives, and hundreds of thousands of others have been displaced by the fighting.[109] In February 2019, the CAR government and fourteen armed groups signed a political agreement negotiated over the previous ten days in Khartoum, Sudan.[110] However, whilst the agreement provides for a cessation of hostilities among the parties, violence has continued to occur in the country. For example, as of June 2020, the UN was reporting that 'armed groups and militia continued to pose [a] serious threats to the civilian population and national stability'.[111] The organization detailed numerous instances of killing and injuring of civilians, one case of killing of a MINUSCA peacekeeper[112] and several cases of sexual violence against women, girls and men.[113] Just like the HCSS in South Sudan, the SCC is operating in an environment of continued violence. In fact, Human Rights Watch (HRW) has questioned 'how the SCC can continue operating in a country where conflicts persist ... and abuses

[108] International Crisis Group (ICG) *Making the Central African Republic's Latest Peace Agreement Stick*, Africa Report N°277 (18 June 2019) 2, https://d2071andvip0wj.cloudfront.net/277-making-cars-latest-peace-agreeement-stick.pdf (accessed 20 February 2021).

[109] As above.

[110] UN Security Council '*Letter dated 14 February 2019 from the Secretary-General addressed to the President of the Security Council*, S/2019/145' (15 February 2019), https://reliefweb.int/sites/reliefweb.int/files/resources/S_2019_145_E.pdf (accessed 20 February 2021).

[111] UN Security Council '*Central African Republic-Report of the Secretary-General, S/2020/545*' (16 June 2020) para 29, https://undocs.org/S/2020/5455 (accessed 20 February 2021).

[112] As above, paras 29–39.

[113] As above, para 70.

continue to be perpetrated'.[114] According to Fabricius, it is no wonder that so far, the Court has laid no charges or made any arrests.[115]

b. Funding

In order to kick start the operations of the HCSS and other justice and accountability institutions in South Sudan, the United States of America (USA) pledged 5 million dollars in 2015.[116] Under the R-ARCSS, the AU has the mandate of determining the key aspects of the Court including funding. Since the Court has not yet been established, as of now the challenge of its funding is just moot. Nevertheless, it is not clear whether the USA's financial pledge still exists, since five years have now passed.

HRW has observed that the financial situation of the SCC remains extremely challenging.[117] As a matter of fact, the institution is dependent on voluntary contributions and its budget is complex because funds are made available from a patchwork of sources, some of which restrict the types of work that may be supported with the funding.[118] According to the budget drawn up by the UN in July 2018, the SCC required between US$10 million and US$13.3 million per year to operate over the next five years.[119] Whilst individual government donations worth US$5 million

[114] n 83 above, 22.

[115] P Fabricius 'Can Justice Prevail in the Midst of a War? The Central African Republic's Special Criminal Court Is a Huge Test Case in Balancing Peace and Justice' *ISS Today* 25 July 2019, https://issafrica.org/iss-today/can-justice-prevail-in-the-midst-of-war (accessed 20 February 2021).

[116] PBS News Hour 'Kerry Makes Emotional Appeal to South Sudan's Warring Leaders' 4 May 2015, https://www.pbs.org/newshour/world/kerry-makes-emotional-appeal-south-sudans-warring-leaders (accessed 21 February 2021); NL Yak 'Kerry Reiterate Formation of Hybrid Court on South Sudan' *Ngokland* 5 May 2015, http://www.ngokland.com/kerry-reiterate-formation-of-hybrid-court-on-south-sudan/ (accessed 21 February 2021).

[117] n 83 above.

[118] As above.

[119] As above.

have come from the USA, France, the Netherlands, among others,[120] the Court has continued to suffer from funding shortfalls. Fabricius noted that the Court's operations faced a funding gap of about US$1 million in the year 2019.[121]

iii. Political leadership reluctant on issues of justice and accountability in South Sudan

According to the Revitalized Agreement, the R-TGoNU is supposed to initiate legislation establishing the HCSS including its mandate, jurisdiction, among others.[122] However, as it has been observed, so far the government has 'delayed and obstructed'[123] the formation of the Court. It has done this by specifically failing to enact the envisaged legislation for the establishment of the Court. Pervasive impunity still remains the norm[124] in South Sudan. As Akech has observed, in South Sudan, 'the focus has historically been on reconciliation and amnesty through a 'big tent' approach that rewards belligerents with political and military power'.[125] Thus, the current political leadership in South Sudan has used all tricks to delay the enactment of the necessary legislation to establish the HCSS. I will cite two instances.

Firstly, at the beginning of June 2016, an opinion piece appeared in *The New York Times* newspaper purportedly written by President Kiir and First Vice President Machar, promoting truth (telling) and not trials

[120] E Bussey 'Progress and Challenges in Establishing the Special Criminal Court in the Central African Republic' 2 October 2017, https://www.amnesty.org/en/latest/campaigns/2017/10/progress-and-challenges-in-establishing-the-special-criminal-court-in-the-central-african-republic/ (accessed 21 February 2021).

[121] n 115 above.

[122] IGAD (n 60 above) para 5.1.1.

[123] C du Plessis 'UN Human Rights Report: Accountability Long Overdue in South Sudan' *Africa Portal* 27 February 2020, https://www.africaportal.org/features/un-human-rights-report-accountability-long-overdue-south-sudan/ (accessed 22 February 2020).

[124] UN Human Rights Council '*Report of the Commission on Human Rights in South Sudan, A/HRC/40/69*' 21 February 2019, https://www.securitycouncilreport.org/atf/cf/%7B65BFCF9B-6D27-4E9C-8CD3-CF6E4FF96FF9%7D/A_HRC_40_69.pdf (accessed 22 February 2021).

[125] n 62 above.

(prosecutions) for crimes committed in the RoSS.[126] In the opinion piece, the two leaders promised to 'create a national truth and reconciliation commission modeled on those of South Africa and Northern Ireland … with wide-ranging powers including that to grant amnesty'.[127] The two leaders also argued that, '… disciplinary justice — even if delivered under international law — would destabilize efforts to unite [the] nation by keeping alive anger and hatred among the people of South Sudan'.[128] Thus, they called on '… the international community, and the United States and Britain in particular, to reconsider … [its] support for a planned international tribunal, the HCSS'.[129] However, soon after the opinion piece was published, Machar disavowed its contents saying he had not been consulted about the essay, a position that was opposed by Kiir's spokesman.[130] This incident demonstrated to all and sundry how the political leadership (especially President Kiir) in South Sudan feels about the proposed HCSS. Were political leadership to have its way, the HCSS would not be established.

Secondly, at the end of April/beginning of May 2019, reports emerged indicating that the Kiir government had signed a contract hiring a USA lobby firm, Gainful Solutions Inc., for a whopping US$3.7 million to inter alia '…delay and ultimately block the establishment of the hybrid court envisaged in R-ARCSS'.[131] Subsequently, Gainful Solutions and the government of South Sudan revised the terms of the contract after a public outcry condemning the attempts to undermine the justice and accountability measures in the R-ARCSS. Thus, in the new contract, the

[126] S Kiir & R Machar 'South Sudan Needs Truth, not Trials' *The New York Times* 7 June 2016, https://www.nytimes.com/2016/06/08/opinion/south-sudan-needs-truth-not-trials.html (accessed 15 February 2021); TY Mccormick & S O'grady 'The New York Times Op-ed That Wasn't' *Foreign Policy* 9 June 2016, https://foreignpolicy.com/2016/06/09/the-new-york-times-south-sudan-op-ed-that-wasnt/ (accessed 15 February 2021).

[127] As above.

[128] As above.

[129] As above.

[130] As above.

[131] US Department of Justice 'Consulting Contract Agreement' 2 April 2019, https://efile.fara.gov/docs/6667-Exhibit-AB-20190418-2.pdf (accessed 15 February 2021).

aspect of undermining the establishment of the HCSS was removed.[132] Partly as a result of the government of South Sudan machinations, a group of civil society organizations (CSOs) in July 2020 addressed a letter to the members of the AU Peace and Security Council (AU PSC) on the establishment of the HCSS.[133] In the letter, the CSOs urged the PSC members to inter alia '... take unilateral action to enable the [HCSS] creation immediately'.[134] They also warned that, 'delays in establishing the HCSS threatens the future of the peace deal and protection of civilians, and [do not] prevent survivors and families of victims from seeking justice for themselves and their loved ones'.[135] In terms of what has been done towards the establishment of the HCSS, the AU held consultations with the government of the RoSS in July 2017[136] and convened expert consultations in December 2019 in Dar es Salaam, Tanzania, which reviewed the Court's legal instruments prepared by the Office of the Legal Counsel of the AU. Notwithstanding this progress however, generally the UN Human Rights Council (2019) has concluded that 'the process of establishing the HCSS has stalled',[137] with 'lack of political will ... by the government contribut[ing] to this'.[138]

The procrastination to establish seems to have been ended by the announcement at the end of January 2021 that the Cabinet of the R-TGoNU had approved a plan by the justice ministry to start setting up institutions for peace and reconciliation spelled out in Chapter Five of

[132] US Department of Justice 'Consulting Contract Agreement' 7 May 2019, https://efile.fara.gov/docs/6667-Exhibit-AB-20190507-3.pdf (accessed 15 February 2021).

[133] South Sudan Civil Society Forum et al., *Letter to the AU Peace and Security Council Regarding the Session on South Sudan* 15 July 2021, https://www.hrw.org/news/2020/07/15/letter-au-peace-and-security-council-regarding-session-south-sudan (accessed 16 February 2021).

[134] As above.

[135] As above.

[136] AU '*African Union Commission and the South Sudan Transitional Government Advance on Establishment of the Hybrid Court for South Sudan*' 25 July 2017, https://au.int/en/pressreleases/20170725/african-union-commission-and-south-sudan-transitional-government-advance (accessed 16 February 2021).

[137] UN Human Rights Council 'Report of the Commission on Human Rights in South Sudan' *A/HRC/40/69*, 21 February 2019, https://www.securitycouncilreport.org/atf/cf/%7B65BFCF9B-6D27-4E9C-8CD3-CF6E4FF96FF9%7D/A_HRC_40_69.pdf (accessed 16 February 2021).

[138] As above.

the Revitalized Agreement.[139] The decision was immediately welcomed by the Chairperson of the AU who noted that '... the decision put an end to the delays in establishing [inter lia the HCSS]'.[140] He concluded by observing that '... he looked forward to work[ing] with the Government of South Sudan to ensure the finalization and signing of the MoU on the establishment of the Court at the earliest opportunity'.[141] As at the end of April 2021, the South African-based think tank-Institute for Security Studies (ISS) reported that the MoU to establish the HCSS has not been signed.[142]

iv. The SCC and ICC in the CAR

The CAR signed the Rome Statute on 7 December 1999 and ratified it on 3 October 2001. On 22 December 2004, the government requested the Prosecutor 'to investigate the situation of crimes within the jurisdiction of the Court committed anywhere on the territory of the CAR since 1 July 2002, the date of entry into force of the Rome Statute'.[143] The CAR's request was made after the country's *Cour de Cassation* had concluded that 'the national judicial system was unable to carry out the necessary criminal proceedings, in particular to collect

[139] Takpiny, B 'South Sudan Approves Establishment of Hybrid Court' 30 January 2021 https://www.aa.com.tr/en/africa/south-sudan-approves-establishment-of-hybrid-court/2127899 (accessed 27 April 2021); Jale, R 'Cabinet Approves Establishment of Hybrid Court' *Eye Radio* 30 January 2021 https://eyeradio.org/cabinet-approves-establishment-of-hybrid-court/ (accessed 27 April 2021).

[140] AU 'Statement by H.E. Mr. Moussa Faki Mahamat, Chairperson of the African Union Commission, on African Union Hybrid Court of South Sudan' 30 January 2021 https://au.int/en/pressreleases/20210130/statement-he-mr-moussa-faki-mahamat-chairperson-african-union-commission (accessed 28 April 2021).

[141] As above.

[142] A Ngari & M Mahdi 'Missteps by South Sudan's Government Keeps the Country in Conflict' 27 April 2021 https://issafrica.org/iss-today/missteps-by-south-sudans-government-keep-the-country-in-conflict?utm_source=BenchmarkEmail&utm_campaign=ISS_Weekly&utm_medium=email (accessed 30 April 2021).

[143] International Criminal Court (ICC) 'Prosecutor Received Referral concerning Central African Republic, ICC-OTP-20050107-86' 7 January 2005, https://www.icc-cpi.int/Pages/item.aspx?name=otp+prosecutor+receives+referral+concerning+central+african+republic (accessed 16 February 2021).

evidence and obtain the accused'.[144] Thus, the ICC Prosecutor formally announced the opening of the investigation in the CAR situation on 22 May 2007.[145] As at the time of writing, the ICC has two investigations into the CAR with the first focused on crimes committed during the conflict in 2002 and 2003, and the second focusing on crimes committed since 2012. As a result of the first investigation, former DRC Vice President Jean Pierre Bemba Gombo was tried and convicted of war crimes and crimes against humanity, and sentenced to 18 years in prison.[146] On appeal, however, the sentence was quashed.[147] The second investigation has to-date not resulted in any suspects being charged. Thus, it is in this context that the SCC is operating. Both the ICC and the SCC (and also the ordinary courts) share concurrent jurisdiction over international crimes which may also pose a challenge. Labuda has observed that the concurrent existence of the SCC and ICC marks the first time that the two courts [are] investigat[ing] crimes in the same country'.[148] The challenge may arise around the issue of complementarity under which the ICC is a court of last resort, stepping in a situation only where national authorities are unable or unwilling to try cases domestically. The danger in the CAR is that the SCC and ICC might start competing for jurisdictional space.[149] Moreover, the SCC law purports to give jurisdictional primacy

[144] ICC 'Background-Situation in the Central African Republic, ICC-OTP-BN-20070522-220-A_EN' 22 May 2007, https://www.icc-cpi.int/NR/rdonlyres/B64950CF-8370-4438-AD7C-0905079D747A/144037/ICCOTPBN20070522220_A_EN.pdf (accessed 17 February 2021).

[145] ICC 'Prosecutor Opens Investigation in the Central African Republic' 22 May 2007, https://www.icc-cpi.int/Pages/item.aspx?name=prosecutor+opens+investigation+in+the+central+african+republic&ln=en&lan=en-GB (accessed 17 February 2021).

[146] J Burke 'Jean-Pierre Bemba Sentenced to 18 Years in Prison by International Criminal Court' *The Guardian* 21 June 2016, https://www.theguardian.com/law/2016/jun/21/jean-pierre-bemba-sentenced-to-18-years-in-prison-by-international-criminal-court (accessed 17 February 2021).

[147] O Bowcott 'Jean-Pierre Bemba's War Crimes Conviction Overturned' *The Guardian* 8 June 2018, https://www.theguardian.com/global-development/2018/jun/08/former-congo-leader-jean-pierre-bemba-wins-war-crimes-appeal-international-criminal-court (accessed 17 February 2021).

[148] n 93 above.

[149] In March 2018, the ICC Prosecutor and the SCC Special Prosecutor exchanged letters on cooperation. See HRW (n 83) 30.

to the ICC,[150] a fact that may give rise to confusion of roles of the two institutions. Nevertheless, so far, this challenge has not materialized.

e. Individual prosecutions for mass crimes, the best way forward?

As has been noted above, there is no agreed common approach on how accountability for mass atrocity crimes should be achieved. In fact, it has been observed that 'there is no approach which should have a monopoly over the provision of [mass atrocities] accountability'.[151] Whilst the merits of the liberal-prosecutorial model (of which the hybrid tribunal is one of the kind) have been advanced, some have doubted its capacity to address mass atrocity crimes which are essentially political. Minnow has inter alia first argued that 'prosecutions … may be viewed as obstacles to reconciliation and to nation building …'[152] The patent selectivity in prosecution—the simple difficulty of justifying why some people are prosecuted and others are not—does not bode well for the promotion of reconciliation. The prosecution of some and not others has the potential of promoting a sense of injustice and victimhood in sections of the society. Secondly, prosecutions following mass atrocities can never establish a complete historical record, despite all hopes.[153] Defendants in war crimes trials tell their version of the story at trials, and like other defendants, they often lie, further compromising the historical record.[154] In the end, Minow cautions that, 'trials should not be pursued where there is no chance for fairness or perceptions of fairness; where the tribunal is entirely subject to a particular nation's self-interest; or where there are overwhelming disparities between the resources and will needed to undertake trials…'[155] As we have observed above, the current situations

[150] Article 37, Loi. No. 15/003.

[151] Kersten, M 'On the Rebirth of Hybrid Tribunals' *Justice in Conflict* 22 January 2016 https://justiceinconflict.org/2016/01/22/on-the-rebirth-of-hybrid-tribunals/ (accessed 28 April 2021).

[152] M Minow, *Between Vengeance and Forgiveness: Facing History after Genocide and Mass Violence* (1998) 128.

[153] As above, 47.

[154] As above.

[155] As above, 50.

in South Sudan and even CAR may not be conducive to hold trials for mass atrocity crimes.

Moreover, the deterrence aspects of trials have also been doubted. The trials at the international criminal tribunal for former Yugoslavia (ICTY) and the International Criminal Tribunal for Rwanda (ICTR) did not deter subsequent abuses in the former Yugoslavia and Central Africa. In the same vein, it is observed that 'the prosecution of perpetrators of atrocities according to universal standards, risks causing more atrocities than it would prevent, because it pays insufficient attention to political realities'.[156] As noted above, this is exactly what Mamdani has observed in the case of South Sudan. Moreover, the deterrence value of trials for mass atrocity crimes has also been doubted. The trials at the international criminal tribunal for former Yugoslavia (ICTY) and the International Criminal Tribunal for Rwanda (ICTR) did not deter subsequent abuses in the former Yugoslavia and Central Africa.[157] So, from the foregoing, the work of the envisaged HCSS and the ongoing SCC trials may not necessarily lead to peace in South Sudan and CAR, respectively.

6 Conclusion

This chapter has examined the attempts at addressing human rights violations arising out of the civil wars in South Sudan and the CAR, which civil wars are yet to come to an end. In the former, the HCSS has been proposed as one of the measures to address international crimes committed since the start of the civil war in December 2013. At the end of January 2021, the R-TGoNU finally announced that it was ready to establish the court after much procrastination. On the other hand, the SCC in the CAR is operational and addressing international crimes that have occurred in the country since 2003. Since it started operating in the second half of 2018, however, it has not yet handed down indictments. The HCSS and SCC epitomize the view that human rights crimes (especially international ones) committed during conflict must be punished, a view promoted by the liberal-prosecution theorists. But the liberal-prosecution model has been criticized for not being appropriate to

[156] J Snyder & L Vinjamuri 'Trials and Errors: Principle and Pragmatism in Strategies of International Justice' 28 *International Security* (2003–2004) 5–44.

[157] As above.

address mass atrocity crimes, which are essentially political. It is argued that societies emerging from civil conflict, in which mass crimes have been committed, first need to engage in collective national reconciliation as a precursor for individual accountability. Nevertheless, there is no agreement on the sequencing of these processes; thus, a dilemma remains.

Be that as it may, we have highlighted the challenges that the SCC is facing, which most likely the HCSS will also face when it is finally made operational. Whilst some of the challenges such as political will and ensuring adequate funding among others may be resolved in the short term, ending the ongoing conflicts in South Sudan and CAR on the other hand will be in the long run. For example, since the signing of the Revitalized Agreement, 'staggering levels of violence'[158] continue to characterise South Sudan, whilst insurgents in CAR have in the immediate past threatened to attack the capital Bangui.[159] Thus, the continued instability in the two countries will continue to impact the operations of the mass crimes accountability institutions of the HCSS and SCC, respectively. In the end, it is the conclusion of this chapter that the yet to be oprationalized HCSS and the SCC are just parts of the puzzle towards addressing mass atrocity crimes in South Sudan and the CAR.

References

AFP 'At Least 300 Killed in Latest South Sudan Violence: UN' *Mail Online* 15 July 2016 http://www.dailymail.co.uk/wires/afp/article-3691844/At-300-killed-latest-South-Sudan-violence-UN.html.

Africanews 'Rebels Attack Central African Republic's Capital' 13 January 2021 https://www.africanews.com/2021/01/13/rebels-attack-central-african-republic-s-capital/.

Akech, JG 'Rethinking Transitional Justice in South Sudan: Critical Perspectives on Justice and Reconciliation' (2020) *International Journal of Transitional Justice* 1.

[158] See UN Human Rights Council 'Despite Renewed Political Commitment, Staggering Levels of Violence Continued Across South Sudan for the Second Successive Year, UN Experts Note' 19 February 2021 https://www.ohchr.org/EN/HRBodies/HRC/Pages/NewsDetail.aspx?NewsID=26761&LangID=E (accessed 30 April 2021).

[159] See Africanews 'Rebels Attack Central African Republic's Capital' 13 January 2021 https://www.africanews.com/2021/01/13/rebels-attack-central-african-republic-s-capital/ (accessed 1 May 2021).

Akpasom, Y & Okeke, JM 'From MISAB to MISCA: Protracted Conflicts and the Unending Regional Response to the Crises in Central African Republic' in Aboagye, FB (ed) *A Comprehensive Review of African Conflicts and Regional Interventions [CRACRI]* (Addis Ababa: AU & APSTA 2016).

Apuuli, KP 'IGAD's Mediation in the Current South Sudan Conflict: Prospects and Challenges' (2015) 8 *African Security* 120.

Arnould, V (2006). 'Justice After Civil Wars: Truth Commissions' and War Crimes Tribunals' Contribution to Post-Conflict Reconciliation' (2006) LIX *Studia Diplomatica* 141.

Arnould, V 'The Uncertain Promise of Hybrid Justice in the Central African Republic' *African Policy Brief no. 14* (Egmont Royal Institute for International Affairs September 2015).

AU 'Communiqué of the 380th PSC Meeting on the Situation in the Central African Republic (CAR)' (17 June 2013) http://afcone.peaceau.org/en/article/communique-of-the-380th-psc-meeting-on-the-situation-in-the-central-african-republic-car.

AU 'Communiqué of the Peace and Security Council 411th meeting at the Level of Heads of State and Government, PSC/AHG/COMM.1 (CDXI)' (Banjul 30 December 2013) http://www.peaceau.org/uploads/psc-com-411-southsudan-30-12-2013.pdf.

AU *Commission of Inquiry on South Sudan, Final Report of the African Union Commission of Inquiry on South Sudan* (Addis Ababa 15 October 2014).

AU *Report of the Chairperson of the Commission on the situation in the Central African Republic and the activities of the African-led International Support Mission in the Central African Republic' PSC/AHG/4(CDXVI)* (Addis Ababa 29 January 2014) http://www.peaceau.org/uploads/auc.rpt.car.misca.activities.pdf.

AU 'African Union Commission and the South Sudan Transitional Government Advance on Establishment of the Hybrid Court for South Sudan' (25 July 2017) https://au.int/en/pressreleases/20170725/african-union-commission-and-south-sudan-transitional-government-advance.

AU 'Statement by H.E. Mr. Moussa Faki Mahamat, Chairperson of the African Union Commission, on African Union Hybrid Court of South Sudan' 30 January 2021 https://au.int/en/pressreleases/20210130/statement-he-mr-moussa-faki-mahamat-chairperson-african-union-commission.

Bassiouni, MC (1996). 'Searching for Peace and Achieving Justice: The Need for Accountability' (1996) 59 *Law & Contemporary Problems* 9.

BBC News 'Jacob Zuma: 13 South African Soldiers Killed in CAR' 25 March 2013 https://www.bbc.com/news/world-africa-21923624.

Benomar, J 'Justice After Transitions' in Kritz, NJ (ed) *Transitional Justice: How Emerging Democracies Reckon with Former Regimes* (vol. 1) (Washington: United States Institute for Peace 1995).

Birhanu, FM 'Balancing the Rights of the Accused with Measures for Protection of Victims and Witnesses in International Criminal Tribunals: The Case of the International Criminal Tribunal for Rwanda' unpublished LLM dissertation Makerere University 2002.

Blanchard, LP 'South Sudan's Civil War: Nearly 400,000 Estimated Dead' *CRS Insight* 28 September 2018 https://fas.org/sgp/crs/row/IN10975.pdf.

Bowcott, O 'Jean-Pierre Bemba's War Crimes Conviction Overturned' *The Guardian* 8 June 2018 https://www.theguardian.com/global-development/2018/jun/08/former-congo-leader-jean-pierre-bemba-wins-war-crimes-appeal-international-criminal-court.

Burke, J 'Jean-Pierre Bemba Sentenced to 18 Years in Prison by International Criminal Court' *The Guardian* 21 June 2016 https://www.theguardian.com/law/2016/jun/21/jean-pierre-bemba-sentenced-to-18-years-in-prison-by-international-criminal-court.

Bussey, E 'Progress and Challenges in Establishing the Special Criminal Court in the Central African Republic' (2 October 2017) https://www.amnesty.org/en/latest/campaigns/2017/10/progress-and-challenges-in-establishing-the-special-criminal-court-in-the-central-african-republic/.

Cockayne, J 'The Fraying Shoestring: Rethinking Hybrid War Crimes Tribunals' (2005) 28 *Fordham International Law Journal* 616.

Crocker, D 'Truth Commissions, Transitional Justice and Civil Society' in Rotberg, R & Dennis, T (eds) *Truth v. Justice* (Princeton: Princeton University Press 2000).

Cryer, R 'A Special Court for Sierra Leone?' (2001) 50 *International & Comparative Law Quarterly* 435.

Dersso, S *Annual Review of the African Union Peace and Security Council 2013/2014* (Pretoria: ISS 2014).

Dickinson, LA 'Transitional Justice in Afghanistan: The Promise of Mixed Tribunals' (2002) 31 *Denver Journal of International Law & Policy* 23 file:///C:/Users/USER/Downloads/SSRN-id1427509.pdf.

Dickinson, LA 'The Promise of Hybrid Courts' (2003) 97 *American Journal of International Law* 295.

du Plessis, C 'UN Human Rights Report: Accountability Long Overdue in South Sudan' *Africa Portal* 27 February 2020 https://www.africaportal.org/features/un-human-rights-report-accountability-long-overdue-south-sudan/.

Fabricius, P 'Can Justice Prevail in the Midst of a War? The Central African Republic's Special Criminal Court Is a Huge Test Case in Balancing Peace and Justice' *ISS Today* 25 July 2019 https://issafrica.org/iss-today/can-justice-prevail-in-the-midst-of-war.

Gabara, N '13 SA Soldiers Confirmed Dead in CAR' *SA News* 25 March 2013 https://www.sanews.gov.za/africa/13-sa-soldiers-confirmed-dead-car.

Galligan, DJ *Due Process and Fair Procedures: A Study of Administrative Procedures* (Oxford: Clarendon Press 1996).

Goldstein-Bolocan, M 'Rwandan *Gacaca*: An Experiment in Transitional Justice' (2004) 2004 *Journal of Dispute Resolution* 355 https://scholarship.law.missouri.edu/cgi/viewcontent.cgi?article=1471&context=jdr

Harrell, PE *Rwanda's Gamble: Gacaca and A New Model of Transitional Justice* (New York: Writers Club Press 2003).

HRW '"Looking for Justice"- The Special Criminal Court, a new Opportunity for Victims in the Central African Republic' (17 May 2018) https://www.hrw.org/report/2018/05/17/looking-justice/special-criminal-court-new-opportunity-victims-central-african.

ICC 'Prosecutor Received Referral Concerning Central African Republic, ICC-OTP-20050107-86' (7 January 2005) https://www.icc-cpi.int/Pages/item.aspx?name=otp+prosecutor+receives+referral+concerning+central+african+republic.

ICC 'Background-Situation in the Central African Republic, ICC-OTP-BN-20070522-220-A_EN' (22 May 2007) https://www.icc-cpi.int/NR/rdonlyres/B64950CF-8370-4438-AD7C-0905079D747A/144037/ICCOTPBN20070522220_A_EN.pdf.

ICC 'Prosecutor Opens investigation in the Central African Republic' 22 May 2007 https://www.icc-cpi.int/Pages/item.aspx?name=prosecutor+opens+investigation+in+the+central+african+republic&ln=en&lan=en-GB.

IGAD *Agreement on the Resolution of the Conflict in the Republic of South Sudan* (Addis Ababa 17 August 2015).

IGAD *Revitalized Agreement on the Resolution of the Conflict in the Republic of South Sudan (R-ARCSS)* (Addis Ababa 12 September 2018).

ICG *Making the Central African Republic's Latest Peace Agreement Stick*, Africa Report N°277 (Nairobi/Brussels 18 June 2019) https://d2071andvip0wj.cloudfront.net/277-making-cars-latest-peace-agreeement-stick.pdf.

Jale, R 'Cabinet Approves Establishment of Hybrid Court' *Eye Radio* 30 January 2021 https://eyeradio.org/cabinet-approves-establishment-of-hybrid-court/.

Katshung, JY 'Prosecution of Grave Violations of Human Rights in Light of Challenges of National Courts and the ICC: The Congolese Dilemma' (2006) 7 *Human Rights Review* 5.

Kersten, M 'On the Rebirth of Hybrid Tribunals' *Justice in Conflict* 22 January 2016 https://justiceinconflict.org/2016/01/22/on-the-rebirth-of-hybrid-tribunals/.

Kiir, S & Machar, R 'South Sudan Needs Truth, not Trials' *The New York Times* 7 June 2016 https://www.nytimes.com/2016/06/08/opinion/south-sudan-needs-truth-not-trials.html.

Kindiki, K 'Prosecuting the Perpetrators of the 1994 Genocide in Rwanda: Its Basis in International Law and the Implication for the Protection of Human Rights in Africa' (2001) 1 *African Human Rights Law Journal* 64.

Labuda, PI 'UN Peace Operations: Tracking the Shift from Peacekeeping to Peace Enforcement and State Building' *EJIL: Talk!* 2 September 2015 https://www.ejiltalk.org/un-peace-operations-tracking-the-shift-from-peacekeeping-to-peace-enforcement-and-state-building/.

Labuda, PI 'The Special Criminal Court in the Central African Republic-Failure or Vindication of Complementarity?' (2017) 15 *Journal of International Criminal Justice* 175.

Labuda, PI 'The Special Criminal Court in the Central African Republic' (22 January 2018) 22 *ASIL Insights* https://www.asil.org/insights/volume/22/issue/2/special-criminal-court-central-african-republic.

Labuda, PI 'Open for Business': The Special Criminal Court launches investigations in the Central African Republic', *EJIL: Talk*! 8 February 2019 https://www.ejiltalk.org/open-for-business-the-special-criminal-court-launches-investigations-in-the-central-african-republic/.

Landsman, S 'Alternative Responses to Serious Human Rights Abuses: Of Prosecution and Truth Commissions' (1996) 59 *Law & Contemporary Problems* 81.

Lipscomb, R 'Restructuring the ICC Framework to Advance Transitional Justice: A Search for a Permanent Solution in Sudan' (2005) 106 *Columbia Law Review* 182.

May, L *Crimes Against Humanity: A Normative Account* (Cambridge: Cambridge University Press 2005).

Mccormick, TY & O'grady, S 'The New York Times Op-ed That Wasn't' *Foreign Policy* 9 June 2016 https://foreignpolicy.com/2016/06/09/the-new-york-times-south-sudan-op-ed-that-wasnt/.

Mednick, S 'Nearly 400,000 'Excess Deaths' Caused by South Sudan War' *AP News* 26 September 2018 https://apnews.com/4f5a8681027c4ee7894289c058805b3e/Nearly-400,000-'excess-deaths'-caused-by-South-Sudan-war.

Memorandum d'entente entre la Mission Multidimensionnelle intégré e des Nations Unies pour la stabilization en République centrafricaine et le Gouvernement de la République centrafricaine, signed 5 August, Ms. Isabelle Gaudeuille, Minister of Justice, 5 August 2014 and Mr. Babacar Gaye, Special Representative of Secretary General (7 August 2014), https://www.fidh.org/IMG/pdf/mou_minusca_-_rca_concernant_la_cps.pdf.

Minow, M *Between Vengeance and Forgiveness: Facing History After Genocide and Mass Violence* (Boston: Bacon Press, 1998).

Ngari, A & Mahdi, M 'Missteps by South Sudan's Government Keeps the Country in Conflict' 27 April 2021 https://issafrica.org/iss-today/missteps-by-south-sudans-government-keep-the-country-in-conflict?utm_source=BenchmarkEmail&utm_campaign=ISS_Weekly&utm_medium=email.

Njoroge, ASK *Report on the Status of Implementation of the Revitalized Agreement on the Resolution of the conflict in the Republic of South Sudan for the Period 1 January to 31 March 2020, Report No. 006/20* (Juba South Sudan 2020).

Oduro, F 'Reconciling a Divided Nation Through a Non-Retributive Justice Approach: Ghana's National Reconciliation Initiative' (2005) 9 *International Journal of Human Rights* 327.

PBS News Hour 'Kerry Makes Emotional Appeal to South Sudan's Warring Leaders' 4 May 2015 https://www.pbs.org/newshour/world/kerry-makes-emotional-appeal-south-sudans-warring-leaders.

Ratner, SR & Abrams, JS *Accountability for Human Rights Atrocities in International Law: Beyond the Nuremberg Legacy* (2nd edn.) (Oxford: Oxford University Press 2001).

Republique Centrafricaine, 'Loi organique portant creation, organization et fonctionnement de la Cour penale special, Loi no. 15/003' (3 June 2015), https://www.fidh.org/IMG/pdf/loi_organique_portant_creation_organisation_et_fonctionnement_de_la_cps.pdf.

Snyder, J & Vinjamuri, L 'Trials and Errors: Principle and Pragmatism in Strategies of International Justice' (2003–2004) 28 *International Security* (2003–2004) 5.

South Sudan Civil Society Forum et al. 'Letter to the AU Peace and Security Council regarding the session on South Sudan' (15 July 2020) https://www.hrw.org/news/2020/07/15/letter-au-peace-and-security-council-regarding-session-south-sudan.

Takpiny, B 'South Sudan Approves Establishment of Hybrid Court' 30 January 2021 https://www.aa.com.tr/en/africa/south-sudan-approves-establishment-of-hybrid-court/2127899.

UN Human Rights Council 'Despite Renewed Political Commitment, Staggering Levels of Violence Continued Across South Sudan for the Second Successive Year, UN Experts Note' (19 February 2021) https://www.ohchr.org/EN/HRBodies/HRC/Pages/NewsDetail.aspx?NewsID=26761&LangID=E.

UN Human Rights Council 'Report of the Commission on Human Rights in South Sudan, A/HRC/40/69' (21 February 2019) https://www.securitycouncilreport.org/atf/cf/%7B65BFCF9B-6D27-4E9C-8CD3-CF6E4FF96FF9%7D/A_HRC_40_69.pdf.

UN Security Council 'Report of the Secretary General of the UN on the situation in Central African Republic, UN Doc. S/2013/261 (3 May 2013)' (2013) https://undocs.org/S/2013/261.

UN Security Council 'Resolution 2149 (2014) Adopted by the Security Council at its 7153rd Meeting, on 10 April 2014, S/Res/2149 (2014)' (10 April 2014) https://undocs.org/S/RES/2149 (2014).

UN Security Council 'Letter dated 14 February 2019 from the Secretary-General Addressed to the President of the Security Council, S/2019/145' (15 February 2019) https://reliefweb.int/sites/reliefweb.int/files/resources/S_2019_145_E.pdf.

UN Security Council 'Central African Republic-Report of the Secretary-General, S/2020/545' (16 June 2020) https://undocs.org/S/2020/5455.

UN Security Council 'Situation in South Sudan-Report of the Secretary-General, S/2020/890' (9 September 2020) https://undocs.org/S/2020/890.

US Department of Justice 'Consulting Contract Agreement' (2 April 2019) https://efile.fara.gov/docs/6667-Exhibit-AB-20190418-2.pdf.

US Department of Justice 'Consulting Contract Agreement' (7 May 2019) https://efile.fara.gov/docs/6667-Exhibit-AB-20190507-3.pdf.

Wright, Q (1949) 'International Law and Guilt by Association' (1949) 43 *American Journal of International Law* 746.

Yak, NL 'Kerry Reiterate Formation of Hybrid Court on South Sudan' *Ngokland* 5 May 2015 http://www.ngokland.com/kerry-reiterate-formation-of-hybrid-court-on-south-sudan/.

Zalaquett, J 'Confronting Human Rights Violations Committed by Former Governments: Principles Applicable and Political Constraints' in Kritz, NJ (ed) *Transitional Justice: How Emerging Democracies Reckon with Former Regimes* (vol. 1) (Washington: United States Institute for Peace 1995).

A Critical Assessment of the International Crimes Division of the High Court of Uganda

Josephine Ndagire

1 Introduction

The duty to prosecute "international crimes" domestically is a relatively recent endeavour.[1] Indeed, the adoption of the Rome Statute of the International Criminal Court (Rome Statute), in the early 2000s, and the novel concept of "complementarity" that it embodies, introduced the idea of prosecuting conflict-related crimes at the national level.[2] While this is an important step in the fight against impunity for the most heinous crimes, the majority of national criminal systems were

[1] C Meinicke "Domestic Prosecution of International Crimes-Africa" *Public International Law Policy Group*, 15 May 2019.

[2] SDD Bachmann & EL Nwibo, "Pull and Push- Implementing the Complementarity Principle of the Rome Statute of the ICC within the AU: Opportunities and Challenges" (2018) 43 *Brooklyn Journal of International Law* 457.

J. Ndagire (✉)
School of Law, Makerere University, Kampala, Uganda
e-mail: josephine.ndagire@mak.ac.ug

E. C. Lubaale and N. Dyani-Mhango (eds.), *National Accountability for International Crimes in Africa*,
https://doi.org/10.1007/978-3-030-88044-6_12

not designed with these crimes in mind.[3] As such, efforts to that end are often met with tremendous legal and structural barriers. Before the advent of the contemporary international criminal system, the doctrine of state sovereignty shielded offenders in war/conflict from external prosecution.[4] The common practice was to prosecute offenders—often, members of the national army in a military tribunal under martial law. Indeed, states resented the idea of extending outside jurisdiction to their nationals.[5] International law only had jurisdiction over crimes of an "international character". In essence, crimes of an international character were committed between "lawful combatants", that is, combatants acting on behalf of a state. The Geneva Conventions and Additional Protocols, thereto, make very little reference to crimes of an unlawful nature, that is, crimes committed by unlawful combatants.

The evolution of war—from conflict between states—to conflicts between states and militias, rebel groups or terrorist organizations, posed significant accountability challenges. Because the categories outlined above are not regarded as lawful combatants in international law, to the extent that they neither carry arms openly nor have a known and legally recognized structure, as prescribed. As a new field, international criminal law (ICL) seeks to primarily regulate these unlawful combatants. Under ICL, individuals are personally responsible for the crimes they commit.[6] By design, the International Criminal Court (ICC) exercises jurisdiction over the most responsible, and in other cases, if the state is unwilling or unable to prosecute the perpetrators.[7] Hence, the jurisdiction of the ICC is complementary to that of states.[8] While this arrangement is the most

[3] R Dicker & H Duffy "National Courts and the ICC" (1999) 6(1) *Brown Journal of World Affairs* 53.

[4] G Roberts "Assault on Sovereignty: The Clear and Present Danger of the New International Criminal Court" (2001) 17(1) *American University International Law Review* 35.

[5] N Hogan "State Sovereignty in the Post-Cold War Era" (2012) *E-International Relations*, available at https://www.e-ir.info/2012/07/01/state-sovereignty-in-the-post-cold-war-era/.

[6] E Greppi "The Evolution of Individual Criminal Responsibility Under International Law" (1999) 81 (835) *International Review of the Red Cross* 531.

[7] S Song "The Role of the International Criminal Court in Ending Impunity and Establishing the Rule of Law" *UN Chronicle* available at https://www.un.org/en/chronicle/article/role-international-criminal-court-ending-impunity-and-establishing-rule-law.

[8] As above.

reasonable and logical, because states have the primary duty to prosecute crimes committed on their territory, national legal systems were generally not designed to prosecute international crimes. Decades after Rome Statute of the International Criminal Court (Rome Statute) came into force; several states still lack the capacity to prosecute international crimes, despite being party.[9] The Rome Statute does not provide a definition of ***unwillingness or inability*** to prosecute, although some indicators have been articulated over the years, including the length of the trial, victim participation and inclusivity.[10]

At the regional level, the African Union (AU) is intent on safeguarding the constitutional order, stability and integrity of its member states.[11] This, in essence, includes protecting sitting heads of state on the continent from prosecution by the ICC.[12] This assertion is contested, and divergent views argue that the idea of a regional criminal court preceded the ICC indictment of Bashir.[13] This notwithstanding, the events preceding the adoption of the Malabo Protocol, and the politics of the day, suggest otherwise. It should be noted that the Malabo Protocol needs at least 30 ratifications by members of the AU and is yet to come into force.

National legal systems face several legal and structural barriers to prosecution of international crimes. While several state parties to the Rome Statute have enacted legislation that would allow for the prosecution of international crimes, the structures within which these laws must work are not aligned.[14] As such, the police, prosecution, investigators, and judiciary face significant constraints, when dealing with international crimes.[15] It is therefore not uncommon for international crimes to be treated as ordinary crimes, and to be investigated and prosecuted, as such.

[9] EY Omorogbe "The Crisis of International Criminal Law in Africa: A Regional Regime in Response?" (2019) 66 *Netherlands International Law Review* 287.

[10] P Hobbs "The Catalysing Effect of the Rome Statute in Africa: Positive Complementarity and Self-Referrals" (2020) 31 *Criminal Law Forum* 345.

[11] n 9 above.

[12] K Mills '"Bashir Is Dividing Us": Africa and the International Criminal Court' (2012) 34 *Human Rights Quarterly* 404.

[13] VO Nmehielle "'Saddling' the New African Regional Human Rights Court with International Criminal Jurisdiction: Innovative, Obstructive, Expedient?" (2014) 7 *African Journal of Legal Studies* (2014) 7, 8.

[14] n 9 above.

[15] n 9 above.

This tendency undermines the essence of international crimes and the very reason why they are categorized as such. International crimes are a grave affront to interests protected by international law and must be accorded such seriousness. This distinction calls for a separate form of accountability processes and mechanisms.

At the peak of the conflict in Northern Uganda, it was apparent that the heinous crimes could not go unpunished. While the leadership of the rebel group was referred to the ICC by the government, there was need to ensure accountability for thousands more. This chapter provides insight into the workings of the ICDHC. Part 1 embodies an introduction; Part 2 discusses the concept of individual criminal responsibility; Part 3 examines prosecution of international crimes domestically, while Part 4 considers the specific case of Uganda and the plausibility of prosecution of international crimes. Part 5 discusses the *Kwoyelo case*.

2 Individual Criminal Responsibility Under International Law

In the aftermath of the First World War, there were unanimous calls for the prosecution of perpetrators of international crimes, particularly, German military officials. Consequently, the Versailles Peace Treaty and Regulations (Versailles Treaty) set out to ensure some form of accountability for atrocities committed by the Germans. At this point, international crimes were not clearly articulated but nonetheless, Article 227 set up a mechanism to prosecute German's former emperor of "\'a supreme offence against international morality and the sanctity of treaties". Both offences were proscribed but largely vague and unknown. In a similar fashion, Article 228, bestowed upon states, powers to prosecute perpetrators of war crimes in military tribunals.

An expert body (Commission on the Responsibilities of the Authors of War and on Enforcement of Penalties) was tasked with enforcing individual criminal liability for war crimes. A report issued by this Commission held individuals personally liable for crimes against humanity, specifically, rape, massacres and torture, as well as war crimes. The prosecution of individuals was left to Germany. In reality, Germany only prosecuted 12 individuals and convicted six. This, despite the fact the report of the Commission implicated 20,000 individuals.

It is only after the Second World War that individual responsibility for international crimes took hold. The establishment of the International

Military Tribunal (Nuremberg Tribunal) and the International Military Tribunal for the Far East (Tokyo Tribunal), by the allied powers, was a watershed moment in international law. Article 6 of the Charter of the Nuremberg Tribunal, for instance, bestowed upon the Tribunal, over persons who, in the interest of the European Axis states and acting either as individuals or members of organizations, perpetrated crimes of an international nature (Article 6 (a)-(c)). It is these tribunals that cemented the concept of individual responsibility for international crimes. Indeed, the argument by the accused that the subjects of international law are states, and not individuals, was rejected outright. States would no longer be held vicariously liable for the acts of men. In response, the Nuremberg Tribunal famously declared, "[T]hat international law imposes duties and liabilities upon individuals as well as upon States has long been recognized. Crimes against international law are committed by men, not by abstract entities, and only by punishing individuals who commit such crimes can the provision of international law be enforced".[16] This declaration, along with others, was embodied in what came to be known as, "Principles of International Law Recognized in the Charter of the Nuremberg Tribunal and the Judgment of the Tribunal"[17] (Nuremberg Principles). The declaration relating to individual responsibility for international crimes is, Principle 1, and is to the effect, "Any person who commits an act which constitutes a crime under international law is responsible therefore and liable to punishment".

The principle of individual criminal responsibility is, today, a matter of customary international law.[18] However, despite this momentous milestone in international law, the post-Second World War tribunals did not address the individual criminal responsibility of non-state actors. All those prosecuted by the Nuremberg and Tokyo tribunals had committed crimes in an official capacity, either as members of the armed forces or some other official designated role. This matter was raised by the International Law Commission in 1996. The International Law Commission Draft Code

[16] Trial of the Major War Criminals before the International Military Tribunal, vol. I, Nuremberg 1947, page 223.

[17] Text of the Nuremberg Principles Adopted by the International Law Commission, A/CN.4/L.2, Extract from the Yearbook of the International Law Commission: - 1950, vol. II.

[18] Y Tan, "The Identification of Customary Rules in International Criminal Law" (2018) 34(2) *Utrecht Journal of International and European Law*, pp. 92–110, 92.

of Crimes against the Peace and Security of Man-kind expounded the principle of individual criminal responsibility, by expressly articulating the *personal* responsibility of *any* individual for international crimes.

The onslaught of brutal conflicts within states in recent decades hastened the need for a permanent international criminal court. Prior to its establishment, the world had witnessed atrocities of a magnitude comparable to the world wars. In Rwanda, Cambodia, Sierra Leone, Yugoslavia and East Timor, heinous crimes such as genocide, crimes against humanity and war crimes were committed in modern times. Although hybrid (Sierra Leone) and internationalized judicial mechanisms—the International Criminal Tribunal for the former Yugoslavia (ICTY) and the International Criminal Tribunal for Rwanda (ICTR), this model proved unsustainable, particularly, in terms of associated expenses.[19] With conflicts brewing in Sudan, Uganda, the Democratic Republic of the Congo, Central African Republic and elsewhere, the actualization of a criminal court of an international nature seemed timely. The establishment of the ad hoc tribunals (ICTY and ICTR) coincided with the process leading to the establishment of the ICC. It should be noted that calls for the establishment of a permanent criminal court preceded the world wars,[20] although the UN first acknowledged the need for the court in 1948.[21] Efforts by the International Law Commission on a permanent criminal court continued on and off, until 1994. And the Ad Hoc Committee on the Establishment of the International Criminal Court met two times in 1995.

The United Nations Security Council resolutions that established both the ICTY and ICTR clearly articulated the principle of individual criminal responsibility for state and non-state actors, alike. Article 1 of the ICTY Statute established the jurisdiction over natural persons responsible for serious violations of international humanitarian law committed in the territory of former Yugoslavia since 1991. Under Article 6(1) of the ICTR

[19] See, D Wippman "The Costs of International Justice" (2006) 100 (4) *The American Journal of International Law* 861.

[20] C Remigius "United States Objection to the International Criminal Court: A Paradox of—Operation Enduring Freedom" (2003) 9 *Annual Survey of International & Comparative Law* 19, 23.

[21] UN General Assembly, *Convention on the Prevention and Punishment of the Crime of Genocide*, 9 December 1948, United Nations, Treaty Series, vol. 78, p. 277, available at: https://www.refworld.org/docid/3ae6b3ac0.html [accessed 14 December 2020].

Statute, individual responsibility is vested on a person who planned, instigated, ordered, committed, aided or abetted the planning, execution or preparation of an international crime. The principle of Individual Criminal Responsibility was further crystallized by the Rome Statute which articulated that liability for a crime is solely based on conduct of an individual through its commission and the other modes of participation [ordering, instigation, aiding and abetting] are accessory individual liabilities.[22] Therefore, Section 6 of the High Court (International Crimes Division) Practice Directions of 2011 doesn't come as a shock to Uganda when it also introduces individual criminal responsibility for those who have committed serious crimes in Uganda. This is because there is enough precedent that has been established over the years through the UNSC and the ICC.

3 Prosecution of International Crimes Domestically

States can exercise universal jurisdiction over international crimes. International crimes are so heinous and threaten the international order that their proscription is a matter of consensus.[23] States, in fact, have a duty to do so. The duty to prosecute perpetrators of international crimes forms part of customary international law.

The duty to prosecute can be traced to several major conventions such as the Convention on the Prevention and Punishment of the Crime of Genocide (Genocide Convention).[24] States undertake to punish and prevent genocide in Article 1. Article 6 of the Genocide Convention states perpetrators of genocide "shall be tried by a competent tribunal of the State in the territory of which the act was committed, or by

[22] See Article 25 (1) of the ICC Statute. See also, Eduardo, Greppi, "The Evolution of Individual Criminal Responsibility Under International Law" *IRRC*, vol. 8, No. 835, September 1999.

[23] A Slaughter "Defining Limits: Universal Jurisdiction and National Courts" *Universal Jurisdiction: National Courts and The Prosecution of Serious Crimes Under International Law*, vol. 196 (Stephen Macedo, ed. 2006). See, also, PJCS van der Oije "A Surinam Crime Before a Dutch Court: Post-Colonial Injustice or Universal Jurisdiction?" (2001) 14(2) *Leiden Journal of International Law* 455, 457.

[24] UN General Assembly, *Convention on the Prevention and Punishment of the Crime of Genocide*, 9 December 1948, United Nations, Treaty Series, vol. 78, p. 277, available at: https://www.refworld.org/docid/3ae6b3ac0.html [accessed 7 December 2020].

such international penal tribunal as may have jurisdiction".[25] Clearly, the Genocide Convention establishes a duty to prosecute acts of genocide by a state on whose territory the crimes were committed. The International Court of Justice has interpreted this provision to include jurisdiction by other states.[26] In *Bosnia and Herzegovina v. Serbia and Montenegro*, the International Court of Justice opined that states have a duty to prevent genocide, which is "normative and compelling". It has been argued that the duty to prosecute under the Genocide Convention is a norm of jus cogens.[27] In Article IV, the Genocide Convention makes no exception to prosecutions and specifically lists "rulers, public officials or private individuals".[28] To ensure accountability for genocide, states must enact laws that allow for its prosecution domestically (Article V). Article 146 of Geneva Convention IV reiterates this provision in Article 146 and asserts that states have a duty to prosecute persons alleged to have committed grave breaches, regardless of their nationality.[29]

Similarly, the United Nations Convention against Torture and Other Cruel Inhuman or Degrading Treatment or Punishment, 1984 (UNCAT), establishes universal jurisdiction over torture and similar acts (Articles 5, 14). Article 2 (1) of UNCAT requires states to "... take effective legislative, administrative, judicial or other measures to prevent acts of torture in any territory under its jurisdiction". States must extradite perpetrators or submit their cases to competent authorities for prosecution (Article 7).

Despite the International Covenant on Civil and Political Rights (ICCPR), not explicitly establishing a duty to punish rights violations,

[25] Article 6, Genocide Convention.

[26] *Bosnia and Herzegovina v. Serbia and Montenegro (Application of the Convention on the Prevention and Punishment of the Crime of Genocide)* Judgment, 26 February 2007 [2007] ICJ 2.

[27] See, LA Steven "Genocide and the Duty to Extradite or Prosecute: Why the United States is in Breach of Its International Obligations" (1998–1999) 39 *Virginia Journal of International Law* 425. See also, O Ben-Naftali & M Sharon "What the ICJ did not say about the Duty to Punish Genocide: The Missing Pieces in a Puzzle" (2007) 5(4) *Journal of International Criminal Justice* 859.

[28] Principles of international cooperation in the detention, arrest, extradition and punishment of persons guilty of war crimes and crimes against humanity General Assembly adopted resolution 3074 (XXVIII).

[29] D Orentlicher "Settling Accounts: The Duty to Prosecute Human Rights Violations of the Prior Regime" (1991) 100 *Yale Law Journal* 2537, 2561.

the Human Rights Committee has interpreted state duties under the Covenant to include investigation and punishment of human rights violations.[30] In addition, the Principles of International Co-operation in the Detection, Arrest, Extradition and Punishment of Persons Guilty of War Crimes and Crimes against Humanity (Principles of International Co-operation) require states to take measures to prevent and punish international crimes and to cooperate in their prosecution (Principles 3 and 4). Principle 1 establishes a duty to investigate, arrest, prosecute and punish persons alleged to have committed war crimes and crimes against humanity.[31] The Principles of International Co-operation specifically require investigation, prosecution and punishment to take place in the country where the crimes were committed (Principle 5).

The duty to prosecute international crimes is entrenched in the Rome Statute. Starting in the Preamble, the Rome Statute proclaims that every state has a duty to exercise criminal jurisdiction over perpetrators of international crimes (Paragraph 6). Kreicker argues that Paragraph 6 only re-affirms an existing duty to prosecute international crimes—a customary international law obligation.[32] Indeed, Paragraph 6 reads in full, "*Recalling* that it is the duty of every State to exercise its criminal jurisdiction over those responsible for international crimes...", which presupposes an existing duty. Still, Paragraph 4 of the Preamble reiterates the seriousness of international crimes and besieges states to take measures at the national level to ensure that such crimes are punished. In this respect, the Rome Statute lays the foundation for its complementarity in Paragraph 10.[33] The term complementarity, while not defined by the Rome Statute, has been the subject of immense discussion in scholarly literature.[34] The gist of the principle is that the role of the

[30] Article 2 (1) Convention against Torture and Other Cruel, Inhuman or Degrading Treatment or Punishment (CAT), see also, Article 5, CAT.

[31] Principles of international co-operation in the detection, arrest, extradition and punishment of persons guilty of war crimes and crimes against humanity, Adopted by General Assembly resolution 3074 (XXVIII) of 3 December 1973.

[32] H Kreicker "National Prosecution of International Crimes from a Comparative Perspective: The Question of Genocide" (2005) 5 *International Criminal Law Review* 313.

[33] See, JD Van der Vyver, "Personal and Territorial Jurisdiction of the International Criminal Court" (2000) 14 *Emory International Law Review* 1, 66.

[34] Seils Paul, "Handbook on Complementarity; An Introduction to the Role of National Courts and the ICC in Prosecuting International Crimes." *International Center for Justice*

ICC is secondary to that of domestic courts or national jurisdiction.[35] In contrast, specialized international tribunals have primary jurisdiction over crimes they were established to prosecute and could, in fact, take over a case before a domestic court.[36]

That states have a duty to prosecute international crimes committed on their territory is now a matter of international consensus. Increasingly, this duty is being interpreted as not only applicable to the state on whose territory an international crime is committed, but other states, too. The duty to prosecute must be undertaken in a manner consistent with international law. Hence, international crimes must not be prosecuted as domestic crimes. Claims about sovereignty of a state and its prerogative to prosecute international crimes in accordance with its own laws cannot hold—if such laws do not conform to the global understandings of genocide, crimes against humanity, war crimes and aggression.

4 Legal Basis for Prosecution of International Crimes

A former protectorate of Britain, Uganda, too has a common law heritage and follows the tradition of judicial precedent. As in most common law jurisdictions, international law is not directly enforceable, unless "domesticated" or incorporated into domestic law by an Act of Parliament.[37] States, however, have a duty to align their laws with international law

Transformation available at: https://www.ictj.org/complementarity-icc/ see also, Sarah, Nouwen, "Complementarity in Uganda: Domestic Diversity or International Imposition?" Cambridge University Press, pp. 1120–1154 available at: https://doi.org/10.1017/CBO9781316134115.047.

[35] n 30 above.

[36] JJ Llewellyn & S Raponi, "The Protection of Human Rights Through International Criminal Law: A Conversation with Madam Justice Louise Arbour, Chief Prosecutor of the International Criminal Tribunals for the Former Yugoslavia and Rwanda" (1999) 57(1) *University of Toronto Faculty Law Review* 83, 94–95 cited in JJ Llewellyn "A Comment on the Complementarity Jurisdiction of the International Criminal Court: Adding Insult to Injury in Transitional Contexts?" (2001) 24 *Dalhousie Law Journal* 192, 194.

[37] Speech of the Honourable AG. Chief Justice at the Official Opening of the Round Table Discussion for Judges from the East African Region and Southern Sudan, July 29, 2010.

and to interpret their laws in accordance with the international law.[38] Objective XXVIII (b) of the National Objectives and Directive Principles of State Policy of the Constitution of the Republic of Uganda (Constitution) call for an alignment of foreign policy with international obligations, including treaty obligations.[39]

Uganda accented or ratified several international instruments that proscribe international crimes, including the Genocide Convention on November 14, 1995; Geneva Conventions of 1949 on May 18, 1964; the Additional Protocol (I) to the Geneva Conventions of 1977 on March 13, 1991; Additional Protocol (II) to the Geneva Conventions of 1977 on March 13, 1991; Optional Protocol on the involvement of children in armed conflict, on May 6, 2002 (with a declaration on the minimum age of recruitment); Additional Protocol (III) to the Geneva Conventions of 2005 on May 21, 2008; Rome Statute on June 14, 2002; and the OAU Convention on Mercenaries on July 2, 2004.

The process of domesticating the International Criminal Court Act (ICC Act) began in 2004. The delays and controversies surrounding its tabling in the floor of Parliament for debate raised questions about the government's commitment to prosecute international crimes. Interestingly, prior to its enactment, the government referred the situation in Northern Uganda to the ICC, causing the indictment of the LRA top leadership, including rebel leader, Joseph Kony. The ICC Act was eventually enacted on June 25, 2010, around the time Uganda was hosting the ICC Review Conference in Kampala. Among its aims is the enforcement of the Rome Statute in Uganda (Section 2 (a)) and "to make further provision in Uganda's law for the punishment of the international crimes of genocide, crimes against humanity and war crimes" (Section 2 (c)). The latter provision presupposes that there was already provision in Ugandan law to prosecute and punish international crimes.[40]

[38] H Onoria, "Application of International Law in Domestic Courts: Perspectives from Practice, Round Table Discussion for Judges from the East African Region and Southern Sudan," July 29, 2010, 21.

[39] Objective XXVIII (b) of the National Objectives provides that the—the foreign policy of Uganda shall be based on the principles of—(b) respect for international law and treaty obligations.

[40] Under Section 2 of the International Criminal Court Act, other purposes include arrest and surrender of persons to the ICC; enabling the courts in Uganda to try international crimes; provision of various forms of assistance to the ICC; enabling the ICC to conduct proceedings in Uganda; and enforcement of ICC sentences.

As such, the ICC Act effectively submerges international criminal law into Uganda's criminal law.[41] Under Section 3, it defines an international crime, as "a crime in respect of which the ICC has jurisdiction under article 5 of the Statute". This, in essence includes genocide, crimes against humanity, war crimes and aggression. Uganda may exercise jurisdiction over nationals or persons employed by Uganda; persons who commit an offence against citizens or permanent residents of Uganda; and persons present in Uganda after committing an offence (universal jurisdiction) (Section 8, ICC Act). Sections 4 and 5 of the ICC Act adopt aspects of Part 2 of the Rome Statute relating jurisdiction, applicable law and admissibility. Interestingly, Article 21 of the Rome Statute, which falls under Part 2, states that the applicable law includes "... applicable treaties and the principles and rules of international law, including the established principles of the international law of armed conflict". The "principles and rules of international law' unmistakably refer to customary international law.

Although the Director of Public Prosecutions must sanction charges in ordinary trials (offences of a non-international character), the law allows private prosecutions, which the DPP may take over. However, with regard to the international crimes, the DPP must *always* consent to all prosecutions (Section 17, ICC Act). In that respect, a person suspected of committing international crimes can only be arrested and remanded but no further action is permitted without the express consent of the DPP. This provision is significant in several ways. First, the DPP is a political appointee and head of prosecutions in Uganda. Secondly, international crimes are political in nature and motivated by political reasons. Thirdly, and more important, Uganda government and army officials are alleged to have committed international crimes themselves. So, the insistence on the DPP's consent before prosecutions can be instituted is telling. This appears to be the first step of the ICC Act to shield would-be accused persons.

[41] Human Rights Network (Uganda), "Analysis of the International Criminal Court Bill (No. 10/2004) in the Context of Uganda's Obligations under the Statute of the International Criminal Court," January 17, 2005. See also, H Singh "Crimes Against Humanity Draft Bill of 2009: The International Implications of Addressing Impunity Through National Legislation" (2010–2011) 17 *ILSA Journal of International & Comparative Law* 23.

The practicability of complementarity in the Uganda case is complicated, at best. The ICC Act notoriously excludes Article 27 of the Rome Statute. Article 27 of the Rome Statute subjects all persons to the Rome Statute, without exemptions. The Rome Statute specifically singles out heads of state or government, representatives to a legislative body and other elected officials or government officials. In addition, official capacity cannot be a ground for mitigating a sentence. Read together, Section 17 ICC Act and the omission of Article 27 of the Rome Statute effectively shield the president and other high-ranking officials from prosecution. In terms of Article 17 of the Rome Statute, it would appear that Uganda demonstrated unwillingness to try high-ranking civilian and military officials, or at the very least, seeks to manage and/or influence prosecutorial decisions. To complicate the situation further, the Amnesty Act shields several perpetrators from prosecution.[42] The decade-long trial of Thomas Kwoyelo for acts committed as part of the LRA espoused several challenges related to prosecution of international crimes in Uganda.

5 Analysis of the *Thomas Kwoyelo* Case

Since inception, the ICDHC has only heard one case related to the war in Northern Uganda. A colonel in the LRA, Thomas Kwoyelo was captured in March 2009 while in the Democratic Republic of the Congo and handed over to the Ugandan forces. In 2010, he was charged with 12 counts under the Fourth Geneva Conventions Act, including wilful killing, taking hostages and extensive destruction of property in Northern Uganda. His trial started on the July 11, 2011. The Prosecution submitted an amended charge sheet with 53 alternative charges under the Penal Code Act—Uganda's criminal code. The amended charge sheet included offences, such as murder contrary to Sections 188 and 189, kidnap with intent to murder contrary to Section 243(1) (a), robbery with aggravation contrary to Sections 285 and 288 of the Penal Code Act.

[42] AKA Greenawalt "Complementarity in Crisis: Uganda, Alternative Justice, and the International Criminal Court" (2009) 50 *Virginia Journal of International Law* 107. His Worship Asiimwe Tadeo, "Effecting Complementarity; Challenges and Opportunities: A Case Study of the International Crimes Division of Uganda" 30 July 2012, pages 1–10. See also, Katherine A. Marshall "Prevention and Complementarity in the International Criminal Court: A Positive Approach" (2010) 17(2) *Human Rights Brief* 21.

No charge was brought under the ICC Act of 2010 because all crimes Kwoyelo allegedly committed took place before it was enacted.

Article 3, common to the four Geneva Conventions, covers situations of non-international armed conflicts. These types of conflicts include civil wars, internal armed conflicts that spill over into other states or internal conflicts in which third state intervenes. A number of rules and principles contained in the four Geneva Conventions of 1949 also exist under customary law. As part of customary international law, these rules and principles are applicable to all states. In addition to Common Article 3, the prosecution could have relied on customary international law. Customary international law has historically played a very significant role in domestic systems, especially in regard to filling gaps in domestic law.[43] In many legal systems, customary international law is also invoked to interpret domestic law. Since the ICC Act domesticates the Rome Statute, the crimes proscribed therein are crimes under customary international law. Unfortunately, customary international law is largely unknown in the Uganda legal system.

The Kwoyelo trial has been impeded by significant delays, for various reasons. The trial was halted pending reference to the Constitutional Court in respect of the constitutionality of his trial.[44] The reference culminated into an appeal to the Supreme Court of Uganda.[45] This took close to 4 years as his pre-trial started in 2016. To date, the trial is ongoing with no clear indication as to when judgement will be delivered. As May 2021, the trial has lasted about ten years. This therefore raises questions of due process in respect of this particular case. Efficiency in justice dispensation is a great component of a fair trial. Article 28 (1) of the Constitution of Uganda requires a fair and speedy hearing in all criminal and civil matters.[46] However, what constitutes a speedy trial is no

[43] H Vallikivi "Domestic Applicability of Customary International Law in Estonia" (2002) VII *Juridica International* 28, available at: http://www.juridicainternational.eu/public/pdf/ji_2002_1_28.pdf, last accessed May 13, 2021. See also, D Sloss & M Van Alstine "International Law in Domestic Courts" (2015), available at: http://digitalcommons.law.scu.edu/facpubs/889, last accessed, May 16, 2021, also available in W Sandholtz & CA Whytock (eds) *Research Handbook on the Politics of International Law* (2017) 79.

[44] *Thomas Kwoyelo alias Latoni v. Uganda*, Constitutional Court, Constitutional Petition No. 36/2011.

[45] *Uganda v. Thomas Kwoyelo alias Latoni*, Constitutional Appeal, No. 1/2012.

[46] Article 28, Constitution of the Republic of Uganda, 1995.

defined in law. This notwithstanding, ten years is an unreasonable period of time for both Kwoyelo and the victims.

The law on amnesty allows rebels who renounce and abandon involvement in the war or an armed rebellion to receive amnesty. The Amnesty Act defines "amnesty" to mean a pardon, forgiveness, exemption or discharge from criminal prosecution or any other form of punishment by the state.[47] It was aimed at encouraging members of the LRA to abandon hostilities. Over 12,000 LRA members have applied and have been granted amnesty since the enactment of the Amnesty Act in 2000. The Amnesty Act violates Uganda's international obligations because amnesties for genocide, war crimes and crimes against humanity are inconsistent with international law, which mandates that such crimes should be punished.

Kwoyelo applied for amnesty while in prison, but the Director of Public Prosecutions (DPP) did not respond to his request. He petitioned the Constitutional Court arguing that the Amnesty Act was implemented in a discriminatory manner in contrary to the Constitution. The Constitutional Court established that there was discrimination against Kwoyelo.[48] The Attorney General appealed against the decision in the Supreme Court. The Supreme Court clarified that the amnesty does not apply to offences (grave breaches) Kwoyelo was charged with, and that the DPP was under no obligation to give reasons for not certifying an individual for amnesty. There are two aspects to the role of the Director of Public Prosecutions. Where the DPP investigates and is satisfied that the offence is eligible for amnesty under Section 2, he or she may issue a certificate for grant of amnesty. However, if the DPP is not satisfied that the offences committed do not fall under the Amnesty Act, he or she may certify and may commence prosecution proceedings against that person.[49]

6 A Critical Review of the International Crimes Division

Following a referral of the conflict in Northern Uganda to the ICC, the Court issued indictments against the LRA leadership. The indictments

[47] Section 2, Amnesty Act.

[48] n 44, *above*.

[49] n 45.

coincided with negotiations between the LRA and the Uganda government. During the negotiations, the ICC indicted the LRA top leaders. The indictments quickly became a sticking point in the negotiations, with the LRA threatening to withdraw from the negotiation process, unless they were dropped.[50] It is against this backdrop that the government agreed to establish a mechanism to try the LRA.[51] The negotiations culminated into Juba Agreement on Accountability and Reconciliation and its Annexure (Juba Agreement). The Agreement on Accountability and Reconciliation which was signed on June 29, 2007, was intended to prevent impunity and promote redress in accordance with the Constitution and International Obligations in connection with the requirements of the Rome Statute. The Preamble to the Juba Agreement highlights the importance of local judicial processes as central to the principle of complementarity in the Rome Statute, made provision for local trials. The Preamble of the Juba Agreement makes a reference to the principle of complementarity and the need for appropriate justice mechanisms including customary processes.[52] The Juba Agreement specifically makes provision for civil and criminal accountability mechanisms (Clause 4.1).

In a bid to establish criminal accountability mechanisms, the International Crimes Division of the High Court (formerly War Crimes Division) was established by an administrative decree in 2008. Legal Notice Number 10 of 2011 (Legal Notice 10) extended the jurisdiction of the International Crimes Division of the High Court, without prejudice to Article 139 of the Constitution, under Section 6, to include any offence related to genocide, crimes against humanity, war crimes, terrorism, human trafficking, piracy and any other international crimes as provided for by the Penal Code Act, the Geneva Conventions Act, International Criminal Court Act or under any penal enactment.[53] Article 139(1) of the Constitution provides that the High Court shall have unlimited original jurisdiction in all matters, subject to the provisions

[50] Open Society Foundations "Putting Complementarity into Practice: Domestic Justice for International Crimes in DRC, Uganda, and Kenya" January 2011, available at:http://www.soros.org/initiatives/justice/articles_publications/publications/comple mentarity-in-practice20110119/putting-complementarity-into-practice-20110120.pdf.

[51] n 47, *above*.

[52] Sections 3 - 4 Preamble to the Juba Agreement on Accountability and Reconciliation (Juba Agreement).

[53] High Court (International crimes Division) Practice Direction, 2011 para 6.

of the Constitution (the ICDHC is a specialized division of the High Court).

6.1 ICDHC Structure

The ICDHC sits as a bench of three judges in war crimes proceedings but there are five judges appointed to the ICDHC.[54] The judges are appointed by the Principal Judge in consultation with the Chief Justice.[55] There is the head of Division and a registrar for administration.[56] It has been noted that there is a rotation of registrars and judges almost every two years and four years, respectively, at the ICDHC.[57] Blakely argues that job rotation is costly in the long run and causes entities to suffer.[58] This is very visible with the impact created by rotation of staff at the ICDHC which has resulted in numerous trainings of different staff members on matters of law hence making victims weary of waiting for justice.[59] The judges that constitute the court are not appointed full-time to its work. For instance, the pre-trial judge has to combine her task with her daily management of the Mbale High Court. Changes in quorum of the bench that hears the Kwoyelo case are confusing and lead to misinterpretation of evidence and inconsistencies in important aspects such as the demeanour of the accused and the witnesses.

This raised a concern on the ability of the ICDHC to comply with international standards in international crimes. In 2016, a pre-trial

[54] K McNamara "Seeking Justice in Ugandan Courts: Amnesty and the Case of Kwoyelo" (2013) 12(3) *Washington University Global Studies Law Review* 653. Currently, these Judges hold different positions in other divisions of the High Court and they include: Justice Steven Mubiru who is the Resident Judge at Gulu, Justice Jane Kiggundu, Justice Duncan Gaswaga who is also the Deputy Head of the Commercial Division and Justice Michael Elubu who is the Acting Head of the Civil Division.

[55] ICDHC Practice Directions, para 4 and 5.

[56] Kenyans For Peace, Wise Truth and Justice, "Domestic Prosecution of International Crimes, Lessons for Kenya."

[57] S Nakandha "Complementarity Reality Check: The Case of Uganda's International Crimes Division" *International Justice Monitor*, June 21, 2020 Also accessed at www.ijmonitor.org.

[58] RB Gray "5 Advantages and Disadvantages of Job Rotation Program" accessed at www.patriotsoftware.com.

[59] Lady Justice Susan Okalany "Specialized Teams in the investigation, prosecution and Judgment of International Crimes; The Ugandan Experience" 3rd July 2019.

judge granted Kwoyelo's alleged victims the right to participate at all stages of the proceedings. This followed international standards where victim participation is integral to the trials. However, victim participation requires access to technical and material resources. Despite efforts from the civil society activists and development partners, these resources remain limited and largely unavailable.[60]

The ICC on the other hand is composed of 18 Judges who are elected to a 9-year term in office by the Assembly of State Parties to the Rome Statute. These Judges usually have moral character integrated with impartiality and integrity.[61] These Judges have an established competence in criminal law and procedure equipped with the necessary experience in the relevant areas of International Humanitarian Law and Human Rights Law.[62] The Judges' election is by secret ballot at a meeting of the ASP convened for that purpose. Because of the nature of the Court, the judges are barred from indulging in activities which may alternate their judicial functions or question their confidence in their independence.[63]

Matters before the ICDHC are instituted by the Office of the Director of Public Prosecutions.[64] This office has the International Crimes Department, formerly the War Crimes and Anti-Terrorism Section, which, specifically, handles prosecution of international crimes.[65] Appeals from the ICDHC lie to the Court of Appeal as a first appellate Court and the Supreme Court of Uganda as the final appellate Court.[66] Since its inception, the ICDHC has not registered any appeal relating to war crimes basically because it hasn't yet passed a decision on war crimes and crimes against humanity.

The office relies heavily on support from other government agencies and NGOs during interviews and very underequipped in terms of human

[60] R Ravet "Thomas Kwoyelo in Uganda: Victim's Participation Brings Hope and Challenges" https://www.ijmonitor.org/2018/10/thomas-kwoyelo-in-uganda-victims-participation-brings-hope-and-challenges/ accessed on 12th December 2020.

[61] The Bangalore Principles of Judicial Conduct.

[62] International Criminal Court, "The Judges of the Court," available at www.icc-cpi.int.

[63] n59 above.

[64] Article 120 (3) of the Constitution of the Republic of Uganda, 1995, as amended.

[65] Accessed at www.dpp.go.ug. Also see KPTJ, *above*.

[66] Article 132 and 134 of the Constitution of the Republic of Uganda, 1995 as amended.

resource and funding.[67] Investigations are carried out by the Criminal Investigation Department (CID) of the Ugandan Police Force. Senior police officers address ICDHC-related investigations.[68] This arrangement has adversely affected the efficiency of the office in executing its mandate. In the trial of Kwoyelo, the wheels of justice are slowed by numerous delays related to insufficient funding of the court process. Heavy reliance on external support compromises the efficacy and consistency of the office in its operations.

The Rome Statute establishes the Office of the Prosecutor which is equipped with approximately 380 staff members in different fields: the legal profession, investigators, analysts, psycho-social experts, individuals with experience in diplomacy and international relations.[69] The office has three complementary divisions which help advance its mandate, and they include jurisdiction, complementarity and the cooperation division whose core mandate is to carry out preliminary examinations and issue advice on issues of jurisdiction as well as admissibility and external relations with the OTP. The investigation division issues protection policies and investigates crime and analysis. The OTP benefits from the services of approximately 380 dedicated staff members from over 80 countries, including members of the legal profession, investigators and analysts, psycho-social experts, public information and communication and more.[70] The OTP is therefore adequately staffed to execute its mandate under Article 42 of the Rome Statute. This contrast depicts an ill-equipped department ready to take on one of the most decried and heinous atrocities against humanity, yet so unready pausing a serious and unsettling question of what if the system works against the victims?

An accused has a right to a private lawyer or one provided under the state brief system. Lawyers on state brief are usually instructed late in the process, allowing little time for preparation of a defence, contrary to constitutional guarantees on due process (Article 28 Constitution). In

[67] Interview with Lino Anguzu, Head, International Crimes Department, Office of the Director of Public Prosecutions.

[68] Human Rights Watch, Justice for Serious Crimes before National Courts; Uganda's International Crimes Division, at: https://www.hrw.org/sites/default/files/reports/uganda0112ForUpload_0.pdf, last accessed, June 4, 2021.

[69] Articles 13-14 Rome Statute.

[70] Office of the Prosecutor, available at: https://www.icc-cpi.intl/about/otp, last accessed, June 4, 2021.

cases before the ICDHC, thorough investigations must be undertaken by both the prosecution and defence; however in the latter case, the scarcity of funds renders this impossible.[71] This generally calls into question the ability of the ICDHC to conduct a fair hearing. It should be noted that at the ICC, the defence is independent, although it benefits from the services of the registry, to enable adequate preparation by the defence.

6.2 *Rules of Procedure*

Victim participation is central to proceedings before the ICC (Article 68 Rome Statute).[72] The high probability of re-victimizing survivors justifies the need to protect their mental health.[73] Therefore, the acknowledgement of victims' rights is among the greatest achievements advanced by the ICC.[74] This was aimed at taking victims' interests and views into consideration during trial.[75] Such interests, views and concerns may be presented by the legal representative of the victims in accordance with the Rules of Procedure and Evidence. Victims are those who have suffered harm as a result of the commission of any crime within the jurisdiction of the court. These may include individual people, but also organizations or

[71] Nakandha (n57 above) the defence counsel Caleb Alaka stated that he took up Thomas Kwoyelo's case 9 years ago purely on a Pro-bono Basis and on a humanitarian ground because he had seen children soldiers in his home area run away from camps to join the streets since the streets were easier compared to being a child soldier in a camp.

[72] Article 68 of the Rome Statute. See also, H Olasolo and A Kiss "The Role of Victims in Criminal Proceedings before the International Criminal Court" (2010) 81 *International Review of Penal Law* 126.

[73] "Developments in Law-International Criminal Law II: The Promises of International Prosecution" (2001) 114(7) *Harvard Law Review* 1943, 1957, 1972, 1980–1983.

[74] PV Gonzalez "The Role of Victims in International Criminal Court Proceedings: Their Rights and the First Rulings of the Court" (2006) 5 *International Journal on Human Rights* 19.

[75] S SaCouto "Victim Participation at the International Criminal Court and the Extraordinary Chambers in the Courts of Cambodia: A Feminist Project" (2012) 18 *Michigan Journal of Gender and Law* 297, accessed at https://repository.law.umich.edu/mjgl/vol18/iss/2. See also Rule 85 of the ICC Rules of Procedure and Evidence on the definition of a victim, as a natural person who has suffered harm as a result of the commission of a crime or an organization or institution that has sustained direct harm to any of their property which is dedicated to religion, education, art or science or charitable purposes and historic monuments for humanitarian purposes.

institutions that have sustained direct harm to property dedicated to religion, education, art, sciences or charitable purposes, and to their historic monuments, hospitals, and other places and objects for humanitarian purposes.[76] The victims through their legal representative can then attend and participate in the hearings, make opening and closing statements and intervene on how best they can be compensated. This is enabled by the Office of the Public Counsel for Victims.[77] In the Lubanga case, the Trial Chamber noted that victims have very general and wide-ranging interests and in being allowed to express their concerns, protecting their dignity and ensuring their safety is paramount.[78] The responsibility for the right to protection lies with all the organs of Court.[79]

The ICDHC Rules of Procedure and Evidence provide for the rights to protection and information but are silent on the right to participate fully at the pre-trial stage.[80] Pre-trial judge considers the status of victims (Rule 6(2) (e)) and as per Rule 7(1)(c), can issue orders for protection and privacy of victims on his or her own motion or upon request by the Prosecution. It is commendable that the Rules consider victim protection at this early stage. However, the victims' right to protection also encompasses the need to be consulted on the necessity and details of protection.[81] In the Kwoyelo case, the ICDHC invoked ICC Rules of

[76] Victims, available at: https://www.iccc-cpi.int/about/victims (last accessed on 12 December 2020).

[77] L Moffet "Victims at the ICC-Who's Representing Who?", available at: https://justiceinconflict.org/2015/05/05/victims-at-the-icc-whos-representing-who/, last accessed, May 24, 2021.

[78] *The Prosecutor v Thomas Lubanga Dyilo*, ICC-01/04-01/06. See Article 68(1) of the Rome Statute which assigns the responsibility for witness protection to the Court as a whole, "The Court shall take appropriate measures to protect the safety, physical and psychological well-being, dignity and privacy of the victims and witnesses. In doing so, the Court shall have regard to all relevant factors including age, gender, health and the nature of the Crime...."

[79] Gonzalez (n74 above).

[80] Article 68(3) of the Rome Statute grants victims the right to participate before the International Criminal Court by allowing their views and concerns to be advanced at various stages of the proceedings including the pre-trial stage.

[81] Uganda International Crimes Division (ICD) Rules 2016: Analysis on Victim Participation Framework, final version August 2016 pg 3.

Procedure and Evidence to enable victims to participate fully in all the stages of the case.[82]

The ICDHC is expected to take into consideration the interests of the victims.[83] It must be noted that for the victims to be allowed to participate in the proceedings, they ought to apply to the registrar of the ICD through a letter expressing their interest to do so. The registrar is then mandated to refer the victims to a list of lawyers maintained at the registry or suggest one or more common legal representative. It is then up to the judges to apportion time for victim participation as the proceedings go on. The ICC on the other hand has "The Victims Participation and Reparation Section which assists and facilitates victims" access to the ICC.[84] It equally serves as an entry point for victims' applications to participate in the proceedings. This Section presents a victims' report at the commencement of the investigations to the Pre-Trial Chamber. It is the judges of the ICC who will examine each application and decide whether or not the applicant is entitled to participate in ICC proceedings and at what stages; it is also for the judges to decide which applicants are entitled to receive reparations in case of a conviction.[85] ICDHC is not conscious of the importance of victims' participation, which perhaps explains the general hostility of witnesses and victims to formal justice. In contrast, the preferred traditional justice mechanisms are highly participatory and inclusive.

The protection of the identity of witnesses and victims is fundamental in criminal proceedings, especially, for political/international crimes.[86] The duty to put in place protective measures for victim protection is

[82] Lady Justice Susan Okalany, "Specialized Teams in the Investigation, Prosecution and Judgment of International Crimes: The Ugandan Experience", 3rd July 2019.

[83] Rule 35 of the ICD Rules. See also Clause 8 of the Agreement on Accountability and Reconciliation.

[84] REDRESS, "Victim Participation at the International Crimes Division in Uganda-Stakeholder Roundtable Report", 16th and 17 January 2017.

[85] Victims before the International Criminal Court: "A guide for the participation of victims in the proceedings of the ICC," pg 16.

[86] REDRESS, "Victim Participation at the International Crimes Division in Uganda-Stakeholder Roundtable Report", 16 and 17 January 2017, *above*, Victim Protection measures include expunging names and identifying information from Court records, testimonies under pseudonyms, electronic facial distortion, voice distortion and closed sessions.

central to criminal justice.[87] The ICC established the Victims and Witness Unit to protect and support the victims and witnesses.[88] Uganda is yet to get a Witness Protection Program, having tabled the Witness Protection Bill of 2015 numerous times before the Parliament without success. The bill envisages the creation of a Witness Protection Agency.[89] In 2019, the Office of the Director of Public Prosecutions launched the Witness Protection Guidelines whose mandate is to ensure that prosecution witnesses and victims are protected from harm or threat during proceedings.[90] However, these guidelines are directory and not mandatory as there is no enabling national law.

6.3 Evidentiary Matters

Once an accused person is committed to trial before the ICDHC, the trial is prepared through a series of hearings at the pre-trial stage. The pre-trial hearing includes the disclosure of the evidence by the prosecution to the defence. The Evidence Act guides evidentiary hearings in Uganda and it places the burden of proof beyond reasonable doubt on the prosecution in criminal matters (Section 101).[91] It is worth noting that evidence before the ICDHC must either be direct evidence, followed by circumstantial evidence and hearsay according to the Rules of Procedure and Evidence.[92] However, these rules work best in circumstances where there is individual commission of a crime. These same rules of evidence have not been proved to work effectively in trying war crimes and crimes against humanity because of the command responsibility.

[87] UNODC, "Victim Assistance and Witness Protection", available at www.unodc.org, See also "Prosecutor v. Katanga and Ngudjolo" ICC-01/04-01/07-475 (13 May 2008) pages 13–14 where the Appeals Chamber determined that the obligation to protect extends to all persons at risk by the investigation of the Prosecutor.

[88] Article 43(6) of the Rome Statute, See also, Mackay Fiona, "Victim Participation in Proceedings before the International Criminal Court" (2008) 15(3) *Human Rights Brief* 2.

[89] Olive Nakatude, *Expedite Witness Protection Bill-Law Reform Commission*, n.d.

[90] The Witness Protection Guidelines, 2019, See also Guideline 3.6.

[91] Section 101 of the Evidence Act Cap 6.

[92] Circumstantial evidence is often the best evidence as it is evidence of surrounding circumstances which by intensified examination is capable of proving a proposition with the accuracy of mathematics. See *Thaika v. Republic* [2006] EA 362.

For evidence to be admitted before the ICC, it must satisfy the test of relevance, probative value and absence of prejudicial effect.[93] The Bangladesh War Crimes Tribunal was not strictly bound by technical rules when considering evidence.[94] There is need for the ICDHC to relax evidentiary requirements for international crimes. Kwoyelo was charged with both ordinary crimes and crimes under the ICC Act, including murder. Proof of murder under the Penal Code Act requires that evidence must be adduced that there was death of a person, which was unlawfully caused with malice aforethought by the accused person.[95] Again, in the context of conflict, this requirement seems rigid and impractical. In the first place, victims or survivors may not know where the body of the deceased person was buried, especially, where they are abducted and moved from place to place, in unfamiliar territory. The abductees of the LRA moved between remote parts of Uganda and South Sudan. Secondly, victims or survivors may not recall such minute details due to trauma. It is therefore important to acknowledge these peculiarities and to apply evidentiary rules with appropriate modification.

Identification of an accused person is a core rule of evidence in Uganda. Identification is the process through which a witness or a victim is able to recognize a suspect from a group of people as the alleged perpetrator of a crime. This is normally done through an identification parade which is carried out at the police station. This process involves parading a suspect with a number of other similar looking persons to be identified by the victim or witness sequentially. Pertinent to note is that identification parades are held as a means of corroborating any identification claim made by the victim or witness.[96] However, to be able to identify the suspect/accused, the witness or victim should have identified them at the scene of the crime. This therefore requires that some factors have to be taken into consideration, for example, the length of time of commission of the offence, time the offence was committed, as well as proximity and

[93] N Mehandra and A Koenig "Open Source Evidence and the International Criminal Court" (2019) *Harvard Human Rights Journal*, 15 April 2019, available at https://harvardhrj.com/2019/04/open-source-evidence-and-the-international-criminal-court/.

[94] Section 19(1) of the International Crimes Tribunal Rules of Evidence.

[95] Section 188 of the Penal Code Act, Cap 120, See Article 7(1) (a) of the Rome Statute.

[96] *Mubangizi v. Uganda* (Criminal Appeal No. 0012 of 2012), See also, *Bogere Moses & another v. Uganda* SCCA No. 1 of 1997.

relationship between the identifier and the accused.[97] Where any of the listed factors is not fulfilled, it becomes very hard to point to the participation of the accused in the crime. This rule is not practical for trials before the ICDHC, for several reasons, especially in the light of the fact that international crimes are prosecuted decades after cessation of hostilities. Specifically, in the case of Northern Uganda, the raids were conducted by masked raiders in the night, and in villages that they were unknown.[98]

7 Conclusion

The duty to prosecute international crimes precedes contemporary international law. It is a solid norm under customary international law. This duty has been articulated and interpreted over the years. The Rome Statute has been instructive to that end. Prosecutions of international crimes domestically must meet international standards. Indeed, in addition to the ability to prosecute international crimes, states must demonstrate a genuine willingness to do so. In part, this willingness may be demonstrated by enacting legislation to prosecute these crimes and establishing an appropriate mechanism. The critical factor, however, is to ensure that these mechanisms are functional, and well resourced, in terms of staffing and facilities. In addition, these mechanisms must be situated in an enabling or friendly environment. While Uganda established a mechanism to adjudicate international crimes and enacted a law to enable the prosecution thereof, in real terms, the mechanism faces significant structural and systemic hurdles.

The jurisdiction of the ICDHC is not only limited in terms of the crimes it can hear—crimes committed after 25 June 2010, it is also facing restrictions on who can appear before it. The ICC Act seemingly increases the power of the DPP and removes any possibility of private prosecutions. Arguably, the ICC Act appears to shield high-ranking officials from the jurisdiction of the ICDHC, including the head of state. It is therefore of little surprise that no official of the Uganda government has been investigated or charged before the ICDHC, despite credible evidence pointing towards the involvement of the regime in the commission of international

[97] *Abdallah Nabulele & Anor v. Uganda* (CA No.9 of 1978).

[98] Human Rights Watch, "Abducted and Abused: Renewed War in Northern Uganda", 15 July 2003, A1512, available at: https://www.refworld.org/docid/45dac8872.html, accessed 12 December 2020.

crimes during the war. Be that as it may, only one member of the LRA, Kwoyelo, has been charged before the ICDHC. And the trial has lasted several years, despite it being the only case being handled in that realm.

The aforementioned issues coupled with the frequent rotation of judges weaken the functionality of the ICDHC. Each time a judge who has benefitted from training is moved to another court, the ICDHC moves a step backward. Staff, including judicial officers, should serve at the court on permanent terms or a reasonable fixed period to avoid unnecessary disruptions.

The absence of a victim and witness protection mechanism or avenues that allow victims an active role in the proceedings raises doubt as to the ability of the ICDHC to meet the demands of justice, expected of crimes of this nature. While the 2019 Guidelines on Witness Protection are an important first step, witness protection, particularly for international crimes, should be a matter of policy and law.

Finally, as the trial of Kwoyelo draws to conclusion, there are reservations about the manner in which it has been conducted. It also remains to be seen whether the ICDHC will hear more cases, including those of government officials. It is only after the ODPP demonstrates impartiality and vigilance in prosecuting LRA-related crimes, that Uganda can be said to be fulfilling its responsibility to prosecute international crimes.

References

A Liang, "International Criminal Court Is 'Hunting' Africans" *Daily Telegraph*, 27 May 2013.

Abdallah Nabulele & Anor v. Uganda *(CA No.9 of 1978)* [1978] UGCA 14 (5 December 1978).

Alexander KA Greenawalt, Complementarity in Crisis: "Uganda, Alternative Justice, and the International Criminal Court" 50 *Virginia Journal of International Law* 107 (2009).

Anna Macdonald & Holly Porter, The Trial of Thomas Kwoyelo: "Opportunity or Spectre? Reflections from the Ground on the First LRA Prosecution" *Africa* 86, no. 4 (2016).

Anne-Marie Slaughter, "Defining the Limits: Universal Jurisdiction and National Courts" University of Pennsylvania Press, 2004. Available at http://www.upenn.edu/penpress [accessed on 12 December 2020]

Application of the Convention on the Prevention and Punishment of the Crime of Genocide (Bosnia and Herzegovina v. Yugoslavia (Serbia and Montenegro)); Order of the Court on Provisional Measures, *International*

Court of Justice (ICJ), 13 September 1993. Available at https://www.refworld.org/cases,ICJ,3ae6b6721c.html [accessed on 17th December 2020].

Attorney General v. Suzan Kigula and 417 others, *Constitutional Appeal No. 3 of 2006*, Uganda: Supreme Court, 21 January 2009.

Barker v. Wingo, *407 U.S 514* (1972).

Bogere Moses & another v. Uganda, *Uganda Legal Information Institute* (Criminal Appeal No. 1 of 1997) [1998] UGHC 15 (6 July 1998).

Cleo Meinicke, "Domestic Prosecution of International Crimes-Africa" *PILPG* May 15, 2019

David Wippman, "The Costs of International Justice" *The American Journal of International Law* 100, no. 4 (2006). Available at https://doi.org/10.1017/S00029300000319 [accessed on 19 December 2020].

"Developments in Law-International Criminal Law II: The Promises of International Prosecution" 114 *Harvard Law Review* 1957, 1972 (2000). Available at https://doi.org/10.2307/1342499 or https://www.jstor.org/stable/1342499 [accessed on 16 December 2020].

Diane Orentlicher. "Settling Accounts: The Duty to Prosecute Human Rights Violations of the Prior Regime" 10 *Yale Law Journal* 100, no. 8 (1991): 2537–2615. Available at https://doi.org/10.2307/796903 or https://www.jstor.org/stable/796903 [accessed on 4 December 2020].

Dr. Heike Gramckow & Barry Walsh, "Developing Specialized Court Services, International Experience and Lessons Learned" *Justice and Development Working Paper Series* 24/2013 World Bank, Washington DC. Available at https://openknowledge.worldbank.org/handle/10986/16677 [accessed on 17 December 2020].

Edoardo Greppi, "The Evolution of Individual Criminal Responsibility under International Law" *International Review of the Red Cross, no. 835*. Available at www.icrc.org.

EY Omorogbe, "The Crisis of International Criminal Law in Africa: A Regional Regime in Response?" *Netherlands International Law Review* 66, 287–311. Available at https://doi.org/10.1007/s40802-01900143-5.

Fiona Mackay, "Victim Participation in Proceedings before the International Criminal Court" *Human Rights Brief* 15, no. 3 (2008): 2–5.

"Genocide and the Duty to Extradite or Prosecute: Why the United States is in Breach of Its International Obligations" 39 *Virginia Journal of International Law* 425 (1998–1999) [accessed on 29 December 2020].

Guy Roberts, "Assault on Sovereignty: The Clear and Present Danger of the New International Criminal Court" *American University International Law Review* 17, no. 1 (2000): 35–77.

Hannes Vallikivi, "Domestic Applicability of Customary International Law in Estonia". Available at http://www.juridicainternational.eu/public/pdf/ji_2002_1_28.pdf.

Hansdeep Singh, "Crimes Against Humanity Draft Bill of 2009: The International Implications of Addressing Impunity Through National Legislation" 17 *ILSA Journal of International and Comparative Law* 23.

Hector Olasolo & Alejandro Kiss, "The Role of Victims in Criminal Proceedings Before the International Criminal Court" *International Review of Penal Law* 81 (2010).

Helmut Kreicker, "National Prosecution of International Crimes from a Comparative Perspective, The Question of Genocide" 5, 2003.

Henry Onoria, "Application of International Law in Domestic Courts: Perspectives from Practice, Round Table Discussion for Judges from the East African Region and Southern Sudan" July 29, 2010.

His Worship Asiimwe Tadeo, "Effecting Complementarity; Challenges and Opportunities: A Case Study of the International Crimes Division of Uganda" 30 July 2012 https://www.icrc.org/en/doc/resources/documents/misc/customary-law-q-and-a-150805.htm.

Human Rights Network (Uganda), "Analysis of the International Criminal Court Bill (No. 10/2004) in the Context of Uganda's Obligations Under the Statute of the International Criminal Court" January 17, 2005.

Human Rights Watch, "Abducted and Abused: Renewed War in Northern Uganda" 15th July 2003, A1512. Available at https://www.refworld.org/docid/45dac8872.html [accessed on 12 December 2020].

Human Rights Watch, "Justice for Serious Crimes Before National Courts; Uganda's International Crimes Division" at www.hrw.org.

International Crimes Division High Court Practice Directions.

International Criminal Court, "The Judges of the Court." Available at www.icc-cpi.int.

JD Van der Vyver, "Personal and Territorial Jurisdiction of the International Criminal Court" 14 *Emory International Law Review* 1 (2000).

JJ Llewellyn & S Raponi, "The Protection of Human Rights Through International Criminal Law: A Conversation with Madam Justice Louise Arbour, Chief Prosecutor of the International Criminal Tribunals for the Former Yugoslavia and Rwanda" 57 *University of Toronto Faculty of Law Review* 83 (1999).

James Nyawo, "Right to a Fair Trial in the International Criminal Accountability: Are the Judges at the ICC Charming the Critics?" *Knowledge Platform Security & Rule of Law.*

Jennifer J Llewellyn, A Comment on the Complementarity Jurisdiction of the International Criminal Court: Adding Insult to Injury in Transitional Contexts? 24 *Dalhousie Law Journal* 192, 194.

JLOS, "International Crimes Division: Frequently Asked Questions" *Journal of International Criminal Justice* 5, no. 4 (September 2007). Available at www.jlos.go.ug.

Katherine A Marshall, "Prevention and Complementarity in the International Criminal Court: A Positive Approach" *Human Rights Brief* 17, no. 2 (2010).

Kenyans For Peace, Wise Truth and Justice, "Domestic Prosecution of International Crimes, Lessons for Kenya" *KPTJ*. Available at media.africaportal.org [accessed on 3 December 2020].

Kristy McNamara, "Seeking Justice in Ugandan Courts: Amnesty and the Case of Kwoyelo" 12 *Washington University Global Studies Law Review* 653 (2013). Also available at https://openscholarship.wustl.educ/law_globalstudies/vol12/iss3/19 [accessed on 6 December 2020].

Lady Justice Susan Okalany, "Specialized Teams in the Investigation, Prosecution and Judgment of International Crimes; The Ugandan Experience" *Working Group on the Fight Against Impunity in Africa*, National Assembly of Gambia, 3rd July 2019. Available at www.pgaction.org [accessed on 9 December 2020]

Looking Beyond Amnesty and Traditional Justice and Reconciliation Mechanisms in Northern Uganda: A proposal for Truth Telling and Reparations, 28 B.C. *Third World Quarterly* 345, 357 (2008).

Luke Moffet, "Victims at the ICC-Who's Representing Who?" 2014 *Justice in Conflict*. Available at justiceinconflict.org.

Mubangizi v. Uganda (*Criminal Appeal No. 0012 of 2012)*

Mehandra Nikita & Koenig Alex, "Open Source Evidence and the International Criminal Court" *Harvard Human Rights Journal*, April 15, 2019. Available at harvardhrj.com.

Nigel Hogan, "State Sovereignty in the Post-Cold War Era" *E-International Relations* (2012).

Office of the Prosecutor https://www.icc-cpi.intl/about/otp.

OHCHR Uganda Thematic Briefing Note: "A Step Towards Abolition in Uganda; Assessing the Implications of the Law Revision (Penalties in Criminal Matters) Miscellaneous Amendment Act, 2019."

Olive Nakatude, "Expedite Witness Protection Bill-Law Reform Commission" *URN*, 27 April 2018. Available at https://ugandaradionetwork.net or www.parliament.go.ug [accessed on 3 December 2020].

Open Society Foundations, "Putting Complementarity into Practice: Domestic Justice for International Crimes in DRC, Uganda, and Kenya" *Open Society Foundations*, January 2011. Available at www.justiceinitiative.org [accessed on 19 December 2020].

OrnaBen-Naftali, Miri Sharon, "What the ICJ Did not Say About the Duty to Punish Genocide: The Missing Pieces in a Puzzle" *Journal of International Criminal Justice* 5, no. 4 (September 2007). Available at https://doi.org/10.1093/jicj/mqm041 [accessed on 29 December 2020].

P Hobbs, "The Catalysing Effect of the Rome Statute in Africa: Positive Complementarity and Self-Referrals" *Crim Law Forum* 31 (2020): 345–376. Available at https://doi.org/10.1007/s10609-020-09398-7.

Paulina V Gonzalez, "The Role of Victims in International Criminal Court Proceedings: Their Rights and the First Rulings of the Court" *International Journal on Human Rights*, no. 5 (2006).

Pita JC Schimmelpenninck van der Oije, "A Surinam Crime Before a Dutch Court: Post-Colonial Injustice or Universal Jurisdiction?" *Leiden Journal of International Law* 14, no. 2 (2001) [accessed on 2 December 2020].

Principles of International Cooperation in the Detention, Arrest, Extradition and Punishment of Persons Guilty of War Crimes and Crimes Against Humanity General Assembly Adopted Resolution 3074 (XXVIII).

Prosecutor v. Jean-Pierre Bemba *ICC-01/05-01/08.*

Prosecutor v. Katanga and Ngudjolo *ICC-01/04-01/07-475* (13 May 2008).

R v. Askov *[1990]2 SCR 1199.*

Rachel B. Gray, "5 Advantages and Disadvantages of Job Rotation Program." Available at www.patriotsoftware.com [accessed on 15 December 2020].

REDRESS, "Uganda International Crimes Division (ICD) Rules 2016: Analysis on Victim Participation Framework, Final Version" August 2016. Available at redress.org [accessed on 14 December 2020].

REDRESS, "Victim Participation at the International Crimes Division in Uganda-Stakeholder Roundtable Report", 16th and 17th January 2017. Available at redress.org [accessed on 16 December 2020].

Remigius Chibueze, "United States Objection to the International Criminal Court: A paradox of Operation Enduring Freedom" 9 *Annual Survey of International & Comparative Law* 19, 23.

Richard Dicker and Helen Duffy, "National Courts and the ICC" *Brown Journal of World Affairs* 6, no. 1. Available at https://www.jstor.org/stable/245 90221.

Romain Ravet, "Thomas Kwoyelo in Uganda: Victim's Participation Brings Hope and Challenges." Available at https://www.ijmonitor.org/2018/10/ thomas-kwoyelo-in-uganda-victims-participation-brings-hope-and-challenges/ [accessed on 12 December 2020].

"Rwanda's Paul Kagame Accuses ICC of Bias Against Africa" *Aljazeera*, 29 April 2018. Available at https://www.aljazeera.com/news/2018/04/rwanda-kag ame-accuses-icc-bias-africa-180429050656022.html.

Sarah Nouwen, "Complementarity in Uganda: Domestic Diversity or International Imposition?" Cambridge University Press, pp. 1120–1154. Available at https://doi.org/10.1017/CBO9781316134115.047.

Sascha Dominik D. Bachmann & Eda L. Nwibo, "Pull and Push- Implementing the Complementarity Principle of the Rome Statute of the ICC within the AU: Opportunities and Challenges" 43 *Brooklyn Journal of International Law* 457 (2018). Available at https://brooklynworks.brooklaw.edu/bjil/vol43/iss 2/10.

Seils Paul, "Handbook on Complementarity; An Introduction to the Role of National Courts and the ICC in Prosecuting International Crimes" *International Center for Justice Transformation*. Available at https://www.ictj.org/complementarity-icc/.

Sharon Nakandha, "Complementarity Reality Check: The Case of Uganda's International Crimes Division" *International Justice Monitor*, June 21, 2020. Available at www.ijmonitor.org [accessed on 30 November 2020].

Song Sang-Hyun, "The Role of the International Criminal Court in Ending Impunity and Establishing the Rule of Law" *UN Chronicle*. Available at www.un.org.

Susan SaCouto, "Victim Participation at the International Criminal Court and the Extraordinary Chambers in the Courts of Cambodia: A Feminist Project" 18 *Michigan Journal of Gender & Law* 297 (2012). Available at https://repository.law.umich.edu/mjgl/vol18/iss/2 [accessed on 5 December 2020].

Text of the Nuremberg Principles Adopted by the International Law Commission, A/CN.4/L.2.

The Bangalore Principles of Judicial Conduct, 2002. Available at www.un.org.

The Constitution of the Republic of Uganda, 1995 as amended.

The Evidence Act Cap 6.

The High Court (International Crimes Division) Practice Direction, 2011.

The International Crimes Tribunal Rules of Procedure and Evidence of the Former Yugoslavia.

The International Criminal Court Act, 2010.

The International Criminal Court Rules of Procedure and Evidence.

The Juba Agreement on Accountability and Reconciliation (Juba Agreement), *United Nations Security Council*, 29/06/2007. Available at www.securitycouncilreport.org [accessed on 2 December 2020].

The New Vision Newspaper, "Judge Faults War Crimes Court" *The New Vision Newspaper*, July 5, 2011. Available at http://www.newvision.co.ug/D/8/12/759378.

The Prosecutor V Thomas Lubanga Dyilo, *ICC-01/04-01/06*.

The Witness Protection Guidelines, 2019. Available at www.dpp.go.ug or www.jlos.go.ug.

Trial of the Major War Criminals Before the International Military Tribunal, vol. I, Nuremberg 1947.

Uganda Law Reform Commission; *Development Model Law on Amnesty for Uganda*.

Uganda v. Thomas Kwoyelo (Constitutional Appeal No. 10 of 2012*) [2015] UGSC* 5 (8 April 2015) [accessed on 4 December 2020].

Uganda: "Q&A on the Trail of Thomas Kwoyelo" July 7, 2011, accessed on www.hrw.org.

UN General Assembly, Convention against Torture and Other Cruel, Inhuman or Degrading Treatment, 10 December 1984, *United Nations*, Treaty Series, vol. 1465, p. 85. Available at https://www.refworld.org/docid/3ae6b3a94.html [accessed on 21 December 2020].

UN General Assembly, Principles of International Co-operation in the Detention, Arrest, Extradition and Punishment of Persons Guilty of War Crimes and Crimes Against Humanity, 3 December 1973 A/RES/3074(XXVIII). Available at https://refworld.org/docid/3b00f1c034.html [accessed on 17 December 2020].

UN General Assembly, "Convention on the Prevention and Punishment of the Crime of Genocide" 9 December 1948, United Nations, Treaty Series, vol. 78, p. 277. Available at https://www.refworld.org/docid/3ae6b3ac0.html [accessed on 14 December 2020].

Universal Jurisdiction: National Courts and The Prosecution of Serious Crimes Under International Law, vol. 196 (Stephen Macedo, ed. 2006).

UNODC, "Victim Assistance and Witness Protection", Accessed at www.unodc.org

Victims Before the International Criminal Court: "A Guide for the Participation of Victims in the Proceedings of the ICC" *International Criminal Court*. Available at https://www.iccc-cpi.int/about/victims [accessed on 12 December 2020].

Vision Reporter, "Judge Faults War Crimes Court" *The New Vision Newspaper*, July 5, 2011. Available at http://www.newvision.co.ug/D/8/12/759378 [accessed on 31 November 2020].

X. v. France. *European Court of Human Rights Application No. 18020/91*

Y Tan, "The Identification of Customary Rules in International Criminal Law" *Utrecht Journal of International and European Law* 34, no. 2 (2018) [accessed on 17 November 2020].

Wild Goose Chase, or a Quest for Genuine Prosecution? Lessons from Uganda's Ongoing Trial of Thomas Kwoyelo

Daniel Ronald Ruhweza

1 Introduction

The trial of Kwoyelo (*Kwoyelo Trial*), also known as *Latoni*, has been central to the justice versus peace debate in Uganda.[1] The trial has been problematised by several factors both external and internal which have inadvertently affected the judicial process by exponentially prolonging

[1] For a detailed discussion on the peace vs. Justice debate, see Unpublished: Ruhweza, Daniel Ronald (2016) '*Situating the Place for Traditional Justice Mechanisms in International Criminal Justice: A Critical Analysis of the Implications of the Juba Peace Agreement on Reconciliation and Accountability.*' *Unpublished*, thesis, University of Kent (KAR id:56,646); See, for example, Katy Glassborow, 'See Peace Versus Justice in Uganda: Can the International Criminal Court's Demand That Ugandan Rebel Leaders Face Trial Coexist with the Need to Achieve a Workable Peace Deal?' *Special Report, Institute for War and Peace Reporting*, available at https://iwpr.net/global-voices/peace-versus-justice-uganda, last accessed 16 June 2021.

D. R. Ruhweza (✉)
Department of Law and Jurisprudence, School of Law, Makerere University, Kampala, Uganda

E. C. Lubaale and N. Dyani-Mhango (eds.), *National Accountability for International Crimes in Africa*,
https://doi.org/10.1007/978-3-030-88044-6_13

it.[2] The resultant narrative has therefore been one of a flawed incapacitated justice system as advanced by several authors for its failure, firstly to successfully prosecute Thomas Kwoyelo in a timely manner since he was arrested in March 2009, and secondly for its failure to take into account the various dynamics surrounding the notions of victim's justice and victim-perpetrator justice.[3] This chapter attempts to give consideration to the historical underpinnings that have in one way or the other influenced violence in Uganda ranging from political to ethnic differences. These two forces have been central to Uganda's heritage of violence and continue in subtle ways to undermine institutions and trust up to date.

The question at the core of this study is whether it is possible to reconcile the interests of justice and peace without compromising either. This means the pursuit of holistic justice is necessary in order to provide accountability on the one hand and foster reconciliation among victims and perpetrators (including victim-perpetrators), on the other. It is argued that 'restorative[4] and retributive justice alone may not lead to a stable peace, because it does not resolve underlying grievances that led to violent conflict. Therefore, transitional justice should incorporate conflict resolution, civil rights, and participation, as well as socioeconomic and redistributive justice to address historical marginalization.'[5] To this list,

[2] 'Q & A on the Trial of Thomas Kwoyelo' *Human Rights Watch'* https://www.hrw.org/news/2011/07/07/uganda-qa-trial-thomas-kwoyelo (accessed 16 June 2021).

[3] A Macdonald and H Porter, 'The Trial of Thomas Kwoyelo: Opportunity or Spectre? Reflections from the Ground on the First LRA Prosecution' (2016) 86 (4) 698–722, available at https://core.ac.uk/download/pdf/196594978.pdf (accessed 16 June 2021).

[4] Quinn has defined restorative justice as '...a process of active participation in which the wider community deliberates over past crimes, giving centre stage to both victim and perpetrator in a process which seeks to bestow dignity and empowerment upon victims, with special emphasis placed upon contextual factors.' See JR Quinn. '*Are Truth Commissions Useful in Promoting Restorative Justice? In Crosscurrents: International Relations.'* 4th ed. Ed. Mark Charlton. Toronto: Nelson Canada, 2005, 402–408.

[5] L Laplante 'Plural Justice: A Holistic Approach to Transitional Justice and Peacebuilding,' 31 October 2018, available at https://peacelab.blog/2018/10/plural-justice-a-holistic-approach-to-transitional-justice-and-peacebuilding (accessed 16 June 2021).

Besmel adds amnesties[6] as well as truth and reconciliation truth commissions.[7] Whereas the State of Uganda challenged the constitutionality of its own Amnesty Act, the Supreme Court of Uganda did not find the Act to be unconstitutional. This was a bold move against the global tide against amnesties with authors like McNamara contesting its legality and international law acceptability. It is here that the chapter seeks to contribute to the existing literature.

The chapter responds to these questions by placing the State at the centre of the narrative as having the power and machinery at its disposal to create an atmosphere for the realisation of holistic justice. Authors like Bradfield have argued that the push against the Amnesty Act and the subsequent prosecution of Kwoyelo does have an effect for would-be rebels who would want to abandon the rebellion and return home. However, the fear of trial in Uganda—which also still has the death penalty—would deter this. It is, however, noted that the inefficiency and inability of the State in failing to prosecute the case in a timely manner while at the same time not giving considerable attention to the wider notions of holistic justice have impaired its critical contribution in building an understanding of justice that goes beyond retribution. Nonetheless, this should not remove the obligation on the State to protect and ensure the realisation of justice.

This chapter traverses three main arguments. First, that holistic justice as opposed to retributive justice is a better approach to dealing with post-conflict dynamics. Secondly, that justice is not an abstract concept and should adhere to the context in which it operates. Lastly and more specifically, that the prosecution of Thomas Kwoyelo is simply a 'wild goose chase'—a hopeless search for or pursuit of something unattainable—in this case, an attempt at checking the boxes of justice as defined by international law and State obligations as opposed to a genuine pursuit for redress for the victims of his alleged actions. The purpose of the chapter is therefore to argue for the realisation of holistic justice—a form of justice

[6] A O'Shea *Amnesty for Crime in International Law and Practice* (2002) 23, The role of amnesty as a mode of fostering transition, peace, reconciliation, forgiveness, and truth cannot not be understated in this light being seen as 'a more appropriate means of achieving this goal than punishment.'

[7] P Besmel 'A Holistic Approach to Transitional Justice for Afghanistan' in LJ Leonard (ed) *Global Perspectives on People, Process, and Practice in Criminal Justice* (2021) 195–213.

alive to the dynamics surrounding the violence that transpired in the war against the Lord's Resistance Army. Before the chapter embarks on the *Kwoyelo Trial*, it analyses the literature on prosecutorial or retributive justice versus a restitutive or rehabilitative form of justice.

2 Literature Review on Prosecutorial or Retributive Justice Versus a Reconciliatory, Restitutive or Rehabilitative Form of Justice

As noted above, the *Kwoyelo Trial* currently at the International Crimes Division (ICD) in Uganda has been the subject of several discourses in the local and international arena as a point of criticism, especially from the perspective of post-conflict dispute resolution. Central to some of these discourses has been the question of prosecutorial or retributive justice[8] versus a restitutive or rehabilitative form of justice. The case for reconciliatory justice has been strongly made by authors like Beitzel and Castle,[9] Besmel,[10] and Llorente,[11] among others. These authors argue that post-conflict justice has to include more than just punishment of the offenders. It has to include reconciliation, truth telling, and peace-building. However, authors such as Allen have been at the forefront of presenting the case for prosecutorial justice. They have heavily criticised non-prosecutorial justice generally and traditional justice mechanisms in particular.[12] In his *Independent Report* about the conflict in northern Uganda, Allen argued that the 'people of northern Uganda required the

[8] M Maiese 'Retributive Justice,' available at https://www.beyondintractability.org/essay/retributive.justice (accessed 16 June 2021).

[9] T Beitzel and T Castle, 'Achieving Justice Through the International Criminal Court in Northern Uganda: Is Indigenous/Restorative Justice a Better Approach?' *International Criminal Justice Review*, 2013, 23(1): 41–55. https://doi.org/10.1177/1057567712475306 (accessed 16 June 2021).

[10] Besmel (n. 7 above) 195–213.

[11] R Vazquez Llorente, 'Striking a Balance Between Restorative and Retributive Justice: A New Challenge for International Prosecutors,' available at https://www.law.ox.ac.uk/sites/files/oxlaw/striking_a_balance_between_restorative_a.pdf (accessed 16 June 2021).

[12] T Allen, War and Justice in Northern Uganda (draft) (London: Crisis States Research Centre, February 2005), 58–59; https://www.files.ethz.ch/isn/56421/2005-02_AllenICCReport.pdf (accessed 8 October 2021).

same kind of conventional legal mechanisms as everyone else living in the modern states.'[13]

However, whereas Allen's criticism was against traditional justice mechanisms, it should be remembered that they too are part and parcel of the reconciliatory justice[14] and therefore the idea that states which practice such are not 'modern' is not necessarily correct. More so, Drumbl and Kelsall also dispute the assumption made by Allen that the retributory or punitive justice systems adopted by Uganda are 'value neutral and universal.'[15] These authors instead argue that these procedures are actually heavily informed by a specific cultural understanding—be it western or even subaltern.[16] To this end, Afako argues that for northern Uganda, the peace negotiations between the LRA and the Government of Uganda sought to have a middle ground by having a 'comprehensive and integrated package of measures ... to establish the domestic processes which would take over the conduct of the LRA cases, while also promoting reconciliation and restorative justice values. This dual approach was reflected, amongst other things, in the emphasis placed on reconciliation, the needs of victims and the rehabilitation of offenders.'[17]

The claim that the ICC promoted both prosecutorial/retributive and restorative justice, have also been made by persons such as the then President of the International Criminal Court (ICC), Judge Sang-Hyun Song.[18] This is, however, not only contradicts the preamble of the Rome Statute that emphasises retribution, but is also disputed by Garbett who

[13] Note 6 at p. 66. See also Greenawalt KA Alexander, 'International Criminal Law for Retributivists,' *University of Pennsylvania Journal of International Law (JIL) 35:4* 2014, 969.

[14] Transitional justice as a vital element of 'contemporary peace processes,' See Graeme Young 'Transitional Justice in Sierra Leone: A Critical Analysis' (2019) 1 The United Nations University Graduate Student Journal 4.

[15] MA Drumbl, 'Collective Violence and Individual Punishment: The Criminality of Mass Atrocity.' Northwestern University Law Review [2005] 99 (2) 539, 551 in See T Kelsall *Culture Under Cross-Examination: International Justice and the Special Court for Sierra Leone* (2009) 9.

[16] n. 14 above.

[17] B Afako, 'Negotiating in the Shadow of Justice' (2010) *A Supplement to Accord Issue 11, Protracted Conflict, Elusive Peace: Initiatives to End the Violence in Northern Uganda (2002)* 21.

[18] ICC Press Release (International Criminal Court Press Release). (2012). ICC President tells World Parliamentary Conference 'ICC brings retributive and restorative justice

argues that the 'ICC's proceedings are better understood to comprise a retributive approach with the additional participants of legal representatives of victims, and not a typical restorative justice approach.'[19] Writing about the situation in Uganda, Branch thus argues that none of these systems is perfect. Indeed, Anna Macdonald and Holly Porter agree that 'there are mixed reactions to the trial of Kwoyelo which include '(1) something central to Acholi perceptions and practices concerning wrongdoing and justice in general; (2) the complexity of people's attitudes towards LRA crimes; and (3) the relationship between many Acholi people and the various state, non-state and hybrid institutions involved in justice endeavours.'[20] Macdonald and Holly further argue that 'a very powerful narrative, espoused by local political, religious and cultural leaders, as well as by supportive NGOs, emphasizes that the vast majority of LRA fighters, even those in senior ranks, were abducted against their will, and so, for the duration of their time in the LRA, their personal autonomy was entirely suspended. They cannot, therefore, be held culpable for their actions. In this historically contingent narrative, victims could easily have been perpetrators and the perpetrators themselves were victims. Thus, characters such as Kwoyelo no longer have an individual identity; rather, they take on a broader social and collective identity – that of the innocent child, abducted against his or her will, deprived of personal agency, forced to commit terrible crimes, and whose fate is now subject to the vicissitudes of a hostile central state.'[21] This therefore calls for a deeper reflection of ensuring that a form of holistic justice that addresses all these nuances is adopted. Such a reflection cannot do away with truth telling, apologies, memorialisation, reparations, and economic restitution. Indeed, Greenawalt also acknowledges that 'retributivism cannot provide a complete theory of ICL, but must

together with the prevention of crimes,' 11 December 2012. ICC-CPI-20121211-PR860, available at https://www.icc-cpi.int/Pages/item.aspx?name=pr860 (accessed 16 June 2021).

[19] C Garbett, 'The International Criminal Court and Restorative Justice: Victims, Participation and the Processes of Justice' (2017) 5(2) *Restorative Justice: An International Journal*, 198, 198.

[20] Anna Macdonald and Holly Porter, 'The Trial of Thomas Kwoyelo: Opportunity or Spectre,' 17 November 2016, available at https://blogs.lse.ac.uk/africaatlse/2016/11/17/the-trial-of-thomaskwoyelo-opportunity-or-spectre/ (last accessed 24th June 2021).

[21] ibid.

instead co-exist with non-retributive rationales ... (which)[22]... reflects the general limitations of retributivism as a real-world institutional theory.'[23] It is this holistic approach as noted by Laplante, that this chapter seeks to explore.

Akhavan[24] has argued that unconscionable atrocities act as an effective accelerant for standard setting and institution building in the human rights system. However, this has not necessarily happened in Uganda, as seen by the prolonged and ongoing *Kwoyelo Trial* amidst the divergent views on the meaning of justice. Clarke further notes that there are several interpretations of justice and pressures mounted from several actors onto a community like Uganda which is torn by violence.[25] Kyomuhangi also highlights a long history of Uganda's cycles of violence and political turmoil, and shows how some victims blame the government for its lacklustre approach to their perils and showing how these play a part in determining how people perceive state-procured retributive justice. These varied interpretations of justice are exemplified by the way in which various reports have represented heterogeneous needs of the victims and affected persons.[26] These varied judicial needs therefore clearly show that transitional justice after conflict cannot be sequenced but needs to be applied at the same time and space. Kamari also notes that there has been subversion of agency from Ugandans by the international community through the International Criminal Court.[27] This was done through the solicitation of referrals of the Lord's Resistance Army cases from Uganda in a bid to preserve the legitimacy of the ICC in the light of

[22] Insertion mine.

[23] n. 12 above.

[24] P Akhavan, 'The International Criminal Tribunal for Rwanda: The Politics and Pragmatics of Punishment.' (1996) 90 *The American Journal of International Law* 501.

[25] KM Clarke, *Fictions of Justice; The International Criminal Court and the Challenge of Legal Pluralism in Sub-Saharan Africa* (2009).

[26] Compare, for example, P Pham, P Vinck, M Wierda, E Stover, and A di Giovanni *Forgotten Voices: A Population—Based Survey of Attitudes About Peace and Justice in Northern Uganda,* International Center for Transitional Justice and Human Rights Center, University of California, Berkeley, July 2005, with JR Quinn 'Tried and True: The Role of Informal Mechanisms in Transitional Justice,' A Paper Presented at the International Society of Political Psychology Annual Meeting, Toronto, 6 July 2005.

[27] Clarke n. 23 above.

resistance it was receiving from the United States of America (USA).[28] On the one hand, this referral confirms that the organs of the State of Uganda did have legitimacy issues in so far as some of the victims queried their genuineness they were looked at with suspicion As such the referral of the situation in northern Uganda to the ICC-privileged prosecution over other forms of justice and in so doing, denied the other justice mechanisms the necessary leverage they needed for legitimacy.

Kamari's view, which is supported by authors such as Branch[29] and Schabas[30] inevitably has meant that other mechanisms of post-conflict justice have taken a back seat and denied the would-be beneficiaries, the much-needed interventions they needed. In the specific case of Kwoyelo, the resort to the use of customary international law to ensure that he was prosecuted was a novel move by the Government of Uganda which more or less sealed the fate for Kwoyelo. Whereas authors such as Seelinger have supported this approach, it does open up a pandora's box to try government and political leaders for historical injustices which might be an unforeseen possibility. This further states that holistic justice does not include an either-or dimension but encompasses all mechanisms of transitional justice that can address the varied needs of the victims and victim perpetrators and interested parties—which are clearly homogenous, and the State has the primary responsibility to ensure that this happens.

[28] H Patrick 'The Monkey Cannot Preside Over a Case Concerning the Jungle: Why the International Justice Is Guilty of Overreach in Northern Uganda,' Paper Presented at the International Conference on 'Spheres of Justice' held by the Mahanirban Calcutta Research Group in September 2007, available at http://restorativejustice.org/rj-library/even-should-the-heavens-falltiming-and-sequencing-of-transitional-justice-a-gap-in-the-rome-statute-or-towards-a-flexible-transitional-justice-scheme-for-the-21st-century/10968/#sthash.swo013iN.dpbs (accessed 8 October 2020).

[29] KA Rodman and P Booth 'Manipulated Commitments: The International Criminal Court in Uganda' (2013) 35(2) *Human Rights Quarterly* 271.

[30] Schabas quotes that the Prosecutor '[W]hile *proprio motu* power is a critical aspect of the Office's independence, the Prosecutor adopted the policy of inviting and welcoming voluntary referrals by territorial states as a first step in triggering the jurisdiction of the Court,' See Office of the Prosecutor, 'Report on the Activities Performed During the First Three Years (June 2003–June 2006),' 12 September' 2006, p. 7. Cited in WA Schabas 'Complementarity in Practice: Creative Solutions of a Trap for the Court?' For presentation at the 20th Anniversary Conference of the International Society for the Reform of Criminal Law, Vancouver, 23 June 2007, available at https://www.icc-cpi.int/RelatedRecords/CR2010_02017.PDF (accessed 3 October 2020). Also cited in M Politi and F Gioia (eds) *The International Criminal Court and National Jurisdictions* (2008) 25.

Additionally, Stahn and El Zeidy[31] as well as Burke-White and Kaplan[32] also criticise the privileging of prosecution by way of solicitation of referrals in the light of the fact that the State of Uganda had a well-functioning judiciary which is 'among the best in Africa.'[33] The State seems to have fallen into the trap of political expediency by trying to avoid the risk of being perceived negatively by the Acholi population so as to avoid the possibility of tainting the courts as 'an extension of the conflict by other means' hence the 'resort to the ICC as a disinterested third party.'[34] In essence, it is argued that in the light of the fact that the ICC does not even have a police force (and still relies on the State or other actors), if the State had not succumbed to any pressure, it would have been able to prosecute the case itself. However, that in itself would not be enough as prosecution by itself does not address other issues such as those dealing with the historical injustices, reconciliation, forgiveness, psychosocial needs, memorialisation, and peacebuilding both within the directly affected communities and those in the wider nation. Regarding the specific *Kwoyelo Trial*, Bako highlights the challenges faced by the ICD in lacking the necessary funds to conduct its affairs.

In the light of the above review, it is clear that the State needs to take a more central role in pursuing a more holistic form of justice—one that does not privilege one theory of justice over the other, but rather uses its resources and political will to address the diverse needs of its citizens after violent conflict—be they victims or victim perpetrators. This means going beyond striking 'a balance between restorative and retributive justice' but also addressing the other varied needs that remain glaringly unaddressed.

[31] C Stahn and M Zeidy, *The International Criminal Court and Complementarity: From Theory to Practice* Vol 1 (2011) 299 in S Ndagire 'Complex Complementarity: An Analysis of the Legal Challenges Crippling the International Crimes Division (ICD) of the Uganda High Court From Prosecuting International Crimes Committed in Northern Uganda.' (Advanced Degree of Master of Laws in Public International Law (with a specialization in International Criminal Law), Leiden University 2012) (Copy on file) at 42.

[32] W Burke-White and S Kaplan, 'Shaping the Contours of Domestic Justice: The ICC and an Admissibility Challenge in the Ugandan Situation,' (2009) 7 *Journal of International Criminal Justice* 257, 259.

[33] n. 12 above.

[34] Stahn and Zeidy n. 29 above.

Now that the literature on prosecutorial or retributive justice versus a restitutive or rehabilitative form of justice has been discussed, the chapter moves to the discussion of the *Kwoyelo Trial*.

3 Background to the *Kwoyelo Trial*

The State of Uganda has for the last decade sought to try Thomas Kwoyelo for offences allegedly committed when he was part of the Lord's Resistance Army (LRA) rebellion that ravaged the northern part of Uganda for the greater part of 1990's.[35] Uganda, which had earlier on passed the Amnesty Act in 2000 not only referred the situation in northern Uganda to the ICC, but also commenced a peace process with the rebels.[36] The subsequent arrest of Thomas Kwoyelo—a former child soldier who was allegedly abducted in 1987—inadvertently placed the State in a precarious situation. On the one hand, was the demand by some sections of the population—especially the leaders of the people most affected by the conflict—for the continued use of the Amnesty laws,[37] rehabilitation and the push to have peaceful coexistence of citizens after conflict, while on the other was the demand for punishment and the trial of Kwoyelo even if it was at the expense of abandoning the Government's Amnesty law.

[35] CSIS, 'Critical Questions—The Lord's Resistance Army', available at https://www.csis.org/analysis/lord%E2%80%99s-resistance-army (accessed 8 October 8 2020). Avocats Sans Frontières 2016. Avocats Sans Frontières. 2016. 'A Trial for History: Thomas Kwoyelo in Uganda.' Avocats Sans Frontières. September. https://www.asf.be/blog/2018/09/20/thomas-kwoyelo-in-uganda-a-trial-for-history/ (accessed 6 October 2020) See also Parliamentarians for Global Action 2020. Parliamentarians for Global Action. 2020. 'Uganda Campaign for the Rome Statute of the ICC.' Parliamentarians for Global Action, available at https://www.pgaction.org/ilhr/rome-statute/africa/uganda.html (accessed 6 October 2020).

[36] B Afako, 'Undermining the LRA: Role of Uganda's Amnesty Act' *Conciliation Resources,* August 2012, available at https://www.c-r.org/news-and-views/comment/undermining-lra-role-ugandas-amnesty-act (accessed 24 June 2021); and B Afako, 'Reconciliation and Justice: "Mato oput" and the Amnesty Act' (2002) 11 *Accord* 64.

[37] Afako 'Understanding the LRA: Role of Uganda's Amnesty Act' n. 34 above.

3.1 *Thomas Kwoyelo and the Lord's Resistance Army*

The Lord's Resistance Army (LRA), led by Joseph Kony, has been active in destabilising northern Uganda since 1987.[38] He claimed to be cousin of Alice Lakwena, a leader of another rebel force—Alice Lakwena's Holy Spirit Movement.[39] After her defeat, Kony decided to continue her agenda and recruited several of her soldiers.[40] The rationale behind the LRA rebellion is not clearly understood as most believe that he is engaged in the occult which directed his random sporadic attacks against the government, and others believe the conflict is a result of serious and legitimate complaints carried by mainly the Acholi and other tribes in the north region of Uganda against the central government.[41] It is argued that the conflict in northern Uganda is deeply rooted in inter-ethnic competition for power as a result of a north and south economic divide.[42] Such differences continue to foster fear and mistrust thus creating more division in society to date. Questions remain unanswered as to why the State failed to stop the war with many groups, with suggestions that the State

[38] KC Dunn 'The Lord's Resistance Army' (2004) 31 (99) *Review of African Political Economy* 139–142.

[39] For a detailed background to the LRA War, see RR Atkinson *Operation Lightning Thunder, December 2008–March (2009)* International Peace Institute, 13–16. 'From *Uganda to the Congo and Beyond: Pursuing the Lord's Resistance Army*,' www.jstor.org/stable/resrep09604.8 (accessed 6 October 2020).

[40] Dunn, Kevin n. 21 above.

[41] Ethnicity has played a big role in the political history of Uganda, being one of the most ethnically diverse countries in Africa, with roles split along lines of region and tribe. Mamdani Mahmood. 'Imperialism and Fascisim in Uganda. London: Heineman' (1983). States *'it became saying that a soldier was from the north, civil servant from the south and a merchant an Asian.'*

[42] Conflict, mistrust, and deception have been passed down generations due to the phenomenon of ethnic hierarchy that has existed in Uganda since its early colonial days, with various ethnic groups seeking a dominant position at the cost of others, this led to revolt by other groups who sought to counter the demands of such groups, such revolt usually culminated into savage barbarism. See NA, Foreign Commonwealth Office, FCO 31/716 Letter from British High Commissioner in Kampala to Minister of Foreign Affairs and Commonwealth Organisation, 28/08/70. Those in power stirred all forces available to favour them. As such, the army became and has always been a key player in the role of governing Uganda, especially given the fact that most of the army consisted of fighters from a common ethic origin. It became easy to gather and sustain support and

benefited from the war politically and economically.[43] The conflict which mainly affected children, saw thousands of them being kidnapped.[44] They were often forced to become child soldiers or sexual concubines for LRA officers.[45]

For more than twenty years, the LRA meted unimaginable forms of violence, suffering, and killings on the people of northern Uganda and in the process displaced more than 1.5 million of them. The State continually pursued both a carrot and stick as well as a confrontational approach to address the conflict, the latter only making matters worse.[46] The international community intervened to aid the State in resolving the conflict, with the goal of finding an amicable end to it. Well aware that neither party had the means to induce the LRA fighters into a negotiation, and with the efforts at peace frustrated by negative rebel sentiments, the United States started providing military aid.[47]

control for the regime at the time. Nyombi, Chrispas and Ronald Kaddu. 2015. 'Ethnic Conflict in Uganda's Political History.' Papers. SSRN. 17 August, available at https://papers.ssrn.com/sol3/papers.cfm?abstract_id=2645055 (accessed 7 October 2020). For a deeper understanding of the roots of violent conflict in Uganda generally and Northern Uganda in particular, please see T.V, Sathyamurthy, 'Uganda Politics: Convoluted movement from tribe to nation.' (1972) Economic and Political weekly (Economic and political weekly) 2122–2128; Hancock, Glenworth G and Ian Hancock, 'Obote and Amin: Change and Continuity in Mordern Uganda Politics.' *African Affairs* (1973) 237–255, 238; Mamdani, Mahmood. 'The Uganda Asian Expulsion Twenty Years After.' (1993) Economic & Political Weekly 93–96, 94; Phares Mutibwa, '*Uganda Since Independence: A Story of Unfulfilled Hopes, Africa World*' (1992) PR; First Ugandan Edition.; Prunier, Gerard. 'Rebel Movements and Proxy Warfare: Uganda, Sudan and the Congo (1986–1999).' (2004) *African Affairs*, 359–383, 372.

[43] 'Economic Cost of the Conflict in Northern Uganda, ReliefWeb,' available at https://reliefweb.int/report/uganda/economic-cost-conflict-northern-uganda (accessed 16 June 2021).

[44] Amnesty International 2001: 2.

[45] Cederna, Giulio. 2003. 'Gulu's Night Commuters' Walk to Escape Kony's Murderous Campaign.' The East African, 2–8 June.

[46] Crisis Group, 'Northern Uganda: Understanding and Solving the Conflict.' Crisis Group. 14 April, available at https://www.crisisgroup.org/africa/hor-africa/uganda/northern-uganda-understanding-and-solving-conflict (accessed 11 October 2020.).

[47] n. 44 above.

3.2 *Commencement of Peace Talks—The Start of a New Era*

On 14th July 2006, peace talks between the Government of Uganda (GoU) and the Lord's Resistance Army (LRA) formally started in Juba after a period of prolonged unsuccessful attempts, with one goal in mind—to end the fierce 20-year conflict desolating northern Uganda.[48] To achieve this goal, a comprehensive agreement to address the long-term economic, political, and social issues that afflict northern Uganda was drafted.[49] Calls for a robust justice mechanism were prominent, and a proper framework for domestic justice to resolve the impacts of the war was needed.[50]

In a bid to achieve the above, annexes to the Agreement on Accountability and Reconciliation were signed on 29th June 2007. The Agreement acknowledged the human rights violations and adverse socio-economic and political impacts of the conflict and the need to honour the suffering of the victims by promoting lasting peace and justice, with a commitment to promote redress in accordance with the Constitution of Uganda and international obligations.[51] However, difficulties soon arose during the Juba process. The rebels' reluctance to sign the final Peace Agreement signalled to many that the LRA had no interest in amicable settlement given the fact that all previous talks had ended unsuccessfully. It remains important to note that violence also would not solve the crisis given the events that unfolded in the following years.[52]

[48] The New Humanitarian, 'LRA Peace Talks Kick Off.' https://www.thenewhumanitarian.org/news/2006/07/14/lra-peace-talks-kick (accessed 7 October 2020). Also see Lamwaka, Caroline. n.d. 'The Peace Process in Northern Uganda 1986–1990 (2002).' https://www.c-r.org/accord/northern-uganda/peace-process-northern-uganda-1986-1990-2002 (accessed 10 October 2020).

[49] International Crisis Group. 'Northern Uganda Peace Process: The Need to Maintain Momentum.' (2007) Policy Briefing, Kampala/Nairobi/Brussels: Crisis Group Africa Briefing. 1.

[50] Betty Bigombe arranged face to face peace talks and helped create a multi-prong effort that included traditional leaders, women, youth, and the international community in a push to end the 20-year-old war. See BBC News, Betty Bigombe: 'The Woman Who Befriended a Warlord' 8 August 2019, available at https://www.bbc.com/news/world-africa-49269136 (accessed 24 June 2021).

[51] Government of Southern Sudan. 'Annexure to the Agreement on Accountability and Reconciliation. Annexure to the Agreement on Accountability and Reconciliation. Juba' (2007) Government of South Sudan, 29 June.

[52] Stahn and El Zeidy n. 32 above.

A failure of peace talks resulted into continuation of the war between 2008 and 2009. The LRA carried out massacres in Makombo (DRC), and in Uganda where about 1300 civilians lost their lives in 2008–2009. This prompted the signing of the Lord's Resistance Army Disarmament and Northern Uganda Recovery Act,[53] who reaffirmed the US Government's commitment to ending the LRA rebellion.[54] A coordinated strike dubbed '*Operation Lightning Thunder*' by the Uganda People's Defence Forces against the LRA resulted in losses on both sides as well as the loss of a number of civilian lives, but a few rebel commanders were captured, including Thomas Kwoyelo.[55]

Military efforts have more or less created a situation of negative peace, with the LRA being reduced to minimal numbers that are allegedly roaming in the deep forests of the Central Africa Republic. The LRA has since been rooted out of Uganda.[56] The UPDF has always argued that with the right technical help of the international community, enforcing peace is possible even when doubts exist as to whether such attempts will yield satisfactory results.[57] In February 2021, another rebel commander, Dominic Ongwen, Brigade Commander of the Senior Brigade of the LRA found guilty by the ICC of committing sixty one crimes against

[53] According to (then) President Obama 'the legislation crystallizes the commitment of the United States to help bring an end to the brutality and destruction that have been a hallmark of the LRA across several countries for two decades, and to pursue a future of greater security and hope for the people of central Africa.' See 'Statement by the President on the Signing of the Lord's Resistance Army Disarmament and Northern Uganda Recovery Act of 2009', available at https://obamawhitehouse.archives.gov/the-press-office/statement-president-signing-lords-resistance-army-disarmament-and-northern-uganda-r, last accessed 24 June 2021. See also 'Lords of Woe' *The Economist*, 11 November 2010, available at https://www.economist.com/middle-east-and-africa/2010/11/11/lords-of-woe?story_id=17472814 (accessed 24 June 2021).

[54] n. 51 above.

[55] Atkinson n. 37 above.

[56] Human Rights Watch 'Q&A on Joseph Kony and the Lord's Resistance Army', available at https://www.hrw.org/news/2012/03/21/qa-joseph-kony-and-lords-resistance-army (accessed 16 June 2021). See also BBC News, 'Uganda Ends Hunt for LRA Leader Joseph Kony,' 19 April 2017, available at https://www.bbc.com/news/world-africa-39643914 (accessed 16 June 2021).

[57] J Hemmer with N Frencken *Expert Meeting Report: The Lord's Resistance Army: In Search for a New Approach. Conflict Research Unit*, Conflict Research Unit, Clingendael Institute, 25 June 2010.

humanity and war crimes in northern Uganda between 1 July 2002 and 31 December 2005.[58] He was sentenced to imprisonment for 25 years.

4 The Pursuit of Justice and the *Kwoyelo Trial*

By the end of the conflict in northern Uganda, there were competing demands from various power centres—the international community which mainly sought for retributive justice,[59] some opposition by the Resistance local communities which sought restorative (and rehabilitative) justice (including the use of traditional justice mechanisms),[60] demands of the victims (which are/were not necessarily limited to the court room experience), the requests from women's groups to address the question of sexual and gender-based crimes,[61] and the desire by the State and religious institutions only to heal society but also unite its people once again (or even for the first time).[62] It is the position in this chapter, that while the State was endowed with all means at its disposal to critically interrogate the Kwoyelo question, a holistic approach that focused on both the victims and perpetrator would present a higher chance of justice and peace, especially for victims who barely relate with western modes or conceptions of Justice.

[58] Press Release: Dominic Ongwen declared guilty of war crimes and crimes against humanity committed in Uganda, 4 February 2021 ICC-CPI-20210204-PR1564, available at https://www.icc-cpi.int/Pages/item.aspx?name=pr1564 (accessed 16 June 2021).

[59] Bernard 2018, (CC); Marieke Wierda 2008. Bernard, Okot Kasozi. 2018. 'The Venom of War in Northern Uganda.' Justice Hub. 16 September, available at https://justicehub.org/article/the-venom-of-war-in-northern-uganda/ (accessed 6 October 2020).

[60] Gabagambi, Julena Jumbe. 'A Comparative Analysis of Restorative Justice Practices in Africa.' (2018) GlobaLex. October. Available at https://www.nyulawglobal.org/globalex/Restorative_Justice_Africa.html#_3.4._Uganda (accessed 6 October 2020). See also Porter 2016. Porter, Anna Macdonald and Holly. 2016. 'The Trial of Thomas Kwoyelo: Opportunity or Spectre? Reflections from the Ground on the first LRA Prosecution.' Africa 698–722. He highlights that the religious groups, and some politicians vehemently advocated for traditional modes of dispute resolution strongly emphasising one part only(reconciliation), yet the entire traditional setup was equally harsh, yet Kwoyelo could not be subjected to part of the tradition while ignoring the other on grounds of its harshness.

[61] Building Back Better. 2015. 'Northern Uganda.' Building Back Better. https://www.buildingbackbetter.org/case-studies-2/northern-uganda, last accessed 7 October 2020.

[62] C Rodriguez 'The Role of Religious Leaders.' (2002) 11 *Accord* 58–59.

The *Kwoyelo Trial* has attracted both local and international attention, being one of the first relating to international crimes in Uganda. Conflicts existing within the legal regime have resulted into a convoluted process that has seen Kwoyelo in and out of court ever since his arrest to present. It is key that one understands the underpinnings in this case and why this trial seems to appear as a wild goose chase that has not yielded results despite the existence of both formal and non-formal justice mechanisms in place. Therefore, using the ongoing trial of Kwoyelo currently at the High Court and the various events leading up to the trial, the next sections of this chapter analyse the competing demands placed before a State when conducting a national prosecution as demanded by international criminal law while at the same time covering its own failure to honour the responsibility to protect its own citizens who were abducted and allegedly conditioned to become killing machines.[63] Specifically, the analysis explores the various twists and turns that the Kwoyelo ordeal has taken to date; from the refusal to grant him amnesty, to keeping him in custody since 2009, the lengthy court cases and constitutional petitions that saw the Government reneging on its own amnesty law, the absence of a copy of the ruling of court on applicability on customary international law, the ruling of the African Commission on Human and People's Rights regarding his illegal detention, among others.[64]

4.1 Arrest and Pre-Trial Proceedings

Thomas Kwoyelo was a commander in the Lord's Resistance Army. He was captured by the Uganda People's Defence Forces in 2005 and detained at Luzira Prison. While in detention, he made a declaration on the 12th of January 2010, pursuant to the Amnesty Act, before an officer in charge of the prison renouncing rebellion and seeking amnesty. The declaration was submitted to the Amnesty Commission under the

[63] Article 120 (3) of the 1995 constitution of the Republic of Uganda; See also Section 2 The Geneva Conventions Act Cap 363; Article 1 of the Rome Statute of the International Criminal Court that establishes complementary jurisdiction in criminal matters. See Article 17 of the Rome Statue.

[64] *Kwoyelo v Uganda* 2018: In October 2018, the African Commission ordered the government of Uganda to compensate Thomas Kwoyelo for violating his rights under the African Charter such rights included the right to a fair trial.

Amnesty Act.[65] The commission stated that in its view, Kwoyelo qualified for amnesty under the provisions of the Act and forwarded the application to the Director of Public Prosecutions (DPP). However, on 6th September 2010, the DPP preferred criminal charges against him before the Chief Magistrates court.[66]

The charges were in respect of various offences under Article 147 of the Fourth Geneva Conventions Act, Cap. 363 (Laws of Uganda)[67] and Kwoyelo was subsequently committed for trial to the International Crimes Division of the High Court. A reference to the Constitutional Court was then requested on the contention that the offence for which he was indicted qualified him for amnesty under the Amnesty Act.[68]

1. Three questions were presented for the court's determination: whether the failure by the DPP and Amnesty Commission to act on the application by the accused for grant of a certificate of Amnesty

[65] Section 2 of the Amnesty Act.

[66] Beitzel T, Castle T. no. 9 above, 2.

[67] Uganda acceded to the Conventions and accordingly enacted The Geneva Conventions Act, Cap. 363, Laws of Uganda which commenced on 16th October 1964. The purpose of the Act is given as 'to enable effect to be given to certain international conventions done at Geneva on the twelfth day of August, one thousand nine hundred and forty-nine.' Article 147 of the Fourth Geneva Convention provides for grave breaches, which were incorporated in the Geneva Convention Act, Cap. 363 of the Laws of Uganda as follows:

> Grave breaches to which the preceding Article relates shall be those involving any of the following acts, if committed against persons or property protected by the present Convention: willful killing, torture or inhuman treatment, including biological experiments, wilfully causing great suffering or serious injury to body or health, unlawful deportation or transfer or unlawful confinement of a protected person, compelling a protected person to serve in the forces of a hostile Power, or wilfully depriving a protected person of the rights of fair and regular trial prescribed in the present Convention, taking of hostages and extensive destruction and appropriation of property, not justified by military necessity and carried out unlawfully and wantonly.

[68] The trial came up for hearing first in a lower court (the Chief Magistrate's Court) and was later committed to a Division of the High Court specialised in the nature of offences Kwoyelo was charged with—the International Crimes Division. Kwoyelo then requested for a reference to the Constitutional Court to challenge the constitutionality of the acts by the Director of Public Prosecutions that allegedly infringed on his rights. The decision of the constitutional court was then appealed to the Supreme Court.

was discriminatory and in contravention of the provisions of the Constitution of the Republic of Uganda; whether indicting the accused under Article 147 of the 4th Geneva Conventions Act of the offences allegedly committed in Uganda between 1993 and 2005 was inconsistent with and in contravention of the Constitution; and whether the alleged detention of the accused in the private residence of an unnamed officials of the Chieftaincy Military Intelligence was in contravention of and inconsistent with the provisions of the Constitution.

2. The Constitutional Court unanimously agreed with Kwoyelo's defence highlighting that he had acquired a legal right to amnesty under Section 3 of the Act, and also faulted the Amnesty Commission for its failure to process his certificate yet they had processed the same for other senior ex-commanders.[69] On appeal, the Attorney General raised thirteen grounds of appeal for the determination of the Supreme Court, mostly directed towards reconciliation of the Amnesty Act with provisions of the Constitution, the prosecution powers, and independence of the DPP against the plea of pardon and the provision for amnesty, as well as the status and effect of the Geneva Conventions Act in relation to the Amnesty Act and Uganda's obligations under international treaties and conventions.[70]
3. The Supreme Court summarised the issues raised by both parties into three key questions i.e. whether the Amnesty Act is inconsistent with the Constitution of Uganda; whether the Amnesty Act is inconsistent with Uganda's international law obligations on account that it purports to grant blanket amnesty for all crimes including those stipulated in the Geneva Conventions Act; whether the Respondent was discriminated against.

[69] KS Kihika and M Regue, 'Pursuing Accountability for Serious Crimes in Uganda's Courts Reflections on the Thomas Kwoyelo Case' 2015. 'ICTJ Briefing.' *ICTJ*, January 2015, available at https://www.ictj.org/sites/default/files/ICTJ-Briefing-Uganda-Kwoyelo-2015.pdf (accessed 7 October 2020).

[70] Before the decision of the Supreme Court of Uganda, the Constitutional Court had earlier halted the trial on grounds that it was unconstitutional, having found that the Amnesty Act was consistent with the constitution and that Kwoyelo was indeed entitled to protection by the Act. See *Thomas Kwoyelo alias Latoni v. Uganda* 2011 Constitutional Petition No. 036 of 2011.

The Supreme Court found that the Act did not grant blanket Amnesty as asserted by the Attorney General. While resolving this question, the court observed that the Act targeted people who have participated in acts of war or rebellion, specifically Acts in furtherance of the war. Drawing attention to the definition of amnesty in the Act, the court was of the view that it targeted political crimes and those incidental to such acts or crimes, but it did not include granting amnesty to grave crimes committed by an individual or group for other purposes. The effect of Section 2A of the Amnesty (Amendment Act) 2006 implied that the Act could not extend a blanket Amnesty, as it placed a requirement of certification from the DPP as to whether one qualified for Amnesty or not. For those reasons, the Court found that the Amnesty Act was neither inconsistent with the Constitution of the Republic of Uganda nor inconsistent with Uganda's international law obligations.

Rearding whether Kwoyelo had been subjected to discrimination or unequal treatment, ti had been argued for him that the office of the DPP had earlier granted over two hundred fighters (and some commanders who were higher in rank to the Kwoyelo amnesty) and that failure to grant him amnesty constituted discriminatory treatment. The court held that the number of people the DPP sanctioned for grant of amnesty was immaterial, and what was important was that the DPP studied each case and was satisfied that they could be granted immunity. In the same light, the DPP therefore did not have to give any reasons or explanations as to why he did not certify the respondent for amnesty. The Supreme Court then sent the case back to the International Crimes Division of the High Court to proceed with the hearing on the merits.

4.2 *Implications of the Pre-trial Findings of the Supreme Court*

The Supreme Court decision raises some serious concerns to note. In the first instance, whereas the court found that the DPP had the discretion as to whether or not it could grant a certificate to Kwoyelo, there remains the glaring uncertainty with regards to who may or may not be granted the certificate from the office of the DPP. Moreover, the finding that the office of the DPP need not give an account to anyone regarding the decision to grant or deny amnesty simply elevates this uncertainty. In a free and democratic society, it is expected that certain rules or principles guide the exercise of discretion in decision-making and that those principles be made known for purposes of accountability and transparency.

Absence of that check leaves room for abuse as the DPP could easily be viewed as cherry picking on who he or she wants to prosecute. While the need to give reasons is not absolute,[71] provision should have been made for extremely volatile situations such as this one especially in the light of the conflicting legal obligations that courts uphold in order to meet the interests of justice.

Secondly, when the court held that it was immaterial for it to consider the number of persons who were granted amnesty before and after Kwoyelo, it exposed the limitation of the powers of the Supreme Court and any Court of Justice in delivering holistic justice. The rationale for the Amnesty Act (and the Amnesty Commission) was to help encourage many of those in rebellion to return home. To ignore these numbers meant that the court chose to ignore the realities on ground such as how many people have actually been successfully integrated into society after the societies where these crimes were committed carried out their own versions of rehabilitative justice. To ignore this reality and the general movement towards transitional justice and instead insist on the prosecution of one individual who is also a victim was restrictive and short-sighted. While the offences committed by Kwoyelo cannot be downplayed, it remains controversial that one individual is on trial to date. It begs the question as to whether the prosecution is genuine or a mere attempt at ticking the box, a move meant satisfy a specific group of persons mainly from the Global North that demand a certain type of justice.[72]

In spite of the above, it is true that Uganda and her people remain divided to date regarding the trial (or not) of Kwoyelo. There are loud voices on each side of the divide with victim groups having to be confronted by friends, relatives, politicians, and the international community that are strongly opposed to his trial.[73] These political sentiments and undertones cement the view that a middle way should be found—one that not only seeks to address the retributive needs of individuals,

[71] *Brayhead (Ascot) Ltd v Berkshire County Council* 1968 [1964] 1 ALL ER 149, [1964] 2 QB 303 (Court of Appeal).

[72] Ruhweza n. 1 above See generally.

[73] Porter n. 70 above noted that victims argue that politicians and religious leaders misfired advocating for Amnesty for Thomas Kwoyelo without even bothering to cross-check with the Victims of his violent actions carried out during the war not only against random person in the north but also his own neighbours and some family members.

but also seeks to find a way in which society will heal. A rehabilitative and reconciliatory justice.

4.3 The Role of the International Crimes Division of the High Court of Uganda—Trial on the Merits

The International Crimes Division (ICD) is a special division in the High Court of Uganda that was established in 2008. It was specially established by the Government to fulfil its commitment towards its obligations created at the Juba Agreement on Accountability and Reconciliation. The central role of the International Crimes Division was to try the perpetrators of war crimes and was the first clear line of judicial redress created in municipal law for the purpose of prosecuting war crimes.[74] This is in line with the principle of complementarity that gives the International Criminal Court secondary jurisdiction.[75]

The ICD has jurisdiction to try offences relating to genocide, crimes against humanity, war crimes, terrorism, human trafficking, piracy, and other international crimes as may be provided under the Penal Code Act, the Geneva Conventions Act, The International Criminal Court Act No. 11 of 2010, or any other penal enactment.[76] When the ICD commenced *Kwoyelo Trial* in 2018, there was a lot of uncertainty surrounding how long the trial would take, issues of victim participation, and questions around the lengthy process leading up to his trial at since his capture in 2008.[77] The ICD was essential in confirming Kwoyelo's charges, a process that took more than two years. In 2016, three pre-trial hearings were held, and more pre-trial hearings were held in 2017 until final confirmation of the charges in 2018.[78]

[74] Judiciary. n.d. 'International Crimes Division'. https://judiciary.go.ug/data/smenu/18/international%20Crimes%20division.html (accessed 14 October 2020). See also KT Seelinger, 'Uganda's Case of Thomas Kwoyelo: Customary International Law on Trial' (2017) 8 *California Law Review Online* 19.

[75] Article 1 Rome Statue of the International Criminal Court.

[76] Section 6 of the High Court (International Crimes Division) Practice Directions No. 10 of 2011.

[77] Ogora Lino Owor, 'Thomas Kwoyelo's Trial Commences in Uganda' 25th September 2018, available at https://www.ijmonitor.org/2018/09/thomas-kwoyelos-trial-commences-in-uganda/ (accessed 8 October 2020).

[78] n. 75 above.

The *Kwoyelo Trial* was the first to be tried under the ICD new Rules of Procedure, and due to a number of Constitutional Court petitions and appeals to the Supreme Court, the hearing of the case by the ICD on its merits is still pending since 2016. The most recent proceeding was held in March 2020 and due to the effects of the Corona Virus pandemic its hearing remains undetermined.[79] Looking at the convoluted trial process, it becomes impossible to understand whether justice is being done and if so, for whom.

It has also been argued that all the pre-trial processes simply show that the International Crimes Division lacks the means to fully achieve the task presented before it.[80] The judges that made up the court were not appointed full time, and yet there was a need to also interpret and implement new concepts and processes due to the unique nature of international crimes.[81] Many Civil Society representatives have expressed mixed reactions over the trial, as to whether or not it will be effective in dispensing justice. It has also been stated that the delay in Kwoyelo's trial is certainly a denial of justice whether or not a conviction is secured, as there remains the question of reparation to the victims and whether a conviction would actually provide satisfaction for those who suffered

[79] See Avocats Sans Frontières, 'Kwoyelo, Thomas (ICD-002/2010)' available at https://www.asf.be/blog/trialobservation/kwoyelo-thomas-icd-002-2010/ (accessed 8 October 2020).

[80] See challenges highlighted by His Worship Asiimwe Tadeo-Registrar of the International Crimes Division of Uganda in 'Effecting Complementarity: Challenges and Opportunities: A Case Study of the International Crimes Division of Uganda' A Paper Presented by His Worship Asiimwe Tadeo-Registrar of the International Crimes Division of Uganda at a Regional Forum on International and Transitional Justice organised by Avocats Sans Frontières-Uganda Mission and the Uganda Coalition of the International Criminal Court on 30th July 2012 at Imperial Botanical Beach Hotel, Entebbe, available at https://www.asf.be/wp-content/uploads/2012/10/Case-Study-of-the-International-Crimes-Division-of-Uganda.pdf, 8–10 (accessed 8 October 2020). See also comments by lawyer Caleb Alaka where he highlights the challenges faced by the ICD in S Nakandha, 'Complementarity Reality Check: The Case of Uganda's International Crimes Division,' 21 June 2020, available at https://www.ijmonitor.org/2020/06/complementarity-reality-check-the-case-of-ugandas-international-crimes-division/ (accessed 8 October 2020).

[81] Avocats Sans Frontières 2016 '*…such concepts included participation of victims, which required access to specific technical and material resources. Despite all these efforts from INGO's and development, these resources remain limited.*'

and lost their lives.[82] Elongated processes only make it harder for the victims who continuously advocated for transitional, local dispute resolution mechanisms that provide a distinctive but appreciated understanding of the concept of justice i.e. forgiveness, reconciliation, and restoration.

The ICD faced a number of challenges in terms of Rules of Procedure and evidence, because its administrative setup in the High Court enabled it to set its own rules which were not provided for in domestic legislation.[83] The Rules of Procedure and evidence put in place were still quite new and unexplored which meant that the judges had to navigate the challenge of interpreting the provisions. Another concern arose in the determination of the role of victims during pre-trial procedures as the rules remain silent as to what procedure a trial judge should adopt to determine an applicant's eligibility to participate neither do they set out a formal procedure of application to victims who have an interest in matters before the court.[84] Other delays in the trial arose from repeated amendments of the indictment to include sexual gender-based violence cases and to reclassify the conflict from one of an international nature to a non-international armed conflict which had implications on the applicability of international law.[85]

[82] Ogora, Uganda: Civil Society in Uganda Express Mixed Reactions Over Kwoyelo Trial As Proceedings Remain On Hold 2020, available at https://www.ijmonitor.org/2020/06/civil-society-in-uganda-express-mixed-reactions-over-kwoyelo-trial-as-proceedings-remain-on-hold/ (accessed 8 October 2020).

[83] Asiimwe, Tadeo. 2012. Effecting Complementarity: Challenges and Opportunities: A Case Study of the International Crimes Division of Uganda. Kampala, July 30, available at https://www.asf.be/wp-content/uploads/2012/10/Case-Study-of-the-International-Crimes-Division-of-Uganda.pdf (accessed 8 October 2020).

[84] REDRESS. 2016. Uganda International Crimes Division (ICD) Rules 2016 Analysis on Victim Participation Framework. Kampala, August.

[85] Preethi Lolasksha Nagaveni, Amit Anand. n.d. 'International and Non-International Armed Conflicts and Application of International Humanitarian Law as Lex Specialis.' eprints. https://eprints.lancs.ac.uk/id/eprint/125074/1/International_and_Non_International_Armed_Conflicts_and_Application_of_International_Humanitarian_Law_as_Lex_Specialis.pdf (accessed 31 October 2020). Non-international conflicts generally take place within the boundaries of a State and comprise of armed conflict between a State and armed group or among groups that do not operate under the State's authority.

5 International and Domestic Law Obligations Applicable in the *Kwoyelo Trial*

The DPP preferred several charges against Thomas Kwoyelo, comprised of offences recognised both under domestic and international customary law with the view of possibly increasing the chances of conviction.[86] This section, therefore, explores international and domestic obligations in relation to the *Kwoyelo Trial.*

5.1 The Place of International Law in Uganda's Legal Framework

Customary international law (CIL) is recognised by the Statute of International Justice as 'a source of international law requiring 'evidence of a general practice accepted as law.'[87] Sellinger notes that CIL

> has both an objective element (of) 'state practice' and a subjective element (of) '*opinio juris*, or the belief that a state is obliged to follow the rule of law in question. Taken together, one might say that customary international law consists of state practice that is consistent, widespread, and obeyed out of a sense of legal obligation.[88]

CIL is therefore recognised as a system of rules established by universal consent among civilised inhabitants of the world and all the people.[89] Customary international law is unwritten and is derived from practice accepted as law.[90] International law has been applied in Uganda's jurisprudence before, albeit mostly as a guide to constitutional interpretation.[91] Judges have gradually shown approval of its applicability in case

[86] Seelinger n. 72 above.

[87] Statute of the International Court of Justice, 26 June 1945, art. 38(1)(b).

[88] Seelinger n. 72 above.

[89] JJ Paust, 'Customary International Law: Its Nature, Sources and Status as Law of the United States' (1990). *Michigan Journal of International Law* 59–91.

[90] United Nations. 2018. Draft Conclusions on Identification of Customary International Law, with commentaries. Report, New York: United Nations.

[91] B Kabumba, 'The Application of International Law in the Ugandan Judicial System: A Critical Enquiry' (2010) International Law and Domestic Human Rights Litigation in Africa 83–107.

law.[92] The courts have also relied on international law to give effect to provisions of domestic legislation by giving them a broader interpretation than domestic jurisprudence would ordinarily allow.[93]

However, the preferred approach has always been that which prioritises protection and enforcement of human rights. The trial of Thomas Kwoyelo was the first of its kind to take a prosecutorial turn in the application of international law in Uganda. Jurisdictions outside Uganda have also taken on a similar approach to international law, evoking its significance mostly in the interpretation of ambiguous statutes especially or particular to human rights.[94]

The decision to apply international customary law in Uganda's domestic pre-trial procedures was dependent on whether the crimes Kwoyelo was charged with under customary international law were recognised as war crimes and crimes against humanity at the time of their alleged commission. The decision highlighted the three main sources of international law as treaties, customs, and generally accepted principles of laws derived from national and international legal systems and emphasised the need for such provisions to pass the repugnancy test before their application.[95] Citing Article 28 of the Constitution and Section 15(1) of

[92] *Tinyefuza v Attorney General* Constitutional Petition No. 1 of 1996 (Court of Appeal, 25 April 1997). 18, where the words of the constitution or other law are ambiguous or unclear or capable of several meanings, resort may be made to aids of construction and these include international instruments to which this court has acceded and thus elected to be judged in the community of nations.

[93] See, *Charles Onyango Obbo and Another v Attorney General* Constitutional Appeal No. 2 of 2002 (Court of Appeal, 2002). Is one example of Court's use of customary international law to broaden the scope of rights? The court broadened the scope of the right to freedom of expression relying on the European Court of Human Rights case Handyside v The United Kingdom to find that the right to freedom of expression is an inherent concept in a democratic and diverse society.

[94] J Dugard 'The Application of Customary International Law Affecting Human Rights by National Tribunals.' (2004) *Proceedings of the Annual Meeting (American Society of International Law)* 245–251 cites *Lareau v Manson* 507 F.Supp. 1177 (D. Conn. 1980) and *Sterling v. Cupp* .290 Or. 611, 625 P.2d 123 (1981). Where municipal courts in the United States relied on the Universal declaration of Human rights as evidence of international standards or contemporary expressions of concern.

[95] *Pre-Trial Hearing in the Case of Thomas Kwoyelo,* 2018. Case No. 2 of 2010 (International Crimes Division of the High Court in Uganda, 30 August).

the Judicature Act,[96] Justice Okalany ruled that the ICD was accordingly empowered to apply international customary law as well other authorities or jurisprudence from the International Court of Justice (ICJ) as they passed the repugnancy test and the nature of crimes constituted war crimes and crimes against humanity.[97] The question of whether the principle of legality as enshrined in Article 28(7)[98] and 28(12)[99] of the Constitution had been violated could not arise in the circumstances of Kwoyelo's case given that the crimes complained of had already been recognised under international law.[100]

In dualist States like Uganda, the application of customary international law in a domestic situation does not nullify or render useless the provisions of domestic legislation but rather reinforces the State's prosecutorial capacities and its enforcement of critical human rights provisions within domestic legislation.[101] Customary international law is cognisant to patterns or practice and patterns of legal expectation.[102] The overall context, the nature of the rule and the particular circumstances in which

[96] The Judicature Act Cap 13. Section 15(1) allows the High Court to apply laws that are not repugnant to natural justice, equity and good conscience, and not incompatible either directly or by implication with any written law in the land.

[97] Supra 89.

[98] Article 28(7) of the Constitution 1995 is to the effect that no person shall be charged with or convicted of a criminal offence which is founded on an act or omission that did not at the time it took place constitute a criminal offence.

[99] Article 28(12) of the constitution 1995 is to the effect that Except for contempt of court, no person shall be convicted of a criminal offence unless the offence is defined and the penalty for it prescribed by law.

[100] The principle of legality 'is applicable where a new offence is created... offences that were criminalised under international law at the time of their commission and domestically criminalized on a later date would not offend this principle.'

[101] *R v Jones (Maragret and others)* 2006: 'war crimes as recognized in customary international law would be triable and punishable under domestic criminal law of this country irrespective of any domestic statue.' Page 22 See also Rono v Rono (2008) 1K.L.R. 803 'Customary international law is applicable even in the absence of implementing legislation along as it is consistent with domestic legislation.'

[102] General practice refers primarily to the practice of States that contributes to the formation, or expression, of rules of customary international law. In some instances, practice of international organizations also contributes to the formation, or expression of rules of customary international law. State practice consists of the conduct of the State, whether in exercise of its legislative, judicial, or other functions while practice itself includes both verbal and physical acts and some circumstances inaction as well, however with no predetermined hierarchy among the various forms of practice.

the evidence in question is to be found must be held in regard as well. To that extent, the court was and is at liberty to apply customary international law directly as it provides sufficient clarity, definitions, and elements underlying each crime. In that sense, acts such as murder or rape that could be part of domestic penal statutes qualify as war crimes and crimes against humanity when performed in particular context. The assumption is that the DPP's office is technically and intellectually equipped to handle indictment and prosecution even where the domestic legal regime may not provide specifically for such scenarios.

The danger of applying international customary law surfaces when municipal law is placed at crossroads or contradicted as a result.

5.2 *The International Law Vs. Municipal Law Paradigm Addressing in War Crimes—A Quest for Peace, Justice, or Compliance?*

When considering the State's domestic and international law obligations, courts should pay close attention to the impact international law obligations could have on the demands of the domestic legal regime. Domestic dispute resolution apparatus at times does have the capacity to provide redress where rights have been violated in an existing crisis. Rushing to alien modes instead not only exasperates the domestic legal process but brings with it both necessary and unnecessary complexities that could all together set courts on a proper, or rather a misguided quest for justice. There is need therefore for a sceptical approach while attempting to merge municipal and international law within a State to resolve a local dispute.

In its judgement of 22 November 2017, for example, the International Crimes Division of the High Court confirmed that customary international law is applicable in domestic courts of Uganda.[103] This decision had the effect of undermining the input of the Amnesty Act, a move that would have extended the vision of peace foreseen under the 2007 Peace Agreement. And yet, the *Kwoyelo Trial* plays a pivotal role in understanding the spirit behind the Peace Agreement in the light of the purpose and effect of the Amnesty Act. The case concerns the two key issues highlighted at the 2007 Accountability and Reconciliation Agreement and the

[103] Ogora, Lino Owor, 'International Justice Monitor.' https://www.ijmonitor.org/2017/12/judge-rules-that-customary-international-law-is-applicable-in-ugandas-domestic-courts/ (accessed 8 October 2020).

Amnesty Act: peace and reconciliation. One could only expect then that the courts would channel effort towards ensuring the realisation of the spirit contained in their provisions since that particular agreement became binding on both parties having been signed by both the Government and the rebel group.

Therefore, the application whether of domestic or international law in addressing war crimes should not be isolated from the vision fronted by the 2007 Peace Agreement and Amnesty Act. This vision advocated for peace, reconciliation, and accountability in the light of sceptical sentiments towards the utility of formal court processes in delivering a sense of justice, especially since a traditional approach would guarantee some form of direct compensation and hence provide a tangible sense of justice to the victims.[104] The significance and effect of the 2007 Peace Agreement and the Amnesty Act could have been instructive in building a special character of the *Kwoyelo Trial*.

That is a clear example of the struggle for justice between not just the State and the international community but also one for the victims. This is why a special approach was required from the start; not one hell-bent on simply fronting or achieving retributive aspects of justice, but one that wholesomely considered the needs of all the victims, a divided nation, and victim perpetrators. The absence of this resulted into many questions about the true purpose of the prosecution, with concerns raised about its genuineness or whether it was simply conducted by the State to show that it tried to do something.

Courts as institutions of justice should be alive to all the facts surrounding a case before strictly applying provisions whether in domestic or international legislation. Focusing on only one side of the facts and undermining the significance or implication of the other side can only foster injustice, for example, in such a case where the particular justification of amnesty for the LRA rebels was that the fighters themselves like Thomas Kwoyelo were also victims of the war. By crumbling under pressure from the international community and even from within, Uganda backtracked on its obligations both under the Peace Agreement and the

[104] International Justice Monitor. 2018. 'Thomas Kwoyelo in Uganda: Victims' Participation Brings Hope and Challenges,' International Justice Monitor. 17 October. https://www.ijmonitor.org/2018/10/thomas-kwoyelo-in-uganda-victims-participation-brings-hope-and-challenges/ (accessed 8 October 2020).

Amnesty Act, crucial frameworks that could have provided a form of justice grounded in reconciliation and accountability.[105]

Domestic legal obligations do not stand on their own. However, there is good reason for their existence such that to side-line them could easily render domestic legislation useless—if the courts will as of priority turn to an international law framework to remedy a domestic crisis. Caution must be exercised by States in integrating international law into their justice framework. Careful steps and consideration should be made deliberately, especially where the decision is likely to more significantly affect the victims who may not understand the complexities of a somewhat foreign justice framework. Therefore, whereas the application of customary international law brings with it a sense of clarity to the prosecution capacity of the State, it also creates a Pandora's box with dire consequences on domestic legislation or policy—potentially depriving it of its relevance. The courts then have an extra obligation to be extremely cautious during application of international customary law paying due regard to the possible negative effects of its application overshadowing its usefulness.

5.3 The Question of Selective Justice

While international law also affords prosecution as a means of redress, it is argued that this is of little relevance to the victims given that some of them also view the State as being responsible for the war and atrocities that occurred.[106] More problematically, the scope of its application has been limited to those considered rebels and arrested by the State, but not to the government agents. It therefore begs the question whether the State was intent on moving fast to protect its own from prosecution for gross human rights violations by fronting and 'weighing down heavily' on the first scapegoat. Generally, selective prosecution that targets non-state actors is bound to undermine the credibility of the criminal justice system.[107]

[105] Stephen. 'In the Shadow of Kwoyelo's Trial' (2015) Contested Justice 147–170, 158.

[106] n. 103 above.

[107] For example, former President of the Uganda People's Congress Political Party, Mr. Olara Otunnu criticised the ICC over what he described as trials of 'soft' suspects for war crimes against humanity, leaving out 'the big fish.' He further noted that 'There are other perpetrators who were not in the LRA who have committed worst atrocities, but

In Kwoyelo's scenario, for example, it then becomes unfair to only subject him to it, while other known perpetrators are protected by amnesty laws or their institutions. The whole process therefore needs to be rethought—trials should not directed to only commanders but also their subordinates, members of the UPDF, as well as perpetrators of other crimes that might constitute war crimes. The *Kwoyelo Trial* also raises concerns about selective application of international customary law.[108] While it provided a basis for some of the charges preferred against him, it is argued that he was selectively subjected to it while other perpetrators of the same crimes, both LRA and UPDF fighters, continue to walk scot free.[109] If its application happens selectively despite the existence of overwhelming evidence against other parties, CIL may then be viewed as a State weapon that is pointed at specific groups.

6 The Case for Holistic Justice

The Office of the United Nations High Commissioner for Human Rights encourages people to think of justice, peace, and democracy as mutually reinforcing imperatives that must be extended in delicate post-conflict settings.[110] Transitional justice mechanisms have played a big role in

have been left free,' See Otunnu raps ICC over 'soft' target trials, 28 January 2016, available at https://www.monitor.co.ug/uganda/news/national/otunnu-raps-icc-over-soft-target-trials-1638530 (accessed 24 June 2021). See also David Lanz, 'The ICC's Intervention in Northern Uganda: Beyond the Simplicity of Peace vs. Justice, *The Fletcher School of Law and Diplomacy*,' May 2007, available at https://reliefweb.int/sites/reliefweb.int/files/resources/EC66215A0071F156C12573910051D06D-Full_Report.pdf last accessed 24 June 2021. See generally, United Nations Office on Drugs and Crime (UNODC). 'Handbook of Basic Principles and Promising Practices on Alternatives to Imprisonment', available at https://www.unodc.org/pdf/criminal_justice/Handbook_of_Basic_Principles_and_Promising_Practices_on_Alternatives_to_Imprisonment.pdf (accessed 24 June 2021).

[108] The Fourth Geneva Convention of 12th August 1949 see also Amended Indictment: Uganda versus Kwoyelo Thomas alias Latoni. 2010. Case No. 02 (International Crimes Division of the High Court of Uganda).

[109] Adam Branch, 'Dominic Ongwen on Trial: The ICC's African Dilemmas' (2017) *International Journal of Transitional Justice*, 11, 30–49. https://doi.org/10.1093/ijtj/ijw027.

[110] Office of the United Nations High Commissioner for Human Rights. 'Rule-of-Law Tools for Post-Conflict States, National Consultations on Transitional Justice.' (2009) Rule-of-Law Tools for Post-Conflict States, National Consultations on Transitional Justice. New York: United Nations Publications.

trying to address the effects of the war in northern Uganda.[111] These transitional justice policies and frameworks have been streamlined by the National Transitional Justice Policy (NTJP) of 2019. The enactment of the policy stemmed from the need to address years of trauma visited on the people of Uganda over years of violence.

The NTJP is a model that envisions delivery of substantive justice, sustainable peace and conflict resolution. It utilises available justice mechanisms with the aim of providing long-lasting solutions in post-conflict situation. It recognises the limitations in formal justice mechanisms that frustrate the justice process such as the lack of victim participation and witness protection which both constitute key elements for the realisation of transitional justice. It also recognises the complementary role of traditional justice mechanisms.[112]

In the context of the LRA war, transitional justice mechanisms took shape in three different phases. First, the commencement of criminal proceedings under the International Criminal Court Statute which resulted in the issuance of arrest warrants for the LRA top commanders. Secondly, peace and reconciliation, which phase was codified by the Agreement on Accountability and reconciliation and its annexure.[113] This phase was aimed at compensation, reconciliation and rehabilitation, and truth telling rather than the traditional retributive approach. This would be materialised by traditional dispute mechanisms such as Mato Oput, which therefore created the need for amnesty for some of the fighters. Emphasis was placed on the importance of the traditional ritual of Mato Oput, which through its element of social restoration sought to mend broken relationships and vanquish misfortune from the land.[114]

[111] Macdonald, Anna. 'Transitional Justice and Political Economies of Survival in Postconflict Northern Uganda.' (2017) LSE Research Online. http://eprints.ise.ac.uk/68314/ (accessed 11 October 2020).

[112] Ruhweza n. 70 above.

[113] UCDP. Agreement on Accountability and Reconciliation Between the Government of the Republic of Uganda and the Lord's Resistance Army/Movement. (2007). And the Annexure to the Agreement on Accountability and Reconciliation. Juba: Government of South Sudan, 29 June.

[114] Wright, Tessa. 'The Search for Transitional Justice in Uganda.' Thesis, University of Canterbury. https://ir.canterbury.ac.nz/handle/10092/6562.

The truth telling process is essential in re-establishing peace in a community.[115] Within the field of transitional justice, truth-telling is considered a vital process in the reconciliation of violently divided societies and the consolidation of peace after violent conflict (Huyse & Salter 2008). The ultimate goal of Mato- Oput is to restore relations between the offended clans. Truth telling remains an integral part of the practice. It is a voluntary process that consists of a cooling-off period after which representatives of the clans engage in shuttle diplomacy in order to collect confessions and establish the truth.[116]

However, the truth telling process alone is itself insufficient to settle the quest for holistic justice given the complexities that come with conflict such as notions of victim-perpetrators. This is where formal processes with elaborate criteria would intervene to balance the interests of peace vis-à-vis those of justice. While Kwoyelo is a former abductee whose actions arguably lacked moral agency, there are many victims hungry for justice by prosecution, especially those falling outside the 'moral Acholi jurisdiction of responses to wrongdoing.'[117] However, an alternative argument has been made thus:

> Mato Oput's wider application in this context would address an important, emerging reality: that the ICC cannot investigate and prosecute many of the worst perpetrators, many of whom are children that the Lord's Resistance army (LRA) forcibly conscripted. Not only would it expand the scope for administering justice on the local level: it might also complement ICC's activities by allowing more perpetrators to voluntarily confess their guilt.[118]

The input of transitional justice and traditional justice processes like *Mato Oput (a ritual ceremony and process aimed at restoring relationships between clans)* is helpful in settling psychological effects of the war. Given a strong inclination and attachment to particular belief systems, many of

[115] Ketty Anyeko et al., 'The Cooling of Hearts: Community Truth-Telling in Northern Uganda.' (2012) *Human Rights Review*, 107–124.

[116] Wright n. 112 above, 111 and 114.

[117] Bradfield, Paul, 'Reshaping Amnesty in Uganda.' (2017) *Journal of International Criminal Justice*, 827–855.

[118] Roach, Steven C, 'Multilayered Justice in Northern Uganda: ICC Intervention and Local Procedures of Accountability.' (2013). *International Criminal Law Review*, 249–268.

the victims still identify and hold onto them and continue to suffer in the belief that it is only by appeasing the spirits of the dead that they can find true forgiveness and settlement. To this extent, the role of Mato Oput and related ceremonies cannot be under looked given their potential to harness the power in the belief systems held in a community to create a sense of peace and justice.[119]

The third phase involved an agreement on comprehensive solutions. This phase in particular was designed to address the root causes of the conflict, which was to be attained through political and economic reforms.[120] There was need to address the numerous dimensions of violence afflicted on victims of the war in northern Uganda avail redress that would provide a sense of justice. For example, certain forms of compensation may not necessarily remedy groups that have experienced sexual violence.[121] In 2010, the Refugee Documentation Centre of Ireland issued a report highlighting the sexual violence against women and girls and women in northern Uganda perpetrated not only by LRA insurgents but the Uganda People's Defence Forces (UPDF).[122] Such victims have faced numerous hurdles in trying to bring those responsible to book.[123] More than 32,000 children were abducted and used as child combatants and sex slaves. The report also highlights the State's inaction in form of failure to facilitate avenues through which such victims can access redress.[124] This has only worsened already existing community

[119] Baines, Erin K, 'The Haunting of Alice: Local Approaches to Justice and Reconciliation in Northern Uganda.' (2007). *The International Journal of Transitional Justice*, 91–114.

[120] Unpublished: Iversen, Anne Kirstine. 'Transitional Justice in Northern Uganda: A Report on the Pursuit of Justice in Ongoing Conflict.' Unpublished Thesis, Trekroner: Roskilde University, 36.

[121] Amnesty international also notes that the conflict in was characterised by sexual and gender-based violence. See Amnesty International 2007.

[122] Refugee Documentation Center (Ireland). 'Are There Reports of Sexual Violence Against Women and Girl Children in Uganda? Are There Reports of Sexual Violence Against Women and Girl Children in Uganda?' (2010). Legal Aid Board, 16 June.

[123] n. 121 above.

[124] n. 122 above.

hostility and ridicule. It should be noted that women or girls were not the only ones at the receiving end of these actions.[125]

Whereas the UN Basic Principles highlight five forms of reparations i.e. restitution, rehabilitation, compensation, satisfaction, and guarantees of non-repetition, more emphasis should be placed on the justice system to push also for the prosecution of such heinous crimes as they constitute crimes against humanity and a gender-based form of war crimes.[126] The State should consider a victim and gender-specific approach.[127] This will enable effective gender-sensitive implementation guidelines that will enable victims to gain not only rehabilitation services or compensation alone but also prosecute perpetrators. A gender-sensitive approach addresses concerns peculiar to a particular gender bracket enabling the victims to better address issues of trauma. The communities should be encouraged to embrace and support victims of sexual violence. Processes of rehabilitation and community sensitization will be instrumental in establishing social bonds in society and fostering peace and understanding.

The violent nature of Uganda's history prompted the intervention of various groups that highlight the injustices visited upon the different kinds of victims in wars like the LRA war.[128] The cost of war also reshaped the approaches to conflict resolution, with a shift towards reconciliation and peaceful settlement and away from violence. Calls were made for dialogue, and amnesty to help in confidence building as well as traditional dispute resolution mechanisms.[129] With the help of the Uganda Human Rights Commission that initiated the Human Rights Documentation project, human rights violations that were committed between

[125] Agabo, Winifred. n.d. 'Response to Sexual Violence in Northern Uganda. Whose Responsibility?' https://www.refugeelawproject.org/blog-menu/operation-and-support-blog/response-to-sexual-violence-in-northern-uganda-whose-responsibility.html (accessed 19 October 2020). See also Refugee Law Project 2017 page 12. Refugee Law Project. 2017. 'Hidden Realities.' Screening for Experiences of Violence among War-Affected South Sudanese Refugees In northern Uganda. Refugee Law Project, August. The working paper highlights various forms of sexual and physical violence visited on both male and female participants by insurgents.

[126] Kallweit et al. 'Building Blocks for Reparations Providing Interim Relief to Victims Through Targeted Development Assistance.' *ICTJ Research Report,* 15 September 2020.

[127] As above.

[128] As above.

[129] n. 61 above, Article 120 (3).

1986 and 2007 were documented for the purpose of providing technical assistance and ensuring victim participation.[130] The International Centre for Transitional Justice (ICTJ) was also instrumental in the formation of an effective, integrated, and victim-cantered national-transitional justice policy framework.[131] While the country continued to recover from the brutal conflict, special attention had to be paid to victims of sexual violence and children born of war. The recently adopted National Transitional Justice Policy (NTJP) doesn't make specific mention of the latter which raises concerns about them missing out.[132]

The concept of restorative justice in Acholi and other tribes has been welcomed by some given the inadequacies portrayed by the formal justice processes. This has placed tradition at the centre of conflict resolution, rehabilitation, and settlement for both victims and perpetrators, keeping in mind that traditional dispute modes do not only offer forgiveness but also impose punishment.[133] There is need for provisional relief to victims of the war, and not just forms of compensation alone but an assurance that the State is pursuing justice for the victims.

The pursuit for justice in the *Kwoyelo* case ought to traverse the needs of the aforementioned key victims generally and the case for women and children in particular. Clearly, the court on its own is unable to address and provide holistic remedies or adequate answers to all the various nuances, hence the call for a holistic justice that encompasses economic, social, political, and cultural interventions. The NTJP is therefore a viable step in the right direction in so far as it attempts to address all these.

[130] n. 127 above.

[131] n. 127 above.

[132] Kirabira et al., 'Transitional Justice in Uganda: The Dilemma of Children Born of War.' *International Law Blog* 24 July 2020, available at https://internationallaw.blog/2020/07/24/transitional-justice-in-uganda-the-dilemma-of-children-born-of-war/ (accessed 11 October 2020).

[133] Meinert, Lotte and Susan Reynolds Whyte, 'Legacies of Violence: The Communicability of Spirits and Trauma in Northern Uganda.' (2020) J Ineeberg, A Roepstorff, and L Meinert (Eds) *Biosocial Worlds: Anthropology of Health Environments Beyond Determinism* (2020) 168–190.

7 Conclusion

The *Kwoyelo Trial* exposes several conflicting interpretations of justice and a struggle to have one concept override another. The arrest and trial of Thomas Kwoyelo provided a glimmer of hope to the victims. However, the failure to manage the expectations of the victims, the technical details of the trial process, as well as inadequate attention paid to victim perpetrators, have all dimmed that ray of hope. The fact that Kwoyelo was also abducted and recruited as a child has also complicated the trial process. These challenges indeed show that the criminal justice formal framework is susceptible to a number of forces, highlighting the need for uniform consensus on such situations, not only among top State officials but also among the victims who demand or expect more from the case.

The justice and peace dilemma must be given a wholesome approach. Courts and States should always pay close attention to the particular facts of the case in such situations, taking into account the views and demands of the victims, the history of the conflict, the history of the perpetrators, and other legally recognised modes of dispute resolution that can offer justice not just by retribution alone but also through reconciliation, rehabilitation, and compensation, and harness the power within the available systems to create a sense of justice and peace both for the victims and the perpetrators.

The *Kwoyelo* trial process shows that it is possible to have a fusion of municipal law and international law for the purpose of enabling court to come to a just decision, especially in the context of crimes that some individual countries may not have fully appreciated within municipal law. In essence, courts must be willing to navigate across several dimensions of law and jurisprudence to meet the cost of holistic justice. This, however, is not without its challenges as traversed by this chapter. Kwoyelo legal team remains eager to appeal against the ruling by the trial judge on the retrospective applicability of criminal law under international law. The victims and the general public still await the conclusion of this trial and the final result of any subsequent appeals. When all curtains eventually close on the trial of Thomas Kwoyelo, the important question shall still be whether justice was achieved and if so, for whom.

Acknowledgements I am deeply grateful to Mwondha Dean Michael for the research assistance rendered in putting this chapter together. I am equally grateful for the helpful comments from Ms. Ruth Muhawe, Charles Kaamuli, Edgar Baguma and the anonymous reviewers of this chapter.

References

Acirokop, Prudence. 2012. *Accountability for Mass Atrocities the LRA Conflict in Uganda*. PHD Thesis, University of Pretoria. https://repository.up.ac.za/bitstream/handle/2263/23898/04chapter4.pdf?sequence=5. Accessed October 8, 2020.

Afako, Barney. 2002. "Reconciliation and Justice: 'Mato oput' and the Amnesty Act (2002)." *Conciliation Resources*. May. https://www.c-r.org/accord/northern-uganda/reconciliation-and-justice-%E2%80%98mato-oput%E2%80%99-and-amnesty-act-2002. Accessed October 8, 2020.

Afako, Barney. 2002. "Reconciliation and Justice." *Accord Protracted Conflict, Elusive Peace Initiatives to End the Violence in Northern Uganda*, 64–67.

———. 2012. "Undermining the LRA: Role of Uganda's Amnesty Act." *Conciliation Resources*. August. https://www.c-r.org/news-and-views/comment/undermining-lra-role-ugandas-amnesty-act. Accessed October 11, 2020.

Agabo, Winifred. n.d. *Response to Sexual Violence in Northern Uganda. Whose Responsibility?* https://www.refugeelawproject.org/blog-menu/operation-and-support-blog/response-to-sexual-violence-in-northern-uganda-whose-responsibility.html. Accessed October 19, 2020.

Amnesty International. 2001:2. *Amnesty International Report*. Report, London: Amnesty International Publishers.

Amnesty International. 2007. "Amnesty International." *Uganda: Doubly Traumatised: The Lack of Access to Justice by Women Victims of Sexual and Gender-Based Violence in Northern Uganda*. Amnesty International, November 30.

Asiimwe, Tadeo. 2012. *Effecting Complementarity: Challenges and Opportunities: A Case Study of the International Crimes Division of Uganda*. Kampala, July 30.

Atkinson, Ronald R. 2008. *Operation Lightning Thunder*. International Peace Institue.

Avocats Sans Frontières. 2016. "A Trial for History: Thomas Kwoyelo in Uganda." *Avocats Sans Frontières*. September. https://www.asf.be/blog/2018/09/20/thomas-kwoyelo-in-uganda-a-trial-for-history/. Accessed October 6, 2020.

———. n.d. "Kwoyelo, Thomas (ICD-002/2010)." *Avocats Sans Frontières.* https://www.asf.be/blog/trialobservation/kwoyelo-thomas-icd-002-2010/. Accessed October 10, 2020.

Baines, Erin K. 2007. "The Haunting of Alice: Local Approaches to Justice and Reconciliation in Northern Uganda." *The International Journal of Transitional Justice,* 91–114.

Bernard, Okot Kasozi. 2018. "The Venom of War in Northern Uganda." *Justice Hub.* September 16. https://justicehub.org/article/the-venom-of-war-in-northern-uganda/. Accessed October 6, 2020.

Bradfield, Paul. 2017. "Reshaping Amnesty in Uganda." *Journal of International Criminal Justice,* 827–855.

Brayhead (Ascot) Ltd v Berkshire County Council. 1968. [1964] 1 ALL ER 149, [1964] 2 QB 303 (Court of Appeal).

Building Back Better. 2015. "Northern Uganda." *Building Back Better.* https://www.buildingbackbetter.org/case-studies-2/northern-uganda. Accessed October 7, 2020.

Cederna, Giulio. 2003. "'Gulus Night Commuters' Walk to Escape Kony's Murderous Campaign." *The East African*, June 2–8.

Charles Onyango Obbo and Another V Attorney General. 2002. Constitutional Appeal No. 2 of 2002 (Court of Appeal).

Crisis Group. 2004. "Northern Uganda: Understanding and Solving the Conflict." *Crisis Grouo.* April 14. https://www.crisisgroup.org/africa/hor-africa/uganda/northern-uganda-understanding-and-solving-conflict. Accessed October 11, 2020.

Dugard, John. 2004. "The Application of Customary International Law Affecting Human Rights by National Tribunals." *Proceedings of the Annual Meeting (American Society of International Law).* London: Cambridge University Press, 245–251.

Dunn, Kevin C. 2004. "The Lord's Resistence Army." *Review of African Political Economy,* 139–142.

Gabagambi, Julena Jumbe. 2018. "A Comparative Analysis of Restorative Justice Practices in Africa." *GlobaLex.* October. https://www.nyulawglobal.org/globalex/Restorative_Justice_Africa.html#_3.4._Uganda. Accessed October 6, 2020.

Government of Southern Sudan. 2007. "Annexure to the Agreement on Accountability and Reconciliation." *Annexure to the Agreement on Accountability and Reconciliation.* Juba: Government of South Sudan, June 29.

Hemmer, Jort and Niki Frencken. 2010. *The Lord's Resistance Army: In Search for a New Approach.* Conflict Research Unit.

Hancock, Glenworth G and Ian Hancock. 1973. "Obote and Amin: Change and Continuity in Mordern Uganda Politics." *African Affairs,* 237–255.

Huyse, Luc and Mark Salter. 2008. *Traditional Justice and Reconciliation after Violent Conflict: Learning from African Experiences*. https://www.idea.int/sites/default/files/publications/traditional-justice-and-reconciliation-after-violent-conflictlearning-from-african-experiences_0.pdf.

ICTJ. n.d. "Uganda abd Transitional Justice." *ICTJ*. https://www.ictj.org/our-work/regions-and-countries/uganda. Accessed October 11, 2020.

International Crisis Group. 2004. *Northan Uganda: Understanding and Solving the Conflict*. Nairobi/Brussels: ICG Africa.

International Crisis Group. 2007. *Norther Uganda Peace Process: The Need to Maintain Momentum*. Policy Briefing, Kampala/Nairobi/Brussels: Crisis Group Africa Briefing.

International Justice Monitor. 2018. "Thomas Kwoyelo in Uganda: Victims' Participation Brings Hope and Challenges." *International Justice Monitor*. October 17. https://www.ijmonitor.org/2018/10/thomas-kwoyelo-in-uganda-victims-participation-brings-hope-and-challenges/. Accessed October 8, 2020.

Iversen, Anne Kirstine. 2009. *Transitional Justice in Northern Uganda: A Report on the Pursuit of Justice in Ongoing Conflict*. Thesis, Trekroner: Roskilde University.

Judiciary. n.d. *International Crimes Division*. https://judiciary.go.ug/data/smenu/18/international%20Crimes%20division.html. Accessed October 14, 2020.

Kabumba, Busingye. 2010. "The Application of International Law in the Ugandan Judicial System: A Crtical Enquiry." *International Law and Domestic Human Rights Litigation in Africa*, 83–107.

Ketty Anyeko, Erin Baines, Emon Komakech, Boniface Ojok, Lino Ogora, Letha Victor. 2012. "The Cooling of Hearts: Community Truth-Telling in Northern Uganda." *Human Rights Review*, 107–124.

Kihika, Kasande Sarah and Eva Kallweit. 2020. *Building Blocks for Reparations Providing Interim Relief to Victims Through Targeted Development Assistance*. Research Reoprt, September.

Kihika, Kasande Sarah and Meritxell Regue. 2015. "ICTJ Briefing." *ictj*. January. https://www.ictj.org/sites/default/files/ICTJ-Briefing-Uganda-Kwoyelo-2015.pdf. Accessed October 7, 2020.

Kirabira, Mugero Jesse and Tonny Raymond. 2020. "Transitional Justice in Uganda: The Dilemma of Children Born of War." *International Law Blog*. July 24. https://internationallaw.blog/2020/07/24/transitional-justice-in-uganda-the-dilemma-of-children-born-of-war/. Accessed October 11, 2020.

Kwoyelo V Uganda. 2018. Communication (431/12) [2018] ACHPR 129 (ACHPR, October 17).

Lamwaka, Caroline. n.d. "The Peace Process in Northern Uganda 1986–1990 (2002)." *Conciliation Resources*. https://www.c-r.org/accord/northern-uganda/peace-process-northern-uganda-1986-1990-2002. Accessed October 10, 2020.

Macdonald, Anna. 2017. "Transitional Justice and Political Economies of Survival in Postconflict Northern Uganda." *LSE Research Online*. http://eprints.ise.ac.uk/68314/. Accessed October 11, 2020.

Macdonald, Anna and Holly Porter. 2016. "The Trial of Thomas Kwoyelo: Opportunity or Spectre." November 17th 2016. https://blogs.lse.ac.uk/africaalse/2016/11/17/the-trial-of-thomas-kwoyelo-opportunity-or-spectre/ last. Accessed 28th December 2021.

Mamdani. 1983. *Imperialism and Fascisim in Uganda*. London: Heineman.

Mamdani, Mahmood. 1993. "The Uganda Asian Expulsion Twenty Years After." *Economic & Political Weekly*, 93–96.

Marieke Wierda, Michael Otim. 2008. "Justice at Juba: International Obligations and Local Demands in Northern Uganda." *Court Conflict? Justice, Peace and the ICC in Africa*, 21–28.

Meinert, Lotte and Susan Reynolds Whyte. 2020. "Legacies of Violence: The Communicability of Spirits and Trauma in Northern Uganda." In *Biosocial Worls*, 168–190. UCL Press.

Ministry of Defence and Veteran Affairs. n.d. *Uganda People's Defence Forces (UPDF)*. http://www.defence.go.ug/updf. Accessed May 14, 2021.

Nyombi, Chrispas and Ronald Kaddu. 2015. "Ethnic Conflict in Uganda's Political History." *Papers. SSRN*. August 17. https://papers.ssrn.com/sol3/papers.cfm?abstract_id=2645055. Accessed October 11, 2020.

Office of the United Nations High Commissioner for Human Rights. 2009. "Rule-of-Law Tools for Post-Conflict States, National Consultations on Transitional Justice." *Rule-of-Law Tools for Post-Conflict States, National Consultations on Transitional Justice*. New York: United Nations Publications.

Ogora, Lino Owor. 2017. "International Justice Monitor." *ijmonitor*. December 3. https://www.ijmonitor.org/2017/12/judge-rules-that-customary-international-law-is-applicable-in-ugandas-domestic-courts/. Accessed October 8, 2020.

———. 2018. "Thomas Kwoyelo's Trial Commences in Uganda." *International Justice Monitor*. September 25. https://www.ijmonitor.org/2018/09/thomas-kwoyelos-trial-commences-in-uganda/. Accessed October 10, 2020.

———. 2020. "Uganda: Civil Society in Uganda Express Mixed Reactions Over Kwoyelo Trial as Proceedings Remain on Hold." *allAfrica*. June 22. https://allafrica.com/stories/202006230267.html. Accessed October 10, 2020.

Oola, Stephen. 2015. "In the Shadow of Kwoyelo's Trial." *Contested Justice*, 147–170.

Parliamentarians for Global Action. 2020. "Uganda Campaign for the Rome Statute of the ICC." *Parliamentarians for Global Action*. https://www.pgaction.org/ilhr/rome-statute/africa/uganda.html. Accessed October 6, 2020.

Paust, Jordan J. 1990. "Customary International Law: Its Nature, Sources and Status as Law of the United States." *Michigan Journal of International Law*, 59–91.

Porter, Anna Macdonald and Holly. 2016. "The Trial of Thomas Kwoyelo: Opportunity or Spectre? Reflections from the Ground on the First LRA Prosecution." *Africa*, 698–722.

Pre Trial Hearing in the Case of Thomas Kwoyelo. 2018. Case No. 2 of 2010 (International Crimes Division of the High Court in Uganda, August 30).

Preethi Lolasksha Nagaveni, Amit Anand. n.d. "International and Non-International Armed Conflicts and Application of International Humanitarian Law as Lex Specialis." *eprints*. https://eprints.lancs.ac.uk/id/eprint/125074/1/International_and_Non_International_Armed_Conflicts_and_Application_of_International_Humanitarian_Law_as_Lex_Specialis.pdf. Accessed October 31, 2020.

Prunier, Gerard. 2004. "Rebel Movements and Proxy Warfare: Uganda, Sudan and the Congo (1986–1999)." *African Affairs*, 359–383.

R v Jones (Maragret and Others). 2006. UKHL 16 [28] (House of Lords).

REDRESS. 2016. *Uganda International Crimes Division (ICD) Rules 2016 Analysis on Victim Participation Framework*. Kampala, August.

Refugee Documentation Center (Ireland). 2010. "Are There Reports of Sexual Violence Against Women and Girl Children in Uganda?" *Are There Reports of Sexual Violence Against Women and Girl Children in Uganda?* Legal Aid Board, June 16.

Refugee Law Project. 2017. "Hidden Realities." *Screening for Experiences of Violence Amongst War-Affected South Sudanese Refugees in Northern Uganda*. Refugee Law Project, August.

Roach, Steven C. 2013. "Multilayered Justice in Northern Uganda: ICC Intervention and Local Procedures of Accountability." *International Criminal Law Review*, 249–268.

Rodriguez, Carlos. 2002. "The Role of Religious Leaders." *Accord Protracted Conflict, Elusive Peace Initiatives to End the Violence in Northern Uganda*, 58–59.

Sathyamurthy, T.V. 1972. "Uganda Politics: Convoluted Movement from Tribe to Nation." *Economic and Political Weekly* (Economic and Political Weekly), 2122–2128.

Seelinger, Kim Thuy. 2017. "Uganda's Case of Thomas Kwoyelo: Customary International Law on Trial." *California Law Review Online*, 19–39.

The New Humanitarian. 2006. "LRA Peace Talks Kick Off." *The New Humanitarian*. July 14. https://www.thenewhumanitarian.org/news/2006/07/14/lra-peace-talks-kick. Accessed October 7, 2020.

Thomas Kwoyelo alias Latoni v. Uganda. 2011. Constitutional Petition No. 036 of 2011 (Constitutional Court).

Tinyefuza v Attorney General. 1997. Constitutional Petition No. 1 of 1996 (Court of Appeal, April 25).

UCDP. 2007. *Agreement on Accountability and Reconciliation Between the Government of the Republic of Uganda and the Lord's Resistance Army/Movement*. Juba, June 29.

Uganda v Kwoyelo Thomas alias Latoni. 2010. Case No. 02 (International Crimes Division of The High Court of Uganda).

Uganda v Thomas Kwoyelo. 2015. Constitutional Appeal No. 01 of 2012 (Supreme Court of Uganda, April 8).

United Nations. 2018. *Draft Conclusions on Identification of Customary International Law, with Commentaries*. Report, New York: United Nations.

Wright, Tessa. Global Dimensions. *The Search for Transitional Justice in Uganda*. Thesis, University of Canterbury.

PART IV

Reflecting on National Accountability for Pre-Rome Statute International Crimes

South Africa's Accountability for International Crimes: Revisiting the (Non) Prosecution of Perpetrators of Apartheid for Crimes Against Humanity

Ntombizozuko Dyani-Mhango

1 Introduction

> I don't fully agree with that. I'm not justifying apartheid in any way ... I apologised for that, profusely apologise for that, but there's a difference between calling something a crime. Genocide is a crime, apartheid cannot be, that's why I'm saying this. Apartheid cannot be compared to genocide.[1]

The last apartheid president of South Africa, FW De Klerk made the above controversial statement denying that apartheid is a crime against

[1] SABC 'FW de Klerk's Statement on Apartheid Sparks Condemnation from All Sectors' *SABC News*, 17 February 2020, available at https://www.sabcnews.com/sabcnews/fw-de-klerks-controversial-stance-on-apartheid/ (last accessed on 28 January 2021).

N. Dyani-Mhango (✉)
Faculty of Law, University of Pretoria, Pretoria, South Africa
e-mail: ntombizozuko.dyani-mhango@up.ac.za

E. C. Lubaale and N. Dyani-Mhango (eds.), *National Accountability for International Crimes in Africa*,
https://doi.org/10.1007/978-3-030-88044-6_14

humanity. This statement was condemned[2] de Klerk, through his foundation, later issued an apology.[3] However, this statement has reopened the conversation about the crimes that were committed during the legally sanctioned apartheid in South Africa, and the need to prosecute its perpetrators for crimes against humanity.

An immense literature is written about South Africa's international and constitutional obligations under the Rome Statute[4] and its subsequent breach of those obligations. A search on Google Scholar returned 67,800 results in zero point ten (0.10) seconds![5] Most of the literature deals with the Al Bashir's visit to South Africa[6] and South Africa's failure to apprehend him and surrender him to the ICC, and South Africa's attempted

[2] U Nkanjeni 'Zindzi Mandela 'Heartbroken' About ANC's 'Defence' of FW de Klerk' *Times Live,* 17 February 2020, available at https://www.timeslive.co.za/politics/2020-02-17-zindzi-mandela-heartbroken-about-ancs-defence-of-fw-de-klerk/ (last accessed on 28 January 2021); BBC 'FW de Klerk and the South African Row Over Apartheid and Crimes Against Numanity' *BBC* News, 18 February 2020, available at https://www.bbc.com/news/world-africa-51532829 (last accessed on 28 January 2021); and Times Live 'Tutu Takes on De Klerk: Withdraw Your Statement About Apartheid' 16 February 2020, available at https://www.timeslive.co.za/politics/2020-02-16-tutu-takes-on-de-klerk-withdraw-your-statement-about-apartheid/ (last accessed on 9 June 2021).

[3] See, A Makinana 'FW de Klerk Apologises for Statement that Apartheid Was Not a Crime Against Humanity' *Times Live*, 17 February 2020, available at https://www.timeslive.co.za/news/south-africa/2020-02-17-fw-de-klerk-apologises-for-statement-that-apartheid-was-not-a-crime-against-humanity/ (last accessed on 28 January 2021).

[4] See, for example, M du Plessis 'South Africa's Implementation of the ICC Statute' (2007) 5 *Journal of International Criminal Justice* 460.

[5] The search words were 'South Africa Rome Statute' https://scholar.google.com/scholar?hl=en&as_sdt=0%2C5&authuser=1&q=south+africa+and+rome+statute&btnG= (last accessed on 06 July 2021).

[6] See, for example, D Tladi 'The Duty of South Africa to Arrest and Surrender Al Bashir under South African and International Law: A Perspective from International Law' (2015) 13 (5) *Journal of International Criminal Justice* 1027; MJ Ventura, 'Escape from Johannesburg: Sudanese President Al Bashir Visits South Africa, and the Implicit Removal of Head of State Immunity by the United Nations Security Council in Light of Al Jedda', (2015) 13 *Journal of International Criminal Justice* (2015) 995; and E De Wet 'The Implications of President Al-Bashir's Visit to South Africa for International and Domestic Law' (2015) 13 (5) *Journal of International Criminal Justice* 1049.

withdrawal from the Rome Statute.[7] This author has also written extensively on those aspects.[8] The chapter adds to the existing literature that has considered the crime of apartheid as a crime against humanity[9] and the prosecution of persons who are alleged to have committed those crimes during the height of apartheid in South Africa for crimes against humanity. However, the literature consulted does not examine the underlying reasons for failure to prosecute such as political interference over the prosecuting authority by the national executive branch of government. This chapter, therefore, shifts focus to explore reasons for failure to apartheid as a crime against humanity before the South African courts as South Africa seemingly has the laws and the institutions to make this happen.[10] In this regard, the purpose of this chapter is to explore South Africa's accountability for international crimes in the context of its

[7] See for example, M Ssenyonjo 'State Withdrawal Notifications from the Rome Statute of the International Criminal Court: South Africa, Burundi and the Gambia' (2018) 29 *Criminal Law Forum* 63; M du Plessis & G Mettraux 'South Africa's Failed Withdrawal from the Rome Statute: Politics, Law, and Judicial Accountability' (2017) 15(2) *Journal of International Criminal Justice* 361; MM Wabwile 'South Africa's Proposed Exit from the Rome Statute: Alternative Perspectives' (2018) 11 *African Journal of Legal Studies* 117; and L Stone 'A Sign of the Times: South Africa's Politico-Legal Retrogression as Illustrated Through the Intention to Withdraw from the Rome Statute' (2018) 33 *Southern African Public Law* 1.

[8] S Lungu & N Dyani-Mhango 'Ensuring that State Parties to the Rome Statute Cooperate with ICC Requests to Arrest and Surrender Suspects: Reflecting on the Role of the Security Council through the Lens of the Responsibility to Protect (R2P)' (2018) *African Yearbook of International Humanitarian Law* 119; N Dyani-Mhango 'South Africa's (Unconstitutional) Withdrawal from the Rome Statute: A Note on *Democratic Alliance v Minister of International Relations and Cooperation*' (2018) 34(2) *South African Journal on Human Rights* 268; N Dyani-Mhango 'The ICC Pre-Trial Chamber's Decision on South Africa's Failure to Arrest and Surrender South Africa: South Africa Escapes 'Sanctions' 2017 *African Yearbook of International Humanitarian Law* 37; and N Dyani-Mhango 'South Africa's Dilemma: Immunity Laws, International Obligations and the Visit by Sudan's President Omar Al Bashir' 26 (3) *Washington International Law Journal* 535.

[9] See, N Boister & R Burchill 'The Implications of the Pinochet Decisions for the Extradition or Prosecution of Former South African Heads of State for Crimes Committed under Apartheid' (1999) 11(4) *African Journal of International and Comparative Law* 619; R Slye 'Apartheid as a Crime Against Humanity: A Submission to the South African Truth and Reconciliation Commission' (1999) 20 *Michigan Journal of International Law* 267; and C Gevers 'Prosecuting the Crime Against Humanity of Apartheid: Never, Again' (2018) *African Yearbook on International Humanitarian Law* 25.

[10] See, generally, N Dyani-Mhango 'South Africa's Contribution to the International Criminal Justice' in M Ndulo & C Emeziem (eds) *Handbook on African Law* (2021).

violent past. It explores the question whether South Africa is capable of prosecuting persons accused of apartheid for crimes against humanity.

It has been argued that South Africa is capable to prosecute perpetrators of international crimes for two reasons.[11] Firstly, the judiciary has been resistant and demonstrated its fierce independence[12] despite criticism from the governing political elite.[13] There are several judgments that are politically fraught that the judiciary has and continues to hand down irrespective of how these judgments will be received by the public.[14] Other branches of government have so far generally adhered to the courts' judgments. For example, in *Democratic Alliance v Minister of International Relations and Cooperation*, the executive branch of government revoked the notice of withdrawal that was already deposited to the

[11] Dyani-Mhango (note 10 above).

[12] See, section 165 of the Constitution which stipulates that '[t]he courts are independent and subject only to the Constitution and the law, which they must apply impartially and without fear, favour or prejudice'. See also *Justice Alliance of South Africa v President of Republic of South Africa and Others, Freedom Under Law v President of Republic of South Africa and Others, Centre for Applied Legal Studies and Another v President of Republic of South Africa and Others* 2011 (5) SA 388 (CC), para 36, where the Court remarked that '[j]udicial independence is crucial to the courts for the fulfilment of their constitutional role. It is 'foundational to and indispensable for the discharge of the judicial function in a constitutional democracy based on the rule of law'. What is vital to judicial independence is that 'the Judiciary should enforce the law impartially and that it should function independently of the Legislature and the Executive.'.

[13] See for example, 'Nzimande slams 'judicial dictatorship'' News24, 18 December 2011, available at https://www.news24.com/News24/Nzimande-slams-judicial-dictatorship-20111217-2 (last accessed on 19 January 2021) (criticizing the Supreme Court of Appeal's judgment for setting aside President's Zuma's appointment of Simelane as the National Director of Public Prosecutions); and Gwede Mantashe singles out 'problematic courts' News24, 22 June 2015, available at https://www.news24.com/News24/Gwede-Mantashe-singles-out-problematic-courts-20150622 (last accessed on 19 January 2021) (criticizing the Gauteng High Court's judgment for instructing the officials to arrest and surrender former Sudanese President Al Bashir to the International Criminal Court).

[14] For example, Economic Freedom Fighters and Others v Speaker of the National Assembly 2018 (2) SA 571 (CC) (about the removal of the president from office); *Economic Freedom Fighters v Speaker of the National Assembly and Others; Democratic Alliance v Speaker of the National Assembly and Others* 2016 (5) BCLR 618 (CC); 2016 (3) SA 580 (CC) (about whether the president violated his oath of office); *President of the Republic of South Africa and Others v South African Rugby Football Union and Others* 2000 (1) SA 1 (about the review of presidential powers; and *Zuma v Public Protector*); and *President of the Republic of South Africa v Office of the Public Protector and Others* 2018 (2) SA 100 (GP) (instructing the president to establish a commission of inquiry on allegation of corruption and other related impropriety matters involving the president).

United Nations Secretary-General.[15] Further, when the Constitutional Court (the Court)[16] directed the President to withdraw his signature to the 2014 Protocol on the Tribunal in the Southern African Development Community, the President obliged.[17]

Secondly, it is argued that the Constitution makes provisions for the National Prosecuting Authority (NPA)[18] headed by an independent National Director of Prosecutions (NDPP)[19] to be able to prosecute international crimes.[20] The structure of the NPA[21] and the powers of the NDPP[22] are fully expanded in the NPA Act. After many years of instability in the office of the NDPP, where no NDPP has ever served

[15] United Nations, *Rome Statute of the International Criminal Court Rome, 17 July 1998 South Africa: Withdrawal of Notification of Withdrawal,* Reference: C.N.121. 2017.TREATIES-XVIII.10 (Depositary Notification), 7 March 2017, available at https://treaties.un.org/doc/Publication/CN/2017/CN.121.2017-Eng.pdf (last accessed 19 January 2021).

[16] Apex court with a broad jurisdiction and is the highest court of the land. See section 165(3) of the Constitution.

[17] *Law Society of South Africa and Others v President of the Republic of South Africa and Others* 2019 (3) BCLR 329 (CC); 2019 (3) SA 30 (CC). See also, SADC *Communique of the 39th SADC Summit of Heads of State and Government*, 18 August 2019, at para 20, available at www.sadc.int/files/1915/6614/8772/Communique_of_the_39th_SADC_Summit-English.pdf (last accessed on 19 January 2020).

[18] Section 179(1)(a) of the Constitution stipulates that: '[t]here is a single national prosecuting authority in the Republic, structured in terms of an Act of Parliament, and consisting of—a [NDPP], who is the head of the prosecuting authority, and is appointed by the President, as head of the national executive'. The Act of Parliament is the National Prosecuting Authority Act 32 of 1998 (NPA Act).

[19] See section 179(4) of the Constitution (which requires national legislation 'to ensure that the prosecuting authority exercises its functions without fear, favour or prejudice') read with the NPA Act, section 32(2)(1)(a) (which stipulates that '[a] member of the prosecuting authority shall serve impartially and exercise, carry out or perform his or her powers, duties and functions in good faith and without fear, favour or prejudice and subject only to the Constitution and the law'. For a thorough discussion on the independence and impartiality of the NDPP and the prosecutors, see N Dyani-Mhango 'Reflections on Prosecutorial Independence and Impartiality in South Africa: The Recent Jurisprudence of the Courts' (2020) 35(2) *SA Public Law* 1.

[20] Section 5(1) of the ICC Act requires the NDPP to give consent before a prosecution is instigated against the accused.

[21] Sections 2–7 of the NPA Act.

[22] Section 22 of the NPA Act.

their non-renewable term of 10 years,[23] and with several court judgments dealing with the issues in that office,[24] President Ramaphosa appointed a new NDPP in December 2018.[25]

Consequently, the chapter reads as follows. Firstly, it explores the prosecution of perpetrators of apartheid for a crime against humanity. This part first gives a brief background on crimes against humanity in international law to understand how the crime of apartheid fits into the crimes against humanity scheme. Then it considers apartheid as a crime against humanity. Secondly, the chapter gives a general overview of the South African law on South Africa's international and constitutional obligations to investigate and prosecute perpetrators of international crimes before the national courts. Thirdly, the chapter explores reasons for South Africa's failure to prosecute perpetrators of apartheid for crimes against humanity in the aftermath of the Truth and Reconciliation Commission's recommendation that to investigate and prosecute persons who failed to apply for amnesty for apartheid crimes committed during the apartheid era. The chapter finds that there has been political interference that led to this failure to prosecute. Finally, the chapter investigates consequences for political interference with the NPA's duty to prosecute perpetrators of apartheid for crimes against humanity. The chapter argues that for any accountability for international crimes to be achieved in South Africa, there first needs to be a willingness from the governing political elite to prosecute perpetrators of apartheid for crimes against humanity, and for parliament to exercise its duty to hold the executive accountable should the executive interferes with the NPA's prosecutorial duties.

[23] Section 12(1) of the NPA Act stipulates that the NDPP occupies the office for a non-renewable period of ten years as she has not reached the age of 65.

[24] See, *Democratic Alliance v President of South Africa* 2013 (1) SA 248 (CC), (removing Menzi Simelane from office as it was found he was not fit and proper to hold office); *Corruption Watch NPC & Others v President of the Republic of South Africa & Others; Nxasana v Corruption Watch NPC & Others* 2018 (10) BCLR 1179 (CC) ('*Corruption Watch NPC*') (about the suspension of Mxolisi Nxasana who later reached a settlement with the president, which was invalidated by the judgment, and about Shaun Abrahams, who was removed from office after this judgment). See also, V Pikoli and M Wiener *My Second Initiation: The Memoir of Vusi Pikoli* (2013) 231, where Vusi Pikoli gives an account of what led to his suspension as NDPP).

[25] R Pather 'The First Woman NDPP: Shamila Batohi Is the New NPA Boss' *Mail & Guardian* 4 Dec 2018, available at https://mg.co.za/article/2018-12-04-the-first-woman-ndpp-shamila-batohi-is-the-new-npa-boss/ (last accessed on 19 January 2021).

2 Apartheid as a Crime Against Humanity

Before embarking on a discussion on apartheid as a crime against humanity, it is important to first discuss what is meant by crimes against humanity to give context.

2.1 A Brief Overview of Crimes Against Humanity

It is widely accepted that crimes against humanity originate from the preamble of the Hague Regulations of 1907, which made references to the 'laws of humanity'.[26] Further, the term 'crimes against humanity' was first used in 1915 to condemn the atrocities committed against the Greek and the Armenians by the Turkish forces.[27] However, it was after the World War II that crimes against humanity were included in the Nuremberg Charter[28] and Tokyo Charter[29] to prosecute major war criminals. The rationale for this inclusion was to ensure that the types of acts amounting to war crimes could also be punished when the victim and the perpetrator have the same nationality.[30] Hence, when the Nuremberg Charter was drafted, the atrocities committed by the Germans against their own nationals were amongst the actions the international community sought to address.[31] The Nuremberg Tribunal had jurisdiction over

[26] K Ambos 'Crimes Against Humanity and the International Criminal Court' in LN Sadat *Forging a Convention for Crimes Against Humanity* (2011) 279, 280.

[27] M du Plessis and E Cohen 'International Criminal Courts, the International Criminal Court, and South Africa's Implementation of the Rome Statute' in J Dugard, M du Plessis, T Maluwa and D Tladi *Dugard's International Law: A South African Perspective* (5th Ed, 2018) 245, 254.

[28] Annex to Agreement for the Prosecution and Punishment of Major War Criminals of the European Axis (London Agreement), London, Aug. 8, 1945, 82 U.N.T.S. 279, 59 Stat. 1544, E.A.S. No. 472 *Reprinted* in (1945) 39 *American Journal of International Law* 257 (Supp.) (Nuremberg Charter).

[29] Charter of the International Military Tribunals for the Far East, Jan. 19, 1946, T.I.A.S. 1589 (Tokyo Charter). For a thorough discussion of crimes against humanity, see MC Bassiouni *Crimes Against Humanity in International Criminal Law* (1999).

[30] JG Gardam and MJ Garvis *Women, Armed Conflict and International Law* (2001) 197.

[31] Bassiouni (note 37 above) 2.

crimes against humanity 'whether or not in violation of the domestic law of the country where perpetrated'.[32]

Equally, in the early 1990s, the United Nations (UN) established ad hoc international criminal tribunals for the former Yugoslavia and for Rwanda, following the atrocities that materialized in their respective territories. Acting in accordance with its powers under Chapter VII of the UN Charter,[33] the Security Council established the International Criminal Tribunal for the former Yugoslavia (ICTY)[34] and the International Criminal Tribunal for Rwanda (ICTR)[35] to 'maintain or restore international peace and security'.[36] Like the Nuremberg and the Tokyo Charters, the ICTY Statute requires a link between crimes against humanity and an armed conflict. In this regard, the ICTY Statute provides that '[the ICTY] shall have the power to prosecute persons responsible for [crimes against humanity] when committed *in armed conflict* ... and directed against any civilian population'.[37] The ICTR Statute, on the other hand, does not require a link with armed conflict but it requires that the acts be committed on discriminatory grounds.[38] Nevertheless, the Appeals

[32] See art 6(c) of the Nuremberg Charter. See also art 5(c) of the Tokyo Charter, which defines crimes against humanity to include '... murder, extermination, enslavement, deportation, and other inhumane acts committed before or during the war, or persecutions on political or racial grounds in execution of or in connection with any crime within the jurisdiction of the Tribunal, whether or not in violation of the law of the country where perpetrated'.

[33] United Nations, *Charter of the United Nations*, 1945, 1 UNTS XVI (UN Charter), available at https://treaties.un.org/doc/publication/ctc/uncharter.pdf (last accessed on 19 June 2021).

[34] The ICTY was established to prosecute 'Persons Responsible for Serious Violations of International Humanitarian Law Committed in the Territory of the Former Yugoslavia since 1991', S.C. Res. 827 (25 May 1993). The Statute of the ICTY is contained in the UN Doc. S/25704, Anne x (3 May 1993).

[35] The ICTR was established for the 'Prosecution of Persons Responsible for Genocide and Other Serious Violations of International Humanitarian Law Committed in the Territory of Rwanda and Rwandan Citizens Responsible for Genocide and Other Violations in the Territory of Neighboring States, between 1 Jan. 1994 and 31 Dec. 1994', SC Res. 955 (8 Nov. 1994). The Statute of the ICTR is attached to SC Res. 955 as an annex.

[36] Art 39 of the UN Charter provides that '[t]he Security Council shall determine the existence of any threat to the peace, breach of peace, or act of aggression and shall make recommendations, or decide what measures shall be taken'.

[37] Art 5 of the ICTY Statute (emphasis added).

[38] Art 3 of the ICTR Statute states that '[the ICTR] shall have the power to prosecute persons responsible for [crimes against humanity] when committed as part of a widespread

Chamber of the ICTY in the *Tadic Case*[39] held that crimes against humanity be committed even in the absence of an armed conflict. The Rome Statute does not require crimes against humanity to be connected to an armed conflict, nor does it require the existence of discriminatory grounds.[40] This means that crimes against humanity can also be committed during peacetime *against any civil population*.[41]

For a crime to be considered a crime against humanity, it must be an act 'committed as part of a widespread or systematic attack directed against any civilian population'.[42] The Trial Chamber in *Akayesu* has defined the terms 'widespread' and 'systematic' as follows:

> The concept of widespread' may be defined as massive, frequent, large-scale action, carried out collectively with considerable seriousness and directed against a multiplicity of victims. The concept of systematic' may be defined as thoroughly organised and following a regular pattern on the basis of a common policy involving substantial public or private resources. There is no requirement that this policy must be adopted formally as the policy of a state. There must however be some kind of preconceived plan or policy.[43]

or systematic attack against any civilian population *on national, political, ethnic, racial or religious grounds*'. (Emphasis added).

[39] See *Prosecutor v Tadic Decision on the Defence Motion for Interlocutory Appeal on Jurisdiction*, Case No IT-94-1, para 141.

[40] Art 7(1) of the Rome Statute.

[41] The ICTR Trial Chamber in *Prosecutor v Akayesu*, Case No. ICTR-96-13-T defined members of the civilian population to mean 'people who are not taking any active part in the hostilities, including members of the armed forces who laid down their arms and those persons placed *hors de combat* by sickness, wounds, detention or any other cause'. See also, *Prosecutor* v *Dragoljub Kunarac, Radomir Kovac and Zoran Vukovic* Case No.: IT-96-23-T & IT-96-23/1-T paras 421 and 425 also explained that that '[t]he civilian population must not be the primary object of the attack' and that '[t]he "civilian population" comprises, as suggested by the Commentary to the two Additional Protocols of 1977 to the Geneva Conventions of 1949, all persons who are civilians as opposed to members of the armed forces and other legitimate combatants'; and *Prosecutor v Jean-Pierre Bemba Gombo, Judgment pursuant to Article 74 of the Statute*, Case No. ICC-01/05-01/08 para 154.

[42] Art 7(1) of the Rome Statute. See also, *Tadic* para 644, (stating that 'there must be some form of a governmental, organizational or group policy to commit these acts'); and *Akayesu* para 580, (stating that '[t]here must however be some kind of preconceived plan or policy').

[43] *Akayesu* para 580. See also, Art 5 of the ICTY Statute and Art 3 of the ICTR Statute.

The Prosecutor does not have to satisfy both elements to prove that an accused has committed crimes against humanity.[44] So, the attack may either be widespread or systematic. The term 'attack' means 'a course of conduct involving the ***multiple commission of acts*** … against any civilian population, pursuant to or in furtherance of a State or organizational *policy* to commit such attack'.[45] The Rome Statute, therefore, requires 'some minimal level of scale ('multiple' acts) and 'some minimal level of collectivity' (the 'policy' element).[46] It is important to note that there is no consensus amongst scholars on whether the policy element is necessary to prove the existence of an attack that constitutes a crime against humanity.[47] That discussion goes beyond the scope of this chapter. For the purposes of this discussion, the passage from *Prosecutor v Laurent Gbagbo, Decision on the confirmation of charges against Laurent Gbagbo*,[48] will suffice:

> the policy to carry out the attack against the civilian population must be attributed to a State or an organisation. With respect to the latter, Chambers of the Court have consistently held that the policy may be linked to groups that govern a specific territory or to an organisation that has the capability to commit a widespread or systematic attack against the civilian population. A view has also been expressed that the organisation within the meaning of article 7(2)(a) of the Statute must partake of some characteristics of a State, which "eventually turn the private 'organization' into an entity which may act like a State or has quasi-State abilities".

[44] In *Prosecutor v Tadic, Opinion and Judgment,* Case No. IT-94-1, 7 May 1997, para 646, the ICTY Trial Chamber stated that 'it is now well established that the requirement that the acts be directed against a civilian 'population' can be fulfilled if the acts occur in either a widespread basis or in a systematic manner. Either one of these is sufficient to exclude isolated or random acts'.

[45] Art 7(2)(a) of the Rome Statute.

[46] R Cryer, H Friman, D Robinson & E Wilmshurst *An Introduction to International Criminal Law and Procedure* (3rd Ed) (2014) 235. See also, *Prosecutor v Laurent Gbagbo, Decision on the Confirmation of Charges Against Laurent Gbagbo*, ICC-02/11-01/11-656-Red 12-06-2014 2/131 NM PT, paras 209 and 210.

[47] For more on this, see, generally, CC Jalloh 'What Makes a Crime Against Humanity and Crime Against Humanity' (2013) 28(2) *American University International Law Review* 381.

[48] ICC-02/11-01/11-656-Red 12-06-2014 2/131 NM PT para 217.

The crimes that fall into the category of crimes against humanity include: '(a) Murder; (b) Extermination; (c) Enslavement; (d) Deportation; (e) Imprisonment; (f) Torture; (g) Rape; (h) Persecutions on political, racial and religious grounds; (i) Other inhumane acts'.[49] Article 7 of the Rome Statute which consists of all the list found in the ICTR and ICTY statutes and has added enforced disappearance,[50] and the crime of apartheid.[51] The Rome statute also extends the crime of rape to include other forms of sexual violence 'of comparative gravity',[52] and extends the crime of imprisonment to include 'other severe deprivation of physical liberty in violation of fundamental rules of international law'.[53] The ICTY, ICTR and ICC have found several persons guilty of perpetrating crimes against humanity on one or more of these grounds.[54]

Unlike international crimes such as genocide, war crimes and torture, there is no treaty that is solely dedicated to crimes against humanity yet. However, there are attempts to adopt a convention for crimes against humanity.[55] In fact, the International Law Commission has recommended Draft Articles on Prevention and Punishment of Crimes Against Humanity to the UN General Assembly.[56]

It is important to highlight that it is generally accepted that the prohibition of crimes against humanity has acquired the status of customary

[49] See arts 3 and 5 of the ICTR and ICTY Statutes, respectively.

[50] Art 7(i) of the Rome Statute.

[51] Art 7(k) of the Rome Statute.

[52] Art 7(g) of the Rome Statute.

[53] Art 7(e) of the Rome Statute. See also, draft article 2 of the ILC on the proposed 'draft articles on prevention and punishment of crimes against humanity', which has copied art 7 of the Rome Statute verbatim.

[54] For example, *Akayesu*, *Furundzija*, and *Bemba*.

[55] See, Sadat (note 34 above); and M George 'Prospect for a Convention and Prevention and Punishment of Crimes Against Humanity' *Opinio Juris* (08 October 2019), available at http://opiniojuris.org/2019/10/08/prospects-for-a-convention-on-the-prevention-and-punishment-of-crimes-against-humanity/ (last accessed on 14 March 2021).

[56] See, United Nations International Law Commission, *Report of the International Law Commission on the Work of the Seventy-First Session* (29 April–7 June and 8 July–9 August 2019), Chapter IV: Crimes Against Humanity, where the International Law Commission recommends the 'draft articles on prevention and punishment of crimes against humanity to the General Assembly'.

international law.[57] To prove that a rule or norm has acquired the status of customary international law, it has 'to be found that there exists a settled practice which is widespread and extensive (i.e., recognized by a majority of states) (the *usus*) and that the practice occurs out of a sense of legal obligation by the states (the *opinio juris*)'.[58] The most obvious significance of a norm of a customary character is that it binds states that are not parties to the treaty in which the norm is restated.[59] Further, it is generally accepted that the prohibition of international crimes that fall under the Rome Statute such as war crimes, crimes against humanity and genocide, has acquired the peremptory norm status.[60] A peremptory norm is 'a norm [of general international law] accepted and recognized

[57] See also *Federal Republic of Germany v Denmark; Federal Republic of Germany v Netherlands (North Sea Continental Shelf Case)*, I.C.J. Rep. 1969, p. 3, paras 70–71, where the ICJ held that treaty provisions could apply to non-signatories if the provisions qualify as customary international law. This will happen if a provision is of a 'fundamentally norm-creating character such as could be regarded as forming the basis of a general rule of law' (paras 41–42).

[58] *Democratic Alliance v Minister of International Relations and Co-operation and Others; Engels and Another v Minister of International Relations and Co-operation and Another* 2018 (2) SACR 654 (GP), para 21; see also art 38 of the Statute of the International Court of Justice, United Nations, *Statute of the International Court of Justice*, 18 April 1946, which defines customary international law 'as evidence of a general practice accepted as law'.

[59] T Meron *Human Rights and Humanitarian Norms as Customary Law* (1989) 3.

[60] *See for example, Prosecutor v Kupreškić* et al., Judgment, Case Number IT-95-16, 14 January 2000, para 520 confirming that most norms of international humanitarian law, especially those prohibiting war crimes, *crimes against humanity* and genocide, are also peremptory norms of international law or *jus cogens*; and *Prosecutor v Furundzija*, Case No. IT-95-17/1, Judgment, 10 December 1998, para 147, holding that the prohibition on torture, genocide, slavery, racial discrimination, aggression, the acquisition of territory by force and the forcible suppression of the right of peoples to self-determination have acquired 'a particularly high status in the international normative system'. See also, the fourth preambular to the Draft Articles on prevention and punishment of crimes against humanity which recalls 'that the prohibition of crimes against humanity is a peremptory norm of general international law (jus cogens)'. Commentary (5) explains that:

> (5) The fourth preambular paragraph recalls also that the prohibition of crimes against humanity is not just a rule of international law; it is a peremptory norm of general international law (jus cogens). As such, this prohibition is accepted and recognized by the international community of States as a whole as a norm from which no derogation is permitted and which can be modified only by a subsequent norm of general international law having the same character. The Commission has previously indicated that the prohibition of crimes against humanity is "clearly

by the international community of States as a whole as a norm from which no derogation is permitted and which can be modified only by a subsequent norm of general international law having the same character'.[61] Peremptory norms enjoy a higher status than other norms and may only be modified by a new norm having the same status.[62] A peremptory norm creates legal obligations for the international community as a whole.[63] Consequently, there are two requirements to be met before a norm can be said it has acquired the status of peremptory norms: it must be a norm of general international law; and that it must be accepted by the international community of states as a whole that can only be modified by a norm of a similar status.

This brief overview demonstrates that crimes against humanity are prohibited by both treaty law and customary international law, and that such prohibition has acquired the peremptory norm status. The next section deals with the crime of apartheid as a crime against humanity.

> accepted and recognized" as a peremptory norm of international law. The International Court of Justice has found that the prohibition on certain acts, such as torture, has the character of jus cogens, which a *fortiori* suggests that a prohibition of the perpetration of such acts on a widespread or systematic basis amounting to crimes against humanity would also have the character of jus cogens.

[61] See Draft conclusion 2 [3(1)], Annex, the Draft Conclusions on Peremptory Norms of General International Law (Jus Cogens) adopted on first reading, *Report of the international Law Commission,* Seventy-First Session, General Assembly Official Records (A/74/10) (2019).

[62] See, *Case Concerning Armed Activities on the Territory of the Congo (New Application: 2002) (the Democratic Republic of the Congo v Rwanda)* 2006 ICJ Rep 6 (Separate Opinion of Judge Ad Hoc Dugard) para 10, where Judge Ad Hoc Dugard explains that peremptory norms 'enjoy a hierarchical superiority to other norms in the international legal order'. See also, art 53 of the Vienna Convention on the Law of Treaties (with annex), opened for signature 23 May 1969, 1155 *UNTS* 331 stipulating that:

> [a] treaty is void if, at the time of its conclusion, it conflicts with a peremptory norm of general international law. For the purposes of the present Convention, a peremptory norm of general international law is a norm accepted and recognised by the international community of states as a whole as a norm from which no derogation is permitted, and which can be modified only by a subsequent norm of general international law having the same character.

[63] See, K Hossain 'The Concept of Jus Cogens and the Obligation Under the U.N. Charter' (2005) 3 *Santa Clara Journal of International Law* 72 78.

2.2 *Apartheid as a Crime Against Humanity in International Law*

The crime of apartheid originates from southern Africa, and in particular, South Africa, where apartheid was sanctioned by the state. Gibson explains apartheid in South Africa as

> a system of legalized racial segregation and institutionalized White supremacy enforced by the National Party government of South Africa between 1948 and 1990. Apartheid had its roots in the history of European colonization and settlement of southern Africa, with the development of practices and policies of separation along the racial lines and domination by European's settlers and their descendants. The White-only apartheid government segregated education, medical care, transportation, and other public services, and provided Black people with services greatly inferior to those of Whites.[64]

It is interesting to note that South Africa played a significant role in the global stage and most notable in the creation of the League of Nations[65] and subsequently the UN despite this sanctioned violence.[66] It was only later that apartheid was condemned and declared a crime against humanity by the international community including the UN General

[64] JR Gibson *The Mis-Education of the Bantu: The Psychohistorical Evolution and Perpetuation of White Supremacy in South Africa* (2004) 3.

[65] See, the list of original members available at https://www.britannica.com/topic/League-of-Nations/Members-of-the-League-of-Nations (last accessed on 27 January 2021).

[66] See the original signatories of the UN Charter.

Assembly[67] and the UN Security Council.[68] In the African region, the Organization of the African Unity (OAU), the predecessor to the African Union (AU) also passed several resolutions condemning racial domination in the Southern African region.[69] Consequently, the international

[67] See, for example, UN General Assembly, *The Policies of Apartheid of the Government of the Republic of South Africa*, 13 December 1967, A/RES/2307, paras 1& 2, (condemning 'the policies of apartheid practised by the Government of South Africa as a crime against humanity', and further recognizing 'the legitimacy of the struggle of the people of South Africa for human rights and fundamental freedoms for all the people of South Africa irrespective of race, colour or creed'); UN General Assembly, *Question of Race Conflict in South Africa Resulting from the Policies of Apartheid of the Government of the Union of South Africa*, 30 January 1957, A/RES/1016; UN General Assembly, *The Policies of Apartheid of the Government of the Republic of South Africa*, 16 December 1966, A/RES/2202; UN General Assembly, *The Policies of Apartheid of the Government of South Africa*, 2 December 1968, A/RES/2396; UN General Assembly, *The Policies of Apartheid of the Government of South Africa1*, 8 December 1970, A/RES/2671 F, (declaring that 'the policies of *apartheid* of the Government of South Africa are a negation of the Charter of the United Nations and constitute a crime against humanity'); UN General Assembly, *International Convention on the Suppression and Punishment of the Crime of Apartheid*, 30 November 1973, A/RES/3068(XXVIII), (adopting the Apartheid Convention); UN General Assembly, *Policies of Apartheid of the Government of South Africa*, 28 November 1975, A/RES/3411 C & G; UN General Assembly, *Policies of Apartheid of the Government of South Africa*, 17 December 1979, A/RES/34/93 A-R; UN General Assembly, *Policies of Apartheid of the Government of South Africa*, 16 December 1980, A/RES/35/206.

[68] For example, UN Security Council, *Security Council Resolution 134 (1960) [Question Relating to the Situation in the Union of South Africa]*, 1 April 1960, S/RES/134 (1960); UN Security Council, *Security Council Resolution 181 (1963) [Policies of Apartheid of the Government of the Republic of South Africa]*, 7 August 1963, S/RES/181 (1963); UN Security Council, *Security Council Resolution 182 (1963) [Policies of Apartheid of the Government of the Republic of South Africa]*, 4 December 1963, S/RES/182 (1963); UN Security Council, *Security Council Resolution 392 (1976) [South Africa]*, 19 June 1976, S/RES/392 (1976); UN Security Council, *Security Council Resolution 417 (1977) [South Africa]*, 31 October 1977, S/RES/417 (1977); UN Security Council, *Security Council Resolution 418 (1977) [South Africa]*, 4 November 1977, S/RES/418 (1977); UN Security Council, *Security Council Resolution 473 (1980) [South Africa]*, 13 June 1980, S/RES/473 (1980); and UN Security Council, *Security Council Resolution 554 (1984) [South Africa]*, 17 August 1984, S/RES/554 (1984).

[69] For example, see OAU, First Summit Conference of Independent African States Meeting, CIAS/PLEN. 2/REV.2, Addis Ababa, Ethiopia, May 22–25, 1963 (agenda items including decolonization, and apartheid and racial discrimination); OAU, Resolution on Apartheid and Racial Discrimination in South Africa, First Ordinary Sess. Assembly of Heads of State and Government, AHG/Res. 6(I), Cairo, UAR, July, 17–21 1964, noting with grave concern the consistent refusal of the South African government to give consideration to appeals by every section of world opinion and in particular the resolutions

community adopted the Declaration on the Elimination of All Forms of Racial Discrimination[70]; the Convention on the Elimination of All Forms of Racial Discrimination[71]; and the Apartheid Convention.[72]

Both the Declaration on the Elimination of All Forms of Racial Discrimination[73] and the Convention on the Elimination of All Forms of Racial Discrimination[74] condemn apartheid and enjoin states (parties) to eliminate it from their government policies. However, they both do

of the UN Security Council and General Assembly. It therefore '[c]ondemne[d] the South African government policy' (para. 2) as it 'represent[ed] serious threat to peace and security' (para. 1); OAU, Second Ordinary Sess. Assembly of Heads of State and Government, Apartheid and Racial Discrimination in South Africa, AHG/Res. 34 (II), 21–26 October, 1965, calling on all states to institute a strict embargo on the supply of arms and ammunition and other material for use by military and police forces in South Africa (para 4) and inviting 'the South African liberation movements to cert their policies and actions and intensify the struggle for full equality, and appeals to all States to lend moral and material assistance to the liberation movements in their struggle' (para 10); Resolution on Southern Rhodesia, First Ordinary Sess., ibid, requesting the African states to take a vigorous stand against a Declaration of Independence of Southern Rhodesia by a European minority government and to pledge themselves to take appropriate measures, including the recognition and support of an African nationalist government in exile should such eventuality arise, para 1; OAU, Southern Rhodesia, Second Ordinary session, ibid, resolved 'to use all possible means including force to oppose a unilateral declaration of independence' (para 6(b)) and to 'give immediate assistance to the people of Zimbabwe with a view to establishing a majority government in the country' (para 6(c)); and OAU, First Ordinary Session, ibid, Territories under Portuguese Domination, AHG/Res. 13 (I), condemning Portugal for its persistent refusal to recognize the right of the peoples under its domination to self-determination and independence, ibid para 1.

[70] UN General Assembly, *United Nations Declaration on the Elimination of All Forms of Racial Discrimination*, 20 November 1963, A/RES/1904 (1963).

[71] International Convention on the Elimination of All Forms of Racial Discrimination, adopted and opened for signature and ratification by General Assembly resolution 2106 (XX) of 21 December 1965 entry into force 4 January 1969.

[72] International Convention on the Suppression and Punishment of the Crime of Apartheid G.A. res. 3068 (XXVIII)), 28 U.N. GAOR Supp. (No. 30) at 75, U.N. Doc. A/9030 (1974), 1015 U.N.T.S. 243, entered into force July 18, 1976 (Apartheid Convention).

[73] Art 5 enjoins states to eliminate 'governmental and other public policies of racial segregation and especially policies of apartheid, as well as all forms of racial discrimination and separation resulting from such policies'.

[74] Art 3 provides that '[s]tates Parties particularly condemn racial segregation and apartheid and undertake to prevent, prohibit and eradicate all practices of this nature in territories under their jurisdiction'.

not declare apartheid as a crime against humanity. It is the Apartheid Convention that stipulates that

> The States Parties to the present convention declare that *apartheid* is a *crime against humanity* and that inhuman acts resulting from the policies and practices of *apartheid* and similar policies and practices of racial segregation and discrimination, as defined in article II of the Convention, are crimes violating the principles of international law, in particular the purposes and principles of the Charter of the United Nations, and constituting a serious threat to international peace and security.[75]

The definition of 'the crime of apartheid' found in article II of the Apartheid Convention provides that it 'shall include similar policies and practices of racial segregation and discrimination as practised in southern Africa, [and] shall apply to the following inhuman acts committed for the purpose of establishing and maintaining domination by one racial group of persons over any other racial group of persons and systematically oppressing them'. The inhuman acts listed in article II of the Apartheid Convention are as follows:

a. Denial to a member or members of a racial group or groups of the right to life and liberty of person:
i. By murder of members of a racial group or groups;
ii. By the infliction upon the members of a racial group or groups of serious bodily or mental harm, by the infringement of their freedom or dignity, or by subjecting them to torture or to cruel, inhuman or degrading treatment or punishment;
iii. By arbitrary arrest and illegal imprisonment of the members of a racial group or groups;
b. Deliberate imposition on a racial group or groups of living conditions calculated to cause its or their physical destruction in whole or in part;
c. Any legislative measures and other measures calculated to prevent a racial group or groups from participation in the political, social, economic and cultural life of the country and the deliberate creation of conditions preventing the full development of such a group or groups, in particular by denying to members of a racial group or

[75] Art I(1) of the Apartheid Convention.

groups basic human rights and freedoms, including the right to work, the right to form recognized trade unions, the right to education, the right to leave and to return to their country, the right to a nationality, the right to freedom of movement and residence, the right to freedom of opinion and expression, and the right to freedom of peaceful assembly and association;

d. Any measures including legislative measures, designed to divide the population along racial lines by the creation of separate reserves and ghettos for the members of a racial group or groups, the prohibition of mixed marriages among members of various racial groups, the expropriation of landed property belonging to a racial group or groups or to members thereof;

e. Exploitation of the labour of the members of a racial group or groups, in particular by submitting them to forced labour;

f. Persecution of organizations and persons, by depriving them of fundamental rights and freedoms, because they oppose apartheid.

These inhumane acts describe the events in South Africa during the apartheid period. Laws were enacted to ensure classification[76] and segregation of races[77]; land dispossession[78]; and the suppression of dissent or protests[79] to mention just a few. These laws entrenched apartheid and the subsequent oppression of the Black population in South Africa.

[76] For example, see the Population Registration Act 30 of 1950 where section 5(1) provides that '[e]very person whose name is included in the register shall be classified by the Director [of Census] as a white person, a coloured person, or a native, as the case may be, and every coloured person or native whose name is so included shall be classified by the Director according to the ethnic group or other group to which he belongs'. The definitions section defines a white person as 'a person who in appearance obviously is, or who is generally accepted as a white person, but does not include a person who, although in appearance obviously a white person, is generally accepted as a coloured person;' a coloured person is defined as 'a person who is not a white person or a native;' and a native is 'a person who in fact is or is generally accepted as a member of any aboriginal race or tribe in Africa'. See section 1 (xv), (iii), and (x) respectively.

[77] Group Areas Act 41 of 1950; Promotion of Bantu Self-Governing Act 46 of 1959; The Reservation of Separate Amenities Act 49 of 1953; Prohibition of Mixed Marriages Act 55 of 1949; and Immorality Act 23 of 1957.

[78] Native Land Act 27 of 1913; Native Trust and Land Act 18 of 1936; Group Areas Act; and Stock Limitation Act, 1950.

[79] Suppression of Communism Act 44 of 1950; General Law Amendment Act 76 of 1962; and Terrorism Act 83 of 1967.

It is important to emphasize that article I(1) of the Apartheid Convention also declares apartheid a serious threat to international peace and security. A threat to international peace and security invokes reaction from the international community. In this regard, Chapter VII of the UN Charter delegates the responsibility to maintain international peace and security to the UN Security Council.[80] Article 24 (1) of the UN Charter stipulates the Security Council acts on behalf of the UN member states when carrying out its duties under the UN Charter. In response to this, UN member states are required to comply and fulfil Security Council resolutions adopted pursuant to its Chapter VII powers.[81] Having determined that the UN Charter empowers the Security Council is therefore expected to determine an existence of a threat to peace, breach of peace before it acts.[82] There is no definition of what constitutes a threat to international peace and security. The Security Council determines such existence on a case-by-case basis as evidenced in its numerous resolutions.[83] Once the Security Council determines that there is an existence

[80] See Arts 39–51 under Chapter VII of the United Nations Charter.

[81] See Art 25 of the UN Charter, which states that '[the UN Member States] agree to accept and carry out the decisions of the Security Council in accordance with the [UN] Charter'. See also, ICJ *Legal Consequences for States of the Continued Presence of South Africa in Namibia (South West Africa)*, (Advisory Opinion), [1971] *ICJ Reports* 53 para 115, where the ICJ held that since the UNSC resolution 748 (1992), which was adopted in conformity with the purposes and principles of the UN Charter 'were binding on all [UN Member States], which were under an obligation to accept and carry the decisions of the [Security Council] in accordance with the [...] [UN] Charter'.

[82] See Art 39 of the Charter.

[83] See for example, Resolution 2298 (2016), S/RES/2298 (2016) 22 July 2016 determined 'that the potential for *acquisition by non-State actors of chemical weapons* in Libya represents a threat to international peace and security'); Resolution 2359 (2017), S/RES/2359 (2017), 21 June 2017 ('Recalling that the situation in Mali constitutes a threat to international peace and security, and that the activities in Mali and in the Sahel region of *terrorist organizations* constitute a threat to peace and security in the region and beyond'); Resolution 2315 (2016), S/RES/2315 (2016), 8 November 2016 ('Determining that the situation in the [Former Yugoslavia] continues to constitute a threat to international peace and security'); Resolution 2317 (2016), S/RES/2317 (2016), 10 November 2016 (Expressing concern that *Al-Shabaab continues to pose a serious threat to the peace* and stability of Somalia and the region); Resolution 2177(2014), S/RES/2177 (2014), 18 September 2014 ('Determining that the *unprecedented extent of the Ebola outbreak in Africa* constitutes a threat to international peace and security, [and] Expressing concern about the particular impact of the Ebola outbreak on women'); Resolution 2249 (2015), S/RES/2249 (2015), 20 November 2015 ('Determining that, by *its violent extremist ideology, its terrorist acts, its continued gross systematic and widespread attacks*

of a threat to international peace and security, it then decides on whether to act. Consequently, the Security Council has powers to impose measures against states when discharging its mandate to maintain international peace and security under the UN Charter. Articles 41 and 42 of the UN Charter form the basis for the Security Council to adopt forcible and non-forcible measures.[84] As discussed earlier, there are numerous Security Council Resolutions, where the Security Council determined that apartheid committed in South Africa constituted threat to international peace and security.

Further, the Apartheid Convention creates individual criminal responsibility for perpetrators of apartheid, including individuals who are 'members of organizations and institutions and representatives of the [s]tate'.[85] This is an important provision which may see architects of apartheid, such as De Klerk, being held individually responsible for their perpetration of apartheid as a crime against humanity in South Africa. This is not far fetched as the families of the victims of apartheid recently called de Klerk's prosecution for apartheid crimes.[86] Consequently, states parties to the Apartheid Convention are required to adopt legislative, administrative and judicial measures to prevent perpetration of the crime of apartheid, and to ensure the prosecution of perpetrators of apartheid as a crime against humanity.[87] The Convention also calls for states parties to exercise

directed against civilians, abuses of human rights and violations of international humanitarian law, including those driven on religious or ethnic ground, its eradication of cultural heritage and trafficking of cultural property, but also its control over significant parts and natural resources across Iraq and Syria and its recruitment and training of foreign terrorist fighters whose threat affects all regions and Member States, even those far from conflict zones, the Islamic State in Iraq and the Levant (ISIL, also known as Da'esh), constitutes a global and unprecedented threat to international peace and security') (emphasis added); and SC/RES/181 (1963), 7 August 1963, which stated '[b]eing convinced that the situation in South Africa is seriously *disturbing international peace and security*'.

[84] See the list of the Security Council Resolutions since 1946 to date, United Nations Security Council 'Resolutions' available at https://www.un.org/securitycouncil/content/resolutions (last accessed on 18 June 2021).

[85] Art III of the Apartheid Convention.

[86] See, S Mtshali 'Families of Apartheid Victims Call for FW de Klerk to Face Law for Involvement' *IOL*, 7 July 2021, available at https://www.iol.co.za/news/politics/families-of-apartheid-victims-call-for-fw-de-klerk-to-face-law-for-involvement-0e30dfe7-45fd-4b47-ab1c-57d3f0d405f2 (last accessed on 17 July 2021).

[87] Art IV of the Apartheid Convention.

universal jurisdiction.[88] To date, no state party has attempted to prosecute any South African for perpetrating a crime of apartheid in South Africa. This is despite the existence of the Convention on the Non-Applicability of Statutory Limitations to War Crimes and Crimes Against Humanity,[89] which stipulates that there be no statutory limitation for crimes against humanity including the apartheid.[90]

The Rome Statute criminalizes apartheid and declares it a crime against humanity. The definition of apartheid in the Rome Statute significantly differs from the Apartheid Convention's definition on two grounds. Firstly, the Rome Statute removes reference to the southern African region where apartheid originates. The crime of apartheid can be committed anywhere in the world.[91] Secondly, the crime of apartheid is defined as 'inhumane acts of a character similar to those referred to in paragraph 1, committed in the context of an institutionalized regime of systematic oppression and domination by one racial group over any other racial group or groups and committed with the intention of maintaining that regime'.[92] The acts referred to in paragraph 1 include murder; extermination; enslavement; torture; rape; and persecution. This puts the crime of apartheid in the same category as the heinous crimes mentioned above.[93] The Draft Articles on prevention and punishment of crimes

[88] Art V of the Apartheid Convention provides that '[p]ersons charged with the acts enumerated in article II of the present Convention may be tried by a competent tribunal of any State Party to the Convention which may acquire jurisdiction over the person of the accused or by an international penal tribunal having jurisdiction with respect to those States Parties which shall have accepted its jurisdiction'.

[89] UN General Assembly, *Convention on the Non-Applicability of Statutory Limitations to War Crimes and Crimes Against Humanity*, 26 November 1968, A/RES/2391(XXIII).

[90] Art I (b) Convention on the Non-Applicability of Statutory Limitations to War Crimes and Crimes Against Humanity.

[91] See C Stahn *A Critical Introduction to International Criminal Law* (2019) 69.

[92] Art 7(2)(h) of the Rome Statute.

[93] See A Zahar 'Apartheid as an International Crime' in Antonio Cassese, Dapo Akande & Guido Acquaviva (eds) *Oxford Companion to International Criminal Justice* (2009) 245, 246, (arguing that the crime of apartheid 'is placed under the chapeau of crimes against humanity, at the same logical level as the underlying crimes of murder, deportation, torture, etc.[without any] clarity').

against humanity also recognize apartheid as a crime against humanity with the same definition as that found in the Rome Statute.[94]

There is no doubt that international law condemns and declares apartheid as a crime against humanity, whose prohibition has acquired both the statuses of customary international law and peremptory norms.[95]

3 South African Law on the Prosecution of Perpetrators of Apartheid for a Crime Against Humanity

South Africa is a party to the Convention on the Elimination of All Forms of Racial Discrimination.[96] It is important to note that although the Apartheid Convention is currently ratified by more than 100 states, South Africa is not party to it.[97] The reasons for this missed opportunity are unclear. Further, South Africa is not a party to the Convention on the Non-Applicability of Statutory Limitations to War Crimes and Crimes

[94] Ibid, Draft Articles on prevention and punishment of crimes against humanity 2(1)(j) and 2(2)(h).

[95] See, for example, United Nations International Law Commission, *Report of the International Law Commission on the work of the seventy-first session* (29 April–7 June and 8 July–9 August 2019), Chapter V: Peremptory norms of general international law (jus cogens), Conclusion 23 on non-exhaustive list, listing '(e) The prohibition of racial discrimination and apartheid' as a peremptory norm. See also, para (7) where the International Law Commission make the following commentary:

> The Security Council has also recognized the obligation on States not to recognize the situation created by a *breach of the prohibition of apartheid* and the obligation to respect self-determination. The obligation of non-recognition of acts that are in breach of obligations that arise *under the peremptory norms* of the right of self-determination and the prohibition of apartheid can also be seen in the General Assembly resolution calling for nonrecognition of the Bantustans created by South Africa in the furtherance of apartheid in violation of the right to self-determination.

[96] Signed on 3 October 1994 and ratified on 10 December 1998. See, https://treaties.un.org/Pages/ViewDetails.aspx?\src=IND&mtdsg_no=IV-2&chapter=4&lang=en (last accessed on 22 January 2021.

[97] The Apartheid Convention currently has 31 signatories and 109 ratifications. South Africa has neither signed nor ratified. See, https://treaties.un.org/Pages/ViewDetails.aspx?src=IND&mtdsg_no=IV-7&chapter=4&clang=_en (last accessed on 09 June 2021).

Against Humanity.[98] The question that remains is, how is it possible to hold accountable perpetrators of apartheid and prosecute them for crimes against humanity before the South African national courts?

This section, therefore, discusses relevant laws for the prosecution of international crimes in South Africa. The aim is to demonstrate that South Africa is bound by both international and domestic law to prosecute crimes against humanity. South Africa has an international law friendly Constitution.[99] The Constitution has several provisions that recognize international law as part of the South African law subject to certain conditions,[100] and enjoins courts to prefer an international law friendly interpretation of the legislation[101] and to have regard to the prescripts of international law when interpreting the rights in the Bill of Rights.[102] The Court has also confirmed in various judgments that both treaty and customary international law form an integral part of South African law.[103] In addition, South Africa has incorporated several treaties that it has ratified and that deal with the investigation and prosecution of international

[98] https://treaties.un.org/Pages/ViewDetails.aspx?src=TREATY&mtdsg_no=IV-6&chapter=4&clang=_en (last accessed on 22 January 2021).

[99] D Tladi 'The Interpretation and Identification of International Law in South African Courts (2018) 135 (4) *South African Law Journal* 708.

[100] Sections 231 (on treaty-making) and 232 (on customary international law) of the Constitution of the Republic of South Africa, 1996 ('the Constitution').

[101] Section 233 of the Constitution, which requires the courts to prefer a 'reasonable interpretation of the legislation that is consistent with international law over any alternative interpretation that is inconsistent with international law'.

[102] Section 39(1) of the Constitution enjoins the courts to 'consider international law when interpreting the rights in the Bill of Rights'.

[103] See for example, *S v Makwanyane* para 35, where the Court confirmed that '[c]ustomary international law and the ratification and accession to international agreements is dealt with in ... the Constitution which sets the requirements for such law to be binding within South Africa'. See also, Glenister v President of the Republic of South Africa 2011 (3) SA 347 (CC) (*Glenister II*) para 95, where Ngcobo CJ outlines the process to incorporate treaties into South African law; and Kaunda v President of the Republic of South Africa 2005 (4) SA 235 (CC) para 151, where Ngcobo J confirmed that '[i]t is true that customary international law is part of our law, but it can be altered by our law and, in particular, by our Constitution. Section 232 of the Constitution says that customary international law is the law in South Africa, "unless it is inconsistent with the Constitution or an Act of Parliament"'. See also, section 231 of the Constitution which deals with international agreements and how they can be incorporated into South African law, and section 232 of the Constitution, which recognises customary international law as law of the Republic.

crimes into South African law as contemplated in the Constitution as shown below.[104]

For the purposes of this discussion, the Implementation of the Rome Statute of the International Criminal Court Act[105] (the ICC Act), which incorporates the Rome Statute is the main piece of legislation regulating the investigation and prosecution of international crimes in South Africa. The objectives of the ICC Act create international crimes in accordance with the Rome Statute[106]; give power to the national authorities to investigate and prosecute perpetrators of international crimes[107]; and provide jurisdiction to courts to deal with international crimes,[108] including complementarity[109] and universal jurisdiction[110]; provide for cooperation with the ICC.[111] The ICC Act creates international crimes that are found in the Rome Statute, except for the crime of aggression.[112] It defines the term 'crime' as 'the crime of genocide, crimes against humanity and war crimes'.[113] Consequently, any person who is successfully prosecuted and found guilty of perpetrating an international crime may face a sentence of imprisonment including imprisonment for life or a fine, or both.[114]

The Rome Statute gives primacy to the national jurisdiction to deal with the investigations and prosecutions of international crimes in terms

[104] Section 231(4) of the Constitution stipulates that '[a]ny international agreement becomes law in the Republic when it is enacted into law by national legislation; but a self-executing provision of an agreement that has been approved by Parliament is law in the Republic unless it is inconsistent with the Constitution or an Act of Parliament'. See also, Glenister v President of the Republic of South Africa 2011 (3) SA 347 (CC) (*Glenister II*) paras 89, where Ngcobo CJ outlined section 231 scheme.

[105] Act 27 of 2001.

[106] Section 3(c) of the ICC Act.

[107] Section 3(d) of the ICC Act.

[108] Section 3(d) of the ICC Act.

[109] Section 3(d) of the ICC Act.

[110] Section 3(d) of the ICC Act.

[111] Section 3(e) of the ICC Act.

[112] Section 3(c) of the ICC Act. It must be noted that the ICC Act does mention the crime of aggression in its preamble, however that crime is not provided for in the provision that creates the crime nor is it defined in the definitions section.

[113] Section 1 of the ICC Act read with Schedule 1 parts 1 to 3 of the ICC Act; see also Arts 5, 6, 7 and 8 of the Rome Statute.

[114] Section 4(1) of the ICC Act.

of the complementarity principle.[115] Consequently, section 3(e) of the ICC Act contemplates the application of the complementarity principle in South Africa as it specifies that 'in the event of the national prosecuting authority declining or being unable to prosecute ... persons accused of having committed crimes or offences referred to in the [Rome] Statute'. Most importantly, the ICC Act makes clear that the primacy to prosecute remains with the domestic institutions.[116] The Court in *National Commissioner of the South African Police Service* has also confirmed this.[117]

Another relevant piece of legislation is the Prevention and Combating of Torture of Persons Act,[118] which incorporates the Convention Against

[115] See the preamble to the Rome Statute which states that the ICC 'shall be complementary to national criminal jurisdiction' read with art 1 of the Rome Statute, which further reinforce that the national courts will be given primacy over the ICC to deal with perpetrators of international crimes. See, also, MA Newton '*The Complementarity Conundrum: Are We Watching Evolution or Evisceration?*' (2010) 8 *Santa Clara Journal of International Law* 115, 123, explaining the purpose of the complementarity principle as follows:

> Complementarity is designed to serve as a pragmatic and limiting principle rather than an affirmative means for an aggressive prosecutor to target the nationals of states that are hesitant to embrace ICC jurisdiction and authority. The provisions of the Rome Statute preserve a careful balance between maintaining the integrity of domestic adjudications and authorizing a supranational court to exercise power where domestic systems are inadequate. In preserving this delicate balance, complementarity is best viewed as a restrictive principle rather than an empowering one; while the ICC has affirmative powers as a supranational court, the textual predicates necessary to make a case admissible are designed to constrain the power of the Court.

[116] See Section 5(3) of the ICC Act, which provides that '[t]he National Director must, when reaching a decision on whether to institute a prosecution contemplated in this section, give recognition to the obligation that the Republic in the first instance and in line with the principle of complementarity as contemplated in Art 1 of the Statute has jurisdiction and the responsibility to prosecute persons accused of having committed a crime'.

[117] *National Commissioner of the South African Police Service v Southern African Human Rights Litigation Centre and Another* 2015 (1) SA 315 (CC); 2015 (1) SACR 255 (CC) (*National Commissioner of the South African Police Service*) para 30.

[118] Act 13 of 2013. South Africa has also incorporated the Geneva Conventions of 1949 and Additional Protocols of 1977 through the Implementation of the Geneva Conventions Act 8 of 2012. However, The Geneva Conventions Act is not relevant in this discussion as it deals with war crimes.

Torture and Other Cruel, Inhuman or Degrading Treatment or Punishment ('the Torture Convention').[119] In this regard, the Prevention and Combating of Torture of Persons Act was enacted '[t]o give effect to the Republic's obligations in terms of the [Torture Convention]; to provide for the offence of torture of persons and other offences associated with the torture of persons within or across the borders of the Republic'.[120] The objects of the Act include giving effect to South Africa's obligations under the Torture Convention[121]; providing for prosecution of and penalties for perpetrators of torture[122]; bringing about measures to prevent and to combat torture[123]; and providing for the training of persons involved in the interrogation and detention of persons.[124]

The issue that is relevant in the duty to prosecute international crimes in South Africa is the power of the courts to exercise universal jurisdiction. Universal jurisdiction is 'based on the notion that certain crimes are so harmful to international interests that states are entitled—and even obliged—to bring proceedings against the perpetrator, regardless of the location of the crime or the nationality of the perpetrator or the victim'.[125] The Rome Statute does not expressly provide for the exercise of jurisdiction, instead, in its Preamble, it merely states that 'it is the duty of every State to exercise its criminal jurisdiction over those responsible for international crimes'.[126] In explaining the rationale for states parties to the Rome Statute to elect to exercise universal jurisdiction, Louise Arbor, the former Prosecutor for the ICTY and the ICTR argues that:

[119] UN General Assembly, Convention Against Torture and Other Cruel, Inhuman or Degrading Treatment or Punishment, 10 December 1984, UNTS vol 1465, p. 85.

[120] Long Title of the Prevention and Combating of Torture of Persons Act.

[121] Section 2(1)(a) of the Prevention and Combating of Torture of Persons Act.

[122] Section 2(1)(b) of the Prevention and Combating of Torture of Persons Act. See also section 4, which creates offences and penalties.

[123] Section 2(1)(c) of the Prevention and Combating of Torture of Persons Act.

[124] Section 2(1)(d) of the Prevention and Combating of Torture of Persons Act.

[125] M Robinson 'Foreword' *The Princeton Principles on Universal Jurisdiction* (2001) 16. See also, GP Fletcher 'Against Universal Jurisdiction' (2003) 1 *Journal of International Criminal Justice* 580 (critical of the principle of universal jurisdiction—arguing that it favours the victim and ignores the rights of the accused).

[126] Rome Statute, Preamble, para 6.

> It is ... a fair assumption that States Parties to the ICC Statute will wish to investigate and prosecute crimes falling under their jurisdiction rather than defer to the competence of the ICC. That assumption is certainly likely to hold true for all crimes over which the ICC has competence but in which a national court has a direct interest, such as crimes committed on the territory of that state, or by one of its nationals, or where the victims are nationals of that state, even though they may have suffered elsewhere. Even when the state so involved may have preferred to let the matter rest and not take action (for instance when the accused is a still powerful high-ranking official), it remains a fair assumption that the state will often prefer to proceed domestically rather than have the matter investigated by the ICC.[127]

Consequently, section 4(3) of the ICC Act provides for the exercise universal jurisdiction over persons who perpetrated international crimes outside the borders provided that the alleged perpetrator (a) is a South African citizen; (b) is a South African resident; (c) has committed the alleged international crime against a South African citizen or resident; or (d) is present in the South African territory. The *National Commissioner of Police Service* has confirmed the exercise of universal jurisdiction by the national courts over international crimes.[128] The key issue in this case was whether the principle of universal jurisdiction can be exercised over non-South Africans who perpetrated torture as a crime against humanity against non-South Africans beyond her borders.[129] The Court

[127] L Arbour 'Will the ICC Have an Impact on Universal Jurisdiction' (2003) 1 *Journal of International Criminal Justice* 585, 586.

[128] *National Commissioner of the South African Police Service)* para 42, where the Court reasoned that '[s]ection 4(3) sets the limits to universal jurisdiction. When a person commits an envisaged crime outside of the Republic our courts will have jurisdiction only if at least one of the connecting factors is present. The accused person must be a citizen of, or ordinarily resident in, our country, must have committed the crime against a citizen or a person ordinarily resident within the country, or must be present in the country after the commission of the offence'.

[129] See *National Commissioner of the South African Police Service* para 49, where the Court recalls that '[t]he alleged acts of torture were perpetrated in Zimbabwe, by and against Zimbabwean nationals. None of the perpetrators is present in South Africa. However, the duty to combat torture travels beyond the borders of Zimbabwe'. See also paras 4–11 setting out the facts.

held that international law did not prohibit the exercise of universal jurisdiction,[130] and reasoned that South Africa is bound by its international and domestic law obligations 'where appropriate, to exercise universal jurisdiction in relation to [international] crimes as they offend against the human conscience'.[131]

The Court also confirmed that the accused person needs to be present in the territory before the prosecution can take place.[132] It must be recalled that the Court was called upon to determine whether the relevant authorities can be compelled in terms of their obligations under section 4(3) of the ICC Act to investigate perpetrators of international crimes *in absentia*.[133] In this regard, the Court held that the police may investigate the international crimes extraterritorially even if the perpetrators are not present in South Africa as long as a two-prong test was satisfied. Firstly, it must be clear that the affected state is unwilling and unable to investigate the international crimes on its own; and secondly, it must be reasonable and practical to conduct the investigations extraterritorially.[134]

Like the ICC Act, the Prevention and Combating of Torture of Persons Act provides for the exercise of universal jurisdiction in its provisions. In fact, section 6(1) of the Prevention and Combating of Torture of Persons Act is drafted the same way as section 4(3) of the ICC Act. Therefore, the same interpretation by the Court in *National Commissioner of the South African Police Service* applies, especially since the case dealt with the issue of torture as an international crime in South Africa.[135] It is clear, therefore, that conditional universal jurisdiction is applicable in

[130] *National Commissioner of the South African Police Service* para 26.

[131] *National Commissioner of the South African Police Service* para 39.

[132] See *National Commissioner of the South African Police Service* para 42, where the Court holds that the requirement of presence 'holds true only as far as the prosecution of a crime in a South African court is concerned'.

[133] *National Commissioner of the South African Police Service* para 46 explaining that '[w]e are seized with an enquiry into whether presence is a factor at all when it comes to the exercise of universal jurisdiction for an investigation of an international crime'.

[134] *National Commissioner of the South African Police Service* paras 61–63.

[135] *National Commissioner of the South African Police Service* para 39, where the Court confirmed that 'torture is criminalised in South Africa under section 232 of the Constitution and the [Prevention and Combating of Torture of Persons Act] whilst torture on the scale of crimes against humanity is criminalised under section 232 of the Constitution, the [Prevention and Combating of Torture of Persons Act] and the ICC Act'.

South Africa for both the investigation stage and the prosecution stage of international crimes.

Although South Africa has ratified and domesticated the Rome Statute, it is important to highlight that the Rome Statute only applies to prosecutions of international crimes perpetrated after it came into force.[136] Equally the ICC Act does not apply retrospectively and therefore is inapplicable in the investigation and prosecution of persons accused of committing apartheid crimes before its enactment.[137] Interestingly, the Prevention and Combating of Torture of Persons Act is silent on whether a person who committed the crime of torture (before the Act came into force) can be prosecuted under its provisions. Be that as it may, it is trite law in South Africa that customary international law forms part of domestic law. A rule of customary international law in question must not conflict with a provision of the Constitution or an Act of Parliament.[138] The Court has also confirmed this in various judgments.[139]

It has already been established that the prohibition of apartheid as a crime against humanity has acquired the statuses of customary international law and peremptory norms.[140] This is also confirmed by the Court in *S v Basson* holding that treaty law and *customary law* obliges the state to prosecute perpetrators of the crime of apartheid as 'the practice of apartheid constituted crimes against humanity'.[141] The Court further held in *National Commissioner of South African Police Service* that

[136] See art 11(1) of the Rome Statute, which stipulates that 'The [ICC] has jurisdiction only with respect to crimes committed after the entry into force of this Statute'. However, see T de Souza Dias 'The Retroactive Application of the Rome Statute in Cases of Security Council Referrals and Ad hoc Declarations: An Appraisal of the Existing Solutions to an Under-discussed Problem' (2018) 16 *Journal of Criminal Justice* 65, 66, discussing 'two main instances where the application of the Rome Statute risks being retroactive'.

[137] See also, section 5() of the ICC Act, which provides that '[n]o prosecution may be instituted against a person accused of having committed a crime if the crime in question is alleged to have been committed before the commencement of the Statute'.

[138] Section 232 of the Constitution.

[139] See for example, *S v Makwanyane* para 35; and Kaunda v President of the Republic of South Africa 2005 (4) SA 235 (CC) para 151.

[140] See, J Dugard, M du Plessis and E Cohen 'Jurisdiction and International Crimes' in Dugard et al. (note 35 above) 210, 223, arguing that '[s]uch crimes are limited to piracy, slave-trading, war crimes, *crimes against humanity*, genocide and torture'.

[141] *S v Basson* 2005 para 37 (emphasis added).

apartheid as a crime against humanity has acquired the status of peremptory norms.[142] Therefore, this places an obligation on the South African police to investigate apartheid as a crime against humanity and on the NPA to prosecute such crimes under customary international law.[143]

Despite the confirmation by the Court—that there is an international obligation to prosecute the perpetrators of the crime of apartheid, there has not been any prosecution of perpetrators of this crime in South Africa. The next section explores reasons for the failure to investigate and prosecute perpetrators of apartheid as a crime against humanity.

4 Failure to Hold Accountable Perpetrators of Apartheid Crimes as a Crime Against Humanity in South Africa

As alluded to earlier, South Africa is recovering from a painful past, where the apartheid government perpetrated crimes against humanity against the Black population. During the peaceful negotiations that led to the post-apartheid South Africa, the parties agreed to a truth finding commission of inquiry to deal with the atrocities of the past and with the aim for unity and reconciliation. The rationale for this is found in the epilogue to

[142] *National Commissioner of South African Police Service*, para 37, and later endorsed in *Minister of Justice and Constitutional Development v Southern African Litigation Centre* 2016 (4) BCLR 487 (SCA); 2016 (3) SA 317 (SCA), para 64:

> Along with torture, the international crimes of piracy, slave-trading, war crimes, crimes against humanity, genocide and apartheid require states, even in the absence of binding international treaty law, to suppress such conduct because "all states have an interest as they violate values that constitute the foundation of the world public order".

[143] *National Commissioner of South African Police Service* para 77, where Madjiet JA (as he then was) held:

> The SAPS has misconceived the legal position in its decision not to investigate the torture allegations. It has misconstrued the meaning of its legal duty in terms of the SAPS Act and the ICC Act. It has failed to recognise that the crime of torture has been domesticated into our law by the ICC Act in terms of section 231(4) of the Constitution and that it is law in the Republic in terms of *section 232 of the Constitution due to its status as a peremptory norm of customary international law*'. (emphasis added).

the Constitution of the Republic of South Africa Act 108 of 1993 (the Interim Constitution) which stipulates:

> The adoption of this Constitution lays the secure foundation for the people of South Africa to transcend the divisions and strife of the past, which generated gross violations of human rights, the transgression of humanitarian principles in violent conflicts and a legacy of hatred, fear, guilt and revenge. These can now be addressed on the basis that there is a need for understanding but not for vengeance, a need for reparation but not for retaliation, a need for ubuntu but not for victimisation. In order to advance such reconciliation and reconstruction, amnesty shall be granted in respect of acts, omissions and offences associated Apartheid finally came to an official end on the 27 of April 1994 when South Africa had her first democratic elections that were inclusive of every South African with political objectives and committed in the course of the conflicts of the past. To this end, Parliament under this Constitution shall adopt a law determining a firm cut-off date, which shall be a date after 8 October 1990 and before 6 December 1993, and providing for the mechanisms, criteria and procedures, including tribunals, if any, through which such amnesty shall be dealt with at any time after the law has been passed.

The contemplated law is the Promotion of National Unity and Reconciliation Act 34 of 1995 ('the TRC Act'). The TRC Act established the Truth and Reconciliation Commission ('TRC') with the view to reconcile the nation,[144] and to seek the truth on what happened during apartheid.[145] The objectives of the TRC are set in section 3(1) as follows:

> to promote national unity and reconciliation in a spirit of understanding which transcends the conflicts and divisions of the past by-

[144] See, *Azanian Peoples Organization (AZAPO) and Others v President of the Republic of South Africa and Others* 1996 (8) BCLR 1015 (CC); 1996 (4) SA 672 (CC) ('*AZAPO Case*') para 2, where Mahomed DP explains that 'It was wisely appreciated by those involved in the preceding negotiations that the task of building such a new democratic order was a very difficult task because of the previous history and the deep emotions and indefensible inequities it had generated; and that this could not be achieved without a firm and generous commitment to reconciliation and national unity'. For more discussion on the AZAPO Case, see J Dugard 'Is the Truth and Reconciliation Process Compatible with International Law? An unanswered Question (1997) 13 *SA Journal on Human Rights* 258; D Moellendorf 'Amnesty, Truth and Justice: Azapo' (1997) 13 *South African Journal on Human Rights* 283.

[145] See the Long Title and section 3(1) of the TRC Act.

> *(a)* establishing as complete a picture as possible of the causes, nature and extent of the gross violations of human rights which were committed during the period from 1 March 1960 to the cut-off date, including the antecedents, circumstances, factors and context of such violations, as well as the perspectives of the victims and the motives and perspectives of the persons responsible for the commission of the violations, by conducting investigations and holding hearings;
>
> *(b)* facilitating the granting of amnesty to persons who make full disclosure of all the relevant facts relating to acts associated with a political objective and comply with the requirements of this Act;
>
> *(c)* establishing and making known the fate or whereabouts of victims and by restoring the human and civil dignity of such victims by granting them an opportunity to relate their own accounts of the violations of which they are the victims, and by recommending reparation measures in respect of them;
>
> *(d)* compiling a report providing as comprehensive an account as possible of the activities and findings of the Commission contemplated in paragraphs *(a)*, *(b)* and *(c)*, and which contains recommendations of measures to prevent the future violations of human rights.

The TRC Act also establishes three committees in order 'to achieve the objectives of the [TRC]'[146]—the Human Rights Violations Committee to investigate gross violations of human rights; the Amnesty Committee to deal with amnesty matters; and the Reparation and Rehabilitation Committee to deal with reparations matters.[147]

Interestingly, the Act does not mention the term 'apartheid' in its provisions. Instead, it refers to 'gross violation of human rights', which means 'the violation of human rights through (a) the killing, abduction, torture or severe ill-treatment of any person, or (b) any attempt, conspiracy, incitement, instigation, command or procurement to commit an act referred to in para (a)'.[148] Dugard provides two reasons for this omission. Firstly, he expounds that it was because the TRC did not only deal with the atrocities that were committed by the apartheid state. Instead, even the atrocities that were committed by the national liberation movements such as the governing political party, the African

[146] Section 3(3) of the TRC Act.

[147] Section 3(3)(a)–(c) of the TRC Act.

[148] See section 1 of the TRC Act (the definitions section).

National Congress, were also dealt with.[149] Secondly, Dugard reasons that the crimes under the TRC's jurisdiction were those that constituted crimes under South African law at the time.[150] However, *S v Basson* has confirmed that 'the state's obligation to prosecute offences is ***not limited to offences which were committed after the Constitution came into force*** but also applies to all offences committed before it came into force'.[151] Further, the gross human rights violations listed herein are the same inhumane acts listed in the Rome Statute and the Apartheid Convention as constituting apartheid as a crime against humanity.

The relevant, and perhaps the most controversial issue that stems out of the TRC Act is the provision that grants conditional amnesty to the perpetrators of apartheid crimes as contemplated in the TRC Act.[152] It is, therefore, no surprise that the Azanian Peoples Organization (AZAPO), one of the liberation movements that fought the apartheid regime, together with families of the victims of apartheid such as Steve Biko and Griffiths and Victoria Mxenge challenged the constitutionality of the amnesty provision in the TRC Act.[153] These families challenged the constitutionality of section 20(7) of the TRC Act[154] on the basis that it conflicted with section 22 of the Interim Constitution which provides that everyone is entitled to have their dispute resolved by a

[149] Dugard (note 152 above) 260. See also, The Report of The Truth and Reconciliation Commission - Volume 5, Chapter 6: Findings and Conclusions, para 2, where it is stated that '[t]he new government settled on a compromise. Focusing not only on those violations committed by the former state, the [TRC] Act chose instead to focus on violations committed by all parties to the conflict. It eschewed notions of vengeance or retribution, and instead created a mechanism for the granting of amnesty for politically motivated actions, providing full individual disclosure was made'.

[150] Ibid.

[151] *S v Basson* para 37 (emphasis added).

[152] See section 20 of the TRC Act, in particular section 20(7)(a) which provides that 'No person who has been granted amnesty in respect of an act, omission or offence shall be criminally or civilly liable in respect of such act, omission or offence and no body or organiation or the State, shall be liable; and no person shall be vicariously liable, for any such act, omission or offence'.

[153] *AZAPO Case.*

[154] Section 20(7) of the TRC Act provides:

(a) No person who has been granted amnesty in respect of an act, omission or offence shall be criminally or civilly liable in respect of such act, omission or offence and no body or organisation or the State shall be liable, and no person shall be vicariously liable, for any such act, omission or offence.

court of law or a forum of a similar nature.[155] They argued that the apartheid state agents who committed apartheid crimes against the political activists who fought against apartheid had to be prosecuted, and that victims and dependants of the victims were entitled to institute civil claims for compensation against such perpetrators.[156] The applicants also argued that the impugned provision, which grants conditional immunity to perpetrators of the crime of apartheid was a breach of international law as international law obliges states to prosecute perpetrators of gross human rights violations.[157]

The Court found that section 20(7) of the TRC Act did not conflict with section 22 of the Interim Constitution. The Court reasoned that granting amnesty in terms of section 20(7) of the TRC Act fell squarely on the choice made by Parliament as authorized in the epilogue of the Interim Constitution.[158] The Court refused to discuss whether international law obliged South Africa to prosecute perpetrators of gross human rights violations during the apartheid period. The Court reasoned that it was called upon to deal with the question of whether there was a conflict between section 22(7) of the Interim Constitution and section 20(7) of the TRC. Therefore, 'the enquiry as to whether or not international law prescribes a different duty is irrelevant to that determination'.[159] The Court's failure to deal with this enquiry has been criticized by scholars as the international community had already condemned apartheid as a

(b) Where amnesty is granted to any person in respect of any act, omission or offence, such amnesty shall have no influence upon the criminal liability of any other person contingent upon the liability of the first-mentioned person.

(c) No person, organisation or state shall be civilly or vicariously liable for an act, omission or offence committed between 1 March 1960 and the cut-off date by a person who is deceased, unless amnesty could not have been granted in terms of this Act in respect of such an act, omission or offence.

155 Section 22 of the Interim Constitution stipulates that '[e]very person shall have the right to have justiciable disputes settled by a court of law or, where appropriate, another independent or impartial forum'.

156 *AZAPO Case* para 8.

157 *AZAPO Case* para 25.

158 *AZAPO Case* para 50.

159 *AZAPO Case* para 26.

crime against humanity.[160] The point of this case is that granting conditional amnesty to those who complied with the provisions of section 20 of the TRC Act was found to be constitutionally valid and lawful. The Court, therefore, paved the way for the Amnesty Committee to discharge its duties in the TRC.

Consequently, out of 7112 applications that the Amnesty Committee received, only 849 applicants were granted conditional amnesty with 248 applications refused.[161] Those who were refused amnesty were expected to be prosecuted for the crime of apartheid. The TRC confirmed that 'it has always been understood that, where amnesty has not been applied for, it is incumbent on the present state to have a bold prosecution policy in order to avoid any suggestion of impunity or of contravening its obligations in terms of international law'.[162] Further, when the TRC completed its work and submitted it to President Mbeki, Mbeki confirmed that it was left to the NPA to decide on the prosecution of the perpetrators of the crime of apartheid.[163] The TRC referred many cases in its report to be investigated and prosecuted but there has not been one conviction for, nor prosecution of perpetrators of apartheid for crimes against humanity.[164] There are two reasons for this delay in prosecution. The

[160] See, du Plessis and Cohen (note 21 above) 268, arguing that '[t]he judgment does not ... show concern for the international legal order that condemned apartheid as a crime against humanity, that served as a standard by which the laws of apartheid were measured in the years without hope'.

[161] https://www.justice.gov.za/trc/amntrans/index.htm (last accessed 24 January 2020).

[162] TRC Final Report Volume 6 section 6 Chapter One, 595 para 24.

[163] See, Thabo Mbeki Statement by President Thabo Mbeki to the National Houses of Parliament and the Nation, on the Occasion of the Tabling of the Report of the Truth and Reconciliation Commission, Cape Town, 15 April 2003, where he stated that '[w]e have therefore left this matter in the hands of the [NDPP], for it to pursue any cases that, as is normal practice, it believes deserve prosecution and can be prosecuted. This work is continuing'. See also, Government Gazette, Notice 1539 of 2008, No. 31723, 12 December 2008, para 3.4 confirming that 'the PCLU shall be responsible for overseeing investigations and instituting prosecutions in respect of crimes arising from conflicts of the past'. See also, Pikoli and Wiener (note 18 above) 217 confirming that the PCLU headed by Special Director, Anton Ackerman, was established to deal with the investigation of these crimes.

[164] However, see Pikoli and Weiner (note 18 above) 221, where Pikoli confirms that there have been two successful convictions perpetrators entered a plea with the NPA and were eventually convicted of lesser crimes with lesser sentences.

first reason relates to the amendment of the NPA's prosecutorial policy, whilst the second reason relates to the purported political interference in the prosecution of perpetrators of apartheid arising from the TRC recommendations.

4.1 An Amendment to the Prosecutorial Policy in Response to the TRC Final Report

President Thabo Mbeki made a statement in Parliament in 2003 after the TRC submitted its final report.[165] The gist of President Mbeki's statement was that there was a need to adopt a prosecutorial policy that reflected the recommendations of the TRC considering certain factors. As a result, in 2005 the NPA adopted the *Prosecuting Policy and Directives Relating to the Prosecution of Offences Emanating from Conflict of the Past, and which were committed on or before 11 May of 1994.*[166] This policy was an amendment to the first policy that the NPA had earlier adopted.[167] This amendment became the source of a court challenge in the *Nkadimeng* case. The applicants in this case were the brother to Nokuthula Simelane who was abducted by the security police without trace during the apartheid era and presumed dead[168]; the widows of the 'Cradock Four' whose husbands were killed by the security branch officials[169]; and non-governmental organizations who are 'interested parties in the protection of the constitution'.[170] The Simelane and the Cradock matters were brought before the TRC, where several members of the apartheid security branch were implicated.[171] The applicants challenged the constitutionality of the amended Prosecution Policy of 2005[172] on the grounds that the impugned policy was in conflict with the Constitution; it provided for prosecutorial indemnity; and that it breached the

[165] Statement by President Thabo Mbeki (note 163 above).

[166] See, *Nkadimeng v National Director of Prosecutions and Others* (32,709/07) [2008] ZAGPHC 422 (12 December 2008) ('*Nkadimeng*') Appendix A.

[167] *Nkadimeng* para 6.

[168] *Nkadimeng* paras 2.1–2.3.

[169] *Nkadimeng* paras 2.5–2.7.

[170] Nkadimeng para 3.

[171] *Nkadimeng* paras 2.4 and 2.8.

[172] The reasons for the challenge are set out in *Nkadimeng* paras 9.1–9.2.4.

rule of law, certain rights, and international law.[173] The argument was that this policy allowed the NDPP not to prosecute perpetrators even in cases where there is sufficient evidence to prosecute, and that it was 'a "re-run" of the [TRC] amnesty processes'.[174] The court agreed with the applicants and found the policy amendments to be inconsistent with the Constitution and declared them unlawful and invalid.[175] Most importantly, the high court held that the NDPP had to comply with the constitutional obligation to prosecute perpetrators of international crimes.[176] This policy amendment and the subsequent court case contributed to the delay in prosecuting perpetrators of apartheid for crimes against humanity.

4.2 The Reported Political Interference in the NPA by High-Level Members of the Executive

There are currently few cases that are before the courts only because the families of the victims and non-governmental organizations such as the Foundation for Human Rights have pressured the NPA to investigate and prosecute the perpetrators of the apartheid crimes on certain high-profile cases.[177] It has been reported and confirmed by the high court that there has been political interference in the NPA by high-level politicians in government who do not want these TRC crimes to be prosecuted.[178]

[173] *Nkadimeng* paras 9.1–9.2.4.

[174] *Nkadimeng* para 14.2.

[175] *Nkadimeng* para 18.1.

[176] *Nkadimeng* para 15.4.4.

[177] For further information on these cases see, Foundation for Human Rights, Unfinished Truth and Reconciliation Commission business website detailing the status of these few but high-profile cases available here https://unfinishedtrc.co.za/ (last accessed on 27 January 2021). The current case the Foundation is pushing for are: Nokuthula Simelane (*Nkadimeng* Case); Ahmed Timol (*Rodrigues Case*); Hoosen Haffeje (Waiting for the high court, KwaZulu-Natal to schedule a date for an inquest into the death of Haffejee after the Minister made the request on the insistence of the family. The request was made in August 2019); Imam Haron (the Haron family has requested the re-opening of the inquest and are waiting for an official decision from the Minister of Justice); the Cradock Four (the NPA is slow to deal with this issue even after the son of one of the victims has made representations. One of the accused has since died by suicide in 2016); and Neil Agget (currently before the high court on inquest proceedings into the death of Agget).

[178] See *Rodrigues v National Director of Prosecution of South Africa and Others* 2019 (2) SACR 251 (GJ) (*Rodrigues*).

For example, *Rodrigues*, which deals with Rodrigues, an apartheid agent who is facing prosecution for the murder of Ahmed Timol, who died almost 50 years ago. The Timol matter was brought before the TRC and the TRC found that Rodrigues and others 'were directly responsible for the death of ... Timol'.[179] Rodrigues did not apply for conditional amnesty at the time.[180] Timol's family applied for a second inquest into Timol's death in 2017 in the high court after the first inquest was not satisfactory.[181]

The high court found that Rodrigues 'participated in the cover up to conceal the crime of murder and that he be investigated for being an accessory after the fact in respect of the crime of Timol's murder'.[182] Rodrigues applied for a permanent stay of prosecution citing an infringement of his right to a fair trial and the length of time the NPA took to charge him for the murder of Timol.[183] Rodrigues also argued that 'the [c]ourt should not finalise the application before it but rather use its powers to make an order directing that all relevant information relating to the genesis and the details of the political interference be placed before it before deciding the application'.[184]

On the issue of delay in the prosecution of Rodrigues, Kollapen J found that:

> What occurred in the period from about 2003 until 2017 was that all investigations into TRC cases and other crimes of the past were stopped as a result of an executive decision taken at a high level that purported to interfere with the [NPA]'s prosecutorial decision making.
>
> There was thus what can only be described as high level executive interference on investigating and prosecuting TRC crimes and other crimes of the past in the period from 2003 until about 2017.[185]

[179] *Rodrigues* para 18.

[180] *Rodrigues* para 19.

[181] *Rodrigues* para 15. See also paras 12–14, where the court discusses what happened during the first inquest.

[182] *Rodrigues* para 15.

[183] *Rodrigues* paras 1–2.

[184] *Rodrigues* para 30.

[185] *Rodrigues* paras 21 and 23.

All parties were in agreement that there was political interference in the prosecution of apartheid crimes in light of the TRC recommendation.[186] Kollapen J cited the affidavit of the former NDPP, Vusi Pikoli in the *Nkadimeng* case,[187] which outines how members of the executive branch of government interfered in the investigation and prosecution of apartheid crimes as recommended by the TRC.[188] Kollapen J, whilst confirming that there was a political interference by the executive in the NPA in relation to the prosecution of TRC crimes, he, however, did not agree that the application could not be finalized without seeking details on how the political interference happened. He also held that '[w]hatever form the political interference took, the NPA was enjoined in terms of both its constitutional and legal responsibilities to act on behalf of society and protect the public interest'.[189] There is no doubt that the reported political interference delayed the prosecution of apartheid perpetrators for crimes against humanity.[190] One must ask, what should be the consequences for political interference? It is to that question that this chapter turns.

[186] *Rodrigues* para 32 confirmation by the Court.

[187] *Nkadimeng v National Director of Prosecutions and Others* (32,709/07) [2008] ZAGPHC 422 (12 December 2008) ('*Nkadimeng*'). See also, *Rodrigues* para 23.

[188] The full affidavit of Vusi Pikoli can be found here: https://www.southernafricalitigationcentre.org/wp-content/uploads/2017/08/Vusi-Pikoli-Affidavit-Simelane.pdf (last accessed on 24 January 2021). The detailed affidavit revealed that:

[The then Minister of Justice Bridget Mabandla's] letter disclosed an assumption that the TRC matters will not be prosecuted. I found this to be a disturbing development as it appeared that at a political level there was an expectation that I would not prosecute the TRC cases. I regarded such an expectation as unwarranted interference in my constitutional duty to prosecute without fear, favour or prejudice.

I concluded that there had been improper interference in relation to the TRC cases and that I had been obstructed from taking them forward. I complained that such interference impinged upon my conscience and my oath of office. I indicated that I was unable to deal with these cases in terms of the normal legal processes and sought guidance on the way forward.

[189] *Rodrigues* para 57.

[190] The Supreme Court of Appeal has confirmed the political interference in the prosecution of apartheid crimes but also confirmed that the interference has no bearing on the future prosecution of perpetrators of apartheid committed before May 1994. See, Rodrigues v National Director of Public Prosecutions and Others (1186/2019) [2021] ZASCA 87 (21 June 2021) (*Rodrigues Appeal*), paras 30 and 56.

4.3 *Consequences for Political Interference in the Prosecution of Apartheid as a Crime Against Humanity*

The political interference mentioned above begs the question of what the NPA ought to do when there is a political interference with its work to prosecute apartheid as a crime against humanity. Pikoli claims that there was political interference by the executive in the NPA when it came to the prosecution of the TRC cases in his memoir. The former NDPP states that even though President Mbeki had pronounced that the NDPP had to decide on the prosecution, certain members of Mbeki's Cabinet 'were reluctant to carry out what the president had instructed'.[191] According to Pikoli, the reason for this reluctance was because the NPA was 'simply opening a way that would lead to the prosecution of [African National Congress, the governing political party] people and that there was no malicious intent on the part of the NPA'.[192]

What is interesting and highlighted by Kollapen J is that the NPA did not disclose the political interference that occurred in the TRC cases, instead it was the fourth respondent in this case, who is the nephew of Timol who did.[193] In this regard, Kollapen J held that the NPA had to bear the 'moral and legal consequences of this most serious omission and dereliction of duty on its part'.[194] Kollapen J further made two important instructions in relation to this interference. Firstly, he instructed the NPA to refer the conduct of those involved in the interference to the NDPP to consider taking action in terms of the NPA Act.[195] Secondly, he directed the executive and the NPA to make a public assurance 'that the kind of political interference that occurred in the TRC cases will never occur again'.[196] This also included the executive and the NPA indicating steps they would follow in order to avoid future breaches of the Constitution.[197] The importance of prosecutorial independence in

[191] Pikoli & Weiner 219.

[192] Pikoli & Weiner 218–219.

[193] *Rodrigues* paras 64 and 66. See also, para 4 detailing the respondents in this case.

[194] *Rodrigues* para 64.

[195] *Rodrigues* para 65.

[196] Ibid.

[197] Ibid.

the administration of criminal justice cannot be gainsaid. The Constitution requires that the NPA exercises its duty without any form of interference.[198] The Court has explained that:

> The NPA plays a pivotal role in the administration of criminal justice. With a malleable, corrupt or dysfunctional prosecuting authority, many criminals – especially those holding positions of influence – will rarely, if ever, answer for their criminal deeds. Equally, functionaries within that prosecuting authority may ... 'be pressured ... into pursuing prosecutions to advance a political agenda'. All this is antithetical to the rule of law, a founding value of the Republic.[199]

Kollapen J in *Rodrigues* also recalled the significance of having an independent NPA as contemplated in the Constitution and the NPA Act.[200]

The law is clear on what needs to be done in case there is prosecutorial interference either by a person or an organ of state.[201] There are consequences and penalties. In this regard, the NPA Act states that '[a]ny person who contravenes the provisions of section 32 (1) (b) shall

[198] Section 32(1) of the NPA states

(a) A member of the prosecuting authority *shall serve impartially* and exercise, carry out or perform his or her powers, duties and functions in good faith and *without fear, favour or prejudice* and subject only to the Constitution and the law.

(b) Subject to the Constitution and this Act, no organ of state and no member or employee of an organ of state nor any other person shall improperly interfere with, hinder or obstruct the prosecuting authority or any member thereof in the exercise, carrying out or performance of its, his or her powers, duties and functions.

[199] *Corruption Watch NPC* para 19. See also, *S v Basson* para 33, where the Court has remarked that '[b]y providing for an independent prosecuting authority with the power to institute criminal proceedings, the Constitution makes it plain that the effective prosecution of crime is an important constitutional objective'.

[200] *Rodrigues* paras 58–63. See also, section 179(4) of the Constitution; and section 32 of the NPA Act.

[201] *Corruption Watch NPC* para 21 has confirmed that:

> Improper interference may take any number of forms. Without purporting to be exhaustive, it may come as downright intimidation. It may consist [of] improper promises or inducements. It may take the form of corruptly influencing the decision-making or functioning of the NPA. All these forms and others are proscribed by an Act that gets its authority to guarantee prosecutorial independence directly from the Constitution.

be guilty of an offence and liable on conviction to a fine or to imprisonment for a period not exceeding 10 years or to both such fine and such imprisonment'. Kollapen J has alluded to this when he instructed the NDPP to 'consider whether any action in terms of section 41(1) of the NPA Act is warranted' against those implicated in the interference in the NPA.[202] Further, the NPA Act stipulates that the NPA is 'accountable to Parliament in respect of its powers, functions and duties under this Act, including decisions regarding the institution of prosecutions' and the NDPP 'may, at any time, submit a report to the Minister or Parliament with regard to any matter relating to the prosecuting authority, if he or she deems it necessary'.[203] The Annual Report of the NPA states that the investigations on the interference found in *Rodrigues* are ongoing.[204] It remains to be seen how the NDPP will deal with those implicated. The executive branch of government has been silent on this issue despite being prompted to respond,[205] and there has not been a public assurance from the executive that it will refrain from interfering with the NPA's duty to prosecute apartheid crimes despite being instructed to do so by Kollapen J.

What happens when there is a confirmed case of political interference by the executive branch of government? How is the executive to be held accountable for this interference? The law is clear in this regard. The

[202] *Rodrigues* para 65.

[203] Section 35(1) and (2)(b) of the NPA Act, respectively.

[204] See, NPA Annual Report, 2019/2020, *National Director of Public Prosecutions' Report on the Operations of the National Prosecuting Authority in Terms of section 22(4)(g), Read with section 35(2)(a) of the National Prosecuting Authority Act 32 of 1998*, available at https://www.npa.gov.za/sites/default/files/annual-reports/NPA%20Annual%20Report%202019-2020_0.pdf (last accessed on 27 January 2021), 122.

[205] See, Letter to the President by Former Commissioners of the Truth and Reconciliation Commission Accountability dated 5 February 2019, asking for an apology for the interference in the TRC cases and requesting the president to request a commission of enquiry into the interference. The letter is available at 77307_trc_letter_to_the_president__5_02_2019.pdf (cachefly.net) (last accessed on 27 February 2021). A follow-up letter by the Timol Ahmed Foundation/Trust was also sent. See Letter to President Ramaphosa: Call for an apology.... Dated 23 June 2020, available at Letter to President Ramaphosa: Call for an apology.... - Ahmed Timol (last accessed on 27 January 2021). It is unclear if the president has since responded to these letters.

Constitution requires Parliament to exercise oversight over the executive and to especially hold the executive accountable.[206] The Court has explained this oversight role as follows:

> Parliament is also entrusted with the onerous task of overseeing the Executive. Tyrannical rule is usually at the hands of the Executive, not least because it exercises control over the police and army, two instruments often used to prop up the tyrant through means like arrest, detention, torture and even execution. Even in a democracy, one cannot discount the temptation of the improper use of state organs to further the interests of some within the Executive.[207]

However, one cannot help but wonder if Parliament can play an oversight role over, and to hold the executive accountable for interfering with the NPA in the exercise of its duty to prosecute perpetrators of apartheid crimes. It must be recalled that President Mbeki informed the joint sitting of Parliament that he considered granting pardons to convicted persons whose offences were politically motivated and did not receive amnesty from the TRC.[208] As a result, Mbeki requested the representatives of each political party in Parliament at the time and they agreed to form part of the Reference Group that was tasked to consider the requests for pardon from those persons and make recommendations to the President.[209] The president also made it clear that the ultimate decision would

[206] Section 55(1) of the Constitution, which states that: '[t]he National Assembly must provide for mechanisms—(a) to ensure that all executive organs of state in the national sphere of government are accountable to it; and (b) to maintain oversight of—(i) the exercise of national executive authority, including the implementation of legislation; and (ii) any organ of state'. The Court has explained that '[t]he mechanics of how to go about fulfilling these constitutional obligations is a discretionary matter best left to the National Assembly'. See also, *Economic Freedom Fighters v Speaker of the National Assembly and Others* (note 7 above) para 22 confirming that parliament 'bears the responsibility to play an oversight role over the Executive and State organs and ensure that constitutional and statutory obligations are properly executed'.

[207] *Democratic Alliance v Speaker of the National Assembly and Others* 2016 (3) SA 487 (CC) para 17.

[208] See, Address of the President of South Africa, Thabo Mbeki, to the Joint Sitting of Parliament to Report on the Processing of Some Presidential Pardons: Cape Town, 21 November 2007, available at www.dirco.gov.za/docs/speeches/2007/mbek1121.htm (last accessed on 28 January 2021).

[209] Ibid.

be his in terms of his constitutional obligations in section 84(2)(j) of the Constitution.[210] Although the Court subsequently found the President's decision to pardon these persons,[211] the argument is that if the political parties in Parliament were keen on participating in this Reference Group, how are they to react when there are claims of political interference from the executive on the same issue?

Therefore, it is doubtful that Parliament (at least the political parties that stand to benefit from this) will be keen to see perpetrators of apartheid to be prosecuted for crimes against humanity. The reason for this is simple. It must be recalled that the TRC was mandated to investigate all atrocities that were committed by the agents of the apartheid regime and by the members of the liberation movements resisting the apartheid regime. The Court in *AZAPO* alluded to this when it reasoned that Parliament, when enacting the TRC Act, 'could conceivably have chosen to differentiate between the wrongful acts committed in defence of the old order and those committed in the resistance of it'.[212] However, no such distinction was made. Consequently, any person involved on the either side of the struggle during apartheid, and who did not apply for, or was refused amnesty is eligible for prosecution for gross human rights violations that occurred during that specified period. The prosecution of perpetrators of apartheid for crimes against humanity is only possible through court cases that are prompted by the families of the apartheid victims. In addition, Parliament needs to be forced through court action to exercise its oversight function over the executive to stop interfering with the NPA's duty to deal with these crimes as has been the

[210] Section 84(2)(j) of the Constitution provides that '[t]he President is responsible for—pardoning or reprieving offenders and remitting any fines, penalties or forfeitures'.

[211] See, *Albutt v Centre for the Study of Violence and Reconciliation and Others* 2010 (3) SA 293 (CC) para 71, where Ngcobo CJ found the president's decision that excluded victim of apartheid crimes' participation to be irrational and remarked that '[a] process which permits political party representatives and their members, to the exclusion of the victims, to consider whether a pardon should be granted in an offence with a political motive is entirely inconsistent with the principles and values that underlie our Constitution'.

[212] *AZAPO Case* para 50.

case before. The positive news is that the NDPP has promised to deal with the outstanding TRC cases.[213]

5 Conclusion

This chapter has demonstrated that South Africa has the law that complies with its international and constitutional obligations to ensure that there are investigation and prosecution of international crimes, and in particular apartheid as a crime against humanity. However, this chapter has also demonstrated that there are some doubts on whether South Africa is capable of prosecuting perpetrators of the crime of apartheid for crimes against humanity. This begs the question of whether South Africa is even capable of holding to account the perpetrators of international crimes under the Rome Statute. The unwillingness to prosecute perpetrators of the crimes from South Africa's violent past raises doubts on whether South Africa is capable of prosecuting perpetrators of international crimes that arise from the breach of the ICC Act and the Prevention and Combating of Torture of Persons Act.

5.1 Post-Script

The Supreme Court of Appeal has confirmed the high court judgement in *Rodrigues* and opened way for the NPA and the NDPP to continue with the prosecution of apartheid crimes committed before May 1994 as per the TRC Report.[214] Subsequent to this judgement, the NPA and the Directorate for the Priority Crimes Investigations released a joint statement confirming that there will be prosecution of such perpetrators.[215] The de Klerk Foundation also released a statement condemning

[213] A Makinana 'NPA Looking at Outstanding TRC Cases: Batohi' *Times Live* 9 July 2019, available at https://www.timeslive.co.za/politics/2019-07-09-npa-looking-at-outstanding-trc-cases-batohi/ (last accessed on 27 January 2021).

[214] *Rodrigues Appeal* (note 198 above).

[215] South African Government News Agency 'Hawks, NPA investigate TRC atrocities', *SANews.gov.za,* 28 June 2021, available at https://www.sanews.gov.za/south-africa/hawks-npa-investigate-trc-atrocities, (last accessed on 17 July 2021). See also, Foundation for Human Rights *Press Release—The FHR's statement with respect to the announced dedicated capacity for the apartheid-era crimes*, 28 June 2021, available at https://unfinishedtrc.co.za/press-release-the-fhrs-statement-with-respect-to-the-announced-dedicated-capacity-for-the-apartheid-era-crimes/ (last accessed on 17 July 2021).

such a move and complaining that the prosecution should not be one-sided as the TRC Act makes clear that both sides to the struggle against apartheid will be prosecuted should they fail to apply for amnesty.[216] So, it seems that there may be a long way before we see prosecution of alleged apartheid perpetrators such as de Klerk for crimes against humanity before the South African courts. But only time will tell.

Acknowledgements The author would like to thank Chris Gevers for availing himself to discuss South Africa's failure to prosecute apartheid as a crime against humanity; the South African Reading Group led by Prof Penny Andrews of New York Law School for an opportunity to present the initial draft of this chapter and comments from participants; and the blind reviewers for their comments. All errors remain the author's.

References

Articles

Boister N & Burchill R 'The Implications of the Pinochet Decisions for the Extradition or Prosecution of Former South African Heads of State for Crimes Committed Under Apartheid' (1999) 11(4) *African Journal of International and Comparative Law* 619.

De Souza Dias T 'The Retroactive Application of the Rome Statute in Cases of Security Council Referrals and Ad hoc Declarations: An Appraisal of the Existing Solutions to an Under-discussed Problem' (2018) 16 *Journal of Criminal Justice* 65.

De Wet E 'The Implications of President Al-Bashir's Visit to South Africa for International and Domestic Law' (2015) 13 (5) *Journal of International Criminal Justice* 1049.

Du Plessis M & Mettraux G 'South Africa's Failed Withdrawal from the Rome Statute: Politics, Law, and Judicial Accountability' (2017) 15(2) *Journal of International Criminal Justice* 361.

Du Plessis M 'South Africa's Implementation of the ICC Statute' (2007) 5 *Journal of International Criminal Justice* 460.

Dugard J 'Is the Truth and Reconciliation Process Compatible with International Law? An Unanswered Question (1997) 13 *SA Journal on Human Rights* 258.

[216] De Klerk Foundation Editorial 'The NPA's Decision to Prosecute 'Apartheid Era' Crimes' De Klerk Foundation, undated, available at https://fwdeklerk.org/index.php/en/latest/news/1946-article-the-npa-s-decision-to-prosecute-apartheid-era-crimes (last accessed on 17 July 2021).

Dyani-Mhango N 'Reflections on Prosecutorial Independence and Impartiality in South Africa: The Recent Jurisprudence of the Courts' (2020) 35(2) *SA Public Law* 1.

Dyani-Mhango N 'South Africa's (Unconstitutional) Withdrawal from the Rome Statute: A Note on *Democratic Alliance v Minister of International Relations and Cooperation*' (2018) 34(2) *South African Journal on Human Rights* 268.

Dyani-Mhango N 'South Africa's Dilemma: Immunity Laws, International Obligations and the Visit by Sudan's President Omar Al Bashir' 26 (3) *Washington International Law Journal* 535.

Dyani-Mhango N 'The ICC Pre-Trial Chamber's Decision on South Africa's Failure to Arrest and Surrender South Africa: South Africa Escapes 'Sanctions'' 2017 *African Yearbook of International Humanitarian Law* 37.

Fletcher GP 'Against Universal Jurisdiction' (2003) 1 *Journal of International Criminal Justice* 580.

Gevers C 'Prosecuting the Crime Against Humanity of Apartheid: Never, Again' (2018) *African Yearbook on International Humanitarian Law* 25.

Hossain K 'The Concept of Jus Cogens and the Obligation Under The U.N. Charter' (2005) 3 *Santa Clara Journal of International Law* 72.

Jalloh CC 'What Makes a Crime Against Humanity and Crime Against Humanity' (2013) 28(2) *American University International Law Review* 381.

L Arbour 'Will the ICC Have an Impact on Universal Jurisdiction' (2003) 1 *Journal of International Criminal Justice* 585.

Lungu S & Dyani-Mhango N 'Ensuring That State Parties to the Rome Statute Co-operate with ICC Requests to Arrest and Surrender Suspects: Reflecting on the Role of the Security Council Through the Lens of the Responsibility to Protect (R2P)' (2018) *African Yearbook of International Humanitarian Law* 119.

Moellendorf D 'Amnesty, Truth and Justice: AZAPO' (1997) 13 *South African Journal on Human Rights* 283.

Newton MA 'The Complementarity Conundrum: Are We Watching Evolution or Evisceration?' (2010) 8 *Santa Clara Journal of International Law* 115.

Slye R 'Apartheid as a Crime Against Humanity: A Submission to the South African Truth and Reconciliation Commission' (1999) 20 *Michigan Journal of International Law* 267.

Ssenyonjo M 'State Withdrawal Notifications from the Rome Statute of the International Criminal Court: South Africa, Burundi and the Gambia' (2018) 29 Criminal Law Forum 63.

Stone L 'A Sign of the Times: South Africa's Politico-Legal Retrogression as Illustrated Through the Intention to Withdraw from the Rome Statute' (2018) 33 *Southern African Public Law* 1.

Tladi D 'The Duty of South Africa to Arrest and Surrender Al Bashir Under South African and International Law: A Perspective from International Law' (2015) 13 (5) *Journal of International Criminal Justice* 1027.

Tladi D 'The Interpretation and Identification of International Law in South African Courts (2018) 135 (4) *South African Law Journal* 708.

Ventura MJ 'Escape from Johannesburg: Sudanese President Al Bashir Visits South Africa, and the Implicit Removal of Head of State Immunity by the United Nations Security Council in Light of Al Jedda' (2015) 13 *Journal of International Criminal Justice* (2015) 995.

Wabwile MM 'South Africa's Proposed Exit from the Rome Statute: Alternative Perspectives' (2018) 11 *African Journal of Legal Studies* 117.

Zahar A 'Apartheid as an International Crime' in Cassese A, Akande D & Acquaviva G (eds) *Oxford Companion to International Criminal Justice* (2009) 245.

Books

Bassiouni MC *Crimes Against Humanity in International Criminal Law* (1999).

Cryer, R, Friman H, Robinson D & Wilmshurst E *An Introduction to International Criminal Law and Procedure* (3rd Ed) (2014).

Gardam JG & Garvis MJ *Women, Armed Conflict and International Law* (2001).

Gibson JR *The Mis-Education of the Bantu: The Psychohistorical Evolution and Perpetuation of White Supremacy in South Africa* (2004).

Meron T *Human Rights and Humanitarian Norms as Customary Law* (1989).

Pikoli V and Wiener M *My Second Initiation: The Memoir of Vusi Pikoli* (2013)

Robinson M 'Foreword' *The Princeton Principles on Universal Jurisdiction* (2001) 16.

Stahn C *A Critical Introduction to International Criminal Law* (2019).

Chapters in Books

Ambos K 'Crimes Against Humanity and the International Criminal Court' in Sadat LN *Forging a Convention for Crimes Against Humanity* (2011) 279.

Du Plessis M and Cohen E 'International Criminal Courts, the International Criminal Court, and South Africa's Implementation of the Rome Statute' in Dugard J, M du Plessis M, Maluwa T & Tladi D *Dugard's International Law: A South African Perspective* (5th Ed, 2018) 245.

Dugard J, du Plessis M and Cohen E 'Jurisdiction and International Crimes' in Dugard J, M du Plessis M, Maluwa T & Tladi D *Dugard's International Law: A South African Perspective* (5th Ed, 2018) 210.

Dyani-Mhango N 'South Africa's Contribution to the International Criminal Justice' in Ndulo M & Emeziem C (eds) (2021) *Handbook on African Law: A Historical, Political, Social, and Economic Context of Law in Africa* (2021).

International Agreements

Annex to Agreement for the Prosecution and Punishment of Major War Criminals of the European Axis (London Agreement), London, Aug. 8, 1945, 82 U.N.T.S. 279, 59 Stat. 1544, E.A.S. No. 472 *Reprinted* in (1945) 39 *American Journal of International Law* 257 (Supp.) (Nuremberg Charter).

Charter of the International Military Tribunals for the Far East, Jan. 19, 1946, T.I.A.S. 1589.

Vienna Convention on the Law of Treaties (with annex), Opened for Signature 23 May 1969, 1155 *UNTS* 331. N

United Nations, *Charter of the United Nations*, 1945, 1 UNTS XVI (UN Charter), available at https://treaties.un.org/doc/publication/ctc/uncharter.pdf.

Statute of the International Criminal Tribunal for the Former Yugoslavia, UN Doc. S/25704, Annex (3 May 1993).

Statute of the International Criminal Tribunal for Rwanda, SC Res. 955 as an annex.

Statute of the International Court of Justice, United Nations, *Statute of the International Court of Justice*, 18 April 1946.

UN General Assembly, *Convention on the Non-Applicability of Statutory Limitations to War Crimes and Crimes Against Humanity*, 26 November 1968, A/RES/2391(XXIII).

UN General Assembly, Convention Against Torture and Other Cruel, Inhuman or Degrading Treatment or Punishment, 10 December 1984, UNTS vol 1465, p. 85.

International Convention on the Elimination of All Forms of Racial Discrimination, adopted and opened for signature and ratification by General Assembly resolution 2106 (XX) of 21 December 1965 entry into force 4 January 1969.

International Convention on the Suppression and Punishment of the Crime of Apartheid G.A. res. 3068 (XXVIII)), 28 U.N. GAOR Supp. (No. 30) at 75, U.N. Doc. A/9030 (1974), 1015 U.N.T.S. 243, entered into force July 18, 1976.

Rome Statute of the International Criminal Court 2187 U.N.T.S. 90, *entered into force* July 1, 2002.

Legislation

General Law Amendment Act 76 of 1962.
Group Areas Act 41 of 1950.
Immorality Act 23 of 1957.
Implementation of the Rome Statute of the International Criminal Court Act 27 of 2002.
Native Land Act 27 of 1913.
Native Trust and Land Act 18 of 1936.
Population Registration Act 30 of 1950.
Prevention and Combating of Torture of Persons Act 13 of 2013.
Prohibition of Mixed Marriages Act 55 of 1949.
Promotion of Bantu Self-Governing Act 46 of 1959.
Promotion of National Unity and Reconciliation Act 34 of 1995.
Reservation of Separate Amenities Act 49 of 1953.
Stock Limitation Act of 1950.
Suppression of Communism Act 44 of 1950.
Terrorism Act 83 of 1967.

Caselaw

International

Case Concerning Armed Activities on the Territory of the Congo (New Application: 2002) (the Democratic Republic of the Congo v Rwanda) ICJ Rep. 2006, p. 6.
Federal Republic of Germany v Denmark; Federal Republic of Germany v Netherlands (North Sea Continental Shelf Case), I.C.J. Rep. 1969, p. 3.
Legal Consequences for States of the Continued Presence of South Africa in Namibia (South West Africa), (Advisory Opinion), ICJ Rep. 1971, p. 53.
Prosecutor v Akayesu, Case No. ICTR—96-13-T.
Prosecutor v *Dragoljub Kunarac, Radomir Kovac and Zoran Vukovic* Case No IT-96-23-T & IT-96-23/1-T.
Prosecutor v Furundzija, Case No. IT-95-17/1, Judgment, 10 December 1998.
Prosecutor v Jean-Pierre Bemba Gombo, Judgment pursuant to Article 74 of the Statute, Case No. ICC-01/05-01/08.
Prosecutor v Kupreškić et al, Judgment, Case Number IT-95-16, 14 January 2000.
Prosecutor v Laurent Gbagbo, Decision on the confirmation of charges against Laurent Gbagbo, ICC-02/11-01/11-656-Red 12-06-2014 2/131 NM PT.
Prosecutor v Tadic Decision on the Defence Motion for Interlocutory Appeal on Jurisdiction, Case No IT-94-1.
Prosecutor v Tadic, Opinion and Judgment, Case No IT-94-1, 7 May 1997.

South African

Albutt v Centre for the Study of Violence and Reconciliation and Others 2010 (3) SA 293 (CC).

Azanian Peoples Organization (AZAPO) and Others v President of the Republic of South Africa and Others 1996 (8) BCLR 1015 (CC); 1996 (4) SA 672 (CC).

Corruption Watch NPC & Others v President of the Republic of South Africa & Others; Nxasana v Corruption Watch NPC & Others 2018 (10) BCLR 1179 (CC).

Democratic Alliance v Minister of International Relations and Co-operation and Others; Engels and Another v Minister of International Relations and Co-operation and Another 2018 (2) SACR 654 (GP).

Democratic Alliance v President of South Africa 2013 (1) SA 248 (CC).

Democratic Alliance v Speaker of the National Assembly and Others 2016 (3) SA 487 (CC).

Economic Freedom Fighters and Others v Speaker of the National Assembly 2018 (2) SA 571 (CC).

Economic Freedom Fighters v Speaker of the National Assembly and Others; Democratic Alliance v Speaker of the National Assembly and Others 2016 (5) BCLR 618 (CC); 2016 (3) SA 580 (CC).

Glenister v President of the Republic of South Africa 2011 (3) SA 347 (CC).

Justice Alliance of South Africa v President of Republic of South Africa and Others, Freedom Under Law v President of Republic of South Africa and Others, Centre for Applied Legal Studies and Another v President of Republic of South Africa and Others 2011 (5) SA 388 (CC).

Kaunda v President of the Republic of South Africa 2005 (4) SA 235 (CC).

Law Society of South Africa and Others v President of the Republic of South Africa and Others 2019 (3) BCLR 329 (CC); 2019 (3) SA 30 (CC).

Minister of Justice and Constitutional Development v Southern African Litigation Centre 2016 (4) BCLR 487 (SCA); 2016 (3) SA 317 (SCA).

National Commissioner of the South African Police Service v Southern African Human Rights Litigation Centre and Another 2015 (1) SA 315 (CC); 2015 (1) SACR 255 (CC).

Nkadimeng v National Director of Prosecutions and Others (32709/07) [2008] ZAGPHC 422 (12 December 2008).

President of the Republic of South Africa and Others v South African Rugby Football Union and Others 2000 (1) SA 1 (CC).

President of the Republic of South Africa v Office of the Public Protector and Others 2018 (2) SA 100 (GP).

Rodrigues v National Director of Prosecution of South Africa and Others 2019 (2) SACR 251 (GJ).

Rodrigues v National Director of Public Prosecutions and Others (1186/2019) [2021] ZASCA 87 (21 June 2021).

UN Documents

UN General Assembly, Annex, the Draft Conclusions on Peremptory Norms of General International Law (Jus Cogens) Adopted on First Reading, *Report of the International Law Commission*, Seventy-First Session, General Assembly Official Records (A/74/10) (2019).

UN General Assembly, International Law Commission, *Report of the International Law Commission on the Work of the Seventy-First Session* (29 April–7 June and 8 July–9 August 2019), Chapter V: Peremptory Norms of General International Law (*jus cogens*).

UN General Assembly, *International Convention on the Suppression and Punishment of the Crime of Apartheid*, 30 November 1973, A/RES/3068(XXVIII).

UN General Assembly, *Policies of Apartheid of the Government of South Africa*, 28 November 1975, A/RES/3411 C & G.

UN General Assembly, *Policies of Apartheid of the Government of South Africa*, 17 December 1979, A/RES/34/93 A-R.

UN General Assembly, *Policies of Apartheid of the Government of South Africa*, 16 December 1980, A/RES/35/206.

UN General Assembly, *Question of Race Conflict in South Africa Resulting from the Policies of Apartheid of the Government of the Union of South Africa*, 30 January 1957, A/RES/1016.

UN General Assembly, *The Policies of Apartheid of the Government of the Republic of South Africa*, 13 December 1967, A/RES/2307.

UN General Assembly, *The Policies of Apartheid of the Government of the Republic of South Africa*, 16 December 1966, A/RES/2202.

UN General Assembly, *The Policies of Apartheid of the Government of South Africa*, 2 December 1968, A/RES/2396.

UN General Assembly, *The Policies of Apartheid of the Government of South Africal*, 8 December 1970, A/RES/2671 Fl.

UN General Assembly, *United Nations Declaration on the Elimination of All Forms of Racial Discrimination*, 20 November 1963, A/RES/1904 (1963).

UN International Law Commission, *Report of the International Law Commission on the Work of the Seventy-First Session* (29 April–7 June and 8 July–9 August 2019), Chapter IV: Crimes Against Humanity.

UN Security Council Resolution 181, SC/RES/181 (1963), 7 August 1963.

UN Security Council Resolution 2177(2014), S/RES/2177 (2014), 18 September 2014.

UN Security Council Resolution 2298 (2016), S/RES/2298 (2016) 22 July 2016.

UN Security Council Resolution 2315 (2016), S/RES/2315 (2016), 8 November 2016.

UN Security Council Resolution 2317 (2016), S/RES/2317 (2016), 10 November 2016.

UN Security Council Resolution 2359 (2017), S/RES/2359 (2017), 21 June 2017.

UN Security Council, *Security Council Resolution 134 (1960) [Question Relating to the Situation in the Union of South Africa]*, 1 April 1960, S/RES/134 (1960).

UN Security Council, *Security Council Resolution 181 (1963) [Policies of Apartheid of the Government of the Republic of South Africa]*, 7 August 1963, S/RES/181 (1963).

UN Security Council, *Security Council Resolution 182 (1963) [Policies of Apartheid of the Government of the Republic of South Africa]*, 4 December 1963, S/RES/182 (1963).

UN Security Council, *Security Council Resolution 392 (1976) [South Africa]*, 19 June 1976, S/RES/392 (1976).

UN Security Council, *Security Council Resolution 417 (1977) [South Africa]*, 31 October 1977, S/RES/417 (1977).

UN Security Council, *Security Council Resolution 418 (1977) [South Africa]*, 4 November 1977, S/RES/418 (1977).

UN Security Council, *Security Council Resolution 473 (1980) [South Africa]*, 13 June 1980, S/RES/473 (1980).

UN Security Council, *Security Council Resolution 554 (1984) [South Africa]*, 17 August 1984, S/RES/554 (1984).

UN Security Resolution 2249 (2015), S/RES/2249 (2015), 20 November 2015.

UN, *Rome Statute of the International Criminal Court Rome, 17 July 1998 South Africa: Withdrawal of Notification of Withdrawal*, Reference: C.N.121. 2017.TREATIES-XVIII.10 (Depositary Notification), 7 March 2017, available at https://treaties.un.org/doc/Publication/CN/2017/CN.121.2017-Eng.pdf.

OAU Documents

OAU, First Summit Conference of Independent African States Meeting, CIAS/PLEN. 2/REV.2, Addis Ababa, Ethiopia, May 22–25, 1963.

OAU, Resolution on Apartheid and Racial Discrimination in South Africa, First Ordinary Sess. Assembly of Heads of State and Government, AHG/Res. 6(I), Cairo, UAR, July 17–21, 1964.

OAU, Second Ordinary Sess. Assembly of Heads of State and Government, Apartheid and Racial Discrimination in South Africa, AHG/Res. 34 (II), 21–26 October 1965.

OAU, Territories under Portuguese Domination, AHG/Res. 13 (I).

SADC Documents

SADC *Communique of the 39th SADC Summit of Heads of State and Government*, 18 August 2019, at para 20, available at www.sadc.int/files/1915/6614/8772/Communique_of_the_39th_SADC_Summit-English.pdf (last accessed on 19 January 2020).

Government of South Africa Documents

Address of the President of South Africa, Thabo Mbeki, to the Joint Sitting of Parliament to Report on the Processing of Some Presidential Pardons: Cape Town, 21 November 2007, available at www.dirco.gov.za/docs/speeches/2007/mbek1121.htm.

NPA Annual Report, 2019/2020, *National Director of Public Prosecutions' Report on the Operations of the National Prosecuting Authority in Terms of Section 22(4)(g), Read with Section 35(2)(a) of the National Prosecuting Authority Act 32 of 1998*, available at https://www.npa.gov.za/sites/default/files/annual-reports/NPA%20Annual%20Report%202019-2020_0.pdf.

Report of the Truth and Reconciliation Commission - Volume 5, Chapter 6: Findings and Conclusions.

Thabo Mbeki Statement by President Thabo Mbeki to the National Houses of Parliament and the Nation, on the Occasion of the Tabling of the Report of the Truth and Reconciliation Commission, Cape Town, 15 April 2003.

Websites

BBC 'FW de Klerk and the South African Row Over Apartheid and Crimes Against Humanity' *BBC* News, 18 February 2020, available at https://www.bbc.com/news/world-africa-51532829.

De Klerk Foundation Editorial 'The NPA's Decision to Prosecute 'Apartheid Era' Crimes' *De Klerk Foundation*, undated, available at https://fwdeklerk.org/index.php/en/latest/news/1946-article-the-npa-s-decision-to-prosecute-apartheid-era-crimes.

Foundation for Human Rights *Press Release—The FHR's Statement with Respect to the Announced Dedicated Capacity for the Apartheid-Era Crimes*, 28 June 2021, available at https://unfinishedtrc.co.za/press-release-the-fhrs-statem

ent-with-respect-to-the-announced-dedicated-capacity-for-the-apartheid-era-crimes/, https://www.news24.com/News24/Nzimande-slams-judicial-dictatorship-20111217-2.

Letter to the President by Former Commissioners of the Truth and Reconciliation Commission Accountability dated 5 February 2019, asking for an apology for the interference in the TRC cases and requesting the president to request a commission of enquiry into the interference. The letter is available at 77307_trc_letter_to_the_president__5_02_2019.pdf (cachefly.net).

M George 'Prospect for a Convention and Prevention and Punishment of Crimes Against Humanity' *Opinio Juris* (08 October 2019), available at http://opiniojuris.org/2019/10/08/prospects-for-a-convention-on-the-prevention-and-punishment-of-crimes-against-humanity/.

Makinana A 'FW de Klerk Apologises for Statement That Apartheid Was Not a Crime Against Humanity' *Times Live*, 17 February 2020, available at https://www.timeslive.co.za/news/south-africa/2020-02-17-fw-de-klerk-apologises-for-statement-that-apartheid-was-not-a-crime-against-humanity/.

Makinana A 'NPA Looking at Outstanding TRC Cases: Batohi' *Times Live* 9 July 2019, available at https://www.timeslive.co.za/politics/2019-07-09-npa-looking-at-outstanding-trc-cases-batohi/.

Mtshali, S 'Families of Apartheid Victims Call for FW de Klerk to Face Law for Involvement' *IOL*, 7 July 2021, available at https://www.iol.co.za/news/politics/families-of-apartheid-victims-call-for-fw-de-klerk-to-face-law-for-involvement-0e30dfe7-45fd-4b47-ab1c-57d3f0d405f2.

News24 'Gwede Mantashe Singles Out "Problematic Courts"' *News24*, 22 June 2015, available at https://www.news24.com/News24/Gwede-Mantashe-singles-out-problematic-courts-20150622.

News24 'Nzimande slams 'judicial dictatorship'' *News24*, 18 December 2011, available at https://www.news24.com/News24/Nzimande-slams-judicial-dictatorship-20111217-2 (last accessed on 19 January 2021).

Nkanjeni U 'Zindzi Mandela 'Heartbroken' About ANC's 'Defence' of FW de Klerk' *Times Live,* 17 February 2020, available at https://www.timeslive.co.za/politics/2020-02-17-zindzi-mandela-heartbroken-about-ancs-defence-of-fw-de-klerk/.

Pather R 'The first woman NDPP: Shamila Batohi Is the New NPA Boss' *Mail & Guardian,* 4 December 2018, available at https://mg.co.za/article/2018-12-04-the-first-woman-ndpp-shamila-batohi-is-the-new-npa-boss/.

SABC 'FW de Klerk's Statement on Apartheid Sparks Condemnation from All Sectors' *SABC News*, 17 February 2020, available at https://www.sabcnews.com/sabcnews/fw-de-klerks-controversial-stance-on-apartheid/.

Scholar Google, https://scholar.google.com/scholar?hl=en&as_sdt=0%2C5&authuser=1&q=south+africa+and+rome+statute&btnG=.

South African Government News Agency 'Hawks, NPA Investigate TRC Atrocities', *SANews.gov.za,* 28 June 2021, available at https://www.sanews.gov.za/south-africa/hawks-npa-investigate-trc-atrocities.

Times Live 'Tutu Takes on De Klerk: Withdraw Your Statement About Apartheid' 16 February 2020, available at https://www.timeslive.co.za/politics/2020-02-16-tutu-takes-on-de-klerk-withdraw-your-statement-about-apartheid/.

Timol Ahmed Foundation/Trust, Letter to President Ramaphosa: Call for an Apology.... Dated 23 June 2020, available at Letter to President Ramaphosa: Call for an apology.... - Ahmed Timol.

A History of Atrocity: Patterns, Perpetrators and Prospects for Accountability for International Crimes in Zimbabwe

Siphosami Malunga

1 Introduction

For 37 years, Robert Mugabe and his Zimbabwe African National Union (ZANU-PF) party ruled Zimbabwe with an iron fist, unleashing brutal violence and gross human rights violations against political opponents

S. Malunga (✉)
University of Zimbabwe, Harare, Zimbabwe
e-mail: SiphosamiM@osisa.org

International Law, Univeristy of Oslo, Oslo, Norway

International Law Candidate, University of Witwatersrand, Johannesburg, South Africa

E. C. Lubaale and N. Dyani-Mhango (eds.), *National Accountability for International Crimes in Africa*,
https://doi.org/10.1007/978-3-030-88044-6_15

and government critics.[1] Their most heinous campaign was the genocide in Matabeleland and Midlands between 1983 and 1987, which resulted in the deaths of 20,000 civilians.[2] In 1983, as a strategy to destroy the main opposition party, Patriotic Front-Zimbabwe African People's Union (PF-ZAPU) and create a one-party state, the government deployed the Gukurahundi to Matabeleland and Midlands, ostensibly to fight dissidents.[3] Rather than engage dissidents, the Gukurahundi and other security agencies and Zanu (PF) militia committed gross human rights violations0.4[4] The atrocities ended with the Unity Accord in 1987, accompanied by an amnesty to all perpetrators of gross human rights violations.[5]

The Gukurahundi atrocities would be followed in 1990 by a similarly vicious campaign against the Zimbabwe Unity Movement (ZUM), an

[1] P Zamchiya, 'Inside Competitive Electoral Authoritarianism in Zimbabwe, 2008–2018' in M Tendi, J McGregor and J Alexander (2020) *The Oxford Handbook of Zimbabwean Politics*, Oxford University Press'. E Masunungure 'Zimbabwe's Militarised, Electoral Authoritarianism' (2011) *65* (1) *Journal of International Affairs,* 47–64. Retrieved April 22, 2021, from http://www.jstor.org/stable/24388181; M Nyathi and M Ncube, 'The 2017 Military Coup in Zimbabwe: Implications for Human Rights and the Rule of Law' (2020) 20 *African Human Rights Law Journal* 825–851; S Doran, *Kingdom, Power, Glory: Mugabe, ZANU and the Quest for Supremacy: 1960–1987* (2017) (Sithatha Media).

[2] 'Breaking the Silence—Building True Peace: A Report on the Disturbances in Matabeleland and the Midlands 1980–1988' Catholic Commission for Justice and Peace in Zimbabwe & Legal Resources Foundation (1997) 56; KP Yap, 'Uprooting the Weeds: Power, Ethnicity and Violence in the Matabeleland Conflict' (2001). Doran (n. 1 above); Amnesty International Annual Report, 1984 accessible at POL1000041984ENGLISH.PDF (amnesty.org); SJ Ndlovu-Gatsheni, 'Rethinking Chimurenga and Gukurahundi in Zimbabwe: A Critique of Partisan National History' (2012) 55 *African Studies Review* 1, 1–2.

[3] *Breaking the Silence—Building True Peace* (n. 2 above).

[4] M Killander and M Nyathi, 'Accountability for the Gukurahundi Atrocities in Zimbabwe Thirty Years On: Prospects and Challenges.' (2015) 48 *Comparative and International Law Journal of Southern Africa*, 3, 463–487. Accessed 25 November 2020. http://0-www.jstor.org.innopac.wits.ac.za/stable/26203994. The term Gukurahundi is used expansively to include other-state security agencies that committed atrocities including the Central Intelligence Organization, Police Intelligence Service and Zanu PF youth militia. The term is often used (including in this chapter) interchangeably with 5 Brigade.

[5] *Breaking the Silence—Building True Peace* (n. 2 above).

opposition political party.[6] Gross human rights violations during the 1990 elections, including the attempted murder of a senior ZUM opposition politician by two intelligence officers, were again followed by amnesties.[7] Violence would again be unleashed against white farmers in 2000.[8] Again, the perpetrators of that violence, including murders of white farmers related to the land redistribution programme in 2000, have also enjoyed impunity from accountability0.9[9] The elections in 2000, 2002 and 2008 would be equally bloody.[10] Similarly, perpetrators of political and electoral violence from 2000 to 2008 have also enjoyed impunity from prosecution and punishment. Through state security agencies and party militia, they would continue to commit politically motivated violence, including murders, abductions and torture, targeting political opponents and perceived critics throughout Mugabe's rule until his removal in a coup in 2017.[11]

Mugabe's successor, Emmerson Mnangagwa, would promise a more democratic path that respects human rights.[12] However, the new government would soon resort to politically motivated extra-judicial killings, abductions, torture and rapes by the military, police and intelligence agencies targeting political opponents and critics.[13] More recently, military perpetrators of post-electoral shootings in August 2018 have enjoyed impunity from accountability despite recommendations by the Motlanthe

[6] N Kriger, 'ZANU (PF) Strategies in General Elections, 1980–2000: Discourse and Coercion' (2005) 104, *African Affairs* 1–34. Accessed November 20, 2020. http://0-www.jstor.org.innopac.wits.ac.za/stable/3518631.

[7] As above.

[8] D Coltart, *The Struggle Continues; 50 Years of Tyranny in Zimbabwe* (2016) Jacana 275–276.

[9] RE Howard-Hassmann, 'Mugabe's Zimbabwe, 2000–2009: Massive Human Rights Violations and the Failure to Protect' (2010) 32 *Human Rights Quarterly*, 898–920. Accessed 25 November 2020. http://0-www.jstor.org.innopac.wits.ac.za/stable/409 30339.

[10] Kriger (n. 6 above).

[11] Howard-Hassmann (n. 9 above).

[12] S Malunga, 'A Tale of Broken Promises-Postscript,' in SJ Ndlovu-Gatsheni and P Ruhanya (eds) *The History and Political Transition of Zimbabwe: From Mugabe to Mnangagwa* (2020) 356 (Palgrave Macmillan).

[13] M Kika, 'Blood Chains: The Coup Government's Rights Record Three Years On' *Zimbabwe Independent*, 21 November 2020.

Commission to hold them accountable.[14] The violence did not end in August 2018. There have been ongoing abductions, enforced disappearances, torture of opposition officials, trade union, human rights, democracy activists and civilians seen as opposed to the government and ZANU-PF.[15]The most defining feature of the presidency of Mugabe and Mnangagwa is the impunity enjoyed by known perpetrators of gross human rights violations, including themselves, which prevail.[16]

This chapter demonstrates that the state-sponsored violence that Zimbabweans have experienced since the early 1980s has been so grave as to constitute international crimes, particularly war crimes, crimes against humanity, torture and genocide.[17] The chapter assesses the pattern of interconnected violence over 40 years—from the 1980s to the present—and demonstrates that this violence has been state-sponsored and committed as part of a systematic political agenda and ideology targeting civilians. The chapter also identifies perpetrators responsible for organising, designing, ordering, encouraging and facilitating the atrocities, which should be held individually criminally accountable according to international criminal law. Finally, the chapter makes a case for holding known perpetrators accountable under international criminal law and recommends possible options for doing so. The chapter makes several propositions. The first is that the atrocities committed against civilians by the Zimbabwean government and the ruling Zanu PF over the past 40 years have been pursuant to a political agenda and ideology to systematically attack, persecute, weaken and destroy political opponents, critics and dissenters. The second is that the atrocities constitute international crimes. The third is that a common set of criminally liable perpetrators can be identified and individual criminal responsibility established under international criminal law. The fourth is that prospects and options for accountability exist based on lessons from other experiences worldwide despite some challenges.

[14] 'The Motlanthe Report- What's Next For Victims and the Nation' *ZimRights*, 15 August 2020.

[15] Kika (n. 13 above).

[16] 'Perpetual Fear: Impunity and Cycles of Violence in Zimbabwe' (2011) *Human Rights Watch* accessed November 25, 2020: https://www.hrw.org/report/2011/03/08/perpetual-fear/impunity-and-cycles-violence-zimbabwe.

[17] M Killander and M Nyathi (n. 2 above).

Much of the scholarly research into political violence in Zimbabwe has focused on its impact on political outcomes and democracy. Sociologists have also studied the societal impact of political violence on achieving healing, forgiveness and reconciliation.[18] There is limited legal research into the gravity and propensity of the atrocities and their categorisation under international criminal law and the legal assessment and attribution of criminal responsibility of the alleged perpetrators under international criminal law.[19] There also exists a gap in the analysis of options for holding known perpetrators of atrocities individually criminally responsible. This chapter reviews the patterns of violence in Zimbabwe. It assesses the extent to which the atrocities committed over four decades constitute international crimes, concerning which there is an international legal duty to investigate, prosecute and punish perpetrators who are individually criminally liable. The chapter is expected to advance and contribute knowledge on the subject of accountability of perpetrators for grave crimes in Zimbabwe. It is also expected to assist understanding of the prospects and options for justice for victims whilst reinforcing the international obligation to investigate, prosecute and punish perpetrators. This chapter relies on literature covering a range of important

[18] S Eppel 'Healing the Dead: Exhumation and Reburials as a Tool to Truth Telling and Reclaiming the Past in Rural Zimbabwe' in Borer Tristan Anne (ed) *Telling the Truths: Truth Telling and Peace Building in Post-Conflict Societies* (2006) 259–288; R Murambadoro, 'We Cannot Reconcile Until the Past Has Been Acknowledged: Perspectives on Gukurahundi from Matabeleland, Zimbabwe' (2015) 15 *African Journal on Conflict Resolution* 1 at 33–57; Maurice T Vambe, 'Zimbabwe Genocide: Voices and Perceptions from Ordinary People in Matabeleland and the Midlands Provinces, 30 years on' (2012) 10 *African Identities* 3 at 281–300; D Ngwenya and Geoff Harris, 'The Consequences of Not Healing: Evidence from the Gukurahundi Violence in Zimbabwe' 2015 15 *African Journal on Conflict Resolution* 2; D Dube and D Makwerere, 'Zimbabwe: Towards a Comprehensive Peace Infrastructure' (2012) 2 *International Journal of Humanities and Social Science* 18; C Muchemwa, ET Ngwerume, and M Hove, 'When Will the Long Nightmare Come to an End? Challenges to National Healing and Reconciliation in Post-Colonial Zimbabwe' (2013) 22 *African Security Review* 3 at 145–159; D Ngwenya, *Healing the Wounds of Gukurahundi: A Participatory Action Research Project* (unpublished DTech thesis, Durban University of Technology, 2014); P Machakanja, 'National Healing and Reconciliation in Zimbabwe: Challenges and Opportunities' (2010) *Institute for Justice and Reconciliation,* last accessed from https://www.africaportal.org/publications/national-healing-and-reconciliation-in-zimbabwe-challenges-and-opportunities/ on 5 March 2020; V De Waal, *The Politics of Reconciliation: Zimbabwe's First Decade* (1990); S Mpofu, 'Diasporic New Media and Conversations on Conflict: A Case of Zimbabwe Genocide Debates' in O Ogunyemi, *Media, Diaspora and Conflict* (2017) at 204–221.

[19] M Killander and M Nyathi (n. 2 above).

themes: political and electoral violence, international crimes and international criminal law, transitional justice and accountability for grave crimes, international law of armed conflict and criminal liability.

2 An Overview of Accountability for Atrocities Under International Law

The theory of international crimes provides the conceptual and normative framework for universal jurisdiction for the investigation, prosecution and punishment of international crimes.[20] The theory is supported by a range of instruments, treaties, customary international law, regional and national mechanisms that establish a duty to investigate, prosecute and punish perpetrators of gross violations of human rights, also known as international crimes.[21] An international crime has been described as 'a crime defined by international law, whether customary or conventional.'[22] This includes crimes against humanity, war crimes, genocide, torture, aggression and piracy. International crimes were defined by the US Military Tribunal at Nuremberg as follows:

> An international crime is an act universally recognised as criminal, which is considered a grave matter of international concern and for some valid reason cannot be left within the exclusive jurisdiction of the state that would have control over it under ordinary circumstances.[23]

Every international crime has its specific elements, which must be established in order for an alleged perpetrator to be held accountable. It should be emphasised that war crimes can only be committed

[20] WA Schabas, 'Punishment of Non-State Actors in Non-International Armed Conflict' (2002) 26 *Fordham International Law Journal* 4 at 907–933; D Fleck (ed) *The Handbook of International Humanitarian Law* (2008) 2; M Boothe, *The Handbook of International Humanitarian Law* (2013).

[21] K Kittichisaree, *International Criminal Law* (2001) Oxford University Press. See also M Crettol and AM La Rosa, 'The Missing and Transitional Justice: The Right to Know and the Fight Against Impunity' (2006) 88 *International Review of the Red Cross* 862.

[22] R O'Keefe, *International Criminal Law* (2015) (Oxford University Press, 220).

[23] Hostages Trial, US Military Tribunal at Nuremberg, 19 Feb. 1948 (1953) 15 *Ann. Dig.* 632 at 636.

in armed conflict,[24] whilst genocide and crimes against humanity can be committed in armed conflict and peacetime.[25] The requirement for accountability for international crimes under international law provides for universal jurisdiction for violations of international humanitarian law or gross violations of human rights.[26] It gained traction following at least 50 years of non-action by the international community post the Nuremberg trials of perpetrators of World War II atrocities.[27] A combination of factors, including indifference to war crimes, genocide and crimes against humanity committed in internal and international armed conflict; prevailing Cold War dynamics; and the fact that the majority of victims of atrocities came from developing countries in which the Global North had little or no strategic interests, hindered global action.[28]

The re-emergence of international justice was spurred by the wide-scale violations of international humanitarian law in the former Yugoslavia.[29] The fact that these large-scale atrocities were committed in the full glare of global media and the heart of Europe spurred global action under the auspices of the United Nations, which established the International Criminal Tribunal for the Former Yugoslavia (ICTY) in 1993. Following the genocide in Rwanda in 1994, which resulted in over 800,000 deaths, the United Nations established the International Criminal Tribunal for Rwanda (ICTR).[30] Besides the ICTY and ICTR, the international criminal justice system has recently seen the prosecution of Khmer Rouge leaders before the Extraordinary Chamber for

[24] Protocol Additional to the Geneva Conventions (Protocol I).

[25] Convention on the Prevention and Punishment of the Crime of Genocide, 1951 art 1.

[26] WA Schabas (n. 17 above) 907–933; D Fleck (n. 17 above).

[27] TO Hansen, 'The Vertical and Horizontal Expansion of Transitional Justice: Explanations and Implications for a Contested Field' in S Buckley-Zistel, TK Beck, C Braun and F Mieth (eds) *Transitional Justice Theories* (2014).

25 JE. Stromseth (ed) '*Accountability for Atrocities*': *National and International Responses*' (2003) *Transnational Publishers*, New York.

[28] JE. Stromseth (ed) '*Accountability for Atrocities*': *National and International Responses*' (2003) *Transnational Publishers*, New York.

[29] Stromseth (n. 25 above).

[30] Stromseth (n. 25 above). C Bassiouni, M (ed) '*Post Conflict Justice*' (2002) *Transnational Publishers*, New York; PB Hayner, *Unspeakable Truths: Confronting State Terror and Atrocity* (2001).

Cambodia.[31] More recently, former President of Chad Hissene Habre was prosecuted for atrocities committed during his presidency in the Extraordinary African Chambers in Senegal.[32] Other prosecutions have included former Serbian President Slobodan Milosevic,[33] former Serb General Ratko Mladic,[34] former Liberian President Charles Taylor,[35] former Ivorian President Laurent Gbagbo,[36] former Congolese Vice President Jean Pierre Bemba,[37] Kenyan President, Uhuru Kenyatta and Vice President William Ruto.[38] The International Criminal Court (ICC) also issued an indictment and arrest warrant against Former President of Sudan, Omar Al Bashir, for atrocities in Darfur.[39] In all these instances,

[31] S Williams, 'The Cambodian Extraordinary Chambers: A Dangerous Precedent for International Justice?' (2004) 53 *The International and Comparative Law Quarterly* 227–245. Accessed 25 November 2020. http://www.jstor.org/stable/3663143.

[32] R Adjovi, 'Introductory Note to the Agreement on the Establishment of the Extraordinary African Chambers Within the Senegalese Judicial System Between the Government of the Republic of Senegal and the African Union and the Statute of the Chambers' (2013) 52, no. 4, *International Legal Materials* 1020–1036. Accessed 25 November, 2020. https://doi.org/10.5305/intelegamate.52.4.1020.

[33] GJ Bass, 'Milosevic in The Hague' (2003) 82, no. 3 *Foreign Affairs* 82–96. Accessed 25 November 2020. https://doi.org/10.2307/20033580.

[34] M Dobbs, 'General Mladic in The Hague' (2012) 194 *Foreign Policy* 100–105. Accessed 25 November 2020. http://0-www.jstor.org.innopac.wits.ac.za/stable/23242800.

[35] DC Turack, 'Ending Impunity in Africa: The Charles Taylor Trial at the Special Court for Sierra Leone' (2009) 26, no. 2 *Journal of Third World Studies* 191–202. Accessed 25 November 2020. https://doi.org/10.2307/45194569; CC Jalloh, 'Prosecutor v. Taylor.' (2014) 108, no. 1 *The American Journal of International Law* 58–66. Accessed 25 November 2020. https://doi.org/10.5305/amerjintelaw.108.1.0058.

[36] 'Ex Ivory Coast President Acquitted at ICC', *The Guardian*, 15 January 2019, https://www.theguardian.com/world/2019/jan/15/ex-ivory-coast-president-laurent-gbagbo-acquitted-at-icc.

[37] Y McDermott, 'Prosecutor v. Bemba', *The American Journal of International Law* 110, no. 3 (2016): 526–533. Accessed 25 November 2020. http://0-www.jstor.org.innopac.wits.ac.za/stable/10.5305/amerjintelaw.110.3.0526.

[38] S Brown & CL Sriram, 'The Big Fish Won't Fry Themselves: Criminal Accountability for Post-Election Violence in Kenya' (2012) 111, no. 443 *African Affairs* 244–260. Accessed 25 November 2020. http://0-www.jstor.org.innopac.wits.ac.za/stable/41494487.

[39] *The Prosecutor vs Ahmad Al Bashir* ICC-02/05-01/09.

accountability has been pursued decades after the commission of the crimes.[40]

3 A Pattern of Atrocity

As highlighted above, Zimbabwe's post-independence history is littered with atrocity. Rather than viewing these atrocities as separate, unconnected incidents, this section discusses different episodes of atrocities in the past 40 years and demonstrates that despite being individual, ad-hoc and separate incidents, these atrocities are interconnected, widespread and systematic. Also, the atrocities have been committed pursuant to a political agenda and ideology to destroy, persecute and weaken political opposition, perceived government critics and opponents.

3.1 Gukurahundi (1983–1987)

Between February 1983 and December 1987, civilians in Matabeleland and Midlands endured the most unspeakable atrocities in the history of Zimbabwe.[41] These atrocities, committed by the 5th Brigade of the Zimbabwe National Army (ZNA) and other security agencies under a campaign known as Gukurahundi, resulted in the deaths of thousands of civilians.[42] Many of those killed were abducted and forcibly disappeared, and their bodies thrown into mine shafts or buried secretly in shallow graves.[43] Thousands of people were publicly executed in their villages and buried in mass graves.[44] The 1985 elections took place during the Gukurahundi campaign. At least 80 ZAPU officials and ZIPRA ex-combatants were abducted and then disappeared, and scores of homes of suspected ZAPU supporters were looted and destroyed during the

[40] Habre was tried 26 after he was deposed whilst Khmer Rouge leaders were tried almost 30 years later.

[41] *Breaking the Silence—Building True Peace* (n. 2 above) 56; Yap (n. 2 above).

[42] Doran (n. 1 above), see also Ndlovu-Gatsheni (n. 2 above).

[43] Unpublished: P Santos, 'Representing Conflict: An Analysis of the Chronicle's Coverage of the Conflict in Zimbabwe Between 1983 and 1986', unpublished MA thesis, Rhodes University, 2011; Coltart (n. 8 above).

[44] 'Gukurahundi 5th Brigade Mass Graves in Nkayi', last accessed from https://www.youtube.com/watch?v=Dvx-cxygig8, on 28 November 2020.

campaign.[45] Overall, at least 20,000 people are estimated to have been killed, thousands more starved, tortured, raped, unlawfully detained and their homes and belongings destroyed during the senseless carnage.[46] Those that survived the atrocities bear severe emotional and physical scars.

3.2 Political and Electoral Violence (1990)

The terror campaign during the 1990 elections, barely three years after the end of the Gukurahundi genocide, captures the enduring political agenda behind Zimbabwe's pattern of atrocities. For this reason, it will be discussed in detail. The signing of the Unity Accord in December 1987 ended the conflict in Matabeleland and the Gukurahundi genocide. It also effectively established a de facto one-party state, something that Robert Mugabe and ZANU—had always desired.[47] In October 1988, ZANU-PF expelled its Second Secretary Edgar Tekere for criticising corruption and greed in the party.[48] He responded by forming a new opposition party, ZUM, in April 1989. In a June by-election in Dzivaresekwa, Harare, despite intimidation, disruption, arrests, disruption and illegal detentions by police, ZUM won over 30% of the total votes.[49] In July 1989, police violently disrupted Tekere's first public meeting at the University of Zimbabwe and dispersed thousands of students.[50] Throughout the election campaign, the total weight of the state machinery routinely denied ZUM permission to hold public rallies under the state of emergency regulations. Norma Kriger aptly captures the terror campaign against ZUM during the 1990 election. Almost every rally ZUM convened was violently disrupted.[51] Tekere and ZUM advocated for the complete opposite of what Mugabe and Zanu (PF) wanted: multiparty democracy, clean government, reduced presidential powers and liberal economic policies. In ZUM, Mugabe and Zanu (PF) saw its one-party state agenda under threat. In a reflection of the skewed nature of the political system, ZANU

[45] Kriger (n. 6 above).

[46] *Breaking the Silence—Building True Peace* (n. 2 above) 56.

[47] The Unity Accord contained a specific provision to this effect.

[48] Kriger (n. 6 above).

[49] As above.

[50] As above.

[51] As above.

(PF) won 116 of the 120 elected seats with a 78% share of the vote, whilst ZUM won only two seats, despite getting 17% of the vote.[52] ZUM performed very well in urban areas, winning an average of 26% of the vote and close to 50% in some constituencies.

Mugabe targeted the Conservative Alliance and ZUM with fierce attacks, accusing them of terrorism and racism and threatening to 'chop their heads off.'[53] At a rally in Kadoma, Mugabe warned, 'violence begets violence.' Senior Zanu leaders and Cabinet Ministers like Nathan Shamuyarira urged Zanu supporters to 'clip the wings of whites that voted for ZUM.'[54] Hebert Ushewokunze, former Cabinet Minister and Zanu PF candidate for Highfields called on both ZUM and the CAZ to be destroyed and their candidates killed.[55] A ZANU (PF) campaign advertisement on television claimed that a vote for ZUM, like AIDS, would lead to death, whereas voting for ZANU (PF) would lead to life.[56] No police action was taken against known perpetrators of threats and violence. The most prominent of the attacks was the shooting and attempted murder of the ZUM candidate for Gweru Central, businessman and former Mayor Patrick Kombayi, by Central Intelligence aides of his Zanu (PF) rival, Vice President Simon Muzenda, on whose orders the attempted assassination was carried out. Kombayi's attackers were subsequently arrested, tried and convicted but promptly pardoned by President Mugabe.[57]

Coming after the 1983–1987 attacks on Zapu by the Gukurahundi, the strategies of Zanu (PF) and the government in the 1990 elections reveal a pattern of widespread systematic state-sponsored political and electoral violence in Zimbabwe.[58] They show that the political agenda and ideology to impose a one-party state has always been and continues

[52] As above.

[53] As above.

[54] As above.

[55] As above.

[56] As above.

[57] As above.

[58] See also J Makumbe, 'Electoral Politics in Zimbabwe: Authoritarianism Versus the People' (2006) 31, no. 3 *Africa Development / Afrique Et Développement* 45–61. Accessed November 20, 2020. http://0-www.jstor.org.innopac.wits.ac.za/stable/24483863.

to be the driver of atrocity in Zimbabwe. This agenda and how it has been violently implemented will be discussed further below.

3.3 Land Reform and Election Violence (2000–2002)

At independence, Zimbabwe's newly elected government inherited the 'historical burden of race-based inequalities' in the pattern of access and distribution of land.[59] By 1980, roughly 4% of the population (white farmers) owned over 80% of the land. Reversing the racially skewed distribution of land had been a critical demand that defined the liberation struggle. The Lancaster House Agreement had included a clause that preserved the status quo for ten years and included protection of property rights in the bill of rights section of the Constitution. Precisely ten years after independence, the government passed the Land Acquisition Act. The Act provided for the acquisition of land by the government and its redistribution to the landless blacks without compensation. It also provided for due process in the designation, notification and acquisition, allowing for legal challenges to government acquisition orders. When the constitutionality of the no compensation provision in the Land Acquisition Act was challenged, the court ruled against the government, reinforcing property rights and setting the stage for a confrontation. In 2000, the government commissioned a Constitutional Reform process, which culminated in a referendum in February. A civil society-led effort campaigned for a more people led process. By the 1990 elections, racial tensions had run high with the Zanu (PF) government issuing threats of land reversals and violence to the remnants of the white Rhodesian National Party, the Conservative Alliance of Zimbabwe. The referendum in 2000 further pushed the stakes when, at the last minute, -the government included a clause legalising acquisition of land without compensation and removing land disputes from the jurisdiction of the courts. The non-compensation clause tacked on late in the referendum campaign would still have, if ratified, absolved Zimbabwe from paying compensation for white farms, but it failed to turn the vote. Regardless, two months later, in April, constitutional amendments were

[59] P Alden and J Makumbe, 'The Zimbabwe Constitution: Race, Land Reform and Social Justice', in HG Cornwell and EW Stoddard (eds) *Global Multiculturalism* (2001) 215–237.

passed, permitting the government to expropriate land without paying compensation.[60]

Even with these efforts, the government draft of the Constitution was rejected.[61] Using Zanu (PF)-affiliated war veterans, the government sanctioned violent land invasions throughout the country. The government's strategy on offering land to voters was directly linked to winning the 2000 election against the emergent MDC.[62] The rejection of the compensation clause, perceptions of their support for MDC and the use of land as a voter buying tool precipitated a violent backlash against white commercial farmers, which accompanied the fast-track land reform programme described by Sachikonye as 'violent and chaotic.'[63] As Fisher summarises: 'war veterans set up bases on the commercial farms, from which they, together with the recently formed youth militia and peasants, launched waves of intimidation, violence and in some cases murder, disrupting agricultural work and clearing the farms of their white owners, managers and farm labour. The police refused to intervene, provide protection or lay charges, saying 'it was a political matter.' Judges were threatened and sacked for not toeing the party line, and courts had their rulings ignored.'[64]

By 2006, about sixty white farmers had been killed, and many of their employees had been violently intimidated and tortured.[65] The gruesome and cold-blooded execution-style murders of white farmers illustrate that the attacks were widespread, systematic and political.[66] The brutal murder of David Stevens is illustrative. Stevens farmed tobacco at his Arizona ranch in Macheke. He was openly a supporter of the MDC. On 14 April 2000, a crowd had attacked Stevens's workers who had fought back. On 15 April, the crowd of invaders returned, and Stevens went to the gate to

[60] J Fisher, 'Zimbabwe's Governance and Land Reform Crises—A Postscript.' in J Fisher (ed) *Pioneers, Settlers, Aliens, Exiles: The Decolonisation of White Identity in Zimbabwe* (2010) 201–220. ANU Press. Retrieved 23 November 2020, from http://0-www.jstor.org.innopac.wits.ac.za/stable/j.ctt24hd4n.13.

[61] As above.

[62] As above.

[63] LM Sachikonye, *The Promised Land: From Expropriation to Reconciliation and Jambanja*' (2005) (Weaver Press).

[64] Fisher (n. 57 above).

[65] P Godwin, *When a Crocodile Eats the Sun: A Memoir of Africa* (2007) 81.

[66] Coltart (n. 8 above) 275–276.

negotiate. The crowd seized him, threw him into a truck and took him to the local war veterans' office. A group of fellow white farmers followed and attempted to rescue him but were shot at and decided to report to the police. The police refused to intervene. Whilst they were at the police station, a group of Zanu supporters arrived and seized the farmers from the police threatening to kill them. The group of farmers was separated into two: one taken to the war veterans' office and the other to Zanu PF offices.

Stevens was at the war veterans' office, where he was severely beaten repeatedly and eventually shot dead. The other farmers were beaten, bound with wire, blindfolded and driven some distance, then dumped. Along the way, Steven's body was thrown on the blindfolded group. The next day, on his return from a foreign visit to Cuba, Mugabe was met by the Chairperson of the war veterans, Chenjerai Hunzi, cabinet ministers and scores of jubilant Zanu PF supporters. His State Security Minister, responsible for the CIO, Sidney Sekeramayi, left no doubt about the Stevens murder, saying 'the MDC have slapped a lion in the face and they will be devoured.' Mugabe followed with his unequivocal endorsement of the gruesome murder stating unequivocally, 'he would not order war veterans off the land and that the MDC had started the violence and Zanu PF supporters had a right to defend themselves.'[67] Mugabe would also endorse the murder of Martin Olds a few days later, saying that: 'For them to be banded together to a man in opposition to the government, to have gone much farther in mobilising their labour forces on the farms, to support the one position opposed to the government, has exposed them, not as our friends, but our enemies. Our present state of mind is- you are now our enemies because you have behaved as enemies of Zimbabwe, and we are full of anger.'[68]

The rejection of the government proposed Constitution in a referendum in February 2000 sent Robert Mugabe and Zanu PF into a rage. It also coincided with the formation of the MDC and its announcement

[67] As above, Besides Stevens, other white farmers would be attacked and murdered. In Nyamandlovu, Martin Olds was also murdered by war veterans in cold blood. A gang had driven past a police roadblock to his farm in 13 cars. He had been ambushed when he went to the gate, was shot in the leg and after retreating to his house, it was petrol bombed forcing him out. He was shot and stabbed all over the body within hearing of the police station, which failed to come to his aid. see Coltart (n. 8 above) 275–276.

[68] As above.

that it would contest the forthcoming parliamentary elections in July 2000. Mugabe and Zanu (PF)'s response was swift and brutal. Using the opportunity to arguably 'kill two birds with one stone'—attack the white commercial farmers and the MDC simultaneously, Mugabe and Zanu (PF) unleashed violence unseen since the 1990 elections. The most illustrative incident is the horrific attack of the MDC activists Talent Mabika, Sanderson Makombe and Tichaona Chiminyi, Morgan Tsvangirai's driver, in Buhera Constituency Morgan Tsvangirai was contesting.[69] A vehicle in which the three activists were driving was forced off the road by a vehicle marked 'Zanu (PF) Manicaland Province' on the way to Murambinda Centre. Makombe was sitting at the back and managed to flee, but Chiminya and Mabika were trapped. They were severely beaten and tortured, doused with petrol and set alight and left burning as their assailants—led by CIO officer Joseph Mwale and war veteran Kainos Tom Zimunya together with the Zanu PF candidate's election agents drove off. Makombe emerged from hiding and attempted to save his comrades, but Chiminya was already dead whilst Mabika died a few hours later at the hospital. The police did not arrest Mwale and Zimunya despite the evidence being provided to them on their role by eyewitnesses. In the ensuing court case challenging the election results because of the violence, High Court Judge Devitte ordered Mwale and Zimunya to appear before the court[70] and the police to investigate and prosecute the pair. However, the order was ignored.[71] The police made no effort to arrest them, and the Justice Minister dismissed the High Court decision.[72] Mwale and Zimunya have continued to enjoy impunity from prosecution for the murders.[73] The pervasive political violence, which characterised the

[69] As above.

[70] High Court Order HH 67/2001 HC 8139/2000, 'Buhera North Election Petition'.

[71] 'Government Orders Hitman's Arrest for Killing Political Opponents' see https://www.thenewhumanitarian.org/news/2006/10/16/govt-orders-hitmans-arrest-killing-political-opponents.

[72] 'Chinamasa says High Court Has No Legal Right to Order Prosecutions', *Daily News*, 30 August 2001.

[73] '10 Years On: Chiminya and Mabika Murderers Free', *Zimbabwe Independent*, 23 April 2010: https://www.theindependent.co.zw/2010/04/23/candid-comment-10-years-on-chiminyamabika-murderers-free/.

2000 parliamentary elections, was repeated during the 2002 presidential elections.[74]

3.4 Election and Political Violence (2008–2013)

In the light of the election-related violence in 1985, 1990, 2000 and 2002, violence was anticipated in the harmonised elections in 2008. In the run-up to the election, civil and political rights violations had become so pervasive that Genocide Watch issued a politicide watch, a warning of political mass murder in Zimbabwe.[75] In 2002, the government had passed the Public Order and Security Act and the Access to Information and Protection of Privacy Act, both draconian laws that stifled almost all public political activity and free speech.[76]

In the run-up to the 2008 elections, intimidation, harassment, murder, torture, sexual and other heinous attacks against MDC members and their families intensified.[77] Despite the violence against his supporters, Morgan Tsvangirai, the leader of the MDC, garnered 47.9% of the votes against Robert Mugabe's 43.2% in the 29 March presidential elections.[78] This result was short of the 50% + 1 required to win outright, forcing a run-off. To add to the controversy, the Zimbabwe Electoral Commission inexplicably withheld results for 45 days.[79] By the time they announced them, all trust and confidence in the authenticity of the results had been lost.[80] Between the announcement of the results and the run-off, Zanu PF and the government unleashed an orgy of violence in a military-led operation code-named Operation *Mavoterapapi* (Where Did You Put Your Voter Cross).[81]

[74] J Makumbe, 'Electoral Politics in Zimbabwe: Authoritarianism Versus the People,' 31, no. 3 (2006) *Africa Development/Afrique Et Développement* 45–61.

[75] Genocide Watch, Politicide Warning: Zimbabwe (2008).

[76] J Hammer, 'The Reign of Thuggery' N.Y. Rev. Books, 26 June 2008.

[77] As above.

[78] See Pan-African Parliament, Report of the Pan African Parliament Election Observer Mission: Presidential Run-Off Election and House of Assembly By-Elections, Republic of Zimbabwe (June 27 2008).

[79] 'Bullets for Each of You: State Sponsored Violence Since Zimbabwe March 29 Election', *Human Rights Watch*, 9 June 2008.

[80] As above.

[81] As above.

Due to the violence, Morgan Tsvangirai withdrew from the election, leaving Mugabe as the sole candidate. Torture, beatings, rape and killings of ordinary MDC supporters continued, with police refusing to investigate.[82] At least 153 MDC supporters were killed during Operation *Mavoterapapi* between March and June 2008.[83] As had been the strategy with Gukurahundi, a systematic campaign of gang rapes and sexual attacks against women suspected to be members of the MDC or relatives of MDC members was implemented by members of the CIO, Zanu (PF) youth militia and war veterans.[84] In December 2008, Jestina Mukoko, a human rights activist working on documenting ongoing political violence, and colleagues Broderick Takawira and Pascal Gonzo were abducted by state security agents and held *incommunicado* for three weeks, during which they were tortured.[85] They were released to police custody and detained for another two months. Arrests, intimidation and selective prosecution would be used against MDC officials between 2009 and the July 2013 election, which Zanu PF won after controversially withholding the voters roll until a day or so before the election.[86] After its 2013 election victory and the end of the Government of National Unity, Zanu (PF) intensified its attacks on perceived critics using arrests, torture, enforced disappearances and murder. Notably, journalist and anti-corruption activist Itai Dzamara was abducted and disappeared in March 2015.[87] In 2012, Paul Chizuze, an activist for accountability for Gukurahundi atrocities, was abducted and enforcedly disappeared.[88]

[82] 'False Dawn: The Zimbabwe Power-Sharing Government's Failure to Deliver Human Rights Improvements' *Human Rights Watch* (2009) 5–6.

[83] As above.

[84] AIDS-Free World, Electing to Rape: Sexual Terror in Mugabe's Zimbabwe 8 (2009).

[85] J Mukoko, *The Abduction and Trial of Jestina Mukoko The Fight for Human Rights in Zimbabwe* (David Krut Books, 2016); see also Frontline Defenders: Jestina Mukoko Abducted, accessible at https://www.frontlinedefenders.org/en/case/jestina-mukoko-abducted#case-update-id-8307.

[86] S Muqayi, 'The Strategies Applied by the Zimbabwe African National Union-Patriotic Front (ZANU-PF) to Dominate the 2013 Harmonised Elections in Zimbabwe' (2018) 5, no. 3 *Journal of African Foreign Affairs* 45–64. Accessed 25 November 2020. https://doi.org/10.2307/26664076.

[87] 'Where is Itai Dzamara,' *Amnesty International*, https://www.amnesty.org/en/get-involved/take-action/itai-dzamara-disappearance/.

[88] 'Paul Chizuze—Disappeared': Solidarity Peace Trust, accessible at http://solidaritypeacetrust.org/1145/paul-chizuze-disappeared/.

3.5 *November 2017–2020 Atrocities*

The targeting of perceived political opponents continued up to Mugabe's removal in a military coup in November 2017.[89] The coup itself was another manifestation of Zanu (PF)'s political ideology and policy to retain power.[90] The generals that conducted the coup made it clear that they had done so, amongst other things, to prevent Zanu (PF)'s electoral defeat under Mugabe in the upcoming 2018 elections.[91] This alone illustrated the extent to which the country's military institutions had become politicised and acted as self-appointed arbiters in internal Zanu (PF) party politics. It also stressed the futility of expectations regarding Zanu PF contemplating or even accepting any electoral loss in 2018. The coup followed years of simmering tensions and internal factional fighting within Zanu PF, mainly fuelled by competition over Mugabe's succession. The factional fighting had earlier resulted in the expulsion of former Vice-President Joyce Mujuru by Mugabe.[92] Emmerson Mnangagwa replaced her. Mnangagwa was, in turn, dismissed as Vice President in November 2017, leading to Mugabe's removal in a military coup on 18 November 2017.[93] Most Zimbabweans celebrated the removal of Mugabe, hoping that it would usher in an era of change after many years of toxic politics and declining living conditions.[94] After the removal of Mugabe, he was replaced by his erstwhile deputy Emmerson

[89] 'Zimbabwe's Apparent Coup,' *New York Times*, 15 November 2017.

[90] BM Tendi, 'The Motivations and Dynamics of Zimbabwe's 2017 Military Coup' (2020) 474 Vol 119 *African Affairs* 39–67, https://doi.org/10.1093/afraf/adz024.

[91] In outlining the reasons for Operation Restore Legacy, the generals made it clear that they were saving Zanu PF from defeat in 2018.

[92] 'Mugabe Sacks Vice-President Over Plot': *BBC*, 9 December 2014: https://www.bbc.com/news/world-africa-30400178.

[93] N Beardsworth, N Cheeseman, S Tinhu, 'Zimbabwe: The Coup That Never was, and the Election That Could Have Been,' (2019) 478 Vol 118 *African Affairs*, 580–596, accessible at https://doi.org/10.1093/afraf/adz009; L Thomas-Greenfield and DB Wharton, 'Zimbabwe's Coup: Net Gain or No Gain,' *Military Review*, March/April 2019.

[94] 'Zimbabwe Celebrates as Mugabe Resignation Announced': *The Guardian*, 22 November 2017: https://www.theguardian.com/world/gallery/2017/nov/21/zimbabwe-celebrates-as-mugabe-resignation-announced-in-pictures.

Mnangagwa,[95] who, at his inauguration, promised free and fair elections, political tolerance, respect for human rights, a revived economy, and to fight corruption and normalise relations with the international community.[96] Despite securing the goodwill of millions of Zimbabweans and some foreign governments,[97] Mnangagwa's promises would quickly unravel as Zanu PF returned to factory settings. Whilst the period in the run-up to the 2018 election was less violent than had previously been experienced, Zanu (PF) resorted to other ways to manipulate the process. Amongst them deploying former military and security agents to run the Zimbabwe Electoral Commission (ZEC),[98] relying on extensive vote-buying in rural areas via a government agricultural scheme,[99] deploying the military to rural areas,[100] monopolising the media[101]; and stifling opposition campaigns using the Public Order and Security Act.[102] The looming threat of violence continued to prevail in rural areas providing an advantage to Zanu (PF).[103]

Shortly after the election, as votes were being counted, protests broke out in Harare City Centre regarding delays in releasing the results and

[95] 'Emmerson Mnangagwa Sworn in as Zimbabwe President': *Al Jazeera*, 24 November 2017: https://www.aljazeera.com/news/2017/11/24/emmerson-mnangagwa-sworn-in-as-zimbabwe-president.

[96] 'President Mnangagwa's Inauguration Speech': *The Chronicle*, 25 November 2017: https://www.chronicle.co.zw/president-mnangagwas-inauguration-speech-in-full/.

[97] 'Zimbabwe's New President Mnangagwa Vows to Re-Engage with the World,' *BBC*, 24 November 2017: https://www.bbc.com/news/world-africa-42115622.

[98] S Malunga, 'Six Issues That Must Be Fixed for Elections to Be Free and Fair': *African Arguments*, 14 June, 2017, accessible at https://africanarguments.org/2018/06/14/zimbabwe-election-2018-six-issues-fixed-free-fair/.

[99] European Union: Election Observation Mission Report, http://chrome-extension://oemmndcbldboiebfnladdacbdfmadadm/, http://www.epgencms.europarl.europa.eu/cmsdata/upload/5bb6cf90-4102-4c21-9dab-7f38096a4536/Zimbabwe-General-Elections_2018_final-report.pdf; Siphosami Malunga, 'Were Zimbabwe's Elections Free and Fair: The Final Score Card,' *African Arguments*, 21 August 2018.

[100] 'Zanu PF/Military Deterrence of the Village Vote,' *Zimbabwe Democracy Institute*, 10 July 2018: http://kubatana.net/2018/07/10/zanu-pf-military-deterrence-village-vote/.

[101] M Ndakaripa, 'Zimbabwe's 2018 Elections: Funding, Public Resources and Vote Buying,' *Review of African Political Economy*, 47 (2020):164, 301–312, https://doi.org/10.1080/03056244.2020.1735327.

[102] European Union: Election Observation Mission Report:

[103] 'Zanu PF/Military Deterrence of the Village Vote' (n. 98 above).

suspicions that ZEC was manipulating the results in favour of the Zanu PF presidential candidate, Emmerson Mnangagwa.[104] Some protestors attacked and burned cars at the Zanu (PF) headquarters. The government swiftly responded by deploying the army to the CBD. The army would indiscriminately fire on civilians killing six and wounding dozens.[105] Under pressure, Mnangagwa established an international commission led by former South African President Kgalema Montlhante to investigate the army killings.[106] The commission found that the military had used excessive force and ordered that perpetrators of this atrocity be held accountable.[107] Instead, Mnangagwa would promote the general in charge of the unit that committed the atrocity.[108] After the election, Zimbabwe witnessed an escalation of gross violations of human rights. In response to public protests triggered by an increase in fuel price, the government deployed the army to 'quell' unrests.[109] Under cover of a

[104] T Mungwari, 'Zimbabwe Post-Election Violence, Motlanthe Commission of Enquiry 2018,' *International Journal of Contemporary Research and Review*, Vol 10, Issue 2, accessible at https://www.researchgate.net/publication/331304554_Zimbabwe_Post_Election_Violence_Motlanthe_Commission_of_Inquiry_2018; J. Cotterill, 'Zimbabwe Security Services Blamed for Post-Election Deaths', *Financial Times*, London, 18 December 2018.

[105] 'Zimbabwe: At Least 6 Dead in Post-Election Violence,' *Human Rights Watch,* 3 August 2018, https://www.hrw.org/news/2018/08/03/zimbabwe-least-6-dead-post-election-violence.

[106] 'The Motlanthe Report: What's Next for Victims and the Nation: An Analysis of the Findings and Recommendations of the Motlanthe Report Two Years On', *ZimRights* (2020), http://chrome-extension://oemmndcbldboiebfnladdacbdfmadadm/, http://www.veritaszim.net/sites/veritas_d/files/The%20Motlanthe%20Report.pdf; 'Zimbabwe: Doubts Over Commission of Enquiry's Independence Puts Justice for Post-Election Killings at Risk,' *Amnesty International*, 19 September 2018 https://www.amnesty.org/en/latest/news/2018/09/zimbabwe-doubts-over-commission-of-inquirys-independence-puts-justice-for-post-election-killings-at-risk/.

[107] 'Zimbabwe One Year On, No Justice for Those Killed by Soldiers in Post-Election Demonstrations,' *Amnesty International*, 1 August 2019, https://www.amnesty.org/en/latest/news/2019/08/zimbabwe-one-year-on-no-justice-for-those-killed-by-soldiers-in-post-election-demonstrations/.

[108] 'ED Promotes August 1 Shootings Commander,' *Newsday*, 18 December 2018, 'Mnangagwa Promotes Army Boss Fingered in 1 August 1 Civilian Killings', accessible at https://allafrica.com/stories/201812180073.html.

[109] Solidarity Peace Trust, *Resurgent Authoritarianism: The Politics of the January 2019 Violence In Zimbabwe*, 20 February 2019 (Port Shepstone, SPT, 2019); 'Revolt and Repression in Zimbabwe,' *International Crisis Group,* https://www.crisisgroup.org/africa/southern-africa/zimbabwe/revolt-and-repression-zimbabwe.

countrywide internet shutdown, the army committed heinous atrocities, including torture, rapes and extra-judicial killings.[110] No one would be held to account, and Mnangagwa would boast that 'he had deployed the army himself with instructions to use a whip laced with salt.'[111]

The Mnangagwa led Zanu (PF) government would adapt its tactics against political opposition, critics relying on deploying unidentified gangs to conduct widespread abductions, enforced disappearances, torture and killings.[112] It would use this cloak of anonymity to deny responsibility, arguing that there was a third force conducting the abductions and that the abductions were faked.[113] Zimbabwe would experience a record 106 abductions by state agents,[114] with 64 in one year (2019) and up to 25 extra-judicial killings.[115] Attempts to conceal the identity of the abductors and the state's role would crumble with the release of CCTV footage of a team of state agents and police known as Ferret abducting 22-year-old university student Tawanda Muchehiwa.[116] Muchehiwa would be brutally tortured and only released after a court

[110] Zimbabwe's Troops Accused of 'Systematic Torture' of Protestors, *BBC*, 23 January, 2019, https://www.bbc.com/news/world-africa-46968142.

[111] 'On the Days of Darkness in Zimbabwe: An Updated Report on the Human Rights Violations Committed Between 14 January and 5 February 2019, Zimbabwe Human Rights NGO Forum', http://chrome-extension://oemmndcbldboiebfnladdacbdfmadadm/, http://www.hrforumzim.org/wp-content/uploads/2019/02/Shutdown-Atrocities-Report-6-February-2019.pdf.

[112] This included the abduction, enforced disappearance and torture of MDC member Blessing Toronga later found murdered after the January 2019 protests, doctor Tatenda Mombeyarara for protesting poor working conditions of doctors, Obert Masarira for protesting poor working conditions of teachers, comedian Samantha Kureya (Gonyeti) for her artistic parody about the government, musician Ian Makiwa (Prince Platinum) for a song deemed offensive to the President, MDC politicians Joanna Mamombe, Cecilia Chimbiri and Netsai Marova for protests about the COVID-19 lockdown regulations and university student Tawanda Muchehiwa ahead of a planned protest against corruption on 31 July 2020. Many other activists would be abducted, tortured and dumped.

[113] 'Zimbabwe's MDC Abductees Arrested for Lying About Torture,' *BBC*, 11 June 2020, https://www.bbc.com/news/world-africa-53005447.

[114] Kika (n. 13 above).

[115] As above.

[116] T Muchehiwa, 'I Felt the Gun On the Back of My Head, I Had Made My Peace with Death,' *ZimLive*, 27 August 2020, https://www.zimlive.com/2020/08/27/i-felt-the-gun-on-the-back-of-my-head-i-had-made-peace-with-death/; 'The Brutal Abduction Caught on Camera in Zimbabwe,' *Mail and Guardian*, https://mg.co.za/africa/2020-09-13-the-brutal-abduction-caught-on-camera-in-zimbabwe/.

order to produce him.[117] In the run-up to the 31 July 2020 protests called to protest against corruption, State agents would conduct a blitz on activists and MDC officials, conducting raids, abductions and torture.[118] Like previous attacks against opposition supporters, government critics and activists, the hallmark and motivation were a political agenda, and ideology aimed at destroying, weakening and persecuting perceived political opponents of the government and Zanu (PF).

4 Establishing International Crimes in Zimbabwe

It has been demonstrated that in the past 40 years, the Zimbabwean government has committed a pattern of politically motivated atrocities against the civilian population. This section analyses the pattern of atrocities against prescribed definitions and elements of international crimes and concludes that these atrocities constitute international crimes. As indicated in this chapter's introduction, international crimes are the gravest crimes committed against civilians. They offend certain general principles of law and are a concern of the international community.[119] International crimes are prohibited by customary international law as well as treaties. Customary international law is part of the law of Zimbabwe[120] unless it is inconsistent with the Constitution or an Act of Parliament.[121] Zimbabwe's international obligations thus arise from established international practices in addition to formal written conventions and treaties.[122] Zimbabwe signed and ratified the Convention on the Prevention and

[117] T Moyo, 'Witness to Abduction', *Daily Maverick*, 28 September 2020.

[118] M Heywood, 'Zanu PF Steps Up Repression and Fear to Halt 31 July Anti-Corruption and Poverty Protests,' *Daily Maverick*, 30 July 2020.

[119] Kittichisaree (n. 18 above) 95.

[120] *Minister of Foreign Affairs v Michael Jenrich, Standard Chartered Bank Zimbabwe and Sherriff of Zimbabwe,* Zimbabwe Supreme Court Judgment No. SC 73/18; See also the older cases of *Barker McCormac (Pvt) Ltd v. Government of Kenya*; 1983 (2) ZLR 72, at 77; Judgement of Waddington J who held that '*there is no doubt that customary international law is part of the law of this country,' see also* Sibanda and Another V ICRC (2002 (1) ZLR 364 *which reaffirmed Barker McCormac.*

[121] Section 326 (1) of the Constitution of Zimbabwe.

[122] DJ Harris, *Cases and Materials on International Law 6th Ed* (2004) 20.

Punishment of Genocide, 1948 in 1991.[123] It enacted the Genocide Act in 2000.[124] Zimbabwe also signed and ratified the Geneva Conventions in 1992 and, to date, has not enacted national legislation to domesticate the conventions.[125] The country also signed the Statute of the International Criminal Court in 1998, but it has not ratified it. Also, it has not ratified the Torture Convention.[126] However, all provisions of the above treaties that also constitute customary international law are applicable and binding on the country.[127] This includes the prohibition of torture, war crimes,[128] genocide[129] and crimes against humanity,[130] all of which form customary international law.

The pattern of crimes committed by the Zimbabwean government in the past 40 years and described above readily meets the criteria and elements of the four broad categories of international crimes: war crimes, genocide, crimes against humanity and torture.

[123] ICRC Treaties, State Parties and Commentaries; available at https://ihl-databases.icrc.org/

[124] See Genocide Act (Chapter 9:20) accessible at Genocide Act (Chapter 9:20) - law.co.zw.

[125] The Geneva Conventions of 1949 and their Additional Protocols, accessible at https://www.icrc.org/en/doc/war-and-law/treaties-customary-law/geneva-conventions/overview-geneva-conventions.htm#:~:text=The%201949%20Geneva%20Conventions,soldiers%20on%20land%20during%20war.&text=The%20second%20Geneva%20Convention%20protects,personnel%20at%20sea%20during%20war.

[126] Convention Against Torture and Other Cruel, Inhuman or Degrading Treatment or Punishment, 1984; A/RES/39/46.

[127] A Cassese *International Law* 2nd ed. (2005) Oxford University Press: 157.

[128] *Prosecutor v Dusko Tadic*, Case No. IT-94-1, ICTY App. Chamber, Decision on the Defence Motion for Interlocutory Appeal on Jurisdiction of October 2 1995 ('*Tadic* Jurisdiction Decision') quoted with approval in *Prosecutor v Furundzija*, Case No. IT-95-17/I-T, ICTY.

[129] *Prosecutor v Goran Jelisic*, Case No. IT-95-10, ICTY T. Ch 1, 14 Dec.1999, para 60.

[130] *Tadic* Jurisdiction Decision, As above at para 141.

4.1 War Crimes (1983–1987)

International humanitarian law regulates how armed conflict can be legally conducted. It prohibits certain conduct by parties to an international and internal armed conflict.[131] The violation of the laws of war, especially concerning the treatment of the civilian population by parties to a conflict, can constitute war crimes. War crimes committed in the context of internal armed conflict are governed by Common Article 3 of the Geneva Conventions,[132] Article 1.1 of Additional Protocol II, the Statute of the International Criminal Court[133] and customary international law. As indicated above, Common Article 3 forms part of customary international law.[134] All these instruments prohibit the following acts from being committed against civilians during armed conflict: violence to life and person, in particular murder of all kinds, mutilation, cruel treatment and torture; taking of hostages; outrages upon personal dignity, in particular, humiliating and degrading treatment; the passing of sentences and carrying out of executions without previous judgement pronounced by a regularly constituted court, affording all the judicial guarantees which are recognised as indispensable by civilised peoples.[135]

This characterisation does not apply to mere acts of banditry, internal disturbances and tensions, unorganised and short-lived insurrections, or terrorist activities, which are not subject to international humanitarian law.[136] What determines whether a conflict is just internal strife or an internal armed conflict falling within the scope of Common Article 3 is its intensity and the organisation of the parties.

Zimbabwe is a state party to the Geneva Convention of 1949 and both its Additional Protocols. It should also be emphasised that Common Article 3 forms part of customary international law, making it applicable to and binding on Zimbabwe, as indicated in Section II above. In particular, Common Article 3 of the Geneva Conventions of 1949 and Articles

[131] Fleck (n. 17 above).

[132] As above.

[133] Rome Statute of the International Criminal Court, https://www.icc-cpi.int/resourcelibrary/official-journal/rome-statute.aspx.

[134] (n. 17 above).

[135] Rome Statute (n. 132 above).

[136] *Tadic* Judgement (n. 127 above).

1(1) and 4 of Additional Protocol II Relating to the Protection of Victims of Non-International Armed Conflict (APII) applied to the conflict.

The Matabeleland crisis constituted an internal armed conflict envisaged by international law for several reasons. First, the Zimbabwean government itself characterised the situation as an armed conflict back in 1983 and more recently.[137] Second, the government mobilised and deployed a significant armed forces contingent (the 5th Brigade) and other army units and state security agencies to Matabeleland and Midlands for a prolonged period, further confirming the existence of armed conflict.[138] Third, there was a resort to armed force between, on the one hand, the dissidents as an armed group which was organised (albeit loosely) and the government forces on the other hand. As such, the international law of armed conflict applied to the conflict. Consequently, crimes committed during this conflict constituted violations of the international laws of armed conflict, commonly known as war crimes.[139]

There is compelling evidence that the Gukurahundi atrocities meet the requirements of war crimes (the crimes were committed in the context of an internal armed conflict)[140] and violate the laws of war, especially concerning the treatment of the civilian population by parties to a conflict. According to Common Article 3, Additional Protocol II, the ICC Statute and customary international law, the beatings, cruel treatment, torture, detention, humiliating and degrading treatment and summary executions by the Gukurahundi constituted war crimes.

In addition to a soldier or combatants involved in the armed conflict, civilians can be held individually criminally liable for war crimes if they directly participate in the hostilities or war effort.[141] Thus, in addition to

[137] *Breaking the Silence—Building True Peace* (n. 2 above) 3. Although in establishing the Chihambakwe Commission of Enquiry into the disturbances in Matabeleland—prompted by complaints about Gukurahundi atrocities against civilians, the government did not use the term 'conflict' there was tacit recognition that the deployment of the military was a response to what the government considered an armed conflict; ZimLive, 'Gukurahundi was a conflict situation, Mnangagwa's spokesman says' citing an interview with George Charamba, available at zimlive.com, accessed on 7 March 2020.

[138] *Breaking the Silence—Building True Peace* (n. 2 above) 45.

[139] Common Article 3 of the Geneva Convention.

[140] As above.

[141] *Prosecutor v Kayishema and Ruzindana* -95-1-T (ICTR) 1999 para 175–176.

the soldiers comprising the Gukurahundi and their military commanders, government or party officials, business persons, professionals, healthcare personnel and ordinary people who directly participate in hostilities can be held liable and found guilty of war crimes. As part of their direct participation in the hostilities and the Gukurahundi effort, government officials, including Prime Minister Robert Mugabe,[142] and Enos Nkala and others, would be individually criminally liable if they were still alive. Other civilian government officials who were directly responsible for overseeing the Gukurahundi operation, including then Minister of State Sidney Sekeramayi and Minister of State Security Emmerson Mnangagwa (in charge of the Central Intelligence Organisation (CIO), also meet the requirements of civilians directing, participating and contributing to the war effort. The Director of CIO, Kevin Woods and other CIO officers directly involved, participating and supporting the Gukurahundi operations—all played a crucial role in the torture, rape and murder of civilians at Siwale, Bhalagwe and throughout Matabeleland and Midlands and would be individually criminally liable.

For war crimes to be established, victims of war crimes in internal armed conflict must be civilians or the civilian population.[143] The victims of Gukurahundi atrocities were unarmed civilians not engaged in any hostilities.[144] According to common Article 3, Additional Protocol II, the ICC Statute and customary international law, the beatings, cruel treatment, torture, detention, humiliating and degrading treatment and summary executions by the Gukurahundi constituted war crimes.

4.2 Genocide (1983–1987)

The crime of genocide is the gravest form of international crimes. It is prohibited by the Convention on the Prevention and Punishment of the Crime of Genocide (Genocide Convention),[145] which is now part of

[142] S Doran, 'New Documents Claim to Prove Mugabe Ordered Gukurahundi Killings'.

[143] Geneva Convention (n. 138 above).

[144] *Breaking the Silence—Building True Peace* (n. 2 above) 48.

[145] See Convention of the Prevention and Punishment of Genocide.

customary international law.[146] Zimbabwe is a State party to the Genocide Convention. The country has also enacted the Genocide Act to give effect to the Genocide Convention.[147] Article 2 of the Genocide Convention provides that genocide includes 'any of the following acts committed with intent to destroy in whole or in part a national, ethnical, racial or religious group, as such: killing members of the group; causing serious bodily or mental harm to members of the group; deliberately inflicting on the group conditions of life calculated to bring about its physical destruction in whole or in part; imposing measures intended to prevent births within the group, and forcibly transferring children of the group to another group.' The threshold for proving genocide is exceptionally high and requires an analysis of both the objective and subjective intent of the attackers. The objective elements of the crime of genocide include the commission of any of the enumerated acts with the requisite intent.[148]

The Gukurahundi targeted Ndebeles from Matabeleland and Midlands, who were also considered supporters of the opposition ZAPU political party.[149] To this extent, ZAPU was considered by the Gukurahundi and the government as a Ndebele party linking the political objective of destroying ZAPU and creating a one-party state with a genocidal plan to eliminate Ndebeles-ZAPU supporters.[150] This position is supported by the admission of Colonel Lionel Dyke, who commanded the Paratrooper regiment, which committed widespread atrocities. Dyke acknowledged the targeting of Ndebeles as a deliberate military strategy.[151] Targeting an ethnic group is one of the requirements

[146] CM Bassiouni, 'International Crimes: *Jus Cogens* and *Obligatio Erga Omnes*' (1996) 59 *Law and Contemporary Problems* 4 p68.

[147] Genocide Act, Chapter 9:20.

[148] *Prosecutor vs Jean Kambanda* 97-23-S (ICTR) 1998. *Kambada* was found guilty of genocide, amongst other things, for his omission to fulfil his duty as Prime Minister of Rwanda to take action to stop on-going massacres, which he had become aware of, or to protect the population from possible massacres after he had been personally asked to do so and his omission resulted in massacres.

[149] The term Ndebele is used here to describe a group of collective ethnicities from the region of Matabeleland and Midlands including Kalanga, Sotho, Venda and Tonga amongst others.

[150] We blame the 'Ndebele Party Zapu for Gukurahundi' Mugabe Says: https://www.youtube.com/watch?v=0C1MiDQnQhE.

[151] *Breaking the Silence—Building True Peace* (n. 2 above) 58.

for the crime of genocide according to the Genocide Convention.[152] Whilst the Genocide Convention excludes political groups from protected groups, it is argued that based on the available evidence, including on the methodology of atrocities, the targeting of civilians was multi-dimensional, in which the ethnic element was prominent. The acknowledgement by Col Dyke that the Ndebeles were 'well aware' of the strategy is instructive, whilst the modus operandi of the perpetrators demonstrated an ethnic cleansing agenda.[153]

In many cases, senior government officials made no pretence of the tribal or ethnic nature of the operation.[154] Victims also report being forced all night to sing songs in Shona and beaten if they failed.[155] It is also instructive that the South Africa mission reached the same conclusion that: 'it seems the government has decided to hold the Ndebele as a nation responsible for the dissident problem and act mercilessly against them.'[156] The imposition of a food embargo, a region-wide curfew and the burning of food stocks aimed to starve the entire Ndebele population in Matabeleland and Midlands to death to bring about its destruction further support the genocidal intent of the perpetrators.[157] Also, the predominantly Shona-speaking composition[158] of the 5th Brigade suggests a tribal or ethnic army.

Based on the ethnic composition of the Brigade, the stated intention and conduct of the government of the day, the identity of its victims and the specific acts by the perpetrators, and the large numbers

[152] Genocide Convention (n. 143 above).

[153] *Breaking the Silence—Building True Peace* (n. 2 above) 58.

[154] Doran (n. 1 above) 584: Reflecting on the Bulawayo operation in a discussion with the Norwegians, Acting Commissioner of Police, Henry Mukurazhizha remarked that 'this is not [a] political matter but tribal, that [the] Matabele must be crushed.'.

[155] P Maedza (2017) '*Mai VaDhikondo*': Echoes of the Requiems from the Killing Fields,' *Social Dynamics*, 43:2, 215–229.

[156] Doran (n. 1 above) 420.

[157] H Cameron, 'State-Organized Starvation: A Weapon of Extreme Mass Violence in Matabeleland South, 1984'—Volume 12 Issue 1, Spring 2018, pp. 26–47, *Genocide Studies International Journal*, University of Toronto Press.

[158] *Breaking the Silence—Building True Peace* (n. 2 above) 48. Doran (n. 1 above) 417.

of Ndebeles killed, the Matabeleland atrocities meet the requirements of the international crime of genocide.[159]

4.3 Torture (1980–2020)

Torture is an international crime prohibited by the Convention against Torture and Other Cruel, Inhuman or Degrading Treatment or Punishment (Torture Convention) of 1987[160] and customary international law.[161] Zimbabwe has neither signed nor ratified the Torture Convention but is bound by the provisions of the treaty on the basis that it has become part of customary international law. Torture is defined as 'any act by which severe pain or suffering, whether physical or mental, is intentionally inflicted on a person for such purposes as obtaining from him or a third person information or a confession, punishing him for an act he or a third person has committed.'[162] Torture cannot be justified under any circumstance, nor can an order from a superior officer or public authority be used to justify torture. In the past 40 years, the crime of torture has been the most endemic of all international crimes committed in Zimbabwe. Torture was extensively committed against civilians by the Gukurahundi, the central intelligence organisation, the police and Zanu (PF) militia. This issue is separately addressed in this author's accompanying chapter in this volume. Torture formed a crucial part of the electoral violence against ZUM supporters in 1990, with reports of severe beatings, inhumane and degrading treatment. In 2000, torture was extensively used against MDC supporters and white commercial farmers by Zanu PF affiliated war veterans, Central Intelligence Officers and police. In all cases, reports of

[159] AJ McGregor, and T Ranger (eds) (2000) *Violence and Memory: One Hundred Years in the 'Dark Forests' of Matabeleland*. Oxford University Press; T Dube, 'Gukurahundi Remembered: The Police, Opacity and the Gukurahundi Genocide in Bulilimamangwe District, 1982–1988' *Journal of Asian and African Studies*- February 2021. *Prosecutor v Jean-Paul Akayesu* 96-4-T(ICTR) 1998 para 513; *Prosecutor v Clement Kayishema* and *Obed Ruzindana* 95-I (ICTR) para 98.

[160] Convention against Torture and Other Cruel, Inhuman or Degrading Treatment or Punishment (Torture Convention) of 1987, available at https://treaties.un.org/Pages/ViewDetails.aspx?src=IND&mtdsg_no=IV-9&chapter=4&lang=en.

[161] 'Torture in International Law: A Guide to Jurisprudence': *Association for the Prevention of Torture*; See also: https://ihl-databases.icrc.org/customary-ihl/eng/docs/v1_rul_rule90.

[162] Torture Convention (n. 149 above).

severe beatings, mutilation and dismemberment, rapes and other inhuman and degrading treatment were widespread. In 2008, the post-election Operation Mavoterapapi, described above, was accompanied by the extensive use of torture, beatings, mutilation and rapes of civilians by state security agents, Zanu (PF) militia and war veterans.[163] The operation was aimed at punishing civilians for voting for the MDC. Torture has been deployed extensively against civilians comprising opposition supporters, officials and government critics between 2008 and 2020. As discussed above, abduction, enforced disappearance and torture are a common and preferred strategy of state security agencies (intelligence organisation, military and police) and Zanu PF militia in Zimbabwe. The abduction, enforced disappearance and torture of Tawanda Muchehiwa, Joanna Mamombe, Netsai Marova, Cecilia Chimbiri, Jestina Mukoko, Tendai Mombeyarara, Samantha Kureya are all illustrative of this phenomenon. Further, the Constitutional Court of South Africa has held that there is an obligation on South African authorities to investigate, prosecute and punish torture committed by Zimbabwean government officials against civilians.[164]

4.4 Crimes Against Humanity (1980–2020)

Crimes against humanity are prohibited by customary international law.[165] They are also prohibited by various treaties, including the Rome Statute of the International Criminal Court Statute.[166] Zimbabwe is not a State party to the Rome Statute but is still bound by the customary law prohibition. Article 7(1) of the ICC Statute defines crimes against humanity as '…the following acts when committed as part of a widespread

[163] J Hammer, 'The Reign of Thuggery,' (n. 76 above); see also Bullets for 'Each of You: State Sponsored Violence Since Zimbabwe March 29 Election,' *Human Rights Watch*, June 9 2008 (n 79 above); AIDS-Free World, Electing to Rape: Sexual Terror in Mugabe's Zimbabwe 8 (2009) (n. 84 above).

[164] *National Police Commissioner of the South African Police Service v Southern African Human Rights Litigation Centre Trust (The Torture Docket case)* (CCT 02/14) [2014] ZACC 30; 2015 (1) SA 315 (CC).

[165] Kittichisaree (n. 18 above) See also https://www.un.org/en/genocideprevention/crimes-against-humanity.shtml.

[166] Rome Statute of the International Criminal Court, Art 7 (n. 132 above).

or systematic attack directed against any civilian population with knowledge of the attack[167]: murder, extermination, enslavement, deportation or forcible transfer population, imprisonment or other severe deprivation of physical liberty in violation of fundamental rules of international law, torture, rape, sexual slavery, enforced prostitution, forced pregnancy, enforced sterilisation, or any other form of sexual violence of comparable gravity, persecution against any identifiable group or collectivity on political, racial, national, ethnic, cultural, religious, gender, or other grounds that are universally recognised as impermissible under international law, enforced disappearance of persons, the crime of apartheid, and other inhumane acts of a similar character intentionally causing great suffering, or serious injury to the body or mental health.'

The ICTY has found that the following factors are indicative of a widespread or systematic attack:

1. the existence of a political agenda or ideology to destroy, persecute or weaken a particular community coupled with the institution of efforts to implement that policy;
2. the involvement of political and military authorities at a high level,
3. the extent of financial, military or other means,
4. the extent of the repetitious, uniform and continuous perpetration against the same civilian population.[168]

Each of these factors is discussed below concerning the patterns and incidents of atrocity in the past 40 years:

Existence of a political agenda or ideology to destroy, persecute or weaken a particular community coupled with the institution of efforts to implement that policy

An analysis of the gross violations committed against civilians since 1980 shows a clear pattern of a political agenda or ideology to destroy, persecute or weaken political opposition accompanied by significant mobilisation of efforts to implement and achieve that policy. The design, establishment and deployment of Gukurahundi were pursuant to an ideology to destroy the opposition party ZAPU and persecute, weaken

[167] *Prosecutor v Kupreskic* IT-95-16-A (ICTY) 2000.

[168] *Jelisic* case (n. 129 above) para 53; *Prosecutor v Tihomir Blaskic* IT-95-14 (ICTY) 2000 para 203.

and exterminate its Ndebele supporters to establish a one-party state.[169] The significant mobilisation and deployment of state and military efforts for this purpose prove the existence of this ideology. Likewise, in the run-up to the 1990 election, the persecution of ZUM supporters was undeniably pursuant to a political agenda. This is evident from the deployment of state security apparatus and Zanu (PF) party structures to intimidate, harass and attack ZUM supporters during the election campaign.

Therefore, there is clear evidence of the existence of a political agenda and policy in 1990 to destroy ZUM, persecute, weaken and destroy its supporters.[170] This policy was conceived and directed from the highest levels of government, as demonstrated by the public threats and warnings of physical harm issued by Robert Mugabe and senior officials in the government and Zanu (PF). That Zanu (PF) supporters and government officials carried out the threats demonstrate the institution and mobilisation of efforts to carry out the political agenda. The widespread attacks against ZUM supporters and the attempted murder of senior ZUM official Patrick Kombayi by Central Intelligence Officers (CIO) working for Vice President Simon Muzenda and their subsequent pardon by President Mugabe show the systematic intent and the mobilisation of effort to carry out the political agenda to destroy ZUM, persecute and weaken its supporters and officials.[171]

Similarly, Zanu (PF) carried the same political agenda and ideology to destroy the MDC. From the time the MDC was formed in 2000 to the present, Zanu (PF) has made no secret of its intention to 'crush it' as it did with ZAPU and ZUM. As it did with ZUM, it has accused the MDC of being puppets of the 'whites' and intending to return Zimbabwe to the whites.[172] Mugabe had made a similar allegation about ZUM in 1990, accusing it of aligning with CAZ.[173] The election violence in 2008 forced Morgan Tsvangirai to withdraw from the run-off, which Mugabe won by a landslide.

[169] As above.

[170] Kriger (n. 6 above).

[171] As above.

[172] Zanu PF capitalised on the defeat of the Constitution to argue that the MDC and the white farmers had conspired.

[173] Kriger (n. 6 above).

The role of the Central Intelligence Organisation in abducting, torturing and enforcedly disappearing Jestina Mukoko and her colleagues for their work in documenting political violence by Zanu PF supporters with the involvement of the military demonstrates the significant mobilisation of efforts to implement the political agenda and ideology to destroy the MDC and to silence all critics of the government.

After Mugabe's removal in a military coup in November 2017, the continued targeting of perceived political opponents is another manifestation of Zanu (PF)'s political agenda, ideology and policy to retain power through the use of violence.[174] This is reinforced by the reasons proffered by the generals that conducted the coup that they had done so, amongst other things, to prevent Zanu (PF)'s electoral defeat under Mugabe in the upcoming 2018 elections.[175] The political environment would improve briefly after the coup. However, in the run-up to the election in 2018,[176] Zanu (PF) retained its political ideology, agenda and apparatus of political domination and destruction of the MDC, with the military playing a renewed and increased intimidatory role in the rural areas.[177] The implementation of this policy manifested in the manipulation of the election and the deployment of the military to put down protests against delays in the announcement of election results. The military used live ammunition against unarmed protesters, killing six and wounding dozens of others.[178] Despite the Montlhante International Commission finding the military responsible for the killings and recommending that perpetrators of the shootings be held accountable, the commander of the Brigade that carried out the killings was instead promoted.[179] The military continued to conduct atrocities on behalf of the government and Zanu (PF). In January 2019, in response to public protests over an increase in fuel

[174] BM Tendi, 'The Motivations and Dynamics of Zimbabwe's 2017 Military Coup,' (2020) *African Affairs*, Volume 119 Issue 474, 39–67.

[175] In outlining the reasons for Operation Restore Legacy, the generals made it clear that they were saving Zanu PF from defeat in 2018.

[176] S Malunga, 'Hear the Voice of God', *Africa Report*, 21 December 2019: https://www.theafricareport.com/21549/zimbabwe-hear-the-voice-of-god/.

[177] 'Zanu PF/Military Deterrence of the Village Vote' (n. 98 above).

[178] 'Zimbabwe: At Least Dead in Post-Election Violence', *Human Rights Watch*, 3 August 2018.

[179] 'Zimbabwe: Mnangagwa Promotes Army General Fingered in August 1 Civilian Killings', https://allafrica.com/stories/201812180073.html.

prices, the military was again deployed to put down protest throughout the country. Many civilians were reportedly tortured, raped and killed by the army in the aftermath of the protests.[180] The government blamed the MDC party and civil society, and social media activists for the protests and targeted many for abduction, torture and murder.[181] The courts conducted fast-track trials, convictions and issued lengthy imprisonment sentences against hundreds of civilians accused of participating in the protests.[182]

In August 2019, the government responded with heavy-handed brutality to public protests against deteriorating living conditions by the MDC. Likewise, in July 2020, calls for public protests against corruption and failed governance by the Zanu (PF) government were met with pre-emptive force and excessive violence by the military, police and intelligence agencies. Between 2017 and 2020, there was a marked deterioration of human rights with arrests of journalists and anti-corruption activists, abuse of the courts, record 106 abductions by state agents,[183] 64 in one year (2019) and up to 25 extra-judicial killings.[184] Reminiscent of Gukurahundi abductions and disappearances, 2000, 2002 and 2008 abductions, most of the abductions targeted perceived critics of Zanu (PF) and the government and were carried out by state security teams known as Ferret. In many cases, abductions have been accompanied by torture and sexual abuse, with victims later dumped in the city's

[180] Solidarity Peace Trust, *Resurgent Authoritarianism: The Politics of the January 2019 Violence in Zimbabwe*, 20 February 2019 (Port Shepstone, SPT, 2019). see also Zimbabwe: Ruthless Crackdown on Freedom of Assembly Exposes Intolerance of Dissent, Amnesty International, 9 February 2019, Accessible at https://www.amnesty.org/en/latest/news/2019/02/zimbabwe-ruthless-crackdown-on-freedom-of-assembly/.

[181] For example, Blessing Toronga was abducted on January 24 from Glen Norah C Shopping Centre in Harare. His remains were later found in a mortuary in March 2021.

[182] See Zimbabwe Shutdown Human Rights Update, https://www.hrforumzim.org/news/zimshutdown-human-rights-update-23-january-2019/; Zimbabwe courts convict 375 People over violent January protests, https://www.timeslive.co.za/amp/news/africa/2019-04-03-zimbabwe-courts-convict-375-people-over-violent-january-protests/; Zimbabwean lawyers march to demand return to the rule of law https://www.timeslive.co.za/news/africa/2019-01-29-zimbabwean-lawyers-march-to-demand-a-return-to-the-rule-of-law/.

[183] 'No Fast Track Justice: Zimbabwe Lawyers Petition to Chief Justice': 29 January 2019, accessible at https://newzwire.live/no-fast-track-justice-in-full-zimbabwe-lawyers-petition-to-chief-justice/.

[184] Kika (n. 13 above).

outskirts.[185] In some cases, victims have been killed and dumped, as in the case of Blessing Toronga.[186]

4.5 *The Involvement of Political and Military Authorities at a High Level*

The involvement of political and military authorities in the commission of atrocities in Zimbabwe can be readily established. Concerning Gukurahundi, then Prime Minister Mugabe and his entire cabinet made no secret of their involvement in designing, planning, organising, deploying and directing the Gukurahundi operations. There is evidence of the involvement of the then Prime Minister and Minister of Defence, Robert Mugabe,[187] senior cabinet ministers including Emmerson Mnangagwa (Minister of State Security),[188] Sydney Sekeramayi, (Minister of State), Enos Nkala (Minister of Home Affairs),[189] and senior military officer including Colonel Perence Shiri,[190] high-ranking intelligence officers including Kevin Woods (Central Intelligence Organisation Director)[191] and police commanders,[192] in the formulation of the plan and its implementation.[193] Senior political and security officials have continued to feature in every atrocity since. In 2000, Mugabe, his State Security Minister Sidney Sekeramayi and other senior Zanu (PF) leaders openly encouraged, supported and threatened attacks against MDC civilians and supporters and white commercial farmers and endorsed murders

[185] Joanna Mamombe, Cecilia Chimbiri and Netsai Marova all MDC officials were abducted and tortured in May 2020 for protesting against COVID-19 lockdown regulations.

[186] DNA Tests Confirm MDC Activist's Dumped Body, accessible at https://www.newsday.co.zw/2019/04/dna-tests-confirm-mdc-activists-dumped-body/.

[187] The role of Mugabe and his officials in the Gukurahundi is discussed by the author in the accompanying Chapter.

[188] 'Former CIO Spy, Woods, Implicates Mnangagwa in Gukurahundi' Pindula News, available at https://news.pindula.co.zw/2019/04/14/former-cio-double-agent-woods-implicates-mnangagwa-gukurahundi/, accessed on 7 March 2020.

[189] *Breaking the Silence—Building True Peace* (n. 2 above) 32–45.

[190] As above.

[191] K Woods, *The Kevin Woods Story: In the Shadow of Mugabe's Gallows* (2007) 30.

[192] *Breaking the Silence—Building True Peace* (n. 2 above 56).

[193] As above.

committed by them.[194] CIO operatives and Zanu (PF) election agents were responsible for the horrific murders of Talent Mabika and Tichaona Chiminya.[195] In 2008, the Joint Operations Command comprising the heads of the security institutions were reported to have designed, planned, organised and planned the post-electoral violence in 2008.[196] Likewise, military responses and security clampdown of perceived political opponents and human rights and anti-corruption activists are often preceded by Joint Operations Command meetings and statements warning and threatening action.[197] There is no pretence made of separation between Zanu PF and the national interests and the role of senior military and political personnel in advancing the latter.[198] More recently, the Minister responsible for State Security, Owen Mudha Ncube, has been implicated in directing and overseeing the perpetration of politically motivated human rights abuses against civilians leading to personalised sanctions against him by the government of the United States of America.[199]

4.6 *The Extent of Financial, Military or Other Means*

Since independence, the government has spared no resources to commit atrocities. Starting with Gukurahundi, the size of financial, military and political resources mobilised to advance the political agenda and ideology of crushing ZAPU, destroying and weakening its support base was significant. Before deploying the 5th Brigade (Gukurahundi), the government deployed the 4th and 6th Brigades and the paratrooper regiments under Colonel Dyke to engage and combat dissidents actively.[200] With the

[194] see Coltart (n. 8 above) 275–276.

[195] As above.

[196] 'Bullets for Each of You: State Sponsored Violence Since Zimbabwe March 29 Election' *Human Rights Watch*, 9 June 2008.

[197] 'Zimbabwe Transition in a Muddy Terrain: Political Economy Under Military Capture', *Zimbabwe Democracy Institute* (2017).

[198] 'Army Deals Blow to Mugabe Rival': *BBC*, January 9 2002; 'Army Must Vote Against Tsvangirai: Major General': https://www.politicsweb.co.za/opinion/army-must-vote-against-tsvangirai--major-general.

[199] 'US Sanctions Owen Ncube over protest crackdown,' *Al Jazeera*: https://www.aljazeera.com/news/2019/10/26/us-sanctions-zimbabwes-owen-ncube-over-protest-crackdown.

[200] *Breaking the Silence—Building True Peace* (n 2 above).

arrival of the 5th Brigade in 1983, the total military presence in Matabeleland and Midlands reached 5000 officers. The 5th Brigade alone comprised at least 3500 soldiers, and by 1984, total troop deployment to Matabeleland South reached 15,000.[201] The Gukurahundi operations in Matabeleland also involved various state security agencies, including police, intelligence and militia groups established by the government.[202] The effort undertaken in mobilising the 5th Brigade, allocating significant state resources and contracting the North Korean government to train it,[203] including providing considerable state resources for its accommodation, operations and deploying in Matabeleland for a prolonged duration, all highlight the large extent of state, military and other resources that were assigned.[204] Likewise, the widespread and systematic attacks against white farmers and MDC supporters in rural areas in 2000 and 2002 required the mobilisation of significant resources and personnel in the form of war veterans whose operations were underwritten by Zanu (PF) and the government.[205]

The subsequent operations to destroy the MDC have involved the mobilisations of the entire security cluster under the Joint Operations Command. The electoral violence of 2008 relied on the significant mobilisation of the military, intelligence and police.[206] More recently, the post-coup election of 2018 saw the mobilisation of the military in ways not seen previously. Many have argued that the military has now morphed into the ruling party Zanu (PF) and that the relations are now distinguished from the previous where a 'political party had an army to one where an army has a party.'[207] The mobilisation of the army towards advancing the political agenda and ideology of Zanu (PF) and the government played a vital role in intimidating villagers and securing the

[201] As above.

[202] As above.

[203] As above.

[204] The Gukurahundi was deployed to Matabeleland for over three years.

[205] 'Zimbabwe Government 'Deploying Army' to Help Farm Invaders', *The Guardian*, 20 April 2000. https://www.theguardian.com/world/2000/apr/20/zimbabwe1.

[206] 'Zimbabwe-Transition in a Muddy Terrain: Political Economy Under Military Capture', https://issat.dcaf.ch/ara/Learn/Resource-Library/Policy-and-Research-Papers/Zimbabwe-Transition-in-a-Muddy-Terrain-Political-Economy-Under-Military-Capture.

[207] SJ Ndlovu-Gatsheni and P Ruhanya (Eds) *The History and Political Transition of Zimbabwe: From Mugabe to Mnangagwa* (2020), Palgrave Macmillan.

village vote in 2018.[208] The deployment of the military terrified villagers who would have recalled the military's role in 2008, 2002 and Gukurahundi. Finally, the levels of deployment of the significant military, police and intelligence contingents to quell public protests in January 2019, August 2019 and July 2020 demonstrate a massive commitment to the implementation of the political ideology and agenda to destroy, persecute and weaken civilians in general and especially perceived government opponents or critics and supporters of the MDC.

5 The Extent of the Repetitious, Uniform and Continuous Perpetration Against the Same Civilian Population.

Atrocities have been repeatedly committed throughout Zimbabwe over a long time by the same perpetrators against the civilian population. The civilians targeted have been supporters and officials of opposition political parties and critics of the government or the ruling party, Zanu (PF). The repetitious politically motivated attacks against ZAPU, ZUM and MDC civilian supporters spanning four decades are a testament to a repetitious, uniform and continuous perpetration of crimes against a civilian population. That MDC Alliance opposition supporters and officials, as well as critics of Zanu (PF) and government, continue to suffer abductions, torture and murder in 2020, much the same way ZAPU and ZUM supporters did in the 1980s and 1990s reaffirms that the pattern of atrocities in Zimbabwe shows one series of widespread and systematic attacks against a civilian population over a long time by the same group of perpetrators. These crimes are part of a systematic, interwoven political agenda and continue to be perpetrated by more or less the same perpetrators as a widespread and systematic attack against a civilian population. The objective elements of international crimes against humanity are therefore established.

[208] 'Zanu PF/Military Deterrence of the Village Vote' (n. 98 above).

6 Prospects of Accountability

It has been shown that international crimes carry an international law obligation to investigate, prosecute and punish known perpetrators.[209] This obligation persists long after the commission of an international crime.[210] In the case of continuing crimes, the obligation is to prevent further commission of international crimes.[211]

The fulfilment of the duty to investigate, prosecute and punish crimes has culminated in the prosecution of the Khmer Rouge in Cambodia,[212] the Former President of Chad, Hissene Habre,[213] former President of Liberia Charles Taylor in Sierra Leone,[214] militia leaders in East Timor[215] and elsewhere.[216] The unprecedented ICC prosecution of Kenyan President Uhuru Kenyatta and Vice President William Ruto and Ivorian President Laurent Gbagbo for election-related violence has also broken new ground in international criminal law despite being unsuccessful.[217]

[209] See Rome Statute, Geneva Conventions, Genocide Conventions, Torture Convention; D Orentlicher, 'Settling Accounts: The Duty to Prosecute Human Rights Violations of a Prior Regime,' *The Yale Law Journal*, Vol. 100, No. 8. 1991, p. 253; N. Roht-Arriaza, 'State Responsibility to Investigate and Prosecute Grave Human Rights Violations in International Law,' *California Law Review*, Vol. 78, 1990, p. 451, pp. 458–61, Schabas (n. 17 above) 907–933; Fleck (n. 17 above), J Wouters, 'The Obligation to Prosecute International Crimes.'.

[210] As above.

[211] As above.

[212] Law on the Establishment of the Extraordinary Chamber in Cambodia (ECCC) (2004), accessible at https://www.eccc.gov.kh/en/documents/legal/law-establishment-extraordinary-chambers-amended.

[213] See Statute of the Extraordinary African Chambers, accessible at https://www.hrw.org/news/2013/09/02/statute-extraordinary-african-chambers.

[214] Statute of the Special Court for Sierra Leone, accessible at www.rscsl.org

[215] UNTAET Regulation 2000/15; see also C Reiger and M Wierda, *The Serious Crimes Process in Timor-Leste: In Retrospect*, ICTJ (2006).

[216] The author separately discusses this in the accompanying chapter in this volume: S Malunga, 'Unpacking Gukurahundi Atrocities Against the Ndebeles of Zimbabwe: What Are the Possibilities for Individual Criminal Responsibility of the Perpetrators Under International Criminal Law?'.

[217] *The Prosecutor v. Uhuru Muigai Kenyatta*: ICC-01/09-02/11, accessible at https://www.icc-cpi.int/kenya/kenyatta and *The Prosecutor v. Laurent Gbagbo and Charles Blé Goudé,* ICC-02/11-01/15, https://www.icc-cpi.int/cdi/gbagbo-goude.

The fact that perpetrators in Zimbabwe continue to hold and deploy the political agenda and ideology to destroy, persecute and weaken the civilian population requires urgent action by the Zimbabwean government to stop the ongoing commission of crimes against humanity. However, it is unlikely that the Zimbabwean government, comprised of perpetrators of international crimes, will take any steps to investigate, prosecute and punish these crimes.[218] In designing, encouraging and instigating the commission of the crimes in the past 40 years, followed by repeatedly granting immunity and amnesties to known perpetrators, the government has demonstrated its unwillingness to pursue accountability.[219] With the re-emergence of the international justice system in the past 25 years, a presumption of illegality of amnesties for international crimes has been established.[220] However, this development has not prevented the use of amnesties to facilitate transitions from conflict to peace in several countries worldwide.[221] An amnesty followed the Unity Accord of 1987 between Zanu PF and PF Zapu for Gukurahundi perpetrators.[222] The main difference between the amnesties in Zimbabwe and elsewhere is that they have not been granted to facilitate truth-telling, peaceful and amicable end to conflict and transition

[218] Zimbabwe: Toll of Impunity; Amnesty International, 24 June 2002 AFR 46/034/2002.

[219] In the past 40 years, the Zimbabwean government has received appeals from local and international human rights organisations, including Amnesty International and Human Rights Watch. During Gukurahundi atrocities, the Catholic Conference of Bishops presented Prime Minister Mugabe with evidence of atrocities and called on him to act. In 1997, the Bishops presented President Mugabe with the CCJP Report, 'Breaking the Silence' (n. 2 above), and called for accountability. Mugabe dismissed the report. More recently, the Motlanthe Commission has found that military perpetrators were responsible for the shooting to death of civilians and recommended their prosecution and punishment. Instead, the commander of the unit responsible was promoted.

[220] Princeton Principles on Universal Jurisdiction, adopted by a group of international law experts in 2001, proposed that 'Amnesties are generally inconsistent with the obligation on states to provide accountability for serious crimes under international law'; Principle 7, Princeton Principles on Universal Jurisdiction 28 (2001), Princeton University Program in Law and Public Affairs, *Princeton University*, Princeton, 2001. M Scharf, 'The Amnesty Exception to the Jurisdiction of the International Criminal Court' *Cornell International Law Journal* 8: 32 (1999).

[221] Y Naqvi, 'Amnesty for War Crimes: Defining the Limits of International Recognition,' (2003) *IRRC* 851 Vol 85, 583.

[222] Clemency Order No 1 of 1988 pardoning all people involved in human rights violations committed between 1982 and 1987.

to democratic, inclusive and human rights-respecting societies,[223] but instead to shield perpetrators and facilitate the commission of further crimes.[224] It, therefore, follows that the granting of amnesties to perpetrators by the Zimbabwean government does not absolve them from accountability under international law.[225] Crucially, amnesties have no universal or extraterritorial effect, as they do not affect treaty obligations or entitlements under customary law to prosecute persons accused of international crimes.[226]

In this regard, there is a range of options available to hold known perpetrators accountable according to the international law duty to prevent, investigate, prosecute and punish international crimes. The first option is diplomatic action directed at the Zimbabwean government to stop committing the crimes and hold known perpetrators accountable.[227] If this is unheeded, the international community has the second option to refer the commission of these crimes to the ICC via the Security Council.[228] The option to refer cases to the ICC has been used in the cases of President Omar Al Bashir of Sudan and President Uhuru Kenyatta of Kenya. The Security Council referral can occur irrespective of whether a perpetrator is a national of a country that is not a state party to the

[223] This justification was used by the South African Truth and Reconciliation Commission and upheld by the Constitutional Court of South Africa in *Azanian Peoples Organization (AZAPO) and Others v President of the Republic of South Africa and Others* (1996) ZACC 16. Amnesties have also been negotiated as part of peace deals in Sudan (Sudan Peace Agreement of 21 April 1997), the Democratic Republic of the Congo (1999 Lusaka Ceasefire Agreement) and Sierra Leone (Lome Peace Agreement of 8 July 1999).

[224] The repetition of atrocities by the same perpetrators over 40 years is demonstrative.

[225] Amnesties granted to shield perpetrators have been rejected by some tribunals including in the case of Charles Taylor.

[226] R Boed, 'The Effect of a Domestic Amnesty on the Ability of Foreign States to Prosecute Alleged Perpetrators of Serious Human Rights Violations,' (2000) Vol. 33, No. 2, *Cornell International Law Journal* 297–323.

[227] In the light of the failure to implement Motlanthe Commission recommendation to punish the commission of crimes, and despite calls and targeted sanctions by foreign governments such as the United States of America against known perpetrators, prospects of these measures succeeding are slim.

[228] Rome Statute, Art 13 (b). AS Galand, 'UN Security Council Referrals to the International Criminal Court: Legal Nature, Effects and Limits' in *Leiden Studies in International Law* (Eds): C Stahn, L van den Herik, N Schrijver.

Rome Statute.[229] However, it is limited to crimes that occur after the coming into effect of the Rome Statute in 2002.[230]

The third option is the exercise of universal jurisdiction to investigate, prosecute and punish these crimes.[231] The Genocide Convention, Torture Convention and the Geneva Conventions and Additional Protocol I explicitly set out State obligations to exercise universal jurisdiction over 'grave breaches' of those instruments.[232] The South African Constitutional Court has held that South African authorities—the South African Police Service (SAPS) and National Prosecution Authority (NPA)—have a duty to investigate and prosecute international crimes allegedly committed in Zimbabwe.[233] This decision provides a significant opening for the exercise of universal jurisdiction.

The fourth option is the African Court of Justice. The court is established pursuant to the Malabo Protocol, which extends the jurisdiction of the African Court of Justice to cover individual criminal liability for serious crimes committed in violations of international law.[234] However, Article 46A of the protocol provides immunity to heads of state and any other senior-state officials based on the functions during the tenure of office. The controversial provision effectively shields perpetrators from individual criminal liability and eliminates the African Court of Justice as a mechanism to advance justice for atrocities.

[229] United Nations Charter, Chapter 7.

[230] Rome Statute, Article 11: the ICC jurisdiction is non-retroactive. It has jurisdiction for crimes that occurred after 1 July 2002.

[231] C Bassiouni, 'Universal Jurisdiction for International Crimes: Historical Perspectives and Contemporary' *Practice*, 42 *Va. J. Int'l L.* 81 (2001–2002).

[232] The duty is founded on customary international law as well as treaties such as the Genocide Convention; whose Article V requires States to enact the necessary legislation to give effect to the Genocide Convention and to provide effective penalties for persons found guilty of genocidal acts. See also Articles 49, 50, 129, 146, respectively, of the Geneva Conventions I–IV, Article 85 of Additional Protocol I; for acts constituting grave breaches, see Articles 50, 51, 130, 147, respectively, of the Geneva Conventions I–IV, Article 85 of Additional Protocol I. see also S Ratner and J Abram, 'Accountability for Human Rights Atrocities in International Law: Beyond The Nuremberg Legacy,' (2001) *Oxford University Press* 41.

[233] *National Police Commissioner of the South African Police Service v Southern African Human Rights Litigation Centre Trust (The Torture Docket case)* (CCT 02/14) [2014] ZACC 30; 2015 (1) SA 315 (CC).

[234] African Union, Decision on the Draft Legal Instruments, Assembly AU/Dec.529 (XXIII), Decisions, Declarations and Resolution of the Assembly of the Union, Twenty Third Ordinary Session, June 26–27, 2014.

The fifth option is to investigate, prosecute and punish these crimes before the Zimbabwean national criminal justice system.[235] In the case of Zimbabwe, several challenges militate against this option.[236] Firstly, the alleged perpetrators' continued incumbency, authority and control of political and military power are a significant obstacle to the national justice system holding them accountable.[237] Second, the national legal framework is inadequate to capture the international nature of the crimes. The fact that Zimbabwe is not a party to the Rome Statute means that it has not domesticated the Statute's provisions in its law. The Zimbabwean criminal law criminalises genocide but does not carry explicit prohibitions of crimes against humanity and war crimes.[238] There are no specific legal provisions that criminalise torture. However, the Zimbabwe Constitution prohibits torture.[239] Third, the Zimbabwean judicial system is not, in its current form, able to investigate, prosecute and punish international crimes without significant changes and capacity enhancements.[240] Third, critical concerns regarding the independence, impartiality and allegations of the capture of the judicial system by the government (led by alleged perpetrators) and Zanu (PF) means that its credibility and ability to investigate, prosecute and punish international crimes are questionable.[241]

[235] Presently this can only be done under the Criminal Law (Codification and Reform Act) [Chapter 9:23] https://zimlii.org/zw/legislation/act/2004/23.

[236] Whilst the Zimbabwean Criminal Code criminalises most of the crimes committed in the past 40 years, it does not define the severity and criminal responsibility at the requisite of international criminal law.

[237] The same Zanu (PF), government and military leaders have remained firmly in power and control since the time of the Gukurahundi.

[238] Genocide Act (n. 122 above).

[239] Zimbabwe Constitution Amendment Act No 20 of 2013, Section 53.

[240] The country lacks the specialised prosecutorial capacity to investigate and prosecute international crimes.

[241] M Chifamba, 'Zimbabwe: Mnangagwa's Capture of the Judiciary a Red Flag for State Failure' *Africa Report*, 23 November 2020, accessible at https://www.theafricareport.com/51602/zimbabwe-mnangagwas-capture-of-judiciary-a-red-flag-for-state-failure/; A Magaisa: 'Understanding Judicial Capture in Zimbabwe', accessible at https://www.bigsr.co.uk/single-post/2020/11/14/big-saturday-read-understanding-judicial-capture-in-zimbabwe; 'Judges Confirm Judicial Capture, *NewsDay*,' 29 October 2020, https://www.newsday.co.zw/2020/10/judges-confirm-judicial-capture/.

The sixth option is a hybrid tribunal that combines national with either regional or international justice.[242] Hybrid Tribunals are often the outcome of negotiation between national authorities and the international or regional community.[243] Hybrid Tribunals have been established as a balance or alternative between a fully international or domestic judicial process to hold perpetrators of atrocities accountable.[244] They provide a bridge that combines national and international elements and offers the required flexibility to respond to complex international crimes within a national context.[245] They also provide an opportunity to strengthen the capacity of the national justice system to manage complex international crimes by facilitating collaboration between international and national actors (investigators, prosecutors and judges) in the investigation, prosecution and defence of international crimes.[246] They often provide a negotiated compromise that often allays the concerns of countries reluctant to completely cede sovereignty over the accountability process and of perpetrators reluctant to face justice in international courts.[247] They also provide an opportunity for victims to participate in proceedings conducted within the country's territory directly and more broadly respond to the needs of victims.[248]

[242] CE Caitlin, 'Hybrid Tribunals are the Most Effective Structure for Adjudicating International Crimes Occurring Within a Domestic State' (2013) *Law School Student Scholarship* 90 https://scholarship.shu.edu/student_scholarship/90.

[243] The Sierra Leone, Cambodia, Lebanon, Senegal and East Timor Tribunals were all products of negotiation between the United Nations and the relevant countries including the African Union in the case of the Senegal Tribunal.

[244] SMH Nouwen, 'Hybrid Courts' The Hybrid Category of a New Type of International Crimes Courts' (2006) Volume 2, Issue 2 *Utrecht Law Review*, available at http://www.utrechtlawreview.org/.

[245] https://www.ictj.org/publication/committing-justice-serious-human-rights-violations-lessons-hybrid-tribunals Committing to Justice for Serious Human Rights Violations: Lessons from Hybrid Tribunals, *International Centre for Transitional Justice* (2018), https://www.ictj.org/publication/committing-justice-serious-human-rights-violations-lessons-hybrid-tribunals.

[246] As above.

[247] This would be especially important in the light of the resistance of African countries to the ICC and the geopolitical issues between Zimbabwe and western countries.

[248] The hybrid tribunals in Sierra Leone, East Timor, Cambodia and Lebanon have provided an unprecedented opportunity for victims to participate unlike the cases in the ICC in The Hague.

Recent examples of hybrid tribunals include the Serious Crimes Panel in East Timor,[249] the Special Court for Sierra Leone,[250] the Extraordinary Chamber in Senegal, the Special Tribunal for Lebanon War Crimes Chamber in Bosnia and Herzegovina[251] and the internationalised panels in Kosovo,[252] Extraordinary Chambers in the Courts of Cambodia.[253] Given the limitations of the Zimbabwean national justice system to effectively hold perpetrators of international crimes accountable—described above, a hybrid tribunal provides a strong alternative. The current major constraint to this option is that currently perpetrators remain in power and are unlikely to agree to any accountability process whatsoever. A hybrid tribunal remains an alternative once perpetrators are no longer in power and initiated and supported by the international or regional community.

7 Conclusion

This chapter has demonstrated that the pattern of atrocities committed in Zimbabwe constitutes international crimes, namely war crimes, genocide, crimes against humanity and torture. As demonstrated, atrocities continue to be perpetrated, and perpetrators continue to enjoy state-sanctioned impunity from individual criminal accountability.[254] It has also established that these crimes have been committed pursuant to a political agenda or ideology to destroy, persecute or weaken opposition parties, government critics and activists; and that the ruling Zanu (PF) party and the government have mobilised significant resources and effort

[249] Special Panel of the Dili District Court, https://hybridjustice.com/special-panels-of-the-dili-district-court/.

[250] Special Court for Sierra Leone http://www.rscsl.org/.

[251] War Crimes Chamber in Bosnia; see https://hybridjustice.com/the-war-crimes-chamber-in-bosnia-and-herzegovina/; Special Tribunal for Lebanon: https://www.stl-tsl.org/en.

[252] Silvia Steininger, 'The Kosovo Specialist Chambers—A New Chapter for International Criminal Justice in the Balkans,' *Völkerrechtsblog* (2018), https://voelkerrechtsblog.org/articles/the-kosovo-specialist-chambers/.

L Leicht. 'Kosovo War Crimes Court Can Promote Justice On All Sides' available at https://balkaninsight.com/2020/11/12/kosovo-war-crimes-court-can-promote-justice-on-all-sides/.

[253] Extraordinary Chambers in Cambodia see https://www.eccc.gov.kh/en.

[254] Amnesty-Toll of Impunity (n. 208 above).

to implement its policy over 40 years. Also, the chapter has illustrated that a significant level of financial, military and other means have been deployed in the commission of atrocities. The chapter has also demonstrated the repetitious and uniform nature of the atrocities committed over a long period and targeting the civilian population. The chapter has also demonstrated the involvement and individual criminal liability of senior government and military officials in the perpetration of atrocities in Zimbabwe throughout the entire period. Finally, this chapter has proposed some options for ending atrocities in Zimbabwe and holding known perpetrators accountable.

References

Books

Alexander, J; McGregor, AJ & Ranger, T *Violence and Memory: One Hundred Years in the 'Dark Forests' of Matabeleland* (James Currey 2000)

Bantekas, I *Principles of Direct and Superior Responsibility in International Humanitarian Law* (Manchester University Press 2002)

Bassiouni, CM (ed) *Post Conflict Justice* (Transnational Publishers 2002)

Bassiouni, CM (ed) *Proposed Guiding Principles for Combating Impunity for International Crimes*, in *Post Conflict Justice* (Transnational Publishers 2002)

Buckley-Zistel, S; Beck, TK; Braun C & Mieth F (eds) *Transitional Justice Theories* (Routledge 2014) Cassese, A *International Law* (Oxford University Press 2005)

Coltart, D *The Struggle Continues; 50 Years of Tyranny in Zimbabwe* (Jacana 2016)

Doran, S *Kingdom, Power, Glory: Mugabe, ZANU and the Quest for Supremacy: 1960–1987* (Sithatha Media 2017)

Fleck, D (ed) *The Handbook of International Humanitarian Law* (Oxford University Press 2008)

Godwin, P *When a Crocodile Eats the Sun: A Memoir of Africa* (2007) 81Harris, DJ *Cases and Materials on International Law* 6th ed (Sweet & Maxwell 2004)

Hayner, PB *Unspeakable Truths: Confronting State Terror and Atrocity* (Routledge 2001)

Kittichaisaree, K *International Criminal Law* (Oxford University Press 2001).

Mettraux, G *The Law of Command Responsibility* (Oxford University Press 2009)

Mukoko, J *The Abduction and Trial of Jestina Mukoko, The Fight for Human Rights in Zimbabwe* (David Krut Books, 2016)

Ndlovu-Gatsheni, SJ & Ruhanya, P (Eds) *The History and Political Transition of Zimbabwe: From Mugabe to Mnangagwa* (Palgrave Macmillan 2020).

O'Keefe, R *International Criminal Law* (Oxford University Press 2015)

Ratner, SR; Abrams, J & Bischoff, JL *Accountability for Human Rights Atrocities in International Law: Beyond The Nuremberg Legacy* (Oxford University Press 2001)

Sachikonye, LM *The Promised Land: From expropriation to reconciliation and Jambanja*' (Weaver Press 2005)

Sandoz, Y; Swinarski, C & Zimmermann, B (eds) *Commentary on the Additional Protocols of 8 June 1977 to the Geneva Conventions of 12 August 1949* (Geneva/Dordrecht: ICRC/Nijhoff 1987)

Stromseth, JE (ed) *Accountability for Atrocities: National and International Responses* (Transnational Publishers 2003)

Todd, J *Through the Darkness* (Zebra Press 2007)

Van Sliedregt, E *Individual Criminal Responsibility in International Law* (Oxford University Press 2012)

Woods, K *The Kevin Woods Story: In the Shadow of Mugabe's Gallows* (30 Degrees South 2007)

Journal Articles

Adjovi, R 'Introductory Note to the Agreement on the Establishment of the Extraordinary African Chambers Within the Senegalese Judicial System Between the Government of the Republic of Senegal and the African Union and the Statute of the Chambers.' (2013) 52, 4, *International Legal Materials* 1020–1036

Bassiouni, C 'Universal Jurisdiction for International Crimes: Historical Perspectives and Contemporary Practice' (2001–2002) 42 *Virginia Journal of International Law* 81

Bassiouni, CM 'International Crimes: *Jus Cogens* and *Obligatio Erga Omnes*' (1996) 59, 4 *Law and Contemporary Problems* 68.

Beardsworth, N; Cheeseman, N & Tinhu, S 'Zimbabwe: The Coup That Never was, and the Election That Could Have Been', (2019) 478 Volume 118 *African Affairs*, 580–596

Boed, R 'The Effect of a Domestic Amnesty on the Ability of Foreign States to Prosecute Alleged Perpetrators of Serious Human Rights Violations,' (2000) Vol. 33, No. 2, *Cornell International Law Journal*, 297–323

Caitlin, CE 'Hybrid Tribunals are the Most Effective Structure for Adjudicating International Crimes Occurring Within a Domestic State' (2013) *Law School Student Scholarship* 90

Cameron, H 'State-Organised Starvation: A Weapon of Extreme Mass Violence in Matabeleland South, 1984', Volume 12 Issue 1, Spring 2018, 26–47, *Genocide Studies International Journal*, University of Toronto Press

Chifamba, M 'Zimbabwe: Mnangagwa's Capture of the Judiciary a Red Flag for State Failure' *Africa Report*, 23 November 2020.

Crettol, M & La Rosa, AM 'The Missing and Transitional Justice: The Right to Know and the Fight Against Impunity' (2006) 88 *International Review of the Red Cross* 862.

De Waal, V *The Politics of Reconciliation: Zimbabwe's First Decade* (Africa World Press 1990)

Dube, D & Makwerere, D 'Zimbabwe: Towards a Comprehensive Peace Infrastructure' (2012) 2 *International Journal of Humanities and Social Science* 18.

Dube, T 'Gukurahundi Remembered: The Police, Opacity and the Gukurahundi Genocide in Bulilimamangwe District, 1982–1988' *Journal of Asian and African Studies*- February 2021.

Galand, AS 'UN Security Council Referrals to the International Criminal Court: Legal Nature, Effects and Limits' in (2018) C Stahn, C; Van den Herik & Schrijver, LN (eds) *Leiden Studies in International Law* (Brill Nijhoff 2018)

Howard-Hassmann, RE 'Mugabe's Zimbabwe, 2000–2009: Massive Human Rights Violations and the Failure to Protect.' (2010) 32 *Human Rights Quarterly*, 898–920.

Jalloh, CC 'Prosecutor v. Taylor,' (2014) 108 (1) *The American Journal of International Law* 58–66.

Kriger, N 'ZANU (PF.) Strategies in General Elections, 1980–2000: Discourse and Coercion.' (2005) 104, *African Affairs.*

Killander, M & Nyathi, M 'Accountability for the Gukurahundi Atrocities in Zimbabwe Thirty Years On: Prospects and Challenges.' (2015) 48 *Comparative and International Law Journal of Southern Africa*, 3, 463–87.

Leicht, L 'Kosovo War Crimes Court Can Promote Justice On All Sides' (2020) 12 November, *Balkan Insight*.

Machakanja, P 'National Healing and Reconciliation in Zimbabwe: Challenges and Opportunities' (2010) *Institute for Justice and Reconciliation,* last accessed from https://www.africaportal.org/publications/national-healing-and-reconciliation-in-zimbabwe-challenges-and-opportunities/ on 23 June 2021.

Maedza, P '*Mai VaDhikondo*': Echoes of the Requiems from the Killing Fields (2017) 43 (2) *Social Dynamics* 215–229.

Magaisa, A 'Understanding Judicial Capture in Zimbabwe' *Big Saturday Read* 14 November 2020.

Makumbe, J 'Electoral Politics in Zimbabwe: Authoritarianism Versus the People' (2006) 31 (3) *Africa Development / Afrique Et Développement*, 45–61.

Masunungure, E "Zimbabwe's Militarised, Electoral Authoritarianism.' (2011) 65 (1) *Journal of International Affairs*, 47–64.

McDermott, Y 'Prosecutor v. Bemba' (2016) 110, 3 *The American Journal of International Law* 526–33.

Muchemwa, C; Ngwerume, ET & Hove, M 'When Will the Long Nightmare Come to an End? Challenges to National Healing and Reconciliation in Post-Colonial Zimbabwe' (2013) 22 (3) *African Security Review* 145–159

Mungwari, T 'Zimbabwe Post-Election Violence, Motlanthe Commission of Enquiry (2018) 10 (2) *International Journal of Contemporary Research and Review*.

Muqayi, S 'The Strategies Applied by the Zimbabwe African National Union-Patriotic Front (ZANU-PF) to Dominate the 2013 Harmonised Elections in Zimbabwe' (2018) 5 (3) *Journal of African Foreign Affairs* 45–64.

Murambadoro, R 'We Cannot Reconcile Until the Past Has Been Acknowledged: Perspectives on Gukurahundi from Matabeleland, Zimbabwe' (2015) 15 (1) *African Journal on Conflict Resolution* 33–57.

Naqvi, Y 'Amnesty for War Crimes: Defining the Limits of International Recognition,' (2003) 85 (58) *IRRC* 851

Ndakaripa, M 'Zimbabwe's 2018 Elections: Funding, Public Resources and Vote-Buying,' (2020) (47) 164 *Review of African Political Economy*, 301–312.

Ndlovu-Gatsheni, SJ 'Rethinking Chimurenga and Gukurahundi in Zimbabwe: A Critique of Partisan National History' (2012) 55 (1) *African Studies Review* 1–2.

Ngwenya, D & Harris, G 'The Consequences of Not Healing: Evidence from the Gukurahundi Violence in Zimbabwe' (2015) 15 *African Journal on Conflict Resolution* 2.

Nouwen, SMH 'Hybrid Courts' The Hybrid Category of a New Type of International crimes courts' (2006) Volume 2, Issue 2 Utrecht *Law Review*.

Nyathi, M & Ncube, M 'The 2017 Military Coup in Zimbabwe: Implications for Human Rights and the Rule of Law' (2020) 20 *African Human Rights Law Journal* 825–851.

Orentlicher, D 'Settling Accounts: The Duty to Prosecute Human Rights Violations of a Prior Regime' (1991) 100 *The Yale Law Journal*.

Reiger, C & Wierda, M *The Serious Crimes Process in Timor-Leste: In Retrospect*, (2006) *International Center for Transitional Justice*. Accessed on 23 June 2021: https://www.ictj.org/publication/serious-crimes-process-timor-leste-retrospect.

Roht-Arriaza, N 'State Responsibility to Investigate and Prosecute Grave Human Rights Violations in International Law', *California Law Review*, Vol. 78, 1990 in J Wouters, J *The Obligation to Prosecute International Crimes*.

Schabas, WA 'Punishment of Non-State Actors in Non-International Armed Conflict' (2002) 26 (4) *Fordham International Law Journal* 907–933.

Scharf, M 'The Amnesty Exception to the Jurisdiction of the International Criminal Court' (1999) 8, 32 *Cornell International Law Journal*.

Steininger, S 'The Kosovo Specialist Chambers—A New Chapter for International Criminal Justice in the Balkans' (2018) *Völkerrechtsblog*.

Tendi, BM 'The Motivations and Dynamics of Zimbabwe's 2017 Military Coup' (2020) 474 (119) *African Affairs* 39–67.

Thomas-Greenfield, L & Wharton, DB 'Zimbabwe's Coup: Net Gain or No Gain,' *Military Review*, March/April 2019.

Turack, DC 'Ending Impunity in Africa: The Charles Taylor Trial at the Special Court for Sierra Leone' (2009) 26 (2) *Journal of Third World Studies* 191–202.

Vambe, MT 'Zimbabwe Genocide: Voices and Perceptions from Ordinary People in Matabeleland and the Midlands Provinces, 30 Years On' (2012) 10 *African Identities* 3, 281–300.

Williams, S 'The Cambodian Extraordinary Chambers: A Dangerous Precedent for International Justice?' (2004) 53 *The International and Comparative Law Quarterly* 227–45

Book Chapters

Alden, P & Makumbe, J 'The Zimbabwe Constitution: Race, Land Reform and Social Justice' in Cornwell, HG & Stoddard, EW (eds) (2001) *Global Multiculturalism*, 215–237.

Brown, S & Sriram, CL 'The Big Fish Won't Fry Themselves: Criminal Accountability for Post-Election Violence in Kenya.' (2012) 111 (443) *African Affairs* 244–60.

Eppel, S 'Healing the Dead: Exhumation and Reburials as a Tool to Truth-Telling and Reclaiming the Past in Rural Zimbabwe' in Borer Tristan, A (ed) *Telling the Truths: Truth-Telling and Peacebuilding in Post-Conflict Societies* (2006) 259–288.

Fisher, J 'Zimbabwe's Governance and Land Reform Crises—A Postscript' in Fisher, J (ed) *Pioneers, Settlers, Aliens, Exiles: The Decolonisation of White Identity in Zimbabwe* (ANU Press 2010) 201–220.

Hansen, TO 'The Vertical and Horizontal Expansion of Transitional Justice: Explanations and Implications for a Contested Field', in Buckley-Zistel, S; Beck, TK; Braun C & Mieth F (eds) *Transitional Justice Theories* (Routledge 2014).

Malunga, S 'A Tale of Broken Promises-Postscript,' in Ndlovu-Gatsheni, SJ & Ruhanya, P (eds) *The History and Political Transition of Zimbabwe: From Mugabe to Mnangagwa* 356 (Palgrave Macmillan 2020).

Mpofu, S 'Diasporic New Media and Conversations on Conflict: A Case of Zimbabwe Genocide Debates' in Ogunyemi, O (2017) *Media, Diaspora and Conflict* 204–221.

Reports

AIDS-Free World, Electing to Rape: Sexual Terror in Mugabe's Zimbabwe 8 (2009)

Amnesty International Annual Report, 1984.

'Breaking the Silence—Building True Peace: A Report on the Disturbances in Matabeleland and the Midlands 1980–1988' Catholic Commission for Justice and Peace in Zimbabwe & Legal Resources Foundation (1997)

'Bullets for Each of You: State-Sponsored Violence Since Zimbabwe 29 March Election,' *Human Rights Watch*, 9 June 2008.

Committing to Justice for Serious Human Rights Violations: Lessons from Hybrid Tribunals, (2018) *International Centre for Transitional Justice.*

European Union: Zimbabwe Election Observation Mission Report: 2018.

'False Dawn: The Zimbabwe Power-Sharing Government's Failure to Deliver Human Rights Improvements' (2009) *Human Rights Watch*, 5–6.

Frontline Defenders: Jestina Mukoko Abducted, 5 October 2018.

Genocide Watch, Politicide Warning: Zimbabwe, 24 June (2008).

'On the Days of Darkness in Zimbabwe: An Updated Report on the Human Rights Violations Committed Between 14 January and 5 February 2019,' Zimbabwe Human Rights NGO Forum; 6 February 2019

Pan-African Parliament, Report of the Pan African Parliament Election Observer Mission: Presidential Run-Off Election and House of Assembly By-Elections, Republic of Zimbabwe (27 June 2008).

'Paul Chizuze –Disappeared,' Solidarity Peace Trust, 27 February 2012.

'Perpetual Fear: Impunity and Cycles of Violence in Zimbabwe' (2011) *Human Rights Watch.*

Princeton Principles on Universal Jurisdiction, Adopted by a Group of International Law Experts in 2001, *Princeton University*, Princeton, 2001.

'Revolt and Repression in Zimbabwe,' *International Crisis Group,* 18 January 2019.

Solidarity Peace Trust, *Resurgent Authoritarianism: The Politics of the January 2019 Violence in Zimbabwe*, 20 February 2019.

'The Motlanthe Report: What's Next for Victims and the Nation: An Analysis of the Findings and Recommendations of the Motlanthe Report Two Years On,' *ZimRights* (2020), 15 August 2020.

'Torture in International Law: A Guide to Jurisprudence,' *Association for the Prevention of Torture.*

'Zanu P.F./Military Deterrence of the Village Vote,' *Zimbabwe Democracy Institute*, 10 July 2018.

'Zimbabwe: At Least 6 Dead in Post-Election Violence,' *Human Rights Watch,* 3 August 2018.

'Zimbabwe: Doubts Over Commission of Enquiry's Independence Puts Justice for Post-Election Killings at Risk,' *Amnesty International*, 19 September 2018.

'Where is Itai Dzamara,' *Amnesty International*, 9 September 2015.

'Zimbabwe: At Least Dead in Post-Election Violence,' *Human Rights Watch*, 3 August 2018.

'Zimbabwe: Ruthless Crackdown on Freedom of Assembly Exposes Intolerance of Dissent,' *Amnesty International*, 9 February 2019.

'Zimbabwe Shutdown Human Rights Update,' *Zimbabwe Human Rights Forum*; 23 January 2019.

'Zimbabwe Transition in a Muddy Terrain: Political Economy Under Military Capture' (2017) *Zimbabwe Democracy Institute.*

'Zimbabwe: Toll of Impunity,' *Amnesty International*, 24 June 2002 AFR 46/034/2002.

'Zimbabwe One Year On, No Justice for Those Killed by Soldiers in Post-Election Demonstrations,' *Amnesty International*, 1 August 2019.

Media and Newspaper Articles

'Army Deals Blow to Mugabe Rival,' *BBC*, 9 January 2002.

'Army Must Vote Against Tsvangirai: Major General' *Politics Web*, 31 May 2008.

Bass, GJ 'Milosevic in The Hague' (2003) 82 (3) *Foreign Affairs* 82–96.

'Chinamasa says High Court Has No Legal Right to Order Prosecutions,' *Daily News*, 30 August 2001.

Cotterill, J 'Zimbabwe Security Services Blamed for Post-Election Deaths', *Financial Times*, London, 18 December 2018.

'DNA Tests Confirm MDC Activist's Dumped Body,' *Newsday,* April 2019.

Dobbs, M 'General Mladic in The Hague' (2012) 194 *Foreign Policy* 100–105.

'ED Promotes 1 August Shootings Commander', *Newsday*, 18 December 2018.

'Emmerson Mnangagwa Sworn in as Zimbabwe President,' *Al Jazeera*, 24 November 2017.

'Ex Ivory Coast President Acquitted at ICC' *The Guardian*, 15 January 2019.

'Former CIO Spy, Woods, Implicates Mnangagwa in Gukurahundi,' *Pindula News,* 14 April 2019.

'Gukurahundi Was a Conflict Situation, Mnangagwa's Spokesman Says,' *ZimLive*, 14 April 2019.

Hammer, J, 'The Reign of Thuggery' *NY Rev. Books,* 26 June 2008.

Heywood, M, 'Zanu PF Steps Up Repression and Fear to Halt 31 July Anti-Corruption and Poverty Protests,' *Daily Maverick*, 30 July 2020.

'Government Orders Hitman's Arrest for Killing Political Opponents' *New Humanitarian*, 16 October 2006.

'Gukurahundi 5th Brigade Mass Graves in Nkayi,' last accessed from https://www.youtube.com/watch?v=Dvx-cxygig8.

Judges Confirm Judicial Capture, *NewsDay*, 29 October 2020.

Kika, K, 'Blood Chains: The Coup Government's Rights Record Three Years On' *Zimbabwe Independent,* 21 November 2020.

Malunga, S, 'Hear the Voice of God' *Africa Report*, 21 December 2019.

Malunga, S, 'Six Issues That Must Be Fixed for Elections to Be Free and Fair,' *African Arguments*, 14 June 2017.

Malunga, S, 'Were Zimbabwe's Elections Free and Fair: The Final Score Card,' *African Arguments*, 21 August 2018.

Moyo, T, 'Witness to Abduction,' *Daily Maverick*, 28 September 2020.

Muchehiwa, T, 'I Felt the Gun on the Back of My Head, I had Made My Peace with Death,' *ZimLive*, 27 August 2020.

'Mugabe Sacks Vice-President Over Plot' *BBC*, 9 December 2014.

'No Fast Track Justice: Zimbabwe Lawyers Petition to Chief Justice', *NewsWire,* 29 January 2019.

'President Mnangagwa's Inauguration Speech,' *The Chronicle*, 25 November 2017.

'Ten Years On: Chiminya and Mabika Murderers Free' *Zimbabwe Independent*, 23 April 2010.

'The Brutal Abduction Caught on Camera in Zimbabwe,' *Mail and Guardian*, 13 September 2020.

'US Sanctions Owen Ncube Over Protest Crackdown,' *Al Jazeera,* 26 October 2019.

We Blame the Ndebele Party Zapu for Gukurahundi" Mugabe Says: *SABC (You Tube)* https://www.youtube.com/watch?v=0C1MiDQnQhE.

'Zimbabwe's Apparent Coup,' *New York Times*, 15 November 2017.

'Zimbabwe Celebrates as Mugabe Resignation Announced,' *The Guardian*, 22 November 2017.

'Zimbabwe's New President Mnangagwa Vows to Re-Engage with the World,' *BBC*, 24 November 2017.

'Zimbabwe's Troops Accused of 'Systematic Torture' of Protestors, *BBC*, 23 January 2019.

'Zimbabwe's MDC Abductees Arrested for Lying About Torture,' *BBC,* 11 June 2020.

'Zimbabwe: Mnangagwa Promotes Army General Fingered in 1 August Civilian Killings.' *NewZimbabwe.com,* 18 December, 2018.

'Zimbabwe Courts Convict 375 People Over Violent January Protests,' *Times Live*, 3 April 2019.

'Zimbabwean Lawyers March to Demand Return to the Rule of Law,' *Times Live,* 29 January 2019.

'Zimbabwe Government 'Deploying Army' to Help Farm Invaders,' *The Guardian*, 20 April 2000.

Cases

Azanian Peoples Organisation (AZAPO) and Others v President of the Republic of South Africa and Others (1996) ZACC 16.

Barker McCormac (Pvt) Ltd v Government of Kenya; 1983 (2) ZLR 72.

High Court Order HH 67/2001 HC 8139/2000, 'Buhera North Election Petition'.

Hostages Trial, US Military Tribunal at Nuremberg, 19 February 1948 (1953) 15 *Annual Digest*. 632 at 636.

Minister of Foreign Affairs v Michael Jenrich, Standard Chartered Bank Zimbabwe and Sheriff of Zimbabwe, Zimbabwe Supreme Court Judgment No. SC 73/18.

National Police Commissioner of the South African Police Service v Southern African Human Rights Litigation Centre Trust (The Torture Docket case) (CCT 02/14) [2014] ZACC 30; 2015 (1) SA 315 (CC).

North Sea Continental Shelf Cases, ICJ, 1969, ICJ Reports 1969: accessed on 29 March 2021 at www.icj-cij.org.

Prosecutor v Ahmad Al Bashir ICC-02/05-01/09.

Prosecutor v. Aleksovski IT-95-14/1 (ICTY) 2000.

Prosecutor v Delacic (*Celebici* Case) IT-96-21-A (ICTY) 2001 paras 356–363.

Prosecutor v. Dusko Tadic, Case No. IT-94-1, ICTY App. Ch., Decision on the Defence Motion for Interlocutory Appeal on Jurisdiction of 2 October 1995 ('*Tadic* Jurisdiction Decision').

Prosecutor v Furundija, Case No. IT-95-17/I-T, ICTY T. Ch. II, 10 December 1998.

Prosecutor v Georges Riggiu, ICTR-97-32-1, ICTR Trial Chamber 1, 1 June, 2000.

Prosecutor v Goran Jelisic, Case No. IT-95-10, ICTY T. Ch 1, 14 December 1999.

Prosecutor v Habre, Judgement, Extraordinary African Chamber, 29 July 2016.

Prosecutor v Jean Kambanda 97-23-S (ICTR) 1998.

Prosecutor v Jean-Paul Akayesu 96-4-T(ICTR) 1998.

Prosecutor v Kayishema and Ruzindana -95-1-T (ICTR) 1999.

Prosecutor v Kupreskic IT-95-16-A (ICTY) 2000.

Prosecutor v. Laurent Gbagbo and Charles Blé Goudé, ICC-02/11-01/15.

Prosecutor v Musema 96-13-A (ICTR) 2000 paras 136, 146–148.

Prosecutor v Tihomir Blaskic IT-95-14 (ICTY) 2000.

Prosecutor v Uhuru Muigai Kenyatta: ICC-01/09-02/11.

Prosecutor v Uhuru Kenyatta and Others ICC-01/09-02/11; Dissenting Opinion by Judge Hans-Peter Kaul to Pre-Trial Chamber II's "Decision on the Prosecutor's Application for Summonses to Appear for Francis Kirimi Muthaura, Uhuru Muigai Kenyatta and Mohammed Hussein Ali" in *Sibanda and Another v ICRC* (2002 (1) ZLR 364.

Treaties and Statutes

African Union, Decision on the Draft Legal Instruments, Assembly AU/Dec.529 (XXIII), Decisions, Declarations and Resolution of the Assembly of the Union, Twenty Third Ordinary Session, June 26–27, 2014.
Clemency Order No. 1 of 1988, Zimbabwe.
Constitution of Zimbabwe, Amendment No. 20 of 2013.
Convention on the Prevention and Punishment of the Crime of Genocide, 1951.
Convention Against Torture and Other Cruel, Inhuman or Degrading Treatment or Punishment, 1984; A/RES/39/46.
Criminal Law (Codification and Reform Act) [Chapter 9:23] Zimbabwe.
Geneva Conventions of 1949.
Genocide Act (Chapter 9:20) Zimbabwe.
Law on the Court of Bosnia and Herzegovina 3 July, 2002.
Law on the Establishment of the Extraordinary Chamber in Cambodia (ECCC) (2004).
National Peace and Reconciliation Act [Chapter 10:32] 11 of 2017.
Protocol Additional to the Geneva Conventions of 12 August 1949, and relating to the Protection of Victims of Non-International Armed Conflicts (Protocol II), 8 June 1977.
Rome Statute of the International Criminal Court.
Statute of the Special Court for Sierra Leone.
Statute of the Special Tribunal for Lebanon.
Statute of the International Court of Justice (1945), Art 38 (1) (b): 33 UNTS 993.
Statute of the International Criminal Tribunal for the Former Yugoslavia.
Statute of the International Criminal Tribunal for Rwanda.
Statute of the Extraordinary African Chamber.
United Nations Charter.
UNTAET Regulation 2000/15 on the Special Panel for Serious Crime in East Timor.

Unpublished Theses

Ngwenya, D *Healing the Wounds of Gukurahundi: A Participatory Action Research Project* (unpublished DTech thesis, Durban University of Technology, 2014).

Santos, P, 'Representing Conflict: An Analysis of the Chronicle's Coverage of the Conflict in Zimbabwe Between 1983 and 1986' Unpublished MA thesis, Rhodes University, 2011.

Yap, KP 'Uprooting the Weeds: Power, Ethnicity and Violence in the Matabeleland Conflict' (2001) University of Amsterdam.

Unpacking Gukurahundi Atrocities Against the Ndebeles of Zimbabwe: What Are the Possibilities for Individual Criminal Responsibility of the Perpetrators Under International Criminal Law?

Siphosami Malunga

1 Introduction

In virtually every village in the Zimbabwean provinces of Matabeleland and parts of Midlands, there are constant reminders of unspeakable atrocities perpetrated against defenceless civilians by the government between

---

This chapter forms part of a PhD research thesis by the author.

S. Malunga (✉)
University of Zimbabwe, Harare, Zimbabwe
e-mail: SiphosamiM@osisa.org

International Law, Univeristy of Oslo, Oslo, Norway

International Law Candidate, University of Witwatersrand, Johannesburg, South Africa

E. C. Lubaale and N. Dyani-Mhango (eds.), *National Accountability for International Crimes in Africa*,
https://doi.org/10.1007/978-3-030-88044-6_16

1982 and 1987.[1] In their wake, these atrocities, known as the 'Gukurahundi',[2] were committed by a brigade of the Zimbabwe National Army (ZNA) and other security agencies. The Gukurahundi resulted in the deaths of thousands of Ndebele civilians.[3] Many of those killed were abducted and forcibly disappeared, and their bodies thrown into mine shafts or buried secretly in shallow graves.[4] Thousands of others were publicly executed in their villages and buried in mass graves.[5] At least 20,000 people are estimated to have been killed, thousands more starved, tortured, raped, unlawfully detained, and their homes and belongings

[1] 'Breaking the Silence—Building True Peace: A Report on the Disturbances in Matabeleland and the Midlands 1980–1988' Catholic Commission for Justice and Peace in Zimbabwe & Legal Resources Foundation (1997) 56; KP Yap, 'Uprooting the Weeds: Power, Ethnicity and Violence in the Matabeleland Conflict' (2001); S Doran, *Kingdom, Power, Glory: Mugabe, ZANU and the Quest for Supremacy: 1960–1987* (2017) (Sithatha Media); B Berkeley, 'Wages of War: A Report of Human Rights in Zimbabwe,' *Lawyers Committee for Human Rights*, 1983, Amnesty International Annual Report, 1984 accessible at https://www.amnesty.org/download/Documents/POL1000041984ENGLISH.PDF; SJ Ndlovu-Gatsheni 'Rethinking Chimurenga and Gukurahundi in Zimbabwe: A Critique of Partisan National History' (2012) 55 *African Studies Review* 1, 1–2.

[2] The term Gukurahundi derived from the Shona word that describes the 'early spring rains that wash away the chaff' is commonly used to describe the atrocities that were committed in Matabeleland and Midlands by the 5 Brigade of the Zimbabwe National Army. The term was derived from the mission of the brigade by the then Prime Minister Robert Mugabe. Handing over the Brigade flag emblazoned *'Gukurahundi Brigade'* to its commander, Perence Shiri at its passing out parade in December 1982, he instructed that, in keeping with its name, its mission and purpose was go into to go into Matabeleland and Midlands to *'use the knowledge it had acquired to work with the people, plough and reconstruct'* signalling an explicit targeting of the civilian population. The 5 Brigade was trained by North Korean instructors between August 1981 and September 1982 and deployed to Matabeleland in February 1983.

[3] SJ Ndlovu-Gatsheni 'Rethinking Chimurenga and Gukurahundi in Zimbabwe: A Critique of Partisan National History' (2012) 55 *African Studies Review* 1 at 1–2; S Doran (n 1 above).

[4] P Santos *Representing Conflict: An Analysis of the Chronicle's Coverage of the Conflict in Zimbabwe Between 1983 and 1986* (unpublished MA thesis, Rhodes University, 2011); D Coltart, *The Struggle Continues; 50 Years of Tyranny in Zimbabwe* (2016) Jacana 275–276.

[5] 'Gukurahundi 5th Brigade Mass Graves in Nkayi' https://www.youtube.com/watch?v=Dvx-cxygig8 (accessed on 28 February 2021).

destroyed during the senseless carnage.[6] Those that survived the atrocities bear severe emotional and physical scars because of the physical and psychological abuse.

To date, there has been no individual criminal accountability for these atrocities, and the alleged perpetrators continue to enjoy impunity. Further, neither the Zimbabwean government nor the perpetrators have formally acknowledged the atrocities.[7] Not only have the alleged perpetrators of the atrocities enjoyed impunity for their crimes, but some have also been elevated to higher positions in the public service, including the military.[8] In fact, at the highest levels, the government still primarily comprises the same individuals who oversaw and led the atrocities.[9] This has left victims scarred, emotionally and psychologically traumatised, bitter, helpless, deprived and fearful with no hope of justice, rehabilitation and treatment.[10]

[6] *Breaking the Silence—Building True Peace* (n 1 above) 56.

[7] M Killander and M Nyathi, 'Accountability for the Gukurahundi Atrocities in Zimbabwe Thirty Years On: Prospects and Challenges' (2015) 48 (3) *Comparative and International Law Journal of Southern Africa* 463–487, http://0-www.jstor.org.innopac.wits.ac.za/stable/26203994 (accessed on 25 November 2020); LA Bagnetti 'Ghosts of Gukurahundi Still Haunt Survivors, as Zimbabwe Officials Refuse to Acknowledge' *RFI* 12 March 2019, https://rfi.my/3lts.W (accessed on 7 March 2020); Open letter from Amnesty International to His Excellency the President Robert Mugabe concerning the need for public discussion and action on the disturbances in Matabeleland and the Midlands in the 1980s, 23 May 1997, *Amnesty International*; accessible at https://www.amnesty.org/download/Documents/156000/afr460021997en.pdf.

[8] This includes current President Emmerson Mnangagwa who was Minister of State Security Vice President Constantine Chiwenga who was Commander of the Brady Barracks former Airforce Commander, Perence Shiri who commanded the 5th Brigade; and current Zimbabwe National Army Commander and Lt-General Edzai Chimonyo who was Deputy Commander and later Commander of the 5th Brigade at Bhalagwe.

[9] See Killander and Nyathi (n 7 above).

[10] N Duduzile 'Violence and Memory in Breaking the Silence of Gukurahundi: A Case Study of the ZAM in Johannesburg, South Africa' in I Palmary, B Hamber & L Núñez (eds) *Healing and Change in the City of Gold: Case Studies of Coping and Support in Johannesburg* (2014) 59–77 at 63; N Mlambo 'The Politics of Bitterness: Understanding the Zimbabwean Political Crisis, 1980–2005' (2006) 3 *African Renaissance* 2 at 56; E Masitera 'Creating a Culture of Impunity in Zimbabwe: A Case for Philosophical and Developmental Issues' (2011) 5 *Africana* 2 at 100; A Kunambura 'Zimbabwe: Gukurahundi Carefully Planned' *Zimbabwe Independent* 18 April 2019, available at https://allafrica.com/stories/201904190398.html (accessed on 29 February 2020); BBC News 'Mugabe: Madness of Matabele deaths' *BBC News Online* 2 July 2000, available at http://news.bbc.co.uk/2/hi/africa/816129.stm (accessed on 29 March 2020).

The question of accountability for the atrocities has been debated for many years with little progress.[11] The Constitution of Zimbabwe (2013)[12] provides for the establishment of the National Peace and Reconciliation Commission (NPRC),[13] whose mandate is to address historical crimes and injustices.[14] President Emmerson Mnangagwa (himself implicated in committing the atrocities) has made general promises to address the legacy of the Gukurahundi atrocities and made no effort to ensure that meaningful individual criminal accountability is pursued.[15]

[11] S Eppel 'Healing the Dead: Exhumation and Reburials as a Tool to Truth Telling and Reclaiming the Past in Rural Zimbabwe' in Borer Tristan Anne (ed) *Telling the Truths: Truth Telling and Peace Building in Post-Conflict Societies* (2006) 259–288; R Murambadoro 'We Cannot Reconcile Until the Past Has Been Acknowledged: Perspectives on Gukurahundi from Matabeleland, Zimbabwe' (2015) 15 *African Journal on Conflict Resolution* 1 at 33–57; MT Vambe 'Zimbabwe Genocide: Voices and Perceptions from Ordinary People in Matabeleland and the Midlands Provinces, 30 Years on' (2012) 10 *African Identities* 3 at 281–300; D Ngwenya and G Harris 'The Consequences of Not Healing: Evidence from the Gukurahundi Violence in Zimbabwe' 2015 15 *African Journal on Conflict Resolution* 2; D Dube and D Makwerere'Zimbabwe: Towards a Comprehensive Peace Infrastructure' (2012) 2 *International Journal of Humanities and Social Science* 18; C Muchemwa, ET Ngwerume, and M Hove 'When Will the Long Nightmare Come to an End? Challenges to National Healing and Reconciliation in Post-Colonial Zimbabwe' (2013) 22 *African Security Review* 3 at 145–159; D Ngwenya *Healing the Wounds of Gukurahundi: A Participatory Action Research Project* (unpublished DTech thesis, Durban University of Technology, 2014); P Machakanja 'National Healing and Reconciliation in Zimbabwe: Challenges and Opportunities' (2010) *Institute for Justice and Reconciliation*, https://www.africaportal.org/publications/national-healing-and-reconciliation-in-zimbabwe-challenges-and-opportunities/ (accessed on 5 March 2020); V De Waal *The Politics of Reconciliation: Zimbabwe's First Decade* (1990); S Mpofu 'Diasporic New Media and Conversations on Conflict: A Case of Zimbabwe Genocide Debates' in O Ogunyemi *Media, Diaspora and Conflict* (2017) at 204–221.

[12] Constitution of Zimbabwe, 2013.

[13] See National Peace and Reconciliation Commission, http://www.nprc.org.zw/ (accessed on 29 February 2020).

[14] Constitution of Zimbabwe (n 12 above) s253; National Peace and Reconciliation Act [Chapter 10:32] 11 of 2017; See also National Peace and Reconciliation Commission, http://www.nprc.org.zw/ (accessed on 29 February 2021).

[15] S Alison 'Gukurahundi Ghosts Haunt Mnangagwa' *Mail and Guardian*, 24 November 2017, available at https://mg.co.za/article/2017-11-24-00-gukurahundi-ghosts-haunt-mnangagwa (accessed on 29 February 2020); Ndlovu (n 11), Masitera n 11); Murambadoro (n 11); Vambe (n 11); see also S Malunga 'The False Choice Between Reburials and Justice for the Gukurahundi Victims': *Daily Maverick* 6 May 2019, available at https://www.dailymaverick.co.za/article/2019-05-06-the-false-choice-between-reburials-and-justice-for-the-gukurahundi-victims/ (accessed on 29 February 2021); T Moyo

Besides Killander and Nyathi,[16] who have addressed the challenges and prospects of accountability for Gukurahundi atrocities, much of the scholarly research into Gukurahundi atrocities has focused on the societal impact of the atrocities, on memorialisation, achieving healing, forgiveness and reconciliation.[17] There is a gap in scholarly research regarding individual criminal accountability for the atrocities under international criminal law. Examining these atrocities under international criminal law is necessary for evaluating and identifying the possible national, regional and international accountability mechanisms.[18] Determination of criminal responsibility is essential for attaching individual accountability to alleged perpetrators of these atrocities, thereby advancing the prospects of pursuing individual criminal accountability and combating impunity of perpetrators.

This chapter addresses the existing literature gap on the legal classification of the Gukurahundi atrocities. It seeks to determine whether Gukurahundi atrocities committed against the Ndebeles by the Zimbabwe National Army (ZNA) and other security agencies constitute core international crimes of genocide, crimes against humanity and war crimes. It assesses the application of international criminal and humanitarian law in Zimbabwe and investigates the status of the conflict in Matabeleland under international law. Further, it explores whether perpetrators can be held individually criminally responsible for Gukurahundi atrocities under international law. Finally, this chapter is expected to contribute to understanding Gukurahundi atrocities, perpetrators' role and the victims' demand for justice.

'Digging Up the Graves of Gukurahundi Victims and Burying the Evidence' *Mail and Guardian*, 10 May 2019, available at https://mg.co.za/article/2019-05-10-00-digging-up-the-graves-of-gukurahundi-graves-and-burying-the-evidence/ (accessed on 29 March 2021).

[16] See Killander and Nyathi (n 7 above).

[17] See (n 11 above).

[18] S Eppel *Gukurahundi: The Need for Truth and Reconciliation* (2004) 43–62.

This chapter is grounded in international crimes theory[19] which provides the conceptual and normative framework for international crimes and universal jurisdiction for their perpetration.[20] The theory is supported by a range of instruments, treaties, customary international law, regional and national mechanisms that establish a duty to investigate, prosecute and punish perpetrators of gross violations of human rights, also known as international crimes.[21] An international crime is described as 'a crime defined by international law, whether customary or conventional'[22] This chapter focuses on core international crimes of genocide, crimes against humanity and war crimes. The transitional justice field is also relevant in exploring accountability options but is not the focus of this chapter.[23]

2 Applicability of International Law to Zimbabwe

A determination of the applicability of international law to Zimbabwe is essential to facilitating an examination of whether international crimes

[19] A Chetman, *A Theory of International Crimes: Conceptual and Normative Issues in* KJ Heller et al., *The Oxford Handbook of International Criminal Law* (2020) Oxford University Press. C Bassiouni, M (ed) *Proposed Guiding Principles for Combating Impunity for International Crimes*, in *Post Conflict Justice* (2002) Transnational Publishers; T Meron 'International Criminalisation of Internal Atrocities' (1995) 89 (3) *American Journal of International Law* 554–557.

[20] WA Schabas 'Punishment of Non-State Actors in Non-International Armed Conflict' (2002) 26 *Fordham International Law Journal* 4 at 907–933; D Fleck (ed) *The Handbook of International Humanitarian Law* (2008) 2; M Boothe, *The Handbook of International Humanitarian Law* (2013).

[21] K Kittichaisaree *International Criminal Law* (2001) Oxford University Press; See also M Crettol and AM La Rosa 'The Missing and Transitional Justice: The Right to Know and the Fight Against Impunity' (2006) 88 *International Review of the Red Cross* 862; S Ratner and J Abrams, *Accountability for Human Rights Atrocities in International Law: Beyond The Nuremberg Legacy* (2001) Oxford University Press: 41.

[22] R O'Keefe, *International Criminal Law* (2015) Oxford University Press: 220; KJ Heller, 'What Is an International Crime: (A Revisionist History)' (2017) 58 (2) *Harvard International Law Journal* 353–420.

[23] JE Stromseth (ed) '*Accountability for Atrocities*': *National and International Responses*' (2003) *Transnational Publishers*, New York; CM Bassiouni (ed) '*Post Conflict Justice*' (2002) *Transnational Publishers*, New York; TO Hansen 'The Vertical and Horizontal Expansion of Transitional Justice: Explanations and Implications for a Contested Field' in S Buckley-Zistel, TK Beck, CB and F Mieth (eds) *Transitional Justice Theories* (2014); PB Hayner *Unspeakable Truths: Confronting State Terror and Atrocity* (2001).

have occurred in Zimbabwe and the available legal recourse under international law. International law consists of rules and principles dealing with the conduct of states, and their relations between each other and some of their relations with juridical and natural persons.[24] It is established by customs or treaties recognised by nations as binding in their relations with each other.[25] According to Section 326 (1) of the Constitution of Zimbabwe, customary international law is part of the law of Zimbabwe unless it is inconsistent with the Constitution or an Act of Parliament. The application of customary international law in Zimbabwe has recently been upheld in *Minister of Foreign Affairs v. Michael Jenrich, Standard Chartered Bank Zimbabwe and Sheriff of Zimbabwe,* reaffirming the legal position that was extant at the time of the Gukurahundi atrocities.[26] Section 326(2) requires courts to interpret all legislation in consistency with customary international law, in preference to an alternative interpretation inconsistent with that law. This provision confirms the primacy of customary international law in Zimbabwe. Customary international law is one of the primary sources of international law,[27] and it has two fundamental elements: state practice and the corresponding views of states.[28] International obligations arise from established international practices, as opposed to formal written conventions and treaties.[29]

However, concerning treaties and conventions entered into by the President of Zimbabwe, Section 327 (2) of the Constitution of Zimbabwe provides that they are not binding until approved or ratified by Parliament. In addition, legislation must be enacted by Parliament to give effect to treaties and conventions.[30] However, Section 46 (1) provides

[24] A Cassese *International Law* 2nd ed. (2005) Oxford University Press: 157.

[25] Ibid., 157.

[26] *Minister of Foreign Affairs v Michael Jenrich, Standard Chartered Bank Zimbabwe and Sheriff of Zimbabwe,* Zimbabwe Supreme Court Judgment No. SC 73/18; See also the older cases of *Barker McCormac (Pvt) Ltd v. Government of Kenya*; 1983 (2) ZLR 72, at 77; Judgement of Waddington J who held that '*there is no doubt that customary international law is part of the law of this country', see also Sibanda and Another V ICRC (2002)* (1) ZLR 364 *which reaffirmed Barker McCormac.*

[27] Statute of the International Court of Justice (1945), Art 38 (1) (b): 33 UNTS 993; North Sea Continental Shelf Cases, ICJ, 1969, ICJ Reports 1969: www.icj-cij.org.

[28] A Cassese *International Law* (n 24 above) 157.

[29] DJ Harris, *Cases and Materials on International Law* 6th ed. (2004) 20.

[30] Section 327 (2) Constitution of Zimbabwe (2013).

that when interpreting provisions in the Declaration of Rights, every court, tribunal or forum must consider international law amongst other enumerated sources of law. It should be noted that where a state has signed and ratified a treaty, Article 27 of the Vienna Convention on the Law of Treaties[31] provides that a state party to a treaty may not invoke the provisions of its internal law as justification for its failure to perform the treaty. Based on this provision, any unwillingness or reluctance by Zimbabwe to implement its commitments to ratified international treaties based on Section 327 of the Constitution would itself be in breach of its international law obligations.

However, an Act of Parliament may waive the provision requiring approval or ratification.[32] Parliament may also, by resolution, declare that any international treaty or class of treaties does not require its approval.[33] Finally, when interpreting any legislation, all courts in Zimbabwe are required to adopt a reasonable interpretation consistent with international treaties, conventions or agreements, which are binding on Zimbabwe in preference to interpretations that are inconsistent with such treaty, convention or agreement.[34]

Zimbabwe signed and ratified the Geneva Conventions[35] on 19 October 1992 and, to date, has not enacted national legislation to domesticate the conventions. The ratification of the Geneva Convention, which regulates international and non-international armed conflict, is relevant for the classification of the conflict in Matabeleland and the determination of the State's obligations regarding the conflict. Classifying the conflict is also essential to determine whether violations of the Geneva Conventions, also known as war crimes, were committed. Zimbabwe also signed the Statute of the International Criminal Court, in 1998 but it has not ratified it. The International Criminal Court is the contemporary international criminal tribunal responsible for trying international crimes of genocide,

[31] Geneva Conventions of 1949 available at http://untreaty.un.org/ilc/texts/instruments/english/conventions/1_1_1969.pdf.

[32] Section 327 (4) Constitution of Zimbabwe (2013).

[33] Section 327 (5) Constitution of Zimbabwe (2013).

[34] Section 327 (6) Constitution of Zimbabwe (2013).

[35] See https://www.icrc.org/en/doc/war-and-law/treaties-customary-law/geneva-conventions/overview-geneva-conventions.htm#:~:text=The%201949%20Geneva%20Conventions,soldiers%20on%20land%20during%20war.&text=The%20second%20Geneva%20Convention%20protects,personnel%20at%20sea%20during%20war.

crimes against humanity and war crimes. In addition, Zimbabwe has not ratified the Torture Convention.[36] The Torture Convention was adopted in 1984 to prevent, prosecute and punish all forms of torture.

However, all provisions of the above treaties that also constitute customary international law are applicable and binding on the country.[37] This includes the prohibition of genocide,[38] crimes against humanity,[39] war crimes[40] and torture, all of which form part of customary international law. The absence of national legislation incorporating these international crimes into Zimbabwean law presents a severe obstacle to victims of these crimes who may attempt to seek redress in Zimbabwe because the existing legislation does not contemplate the scale and horrendous nature of the crimes. However, Zimbabwean criminal law, which is not the focus of this chapter, prohibits much of the conduct under such crimes as murder, kidnapping, rape, assault and malicious property damage.

3 The Status of the Conflict in Matabeleland Under International Humanitarian Law

The Gukurahundi atrocities occurred in the backdrop of political fallout and conflict between the then ruling party in Zimbabwe, the Zimbabwe African National Union (ZANU) and the opposition party Zimbabwe African Peoples Union (ZAPU). ZANU had won the first post-independence elections in 1980 with 57 seats. ZAPU obtained 20 whilst 20 were reserved for 'whites'. The UANC won three seats. ZAPU and ZANU had separately spearheaded the armed liberation struggle against the Rhodesian regime. The atrocities were preceded by a series of events over two years. This included the discovery, in 1983, of arms

[36] *Convention Against Torture and Other Cruel, Inhuman or Degrading Treatment or Punishment, 1984*; A/RES/39/46.

[37] A Cassese *International Law* (n 24 above) 157.

[38] *Prosecutor v Goran Jelisic*, Case No. IT-95-10, ICTY T. Ch 1, 14 December 1999, para 60.

[39] *Prosecutor v. Dusko Tadic*, Case No. IT-94-1, ICTY App. Ch., Decision on the Defence Motion for Interlocutory Appeal on Jurisdiction of 2 October 1995 ('*Tadic* Jurisdiction Decision') quoted with approval in *Prosecutor v Furundija*, Case No. IT-95-17/I-T, ICTY T. Ch. II, 10 December 1998, para 141.

[40] *Tadic* Jurisdiction Decision (n 39 above) 59.

caches on ZAPU farms in Matabeleland and Midlands (which ZAPU argued were either planted or known to ZANU). In 1981 armed clashes between former ZANLA and ZIPRA combatants (in the process of being demobilised) in cantonments occurred in Bulawayo and Harare. By 1983 political tensions between ZANU and ZAPU led to the dismissal of ZAPU members from the Cabinet. The arrest of ZIPRA commanders, ZAPU leaders and purges of former ZIPRA combatants from the new Zimbabwe National Army followed the arms caches. Some former ZIPRA members of the army defected with their arms and resorted to banditry. The government response was to deploy the 5th Brigade or Gukurahundi to Matabeleland and Midlands to combat these 'dissidents' ostensibly.

The status of the conflict in Matabeleland and Midlands is crucial for several reasons. First, it determines the application of international humanitarian law to the situation. Second, it determines the country's international legal obligations, and finally, it determines the legal nature of the atrocities committed. The criteria for the classification of non-international armed conflict are set out in the Protocol Additional to the Geneva Conventions of 12 August 1949 and relating to the Protection of Victims of Non-International Armed Conflicts (APII), which is the only treaty dedicated to regulating non-international armed conflict.[41] In order to determine the status, it is essential to analyse existing evidence. These factors would include the government stated position[42], the type, size and extent of military mobilisation,[43] including the training of the

[41] MM Bradley, 'Revisiting the Scope of Application of Additional Protocol II: Exploring the Inherent Minimum Threshold Requirements' (2019) 81 *African International Yearbook of International Humanitarian Law* 83; See also MM Bradley, Unpublished doctoral thesis titled 'An Analysis of the Notions of "Organised Armed Groups" and "Intensity" in the Law of Non-International Armed Conflict' (2018) University of Pretoria. See also Article 1(1) of Protocol Additional to the Geneva Conventions of 12 August 1949, and relating to the Protection of Victims of Non-International Armed Conflicts (Protocol II), 8 June 1977 (hereafter APII).

[42] Despite there being no active conflict at the time, in October 1980, Prime Minister Mugabe signed an agreement with the North Korean President, Kim II Sung that they would train a brigade for the Zimbabwean army. This agreement was soon after Mugabe had announced the need for a militia to "combat malcontents." see *Breaking the Silence—Building True Peace* (n 1 above) 45.

[43] 5th Brigade was drawn from 3500 ex-ZANLA troops at Tongogara Assembly Point. The training of 5th Brigade lasted until September 1982. The equipment assigned to the Brigade was unique and incompatible with the rest of the Zimbabwe National Army with distinctive red berets. Ibid., at 45, 46.

Brigade,[44] duration and size of the military deployment,[45] the hierarchy and seniority of government and military actors,[46] the extent of resources utilised, the nature of hostilities,[47] and the type of actors or groups involved in the conflict and their relationship with each other.

The conduct of armed conflict is regulated by the Geneva Conventions of 1949 and its Additional Protocols. As stated in the previous section, Zimbabwe is a state party to the Geneva Convention of 1949 and its Additional Protocols. It acceded to API in 1983 and APII in 1992. The implication of the non-ratification of APII by Zimbabwe at the time of the Matabeleland will be addressed below. The first Geneva Convention protects wounded and sick soldiers. The second Geneva Convention protects the wounded, sick and shipwrecked at sea during war. The third Geneva Convention protects prisoners of war, and the fourth protects civilians, including those in occupied territories.

Article 3, which is common to all the four Geneva Conventions, covers non-international armed conflict situations. Also known as internal armed conflicts, they include armed conflicts that transcend national borders or spill into neighbouring countries, traditional civil wars, or internal armed conflict in which other states or multinational forces intervene. Common Article 3 establishes the following non-derogable rules

[44] In August 1981, 106 Korean military instructors arrived to train the new Brigade, which Prime Minister Mugabe said was to be used to 'deal with dissidents and any other trouble in the country'. The government met the costs of the training instructors. At this time, there was no unrest or dissident activity in the country. Ibid., at 45.

[45] Apart from the 5th Brigade, the government deployed the 4th and 6th Brigade and the paratrooper regiments to engage actively and combat dissidents. With the arrival of the 5th Brigade, the total military presence in Matabeleland and Midlands reached 5000. Africa Confidential reported estimates of up to 15,000 troops in Matabeleland South in 1984 compared to a maximum of 200 dissidents. However, the 5th Brigade focused its efforts mainly on innocent villagers rather than dissidents. Ibid., at 47.

[46] The Brigade, commanded by Colonel Perence Shiri, operated outside typical army structures and was answerable to the Prime Minister, Robert Mugabe. At its pass out parade in December 1982, he instructed it to '*use the knowledge it had acquired to work with the people, plough and reconstruct*' signalling an explicit targeting of the civilian population. Ibid.

[47] The dissidents were armed and attacked public and private installations in rural Matabeleland and Midlands. The 4th, 5th and 6th Brigades, Zimbabwe Republic Police and intelligence units were deployed to engage and neutralise the dissidents militarily. Ibid., at 115.

of conduct regarding non-international armed conflict: the humane treatment for all persons in enemy hands, without any adverse distinction. It specifically prohibits murder, mutilation, torture, cruel, humiliating and degrading treatment, the taking of hostages and unfair trial; that the wounded, sick and shipwrecked be collected and cared for; grants the ICRC the right to offer its services to the parties to the conflict; that parties to the conflict to bring all or parts of the Geneva Conventions into force through so-called special agreements. Common Article 3 also forms part of customary international law, making it applicable to and binding on Zimbabwe, as indicated in the section above.

APII regulates internal or non-international armed conflict 'which take place in the territory of a state party to the Geneva Convention between its armed forces and dissident forces or other organised armed groups which, under responsible command, exercise such control over a part of its territory as to enable them to carry out sustained and concerted military operations'.[48] APII does not apply to situations of internal disturbances and tensions, such as riots, isolated and sporadic acts of violence and other acts of a similar nature, as not being armed conflicts.[49]

It should be noted that 'AP II does not apply to all and every armed conflict of a non-international character: rather it sets a threshold of application, below which internal armed conflicts remain merely subject to the provisions of Common Article 3 to the Geneva Conventions'.[50] APII provides fundamental guarantees to civilians or all persons not taking part in hostilities, including respect for their person, honour and convictions and religious practices. They shall in all circumstances be treated humanely, without any adverse distinction. It also prohibits orders that there shall be no survivors.[51] The following acts are prohibited: violence to the life, health and physical or mental well-being of persons, in particular, murder as well as cruel treatment such as torture, mutilation or any form of corporal punishment; collective punishments; taking of hostages;

[48] Article 1(1) of APII (n 41 above).

[49] Article 1 (2) of APII.

[50] M Pedrazzi, 'Additional Protocol II and threshold of application' in F Pocar and GL Berute (eds) *International Institute of Humanitarian Law: 'The Additional Protocols 40 Years Later: New Conflicts, New Actors, New Perspectives*; 40th Round Table on Current Issues of International Humanitarian Law (San Remo, 7th–9th September 2017)' available at (accessed on 28 April 2021).

[51] Article 4 (1) of APII.

acts of terrorism; outrages upon personal dignity, in particular humiliating and degrading treatment, rape, enforced prostitution and any form of indecent assault; slavery and the slave trade in all their forms; pillage; threats to commit any of the foregoing acts.[52]

To determine whether the Matabeleland conflict meet the requirements of a non-international armed conflict envisaged by Common Article 3 of the Geneva Conventions and APII, it is necessary to apply the test set out in Article 1 (1) of APII, namely that:

a. hostilities take place in the territory of a state party to the Geneva Convention,
b. hostilities occur between its armed forces and dissident forces or other organised armed groups,
c. armed groups are under responsible command and
d. Armed groups exercise such control over a part of the country's territory as to enable them to carry out sustained and concerted military operations.

The first requirement that hostilities *take place in the territory of a State party to the Geneva Convention* (emphasis added) appears straightforward, but complexities may arise. Clapham argues that 'from a humanitarian perspective, it makes no sense to deny the applicability of the protective measures in the Protocol to conflicts where the state is a party to the Protocol, but the fighting takes place outside its borders. Having reached the threshold for the application of Protocol II, there would be little doubt that customary international humanitarian law applies to the extraterritorial force and the rebel group...'[53] Notwithstanding the foregoing qualification, there is no dispute regarding the territorial requirement of the Matabeleland conflict, which occurred within the territory of Zimbabwe, which acceded to API in 1983 and APII in 1992. The implication of the non-ratification of APII by Zimbabwe at the time of the Matabeleland will be addressed below.

[52] Article 4 (1) of APII.

[53] A Clapham, 'Defining Armed Conflicts Under the Additional Protocols: Is There a Need for Further Clarification? in F Pocar and GL Berute (eds) *International Institute of Humanitarian Law: 'The Additional Protocols 40 Years Later: New Conflicts, New Actors, New Perspectives*; 40th Round Table on Current Issues of International Humanitarian Law (San Remo, 7th–9th September 2017)' available at (accessed on 28 April 2021).

The second requirement in APII of *armed groups under responsible command* (emphasis added) also commonly referred to as *organised armed groups*. Article 1(1) expressly provides that the minimum degree of organisation that an organised armed group must meet under Article 1(1) of APII to become a party to an APII-type non-international armed conflict is an essential element to the classification of such conflict.[54] This requirement and Article 8 of the ICC Statute have received extensive scholarly attention from Martha Bradley.[55] Bradley's work addresses a significant gap in scholarly attention on this issue. She argues that:

> Article 1(1) of Additional Protocol II necessitates a high degree of organisation to be in place for an armed group to qualify as an organised armed group within the scope of application of this treaty. Not every 'band' acting under a 'leader' qualifies as an organised armed group under Additional Protocol II as only those armed groups that satisfy certain criteria are considered to be an armed group for the purposes of Additional Protocol II.[56]

The question of whether the dissidents comprised an organised armed group must be examined. It is estimated that no more than 400 Zapu officers enlisted in the Zimbabwe National Army (ZNA) deserted and individually took up arms and resorted to banditry.[57] The dissidents had various grievances, including the arrest of Zipra commanders, Dumiso Dabengwa and Lookout Masuku, mistreatment and targeted attacks and even killings within the newly formed ZNA. There is, however, no evidence that they were under any organised command.[58] Indeed despite publicly claiming allegiance to the Zapu and Zipra military leadership, the

[54] MM Bradley, 'Revisiting the Scope of Application of Additional Protocol II: Exploring the Inherent Minimum Threshold Requirements' (2019) 81 *African International Yearbook of International Humanitarian Law* 83.

[55] Article 8 (2) (f) the ICC Statute sets out what Bradley argues is a new classification delineating the type of armed conflict that is '*protracted armed conflict*' (emphasis added) which is not contained in APII.

[56] MM Bradley 'Revisiting the Scope of Application of Additional Protocol II: Exploring the Inherent Minimum Threshold Requirements' (n 43 above) 83.

[57] *Breaking the Silence—Building True Peace* (n 1 above) 56.

[58] Ibid., see also 'The Nkomo Affair: Mistrust Never Died' *New York Times*, 12 March 1983 available at https://www.nytimes.com/1983/03/12/world/the-nkomo-affair-mistrust-never-died-news-analysis.html.

dissidents were disowned by senior Zapu and Zipra leaders.[59] Alexander states that:

> dissidents had neither political leaders nor political support but that nonetheless the majority maintained their loyalty to Zapu and tenaciously clung to their liberation war identity as guerrillas, thereby helping to contain South Africa's destabilisation efforts and making the wars' rapid conclusion possible.[60]

However, the government insisted that the dissidents operated under Zapu and Zipra and that unarmed civilians provided support to them. Using the pretext of combating dissidents, the government deployed the Gukurahundi and other units of the ZNA and security agencies.[61] In reality; dissidents essentially acted as 'lone wolves'—not organised armed groups—in committing sporadic acts of banditry and violence and in targeting unarmed civilians.[62] There is also no evidence of 'protracted armed violence *between* (emphasis added) governmental authorities and organised armed groups'. Instead, both the Gukurahundi and dissidents themselves appear to have focused their attacks on civilians and made little effort to confront each other militarily.[63]

The third requirement, namely the *intensity of fighting threshold* (emphasis added) in APII, relates to whether for a non-international armed conflict to be classified as such, it must reach a certain level of intensity. Some scholars suggest that there should be a greater intensity of violence before the APII applies, in addition to the requirement that

[59] Ibid.

[60] J Alexander, 'Dissident Perspectives on Zimbabwe's Post-Independence War' (1998) 68 (2) *Africa: Journal of the International African Institute* 151–182, https://doi.org/10.2307/1161277 (accessed on 29 April 2021). See also J Alexander; JA McGregor; T Ranger (2000) *Violence & Memory: One Hundred Years in the "Dark Forests" of Matabeleland*, James Currey (Oxford).

[61] *Breaking the Silence—Building True Peace* (n 1 above) 56.

[62] J Alexander (n 60 above).

[63] 'Split by Victory in Zimbabwe, Ex Allies Wage a Bitter War' *New York Times*, 18 February 1983, https://www.nytimes.com/1983/02/18/world/split-by-victory-in-zimbabwe-ex-allies-wage-a-bitter-war.html, see also *Breaking the Silence—Building True Peace* (n 1 above) 56.

the organised armed group control territory.[64] However, there is nothing in APII that suggests such a requirement is necessary to trigger Common Article 3 and customary international law. On this basis, there would be no basis to disqualify the hostilities in Matabeleland from the operation of both Common Article 3 and the application of APII to the extent that the relevant content of both corresponds to customary international law.

As explained above, not all the provisions of APII apply to or regulate every non-international armed conflict. Several factors and conditions trigger it. The non-applicability of APII is not a conclusive factor to render or classify a conflict as non-international. There is also convergence that some fundamental aspects of APII, including the basic rules enunciated in Article 13 and relating to the conduct of hostilities, entailing the prohibition to attack the civilian population and individual civilians, are part of customary international law. Other fundamental rules outside the APII, such as the prohibition of indiscriminate attacks, would also be proscribed by customary international law. To that extent, customary international law and not the threshold requirement of the APII would be the most definitive or decisive factor. The international tribunals have outlined a more uncomplicated and more straightforward test for non-international armed conflict. In the *Tadic* Jurisdiction Case,[65] the International Tribunal for the Former Yugoslavia (ICTY) has decided that '[a]rmed conflict exists whenever there is a resort to armed force between States or protracted armed violence between governmental authorities and organised armed groups or between such groups within a State'.[66]

As indicated above, exceptions to this include internal disturbances and tensions, such as riots, isolated and sporadic acts of violence and other acts of a similar nature, which do not constitute an armed conflict.[67] There are compelling arguments and evidence that whilst the armed forces

[64] Y. Sandoz, C. Swinarski, and B. Zimmermann (eds), Commentary on the Additional Protocols of 8 June 1977 to the Geneva Conventions of 12 August 1949 (Geneva/Dordrecht: ICRC/Nijhoff, 1987) at 1343ff; F. Hampson, Direct Participation in Hostilities and the Interoperability of the Law of Armed Conflict and Human Rights Law, 87 International Law Studies (2011) 187–213 at 195–197 and 203; Y. Dinstein, *Non-International Armed Conflicts in International Law* (2014) Cambridge: CUP.

[65] *Tadic* Jurisdiction Decision (n 39 above) 59.

[66] Ibid.

[67] Protocol Additional to the Geneva Conventions of 12 August 1949, and relating to the Protection of Victims of Non-International Armed Conflicts (Protocol II), 8 June 1977, Art *1(2)*.

of Zimbabwe were organised, dissidents were not similarly organised or under responsible command.[68] Applying Common Article 3, provisions of APII that correspond to customary international law and the *Tadic* Jurisdiction case definition,[69] the Matabeleland crisis constituted an internal armed conflict for several reasons. First, the Zimbabwean government itself characterised the situation as an armed conflict back in 1983 and more recently.[70] Second, the government mobilised and deployed a significant armed forces contingent (the 5th Brigade) and other army units and state security agencies to Matabeleland and Midlands for a prolonged period, further confirming the existence of armed conflict.[71] Third, there was a resort to armed force between, on the one hand, the dissidents as an armed group which was organised (albeit loosely) and the government forces on the other hand.[72]

The conflict in Matabeleland was, therefore, a non-international armed conflict as envisaged by international law. The international law of armed conflict, therefore, applied to the conflict. Consequently, crimes committed during this conflict constituted violations of the international law of armed conflict, commonly known as war crimes.

[68] See *Breaking the Silence—Building True Peace*: Notably, whilst some dissidents claimed allegiance to Zapu and the political and military leadership, they were disowned by same. The dissidents also operated as individuals and not as part of an organised group. They also committed sporadic acts of violence and attacks mainly targeting unarmed civilians. There is also no evidence of a 'protracted armed violence *between* (emphasis added) governmental authorities and organised armed groups'. Instead the Gukurahundi appears to have focused its attacks on civilians and made little effort to combat dissidents.

[69] *Tadic* Jurisdiction Decision (n 39 above) 59.

[70] *Breaking the Silence—Building True Peace* at 3. Although in establishing the Commission of Enquiry into the disturbances in Matabeleland—prompted by complaints about Gukurahundi atrocities against civilians, the government did not use the term 'conflict' there was tacit recognition that the deployment of the military was a response to what the government considered an armed conflict; ZimLive, 'Gukurahundi was a conflict situation, Mnangagwa's spokesman says' citing an interview with George Charamba, available at zimlive.com (accessed on 7 March 2020).

[71] see *Breaking the Silence—Building True Peace* (n 1 above) 45.

[72] Ibid.

4 Examining Gukurahundi Atrocities Against the Ndebeles in Terms of International Criminal Law

4.1 An Overview of International Crimes

International criminal law is the body of law that prohibits conduct considered as serious criminal violations of international law. Whilst there is a wide range of international crimes, this chapter focuses on the three core crimes, namely, genocide, crimes against humanity and war crimes. Each of these crimes has its specific elements, which must be established in order for an alleged perpetrator to be held accountable. It is also possible for the same conduct to give rise to several and different international crimes. It should be emphasised that war crimes can only be committed in armed conflict,[73] whilst genocide[74] and crimes against humanity can be committed in armed conflict and peacetime.[75]

4.2 A Synopsis of Gukurahundi Crimes

Within six weeks of deployment to Matabeleland North in late January 1983, the Gukurahundi had murdered over 2000 civilians, hundreds of homesteads had been burnt, and thousands of civilians had been beaten.[76] It would torture, detain and kill thousands more in the months that followed throughout the year and thousands more when it was redeployed to Matabeleland South in February 1984. Some estimates place the death toll from Gukurahundi killings and disappearances at

[73] Protocol Additional to the Geneva Conventions (Protocol I) art 147.

[74] Convention on the Prevention and Punishment of the Crime of Genocide, 1951 art 1.

[75] Article 7 of ICC Statute does not no mention of *when* crimes against are to be committed creating an assumption that it can be in either peacetime or armed conflict. In addition, the crimes against humanity provisions in the ICTY, ICTR, Law on the ECCC statutes do not have wartime-requirement.

[76] *Breaking the Silence—Building True Peace* (n 1 above) 3, 19, 23, 38. See also Zimbabwe Party Reports Attacks, *New York Times*, 8 March 1985 available at https://www.nytimes.com/1985/03/08/world/zimbabwe-party-reports-attacks.html.

20 000.[77] The atrocities were reported by media organisations,[78] religious organisations[79] and human rights organisations.[80] Under pressure, the government established the Commission of Enquiry into the disturbances in Matabeleland (Chihambakwe Commission) to probe the reported abuses.[81] In public meetings, the Commission travelled across Matabeleland and Midlands and received countless reports of torture, rapes and massacres in hearings.[82] It presented its finding to the government, which to date has refused to make them public.[83] In 1997, the Catholic Commission for Justice and Peace released a comprehensive report detailing witness testimonies of the atrocities.[84] To date, the physical and oral evidence of atrocities continues to emerge, including survivor and witness testimonies, mass graves littered across Matabeleland and

[77] *Breaking the Silence—Building True Peace* (n 1 above) 6. The CCJP estimates that between 3500 and 4000 people were killed in only two districts that it accessed. It also reports almost 2000 villagers killed within weeks of the Gukurahundi arriving in Tsholotsho. In view of the fact that the Gukurahundi operated throughout Matabeleland and Midlands, over a period of a year and that it abducted and disappeared thousands of its victims and also the deaths related to the curfew induced food embargo, the death toll could well be beyond 20,000.

[78] 'Split by Victory in Zimbabwe, Ex Allies Wage a Bitter War' *New York Times*, 18 February 1983' This included reports by journalists Donald Trelford of the Observer and BBC's Jeremy Paxman; see Revealed: How British Diplomats Pressured BBC's Jeremy Paxman Over Massacres in Zimbabwe (inews.co.uk).

[79] In 1983, the Catholic Bishop Heinrich Karlen sought a meeting with the then Prime minister and presented a dossier of the abuses see 'Catholic priest who exposed Zim massacre', Sunday Independent 13 November 2012; J Todd *Through the Darkness* (2007) Zebra Press.

[80] Amnesty International Annual Report, 1984 accessible at https://www.amnesty.org/download/Documents/POL1000041984ENGLISH.PDF.

[81] Commission of Enquiry into the disturbances in Matabeleland (Chihambakwe Commission), see https://www.usip.org/publications/1983/09/commission-inquiry-zimbabwe.

[82] *Breaking the Silence—Building True Peace* (n 1 above) 6.

[83] 'Government Should Release Chihambakwe, Dumbutshena Commissions Reports' available at https://www.zimbabwesituation.com/news/govt-should-release-chihambakwe-dumbutshena-commissions-reports/; https://www.zimlive.com/2019/04/19/dumbutshena-chihambakwe-reports-have-been-lost-nprc-chairman/.

[84] *Breaking the Silence—Building True Peace* (n 1 above) 56;

Midlands,[85] and demands for reburials and justice.[86] The establishment of the National Peace and Reconciliation Commission[87] and the explicit attempts by President Mnangagwa—himself implicated in the massacres—to address the Gukurahundi are also a veiled admission of the atrocities by the government. However, he has fallen short of formally acknowledging his role and apologising to the victims personally and on behalf of the government.[88]

Although the scope and breadth of the Gukurahundi atrocities were expansive and covered the entire Matabeleland and Midlands provinces, this section draws on only one prominent and notorious example of Gukurahundi atrocities from each of the Matabeleland provinces to illustrate the international crimes of the Gukurahundi. The Siwale River Massacre in Matabeleland North (1983) and the atrocities committed at the Bhalagwe Detention Camp in Matabeleland South (1984) are considered some of the most heinous committed by the Gukurahundi and provide a sound basis for examining and categorising the atrocities as international crimes (genocide, crimes against humanity and war crimes) and evaluating the criminal responsibility of perpetrators under international law.

4.2.1 The Siwale River Massacre

The most serious of Gukurahundi crimes is mass murder. A key strategy in Matabeleland North was public mass killings or murders targeting

[85] 'Grave Containing Up to 60 People Found at Zimbabwe School' *The Guardian*, 5 October 2011 available at https://www.theguardian.com/world/2011/oct/05/mass-grave-found-zimbabwe-school.

[86] S Malunga 'The False Choice Between Reburials and Justice for the Gukurahundi Victims': *Daily Maverick*, 6 May 2019, available at https://www.dailymaverick.co.za/article/2019-05-06-the-false-choice-between-reburials-and-justice-for-the-gukurahundi-victims/ (accessed on 29 February 2021); T Moyo 'Digging Up the Graves of Gukurahundi Victims and Burying the Evidence' *Mail and Guardian*, 10 May 2019, available at https://mg.co.za/article/2019-05-10-00-digging-up-the-graves-of-gukurahundi-graves-and-burying-the-evidence/ (accessed on 29 March 2021).

[87] National Peace and Reconciliation Commission available at http://www.nprc.org.zw/; see also National Peace and Reconciliation Act [Chapter 10:32] available at https://zimlii.org/zw/legislation/act/2017/11.

[88] 'Zimbabwe President Discusses Exhuming Victims of 1980s Massacres', News24 23 August 2020 available from https://www.news24.com/news24/africa/zimbabwe/zimbabwe-president-mnangagwa-discusses-exhuming-victims-of-1980s-massacre-20200823.

between one and twelve people, and sometimes more.[89] Villagers would be rounded up into groups and publicly executed. One such notable incident is the Siwale River Massacre in Lupane, in which 62 civilians were shot in cold blood on the banks of the river on 5 March 1983 after being severely beaten.[90] Fifty-five died whilst seven survived by pretending to be dead.[91] The following account from a surviving victim and witness of the Siwale River Massacre is illustrative:

> On 5 March 1983, four people were taken from our home. The youngest was myself, then a girl of fifteen. The 5th Brigade took us- there were more than a hundred of them. [T]hey woke us up and accused [...] us - me and my brothers- of being dissidents. They then marched us [...] for about three hours until we reached a camp.
>
> [T]hey took us to a building where there were finally sixty-two (62) people. Then they took us out one by one and beat us. They beat me with a thick stick eighteen inches long all over the body. We were beaten until about 3am.
>
> Then the 5th Brigade marched us to Siwale River, a few hundred metres away. All 62 of us were lined up and shot by the 5th Brigade. One of my brothers was killed instantly, from the bullet through his stomach. By some chance, seven (7) of us survived with gunshot wounds. I was shot in the left thigh. The 5th Brigade finished off some of the others who survived, but my two brothers and I pretended to be dead.
>
> After some time, we managed to get home. The 5th Brigade came looking for survivors of this incident at home - they found my brother R who was badly injured, but they left him. My brother had a gunshot wound in the chest and arm and later had to have his arm amputated first at the elbow, and then later at the shoulder. He had his foot amputated because of a bullet wound.[92]

[89] Examples include the Shashane and Silwane River incidents. See *Breaking the Silence—Building True Peace* (n 1 above) 48: also see Matobo Case Study ibid., at 115–137.

[90] *Breaking the Silence—Building True Peace* (n 1 above) 48.

[91] Ibid.

[92] Ibid.

4.2.2 Bhalagwe Concentration Camp Atrocities

One year after its initial deployment to Matabeleland North, on 2 February 1984, the 5th Brigade was redeployed to Matabeleland South.[93] In addition to mass beatings, torture, rape and burning of villages, curfew and food embargo and deliberate starvation of villagers in the context of a severe drought, it established a mass detention camp at Bhalagwe in Matobo District. Bhalagwe had been a Zimbabwe National Army camp housing mainly former ZIPRA combatants. The excerpt below is drawn from accounts by surviving victims, documented by the CCJP, *Breaking the Silence—Building True Peace Report*[94]:

> Conditions were brutal. Sheds of six-by 12 metres were [each] packed with 136 people who were given no bedding and fed once every two days. Maise meal was served on garbage tin lids, shared at times by 10 and 20 people, and at others by up to 60. One small jam tin of water was provided per day for inmates living in temperatures of over 30 degrees and subjected to multiple forms of physical abuse.When not confined to their sheds or undergoing torture, prisoners were made to do hard labour.
>
> 'The people went through hell at Bhalagwe... Each day brought one near to death through torture' Electric shocks, simulated drownings and beatings were used by the CIO in its attempts to extract confessions of dissident support or activity, while 5 Brigade experimented with a wide variety of tortures... Some prisoners were made to climb trees until their combined weight broke the branches. Another favourite was to force three men into a short pipe, order the two at each end to come out and then beat them so that they kicked and crushed the middle man as he tried to retreat, sometimes resulting in fatalities. Another was to lash prisoners with thorn bushes. Much of the cruelty had a sexual angle to it. Men were forced to attempt sex with donkeys and beaten when they failed to attain erections. A female member of the CIO, who became particularly notorious at Bhalagwe for her 'cruel, ruthless, savage, inhuman' behaviour, would stand astride her victims, asking them what they saw; if too embarrassed to say, they would be 'severely beaten for lying', but if they provided an answer they would receive the same treatment for failing to become aroused and thus 'saying she was not a woman.' In the words of a detainee: 'One day was like a year in hell. ... The perpetrators seemed more of animals than human beings. They laughed and seemed to enjoy people groaning in pain

[93] *Breaking the Silence—Building True Peace* (n 1 above) 119–124;

[94] Ibid., at 119–124; see also Doran (n 1 above) 515–516.

to death [and] women failing to walk after their private parts were poked with sharp objects' Others have also remarked on the mirth that often accompanied torture in the camp: 'They did not care how bad a person was, they laughed always.' Most women were kept for a few days, but some were taken as sex slaves by 5 Brigade and spent a much longer period in the camp. A woman abducted from her home at night described the ordeal she and others suffered at Bhalagwe: "We were beaten daily by the CIO. We were made wives for the officers (girls and young married women). From the forced sex, I am suffering from the disorder of my reproductive organs...I miscarry anytime I am pregnant. I have no children.[95]

4.3 *Unpacking the International Crime of Genocide*

The mass destruction of people, also known as genocide, has been committed several times in the past hundred or so years. The mass killing of the Armenians by the Ottoman Empire in 1915, the Holocaust of the Jews by the Nazis in Germany between 1941 and 1945, the killing of millions of Cambodians by the Khmer Rouge in Cambodia in the 1970 and the mass murder of the Tutsis in Rwanda in 1994 are some the world's most shocking genocide. The crime of genocide is, therefore, one of the gravest international crimes. Its prohibition, by the convention on the Prevention and Punishment of the Crime of Genocide (Genocide Convention),[96] is now part of customary international law and a norm of *jus cogens*.[97] As stated above, Zimbabwe signed and ratified the Genocide Convention and also enacted the Genocide Act. Article 2 of the Genocide Convention defines genocide as follows:

> any of the following acts committed with intent to destroy in whole or in part a national, ethnical, racial or religious group, as such:
>
> (a) Killing members of the group;
> (b) Causing serious bodily or mental harm to members of the group;
> (c) Deliberately inflicting on the group conditions of life calculated to bring about its physical destruction in whole or in part;

[95] BLPC: Case no 3672 RASD.JS, Ref Bhalagwe, April 1984.

[96] Convention on the Prevention and Punishment of the Crime of Genocide, See https://www.un.org/en/genocideprevention/genocide-convention.shtml.

[97] CM Bassiouni 'International crimes: *Jus Cogens* and *Obligatio Erga Omnes*' (1996) 59 *Law and Contemporary Problems* (4) 68.

(d) Imposing measures intended to prevent births within the group;
(e) Forcibly transferring children of the group to another group.[98]

The crime has been prohibited by the statutes of several international criminal tribunals, namely Article 4(2) of the ICTY,[99] Article 2(2) of ICTR[100] and Article 6 of the ICC Statute.[101]

The threshold for proving genocide is exceptionally high and requires an analysis of both the objective and subjective intent of the attackers. The objective elements of the crime of genocide include the commission of any of the enumerated acts with the requisite intent. The crime of genocide requires a specific intent (*dolus specialis*) to destroy in whole or in part one of the protected groups.[102] Failure to prevent the commission of genocide constitutes a crime provided the specific intent to destroy can be proved.[103] A person accused of genocide must be found guilty based on his/her own individual criminal responsibility, without the necessity to establish that genocide has taken place throughout the country.[104] The victim of genocide is the entire protected group itself, not the individual.[105] Although the crime of genocide is usually evident from the destruction of many lives, there is no requirement to establish the precise

[98] Genocide Convention, Art 2 (n 98 above).

[99] ICTY Statute: available at https://legal.un.org/avl/ha/icty/icty.html#:~:text=The%20International%20Criminal%20Tribunal%20for%20the%20former%20Yugoslavia,including%20that%20of%20torture%2C%20extermination%2C%20enslavement%20and%20deportation.

[100] ICTR Stature available at http://www.icls.de/dokumente/ictr_statute.pdf.

[101] Rome Statute of the International Criminal Court, Art 7: https://www.icc-cpi.int/resourcelibrary/official-journal/rome-statute.aspx.

[102] F Chalk, 'Genocide in the 20th Century': Definitions of Genocide and their Implications for Prediction and Prevention, *Holocaust and Genocide Studies*, Volume 4, Issue 2, 1989, Pages 149–160, https://doi.org/10.1093/hgs/4.2.149; G Verdirame 'The Genocide Definition in the Jurisprudence of the Ad Hoc Tribunals' (2000) 49 (3) *International and Comparative Law Quarterly* 578–598.

[103] *Prosecutor vs Jean Kambanda* 97-23-S (ICTR) 1998. *Kambada* was found guilty of genocide, among other things, for his failure to fulfil his duty as Prime Minister of Rwanda to take action to stop on-going massacres, which he had become aware of, or to protect the population from possible massacres after he had been personally asked to do so and his omission resulted in massacres.

[104] *Prosecutor v Jean-Paul Akayesu* 96-4-T(ICTR) 1998.

[105] AKA Greenawalt, 'Rethinking Genocidal Intent: The Case for a Knowledge-Based Interpretation' (1999) 99 (8) Columbia Law Review 2259.

number of victims of an act of genocide attributable to an accused.[106] The necessary element of intent can be inferred from several facts such as words or acts or a pattern of conduct and deliberate and purposeful action that deliberately and consistently and systematically targets victims on account of their membership of a particular group whilst excluding members of other groups.[107] Following the reasoning in Akayesu,[108] the ICTR found in Ruggiu[109] that a person who incites another to commit genocide must himself have specific intent to commit genocide. Akayesu was thus found guilty of the crime of direct and public incitement to commit genocide.

Applying the tests set out above, it is evident that the Gukurahundi targeted Ndebeles from Matabeleland and Midlands, who were also considered supporters of the opposition ZAPU political party.[110] To this extent, ZAPU was considered by the 5th Brigade and the government as a Ndebele party linking the political objective of destroying ZAPU and creating a one-party state with a genocidal plan to eliminate Ndebeles—ZAPU supporters.[111] The deliberate segregation and exclusion of Shona speakers from attacks and mass killings demonstrate a specific genocidal intent to destroy Ndebeles.[112] This position is supported by the admission of Colonel Lionel Dyke. He commanded the Paratrooper regiment, which committed widespread atrocities. Dyke acknowledged the targeting of Ndebeles as a deliberate military strategy.[113] Targeting an ethnic group is one of the requirements for the crime of genocide

[106] *Prosecutor v Goran Jelisic* (n 38 above).

[107] K Kittichaisaree *International Criminal Law* (n 21 above).

[108] *Prosecutor v Jean-Paul Akayesu* (n 106 above).

[109] *Prosecutor v Georges Riggiu*, ICTR-97-32-1, ICTR Trial Chamber 1, 1 June, 2000, para 14.

[110] The term Ndebele is used here to describe a group of collective ethnicities from the region of Matabeleland and Midlands including Kalanga, Sotho, Venda and Tonga among others.

[111] 'We blame the Ndebele Party Zapu for Gukurahundi' Mugabe Says: https://www.youtube.com/watch?v=0C1MiDQnQhE.

[112] Survivors report that members of the Gukurahundi would separate Shona speakers at road blocks and in villages and spare them from beatings, torture and death. See also *Breaking the Silence—Building True Peace* (n 1 above).

[113] *Breaking the Silence—Building True Peace* (n 1 above) 58.

according to the Genocide Convention.[114] While the Genocide Convention excludes political groups from protected groups, it is argued that based on the available evidence, including on the methodology of atrocities, the targeting of civilians was multi-dimensional, in which the ethnic element was prominent, distinguishing, and essential. The acknowledgement by Col Dyke that the Ndebeles were 'well aware' of the strategy is instructive, while the *modus operandi* of the perpetrators demonstrated an ethnic cleansing agenda.[115]

In many cases, senior government officials made no pretence of the tribal or ethnic nature of the operation.[116] Also, victims report being forced all night to sing songs in Shona and being beaten if they failed.[117] It is also instructive that the South Africa mission reached the same conclusion that: 'it seems the government has decided to hold the Ndebele as a nation responsible for the dissident problem and act mercilessly against them'.[118] The imposition of a food embargo, a region-wide curfew and the burning of food stocks aimed to starve the entire Ndebele population in Matabeleland and Midlands to death to bring about its destruction further support the genocidal intent of the perpetrators.[119] More importantly, in addition to other acts, the many public statements by senior officials including Robert Mugabe,[120] Enos

[114] Genocide Convention supra note 48.

[115] See note 92.

[116] Doran (n 1 above) 584: Reflecting on the Bulawayo operation in a discussion with the Norwegians, Acting Commissioner of Police, Henry Mukurazhizha remarked that 'this is not [a] political matter but tribal, that [the] Matabele must be crushed.'

[117] Pedzisai Maedza '"*Mai VaDhikondo*": Echoes of the Requiems from the Killing Fields' (2017) 43 (2) *Social Dynamics* 215–229.

[118] Doran (n 2 above) 420.

[119] H Cameron 'State-Organized Starvation: A Weapon of Extreme Mass Violence in Matabeleland South, 1984' - Volume 12 Issue 1, Spring 2018, pp. 26–47, *Genocide Studies International Journal*, University of Toronto Press.

[120] At the time Mugabe at the time warn that 'Ndebeles must stop voting for Zapu if they wanted to live'.

'New Documents Claim to Prove Mugabe Ordered Gukurahundi Killings' *The Guardian*, 19 May 2015, https://www.theguardian.com/world/2015/may/19/mugabe-zimbabwe-gukurahundi-massacre-matabeleland (accessed on 7 March 2021).

Nkala,[121] Emmerson Mnangagwa[122] and Sydney Sekeramayi,[123] among others, amounted to the crime of direct and public incitement to commit genocide. The predominantly Shona-speaking composition[124] of the 5th Brigade also demonstrates a tribal or ethnic army.

Based on the ethnic composition of the Gukurahundi, the stated intention and conduct of the government of the day, the identity of its victims and the specific acts by the perpetrators, including direct and public incitement, and the large numbers of Ndebeles targeted to the exclusion of Shona speakers, the Matabeleland atrocities readily meet the requirements of the international crime of genocide.[125]

4.4 *Unpacking Crimes Against Humanity*

Crimes against humanity are considered as 'crimes against humaneness' that offend certain general principles of law, and which become the concern of the international community.[126] They have repercussions beyond international frontiers and exceed in magnitude or savagery any limits tolerated by modern civilisation.[127] Unlike genocide, for crimes against humanity, the offender does not need to intend to destroy

[121] On 3 April 1983, Enos Nkala likened dissidents to cockroaches and warned villagers who haboured them that they risked being caught in the crossfire, See 'Reviled in Life and Death' *Mail and Guardian*, 30 August 2013, available at (accessed on 7 March 2020).

[122] S Doran 'Mnangagwa and the Gukurahundi: Fact and Fiction' *Daily Maverick*, 27 November 2017, available at https://www.dailymaverick.co.za/article/2017-11-27-op-ed-mnangagwa-and-the-gukurahundi-fact-and-fiction/ (accessed on 28 February 2021). Mnangagwa ominously warned entire Ndebele communities that those that did not support dissidents would have their lives spared whilst those that did would be killed.

[123] See *Breaking the Silence—Building True Peace* (n 1 above). Doran (n 1 above) generally for inciteful statements issues by senior government officials.

[124] *Breaking the Silence—Building True Peace* (n 1 above) 48. Doran (n 2 above) 417.

[125] AJ McGregor, T Ranger, (eds) (2000) *Violence and Memory: One Hundred Years in the 'Dark Forests' of Matabeleland*. Oxford University Press; T Dube 'Gukurahundi Remembered: The Police, Opacity and the Gukurahundi Genocide in Bulilimamangwe District, 1982–1988' *Journal of Asian and African Studies*- February 2021, *Prosecutor v Jean-Paul Akayesu* 96-4-T(ICTR) 1998 para 513; *Prosecutor v Clement Kayishema* and *Obed Ruzindana* 95-I (ICTR) para 98.

[126] K Kittichisaree *International Criminal Law* at 95.

[127] Egon Schwelb 'Crimes Against Humanity' (1946) 23 *British Yearbook of International Law* 178 at 195–197.

members of a particular group.[128] In the case of the *Prosecutor vs Jean-Paul Akayesu,* the Rwandese mayor,[129] the International Criminal Tribunal for Rwanda (ICTR) set out the difference between genocide and crimes against humanity. Essentially, what differentiates the two crimes is that for genocide, there must be an intent on the part of the perpetrator to target a person on one of the prohibited grounds in the Genocide Convention.[130] Such intent is not required to establish or prove crimes against humanity.[131] The prohibition of crimes against humanity is now part of customary international law.[132] In addition, they are also prohibited in various international legal instruments, including the Rome Statute of the International Criminal Court Statute.[133] Article 7(1) of the ICC Statute defines crimes against humanity as '…the following acts when committed as part of a widespread or systematic attack directed against any civilian population with knowledge of the attack:

> murder, extermination, enslavement, deportation or forcible transfer of population, imprisonment or other severe deprivation of physical liberty in violation of fundamental rules of international law, torture, rape, sexual slavery, enforced prostitution, forced pregnancy, enforced sterilisation, or any other form of sexual violence of comparable gravity, persecution against any identifiable group or collectivity on political, racial, national, ethnic, cultural, religious, gender, or other grounds that are universally recognised as impermissible under international law, enforced disappearance of persons, the crime of apartheid, and other inhumane acts of a similar character intentionally causing great suffering, or serious injury to the body or mental health'.[134]

[128] See *Prosecutor vs. Jean Paul Akayesu* (n 106 above).

[129] Ibid.

[130] R Coalson, 'What's the Difference Between "Crimes Against Humanity" and "Genocide"?' *The Atlantic*, 13 March 2013, https://www.theatlantic.com/international/archive/2013/03/whats-the-difference-between-crimes-against-humanity-and-genocide/274167/.

[131] PM Wald 'Genocide and Crimes Against Humanity'(2007) 6 *Washington University Global Studies Law Review* 621–633.

[132] K Kittichaisaree *International Criminal Law* (n 21 above).

[133] Rome Statute of the International Criminal Court, Art 7: https://www.icc-cpi.int/resourcelibrary/official-journal/rome-statute.aspx.

[134] *Prosecutor v. Kupreskic* IT-95-16-A (ICTY) 2000.

The elements of the offence of a crime against humanity are established when there is evidence that any one or more of the enumerated acts have been committed as 'part of a widespread and systematic attack directed against the civilian population with knowledge of the attack'.[135] In order to prove that an accused person committed the alleged crimes against humanity, both the conditions of applicability for crimes against humanity, that an enumerated act was committed as part of a widespread or systematic attack *as well* as the specific elements of each offence must be established.

The ICTY has found that the following factors are indicative of a widespread or systematic attack:

1. the existence of a political agenda or ideology to destroy, persecute or weaken a particular community coupled with the institution of efforts to implement that policy[136];
2. the involvement of political and military authorities at a high level,[137]
3. the extent of financial, military or other means,[138]
4. the extent of the repetitious, uniform and continuous perpetration against the same civilian population.[139]

In May 2016, the Extraordinary African Chamber convicted Hissene Habre, former President of Chad for crimes against humanity,[140] war crimes, torture and sexual violence and rape.[141] When applying each of these indicative factors to the Gukurahundi atrocities, a clear picture emerges. Each factor is discussed as follows. The Gukurahundi atrocities were linked to an unravelling political crisis in the country at the

[135] See Rome Statute, Art 7 (n 102 above).

[136] *Prosecutor v Goran Jelisic* (n 38 above) para 53; *Prosecutor v Tihomir Blaskic* IT-95-14 (ICTY) 2000 para 203.

[137] Ibid.

[138] Ibid.

[139] Ibid.

[140] The *Prosecutor v Habre*, Jugdement, Extraordinary African Chamber, 29 July 2016.

[141] SA. E. Hogestol 'The Habre Judgement at the Extraordinary African Chambers: A Singular Victory in the Fight Against Impunity' (2016) 34 (3) *Nordic Journal of Human Rights* 147–156.

time. Shortly before the atrocities, the government had fallen out with the opposition ZAPU party, accusing it of caching arms and planning its violent overthrow.[142] The government's response was political and military: detaining senior opposition, military and political leaders,[143] and targeting the opposition and its civilian support base.[144] Retired Colonel Dyke summed up this political ideology as follows:

> I believe the Matabele understand that sort of treatment far better than the treatment I myself was giving them when we would just hunt and kill a man if he was armed] … [t]he fact is that when the 5th Brigade went in; they did brutally deal with the problem. If you were a dissident sympathiser, you died. And it brought peace very quickly.[145]

There is strong evidence of the personal involvement of the then Prime Minister and Minister of Defence, Robert Mugabe,[146] senior cabinet ministers including Emmerson Mnangagwa (Minister of State Security),[147] Sydney Sekeramayi, (Minister of State), Enos Nkala (Minister of Home Affairs),[148] and senior military officer including Colonel Perence Shiri, Brigadier Dominic Chinenge (now Constantine Chiwenga)[149]

[142] *Breaking the Silence—Building True Peace* (n 1 above) 41.

[143] Dabengwa, Masuku, Malunga, and others. See ibid., at 44, 71.

[144] Ibid., at 54, 62.

[145] *Breaking the Silence—Building True Peace* (n 1 above) 58. *The Guardian*, New Documents Claim to Prove Mugabe Ordered Gukurahundi Killings' 19 May 2015, https://www.theguardian.com/world/2015/may/19/mugabe-zimbabwe-gukurahundi-massacre-matabeleland (accessed on 7 March 2020); S Doran (n 1 above); SABC Interview, 'We blame the Ndebele Party, ZAPU for Gukurahundi, says Mugabe, 17 March 2018, available at https://youtu.be/0C1MiDQnQhE (accessed on 29 November 2020).

[146] Ibid., at 32.

[147] Pindula News 'Former CIO Spy, Woods, Implicates Mnangagwa in Gukurahundi' available at https://news.pindula.co.zw/2019/04/14/former-cio-double-agent-woods-implicates-mnangagwa-gukurahundi/ (accessed on 29 November 2020).

[148] Ibid., at 32, 41, 45.

[149] Ibid.

high-ranking intelligence officers including Kevin Woods (Central Intelligence Organisation Director)[150] and police commanders,[151] in the formulation of the plan and its implementation.[152]

Before deploying the 5th Brigade, the government deployed the 4th and 6th Brigades and the paratrooper regiments under Colonel Dyke to engage and combat dissidents.[153] With the arrival of the 5th Brigade in 1983, the total military presence in Matabeleland and Midlands reached 5000 officers. The 5th Brigade alone comprised at least 3500 soldiers, and by 1984, total troop deployment to Matabeleland South reached 15,000.[154]

The Gukurahundi operations in Matabeleland also involved various state security agencies, including police, intelligence and militia groups established by the government.[155] The government effort in mobilising the 5th Brigade, allocating significant state resources, and contracting the North Korean government to train it,[156] providing considerable state resources for accommodating military trainers, deploying, resourcing and supporting operations in Matabeleland for a prolonged duration all demonstrate the extent of the policy and organisation of the State. Evidence of the Gukurahundi atrocities reveals a pattern of repetitious and expansive commission of crimes throughout Matabeleland over a long period. Over at least two years—the 5th Brigade targeted unarmed villagers in Matabeleland North and South, in many cases repeatedly attacking and terrorising the same groups.[157]

An 'attack' typically constitutes one of the enumerated acts when committed as part of a widespread attack; that is, murder, torture, rape, inhumane treatment, deportation, enslavement and other forms of attack.[158] The Gukurahundi committed all these enumerated acts

[150] Kevin Woods: *The Kevin Woods Story: In the Shadow of Mugabe's Gallows* (2007) 30.

[151] *Breaking the Silence—Building True Peace* (n 1 above) 56.

[152] Ibid.

[153] Ibid., at 3.

[154] Ibid., at 46.

[155] Ibid., at 47.

[156] See *Breaking the Silence—Building True Peace* (n 1 above).

[157] See *Breaking the Silence—Building True Peace* (n 1 above).

[158] Rome Statute, Art 7 (n 102 above).

above. As with genocide, this requirement is readily met in the case of the Gukurahundi, where senior political and military leaders, including Prime Minister Mugabe, were notified of atrocities[159] and provided with evidence[160] but still failed to take action to protect innocent civilians,[161] investigate crimes and punish offenders.[162] The term 'civilian population' has been defined by the Trial Chamber of the ICTY in the *Prosecutor vs Blaskic*.[163] In armed conflict, the civilian population consists of all persons not taking part in hostilities.[164] It also includes persons who may at some time have taken part in hostilities but have laid down their arms or have been captured or injured in battle.[165] The fact that there are belligerents amongst the civilian population does not alter its nature as such.[166] The civilian status of the victims of the 5th Brigade is not contested. On the contrary, it has been acknowledged by senior commanders and political leaders in Zimbabwe.[167]

Based on the foregoing, incontrovertible evidence shows that the 5th Brigade atrocities in Matabeleland and Midlands were committed as part of a widespread and systematic attack against a civilian population. These atrocities were, therefore, undeniably crimes against humanity.

4.5 *Unpacking War Crimes*

International humanitarian law regulates how armed conflict is conducted. It prohibits certain conduct by parties to an international and internal armed conflict. The violation of the laws of war, especially concerning the treatment of the civilian population by parties to a

[159] *Breaking the Silence—Building True Peace* (n 1 above) 52.

[160] Ibid.

[161] Ibid., at 52–53.

[162] Ibid.

[163] *Blaskic* Judgment (n 138 above) para 214.

[164] Ibid.

[165] Ibid.

[166] Ibid.

[167] BBC News (n 10 above) In 1983 Prime Minister Mugabe was quoted as saying, 'Where men and women provide food for dissidents, when we get there we eradicate them. We don't differentiate when we fight, because we can't tell who is a dissident and who is not ...' see *Breaking the Silence—Building True Peace* (n 1 above) 44.

conflict, can constitute war crimes. War crimes committed in the context of internal armed conflict are governed by Common Article 3 of the Geneva Conventions,[168] Article 1(1) of APII, the Statute of the International Criminal Court[169] and customary international law. As indicated above, Common Article 3 forms part of customary international law.[170]

All these instruments prohibit the following acts from being committed against civilians during armed conflict: violence to life and person, in particular murder of all kinds, mutilation, cruel treatment and torture; taking of hostages[171]; outrages upon personal dignity, in particular, humiliating and degrading treatment[172]; the passing of sentences and carrying out of executions without previous judgement pronounced by a regularly constituted court, affording all the judicial guarantees which are recognised as indispensable by civilised peoples.[173] These Conventions do not apply to mere acts of banditry, internal disturbances and tensions, unorganised and short-lived insurrections, or terrorist activities, which are not subject to international humanitarian law.[174] What determines whether a conflict is just internal strife or an internal armed conflict falling within the scope of Common Article 3 is its intensity and the organisation of the parties.

In addition to a soldier or combatants involved in the armed conflict, civilians can be held individually criminally liable for war crimes if they directly participate in the hostilities or war effort.[175] Thus, in addition to the soldiers comprising the Gukurahundi and their military commanders, government or party officials, businesspersons, professionals, health care personnel and ordinary people who directly participate in hostilities can be held liable and found guilty of war crimes. As part of their direct participation in the hostilities and the Gukurahundi effort, government officials,

[168] Geneva Convention (n 31 above).

[169] See Rome Statute (n 102 above), see also Geneva Convention (n 31 above).

[170] Ibid.

[171] Ibid.

[172] Ibid.

[173] Ibid.

[174] *Tadic* Jurisdiction Decision (n 39 above) para 59.

[175] *Prosecutor v Kayishema and Ruzindana* -95-1-T (ICTR) 1999 paras 175–176.

including Prime Minister Robert Mugabe,[176] and Enos Nkala and others, would be individually criminally liable if they were still alive. Other civilian government officials who were personally responsible for overseeing the Gukurahundi operation, including then Minister of State Sidney Sekeramayi and Minister of State Security Emmerson Mnangagwa (in charge of the Central Intelligence Organisation, CIO), also meet the requirements of civilians directing, participating and contributing to the war effort. The Director of CIO, Kevin Woods and other CIO officers directly involved, participating and supporting the Gukurahundi operations—all played a crucial role in the torture, rape and murder of civilians at Siwale, Bhalagwe and throughout Matabeleland and Midlands and would be individually criminally liable.

For war crimes to be established, victims of war crimes in internal armed conflict must be civilians or the civilian population.[177] The victims of the Siwale Massacre and Bhalagwe Atrocities were unarmed civilians not engaged in any hostilities.[178] According to Common Article 3, APII, the ICC Statute and customary international law, the beatings, cruel treatment, torture, detention, humiliating and degrading treatment, and summary executions by the Gukurahundi constituted war crimes.

5 Assessing Individual Criminal Responsibility of Perpetrators Under International Law

5.1 An Overview of Individual Criminal Responsibility

This section examines criminal responsibility for international crimes. It draws on the Siwale Massacre and Bhalagwe atrocities and evaluates the types, levels and modes of criminal responsibility of a range of Gukurahundi perpetrators of international crimes, including members of the 5th Brigade, military, political and civilian leaders. Under international criminal law, accountability for atrocities requires that individual criminal responsibility be established with respect to alleged perpetrators. The nature of involvement in perpetrating international crimes is vital in weighing various levels of criminal responsibility, establishing guilt and

[176] S Doran, 'New Documents Claim to Prove Mugabe Ordered Gukurahundi Killings' *The Guardian*, 19 May 2015.

[177] Ibid., at 89.

[178] *Breaking the Silence—Building True Peace* (n 1 above) 48.

meeting appropriate punishment. International criminal law sets out two forms of criminal responsibility: individual responsibility and command or superior responsibility.[179]

Individual criminal responsibility is established for any individual who planned, instigated, ordered, committed or otherwise aided and abetted in the planning, preparation or execution of an international crime.[180] The objective elements for establishing individual responsibility for genocide, crimes against humanity and war crimes are that any of the prohibited acts must be committed with knowledge and intent.[181] While each international crime carries its distinct elements or requirements for individual criminal responsibility, which will be discussed below, there is a common subjective requirement for all crimes. The subjective element requires that the perpetrator knowingly commits the crime in the sense that he/she must understand the overall context in which his/her act occurs.[182] In order to be liable, the perpetrator must have actual and constructive knowledge that his act(s) is or are part of a widespread or systematic attack on a civilian population and pursuant to a plan; or that it is designed to bring about the destruction of a group, and that the crime is committed against civilians for crimes against humanity, genocide and war crimes, respectively.[183] Such knowledge can be inferred or implied from circumstances, and it is not necessary to prove that the perpetrator was aware of the policy or plan. Knowledge can also be inferred from a variety of factors, including political and historical circumstances in which the acts occur, the role and functions of the perpetrator at the time of the commission of the crimes in question, their rank and responsibilities in the political and military hierarchy, the widespread nature and seriousness of the crimes committed, the nature of the crimes and their notoriety.[184]

Applying this to the 5th Brigade atrocities, members of the 5th Brigade who directly committed atrocities, government, intelligence and military

[179] Rome Statute Art 6 (1), 6 (3) (n 135 above).

[180] See Rome Statute supra (n 102 above) Art 25, Statute of the International Criminal Tribunal for the Former Yugoslavia Art 7 (1) and Statute of the International Criminal Tribunal for Rwanda Art 6 (1). E van Sliedregt; Individual Criminal Responsibility in International Law (2012) Oxford Univeristy Press.

[181] *Tadic* Jurisdiction Decision (n 39 above) para 692.

[182] *Akayesu* case op cit note 76 para 469.

[183] Ibid., para 479.

[184] *Blaskic* (n 138 above) para 259.

officials at all levels who designed, planned, ordered and directly or indirectly aided or encouraged the operation could be held liable under this requirement. This category of perpetrators would include all ministers and military commanders involved in conceiving and executing the operation. The criminal responsibility of different actors ranging from political, military, paramilitary, intelligence and civilian will be discussed in relation to each specific international crime committed by the 5th Brigade.

5.2 Unpacking Individual Criminal Responsibility for Genocide

For each of the members of the 5th Brigade that committed the atrocities to be criminally responsible for genocide, they must have had actual and constructive knowledge, in this case, *dolus specialis,* that their actions were designed to bring about the destruction of a group. The murders committed by the Gukurahundi at Siwale and Bhalagwe meet the criteria set out in Article 2 of the Genocide Convention, namely killing members of the group. The kidnapping and torture of the victims meet criteria related to causing serious bodily and mental harm to members of the group. The detentions, starvations and sexual abuse meet the criteria related to deliberately inflicting conditions of life calculated to bring about the physical destruction of the group. The 62 Siwale and thousands of Bhalagwe victims were part of an ethnic group, and their torture and murder were committed by the 5th Brigade with intent to destroy in whole or in part that ethnic group by killing members of the group and causing serious bodily or mental harm to members of the group as envisaged by the Genocide Convention and customary international law.

The summary execution by shooting of such a large number of people at the same time in Siwale and Bhalagwe, and throughout Matabeleland and Midlands over some time (at least four years), across an extensive geographical area (Matabeleland and Midlands) suggests that the perpetrators committed the crime intending to destroy in whole or in part an ethnic group. The subsequent killing of survivors suggests a clear intention to wipe out the entire group as envisaged by the Genocide Convention. All the members of the group that committed the kidnapping, torture, and killings at Siwale and detentions, torture and murders at Bhalagwe had actual and constructive knowledge that their acts of abduction, torture and murder were calculated at bringing the destruction of the Ndebele civilian population in that area.

Based on the *Prosecutor vs Kambanda* ruling, liability for genocide would thus be based on commission. At the same time, there is evidence that Mugabe was personally made aware that the alleged genocide was occurring but failed to stop or prevent them, providing a basis for failure to prevent genocide.

The living, senior government and military officials at all levels who designed, planned, ordered and directly or indirectly aided or encouraged the Gukurahundi operation can be held criminally liable for the Siwale Massacre and other atrocities like Bhalagwe as a genocide. The law does not envisage holding deceased perpetrators, including Robert Mugabe, Enos Nkala and Perence Shiri, criminally liable. The genocidal nature of the atrocities, including at Siwale and Bhalagwe, is demonstrated by the composition of the 5th Brigade (entirely Shona), the behaviour of the direct perpetrators, including informing entire communities that the attacks were revenge for pre-colonial raids by Ndebele kings, Mzilikazi and Lobengula,[185] the orders by perpetrators to villagers to sing Shona songs during the commission of atrocities, and the clearly stated intentions by senior government officials including Enos Nkala (Minister of Home Affairs) who on 12 February 1983 was quoted by the Chronicle as telling villagers at Makwe Irrigation Scheme that: 'People who supported dissidents in their murderous acts, mayhem and rape risked the wrath of the government. If you are one of them, you shall die or be sent to prison'.[186]

The then Prime Minister Mugabe is reported at the time warning during the time that 'Ndebeles must stop voting for Zapu if they wanted to live'.[187] In addition, the then Security Minister, Emmerson Mnangagwa,[188] ominously warned entire Ndebele communities that those that did not support dissidents would have their lives spared whilst those that

[185] *Breaking the Silence—Building True Peace* (n 1 above) 27.

[186] 'Reviled in Life and Death' *Mail and Guardian*, 30 August 2013, available at (accessed on 7 March 2020). On 3 April 1983, Enos Nkala likened dissidents to cockroaches and warned villagers who haboured them that they risked being caught in the crossfire.

[187] 'New Documents Claim to Prove Mugabe Ordered Gukurahundi Killings' *The Guardian*, 19 May 2015, https://www.theguardian.com/world/2015/may/19/mugabe-zimbabwe-gukurahundi-massacre-matabeleland (accessed on 7 March 2021).

[188] S Doran 'Mnangagwa and the Gukurahundi: Fact and Fiction' *Daily Maverick* (n 122 above).

did would be killed.[189] More recently, an admission by former President Mugabe in 2018 that 'Ndebeles wanted to overthrow his government hence the deployment of the Gukurahundi',[190] and the admission by military commanders such as Colonel Dyke that the target of the operation was 'targeted at Ndebeles and that it targeted dissidents as well as civilians'[191] all point to their culpability and genocidal intent.

5.3 *Unpacking Individual Criminal Responsibility for Crimes Against Humanity*

For each of the perpetrators of the Gukurahundi atrocities, including the Siwale Massacre and Bhalagwe atrocities, to be criminally liable for crimes against humanity, they must have had actual and constructive knowledge that their actions were part of a widespread or systematic attack on a civilian population.[192] The 'attacks directed against any civilian population' have to be 'pursuant to or in furtherance of a State or organisational policy to commit such attack'.[193] Even though the Nuremberg Charter did not have specific provisions, the requirement that the crimes are pursuant to an organisational policy was highlighted in the Nuremberg Tribunal judgements, which found that the Nazi inhumane acts were committed as part of the policy of terror and were organised and systematic. The requirement has subsequently been applied by the ICTY and ICC, which explained that it aims to distinguish acts committed by an individual on his own initiative pursuant to his own criminal plan without the involvement, encouragement, and direction of the government group or organisation.[194]

[189] Minister Mnangagwa was quoted as saying 'Blessed are they who will follow the path of the Government laws, for their ~ lays on earth shall be increased. But woe unto those who will choose the path of collaboration with dissidents for we will certainly shorten their stay on earth'. See *Breaking the Silence—Building True Peace* (n 1 above) 54.

[190] SABC Interview, 'We blame the Ndebele Party, ZAPU for Gukurahundi, says Mugabe, 17 March 2018, available at https://youtu.be/0C1MiDQnQhE (accessed on 7 March 2020).

[191] See *Breaking the Silence—Building True Peace* (n 1 above) 58.

[192] Ibid., at Art 7(1) of ICC Statute.

[193] See Article 7 (2) of the ICC Statute.

[194] Prosecutor v Kayeshema and Ruzindana; see also Dissenting Opinion by Judge Hans-Peter Kaul to Pre-Trial Chamber II's 'Decision on the Prosecutor's Application

There is overwhelming evidence of a State and Zanu PF organisational policy to deploy the Gukurahundi to attack civilians. Several government officials were involved in the design of the Gukurahundi operations. As Prime Minister, Robert Mugabe first announced plans to form the Brigade as early as August 1981 while addressing ZANLA ex-combatants at Tongogara cantonment in Chipinge, describing the 5th Brigade; as a 'special unit to combat dissidents and any other trouble in the country.' Following Mugabe's announcement, Mnangagwa reported to Parliament that 106 instructors had arrived from North Korea and would be in the country for 8–12 months to train the 5th Brigade, suggesting in the process that training had already begun.[195] There is evidence from the passing out parade of the Brigade that the then Prime Minister Robert Mugabe instructed its members to go into communities and 'plough and reconstruct'.[196] The significant assignment of state resources and systematic deployment of the Brigade supported by the Central Intelligence Organisation and Zimbabwe Republic Police, firstly to Matabeleland North, then Matabeleland South and parts of the Midlands, demonstrates a State organisational policy to target and attack civilians over a wide geographical area and over time. Throughout its deployment and its commission of atrocities, several government ministers, including Mugabe, Mnangagwa,[197] Nkala and Sekeramayi, would

for Summonses to Appear for Francis Kirimi Muthaura, Uhuru Muigai Kenyatta and Mohammed Hussein Ali' in *Prosecutor v Uhuru Kenyatta and Others* ICC-01/09-02/11; see also; C Kress (2010) 'On the Outer Limits of Crimes against Humanity: The Concept of Organization within the Policy Requirement: Some Reflections on the March 2010 ICC Kenya Decision' (2010) 23 (4) *Leiden Journal of International Law* 855–873. https://doi.org/10.1017/S0922156510000415; Rogier Bartels and Katharine Fortin; Law, Justice and a Potential Security Gap: The "Organization" Requirement in International Humanitarian Law and International Criminal law; *Journal of Conflict & Security Law* (2015), 1–20.

[195] Doran (n 1 above) citing the Hansard, 21 August 1981, Vol 3 pp. 1211–1212.

[196] *Breaking the Silence—Building True Peace* (n 1 above) 45, 47.

[197] Minister Mnangagwa was quoted as saying 'Blessed are they who will follow the path of the Government laws, for their ~ lays on earth shall be increased. But woe unto those who will choose the path of collaboration with dissidents for we will certainly shorten their stay on earth'. See *Breaking the Silence—Building True Peace* (n 1 above) 54. 'Minister defends Five Brigade', *Chronicle*, 5 March 1983 reported on a rally in Victoria Falls in February, where Mnangagwa said that dissidents were like 'cockroaches and bugs', and had reached such 'epidemic proportion' that the government had to bring DDT (5 Brigade) to deal with the problem.

issue incendiary and inciteful statements, threaten civilians and encourage the Gukurahundi to commit crimes as part of this organisational policy to attack civilians.

There is also evidence of a widespread and systematic attack against civilians. In addition to his specific instruction issued to the Gukurahundi at its passing out parade, to target communities and civilians with attacks Mugabe and his ministers would incite and encourage attacks in many public statements. Speaking at a rally, then Prime Minister, Robert Mugabe, was reported in *The Chronicle* as stating that the government's position in eradicating dissidents did not differentiate between armed dissidents and unarmed civilian villagers, whom the government suspected of sympathising with and supported dissidents.[198] Mugabe's Security Minister, Mnangagwa, would re-enforce the policy and plan for a widespread and systematic of civilians in several public statements saying, 'Blessed are they who will follow the path of the Government laws, for their days on earth shall be increased. But woe unto those who will choose the path of collaboration with dissidents for we will certainly shorten their stay on earth'. He also reportedly told a rally near Lupane in March 1983, that the government 'had the option of burning down… all villages infested with dissidents'.[199]

There is also evidence of ethnicisation and politicisation of the 5th Brigade into a ZANU political party paramilitary unit.[200] On this basis, it can be reasonably concluded that each member of the Brigade, wherever deployed, was aware of the systematic plan to attack civilians. In any event, according to international law, there is no requirement to know the detailed specifics of the plan in order to be held criminally responsible.

In conclusion, the group went from homestead to homestead and village to village abducting civilians, forcibly taking them to their camp, systematically beating and torturing them and then summarily executing them; demonstrates knowledge of a systematic plan by the members of the Brigade to attack civilians.

Individual criminal liability can also be attributed to other actors besides the members of the 5th Brigade that directly committed the atrocities at Siwale. Senior government and military officials at all levels who

[198] Ibid., at 44.

[199] *Breaking the Silence—Building True Peace* (n 1 above).

[200] Ibid.

designed, planned, ordered and directly or indirectly aided or encouraged the 5th Brigade operation can be held criminally liable for the Siwale Massacre and Bhalagwe Atrocities as crimes against humanity. In particular, the Prime Minister, who together with his government ministers designed, planned, ordered and encouraged the killings, all meet this requirement.

5.4 *Individual Criminal Responsibility for War Crimes*

For each of the members of the 5th Brigade that committed the atrocities to be criminally responsible for war crimes, they must have had actual and constructive knowledge that their actions were targeted at civilians in the context of an armed conflict. The status of the Matabeleland crisis and an internal armed conflict under international law has been discussed above. As such, all 5th Brigade members, military commanders and government officials at all levels who designed, planned, ordered and directly or indirectly aided or encouraged the Siwale Massacre, Bhalagwe and other crimes are individually criminally responsible for war crimes prohibited by Common Article 3 of the Geneva Conventions,[201] Article 1.1 of APII, the Rome Statute[202] and customary international law. In particular, in the Siwale Massacre and Bhalagwe, the 5th Brigade murdered, mutilated, cruelly treated and tortured, abducted, inflicted outrages upon personal dignity, humiliated, degraded and summarily executed civilians. There is clear evidence that the members of the 5th Brigade that committed the Siwale massacre and atrocities at Bhalagwe were aware of the existence of an armed conflict in that on abducting, torturing, detaining and killing the victims, they accused them of being dissidents. They were also aware of their civilian nature. Similarly, the civilian status of thousands of detainees at Bhalagwe, including female rape victims, was evident to all the perpetrators, including their commanders and civilian political superiors.

In addition to the direct perpetrators of the atrocities in Siwale and Bhalagwe, other living perpetrators who were part of the group that designed, planned, ordered and directly or indirectly aided or encouraged

[201] Geneva Conventions, Common Art 3 (n 31 above).

[202] Rome Statute (n 135 above).

the Siwale Massacre and Bhalagwe atrocities would be individually criminally responsible. This includes former Prime Minister Mugabe, former Home Affairs Minister Enos Nkala, Former Security Minister Emmerson Mnangagwa, former Defence Minister, Sidney Sekeramayi who can all be found individually criminally responsible for the murder, mutilation, cruel treatment and torture, abduction, inflicting outrages upon personal dignity, humiliation, degrading and summary execution of civilians as war crimes. Based on the reasoning in *Kayishema* and *Ruzindana*,[203] it would be possible to establish a link between the different perpetrators of the war crimes at Siwale, Bhalagwe and throughout Matabeleland and Midlands and the war effort from start to finish.

5.5 An Overview of Command or Superior Responsibility

The principle of command or superior responsibility is well established in international law.[204] Under the principle, a superior or commander is criminally responsible for acts committed by their subordinates if they knew or had reason to know that the subordinate was about to commit such acts or had done so and the superior failed to take necessary and reasonable measures to prevent such acts or to punish the perpetrators thereof.[205] Command responsibility is founded on the failure to act in breach of a clear legal duty or moral obligation imposed by international law upon those in authority to act.[206] A person can be found criminally responsible as a superior additionally or alternatively to being individually responsible if the requirements of both forms of responsibility are established.

[203] *Prosecutor v Kayishema and Ruzindana* (n 127 above) para 175.

[204] Rome Statute supra (n 135 above) Art 28, see also Art 7 (3) of ICTY Statute: available at https://legal.un.org/avl/ha/icty/icty.html#:~:text=The%20International%20Criminal%20Tribunal%20for%20the%20former%20Yugoslavia,including%20that%20of%20torture%2C%20extermination%2C%20enslavement%20and%20deportation, see also I Bantekas, *Principles of Direct and Superior Responsibility in International Humanitarian Law*. Manchester, UK: Manchester University Press, 2002; G Mettraux, *The Law of Command Responsibility* (2009) Oxford University Press.

[205] Rome Statute (n 102 above) Art 6(3).

[206] Ibid.

The principle of command responsibility also applies to political leaders, civilian leaders[207] or non-military leaders who wield the required authority. International and national tribunals have found a former civilian prime minister,[208] government ministers, politicians and business leaders or industrialists[209]; guilty under this principle for crimes committed by their subordinates. In determining this level or type of responsibility, it is not the civilian or military status of the superior that matters but the degree of control or authority that such superior exercises or exercised over their subordinates.[210] All that would have to be established in order to impute liability under this category is that the respective political or civilian leader was in a position of authority over the direct perpetrators and exercised effective control and authority, and the perpetrators were their subordinates; and that such commander or superior was aware that the 5th Brigade was about to commit or had committed atrocities and had failed to stop the commission of the crimes or to punish them. In Rwanda, the ICTR found the former prime minister, Kambanda, responsible for genocide and crime against humanity for failing to prevent and punish genocide of hundreds of thousands of Tutsis.[211] The ICTR also found Kayishema,[212] a civilian head of a tea factory and mayor, Jean-Paul Akayesu,[213] criminally responsible under the principle of command or superior responsibility.

As discussed above, international law imposes criminal responsibility on military commanders or superiors for acts committed by their subordinates if such individuals knew or had reason to know that the subordinate was about to commit such acts or had done so and the commander or superior failed to take necessary and reasonable measures to prevent such

[207] *Prosecutor c Delacic* (*Celebici* Case) IT-96-21-A (ICTY) 2001 paras 356–363; *Prosecutor v. Musema* 96-13-A (ICTR) 2000 paras 136, 146–148.

[208] See *Prosecutor v Kambanda* ICTR 97-23-S (ICTR) 1998.

[209] See *Prosecutor v Kayishema and Ruzindana* (n 127 above) paras 213–215.

[210] *Prosecutor v. Aleksovski* IT-95-14/1 (ICTY) 2000, paras 75–78; *Kayishema and Ruzindana* Ibid. para 216; *Akayesu* (n 106 above) para 491.

[211] *Prosecutor v Akayesu* case (n 106 above).

[212] *Prosecutor v Kayishema and Ruzindana* (n 127 above).

[213] *Prosecutor v Akayesu* (n 106 above).

acts or to punish the perpetrators thereof.[214] With command responsibility, criminal liability is founded on the omission or failure to act in breach of a clear legal duty or moral obligation imposed by international law upon those in authority to act,[215] rather than a commission, as is the case for individual responsibility. Under command responsibility, a superior is held liable not because of something they have done but for action they have failed to take when they were aware that their subordinates were about to or had committed crimes. As noted above, a person can be found criminally responsible as a superior additionally or alternatively to being individually responsible if the requirements of both forms of responsibility are established.[216]

Applying these principles to the Siwale Massacre, Bhalagwe and other Gukurahundi atrocities, all civilian, political and military leaders that wielded significant control and authority over the members of the 5th Brigade would be liable for all their crimes (genocide, crimes against humanity and war crimes) under international law. This would include the then Prime Minister, Robert Mugabe,[217] senior ministers Emmerson Mnangagwa, Enos Nkala and Sidney Sekeramayi and government and ZANU officials, and military commanders, including the Commander of the 5th Brigade, Perence Shiri, and then commanders of the Zimbabwe national army and national intelligence, including Rex Nhongo and Kevin Woods, respectively. In addition to command responsibility, the elements of individual responsibility would be objectively met for several of these perpetrators.

6 Conclusion

The primary purpose of this chapter was to examine Gukurahundi atrocities and determine whether they constitute international crimes. This chapter also sought to explore and determine the criminal responsibility of the perpetrators under international law. To that extent, this chapter has analysed the Gukurahundi atrocities committed against Ndebeles

[214] I Bantekas, *Principles of Direct and Superior Responsibility in International Humanitarian Law*, Manchester University Press, 2002; G Mettraux, *The Law of Command Responsibility* (n 205 above).

[215] Rome Statute (n 102 above) Art 6(3).

[216] Ibid., at Art 28.

[217] See *Prosecutor v Kambanda* ICTR 97-23-S (ICTR) 1998.

of Zimbabwe in the 1980s and determined that the atrocities, which included ethnic cleansing, mass murder, enforced disappearances, torture, beatings, mass rapes and destruction of property, were so heinous as to constitute core international crimes of genocide, crimes against humanity and war crimes prohibited by international criminal law. This chapter has reviewed the application of international criminal and humanitarian law in Zimbabwe and classified the Matabeleland as a non-international armed conflict. It has demonstrated that international criminal law establishes individual criminal responsibility on perpetrators of international crimes and determines that perpetrators of Gukurahundi international crimes, therefore, bear individual responsibility for their crimes. It has also illustrated that the perpetrators of these Gukurahundi crimes include known high-level government and military officials who have escaped accountability and continue to enjoy impunity. The chapter has shown that, in addition to being denied justice, victims and survivors of the Gukurahundi continue to bear physical, emotional and psychological scars. This chapter has reiterated that international criminal law imposes a legal obligation to investigate, prosecute and punish perpetrators of international crimes. Finally, this chapter is expected to contribute to understanding Gukurahundi atrocities, the role of perpetrators and the victims' demand for justice, and spur action to hold perpetrators accountable for their heinous crimes.

Bibliography

Books

Alexander, J; McGregor, AJ & Ranger, T *Violence and Memory: One Hundred Years in the 'Dark Forests' of Matabeleland* (James Currey 2000).

Bantekas, I *Principles of Direct and Superior Responsibility in International Humanitarian Law* (Manchester University Press 2002).

Bassiouni, CM (ed) *Post Conflict Justice* (Transnational Publishers 2002).

Bassiouni, CM (ed) *Proposed Guiding Principles for Combating Impunity for International Crimes*, in *Post Conflict Justice* (Transnational Publishers 2002).

Buckley-Zistel, S; Beck, TK; Braun C & Mieth F (eds) *Transitional Justice Theories* (Routledge 2014).

Cassese, A *International Law* (Oxford University Press 2005).

Coltart, D *The Struggle Continues; 50 Years of Tyranny in Zimbabwe* (Jacana 2016).

De Waal, V *The Politics of Reconciliation: Zimbabwe's First Decade* (Africa World Press 1990).

Dinstein, Y *Non-International Armed Conflicts in International Law* (Cambridge University Press 2014).

Doran, S *Kingdom, Power, Glory: Mugabe, ZANU and the Quest for Supremacy: 1960–1987* (Sithatha Media 2017).

Fleck, D (ed) *The Handbook of International Humanitarian Law* (Oxford University Press 2008).

Harris, DJ *Cases and Materials on International Law* 6th ed. (Sweet & Maxwell 2004).

Hayner, PB *Unspeakable Truths: Confronting State Terror and Atrocity* (Routledge 2001).

Kittichaisaree, K *International Criminal Law* (Oxford University Press 2001).

Mettraux, G *The Law of Command Responsibility* (Oxford University Press 2009).

O'Keefe, R *International Criminal Law* (Oxford University Press 2015).

Ratner, SR; Abrams, J & Bischoff, JL, *Accountability for Human Rights Atrocities in International Law: Beyond the Nuremberg Legacy* (Oxford University Press 2001).

Sandoz, Y; Swinarski, C & Zimmermann, B (eds), *Commentary on the Additional Protocols of 8 June 1977 to the Geneva Conventions of 12 August 1949* (Geneva/Dordrecht: ICRC/Nijhoff 1987).

Stromseth, JE (ed) *Accountability for Atrocities: National and International Responses* (Transnational Publishers 2003).

Todd, J *Through the Darkness* (Zebra Press 2007).

Van Sliedregt, E *Individual Criminal Responsibility in International Law* (Oxford University Press 2012).

Woods K, *The Kevin Woods Story: In the Shadow of Mugabe's Gallows* (2007).

Journal Articles

Adjovi, R 'Introductory Note to the Agreement on the Establishment of the Extraordinary African Chambers Within the Senegalese Judicial System Between the Government of the Republic of Senegal and the African Union and the Statute of the Chambers' (2013) 52 (4) *International Legal Materials* 1020–1036.

Alexander, J 'Dissident Perspectives on Zimbabwe's Post-Independence War' (1998) 68 (2) *Africa: Journal of the International African Institute* 151–182. https://doi.org/10.2307/1161277 (accessed 29 on April 2021).

Bartels, R & Fortin, K 'Law, Justice and a Potential Security Gap: The "Organisation" Requirement in International Humanitarian Law and International Criminal law' (2015) *Journal of Conflict & Security Law* 1–20

Bassiouni, CM 'International crimes: *Jus Cogens* and *Obligatio Erga Omnes*' (1996) 59 (4) *Law and Contemporary Problems* 68.

Bassiouni, C 'Universal Jurisdiction for International Crimes: Historical Perspectives and Contemporary Practice' (2001–2002) 42 *Virginia Journal of International Law* 81.

Boed, R 'The Effect of a Domestic Amnesty on the Ability of Foreign States to Prosecute Alleged Perpetrators of Serious Human Rights Violations' (2000) 33 (2) *Cornell International Law Journal* 297–323.

Bradley, MM 'Revisiting the Scope of Application of Additional Protocol II: Exploring the Inherent Minimum Threshold Requirements' (2019) 81 *African International Yearbook of International Humanitarian Law.*

Caitlin, CE, 'Hybrid Tribunals are the Most Effective Structure for Adjudicating International Crimes Occurring Within a Domestic State' (2013) *Law School Student Scholarship* 90.

Cameron, H, 'State-Organised Starvation: A Weapon of Extreme Mass Violence in Matabeleland South, 1984' (2018) 12 (1) *Genocide Studies International Journal* 26–47.

Chalk, F '"Genocide in the 20th Century": Definitions of Genocide and their Implications for Prediction and Prevention' (1989) 4 (2) *Holocaust and Genocide Studies* 149–160.

Chetman, A, *A Theory of International Crimes: Conceptual and Normative Issues in* Heller KJ; Megret F; Nouwen, S; Ohlin JD & Robinson, D, (2020) *The Oxford Handbook of International Criminal Law* (Oxford University Press) 317–340

Clapham, A 'Defining Armed Conflicts Under the Additional Protocols: Is There a Need for Further Clarification?' in Pocar, F & Berute GL (eds) *International Institute of Humanitarian Law: 'The Additional Protocols 40 Years Later: New Conflicts, New Actors, New Perspectives*; 40th Round Table on Current Issues of International Humanitarian Law (San Remo, 7th–9th September 2017)' available at (accessed on 28 April 2021).

Coalson, R 'What's the Difference Between "Crimes Against Humanity" and "Genocide?"' (2013) *The Atlantic.*

Crettol, M & La Rosa, AM 'The Missing and Transitional Justice: the Right to Know and the Fight Against Impunity' (2006) 88 *International Review of the Red Cross* 862.

Dube, T 'Gukurahundi Remembered: The Police, Opacity and the Gukurahundi Genocide in Bulilimamangwe District, 1982–1988' (2021) *Journal of Asian and African Studies.*

Dube, D & Makwerere, D 'Zimbabwe: Towards a Comprehensive Peace Infrastructure' (2012) 2 *International Journal of Humanities and Social Science* 18.

Eppel, S 'Gukurahundi: The Need for Truth and Reconciliation' in Raftopoulous B & Savage T Zimbabwe: *Injustice and Political Reconciliation* (2004) Institute for Justice and Reconciliation 43–62.

Eppel, S 'In Pursuit of Reconciliation from an Intransigent State: An Exercise in Futility, in Tendi, M; McGregor, JA & Alexander, J (2020) *The Oxford Handbook on Zimbabwean Politics.*

Galand, AS 'UN Security Council Referrals to the International Criminal Court: Legal Nature, Effects and Limits' in (2018) C Stahn, C; Van den Herik & Schrijver, LN (eds) *Leiden Studies in International Law* (Brill Nijhoff 2018)

Greenawalt, AKA 'Rethinking Genocidal Intent: The Case for a Knowledge-Based Interpretation' (1999) 99 (8) *Columbia Law Review* 2259–2294.

Hampson, F 'Direct Participation in Hostilities and the Interoperability of the Law of Armed Conflict and Human Rights Law' (2011) 87 *International Law Studies.*

Heller, KJ 'What Is an International Crime: (A Revisionist History)' (2017) 58 (2) *Harvard International Law Journal* 353–420.

Hogestol, SAE 'The Habre Judgement at the Extraordinary African Chambers: A Singular Victory in the Fight Against Impunity' (2016) 34 (3) *Nordic Journal of Human Rights* 147–156.

Jalloh, CC 'Prosecutor v. Taylor' (2014) 108 (1) *The American Journal of International Law* 58–66.

Killander, M & Nyathi, M 'Accountability for the Gukurahundi Atrocities in Zimbabwe Thirty Years On: Prospects and Challenges' (2015) 48 (3) *Comparative and International Law Journal of Southern Africa* 463–487.

Kress, C 'On the Outer Limits of Crimes against Humanity: The Concept of Organization within the Policy Requirement: Some Reflections on the March 2010 ICC Kenya Decision' (2010) 23 (4) *Leiden Journal of International Law* 855–873.

Leicht, L 'Kosovo War Crimes Court Can Promote Justice on All Sides' (2020) 12 November, *Balkan Insight.*

Machakanja, P 'National Healing and Reconciliation in Zimbabwe: Challenges and Opportunities' (2010) *Institute for Justice and Reconciliation*, https://www.africaportal.org/publications/national-healing-and-reconciliation-in-zimbabwe-challenges-and-opportunities/ (accessed on 23 June 2021).

Maedza, P '*Mai VaDhikondo*': Echoes of the Requiems from the Killing Fields, (2017) 43 (2) *Social Dynamics* 215–229.

Masitera, E 'Creating a Culture of Impunity in Zimbabwe: A Case for Philosophical and Developmental Issues' (2011) 5 (2) *Africana* 100.

McDermott, Y 'Prosecutor v. Bemba' (2016) 110 (3) *The American Journal of International Law* 526–533.

Meron, T 'International Criminalisation of Internal Atrocities' (1995) 89 (3) *American Journal of International Law* 554–557.

Mlambo, N 'The Politics of Bitterness: Understanding the Zimbabwean Political Crisis, 1980–2005' (2006) 3 (2) *African Renaissance* 56.

Muchemwa, C; Ngwerume, ET & Hove M, 'When Will the Long Nightmare Come to an End? Challenges to National Healing and Reconciliation in Post-Colonial Zimbabwe' (2013) 22 (3) *African Security Review* 145–159.

Murambadoro, R 'We Cannot Reconcile Until the Past Has Been Acknowledged: Perspectives on Gukurahundi from Matabeleland, Zimbabwe' (2015) 15 (1) *African Journal on Conflict Resolution* 33–57.

Naqvi, Y 'Amnesty for War Crimes: Defining the Limits of International Recognition' (2003) 851 (85) *IRRC* 583.

Ndlovu-Gatsheni, SJ 'Rethinking Chimurenga and Gukurahundi in Zimbabwe: A Critique of Partisan National History' (2012) 55 (1) *African Studies Review* 1–2.

Ngwenya, D & Harris, G 'The Consequences of Not Healing: Evidence from the Gukurahundi Violence in Zimbabwe' (2015) 15 *African Journal on Conflict Resolution* 2.

Nouwen, SMH, 'Hybrid Courts' The Hybrid Category of a New Type of International Crimes Courts' (2006) 2 (2) *Utrecht Law Review* 190–214.

Orentlicher, D 'Settling Accounts: The Duty to Prosecute Human Rights Violations of a Prior Regime' (1991) 100 *The Yale Law Journal*.

Pedrazzi, M 'Additional Protocol II and Threshold of Application' in Pocar, F & Berute GL (eds) *International Institute of Humanitarian Law: 'The Additional Protocols 40 Years Later: New Conflicts, New Actors, New Perspectives*; 40th Round Table on Current Issues of International Humanitarian Law (San Remo, 7th–9th September 2017),' available at (accessed on 28 April 2021).

Reiger, C & Wierda, M *The Serious Crimes Process in Timor-Leste: In Retrospect* (2006) *International Center for Transitional Justice*, https://www.ictj.org/publication/serious-crimes-process-timor-leste-retrospect (accessed on 23 June 2021).

Roht-Arriaza, N 'State Responsibility to Investigate and Prosecute Grave Human Rights Violations in International Law' (1990) *California Law Review* 78.

Schabas, WA 'Punishment of Non-State Actors in Non-International Armed Conflict' (2002) 26 (4) *Fordham International Law Journal* 907–933.

Scharf, M 'The Amnesty Exception to the Jurisdiction of the International Criminal Court' (1999) 8 (32) *Cornell International Law Journal*.

Schwelb E 'Crimes Against Humanity' (1946) 178 (23) *British Yearbook of International Law* 195–197.

Steininger, S 'The Kosovo Specialist Chambers—A New Chapter for International Criminal Justice in the Balkans' (2018) *Völkerrechtsblog*.

Turack, DC 'Ending Impunity in Africa: The Charles Taylor Trial at the Special Court for Sierra Leone' (2009) 26 (2) *Journal of Third World Studies* 191–202.

Vambe, MT 'Zimbabwe Genocide: Voices and Perceptions from Ordinary People in Matabeleland and the Midlands Provinces, 30 Years on' (2012) 10 (3) *African Identities* 281–300.

Verdirame, G 'The Genocide Definition in the Jurisprudence of the Ad Hoc Tribunals' (2000) 49 (3) *International and Comparative Law Quarterly* 578–598.

Wald, PM 'Genocide and Crimes Against Humanity' (2007) 6 *Washington University Global Studies Law Review* 621–633.

Williams, S 'The Cambodian Extraordinary Chambers: A Dangerous Precedent for International Justice?' (2004) 53 *The International and Comparative Law Quarterly* 227–245.

Book Chapters

Eppel, S 'Healing the Dead: Exhumation and Reburials as a Tool to Truth Telling and Reclaiming the Past in Rural Zimbabwe' in Borer TA (ed) (2006) *Telling the Truths: Truth Telling and Peace Building in Post-Conflict Societies* 259–288.

Mpofu, S 'Diasporic New Media and Conversations on Conflict: A Case of Zimbabwe Genocide Debates' in Ogunyemi, O (2017) *Media, Diaspora and Conflict* 204–221.

Hansen, TO 'The Vertical and Horizontal Expansion of Transitional Justice: Explanations and Implications for a Contested Field' in Buckley-Zistel, S; Beck, TK; Braun C & Mieth F (eds) *Transitional Justice Theories* (Routledge 2014).

Brown, S & Sriram, CL 'The Big Fish Won't Fry Themselves: Criminal Accountability for Post-Election Violence in Kenya' (2012) 111 (443) *African Affairs* 244–260.

Duduzile, N 'Violence and Memory in Breaking the Silence of Gukurahundi: A Case Study of the ZAM in Johannesburg, South Africa' in Palmary, I; Hamber B & Núñez, L (eds) (2014) *Healing and Change in the City of Gold: Case Studies of Coping and Support in Johannesburg* 59–77.

Reports

Amnesty International Annual Report, 1984.

Amnesty International Annual Report, 1984 accessible at https://www.amnesty.org/download/Documents/POL1000041984ENGLISH.PDF.

'Breaking the Silence—Building True Peace: A Report on the Disturbances in Matabeleland and the Midlands 1980–1988' Catholic Commission for Justice and Peace in Zimbabwe & Legal Resources Foundation (1997).

Berkeley, B 'Wages of War: A Report of Human Rights in Zimbabwe,' *Lawyers Committee for Human Rights*, 1983, Amnesty International Annual Report, 1984 accessible at https://www.amnesty.org/download/Documents/POL 1000041984ENGLISH.PDF.

Chihambakwe Commission of Enquiry, see https://www.usip.org/publications/1983/09/commission-inquiry-zimbabwe.

Committing to Justice for Serious Human Rights Violations: Lessons from Hybrid Tribunals, (2018) *International Centre for Transitional Justice.*

Open letter from Amnesty International to His Excellency the President Robert Mugabe concerning the need for public discussion and action on the disturbances in Matabeleland and the Midlands in the 1980s, 23 May 1997, *Amnesty International*; accessible at https://www.amnesty.org/download/Documents/156000/afr460021997en.pdf.

Princeton Principles on Universal Jurisdiction, adopted by a group of international law experts in 2001, *Princeton University*, Princeton, 2001.

Media and Newspaper Articles

Alison, S 'Gukurahundi Ghosts Haunt Mnangagwa,' *Mail and Guardian*, 24 November 2017, https://mg.co.za/article/2017-11-24-00-gukurahundi-ghosts-haunt-mnangagwa (accessed on 29 February 2020).

Bass, GJ 'Milosevic in The Hague' (2003) 82, no. 3 *Foreign Affairs* 82–96.

Bagnetti, LA 'Ghosts of Gukurahundi Still Haunt Survivors, as Zimbabwe Officials Refuse to Acknowledge,' *RFI*, 12 March 2019, https://rfi.my/3lts.W (accessed on 7 March 2020).

'Catholic Priest Who Exposed Zimbabwe Massacre,' *Sunday Independent*, 13 November 2012.

Dobbs, M 'General Mladic in The Hague' (2012) 194 *Foreign Policy* 100–105.

Doran, S 'Mnangagwa and the Gukurahundi: Fact and Fiction,' *Daily Maverick*, 27 November 2017, available at https://www.dailymaverick.co.za/article/2017-11-27-op-ed-mnangagwa-and-the-gukurahundi-fact-and-fiction/ (accessed on 28 February 2021).

'Dumbutshena Reports Have Been Lost: NPRC Chairman,' ZimLive, https://www.zimlive.com/2019/04/19/dumbutshena-chihambakwe-reports-have-been-lost-nprc-chairman/ (accessed on 23 June 2021).

'Ex Ivory Coast President Acquitted at ICC,' *The Guardian*, 15 January 2019.

'Former CIO Spy, Woods, Implicates Mnangagwa in Gukurahundi,' Pindula News, 14 April 2019, available at https://news.pindula.co.zw/2019/04/14/former-cio-double-agent-woods-implicates-mnangagwa-gukurahundi/ (accessed on 29 November 2020).

'Government Should Release Chihambakwe, Dumbutshena Commissions Reports,' https://www.zimbabwesituation.com/news/govt-should-release-chihambakwe-dumbutshena-commissions-reports/ (accessed on 23 June 2021).

'Grave Containing Up to 60 People Found at Zimbabwe School,' *The Guardian*, 5 October 2011.

'Gukurahundi 5th Brigade Mass Graves in Nkayi,' https://www.youtube.com/watch?v=Dvx-cxygig8 (accessed on 28 February 2021).

'Gukurahundi was a conflict situation, Mnangagwa's spokesman says' an interview with George Charamba, ZimLive, available at zimlive.com (accessed on 7 March 2021).

Kunambura, A 'Zimbabwe: Gukurahundi Carefully Planned,' *Zimbabwe Independent*, 18 April 2019, available at https://allafrica.com/stories/201904190398.html (accessed on 29 February 2020).

Malunga, S 'The False Choice Between Reburials and Justice for the Gukurahundi Victims' *Daily Maverick*, 6 May 2019, available at https://www.dailymaverick.co.za/article/2019-05-06-the-false-choice-between-reburials-and-justice-for-the-gukurahundi-victims/ (accessed on 29 February 2021).

'Minister defends Five Brigade,' *Chronicle*, 5 March 1983.

Moyo, T 'Digging Up the Graves of Gukurahundi Victims and Burying the Evidence,' *Mail and Guardian*, 10 May 2019, https://mg.co.za/article/2019-05-10-00-digging-up-the-graves-of-gukurahundi-graves-and-burying-the-evidence/ (accessed on 29 February 2021 and 29 March 2021).

'Mugabe: Madness of Matabele deaths,' *BBC News Online*, 2 July 2000, http://news.bbc.co.uk/2/hi/africa/816129.stm (accessed on 29 March 2021).

'New Documents Claim to Prove Mugabe Ordered Gukurahundi Killings', *The Guardian*, 19 May 2015, https://www.theguardian.com/world/2015/may/19/mugabe-zimbabwe-gukurahundi-massacre-matabeleland (accessed on 7 March 2021).

Revealed; How British Diplomats Pressured BBC's Jeremy Paxman over Massacres in Zimbabwe, https://inews.co.uk/news/uk/revealed-british-diplomats-pressured-bbcs-jeremy-paxman-understand-true-perspective-massacres-zimbabwe-61535 (accessed on 23 March 2021).

'Reviled in Life and Death,' *Mail and Guardian*, 30 August 2013, available at (accessed on 7 March 2020).

'Split by Victory in Zimbabwe, Ex Allies Wage a Bitter War,' *New York Times*, 18 February 1983.

'The Nkomo Affair: Mistrust Never Died,' *New York Times*, 12 March 1983.

'We blame the Ndebele Party, ZAPU for Gukurahundi,' says Mugabe, *SABC*, 17 March 2018, https://youtu.be/0C1MiDQnQhE (accessed on 29 November 2020 and 23 June 2021).

'Zimbabwe Party Reports Attacks,' *New York Times*, 8 March 1985.
'Zimbabwe President Discusses Exhuming Victims of 1980s Massacres,' News24, 23 August 2020. https://www.news24.com/news24/africa/zimbabwe/zimbabwe-president-mnangagwa-discusses-exhuming-victims-of-1980s-massacre-20200823 (accessed on 23 June 2021).

Cases

Azanian Peoples Organisation (AZAPO) and Others v President of the Republic of South Africa and Others (1996) ZACC 16.
Barker McCormac (Pvt) Ltd v Government of Kenya; 1983 (2) ZLR 72.
High Court Order HH 67/2001 HC 8139/2000, 'Buhera North Election Petition'.
Hostages Trial, US Military Tribunal at Nuremberg, 19 February 1948 (1953) 15 *Annual Digest*. 632 at 636.
Minister of Foreign Affairs v Michael Jenrich, Standard Chartered Bank Zimbabwe and Sheriff of Zimbabwe, Zimbabwe Supreme Court Judgment No. SC 73/18.
National Police Commissioner of the South African Police Service v Southern African Human Rights Litigation Centre Trust (The Torture Docket case) (CCT 02/14) [2014] ZACC 30; 2015 (1) SA 315 (CC).
North Sea Continental Shelf Cases, ICJ, 1969, ICJ Reports 1969: www.icj-cij.org (accessed on 29 March 2021).
Prosecutor v Ahmad Al Bashir ICC-02/05-01/09.
Prosecutor v. Aleksovski IT-95-14/1 (ICTY) 2000.
Prosecutor v Delacic (*Celebici* Case) IT-96-21-A (ICTY) 2001 paras 356–363.
Prosecutor v. Dusko Tadic, Case No. IT-94-1, ICTY App. Ch., Decision on the Defence Motion for Interlocutory Appeal on Jurisdiction of 2 October 1995 ('*Tadic* Jurisdiction Decision').
Prosecutor v Furundija, Case No. IT-95-17/I-T, ICTY T. Ch. II, 10 December 1998.
Prosecutor v Georges Riggiu, ICTR-97-32-1, ICTR Trial Chamber 1, 1 June, 2000.
Prosecutor v Goran Jelisic, Case No. IT-95-10, ICTY T. Ch 1, 14 December 1999.
Prosecutor v Habre, Judgement, Extraordinary African Chamber, 29 July 2016.
Prosecutor v Jean Kambanda 97-23-S (ICTR) 1998.
Prosecutor v Jean-Paul Akayesu 96-4-T(ICTR) 1998.
Prosecutor v Kayishema and Ruzindana -95-1-T (ICTR) 1999.
Prosecutor v Kupreskic IT-95-16-A (ICTY) 2000.
The Prosecutor v. Laurent Gbagbo and Charles Blé Goudé, ICC-02/11-01/15.
Prosecutor v Musema 96-13-A (ICTR) 2000 paras 136, 146–148.

Prosecutor v Tihomir Blaskic IT-95-14 (ICTY) 2000.
Sibanda and Another v ICRC (2002 (1) ZLR 364.
The Prosecutor v Uhuru Muigai Kenyatta: ICC-01/09-02/11.
Dissenting Opinion by Judge Hans-Peter Kaul to Pre-Trial Chamber II's "Decision on the Prosecutor's Application for Summonses to Appear for Francis Kirimi Muthaura, Uhuru Muigai Kenyatta and Mohammed Hussein Ali" in *Prosecutor v Uhuru Kenyatta and Others* ICC-01/09-02/11.

Treaties and Statutes

African Union, Decision on the Draft Legal Instruments, Assembly AU/Dec.529 (XXIII), Decisions, Declarations and Resolution of the Assembly of the Union, Twenty Third Ordinary Session, June 26–27, 2014.
Clemency Order No 1 of 1988, Zimbabwe.
Constitution of Zimbabwe, Amendment No.20 of 2013.
Convention on the Prevention and Punishment of the Crime of Genocide, 1951.
Convention Against Torture and Other Cruel, Inhuman or Degrading Treatment or Punishment, 1984; A/RES/39/46.
Criminal Law (Codification and Reform Act) [Chapter 9:23] Zimbabwe.
Geneva Conventions of 1949.
Genocide Act (Chapter 9:20) Zimbabwe.
Law on the Court of Bosnia and Herzegovina 3 July, 2002.
Law on the Establishment of the Extraordinary Chamber in Cambodia (ECCC) (2004)
National Peace and Reconciliation Act [Chapter 10:32] 11 of 2017.
Protocol Additional to the Geneva Conventions of 12 August 1949, and relating to the Protection of Victims of Non-International Armed Conflicts (Protocol II), 8 June 1977.
Rome Statute of the International Criminal Court.
Statute of the Special Court for Sierra Leone.
Statute of the Special Tribunal for Lebanon.
Statute of the International Court of Justice (1945), Art 38 (1) (b): 33 UNTS 993.
Statute of the International Criminal Tribunal for the Former Yugoslavia.
Statute of the International Criminal Tribunal for Rwanda.
Statute of the Extraordinary African Chamber.
United Nations Charter.
UNTAET Regulation 2000/15 on the Special Panel for Serious Crime in East Timor.

Unpublished Theses

Bradley, MM Unpublished doctoral thesis titled 'An Analysis of the Notions of "Organised Armed Groups" and "Intensity" in the Law of Non-International Armed Conflict' (2018) University of Pretoria.

Ngwenya, D 'Healing the Wounds of Gukurahundi: A Participatory Action Research Project' (unpublished DTech thesis, Durban University of Technology, 2014).

Santos, P 'Representing Conflict: An Analysis of the Chronicle's Coverage of the Conflict in Zimbabwe Between 1983 and 1986' (unpublished MA thesis, Rhodes University, 2011).

Yap, KP 'Uprooting the Weeds: Power, Ethnicity and Violence in the Matabeleland Conflict' (2001) University of Amsterdam.

Conclusion: Where to, Now?

Ntombizozuko Dyani-Mhango and Emma Charlene Lubaale

Throughout this edited volume, the contributions discussed several issues that concern national accountability for international crimes. The emphasis was always on the rejection of impunity and the call for states to hold perpetrators of international crimes accountable for their role in these atrocities. This volume was enriched with discussions that provide concrete examples of what is happening in various African states that are party to the Rome Statute, and those that are yet to ratify the Statute. The contributions have not only highlighted the challenges faced by these states with regard to national accountability for international crimes but have also provided alternative solutions to deal with these challenges.

There are four major themes that came out of these contributions. The first theme addressed the AU's perspectives on the complementarity

N. Dyani-Mhango (✉)
Faculty of Law, University of Pretoria, Pretoria, South Africa
e-mail: ntombizozuko.dyani-mhango@up.ac.za

E. C. Lubaale
Faculty of Law, Rhodes University, Grahamstown, South Africa
e-mail: e.lubaale@ru.ac.za

E. C. Lubaale and N. Dyani-Mhango (eds.), *National Accountability for International Crimes in Africa*,
https://doi.org/10.1007/978-3-030-88044-6_17

principle in Africa. This theme consists of four chapters that deal with different issues that concern the AU and its member states in relation to ensuring that perpetrators of international crimes face the consequences of their actions. In this regard, Gevers and Mushoriwa[1] gave a historical background to the AU's role in the eradication of international crimes and holding perpetrators to account, while also giving a perspective of why there is currently a tension between the AU and the ICC. In his contribution also under this theme, Lungu[2] was optimistic about the yet to be established International Crimes Division of the African Court on Human and Peoples' Rights and provided recommendations on ways to strengthen this Court's cooperation regime. Mung'omba's chapter[3] highlighted the significance of the concept of universal jurisdiction against the background of Senegal's conviction of Hissène Habré for international crimes. He argued for the adoption of the AU Model Law on Universal jurisdiction by AU member states and claimed that this will demonstrate Africa's seriousness when it comes to holding perpetrators of international crimes accountable. The last chapter in this theme by Samaradiwakera-Wijesundara[4] dealt with national accountability for international crimes by addressing corporate responsibility for international crimes using the examples of South Africa and Nigeria. She argued for the expansion of crimes against humanity to include poverty and inequality, and proposed reforms to hold corporations accountable for international crimes before national courts and regional courts, including the proposed African Court with an international crimes' division.

The second theme from this edited volume addressed the prospects of the complementarity principle and provided alternative approaches to hold perpetrators of international crimes accountable. The chapters in this

[1] C Gevers & L Mushoriwa 'Unable or Unwilling? An Assessment of the African Union's Perspective on the Application of the Complementarity Principle by the International Criminal Court'.

[2] S Lungu 'Cooperation as Complementarity: A Legal Appraisal of the AU's Malabo Protocol'.

[3] I Mung'omba 'Universal Jurisdiction as a Tool in Promoting Accountability for International Crimes in Africa: Exploring the Significance of Hissène Habré's Conviction'.

[4] Samaradiwakera-Wijesundara 'Complementarity and Criminal Liability of Companies in Africa: Missing the Mark?'

theme were by Asaala[5]; Lubaale and Carkeek[6]; and Lubaale.[7] These three chapters discussed different mechanisms to ensure prosecution of perpetrators of international crimes. Assala advocated for a broad interpretation of the complementarity principle, while Lubaale and Carkeek argued that the complementarity principle must include African restorative justice mechanisms using Libya as a case study. Lubaale in her sole-authored chapter discussed the challenges faced by the ICC when requesting state parties to cooperate with its requests to arrest and surrender suspects to it. Lubaale was particularly concerned with the (non) cooperation of state parties whose governments are implicated in the commission of international crimes. She used the example of Uganda as the problematic state in her discussion of what is to come from Sudan as it prepares to cooperate with the ICC post the Al Bashir regime. She was sceptical about the Sudanese commitment to this as the new regime constitutes officials from the Al Bashir regime.

The third theme addressed the prospects and challenges of national accountability for international crimes in Africa with a focus on particular states. Two contributions by Adigun[8] and Onuora-Oguno et al.[9] focused on Nigeria. Adigun explored the relationship between the complementarity principle and federalism, while Onuora-Oguno et al. looked at the accountability for the violation of the rights of internationally displaced persons (IDPs) and argued that that violations of the rights of the IDPs by the Nigerian security agencies constitute crimes against humanity. The authors subsequently called for the ICC to exercise jurisdiction over perpetrators of these crimes based on the complementarity principle since Nigeria is a party to the Rome Statute.

[5] E Asaala 'Towards Lasting Complementarity Among the International Criminal Court, Regional and National Criminal Justice Systems in Africa'.

[6] EC Lubaale & J Carkeek 'African Restorative Justice Approaches as Complementarity: The Case of Libya'.

[7] EC Lubaale 'Now Available but Still not Accessible to the ICC: Al-Bashir and Africa's Politics'.

[8] M Adigun 'Complementarity and Federalism: Prosecuting International Crimes Under the Rome Statute Complementarity Principle in Nigeria as a Federal State'.

[9] Onuora-Oguno et al. 'Accountability for Violations Against Internally Displaced Persons in Nigeria: Finding a Nexus Between International Criminal Justice And Human Rights Violations'.

Apuuli's contribution[10] under this third theme addressed the question of establishing tribunals to deal with the prosecution of perpetrators of atrocities arising from internal conflicts in the respective states while the conflicts are still ongoing. There are also two contributions that focus on Uganda and accountability for international crimes. In her contribution, Ndagire[11] highlighted the challenges faced by the International Crimes Division of the High Court of Uganda in the prosecution of perpetrators of international crimes. She focused her discussion on the Kwoyelo trial which has been ongoing for more than 10 years impacting on both the accused's trial rights and the rights of the victims. In his contribution, Ruhweza[12] takes the discussion on the Kwoyelo trial further and demonstrated that the entire trial process is testament to the fact that the court is not equipped to exercise the task before it.

The last theme of this edited volume dealt with atrocities committed before the Rome Statute came into force and how the states in question fail to deal with those atrocities and questioned whether the concerned states are committed to holding to account perpetrators of international crimes under the Rome Statute regime. In this regard, Dyani-Mhango[13] addressed South Africa's failure to deal with the prosecution of perpetrators of apartheid crimes for crimes against humanity. Dyani-Mhango argued that failure to prosecute is a result of political interference in the National Prosecuting Prosecution's exercise of its prosecutorial duty by the executive branch of government. Dyani-Mhango concluded that there can never be accountability for international crimes perpetrated post the establishment of the ICC and post-apartheid South Africa without first dealing with the perpetrators of apartheid and prosecuting them for crimes against humanity. Equally, Malunga's two chapters[14] discussed the atrocities committed by the post-independence Zimbabwean government

[10] Apuuli 'The Establishment of the Hybrid Court for South Sudan and the Special Criminal Court For Central African Republic: Challenges and Prospects'.

[11] J Ndagire 'A Critical Assessment of the International Crimes Division of the High Court of Uganda'.

[12] D Ruhweza 'Wild Goose Chase, or a Quest for Genuine Prosecution? Lessons From Uganda's Ongoing Trial of Thomas Kwoyelo'.

[13] N Dyani-Mhango 'South Africa's Accountability for International Crimes: Revisiting the (Non) Prosecution of Perpetrators of Apartheid for Crimes Against Humanity'.

[14] S Malunga 'A History of Atrocity: Patterns, Perpetrators and Prospects for Accountability for International Crimes in Zimbabwe'; and S Malunga 'Unpacking Gukurahundi

and the governing political party, Zimbabwe African National Union-Patriotic Front (Zanu PF) in the 1980s against its own citizens, especially the Ndebeles, and against the supporters of the Zimbabwe Unity Movement (ZUM), the Movement for Democratic Change (MDC), white farmers, civil society, human rights, media, and democracy activists. In both chapters, Malunga gave a historical account of the atrocities committed by the Zanu PF and the Zimbabwean government in the past four decades since Zimbabwe gained its independence in 1980. In particular, Malunga focused on the Gukurandi atrocities committed against the Ndebele population in Matebeleland in Zimbabwe. He classified the conflict in Matebeleland as a non-international armed conflict as rules of international humanitarian law so provide. He argued that the atrocities constituted international crimes as they included ethnic cleansing, mass murder, enforced disappearance and torture, and called for international criminal responsibility.

The contributions in this edited volume are clear that accountability for international crimes on an individual level is imperative as the international community acknowledges that these crimes 'shock human conscience' and threaten international peace and security. It is therefore no surprise that the African states profiled in the contributions have one way or the other made strides to ensure that there are mechanisms to hold perpetrators accountable. But national accountability for international crimes is more than just holding individuals accountable, it is also about states being proactive by ensuring that they are not party in the perpetration of international crimes.

1 Where to, Now?

The contributions in this volume only touched the surface on national accountability for international crimes in Africa. There is still a lot more that needs to be explored in shaping the international criminal justice in Africa. What is clear from all the contributions is that there must be national accountability for international crimes. Impunity is not tolerated. The departure is based on the type of accountability the authors expect from states. The peace versus justice debate is still ongoing as we have seen in some of the contributions. The argument from authors is that

Atrocities Against the Ndebeles of Zimbabwe: What Are the Possibilities for Individual Criminal Responsibility of the Perpetrators Under International Criminal Law?'.

there can be no real peace in the post-conflict states without states taking stock of what happened in their politics, and to facilitate meaningful and inclusive reconciliation amongst all those affected by the conflict. The other issue that has come out strongly from these contributions is that there needs to be accountability for atrocities that occurred before the Rome Statute came into force. The argument is that states cannot pretend to be serious about accountability for the Rome Statute crimes when they failed to deal with the pre-Rome Statute crimes.

There is a lot more that still needs to be done in shaping international criminal justice in Africa. With the new ICC Prosecutor coming into office, is there going to be an improvement in the relations between African states and the ICC? Further, towards the conclusion of this edited volume, there are reports on Tigray, Ethiopia, where alleged international crimes which include sexual violence against women are being committed.[15] Yet, there has not been any consequences for the perpetrators of these crimes, despite the calls to do so.[16] In Mozambique, there are also reports of international crimes being committed by ISIS.[17]

[15] United Nations Human Rights, Office of the High Commissioner, 'Ethiopia: Persistent, Credible Reports of Grave Violations in Tigray Underscore Urgent Need for Human Rights Access – Bachelet' Display News, 4 March 2021, available at https://www.ohchr.org/en/NewsEvents/Pages/DisplayNews.aspx?NewsID=26838&LangID=E (last accessed on 26 July 2021); W Akinwotu 'Scale of Tigray Horror Adds to Pressure on Ethiopian Leader' *The Guardian*, 28 March 2021, available at https://www.theguardian.com/world/2021/mar/28/scale-of-tigray-horror-adds-to-pressure-on-ethiopian-leader (last accessed on 26 July 2021); and W Davison 'The Alleged Atrocities in Tigray Risk Tearing Ethiopia Apart' *The Guardian*, 9 May 2021, available at https://www.theguardian.com/commentisfree/2021/may/09/alleged-atrocities-tigray-ethiopia (last accessed on 26 July 2021).

[16] S Nebehay 'U.N. Seeks Access to Ethiopia's Tigray for War Crimes Probe' Reuters, 4 March 2021, available at https://www.reuters.com/article/us-ethiopia-conflict-un-idUSKBN2AW0Z7 (last accessed on 26 July 2021); C Wilmot & S Gebre 'Investigate Crimes in Tigray Now, or Risk a Fragmented Ethiopia' *Mail & Guardian*, 7 March 2021, available at https://mg.co.za/africa/2021-03-07-investigate-crimes-in-tigray-now-or-risk-a-fragmented-ethiopia/ (last accessed on 26 July 2021); and ZM Salih "Don't Betray Women of Tigray': Calls Grow for International Action Against Rape in War' *The Guardian*, 19 June 2021, available at https://www.theguardian.com/global-development/2021/jun/19/dont-betray-women-of-tigray-calls-grow-for-international-action-against-rape-in-war (last accessed on 26 July 2021).

[17] 'Mozambique Insurgency: Children Beheaded, Aid Agency Reports' BBC News, 16 March 2021, available at https://www.bbc.com/news/world-africa-56411157 (last accessed on 26 July 2021); J Burke & P Beaumont 'Isis Claims Deadly Attack in Northern

Further, there are alleged crimes being committed in Eswatini by state security agents.[18] Are there going to be investigations by the ICC on Security Council referrals since both states are not party to the Rome Statute? This also raises the question of accountability for international crimes by non-state actors. Who do we hold responsible for international crimes committed by non-state actors in the territory of African states who are not state party to the Rome Statute? Those are just some of the questions that need to be considered for future research projects on national accountability for international crimes in Africa.

Acknowledgements Emma Charlene Lubaale acknowledges funding from the National Research Foundation (Funding to EC Lubaale, Grant No: 127504) towards the funding of writing retreats that informed the conceptual development of my contributions to this book. Support from the Rhodes University Research Committee Grant is also acknowledged.

References

'Eswatini: Dozens Killed, Tortured, Abducted as Pro-democracy Protests Intensify' Amnesty International, 2 July 2021, available at https://www.amnesty.org/en/latest/news/2021/07/eswatini-dozens-killed-tortured-abducted-as-pro-democracy-protests-intensify/.

'Mozambique Insurgency: Children Beheaded, Aid Agency Reports' BBC News, 16 March 2021, available at https://www.bbc.com/news/world-africa-56411157.

Akinwotu, W 'Scale of Tigray Horror Adds to Pressure on Ethiopian Leader' *The Guardian*, 28 March 2021, available at https://www.theguardian.com/world/2021/mar/28/scale-of-tigray-horror-adds-to-pressure-on-ethiopian-leader.

Burke J & Beaumont, P 'Isis Claims Deadly Attack in Northern Mozambique' *The Guardian*, 29 March 2021, available at <https://www.theguardian.com/world/2021/mar/29/isis-claims-deadly-attack-in-northern-mozambique>.

Mozambique' *The Guardian*, 29 March 2021, available at https://www.theguardian.com/world/2021/mar/29/isis-claims-deadly-attack-in-northern-mozambique (last accessed on 26 July 2021).

[18] 'Eswatini: Dozens Killed, Tortured, Abducted as Pro-democracy Protests Intensify' Amnesty International, 2 July 2021, available at https://www.amnesty.org/en/latest/news/2021/07/eswatini-dozens-killed-tortured-abducted-as-pro-democracy-protests-intensify/ (last accessed on 26 July 2021).

Davison, W 'The Alleged Atrocities in Tigray Risk Tearing Ethiopia Apart' *The Guardian*, 9 May 2021, available at https://www.theguardian.com/commentisfree/2021/may/09/alleged-atrocities-tigray-ethiopia.

Nebehay, S 'U.N. Seeks Access to Ethiopia's Tigray for War Crimes Probe' Reuters, 4 March 2021, available at https://www.reuters.com/article/us-ethiopia-conflict-un-idUSKBN2AW0Z7.

Salih, ZM "Don't Betray Women of Tigray': Calls Grow for International Action Against Rape in War' *The Guardian*, 19 June 2021, available at https://www.theguardian.com/global-development/2021/jun/19/dont-betray-women-of-tigray-calls-grow-for-international-action-against-rape-in-war (last accessed on 26 July 2021).

United Nations Human Rights, Office of the High Commissioner, 'Ethiopia: Persistent, Credible Reports of Grave Violations in Tigray Underscore Urgent Need for Human Rights Access – Bachelet', 4 March 2021, available at https://www.ohchr.org/en/NewsEvents/Pages/DisplayNews.aspx?NewsID=26838&LangID=E.

Wilmot, C & Gebre, S 'Investigate Crimes in Tigray Now, or Risk a Fragmented Ethiopia' *Mail & Guardian*, 7 March 2021, available at https://mg.co.za/africa/2021-03-07-investigate-crimes-in-tigray-now-or-risk-a-fragmented-ethiopia/.

Index

E. C. Lubaale and N. Dyani-Mhango (eds.), *National Accountability for International Crimes in Africa*,
https://doi.org/10.1007/978-3-030-88044-6

H

I

J

K

The manufacturer's authorised representative in the EU is Springer Nature Customer Service Centre GmbH, Europaplatz 3, 69115 Heidelberg, Germany. If you have any concerns regarding our products, please contact ProductSafety@springernature.com

Printed and bound by CPI Group (UK) Ltd, Croydon, CR0 4YY
30/09/2026
02225499-0019